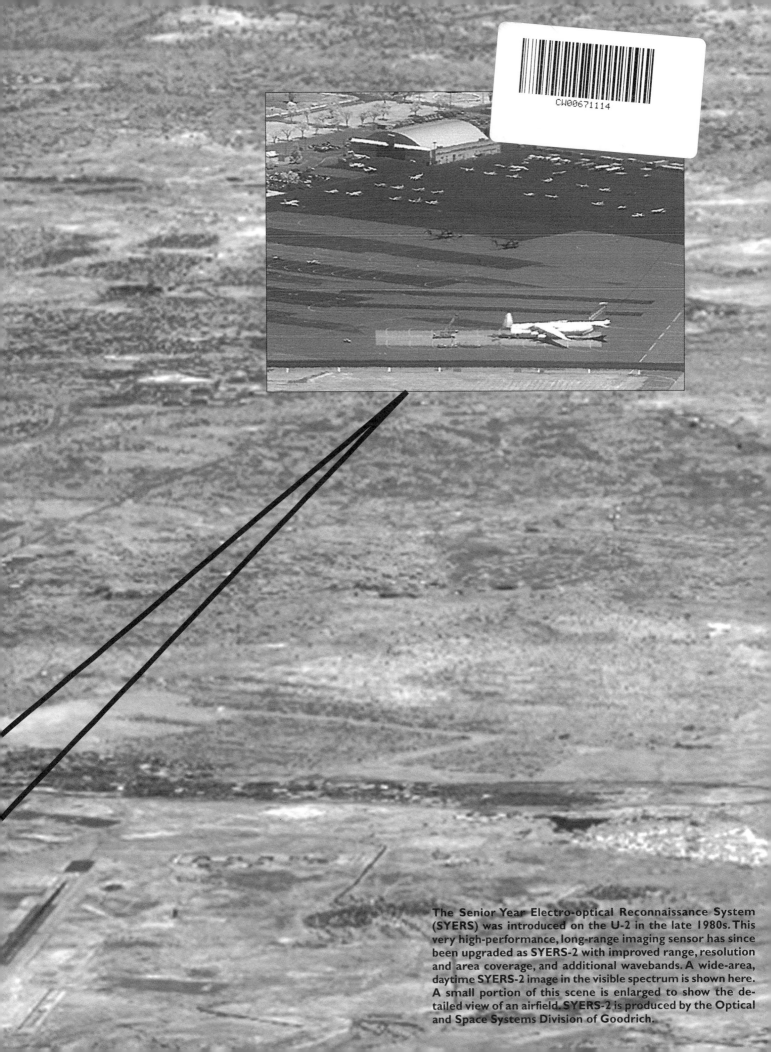

The Senior Year Electro-optical Reconnaissance System (SYERS) was introduced on the U-2 in the late 1980s. This very high-performance, long-range imaging sensor has since been upgraded as SYERS-2 with improved range, resolution and area coverage, and additional wavebands. A wide-area, daytime SYERS-2 image in the visible spectrum is shown here. A small portion of this scene is enlarged to show the detailed view of an airfield. SYERS-2 is produced by the Optical and Space Systems Division of Goodrich.

50 Years of the

U-2

The Complete Illustrated History
of the "Dragon Lady"

*To John
— who has become a great Dragon Lady fan!*

[signature]

Chris Pocock

Schiffer Military History
Atglen, PA

Book Design by Ian Robertson.

Printed in China.
ISBN: 978-0-7643-2346-1

Schiffer Books are available at special discounts for bulk
purchases for sales promotions or premiums. Special editions,
including personalized covers, corporate imprints, and
excerpts can be created in large quantities for special needs.
For more information contact the publisher:

Published by Schiffer Publishing Ltd.
4880 Lower Valley Road
Atglen, PA 19310
Phone: (610) 593-1777; Fax: (610) 593-2002
E-mail: Info@schifferbooks.com

For the largest selection of fine reference books on
this and related subjects, please visit our web site at:
www.schifferbooks.com

We are always looking for people to write books on
new and related subjects. If you have an idea for
a book please contact us at the above address.

This book may be purchased from the publisher. Include $5.00
for shipping. Please try your bookstore first.
You may write for a free catalog.

In Europe, Schiffer books are distributed by
Bushwood Books
6 Marksbury Ave.
Kew Gardens
Surrey TW9 4JF England
Phone: 44 (0) 20 8392-8585; Fax: 44 (0) 20 8392-9876
E-mail: info@bushwoodbooks.co.uk
Website: www.bushwoodbooks.co.uk

Contents

Foreword

by Major General Pat Halloran, USAF (retd.)

Kelly called it the "Angel." The Agency referred to it as the "Article," and the Air Force named it the "Dragon Lady." However, for 50 years, the bad guys of the world simply called it the dreaded U-2 Spy Plane. It was a name that aptly described the design, the mission and the legend.

Of course, those of us who flew the U-2 for the Air Force called it many names, depending on how that Lady responded on the day that we were flying it! Each airframe seemed to have unique flying characteristics and a personality of its own. It was always an interesting experience to ease this marvelous machine above 70,000 feet, and to enjoy the unparalleled view of our private world, while at the same time trying to ignore the drawbacks.

To start with, you had been stuffed into a horribly claustrophobic partial pressure suit. Then, you had spent two hours pre-breathing 100% oxygen, before being squeezed into a very tiny cockpit. Once airborne, you spent a great deal of time attempting to fine tune the autopilot; manage airspeed control inside the 10-knot window of the "coffin corner"; keep over 1,000 gallons of fuel balanced between those floppy wings; shoot and plot celestial navigation fixes; do map pilotage through a drift sight; and wonder how long your bladder would continue to hold on this 9-10 hour flight. That was before they added inflight refueling to extend the range! Oh and yes, you mustn't forget to operate your primary reconnaissance equipment on cue. That's why you're up there. Of course in the back of your mind you were always anticipating the exciting landing which lay in store for you in this strange, bicycle-gear machine.

It was a plane which had an insatiable appetite for eating the lunch of young aviators. Despite those few distractions, there were some extremely rewarding missions that were assigned to U-2 pilots who agreed to go along with this folly. My comments reflect my own experiences in the Air Force side of this program, but friends who flew the U-2 for the CIA, would probably agree with most of them.

I had the great fortune to spend almost 17 years flying Kelly Johnson's spectacular reconnaissance airplanes for the Air Force. First, it was the graceful U-2 for nine years, and then the powerful SR-71 for eight more years. I never dreamed of having such a wonderful opportunity to explore the high altitude flight regimes occupied by those two remarkable vehicles back when I was flying the F-84, my first operational airplane following graduation from pilot training in 1950. There is no question in my mind, that Kelly Johnson was the greatest aeronautical engineer of our time. The aircraft that he produced will always be recognized as some of the greatest designs in modern aeronautical history.

The U-2 was the most demanding, but rewarding airplane I have ever flown in my 34 years in the Air Force. It was single engine (I liked); we flew it solo (I liked); very high (I liked); out of radio contact for most of mission (I really liked); and it had extreme range (necessary, but not a "like" thing). The personal satisfaction in completing some very difficult and hazardous missions in this plane was beyond anything I had ever experienced.

I have had engine failures, dead stick landings, disconnected oxygen at 65,000 feet, and more flameouts than I can count. And talk about a home sick angel...near the end of a mission, with minimum fuel, it would still climb with the throttle in idle! That was a disconcerting experience the first time you encountered it.

All of this excitement came at a high cost. It is interesting to note that of the original 55 airframes that were built back in the '50's, only 10 survived to an honorable retirement in dusty museums. The loss of life, as well as airplanes, was probably the highest, percentage wise, of any operational squadron in the Air Force. Seventeen days after the delivery of our first airplanes, we already had two fatalities, and one of these was on his first flight. Initially, we didn't have an ejection seat, so that didn't help the statistics. Flying this airplane was not exactly fun, but it certainly did have exciting moments. However, every operational mission we flew gave some real professional pay back and every pilot was eager for his next sortie.

It is truly awesome to think that this aircraft, which was originally conceived as a "throw away" machine after a few overflight missions, is still flying today. Several years ago I was tapped to head a study group, with the slightly derogatory name of the "Graybeard Panel," to review the U-2 operations by the Air Combat Command, which had taken over management of the system from the de-activated Strategic Air Command.

As we analyzed the current operations that these aircraft were involved in, I was again impressed with the durability and functional flexibility of the U-2. It has absorbed a long list of upgrades and modifications, such as a fan engine, GPS and a glass cockpit, to enhance its performance and keep it viable for many years to come. The aircraft still performs missions today that are as critical and demanding as any of the ones we flew in the old days. The young men and women (yes, women) who climb into that cockpit today, and head for the fringes of outer space, are as dedicated as any pilots in the history of the aircraft. I am extremely proud to have been one of the original Air Force pilots selected for this program and I share that pride with the pioneers who flew with me, and with those who continue to follow.

We are indeed fortunate to have Chris Pocock as our primary research guru for this program. He has written a number of remarkable books and articles on the U-2. They are my primary source of historical detail on this aircraft and its mission. There is no doubt in my mind, that he knows more about the history of the U-2 than any other person in the world.

I think Kelly Johnson would be awed to read some of the details in this book, of how his Angel has been transformed from the tiny, black world in which it was conceived, to the world wide tactical operations in which it now shines.

1

Genesis

On 30 November 1953, in the development planning office of the Lockheed Corporation in Burbank, California, Jack Carter wrote a memo. The recently retired USAF Colonel titled it Strategic Reconnaissance, classified it "eyes only," and addressed it to his boss, Gene Root. The history of the U-2 began with that memo, in which Carter outlined the urgent need for a new type of manned reconnaissance aircraft, and made some suggestions on how such a plane should be built.

The memo was unambiguous. The Soviet Union was the target, and the aircraft would have to overfly that country at extreme altitude with a payload of up to 500 pounds. Cameras would be one such payload, but Carter also mentioned "new types of sensing equipment," by which he meant radar, infrared, or electronic intelligence. The aircraft should be flown by a single pilot at altitudes between 65,000 and 70,000 feet, at a speed of mach 0.8, and have a radius of action of 1,200 nautical miles. It should be capable of avoiding virtually all Soviet defenses until about 1960.

To build such an aircraft, Carter reckoned, most of the standard rules about structural design would have to be ignored. A maneuver load factor as low as 2.25g might be required—the military norm was more like 7g. Maximum indicated airspeed should be 225-250 knots. To save weight, landing gear should be eliminated. A turbojet, which sacrificed engine life for maximum performance and weight reduction, would be needed.[1]

In addressing his memo to Gene Root, Carter was effectively preaching to the converted, for *both* of them had recently worked for a Pentagon office where U.S. strategic reconnaissance objectives were being redefined. This office, named USAF Development and Advanced Planning (AFDAP), set development planning objectives for various missions. It was headed by Colonel Bernard Schriever, a rising technocrat in the Air Force. Carter had been Schriever's chief-of-staff, and Root was a consultant to AFDAP from the Rand Corporation.[2]

Richard Leghorn

Early in 1952, Bennie Schriever had been impressed by the ideas of Colonel Richard Leghorn, an expert and visionary in the reconnaissance field who had been recalled to military service from Kodak at the start of the Korean War. Leghorn had been drawing attention to the unique political and practical problems involved with peacetime overflights of "denied territory" since 1946. As the Iron Curtain descended on the postwar world,

the requirement outlined by Leghorn and his solution—higher and faster aircraft that would be invulnerable to detection and interception—made ever more sense. Schriever invited Leghorn to join his staff at AFDAP.

The young reconnaissance expert moved from Wright Field, where he had commissioned a proposal from the British manufacturer of the Canberra jet bomber for a radical adaptation of that aircraft to the reconnaissance role.[3] At AFDAP other staffers, such as Gene Kiefer and Major

Colonel Richard Leghorn was a bright, former WWII recon pilot who developed the concept of overflight of "denied territory" behind the Iron Curtain. He also explored possible designs in the early 1950s. (via Cargill Hall)

Bud Wienberg, agreed with Leghorn, that an aircraft designed for overflight could not be built to the usual military specifications, nor operated in the usual military fashion.

But Leghorn's proposal to adapt the Canberra had no takers in the USAF hierarchy, apart from Schriever. This was despite the advice of a group of leading scientists in fields related to reconnaissance, which had confirmed the higher-and-faster requirement in their Beacon Hill Report to USAF in mid-1952. Leghorn was AFDAP's liaison to this study, which was named after the suburb of Boston that was close to Harvard University, MIT, and the Boston University Optical Research Laboratory, where some of the scientists worked.

Meanwhile, wartime-vintage bombers and patrol planes converted for reconnaissance missions were lumbering along—and sometimes across—Soviet borders. They faced an increasing threat of interception from the new Soviet jet fighters, such as the MiG-15, directed by air defense radars. The RB-45C reconnaissance version of America's first jet bomber, the Tornado, was not much of an improvement; its top speed was higher, but its max altitude was still only 40,000 feet. As the risk of detection and interception by the Soviets grew, U.S. military commanders found it increasingly difficult to gain the required political authority for deliberate overflights. A few top-priority missions over European Russia were effectively subcontracted to Britain's Royal Air Force, since Prime Minister Churchill was more willing than President Truman to approve them.[4]

Bald Eagle

Prompted perhaps by these developments, and by the Beacon Hill study, the USAF formally requested design studies for a specialized reconnaissance aircraft on 1 July 1953. At the Wright Air Development Center (WADC) in Ohio, new developments chief Bill Lamar and engine specialist Major John Seaberg had laid the groundwork for this request in the preceding six months. They did not, apparently, refer back to the "unconventional aircraft" work that Leghorn had done there in 1951. But it was

---

BALD EAGLE

The purpose of this design study is to determine the characteristics of an aircraft weapon system having an operational radius of 1500 n mi and capable of conducting pre- and post-strike reconnaissance missions during daylight good visibility conditions.

Performance – Radius 1500 n mi

Speed – Optimum subsonic at altitude of 70,000 feet or higher

Payload – 100 to 700 lbs

Crew – one

Power Plant – current production engines with modifications, if necessary.

Gross Weight – as low as possible

Fuel Requirements – consideration will be given to the glide potential inherent in this type of aircraft. The MIL-C-5011A reserve fuel requirements will be waived. A 10% fuel reserve is considered adequate.

- *Wright Field memo dated 27 March 1953*

---

their idea to bypass the larger aerospace companies (including Lockheed). They thought that this relatively small requirement would get more attention from smaller companies, so they chose Bell and Fairchild. Their superiors at the Air Research and Development Command (ARDC) in Baltimore agreed. In addition, Martin was asked to study a modification of its B-57 light jet bomber, with a larger wing and new engines. The three companies were asked to submit their studies by the end of the year. The codename for the project was Bald Eagle.[5]

Lamar and Seaberg called for an aircraft that could reach 70,000 feet and have a radius of 1,500 nautical miles. They conceded that certain standard military equipment, such as defensive armament and an ejection seat, would have to be eliminated. They hoped that a combination of low wing

The RB-45C (seen here refueling from a KB-29) was the USAF's first medium-range reconnaissance jet, but its maximum altitude was only 40,000 feet. (USAF).

loading and fast-improving turbojet engine technology would meet the requirement, rather than an utterly unconventional airframe. To provide that turbojet, Seaberg favored Pratt & Whitney, where Perry Pratt had designed the highest pressure-ratio engine yet available. It was designated the J57, and it had already been adopted for the B-52 bomber and the F-100 fighter. The J57 was the first 10,000 lbs thrust jet engine, and every pound of that thrust would be needed at 70,000 feet, where only some seven percent of an engine's sea-level thrust could be reproduced.

The Skunk Works

Carter returned to Burbank and wrote his memo to Root. Both newcomers to Lockheed, they soon became aware that the ideal group to work on an unconventional reconnaissance plane was right on their doorstep in Building 82. So the initiative was passed to Kelly Johnson and his Skunk Works.

The Skunk Works had been created in 1943 when Lockheed got the contract to build the P-80, America's first jet fighter. Johnson was a brilliant aeronautical engineer, who had managed to cream off the pick of the Burbank factory's engineering talent into an experimental department where design engineers, mechanics, and assembly workers would work closely together in a streamlined fashion, free from the constraints imposed by the wider company bureaucracy. The department was completely independent from the rest of Lockheed for purchasing and all other support functions.

Walled off from the rest of the plant, and only accessible to the select few staff, it was also a very secure method of building secret prototypes—it built the XP-80 in just 143 days. What on earth were Kelly and Co up to in there? A popular wartime comic strip featured a hairy and eccentric Indian who regularly stirred up a big brew, throwing in skunks, old shoes, and other unlikely raw material. With Johnson's secret shop situated right next to the plastics area, the Skunk Works nickname caught on. The official name for Johnson's operation was Advanced Development Projects (ADP).

In early 1954, the Skunk Works had just completed designing the XF-104, soon to be named the Starfighter. Having heard from U.S. pilots in Korea that speed and altitude were the paramount requirements if you wanted to hassle with MiGs, Johnson had sat down to design a Mach 2 plus hotrod fighter capable of reaching over 60,000 feet. To achieve this with the jet engines then available meant aiming for a gross weight as low as 15,000 lb. Through ruthless pruning of systems and the design of a very short, thin wing this had been achieved.

The CL-282

Johnson realized that the reconnaissance requirement outlined by Carter could be met by modifying the XF-104 fuselage and marrying it to a new high-aspect, low-thickness ratio wing. He set engineers Phil Coleman, Henry Combs, and Gene Frost to work.[6] By 5 March 1954 Johnson and his small team had designed the CL-282 high altitude aircraft. It promised a maximum altitude of 73,000 feet, which would be reached at the end of a cruise-climb from 65,000 feet. The radius of action would be 1,400 nautical miles, measured from the start of cruise-climb. Endurance was therefore more than seven hours. And yet this machine took off at a gross weight of only 13,768 lbs, including a 600 lb allowance for payload.[7]

Some key ideas that Carter had relayed from AFDAP, such as no undercarriage and low maneuver load factor/IAS, were embraced and developed by Johnson and his small team. The CL-282 would take off from a ground cart, and land on a skid attached to the lower fuselage. Otherwise,

Clarence "Kelly" Johnson, Lockheed's brilliant aeronautical engineer, was 44 when he started design of a high-flying reconnaissance aircraft in early 1954 (Lockheed AG2149).

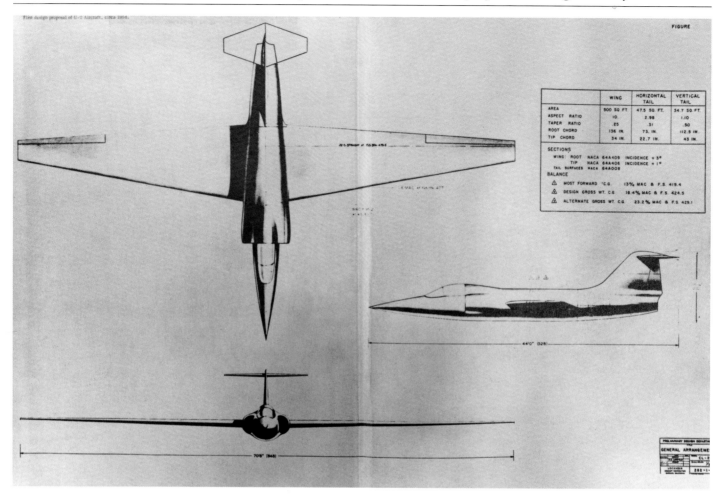

The CL-282 was Kelly Johnson's attempt to adapt the XF-104 for the spyplane requirement. A new, 70-foot wing was the key feature, along with radical weight saving ideas. In early 1955, the 'Angel' evolved from this design (from Lockheed Report LR9732).

The Skunk Works' name derived from a famous wartime comic strip. This logo was later derived from it, and became a trademark.

the fuselage was that of the XF-104 (minus a 62-inch forebody section), and so was the tail. But the engine was changed, from the General Electric J79 turbojet, which Johnson had chosen for the F-104, to the same company's J73-X52.[8] This was an interim engine derived from the first generation J47 that powered the B-47 and the F-86.[9]

The new wing was the key to the CL-282's promised performance. It bolted to the fuselage at ring-frames, with no carry-through structure, just like the XF-104. Wingspan was 70 feet, total area 500 sq feet, and aspect ratio was 10. Although a conventional two-cell construction, this wing boasted a Kelly Johnson innovation which he originally named Span Load Distribution Control. When flying at higher speeds, or in turbulent air, the wing control surfaces could be raised to the gust position (4-degrees for the flaps and 10-degrees for the ailerons). The effect was to reduce bending moments and tail loads by moving the wing center of pressure inboard. This allowed a much lighter wing structure, but one which could still cope with relatively turbulent air. This device—soon to be renamed Gust Control—would later be utilized extensively in transport aircraft.[10]

Rival Contenders

The CL-282 design study was sent to Bennie Schriever at the Pentagon in early March 1954. He was very interested, and requested a specific proposal from Johnson. A month later Johnson was in the Pentagon, promising to take complete responsibility for the program, including the produc-

The 115-ft wingspan of the Bell X-16 design is readily apparent on this model, placed next to an F-86 Sabre for comparison. Funded by the USAF, development of the X-16 was well underway when it was canceled in favor of the CIA's U-2. (via Jay Miller).

tion and field support of 30 airplanes. Two senior civilian officials at that meeting gave him a good reception, but the four USAF Generals present were not so enthusiastic.

They included Lt Gen Donald Putt, the outgoing commander of ARDC. By early April, Putt's staff at Wright Field had completed an evaluation of the industry studies that had been generated by the Bald Eagle request. Following John Seaberg's suggestion, all three contractors had adopted the Pratt & Whitney J57-P37 high altitude engine, and its development was already underway.

Martin had designed a larger wing for the B-57, and replaced its two Wright J65 turbojets with the J57s. Various weight-reducing measures were proposed, including honeycomb-backed skin panels on the wings, reduced spars and wing carry-through structure, and elimination of the flaps. Although this modified B-57 could not reach 70,000 ft, it would nevertheless be a quick and relatively cheap interim solution. Bell also built their Model 67 proposal round two wing-mounted J57s; theirs was a breathtakingly delicate and spindly machine with a super-slim fuselage for maximum drag reduction, and wings with an incredibly high aspect ratio of 12 for maximum lift. They were nearly 115 feet long—nine feet longer than the more conventional airfoil that Martin was proposing. Having decided that a single J57 could do the job, the Fairchild team opted for a much smaller wing, but their M-195 design featured a novel engine installation above and behind the cockpit. Weighing in at a little under 11,000 lbs empty, it was less than half the weight of the Bell.

But Seaberg and his colleagues at WADC could not bring themselves to approve a single-engine design. They picked Bell and Martin instead, and after briefing commanders at ARDC, SAC, and HQ USAF during April, they received immediate approval to proceed with the modified B-57.[11]

Meanwhile, the AFDAP staffers in the Pentagon tried to raise wider interest in Kelly Johnson's unsolicited proposal. They sent it to ARDC for formal evaluation, and briefed SAC commander General Curtis LeMay on their reconnaissance concepts in general, and the CL-282 in particular. LeMay perceived the AFDAP concept (which included the idea of establishing overflight operations in special, dedicated units) as a threat to SAC's primary military mission. He stomped out of the briefing, declaring "This is a bunch of shit! I can do all of that stuff with my B-36!"[12]

CL-282 Rejected

In early June 1954, HQ USAF wrote to Kelly Johnson rejecting the CL-282 because it was too unusual, only single-engined, and they were already committed to the Martin program.[13] This was apparently before ARDC had finished its formal evaluation of the CL-282. But Seaberg's group at Wright Field had reached a similar conclusion a few weeks later.

Colonel (later General) Bennie Schriever was receptive to the Lockheed proposal for a radical solution to the high-altitude reconnaissance requirement, but other USAF officers were not so keen (USAF).

And there the matter might have ended. The U-2 would never have been built, had it not been for a small group of original thinkers: a key civilian in the USAF's leadership; a leading CIA intelligence analyst; and that same group of scientists in the Boston area who had produced the Beacon Hill report. The key USAF civilian was Trevor Gardner, who had been personally appointed as Assistant Secretary of the Air Force for R&D by President Eisenhower. Gardner believed that the U.S. government should be far more concerned than it seemed to be over the threat of a surprise Soviet attack. He had been at the Pentagon meeting when Johnson presented the CL-282 and was impressed. Gardner also knew the business, since he was head of leading reconnaissance camera company Hycon in Pasadena, California, before coming to Washington.

The leading CIA analyst was Philip Strong, the operations chief within the Office of Scientific Intelligence (OSI). Working on the front line of the U.S. effort to gain knowledge of Soviet military developments, Strong was only too aware of how little was known. For instance, a top secret National Intelligence Estimate (NIE) on Soviet guided missile capabilities was full of uncertainties:

"...we have no evidence to confirm or deny current production...firm evidence on the present status of the Kapustin Yar test range is lacking...current intelligence on the particular missiles under development is almost non-existent...."[14]

THE TAXICAB THEORY

You might say that Dr. Land was not exactly an advocate of big government. In fact, he often said that he only believed in groups whose entire membership could fit in the back of a taxicab.

In 1954, Dr. Land put his taxicab theory to the test. Always security-conscious, he sought a secure environment in which to discuss which one of several aircraft prototypes could perform best at high altitude. So six gentlemen piled into a committee member's 1953 Ford. The group spent more than an hour driving through the city, listening to the great aircraft theorist Allen Donovan list the merits of Kelly Johnson's prototype.

- remarks by DCI William Webster at
award ceremony for Dr Land, 1988

And missiles were not the only problem; reports of a Soviet long-range jet bomber had first landed on Strong's desk the previous year. On 1 May 1954 the new bomber flew over Moscow during the Mayday parade, prompting public concern in the U.S. about the growing strategic threat.

The Boston Scientists
The group of mainly Boston-based scientists included Edwin Land, the founder of the Polaroid company; Jim Baker from Harvard University Ob-

Trevor Gardner (left, being sworn in as Assistant Secretary by Secretary of the Air Force Harold Talbott) was the key civilian official who pushed the Lockheed CL-282 design (USAF).

General Curtis LeMay was commander of SAC when the idea of devising a special reconnaissance aircraft and control system was first briefed to him in 1954. He said: "This is a bunch of shit! I can do all of that stuff with my B-36!" (USAF).

servatory; and Allen Donovan from Cornell Aeronautical Laboratory. Land was a widely respected and dynamic pioneer of many optical devices, as well as the inventor of the Polaroid instant camera. He had first been exposed to the airborne recon business as a member of the Beacon Hill study group. Baker was the nation's leading lens designer, and had played a key role in reconnaissance camera development going back to World War Two. Donovan was a bright aeronautical engineer who had refined Dick Leghorn's idea for a specialized aircraft during the Beacon Hill study.

In mid-1953 Baker, Donovan, Land, and a few others were invited to serve on an Intelligence Systems Panel (ISP), part of the USAF's Scientific Advisory Board. Phil Strong became associated, since he was brought in to advise the ISP of the yawning gaps in U.S. intelligence. Since Baker was chairman of the ISP, the USAF asked him to visit some aircraft companies and seek their views on high-altitude aircraft. Strangely, though, Baker was not asked to visit Bell, Fairchild, *or* Lockheed. Baker subsequently paid a long visit to Europe in early 1954, where he learned first hand of operational reconnaissance problems from USAF and RAF commanders.[15]

In mid-May 1954 Trevor Gardner and two colleagues invited Strong to the Pentagon, briefing him on the CL-282 and the Bald Eagle designs. They asked him if the CIA would throw its weight behind the project. Strong discussed the designs with the ISP. Donovan thought the B-57 would be far too heavy; he strongly believed that a single-engined design was vital. Baker suggested that Donovan visit Lockheed to learn more about the CL-282. Donovan was not able to make the trip until early August 1954, when he was briefed by Root and Johnson.[16]

The Land Panel

By that time, the impatient Gardner had managed to energize the Eisenhower administration into commissioning a top-level panel of experts to study the surprise attack issue. It became known as the Technological Capabilities Panel (TCP), and James Killian, the president of MIT, was chosen as its chairman. As an offshoot of the President's own Science Advisory Committee, the TCP members and staff worked in the Executive Office. The TCP reported directly to Eisenhower, and had great authority. Killian subdivided the task into three projects: offensive, defensive, and intelligence

Above: Jim Baker was the Harvard astronomer and expert in optics who served on the Land Panel and conceived the U-2's extraordinary B-camera (James Baker via Cargill Hall). Left: Edwin Land was a brilliant scientist whose drive and vision forged the Polaroid Company and made him a natural choice as a top-level advisor to the US government. More than anyone else, he ensured that the U-2 was actually built (Polaroid Corporate Archive).

capabilities. He invited fellow Bostonian Din Land onto his steering committee, and asked him to head up the intelligence project within the TCP. In turn, Land selected this project's membership, including Jim Baker and physics Nobel Laureate Ed Purcell from Harvard. They became known as the Land Panel.[17]

As soon as Land arrived in Washington on TCP duties Phil Strong approached him with drawings of the CL-282, and told the story of how it had been rejected by the USAF. Strong was lobbying for a flight over Kapustin Yar at this time, but the USAF said it couldn't be done. CIA director Allen Dulles was not very supportive, either. Land intuitively agreed with Strong's frustration. He believed in taking "a clean fresh look at the old, old knowledge." Land saw that Johnson had done just that with the CL-282. He also saw the merit of Leghorn's idea from way back, that such an unconventional plane should also be operated in an unconventional way. Land's innovative mind began to consider alternatives to the standard *modus operandi* of the military services.[18]

Two engines - or one?
In early September, Donovan and Baker paid a visit to Bell Aircraft's Niagara Falls facility to discuss the Model 67.[19] That same month, ARDC designated this aircraft the X-16, and issued a contract for 28 aircraft. But Donovan was unimpressed. He discounted the safety factor that was implied by twin engines. If one engine failed at high altitude during the mission, he noted, the cruise could only be maintained at a lower altitude. There, Donovan argued, the aircraft would be easy prey for Soviet fighters. Donovan still preferred the CL-282, which promised the same or better performance at almost one-third the gross weight.[20]

Land was now lobbying aggressively for the Lockheed plane, and also consulting widely to ensure that it carried the best possible sensor systems. He encouraged Jim Baker to pursue his innovative ideas for reducing camera size and weight, and brought in Richard Perkin of Perkin-Elmer for further advice. Land also persuaded Kodak to continue development of a new plastic film base named Mylar. Because it was so much thinner than existing film bases, a sufficient quantity for long-duration flights could be carried without too great a weight penalty. Land's panel also investigated electronic sensors, with a view to equipping a small high-flyer with a useful signals intelligence (SIGINT) payload.

In October 1954 Baker was sent to Burbank for a detailed discussion on the camera payload weights and bulk. Kelly Johnson fought to keep down both. Every pound added meant two feet of altitude lost, he reminded Baker. The lensman had three different camera configurations in mind: a conventional trimetrogen mapping camera; multiple reconnaissance cameras with focal lengths from 12 to 48 inches in rocking mounts; and a 180-inch design with folded optics for the most detailed coverage of specific targets. The latter was particularly difficult to accommodate in the CL-282's small fuselage.[21]

Land knew that one particular USAF objection to Johnson's plane was the engine. He summoned Perry Pratt and asked him to describe P&W's high-altitude version of the J57. Pratt told how they were modifying the J57's alternator, oil cooler, hydraulic pump, and other key parts. But Johnson was most reluctant to give up the single-shaft GE powerplant, which was

Pratt & Whitney developed a high-altitude version of the J57, and Kelly Johnson was eventually persuaded that it should power the U-2 (via Jay Miller).

almost 1,000 lbs lighter. He knew that changing to the J57 would entail a complete redesign of the CL-282 fuselage, and abandoning the plan to quickly produce it on existing XF-104 jigs.

The CIA as sponsor
By late October 1954, Land's group had not only concluded that the radi-

President Eisenhower gave the go-ahead for development of the secret high-altitude spyplane on 24 November 1954, and approved Din Land's suggestion that it be operated by the CIA, not the Air Force.

cal CL-282 design must be built, they had also made the equally radical decision that its development and operation should *not* be entrusted to the USAF. Together with Trevor Gardner, they met Director of Central Intelligence (DCI) Allen Dulles and suggested that he should sponsor the aircraft. Dulles was dubious; he saw the CIA as an espionage and analysis agency that should not become involved with a major technical development effort such as this. On 5 November, Land wrote to Dulles on behalf of TCP project 3, insisting that "overflight is urgent and presently feasible." With typical *chutzpah*, Land urged Dulles to exercise the CIA's "right" to pioneer scientific techniques for collecting intelligence. The military should not "engage directly in extensive overflight," a task more suited to the CIA which, "as a civilian organization [could] undertake (with the Air Force's assistance) a covert program of selected flights."[22]

Although the TCP was not due to report to the President for another three months, James Killian agreed with Din Land on the urgency of the overflight requirement. The pair went to see President Eisenhower, who asked many hard questions, but endorsed the Land group's approach.[23]

Events now moved quickly. On 18 November General Donald Putt, who had moved up from ARDC to become Deputy Chief of Staff for Development, brought John Seaberg to the Pentagon from Wright Field to brief the TCP scientists on the USAF perspective. Seaberg grudgingly conceded that the Lockheed design was "aerodynamically close" to the Bell and Fairchild designs that he had sponsored. But he insisted that the J73 "would not be good enough to do the job in Kelly's airplane."[24]

Summoned by Trevor Gardner, Kelly Johnson arrived the next day to meet General Putt in the presence of Land's group. Johnson dispelled any lingering doubts the scientists may have had. He reluctantly agreed to re-engine his CL-282 with the J57 engine, and to rethink the lack of a landing gear. At lunch the same day, with Secretary of the Air Force Harold Talbott, DCI Dulles, and his deputy, Lt Gen Pierre Cabell, Johnson was asked how his company could commit to such a tight timescale, when others dared not. "He's already proved it three times on previous projects," Putt intervened. The group told Johnson to go ahead, and emphasized the need for extreme secrecy.[25]

Johnson flew back to California and gained the approval of Lockheed president Robert Gross. While Johnson worked on the redesign, Dulles called a meeting of the U.S. Intelligence Board to ratify the project.[26]

At 8 am on 24 November 1954, Dulles, Cabell, Putt, and Talbott, together with the Secretaries of State and Defense, assembled before President Eisenhower to seek his formal authority to proceed. Ike gave the go-ahead, and told them to report back when the plane was ready for operations. Amazingly, that would be just 17 months later, exactly as Kelly Johnson had promised.

2

Design and Development

Within hours of gaining Presidential approval, DCI Dulles turned the new project over to his Special Assistant for Planning and Co-Ordination, Richard M. Bissell. "RMB"— a brilliant economics professor from Yale and MIT whom Dulles had persuaded to join the CIA the previous February—turned out to be an excellent choice. Although his background was pure East Coast establishment, Bissell had an informal and unorthodox style of management that suited similar spirits like Gardner and Johnson. Although not a scientist or engineer, he was able to quickly assimilate and evaluate technical matters.

Din Land's group of civilian experts continued as important advisors. Assisted by Herb Miller—an Agency specialist on Soviet nuclear programs who became his executive officer—Bissell quickly organized the Development Project Staff (DPS) in one of the old wartime buildings on the "little hill" near the Lincoln Memorial. The DPS reported directly to Dulles, and even within the CIA, its existence was kept on a strict need-to-know basis. The same rules applied at the Pentagon, where R&D chief Don Putt selected Colonel Ozzie Ritland as the USAF's liaison officer to DPS.[1]

On the first working day after Thanksgiving 1954, Kelly Johnson nominated Dick Boehme as his chief assistant for the new project, and together they chose 24 engineers for the detailed design work. The engineers were put on a 45-hour week, and instructed not to tell anyone what they were doing—not even their closest relatives. Johnson had promised to have the first aircraft flying in eight months, but had also been pressured into a significant redesign. Compared with the CL-282, the airframe would have to be scaled up. In consequence, the gross weight would rise, and thus threaten the altitude performance. Johnson said he would trade his grandmother for a 10 pound savings in weight! In the Skunk Works, pounds became known as "grandmothers," as his designers struggled to eliminate every unnecessary ounce.

Who-Does-What

In mid-December Johnson again flew East. In a series of meetings in the Pentagon, a who-does-what agreement was thrashed out. Lockheed's offer to assume total project responsibility was not taken up. The CIA would contract separately for the aircraft, the payloads, and some specialized systems, and the USAF would divert the required number of J57 engines. The CIA would be responsible for communications and security, the USAF for pilot training and logistics. An existing agreement, whereby military personnel were assigned for tours with the CIA's Air Maritime Division for secret covert operations, was extended to cover the new project.[2]

Johnson presented his estimate of $22.5 million to produce, flight test, and support the first six airplanes. He then flew on to the Pratt & Whitney plant at Hartford, CT, where chief engineer Bill Gwynn and his assistant, Wright Parkins, briefed him on the -37 version of the J57, which they were developing for the RB-57D and the X-16. Johnson bluntly told them that its fuel consumption was too high, and its thrust at 70,000 feet—which would be only seven percent of the sea-level value—was too low. In exasperation, Johnson suggested towing his aircraft partway to altitude.[3] But then Perry Pratt promised to make further improvements in a second

Richard Bissell stands close to an enduring symbol of the Cold War, Berlin's Brandenberg Gate. Bissell ran the U-2 project at the CIA, bringing his formidable intellect and management skills to bear (via Frances Pudlo).

> THE AIR FORCE COULD NOT HAVE DONE IT
>
> There was one aspect of the decision with which I disagreed. That was acceptance by the CIA of the leading responsibility for the project. I considered that the Air Force should lead the development phase.... If we were to try it, we would have to duplicate, at least in a small way, a development and procurement structure similar to that of the Air Force.
>
> Dulles overruled my misgivings, and I am glad that he did. Complete success was achieved in the development under our leadership.... I am quite sure that such a degree of security would not have been maintained under standard, or even modified Air Force procurement practices.
>
> *- DDCI General Charles Cabell, "Memoirs of War, Peace and the CIA", Impavide Publications, Colorado Springs, 1997, p318*

high-altitude version of the J57 specifically for the Lockheed plane. It would have higher thrust and lower weight, and be designated the J57-P-31.

Johnson hurried back to Burbank for the initial wind tunnel tests. He pushed his engineers hard. Each specialty was handled by only one or two men, who were trusted to make the right decisions. Under the pressure of time, normally distinct phases of design, tooling, and fabrication were to be merged if necessary. When data was not yet available, inspired estimates would be made.[4]

Design Detail and Changes

In early January, Johnson finally came up with a weight-saving design for the landing gear. The landing skid was abandoned, but not in favor of a conventional undercarriage. Instead, a bicycle-style single main gear and small tail gear would be provided on the centerline. To maintain balance on the ground, compressed rubber wheels on sprung steel legs would protrude from the wing. They would drop out upon takeoff. For landing, a skid was added to each wingtip to protect the airfoil as the aircraft came to rest. The total weight was 250 lbs, only one-third that of a conventional gear for an aircraft of this size.[5]

By the end of January the major drawings were finished. The emerging aircraft was a clever blend of innovation and conservatism. Construction would be mostly aluminum, with the bare minimum of stringers and other forms of structural stiffening, and the skin was wafer-thin—only 0.020 of an inch around the nose, and nowhere thicker than 0.063. Skin panels were to be flush riveted, and the control surfaces would be aerodynamically balanced, with virtually no gap at the hinge point. To save weight in the hydraulic system, none of the primary flight controls were boosted.

Ed Baldwin led the fuselage design. Bifurcated intakes fed the single engine, which Baldwin located at the wing mid-chord for balance. That imperative forced him to place Kelly's single main landing gear between the inlets; further forward than desirable, and posing a significant future challenge for pilots seeking to land the aircraft safely. Ahead of the main gear was a pressurized area for the reconnaissance payloads which was known initially as the equipment bay, and later as the "Q-bay." Ed Martin devised the system, whereby these payloads would be attached to pallets, the pallets mounted on interchangeable hatches, and the hatches fitted flush to the lower fuselage. Another large detachable hatch fitted the top of the payload bay; when both hatches were removed a huge gap in the fuselage

> GETTING STARTED
>
> *6 December 1954*: Cryptonym AQUATONE is assigned to the CL-282 project under Mr.Bissell's direction
> *27 December*: A letter from Mr Trevor Gardner to the DCI promises that the Air Force will furnish jet engines for the CL-282 aircraft
> *29 December*: The Bureau of the Budget approves withdrawal of $35 million from the CIA Contingency Reserve for aircraft and equipment
> *3 January 1955*: Letter contract with Lockheed is signed by General C.P. Cabell (in alias) for the CIA
> *14 January*: Summary of plans and specifications for the photo equipment is presented by Dr. James Baker, Professor of Physics, Harvard University, and a member of the Land Technological Capabilities Panel
> *26 January*: First cover story is promulgated
> *7 February*: Director of the FBI J. Edgar Hoover is briefed. Los Angeles FBI office assigns espionage squad officers to monitor Lockheed Burbank plant
> *2 March*: Definitive contract is signed with Lockheed for 20 aircraft
>
> *- extracts from a CIA Chronology written in 1969*

DISCLOSURE OF INVENTION

PATENT DEPARTMENT
LOCKHEED AIRCRAFT CORPORATION
BURBANK, CALIFORNIA

1. TITLE OF INVENTION Droppable Stabilizing Gear for Aircraft.

2. SKETCH (where necessary) AND DESCRIPTION OF PROCESS OR METHOD OF OPERATION
(Also list and identify herein all attached drawings and descriptions)

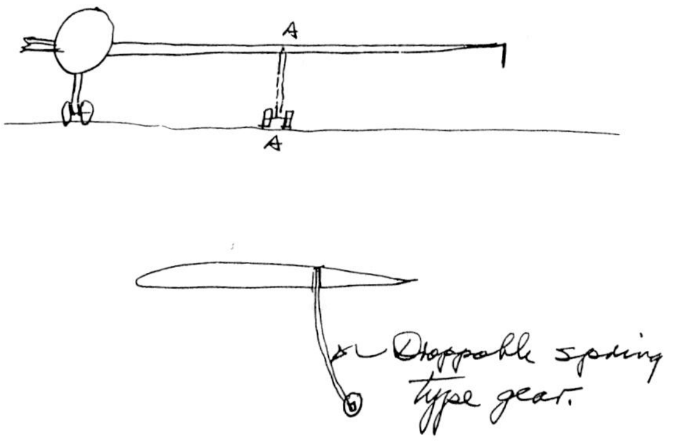

3. PURPOSE of the invention To provide lateral stabilizing for aircraft landing gear for take-off only. By dropping units on take-off (on ground or air) the overall gear wt. can be reduced.

SHOWN and DESCRIBED to me/us on this 7TH day of SEPTEMBER, 1955
Henry Combs
[illegible]
Witnesses' Signatures

14. I (we) hereby certify that, to the best of my (our) knowledge, I am (we are) the first and original inventor(s) of the subject matter hereinbefore described.
SIGNED this 6 day of Sept. 1955
Employee No. 46150
Clarence Johnson Dept. A-1
Inventor's Signature

Kelly Johnson's novel solution to weight-saving, as applied to the Article's undercarriage, is seen here in the patent application that he made for "Droppable Stabilizing Gear for Aircraft." Later, these outriggers were named "pogos."

was apparent, since the cockpit and nose section was supported only by the mid-fuselage spar.[6]

The cockpit was the only part of the fuselage that retained the XF-104 structure. It was therefore very small, and dominated by a large control yoke more typical of a bomber or transport aircraft. The control cables were directly linked to this large yoke, on which was mounted a half-wheel to control the ailerons. The otherwise conventional instrument panel was dominated by the hooded, six-inch display from a driftsight, which Perkin Elmer would provide. Basically a downward-looking periscope, this driftsight allowed pilots to view the scene beneath their aircraft. It had a scanning prism within a nitrogen-purged glass bubble that protruded from the lower fuselage. There was no ejection seat, nor automatic canopy jettison. Pilots in trouble would have to open the canopy themselves before bailing out.

The CL-282's T-tail was replaced by a conventional tail section, to be constructed as a single assembly, including the rear fuselage. This was attached to the forward fuselage by just three 5/8-inch tension bolts. The size of the wing meant placing the tail further aft, and the fuselage was lengthened to 50 feet. But Kelly's gust control innovation reduced the tail loads and allowed a lighter structure.

Bob Wiele did the detail wing design after Johnson specified the section, the limit load factor (still 2.5g), and the aspect ratio (10.67). Compared with the CL-282, the result was a 20% increase in wing area to 600 sq ft, and a 10-foot increase in wingspan to 80 feet. The drawing reached the edge of the boards before the wingtips could be added! The wing had a three-spar construction, but the conventional rib stiffeners were replaced by an unusual lattice-work of aluminum tubing.[7]

The bigger wing allowed more fuel, which was carried in four integral wing tanks, feeding to a fuselage sump tank. The total of 1,335 gallons stretched the aircraft's endurance and range impressively, to 10 hours and over 4,000 nautical miles. The pilot had a fuel quantity gauge for the sump tank only—no indication of how much fuel had been used from the wing tanks. He had to rely on a simple subtractive-type fuel counter that showed him how much was left (in gallons), backed up by a warning light that came on when only 50 gallons remained.

But which fuel to use? At high altitude, the low air pressure would cause the more volatile portions of standard jet kerosene to boil away through the tank vents. After seeking advice from NACA and Colonel Norm Appold at WADC, Johnson turned to General Jimmy Doolittle, who had served on the TCP steering committee and was a board member of the

The innovative design of the wing included "gust control" to allow a much lighter structure than normal. In his patent application, Kelly Johnson named this feature "Span Load Distribution Control."

Colonel Ozzie Ritland was the Pentagon's first liaison officer to the U-2 project, and soon became Richard Bissell's deputy at the CIA itself. Upon promotion in May 1956, he returned to the USAF, much to the dismay of Bissell and Kelly Johnson (AFFTC History Office).

KELLY JOHNSON

There have been many words written about the famous boss of the Skunk Works. Here are some views from Leo Geary, the Colonel who for 10 years from 1956 was the main liaison between the USAF, CIA, and Lockheed; and from Richard Bissell, Project Director:

I probably knew him as well as anyone. Everyone stood in awe of him. But Kelly was very self-critical, so he also questioned the abilities of those around him. Those who were afraid of him didn't understand him. Because if you stood your ground, and won the argument, you sometimes won a quarter from him. Actually, if people were not willing to stand their ground, he did not want them. In some respects, he was a soft-hearted chicken. I have sat down and wept with him, and fought with him on another occasion.

- interview with author

I have paid my tributes to Kelly Johnson as an engineer and organizer. But in addition to that he proved to be, at least in his relationship with me, a remarkable teacher. I started on this project utterly ignorant of engineering and utterly ignorant of anything to do with aviation. And Kelly was articulate enough that, within a year or so, a little engineering had rubbed off on me, at least enough so that I could understand what he was saying in technical discussions.

- Richard Bissell, remarks at AIAA meeting, May 1978

Colonel Leo Geary was in charge of USAF liaison to the CIA's air operations for an unprecedented 10 years (1956-1966). He helped choose the pilots, supply the engines, organize the logistics support, and push for new developments, such as the A-12 (NARA).

Shell Oil company. The famous wartime pilot got Shell to adapt the low vapor pressure kerosene that was used in cigarette lighters as a new jet fuel. It was designated LF-1A. Later, the USAF developed its own specification for a special U-2 fuel, which was designated JP-TS (for Thermally Stable).[8]

The plane did not have a name yet. It was Lockheed model number 185, but the engineers referred to it obliquely as the Article. However, Kelly Johnson began calling it the Angel, since he expected this unique design to soar so close to heaven!

A new pressure suit

Then there was the need to protect the pilot. The new aircraft would be cruising at least 20-30,000 feet above Armstrong's Line, at altitudes where body fluids would start to boil if cockpit pressure was lost. Kelly Johnson's original CL-282 had no cockpit pressurisation at all. The pilot would have to fly the whole mission in an inflated pressure suit! This concept was quickly abandoned. The cockpit would be pressurised to 25-30,000 feet—it could not be a lower value without beefing up the structure and adding more weight.

Bg Gen Don Flickenger, ARDC's expert in pilot protection, was summoned to Trevor Gardner's office in the Pentagon. Flickenger explained that the newly-developed partial pressure suits provided a "get me down" protection until the aircraft reached a physiologically safe altitude of about 10,000 feet. Gardner told him that get-me-down protection wasn't good enough for the long-endurance flights over denied territory that this plane would be flying! Flickenger reckoned it would take three to five years to improve the suits. Gardner gave him 10 months.

The General set to work with the Aeromedical Laboratory at Wright Field, the Lovelace Foundation at Albuquerque, and his favorite pressure suit contractor. This was the David Clark Company in Worcester, MA, which also manufactured some of the nation's finest brassieres and corsets! Flickenger told David Clark to produce a suit that could be worn for up to 12 hours uninflated, and for four hours if it inflated following a cockpit pressurization failure. Clark turned the detailed design work over to his pressure suit specialist, Joe Ruseckas.[9]

Engine troubles

That unforgiving high altitude regime was troubling Pratt & Whitney. They had to produce a powerplant which would be safely operated at the limit of EGT (Exhaust Gas Temperature) for not only takeoff and climb, but also for an eight or nine hour cruise. In early February, Wright Parkins told Kelly Johnson they wanted to abandon the higher thrust, lower-weight -31. Wouldn't the -37 suffice instead? A furious Johnson insisted they continue. He had accepted the -37 as an interim engine for early flight tests only. Johnson had assigned Elmer Gath to engine integration, with Ben Rich doing the inlet design. They were producing a near-perfect ram air distribution within the duct, to ensure the maximum delivery of thin upper air to the compressor face. P&W ploughed on with the -31. They decided to improve the oil seals, halve the oil tank size, and re-examined the oil cooler, alternator and hydraulic pump. They would forge the turbine blades instead of casting them.[10]

Tony LeVier (left), Lockheed's chief test pilot for the F-104, was chosen by Kelly Johnson to fly the U-2 prototype. "I switched from flying the plane with the shortest wings in the world, to the one with longest!" he said (Lockheed AL8068).

Developing the sensors

Not far from Burbank, in Pasadena, CA, a special team led by Bill McFadden began work on the new aircraft's cameras at Hycon—Trevor Gardner's old company. Land's group had recommended that they start by improving some standard USAF K-38 cameras, which had 24-inch focal lengths and exposed 9 x 18-inch frames of film. These were improved by adding thermal stabilization, lightweight barrels, and pre-focused lenses. The film magazines were modified to accept up to 1,800 feet of Kodak's new mylar-based film. In a configuration designated A-1, one of these improved 24-inch cameras would be flown in a rocking mount for medium-scale coverage, alongside three 6-inch wide-angle mapping cameras in a standard trimetrogen arrangement. A second configuration, designated A-2, consisted of three of the 24-inch cameras looking left and right at 37 degrees,

and vertically down. Thanks to the new film, a complete A-2 rig with enough film for a 3,000-mile flight with stereo overlap weighed only 339 lbs.[11]

The real innovation, though, would be the B-camera. By early 1955, Jim Baker had revised his earlier ideas in favor of a unique configuration that violated many of the current rules of the recce business. It combined the area coverage of a panoramic camera with the definition required for target analysis. Hitherto, only large fixed-focal length cameras had been able to provide the latter. A 36-inch focal length lens, together with the lens cone, shutter, and mirror, would rotate to any one of seven overlapping "stop-and-shoot" positions from horizon to horizon. The positions overlapped so that the photo-interpreters could perform stereo measurement. The lens aperture was set at f10 to ensure reliable pre-set focusing at very high altitude. A single swiveling mirror replaced the usual, but much heavier, prism. Two huge film magazines carried 9.5 x 18-inch film, which would wind from opposite directions and be simultaneously exposed to produce an 18 x 18 negative. The contra-winding idea was good news for Kelly Johnson; it meant that the camera's center of gravity remained unchanged through the flight, despite using up to 6,500 feet of film from each magazine. The B-camera weighed 577lbs when this amount of film was carried, but if only 4,000ft of film was loaded on each magazine, a reduction to 484lbs weight was achieved.[12]

Baker turned the concept over to Hycon for detailed design and engineering development. Meanwhile, he began work on the lenses for both A and B camera configurations under a subcontract from Perkin Elmer. Rod Scott of Perkin Elmer devised a 70mm tracking camera by scaling down a 48-inch panoramic camera design. The "tracker" would operate throughout the flight, and its comprehensive (though small-scale) coverage would help the photo-interpreters place the images provided by the 24- and 36-inch lenses in their geographic context.[13]

Baker pioneered the use of computer programs to calculate the optimum lens curvatures and spacings. He used Harvard University's IBM Current Program Calculator, but had to work on it overnight, in order to preserve secrecy. As a result, the Land group's ambitious goal for photo-

The prototype "Angel" or "Article" stands on the hastily-laid tarmac at the Ranch. The strange new plane had been flying for three months before it was formally designated as the U-2 (Lockheed 84-CC-3284).

graphic resolution of 60 line-pairs per millimeter was often achieved once the B-camera went into service. From 60,000 feet, it could resolve objects on the ground as small as 75cm (2.5 feet) across.

At the same time, Baker continued design work on the very long focal length, or C-camera. He argued with Kelly Johnson over the amount of space in the equipment bay that could be allocated to the C's 180-inch folding optics. The aircraft designer wanted more room for batteries and other support equipment. Development of the C-camera fell behind schedule, and it was eventually realized that the A and B camera systems were more than adequate to the task (The prototype C-camera was turned over to the USAF, but was never used operationally).

Land and the TCP had recommended from the outset that the aircraft carry signals intelligence sensors as well as cameras. The task was allocated to Dr. Burt Miller at Ramo-Wooldridge. This was the Los Angeles corporation, recently founded by two former Hughes electronic engineers, that Trevor Gardner had nominated to project-manage the nation's urgent ICBM and satellite developments. (Gen Bennie Schriever, whose AFDAP shop had been instrumental in defining the new spyplane requirement, had transferred to the West Coast to take charge of this effort in mid-1954).

Ramo-Wooldridge faced the same type of challenge as Hycon: they had to radically reduce the size and weight of airborne sensing equipment, and make it run autonomously for up to nine hours. Miller came up with a miniaturized ELINT (electronic intelligence) system that would cover the S-, C-, and X-bands used by Soviet radars. It would determine PRF (Pulse Repetition Frequency) and scan rate, and fit inside the aircraft's nose. The tape recorder used a new type of thin, 1/4-inch tape that was subsequently used in the first mass-market tape recorders.

The wind tunnel tests were completed in early February 1955, and by late March fabrication were well underway, managed by Art Viereck. He used the big presses in Lockheed's main production factory at night, and removed the secret aircraft's parts to the Skunk Works in Building 82 before the dayshift arrived.

Johnson summoned Tony LeVier from Lockheed's new Palmdale facility, where he was working as chief test pilot for the XF-104. LeVier

The first flight of the U-2, with Tony LeVier at the controls. (The image is taken from the film "The Inquisitive Angel" that was made by the CIA in 1957).

ageed to test-fly the Angel before Johnson would reveal the details. When he finally did so, LeVier declared that Kelly was switching him from flying the plane with the shortest wings in the world, to the one with the longest! Johnson then told LeVier and Skunk Works' logistics specialist Dorsey Kammerer to find a remote base where the new aircraft could be flown. The government did not want it tested at Edwards or Palmdale, in full public gaze.

LeVier and Kammerer took the Skunk Works' Beech Bonanza, made a two-week aerial survey of the remote deserts of southern California and Nevada, and came up with a shortlist. None of them appealed to Bissell or Ritland. In mid-April, LeVier flew them and Johnson up to the most likely sites near the Nevada test range. Ritland was already familiar with the area, since he had flown all over it during his previous assignment with the B-29 test squadron that dropped nuclear weapons there. He directed LeVier towards an old World War II airfield that he remembered, just north of the test range and next to the Groom Dry Lake. "We didn't even get a clearance, but flew over it, and within 30 seconds we knew it was *the* place," Ritland said later. They landed on the lakebed. Johnson liked the site, but feared it would prove impossible to get it cleared with the Atomic Energy Commission (AEC).[14]

Ritland took quick care of that, and worked similar miracles from his one-man office in the Pentagon whenever USAF roadblocks had to be cleared.[15] In June he was joined by reconnaissance specialist Col Russ Berg and Lt Col Leo Geary. The latter had previously been responsible for USAF support to the Agency's Air Maritime Division, and was therefore already familiar with the secret world. Over at DPS, meanwhile, Bissell appointed Jim Cunningham as the executive officer. He was a former Marine Corps pilot who had proved to be a smart administrator of various covert projects since joining the CIA. Cunningham and Geary would do the same jobs for the next 10 years, providing valuable continuity and a wealth of experience.[16]

The early U-2 cockpit with its basic flight instruments, and the large yoke and control wheel. The rubber sighting cone for the combined driftsight/sextant is prominent at top (Lockheed PR1627).

Such was the pace of the project, that paperwork always struggled to catch up. Lockheed had been working for two months before it sent a contract to the government! At one stage, Kelly Johnson took out a $3 million bank loan to cover production costs when the CIA's payments fell behind schedule.[17] To preserve secrecy, the CIA's payment checks were made out to "The C & J Manufacturing Company" and sent to Kelly Johnson's home address. Subcontractors also dealt with this "front" company, making deliveries to an unmarked warehouse in downtown Burbank so that their work could not be associated with Lockheed.

There wasn't much paperwork, actually. The monthly progress reports were kept short; unlike regular military business, there were no teams of plant representatives sent in to second-guess the contractors. Bissell told Johnson:

"When you face a decision, I want to know about it and pass judgement. But I rely on you to tell me the potential consequences and costs."

In this atmosphere of trust and dedication the program moved smartly ahead. As it transpired, Lockheed underspent on the first contract worth $22.5 million, which covered the 20 aircraft for the CIA. The corporation returned $2 million to the government, meaning that these airframes cost only just over $1 million each!

In early May, Herb Miller issued contracts from DPS worth $0.8 million for construction of the secret base. Johnson had promised to fly the prototype in August, and doubted whether the base would be ready by then. Washington had turned Kammerer's plan for a small, temporary facility into a larger, permanent facility with a runway, control tower, mess hall, and three hangars. But they were starting from scratch in that desert wasteland: no roads, no water, and no power. With some irony, Johnson named the place Paradise Ranch.[18]

Oilstone and Aquatone

By the third week in May, the prototype "Article" was out of the jigs. But the wing was way behind schedule; aileron design was not yet finished. Johnson put almost everybody on it, and worried about bending instability.[19] He appointed Ernie Joiner to run the flight test program, and sent his contract for Lockheed's role in the subsequent training and deployment phases to the CIA. Cunningham arrived at Burbank to begin the strict security checks on those engineers who had volunteered to go on the deployments.

By late June, it became apparent that the respective roles of the CIA and the USAF in this enterprise needed formal definition. Bissell and Ritland flew to SAC headquarters to brief General LeMay. When LeMay realized how much the regular USAF had been cut out of the loop, he was furious. So was General Thomas Power, the commander of ARDC, when Gardner and Putt briefed him into the project. LeMay and Power enlisted the support of USAF Chief of Staff Nathan Twining and forced a showdown.

The meeting was held in Colorado Springs in early July 1955. CIA Director Dulles and Secretary of the Air Force Harold Talbott rejected LeMay's bid to run the operational phase, and reaffirmed the basic division of responsibilities. But the powerful general insisted that SAC help select the pilots, run the training program, and staff some key operational slots within DPS. The agreement was finally signed by USAF CINC General Twining and DCI Allen Dulles on 3-4 August. The codename for USAF support of the program was changed from Shoehorn to Oilstone. The CIA

was using the cryptonym Aquatone. The secret aircraft still did not have a proper name or designation.[20]

Finish It!

Johnson returned from a short vacation to lead a terrific drive to finish the airplane. Building 82 was working round-the-clock. In early July the static test airframe was ready. Henry Combs, Dick Hruda, and Ray McHenry had done the stress analysis, fuselage landing gear, and wing, respectively. Had they set the correct limit load requirements, or had too much been sacrificed in the desperate quest for altitude? John Henning managed the static tests, and the critical load limits were proved by the end of the month.

CHOOSING GROOM LAKE

The location chosen for flight tests of the U-2 had to be remote, if the secret was to be kept. Lockheed test pilot Tony Levier often claimed that he "discovered" and recommended the location deep in the deserts of Nevada. In fact, it was Colonel Ozzie Ritland who found it:

Kelly had Tony search the western part of the U.S. and make a survey of 50 different airports. Dick Bissell and I reviewed them one day, and none of them looked very good. I told them, "I know a place, and I'll take you up to it." So we got in the Beech Bonanza, and Tony flew Kelly, Dick, and myself up to the area.

We didn't even get an AEC clearance—we went in low. And I went to this little X-shaped field that I had flown over when we dropped the bomb. I'd spent enough time over there.

We flew over it, and within 30 seconds you knew that was the place, because it was a stretched-out thing in the sand, and it was right by a lake. Man alive, we looked at that lake, and we looked at each other. It was another Edwards, so we wheeled around, landed on that lake, taxied up to one end of it, and Kelly Johnson said, "We'll put it right here, that's the hangar."

- USAF Oral History Interview K239.0512-722, March 1974

THE PROCUREMENT PROCESS

In January 1955, Kelly Johnson and CIA General Counsel Lawrence Houston sat down to talk specifics. Instead of giving Lockheed a list of technical specifications, the CIA handed over a list of performance specs. It did not care what the plane looked like, only what it could do.

Johnson opened the negotiations at $26-27 million per plane. Houston responded: "That's too much, I only have $22 million to spend!" The two men dickered for a while and reached a compromise. They set $22 million as the target price. If it looked like Lockheed's costs were running higher, the CIA would simply cut Lockheed's profit percentage. If the planes came in below $22 million, the CIA would raise the company's profit margin. That way, Lockheed had an incentive to save money.

Lockheed delivered all 19 planes as ordered, $3 million below the contract price and $8 million below the estimate.

- article in CIA Studies in Intelligence, Spring 1986, as reported by The Washington Post, 24 July 1988 page C-7

Bob Schumacher was one of four Lockheed pilots who conducted most of the U-2 test flights in 1955-56. He recalled the place they called the Ranch:

It was in the middle of nowhere. I was impressed. There were three T-hangars there, that's all. You could put one airplane in each, with the tail sticking out. We did a lot of maintenance in the open. They had a couple of small dormitories, but the pilots were in a trailer, and there was an eating area with a couple of pool tables at the far end for the evenings. There was one road going out, but we were not supposed to use it. Working away from home was the hardest part. I had a wife and small kids. We would go up Monday morning and get home late Friday or Saturday. Jacky really did not know much about it, other than it was high altitude. I believe Tony Levier told her that.

- interview with the author

The horizontal tail had to be beefed up a little, but the basic design passed the test.[21]

Between 17 and 21 July Johnson made a detailed inspection of the prototype. Three days later, Ritland arrived from Washington to witness loading of the now-disassembled article into a C-124 transport, which would fly it to Paradise Ranch. As part of the contract, Lockheed had designed two wheeled ground carts so that the Article could be easily airfreighted. One carried the aft fuselage, wings, and tail surfaces. The other was adapted from the original CL-282 take-off dolly design, and it carried the forward fuselage, complete with the installed engine. Much of the airplane maintenance could be carried out while it was on these carts, which had self-contained hydraulic and electrical systems.

Secret Base

Incredibly, the secret base in the Nevada desert was at least semi-complete. Herb Miller had organized a large team of construction crews via the Atomic Energy Commission, and they had also worked round-the-clock. The tarmac runway had just been laid. Newly-appointed base commander Dick Newton clashed with Johnson over whether it was ready to accept the heavy C-124. As usual, Johnson won the argument. The Article was flown in, unloaded, wheeled into a semi-complete hangar, and re-assembled.[22]

Soon the Article was ready for engine runs. But the J57 would not start with the special fuel. The ground crew found some five-gallon drums containing JP-4, linked them together, and ran a hose from them into a fuel valve in the J57. Then they lit the engine with the conventional fuel before withdrawing the hose! The proper fix to the starting problem was soon devised—make the engine spark plugs longer—but the interim solution was typical of the "can do" approach that moved the program forward at such a rapid pace.[23]

The Angel Soars

The first taxi trials took place on the lakebed on 1 August 1955. The second run turned into a first flight of sorts when, much to LeVier's surprise, since he had already chopped the power to idle, the aircraft left the ground at around 70 knots and flew for about a quarter of a mile with the flight test crew in hot pursuit. This bird's wing had all the lift expected...and more! It eventually made heavy contact with the ground in a 10- degree left bank. The Article bounced back up, then settled down again under semi-control, and eventually skidded to a halt a mile further on. Both main tires had blown, and the brakes caught fire.

After more taxi tests, the Article was prepared for a proper first flight on 4 August. The day dawned unsettled, with thunderstorms threatening, but Johnson was determined to press on, so in mid-afternoon they wheeled her out again. At 3.55 pm the strange-looking plane with a polished metal

Overhead view of the secret U-2 test site, showing the 6,000-foot runway leading on to the southern edge of Groom Dry Lake. Most project personnel called this place the "Ranch," although the official name during the U-2 days was Watertown Strip (via Mick Roth).

finish soared into the sky. "It flies like a baby buggy!" exclaimed LeVier to fellow test pilot Bob Matye, who was flying chase with a cameraman in a T-33. Kelly Johnson and Henry Combs followed at a safe distance in a C-47, piloted by another Lockheed test pilot, Ray Goudey.

LeVier was less enthusiastic after he brought the Article in to land after an uneventful 20-minute flight to check basic handling qualities. He had previously debated the landing technique with Johnson, who insisted that his Angel be landed tail up, with the main gear touching first, to avoid stalling the wing. The test pilot reckoned it should be brought in to a two-point landing—"just like any taildragger," he said. Johnson prevailed, but on his first landing attempt LeVier ran into exactly the problem he had predicted. Despite partial flaps, fuselage speed brakes extended, and almost idle power, the aircraft had the flattest of glide angles, and when he attempted to grease the main gear at about 90 knots, the porpoising started.

LeVier applied power and went around, only to encounter the same problem again. And again! By now the thunderstorms were closing in, and Johnson was getting very anxious. He even contemplated a belly landing, but LeVier saved the day by trying his taildragger theory, holding the nose up into a flare and executing a perfect two-pointer just as the aircraft neared the stall. The pogos had been locked in position for this first flight, and even at 60 knots with the gear on the runway they were still airborne. The aircraft started to porpoise again. LeVier managed to control it, and the Article finally rolled to a halt at 4.35 pm. Ten minutes later, a downpour flooded the lake with two inches of water! This did not dampen the spirits of the Skunk Works team, who spent the evening celebrating with beer drinking and arm wrestling contests.[24]

LeVier flew again on 6 August and practiced his landing technique. On 8 August at 9 am, the Article made its *official* first flight in front of Bissell, Ritland, and a few more government representatives. It was a spectacular sight, for the power-weight ratio was so great that the take-off roll was just a few hundred feet. The aircraft had to be pulled into a steep climb as soon as it left the ground, to keep below limit speed. After one pass over the spectators, LeVier went on climbing to 32,000 feet as planned. Matye and Johnson struggled unsuccessfully in the T-33 to catch up. The hour-long flight ended with another low pass and a reasonable landing. Kelly had kept his promise, and flown the Angel within just eight months!

Flight Test Problems

An anti-porpoise valve was added to the main gear to help landings, and the flight tests resumed. LeVier expanded the flight envelope at low-medium altitude, and checked out Bob Matye and Ray Goudey in the Angel before being reassigned at the end of August. By then, Matye and Goudey were making one flight nearly every day, and the Angel had soared past 60,000 feet. But the flameouts had begun.[25]

The interim -37 version of the J57 engine was mainly to blame. The fuel control was inadequate, and the bleed valves didn't work properly. One false move with the throttle and the engine would quit. The compressor stalls would occur from 45,000 feet and upwards, with a loud banging noise that startled the pilots. They experienced flameouts under a variety of conditions, such as during a slight yaw or speed reduction, for instance. At first the throttle could not be retarded to idle at all without the engine flaming out. Since the engine could not be restarted in the thin upper air, the aircraft had to descend to 35,000 feet or lower in order to get a relight. At high altitude, the -37 also leaked oil through the high-pressure compressor that ran the cockpit airconditioning. An oily film would accumulate on the inside of the cockpit canopy. The pilots were obliged to take along a swab mounted on the end of a stick in order to wipe the windshield clean! Since cockpit air was also used to pressurize the equipment bay, the oily film was also deposited on the camera windows, making photography useless.

Members of the Skunk Works' U-2 Flight Test Group are shown here in front of a Lockheed Jetstar. They are (from left) flight test engineers Ernie Joiner, Jerry Carney, Bob Klinger; test pilots Bob Schumacher and Ray Goudey; and Kelly Johnson (via Bob Klinger).

Skunk Works engineer Ben Rich came up with a temporary solution: stuff sanitary napkins around the oil filter! Then the bearing seals and oil scavenge system were improved, but the problem was never completely solved in the -37 engine.[26]

The early flight tests also revealed fuel feed problems. The wing had been designed with fore-and-aft fuel tanks, rather than the more usual inboard-and-outboard arrangements. In a steep climb, the aft (auxiliary) tanks would not gravity-feed the sump tank. Pressurization had to be added, and also a ram air scoop to equalize tank pressure in a rapid descent. Uneven fuel feed was another problem, solved eventually by adding a small electric pump.

Flights were restricted to a 200-mile radius of the Ranch. The article could glide at least that far from high altitude and make a deadstick landing if a relight was not possible!

The test pilots developed some standard flight profiles. The aircraft would be climbed rapidly to 55,000 feet, from where a specified speed schedule would be flown. After a somewhat slower climb over the next 10,000 feet, the aircraft would enter a "cruise-climb" for the remainder of the flight, climbing slowly higher as the fuel burned off. The maximum altitude it might reach depended on a number of variables, such as aircraft take-off weight and outside air temperature. But as it crept higher, the precious margin between the aircraft's stalling speed and its maximum speed eroded quickly, so that by about 68,000 feet in an aircraft that had taken off fully-fueled, there could be as little as 10 knots difference between stall buffet and Mach buffet.

In other words, the slowest the aircraft should be flown was approaching the fastest it should be flown! This was "coffin corner," a condition that afflicted all high-altitude flyers, but in the Angel the condition was particularly acute. And it was difficult to tell the difference between stall buffet and Mach buffet. Recovery from a stall could be difficult, since control surface response was poor in the thin upper atmosphere. If the limiting Mach number of 0.8 was exceeded by much, the nose would pitch down and the aircraft would begin accelerating. If the pilot could not regain control, it might eventually break up at lower altitude, where the placard speed was only 260 knots, even with the gust control deployed.

Organizing, Growing

The formal Oilstone-Aquatone agreement was signed by Dulles and a reluctant Twining on 3 August 1955. It specified that Bissell should have a

military deputy with responsibility for deployment and operations. In late August, Ritland moved from the Pentagon to Project HQ and took up this role. By now, DPS had moved out of the CIA's administration building to another address on E Street. Soon, it would move again to "Quarters Eye" on Ohio Street NW, before finally settling into the fifth floor of a downtown office block in 1956. This physical separation from the rest of the CIA added to the strict compartmenting of the project for security purposes—and to the mystique that grew to surround it. The project even had its own secure communications setup. CIA staffers like John Parangosky and John McMahon, who started their CIA careers in DPS as an administration and security officer, respectively, gained the experience and kudos here that would stand them in good stead later in their careers.

In Washington, Kelly Johnson lobbied for more airplanes. He proposed fitting the Westinghouse APQ-56 side-looking reconnaissance radar, already in production for SAC's RB-47Es. He suggested an "intruder version" of the aircraft armed with two small nuclear bombs, and actually got Gardner's permission to start design of a "long range interceptor" version equipped with a Gatling gun in the Q-bay.[27]

As more top commanders were allowed knowledge of the program and its amazing progress, the list of Lockheed fans grew longer. Like LeMay and Powell before them, though, many were upset about previously being denied knowledge of the project. In mid-September, General Al Boyd at Wright Field was finally let in on the secret. The WADC commander insisted that he be allowed to fly the plane—immediately!

Brig Gen Donald Flickenger was the USAF's leading aeromedical expert. He set the requirements for high-altitude flight protection, including the pilots' partial pressure suits, and their rigorous medical examinations (USAF).

It was already obvious that Lockheed had built a winner. Prompted by Gardner, Assistant Secretary of Defense Donald Quarles agreed to buy more aircraft, this time for the USAF. In early October the axe fell on the rival Bell X-16 program.

In early November, Johnson went back to Washington with a recommendation that the interceptor version be put on hold. It was never built, but Johnson returned to Burbank with a provisional agreement to build 29 more of the basic reconnaissance version, this time for the Strategic Air Command (SAC). Leo Geary reckoned it was time to give the Angel a proper military designation. But its true purpose still could not be revealed. Geary called Colonel Jewell Maxwell at ARDC, who dealt with aircraft designations. Geary and Maxwell agreed to put the new aircraft into the U-for-utility category. The first number had already been allocated, so the Angel became the U-2.[28]

The Greek Pilot Plan

The pressure to deploy remained as great as ever. Critics of the Eisenhower administration said that a "bomber gap" was opening up, since the Soviets seemed to be accelerating development and deployment of their nuclear strike force. There was still no sure way of knowing. At a summit conference in Geneva in July 1955, new Soviet leader Nikita Khrushchev had given a frosty reception to President Eisenhower's "Open Skies" proposal for the USA and the USSR to conduct reciprocal aerial reconnaissance flights over each other's territory. In November 1955 the USSR formally rejected the Open Skies proposal.

The CIA's Air Maritime Division had been running covert air operations behind the Iron Curtain since the late forties to insert agents and saboteurs, and drop propaganda leaflets. Defectors and stateless nationals from Eastern Europe were taught to fly these missions under Project Ostiary. Someone suggested that the "Ostiaries" be trained as U-2 pilots for the overflight mission. If one was shot down, it was argued, the U.S. could deny direct involvement. CIA Deputy Director Pierre Cabell didn't like the idea.[29]

Leo Geary, who had supported the CIA's covert flights during a tour at the MAAG in Athens from 1950-53, instead suggested some Greek pilots who had flown specially-modified P-51s over Albania and Bulgaria. Eight of them entered the USAF jet training course at Craig AFB, AL.[30]

Meanwhile, General LeMay selected Colonel Bill Yancey to organize a pilot training program at the Ranch. Like Colonel Marion "Hack" Mixson, whom LeMay had already installed at project HQ to run the deployments, Yancey was an old SAC recce hand. Lt Col Phil Robertson had succeeded him as SAC's reconnaissance branch chief, so Yancey selected Robertson to be operations officer. Yancey and Robertson chose four more pilots from varying backgrounds: Lou Garvin and Bob Mullen from a B-47 wing because they had "taildragger" experience; plus Hank Meierdierck and Lew Setter, who had both been flying jet fighters for SAC. They arrived at Burbank in early November, and the Skunk Works put them through a rudimentary ground school. At the same time, General Boyd and renowned USAF test pilot Colonel Pete Everest made their flight evaluation of the Article at the Ranch. They gave it ARDC's formal seal of approval, though Johnson noted in his diary that "Everest couldn't land the plane."[31]

BILL YANCEY AND HIS GROUP

When General Curtiss LeMay had to pick someone to run the U-2 training program at the Ranch he turned to Bill Yancey, who had been the Chief of Reconnaissance at SAC HQ:

I was told to report to Washington for a series of briefings and get my security clearance, which in itself was mind boggling. There were no more than eight to 10 officers in the entire Air Staff who knew of the CIA program.

A week later I was back in SAC HQ, where General LeMay told me I was to command a small group of hand-picked pilots (five in all), plus a navigator and a smattering of logistic and maintenance personnel.

Our mission was (1) to test the aircraft (which none of us had seen) and report to him its viability, as claimed by Bissell and Johnson; (2) train some 25 jocks drawn from the SAC fighter wings to be CIA recon pilots; and (3) train another 15 SAC pilots to man a squadron for the Air Force.

Working so closely with the Skunk Works and their leader was an experience I will long remember. Kelly Johnson was indeed America's premier aeronautical engineer. He was a genius, brilliant beyond description, yet foremost in his mind was a desire to build the very best airplane for our country.

- correspondence with author

Pressing on with Flight Tests

Lockheed test pilot Bob Sieker had joined the program in early September 1955, replacing LeVier. Goudey, Matye, and Sieker flew intensively, but there were still only two Articles at the Ranch, and many problems to resolve. Ernie Joiner was running flight testing with the help of just four engineers (Paul Deal, Glen Fulkerson, Bob Klinger, and Mich Yoshii). Dorsey Kammerer managed the maintenance, modification, and supply with only another 20 Lockheed men. A fifth test pilot, Bob Schumacher, arrived in mid-November.

Sitting at a ground test rig at the Ranch, Lockheed test pilot Ray Goudey takes instruction on how to use the sextant (Lockheed C88-1447-69).

The prototype Article had strain gages installed in the same locations as the static test article at Burbank. Structural flight tests were initially conducted with the aircraft restricted to 80% of design limit load. Then the measured flight data was correlated with the static test data, before the static tests were extended to ultimate load. Ultimate loads of some 4g were measured, but the limit loads were kept at 2.5g, as originally conceived. The limit loads were duly demonstrated in test flights. The U-2's structure was therefore proved in an orderly fashion, despite the pressure of time. Moreover, the airframe proved stronger than many had thought.

The Mount Charleston crash

To cater to the growing number of commuters, the USAF started a daily shuttle service to the Ranch from March AFB and Burbank with a C-54 transport. At 0700 on the morning of Wednesday, 17 November 1955, it departed Burbank as usual with 14 project personnel onboard, plus five crew. In poor weather, the C-54 smashed into the top of Mount Charleston, near Las Vegas, killing them all. If it had been only 30 feet higher, the lumbering transport would have cleared the 11,000 foot peak. It took three days for rescue parties to reach the wreckage; they were accompanied by a USAF colonel who removed briefcases and top-secret U-2 documents from the charred bodies of the victims.

The dead included project security chief Bill Marr and four of his staff from the CIA; Dick Hruda and Rod Kreimendahl from the Skunk Works design team; and Hycon's vice-president H.C. Silent. In an official statement they were described as civilian technicians and consultants, and the secrecy of Project Aquatone was preserved, as outsiders concluded that the deceased were all working for the Atomic Energy Commission on nuclear weapons projects at the Nevada test range. By sheer chance, some members of the Skunk Works flight test crew missed the flight. They had hangovers from a party the previous night. The USAF shuttle was soon resumed, but Kelly insisted that his own people fly the Skunk Works C-47 to and from the Ranch.

The -37 engines still coughed and "chugged" disconcertingly at higher altitude. There were turbine blade failures. More flameouts and more re-lights, sometimes three per flight. The autopilots were late being delivered from the Lear company. Without them, the aircraft needed constant attention in the cruise-climb. The test pilots managed this, but operational pilots could hardly be expected to monitor the driftsight, take navigation fixes, operate the camera system, and so on at the same time. When the autopilots did finally arrive, the trim had to be frequently reset to fly the cruise-climb airspeed schedule, which was not a constant Mach number. The test pilots encountered sudden temperature changes at the tropopause, which could cause the autopilot to overreact and input too much pitch. They called this phase of flight "the badlands."

Despite these problems, the Angel soared to its design altitude of 70,000 feet, well past the published world record of 65,890 feet.

The CIA recruited the pilots for Project Aquatone from Strategic Air Command fighter wings that were deactivating. This group at Turner AFB, posed in front of an F-84F circa 1954, includes two future CIA U-2 pilots (Frank Powers – left, and Carl Overstreet – right) (via Sue Powers).

BISSELL'S PROGRESS REPORT ON PROJECT AQUATONE

17 November 1955

In order to save time, we have ordered from all of the companies the number of items we would need to mount a major reconnaissance effort, without waiting for prototypes to be developed. Our target is to have a complete weapons system by the end of this calendar year.

In May, we determined to build a secret base...it was ready for use in mid-July, six weeks after it was started.... By mid-December four aircraft will be checked out and in operation with two different kinds of camera configurations.

The most serious technical problem has been that of developing a satisfactory fuel control...appears to be on its way to solution.

The Project is conducted by a joint task force which, although it includes Air Force, remains essentially civilian in character.

We hope to be ready to start operations on or about 1 April 1956

- CIA declassified document

A BIG DISAPPOINTMENT?

Such was the elaborate secrecy surrounding their recruitment by the CIA, that most of the early U-2 pilots really believed they were going to fly a hot new supersonic fighter:

Carmine Vito: On the third floor of a Texas bordello decorated in red and gold, these CIA hoods unveiled a picture of the airplane. Boy, was that a letdown. I thought it was gonna be some supersonic plane capable of flying to the moon. And here was this thing that looked like a glider!

Jim Cherbonneaux: Hell and Damnation! The picture they gave me was of an ungainly glider sitting on a fragile bicycle landing gear. I had to take a real close look to make sure the thing was even jet-powered. This funny-looking airplane obviously was not the hard-flying, fast-fighting aircraft of my dreams.

But later on, they changed their minds:

Carmine Vito: But when I finally saw it at the Ranch, I realized that it was a masterpiece, a Porsche—every rivet was perfect.

Jim Cherbonneaux: I was proud as hell to be one of the few selected for the program out of the whole Air Force.

C-124 transports delivered the finished Articles from Burbank to the Ranch, where they were reassembled and test-flown (Lockheed C88-1447-08).

U-2 PILOTS WERE THE GUINEA PIGS

The early U-2 pilots were effectively the guinea pigs for the intense physical and psychological screening that would later be made famous by the Project Mercury astronauts. "Barium was inserted everywhere you could think of," noted Bill Hall, one of the first U-2 recruits. "We all managed to pass the course, but I thought that breathing into air bags while riding a stationary bicycle would do me in!"

Dr. Don Flickenger had set these demanding physiological requirements, for which he would no doubt have been roundly cursed by the pilots, had they known. But when Flickenger left ARDC in late 1955 for a new post in Europe, his legacy to Project AQUATONE was a radically improved life support system compared with anything else then flying. – C.P.

THE PILOT CONTRACT

Here are extracts from the original contract between the CIA and the U-2 pilots. Despite the careful wording, which gave very little away, the pilots were not allowed to keep a copy!

We wish to engage your services in connection with an activity which has been discussed with you in detail.

1. For the duration of this contract, your services will be reserved exclusively for our activities...
2. You will carry out such instructions as we may from time to time impart to you...
3. For these services, you will be paid monthly...General Duty Status $775, Operational Duty Status $1,500
4. In addition, the amount of $1,000, without interest, will accrue to your credit for each month of satisfactory service in an operational duty status overseas....

   (h) In the event of death incurred in the performance of your duties...we will pay $50,000 to a beneficiary assigned by you in writing....
8. The duration of this contract will be two years. In addition, you may apply for reinstatement in your previous employment at any time when approved by us.

Recruitment

Lockheed's test pilots taught Yancey's training group how to fly the plane. This was inevitably a haphazard affair; most of the U-2's unique flying characteristics could only be experienced first-hand on the initial solo flight. The instructor pilot flew alongside in a T-33 and shouted instructions and encouragement by radio. Landings were still a big challenge: approaching the stall, each aircraft behaved a little differently. Some would roll off in one direction, some in the other. The flight test engineers added small fixed strips to the leading inboard edge of the wing, tailored to each aircraft's individuality as it approached the stall.

Four Greek pilots arrived—the others had been washed out at the training base. It quickly became obvious to the SAC training group that they could not fly the U-2. One nearly wrecked an aircraft by landing it

wing-low. Lt Col Phil Robertson recommended that the project use pilots from SAC's F-84 squadrons instead. Some of these men had combat experience from the Korean War, and had flown long overwater deployments in the single-engined fighter. Flying over hostile territory in the U-2 would not be so different, he reckoned. Conveniently, SAC was disbanding its four Strategic Fighter Wings that flew these F-84s at Bergstrom AFB, TX, and Turner AFB, GA. The security staff at Project HQ liked the idea. The SAC pilots were all facing reassignment, so if some of them disappeared to a secret project, it might not be noticed.[32]

Leo Geary, Hack Mixson, and Jim Cunningham began screening the personnel records for suitable reserve officers. The best candidates were carefully approached and turned over to the Agency for exhaustive interviews, as well as medical and background checks. They wondered at the intense security; initial screening interviews in an off-base motel, false surnames and ID cards, and lie-detector tests. But the money was good: $2,275 a month. This was triple their military pay, although the CIA would retain $1,000 per month until each pilot had completed his two-year contract.[33]

The selected pilots were sent to Wright Field for an altitude chamber test, a ride on the centrifuge, and other stress tests. From there to the Lovelace Clinic at Albuquerque, where they underwent four days of most intrusive medicals, supervised by Dr Donald Kilgore.[34]

Pressure Suits

At the David Clark Company, Joe Ruseckas finished the design of the MC-3 partial pressure suit. Compared with the old T-1 suit they had been using, pilots found the new suit more comfortable, with a pressure bladder and extra sets of adjustable lacing across the chest. They no longer had to "reverse breathe," that is, exhale forcibly in order to take in oxygen. In the early years, each suit was custom-tailored, and the pilots traveled to the Clark factory at Worcester to be fitted. Meanwhile, the Firewel division of Munsingwear Industries in Buffalo, NY, was contracted to provide the oxygen system, regulators, and pilot's seat kit.

The interim life support equipment had already saved the early U-2 pilots' lives more than 20 times after high-altitude flameouts. Before each high-altitude flight, pilots were required to "pre-breathe" oxygen for two hours to eliminate nitrogen bubbles from the bloodstream. Otherwise, they would experience pain equivalent to the "bends" experienced by divers during decompression. Later, it was realized that individuals vary in the rate at which they eliminate nitrogen, and one hour of prebreathing was sufficient for most pilots. A flight surgeon was always on hand to monitor preflight preparations.

As the test flights were extended in duration, it became apparent that the rate of oxygen consumption also differed considerably between pilots. Lou Setter, from the SAC training group, added an oxygen plot to the fuel plot he had already devised. Using these plots, pilots could monitor the rate of consumption of both fuel and oxygen as the flight progressed. On one early flight to high altitude, Phil Robertson noticed from the plots that his oxygen supply was fast-depleting. He quickly initiated a descent, but by 40,000 feet he had only the emergency supply left. By 25,000 feet that, too, was exhausted, and Robertson had to open his helmet faceplate. He landed safely, and the loss of oxygen was traced to a joint in the supply line that deformed and leaked when the pilot sat on the seat pack. Development of the life support system, like most other aspects of the U-2, often proceeded by trial-and-error![35]

The First Group

Six SAC fighter pilots made it through the selection process to form the CIA's first group of U-2 flyers. They were obliged to resign their USAF commissions, but were promised a no-questions-asked return to the military with no break of service upon completion of their contract with the CIA. The procedure was known as "sheep-dipping." As a cover story, the recruits became test pilots with Lockheed, but the CIA really paid their wages.

This first group began training at the Ranch on 11 January 1956. Yancey's men had devised a ground school and flight check-out syllabus. They took the newcomers for three flights in the T-33 to simulate high-altitude flameouts and restarts, and to demonstrate near-stall landings. Then came the first solo in the U-2, a flight to 20,000 feet followed by five practice landings on the lakebed. The awkward pressure suit was worn for the first time on the third flight, lasting three hours and reaching 60,000 feet. A further nine flights progressively introduced high altitude navigation and photography; night flying; eight-hour-plus missions; and runway landings. Having logged 58 hours in the U-2 and flown a final eight-hour check-ride, the new pilot was declared mission-qualified.

The Angel began to venture far from the secret base on endurance-proving flights, now that the test pilots had devised satisfactory climb and cruise speed schedules that accounted for the temperamental -37 engine. On 2 February 1956, Article 344 flew for nine hours and 35 minutes, the longest yet. Bob Schumacher had taken off with a maximum fuel load of 1,362 gallons at a gross weight of 19,900 lbs. He had flown until the fuel low-level warning light came on. But the simple, subtractive fuel counter (which was the only fuel quantity information provided in the cockpit) showed that 1,386 gallons had been consumed—24 more than was loaded! Furthermore, another 15 gallons was drained from the aircraft after landing.

Where had the extra 39 gallons come from? It was discovered that the U-2 had a unique ability to "manufacture" fuel. The kerosene from the wing tanks, which had been "cold-soaking" for hours, was heated—and therefore expanded—as it passed through the fuel-oil heat exchanger! However, for operational flight-planning purposes, it was decided to stick to the original design maximum fuel capacity of 1,335 gallons and gross weight of 17,300 lbs. When fitted with the J57-P-37 engine, the U-2 therefore had a maximum range of about 3,500 nautical miles, and an endurance of eight and a half hours. The -31 engine promised to give the U-2 better range and altitude—when it eventually arrived.

Navigation

The long-range flight tests in early 1956 also served to develop the aircraft's navigation system. The basic navaid was the driftsight; the "downward-looking periscope" provided a 360-degree view beneath the aircraft at two selectable magnifications. But what if it was cloudy below? Dead-reckoning was a viable alternative, since the winds were usually quite light at high altitude. There was also a radio-compass, the AN/ARN-6. But radio stations might be few and far between over denied territory. These three basic means of navigation could not provide the accuracy, reliability, and redundancy that would be required for such long flights.

The known system of long-range, high-frequency ground stations offered a possible alternative, since the pilot could tune into these and determine his position by triangulation. An HF receiver and antenna unit from the Collins Radio company was selected for the U-2, and initially tested successfully in a C-47. But when it was added to a U-2 there were serious problems with the long-wire antenna installation. When the CIA realized that the use of HF could betray the aircraft's position to enemy air defenses, the device (which was designated System II) was dropped.

In mid-October 1955 it was finally decided to adopt celestial navigation. Dr Robert Hills, of the Baird Atomic company in Boston, quickly designed a sextant that could be coupled with the driftsight optics using a levered mirror. Above 50,000 feet, the sky was black from overhead to near the horizon even at midday, allowing star fixes to be taken. The pressure-suited pilot could not perform the necessary calculations in the air, however, so a flight-rated navigator precomputed them before takeoff. Major Ray Burroughs, from SAC HQ, and Jack DeLapp, in the SAC training group at the Ranch, refined these techniques. Like the many U-2 navigators who followed, their preflight work on the ground was vital to the success of the mission.[36]

TOWARD THE UNKNOWN

Lt Col Phil Robertson was one of the first USAF pilots to fly the U-2. He was one of Col Yancey's group who devised the pilot training program, and checked out those who would deploy overseas with Project Aquatone. In those early days, though, the training group was effectively also a flight test group, as they encountered so many unknowns in high-altitude flight, as Robertson recalled:

The original -37 engines limited us to about 65,000 feet. Above that they quit. I was at that altitude over Reno, trying to preclude an engine stall by extending the gear and speedbrakes. Suddenly I hit real turbulence, a 2g gust, the worst I had ever experienced. Suddenly, I was at 71,000 feet! Looking down, I could see the lenticular clouds that formed when the Sierra Wave was active. Luckily the engine didn't quit this time, and I came back home uneventfully. A month or two later I was at a dinner and sat next to a meteorologist. I asked him about the wave. He said it only goes to 45,000 feet. I couldn't tell him that it went much higher!

Right after we got the -31 engines I flew the number five bird. We still did not know much about the high-altitude winds. I flew a straight line to the Great Bear Lake in Canada and returned. When I got back over the Ranch I still had a lot of fuel left, so I went down to San Diego. By now I was indicating 72,500 feet, and my ass was dead tired. The whole flight was 10 hours and five minutes. That evening they recomputed, and my altitude was 74,500 feet. That record stood for three years until they re-engined the airplane.

On one flight, a hydraulic line ruptured and left me with no flaps or speedbrakes. My first attempt at a landing was made with a normal traffic pattern, but I could not slow down to landing speed. The next try, I put the base leg further out, lower and slower, but still no dice. Next I went as low and slow as I could get without dragging a wing in the sage brush, and brought the throttle to idle as I turned final. Halfway across the dry lake, it was clear that idle thrust would keep the bird flying forever, so I stop-cocked the throttle and made my only deadstick landing.

- interview and correspondence with author

KEEPING THE ALTITUDE SECRET

We developed our own brand of humor. On a night flight, I called in my position to ground station. I got a call back from a station very far to the north. The voice said, "NACA Jet ###, what is your position?" I told him where I was, and he said that he had never received a transmission from that far away. "Atmospheric conditions must be very good tonight," I replied, and he said "that must be it!"

We were not allowed to give our actual altitude, and were limited to reporting "forty thousand feet." This caused one of the radar-trackers some concern when he saw me at the top of his scope, way above his B-52s. He asked me to verify my altitude. I told him 40,000 ft. He said 'I read you quite a bit above that." I advised him to have his equipment checked and clicked off.

- Bill Hall, Daedalus Flyer, Winter 1997, p10

OZZIE RITLAND

The first military deputy to Dick Bissell at CIA U-2 Project HQ was promoted and reassigned before the secret aircraft went operational. Therefore, he never received any credit for his contribution outside of the close-knit group that developed the aircraft in 1955-56. But Kelly Johnson obviously held him in the highest regard, as is clear from this letter that the Skunk Work's chief wrote to mark Ritland's departure from Project Aquatone:

Encino, CA
10 April 1956

I never again expect to have such a fine relationship with anyone through such a difficult project and period. It's with a certain feeling of frustration that I write this, because you are leaving just about when the fruits of our labors are becoming ripe. It's not right to have you leave now without getting your full share of credit and satisfaction. You, Dick, and I have paid our full amount in building the Angel project. It's been a big cost. Let's hope it's intelligently used.

Busy flightline scene at the Ranch during pilot training for the CIA detachments (Lockheed C88-1447-21).

Improved Engine Arrives

The prototype of the improved J57-P-31 engine arrived at the Ranch in January 1956 and was fitted to Article 341. Hand-built by Pratt & Whitney engineers, it weighed 450 lbs less and produced 700 lbs more thrust than the 10,500 lb -37. At 70,000 feet and above, it burned just 700 lbs of fuel per hour. And it didn't leak oil, or flameout so readily! Pilots found the -31 much easier to operate, since only one variable (EGT) had to be monitored. However, there was a downside to the new engine: the air restart characteristics were not as good as the -37 because of the lower minimum fuel flow. The -31 could not be restarted above 35,000 feet at all.

Lockheed's pilots completed the basic flight test program at the end of February, although proving of the new engine continued. Remarkably few changes to the basic airframe were required. Although the B-camera was not yet ready the A-camera configurations were flown, and the aircraft proved to be a very stable reconnaissance platform. More milestones were reached. By late March, a maximum altitude of 73,800 feet had been demonstrated, using the new engine. Maximum range was around 4,000 nautical miles, and endurance was nine hours 30 minutes. Total flight time reached 1,000 hours. Nine airplanes had been delivered.[37]

Incredibly, there had been only one serious accident. On 21 March the second Article was damaged when CIA pilot Carmine Vito touched down on the lakebed in a yaw, while trying to correct for gusting winds. The main gear collapsed and punctured the sump tank. Hank Meierdierck, who was acting as mobile officer, dragged the unconscious pilot out of the plane, and Lockheed mechanic Bob Murphy scrambled to shut the engine down.[38]

There had been plenty of potentially serious incidents, though. The engineers were still fiddling with the leading edge, applying layers of duck tape to try and improve the stall characteristics. CIA pilot Marty Knutson was checking this out inflight when the aircraft stalled and entered a spin at 20,000 feet. This had never happened before, and the anxious pilot from the SAC training group, who was flying chase in a T-33, urged Knutson to bail out. He would have done so, had he been physically able to jettison the canopy! Instead, by using rudder against the spin, and with the huge control yoke fully forward, Knutson recovered control and landed safely. A structural check revealed some damage in the wing, where fuel had been forced outboard during the spin by centrifugal force. This aircraft wasn't cleared for spinning![39]

Operational Evaluation

The CIA was arranging a base for the first overseas deployment. The flya-way spares kits had already been designed. The USAF scheduled an operational evaluation at the Ranch. Planes, payloads, procedures, and operational pilots were all evaluated in a six-day "Unit Simulated Combat Maneuvers" (USCM) test from 9-14 April 1956. It went very well, although pilot Jake Kratt was forced to make the first landing away from base during his long-range navigation test. He flamed out over the Mississippi River, relit, flamed out again 600 miles further on, and stretched a glide all the way into Kirtland AFB, Albuquerque, NM.[40] Marty Knutson also had a flameout during his long-range mission, although he managed to relight and recover into the Ranch. He was flying a -37 engine aircraft, and Pratt & Whitney tech reps discovered that some of the turbine blades had failed. Prolonged operation at high EGT and high altitude had caused them to crystallize.

Col Yancey reported to General LeMay that the first group was ready for operations. Bissell and others had their doubts, especially since there were not yet enough -31 engines to fit the deployable aircraft. A compromise was reached: the group would deploy, and the more reliable -31 engines would be shipped to them direct. Until they were installed, no overflights of denied territory would be authorized. In the first days of May four planes and their support gear were loaded into C-124s, which took off. As usual, only those who "needed to know" were aware of the destination.

3

Over the Soviet Union

During a visit to Washington in January 1956, the British Foreign Secretary Selwyn Lloyd met with Allen Dulles, Director of Central Intelligence. Dulles outlined Project Aquatone to his British visitor, and asked for permission to base the first U-2 detachment in the UK. It was an obvious choice; the Anglo-American alliance was particularly strong in intelligence-sharing.

Selwyn Lloyd returned to the UK and recommended the project to Prime Minister (PM) Sir Anthony Eden:

"Allen Dulles promised me that all the intelligence resulting from the operation would be shared with the British authorities," he wrote. "This would be greatly to our advantage, since Soviet airfields which are important to us would be covered."[1]

Eden was dubious. A political flap had just occurred thanks to a USAF attempt to overfly the Iron Curtain countries at high altitude with camera-carrying balloons. After five years of development, and despite opposition from CIA and skepticism from the USAF's own engineers at Wright Field, the project had gone ahead. President Eisenhower approved the operational phase in late December 1955. Over 500 balloons were launched from Western Europe, the theory being that the prevailing jetstreams would carry them west-to-east across the Soviet landmass, so that they could be recovered 8-10 days later in northern Asia.

The scheme was a dismal failure, with less than 10 percent of the camera payloads recovered. Many others were shot down by Warsaw Pact fighters, or simply drifted down to earth. The USSR collected the evidence, displayed it in Moscow, and issued strong protests. The British PM was not impressed. He told aides that he would not approve the proposed U-2 flights for the time being, "in view of the notoriety that the balloons have gained."[2]

But Bissell and Dulles applied pressure via Eisenhower, and Eden reluctantly changed his mind. On 1 May 1956 the first of four U-2s arrived at the USAF's Lakenheath base in East Anglia inside a C-124. By mid-May, they were reassembled and flying. Bissell and Kelly Johnson flew to London to supervise activities. Royal Air Force fighters were tasked to attempt practice intercepts against the U-2s—they didn't get near.[3]

Cover Story

An elaborate cover story had been devised to mask the true purpose of Project AQUATONE. On 7 May a press release was issued in the name of Dr Hugh Dryden, director of the National Advisory Committee for Aeronautics (NACA)—the predecessor of NASA. It announced that the first U-2 aircraft were flying from Watertown Strip, in Southern Nevada, in a new research program. Capable of reaching 55,000 feet, the aircraft would gather research data about the upper atmosphere to help plan future jet airliners that would routinely be flying at the higher levels. Jetstreams, clear air turbulence, cosmic ray particles, the ozone layer, convective clouds—all would be studied by the new aircraft, a few of which had been "made available" to NACA by the USAF. More detailed releases followed, giving full details of the instrumentation being carried aloft, and announcing an extension of the program to the UK and "other parts of the world."

Some of this was true—a weather research package *had* been developed for the U-2, and was to be carried on a special equipment bay hatch during training flights. NACA had a full-time U-2 project officer assigned, but the research agency had no control over where the flights were routed, and received all of its data second-hand.[4] Watertown was now the "official" name for the Ranch. The CIA had named the secret base after the town in upstate New York that was the birthplace of DCI Allen Dulles.

The cover story for Project Aquatone required the co-operation of the National Advisory Committee for Aeronautics (NACA), which became NASA in 1958. The early CIA U-2s all carried the NACA tail marking, supporting the official line that the aircraft was designed for weather research.

For cover purposes, the first U-2 detachment that deployed to the UK was designated Weather Reconnaissance Squadron (Provisional)-1 (WRSP-1). Within the USAF, a provisional squadron did not have to file routine reports to higher headquarters. The real designation was Detachment A, or Det A for short. When two further groups of operational U-2s were formed by the CIA in 1956 they were designated Det B (WRSP-2) and Det C (WRSP-3).[5]

Det A

Det A was an unorthodox mix of USAF and CIA people, and civilian contract employees. General LeMay had ensured that his own men from SAC took most of the USAF slots, including the unit commander, operations officer, and their deputies. About a dozen more USAF officers and a similar number of enlisted men worked in operations, mission planning, provided support aircraft, and so on. There were about 40 CIA staffers looking after administration, security, and communications. Since all of the maintenance—planes, sensors, life support systems—was done under contract, there were upwards of 60 more civilians assigned. Then there were the six "sheep-dipped" operational pilots. They weren't really sure who their boss was—the USAF Colonel who was officially the unit commander, or the GS-12 grade staffer from CIA who was the unit executive officer!

Back in Washington there was a similar division of responsibility between USAF and CIA. The cover designation for the military personnel

---

DON'T APPROACH THIS AIRCRAFT!

The problem about flying a secret aircraft from bases in the UK and Germany was that there were many military pilots and radar controllers who might come across it, and blab! The dilemma for the security people was, how many people should be alerted. In the UK, the RAF produced a basic three-view drawing and showed it to their pilots with strict instruction not to approach or report the aircraft. The Royal Canadian Air Force (RCAF) in Europe took a while to get the message, however:

16 June 1956: Live scramble of Strongbox Zulu Alpha against unknown track 533, position 1545, heading SE at 60,000 feet measured altitude. Finally intercepted in Rhein/Main area during let down. Zulu Alpha lead described the aircraft as having mid-wing jet intakes faired into body, high tail assembly with no gun turret apparent, and tricycle undercarriage with both wheels letting down out of one door in center of fuselage. After some considerable effort, the aircraft number 53166 was finally obtained by the pilot. This aircraft is apparently on the highly classified list, and the COpsO ruled that, in future, all reports on live scrambles would be in classified form (by signal).

- 61st AC&W Squadron, from National Archives of Canada

---

assigned to Project HQ was the 1007th Air Intelligence Service Group, a unit of Headquarters Command (HEDCOM) in the Pentagon. Just as the U-2 deployment began, the military man who had done the most to get the show on the road was reassigned, to Richard Bissell's great disappointment. Colonel Ozzie Ritland was promoted and re-assigned to the Western Development Division. His replacement as Bissell's military deputy was another USAF Colonel with an aeronautical engineering background, Jack Gibbs.

Reluctant Hosts

Det A's stay in Britain was short-lived. Shortly before it arrived, Soviet leaders Bulganin and Khrushchev paid a good will visit to the UK, arriving at Portsmouth dockyard on a Soviet Navy cruiser. Without permission, the British Secret Intelligence Service (MI6) dispatched a frogman to spy on the ship from beneath the water line. He was never seen alive again. The Soviets publicized the incident. The political fallout extended to Project Aquatone. On 18 May, just days before the first overflights were due, Eden called Eisenhower and withdrew his permission for them.[6]

A disappointed Bissell told embarrassed British military and intelligence officials that a base in Germany was his second option. The Brits said they would allow Det A to remain at Lakenheath, but for training flights and maintenance purposes only. No overflights! Bissell and Johnson flew home, pondering their options. Selwyn Lloyd told Eden:

"...should the active operations in Germany ever become the subject of any enquiry, the British government could deny all knowledge of them, since the presence of the special aircraft remaining at Lakenheath could be explained by reference to their meteorological mission."

Although Bissell and company may not have realized it at the time, this episode set the pattern for many future political constraints on U-2

Colonel Jack Gibbs was the senior military officer assigned to the CIA's U-2 Project from 1956 to 1958. He helped Dick Bissell manage the operational debut of the aircraft, and also began the process of developing a successor (via Jim Gibbs).

operations. Even when they were persuaded to grant basing rights, foreign governments were reluctant to give unrestricted permission for illegal overflights.[7]

To Germany

On 11 June, Det A was moved to the busy USAF and CIA base at Wiesbaden, near Frankfurt. At Eisenhower's insistence, Bissell flew to Bonn in late June with CIA Deputy Director Pierre Cabell to get German permission for Soviet overflights. They were relieved to get an enthusiastic response from the "Iron Chancellor," Konrad Adenauer. Bissell decided to make a permanent home for Det A in Germany. Wiesbaden would be temporary, pending construction of suitable facilities at Giebelstadt airfield, 70 miles further east.[8]

The delay in starting overflights did mean that one major improvement could be made: the new and more reliable J-57-31 engines were shipped to Germany shortly after the planes arrived there. By mid-June Det A was ready for business. But President Eisenhower had not yet approved Soviet overflights, pending German approval, and because an official U.S. delegation led by General Nathan Twining, USAF Chief of Staff, had taken up a Soviet invitation to visit Moscow. It did not seem right to invade Soviet airspace while they were there!

The weather was good, so Bissell ordered a flight over the Soviet satellite countries instead. The detailed mission plan was transmitted from Project HQ to Wiesbaden, where Det A's operations staff drew up the flight charts and fuel curve graph that the designated pilot, Carl Overstreet, would take with him.

A strict routine had been established for mission flights. The pilot would be sent to bed some 12 hours before the scheduled launch time, and woken with at least two hours to go. By then, Project HQ would have acquired the latest weather report and forecast for the target areas. If it was good enough, a go signal would be transmitted by the Agency's own secure communications lines to the Det. The pilot would eat a high-protein, "low-residue" meal. (The lavatory arrangements of the partial pressure suit were rudimentary, consisting of a bottle for liquid wastes that the pilot had to connect himself inflight, after much tugging at zips and hoses. How-

ever, some pilots found little call for the bottle even on long flights: the skin-tight pressure suit caused constant perspiration, and much body moisture was eliminated this way rather than through the kidneys. There was no provision for the disposal of solid waste from the body—a messy, uncomfortable, and embarrassing business if the pilot could not restrain himself).

After eating, the pilot would put on long white underwear, seams to the outside so that the tight pressure suit would not impress them indelibly onto the occupant's skin. Now two physiological support technicians helped him into the suit itself for the two-hour prebreathing session. The suit was so restrictive of movement that a fellow pilot would be detailed to perform most of the preflight checks at the waiting aircraft. He would also help the mission pilot strap himself in and connect all the hoses, wires, and so on. This "mobile" pilot would remain on duty throughout the flight. When the U-2 returned he would "chase" it down the runway, calling the height-to-touchdown over the radio, since the pilot's vision was badly restricted in the aircraft's landing attitude.[9]

Overflight

In the early-morning light on 20 June 1956, Overstreet climbed in his plane and taxied to the runway. Since complete radio silence was the rule, he awaited a green "go" light from the tower. Right on schedule, he took off from Wiesbaden on the first-ever operational U-2 mission. His biggest fear was that of screwing up. He flew north and west to gain altitude, before looping back over the base and heading east. Mission 2003 penetrated denied territory where the borders of the two Germanys and Czechoslovakia met. This was by design. If communist radars in either country were detecting the flight, the neighboring countries might fail to coordinate, and lose contact. Overstreet had no indication that he had been detected, however, and Mission 2003 flew on across northern Czechoslovakia before turning north to pass east of Dresden and into Poland. The U-2 completed a tour of every major Polish city before exiting the way it came, flying over Prague and back into West Germany. No screw-up!

After landing, the undeveloped film and the SIGINT tapes were unloaded. After a quick check for quality control they were transferred to a waiting plane, which immediately flew them back to the U.S. The CIA had

Three Bison bombers fly over Moscow during the Tushino airshow, 23 June 1956. This was the first Soviet long-range jet bomber, and Western intelligence had no idea how many were in service (NARA 155107AC).

made arrangements for Eastman Kodak to do the film processing at its plant in Rochester, NY. The original negative was developed and copied. Two duplicate positives were produced—it had been decided that these would allow better photo interpretation of high quality imagery, than working from paper prints.

It was another two days before the film reached Washington. Former U.S. Navy photo-interpreter Art Lundahl had established a Photo Intelligence Division (PID) within the CIA in 1953. When Project AQUATONE was launched, Richard Bissell asked Lundahl to expand his small operation, which was housed in the temporary "M" buildings. Lundahl and his executive officer, Sid Stallings, moved the unit into the top four floors of a nondescript office block at 5th and K Street NW. It was owned by the Steuart Motor Car Company, which operated a car repair workshop on the ground floor. PID's new home was an unlikely location, in one of Washington's least-desirable suburbs. Soon Lundahl's new recruits began to arrive, as did the new photo-exploitation equipment...microstereoscopes, X-ray light tables, and improved mensuration devices. Art Lundahl selected the cryptonym Automat for his expanded operation.[10]

Lundahl's team examined the film from Mission 2003 on 22 June 1956, and compared it with film exposed over the U.S. during the U-2's operational readiness test the previous April. Although all the imagery had been taken by the interim A-2 camera rig, it was excellent quality. Much better than the old wartime German photography that was still the main reference to terrain behind the Iron Curtain! The A-2 system of three 24-inch focal length lenses in a trimetrogen configuration provided stereo overlapping imagery across a 36.5 nautical-mile swath of the ground.

The B-camera was more versatile, as well as higher resolution. If all seven of the "stop and shoot" lens positions were used, it could "see" from horizon to horizon. Since the position of so many U-2 targets behind the Iron Curtain was imprecisely known, this was a big bonus. But there had been development problems with the "B." On test flights, the moving lens assembly would bounce against the stop and cause the next image to blur. The problems were not solved until late 1956. All the early U-2 overflights used the A-2 system instead.

How many Bombers?

After a week as guests of the Soviet Union, General Twining and his group left Moscow. At the Tushino Air Show they had been treated to another spectacular fighter flypast, similar to those flown over the city in the last few Mayday parades. Also flying by was the large, long-range four-engined turboprop bomber that had first been seen a year earlier, and was nicknamed *Bear* by NATO. But there were only four of them, plus three of the big four-jet bombers codenamed *Bison*. So how many *Bisons* and *Bears* were really operational? Twining's hosts were not forthcoming.

Neither did the Soviets talk about their missiles. At a conference in early 1956, British and American intelligence experts had pooled their knowledge of Soviet guided weapons development. It did not amount to much. The only hard evidence came from German scientists who had been co-opted by the USSR in 1945 and obliged to work in Soviet weapons institutes. The USSR let most of them go in the early fifties, and they were thoroughly debriefed by Western intelligence.[11]

By now, therefore, the intelligence community had a huge list of aerial reconnaissance targets behind the Iron Curtain. Bissell had established a new system for prioritizing them the previous December, by organizing the Ad-hoc Requirements Committee (ARC). CIA staff officer Jim Reber

PRESIDENT EISENHOWER

According to John Foster Dulles, who was Secretary of State during the Eisenhower Administration, Ike predicted that a U-2 would come to grief over denied territory as early as 1956, when he approved the overflights of Soviet territory. Dulles quoted the President:

"Well boys, I believe this country needs this information, and I'm going to approve it. But I tell you one thing. Some day one of these machines is going to be caught, and we're going to have a storm...."

chaired this committee, where CIA, Army, Navy, and USAF representatives met to draw up the collection requirements. The top-priority targets were then passed to Project HQ, where mission planners devised potential routes for U-2 flights.

These mission planners knew that they had to cram as many targets as possible into each flight. President Eisenhower had read a detailed brief on Project Aquatone, and told his staff secretary, General Andrew Goodpaster, that he wanted all the vital targets covered as quickly as possible. On 21 June Bissell took James Killian and Din Land with him to the White House, where Goodpaster explained the President's thinking. Eisenhower was going to keep tight control of the flights, and wanted frequent reports. Despite all the CIA's assurances, Ike was worried that the flights might be detected, and that another balloon-type fiasco might ensue. SIGINT reports indicated to project HQ that the first overflight of Czechoslovakia and Poland had indeed been periodically detected by communist radars. Radar operators apparently did not obtain enough data, however, to conclude that an unauthorized intruder was overhead.[12]

On 2 July two U-2s left Wiesbaden in quick succession to fly over eastern Europe again. Jake Kratt flew Mission 2009 south across Austria and into Hungary. After Budapest, he turned south to fly along the Yugoslav border, then all the way across Bulgaria to the Black Sea. Glen Dunaway headed north on Mission 2010 before flying over East Germany, southern Poland, eastern Czechoslovakia and Hungary, and into Romania. This flight

The unlikely location for the CIA's Photo Intelligence Division (PID) was the top four floors of this building at 5th and K Street, in northwest Washington. It was known as the Steuart Building, after the auto dealership which occupied the ground floor (CIA).

UNDERESTIMATING SOVIET RADARS

A U.S. National Intelligence Estimate (NIE) issued while the U-2 was being developed noted that "although the Soviets have made great strides in radar development," their standard S-band V-beam early-warning radar, nicknamed *Token*, had no capability above 60,000 feet. The *Token* coverage was supplemented by two metric (VHF-band) air defense radars nicknamed *Dumbo* and *Knife Rest*, with similar capabilities. British intelligence thought that *Token* could detect bombers at 40,000 feet from 190 miles, but was less impressed with the two metric radars. They were right; the P-3 *Dumbo* and P-8 *Knife Rest* radars could only provide bearing and range. But the West knew nothing about the A-100 radar, which provided early warning for the SAM system around Moscow. And the estimate of the *Token*'s ability proved wrong as soon as the U-2 started overflying the USSR at 70,000 feet—and was detected.

– C.P.

also reached the Black Sea before turning back across southern Romania, Hungary, and Austria. Each aircraft was airborne for nearly seven hours, and they covered nearly 6,000 miles of "denied territory" between them.[13]

Prime Targets

On 3 July, before the postflight analysis of those missions was complete, the President finally gave the go-ahead for 10 days of U-2 flights over the Soviet Union. In Project HQ, Bissell chaired a final review of the mission plans. Everything looked good. Just before midnight, the go signal was transmitted across secure communications to Det A in Germany. Since Wiesbaden was six hours ahead of Washington time, it was 0600 on U.S. Independence Day, 4 July, when Det A pilot Hervey Stockman took off on Mission 2013 in the aircraft marked as NACA 187.

He flew across East Germany and Poland and crossed the Soviet border near Grodno, in Belorus. After flying over known bomber bases around Minsk, Stockman headed north for the prime targets on this flight, which were around Leningrad. But now he had company! Peering down through the driftsight, Stockman saw MiG fighters rising to try and intercept. Contrary to all American hopes, the flight had been detected! Stockman flew steadily on, putting his faith in Kelly Johnson's plane and the intelligence advice that said it could not be reached at altitude by the Soviet fighters. Sure enough, the fighters disappeared. The U-2 pilot flew over the naval shipyards at Leningrad, where Soviet submarines were built, and the three known Soviet long-range bases around the city. Then Stockman turned west, to pass over more suspected Soviet jet bomber bases in the Baltic States before eventually landing back at Wiesbaden after an eight hour 45 minute flight.[14]

The next flight was planned to go all the way to Moscow. When asked to justify such a daring venture by Allen Dulles, Bissell told him that the first time would probably be the safest. The pilot whose turn it was to fly next was told to get some sleep. With Independence Day parties going on all over the base, Carmine Vito did not get much rest. At 0500 the next morning, flying the same aircraft Stockman had flown the previous day (Article 347), Vito took off on U-2 Mission 2014.[15]

His route took him further south than Stockman had flown, over Kracow, Poland, then into the Ukrainian SSR to fly over Brest and Baranovichi, where another of the suspected Bison bomber bases was lo-

cated. There was considerable cloud cover, but it cleared away as Vito turned towards Moscow, virtually following the railroad from Minsk to the Soviet capital. As he crossed the Soviet border, Vito was aware that the air defense system knew he was somewhere above. The MiGs were on his trail, but they were mainly MiG-17s with a maximum altitude of 50,000 feet. Even the newer MiG, nicknamed *Farmer* by NATO, which had just entered service, could only reach 55,000 feet.

Vito flew on over Orsha, where three *Bisons* had been reported earlier in the year by a ground observer. The rolling farmland seemed to stretch forever, divided into a mosaic pattern by stone fences. He neared Moscow, where a new potential danger awaited. The USSR's first surface-to-air missile (SAM) system had been deployed around the capital. That much was already known to Western Intelligence, since U.S. and UK air attachés in Moscow had been monitoring its extensive construction all around the Soviet capital since late 1954.

The Moscow SAM sites

The development of a SAM system around Moscow had aroused intense interest at the CIA's Office of Scientific Intelligence (OSI). Repatriated German rocket scientists had told OSI that the Soviets had been pursuing their wartime "Wasserfall" project, to be capable of knocking down aircraft as high as 65,000 feet. But the characteristics of the Moscow system suggested an entirely new line of development.[16]

Ahead of him, Vito could see the herring bone pattern of the road layout around one of these SAM sites. He flew right over it and on over Moscow, where one of his main objectives was the Fili airframe plant, where the *Bison* bomber was being built. The U-2 then rolled out to the northwest and headed for the science and technology complex just north of Moscow at Kaliningrad, where Soviet missile development took place, and the main Soviet flight test and research airfield at Ramenskoye. In so doing, Vito flew over two more of the SAM sites, but no missiles were fired.[17]

Vito headed for home via his remaining targets: the Khimki rocket engine development and production factory; and more potential bomber bases along the Baltic. The cloud that had obscured some of the targets around Moscow thickened as he flew back, and it was overcast as he passed over the satellite countries. The weather was poor at Wiesbaden, and he needed a ground-controlled approach to land. Underlining the U-2's now-obvious detectability, he was picked up while still way over East Germany and at altitude by the radars that Canada operated as part of its 1st Air Division contribution to NATO.[18]

Detection

But Bissell's hunch about the Soviet air defenses around Moscow had proved correct: they weren't ready for him. In fact, an A-100 radar at Smolensk provided early warning for the Moscow SA-1 SAM system. This radar had detected Vito as he flew overhead on his way towards the capital, and the Soviet operators calculated that he was flying at 20,000 kilometers (65,000 feet). The radar alert proved futile, however, since the missiles for the SA-1 system were not routinely kept at the firing sites. That same evening, Soviet Chief of the General Staff Marshall Sokolovskiy arrived at the command post. He was accompanied by a team of experts from the headquarters of the Voyska Protivovozdushnoy Oborona Strany (PVO, or Troops of the Air Defense Forces). They studied the target tracks of Vito's flight, and concluded that a radar malfunction or operator error had occurred. No aircraft could fly that high! The missile system commander disagreed, and persuaded Sokolovskiy that the missiles should be armed, moved to the launch site, fueled, and placed on alert. It was done that very night.[19]

President Eisenhower had already made it clear he wanted the flights stopped if they could be tracked. Exactly what constituted effective tracking was a matter of interpretation, however. It took some time for the CIA to correlate the SIGINT data from the U-2's own receivers with that obtained by the U.S.-operated SIGINT ground stations in Germany and the UK. Ike was told that the flights were being detected, though still imperfectly. He considered halting the operation, but told Goodpaster it could continue until more definite information was available.[20]

Meanwhile, bad weather prevented further overflights on the three days following Vito's flight. But on 9 July two U-2s took off in quick succession from Wiesbaden to resume the program. Marty Knutson flew Mission 2020 to the north of Berlin and up the Baltic Coast as far as Riga, then turned east and south to cover targets around Kaunas, Vilnius, and Minsk before returning via Warsaw. Carl Overstreet took Mission 2021 along the southern route via Czechoslovakia and Hungary, then turned northeast into the Ukrainian SSR. Flying as far east as Kiev, he made a high-altitude tour of more potential bomber bases (Gomel, Bobrusk, and Baranovichi again) before returning via southern Poland. Unfortunately, a broken shutter ruined much of the photography from Overstreet's flight. When the flight passed Kiev, anti-aircraft artillery fired at it. Of course, the shells exploded harmlessly thousands of feet below. But the barrage attracted plenty of attention in Kiev itself, causing rumors to spread that the city had come under an air attack. When he heard of this, Soviet Premier Khrushchev castigated the anti-aircraft units for their useless action.[21]

Protest

The next day, 10 July, Glen Dunaway made Det A's furthest excursion yet to the East. He flew Mission 2024 all the way to Kerch, on the eastern tip of the Crimean Peninsula, returning via Sevastopol, Simferopol, Odessa, and the satellite countries. Although Dunaway saw fighters beneath him over Odessa, the rest of the flight was uneventful. But while he was airborne, the USSR delivered a protest note about the previous days' flights to the U.S. Embassy in Moscow. After some debate over whether to con-

cede that the flights had taken place, the Soviet leadership decided to swallow its pride.

The protest note described in some detail the "gross violations" of Soviet airspace "for purposes of reconnaissance," and ascribed them to "a twin-engined medium bomber of the USAF." It was clear that the Soviet air defense system had not only detected each flight, but had also tracked them for considerable distances. Although the note admitted that one of them "had penetrated to a significant depth over Soviet territory," it did not mention Moscow. (Thirty-seven years later, two senior former Soviet air defense officers could still not bring themselves to admit that the Soviet capital had been overflown. Their published article on the U-2 flights over the USSR vaguely noted that the aircraft "got 1,000 kilometers deep into the USSR.")[22]

U.S. intelligence concluded that the Soviets were indeed confused, and embarrassed to admit the true extent of the overflights. Handoffs of targets between air defense sectors were (as the U.S. had hoped) inadequate. It seemed that each sector was unwilling to be blamed for failure to intercept, and was therefore reluctant to transmit details of the intruder to

An A-2 camera rig is winched into the U-2 payload bay, which spanned the entire fuselage immediately aft of the cockpit. This interim configuration of three 24-inch focal length units in fixed mounts was used for the first series of overflights (Lockheed C88-1447-52).

the next sector. By referring to a "twin-engined bomber," the Soviets evidently could not believe that a single-engined plane could fly so high.[23] The Czechoslovak and Polish governments also protested the flights, though less specifically.

As far as President Eisenhower was concerned the game was up. When the Soviet protest note reached the White House later on 10 July, U-2 overflights were suspended. Ike was annoyed that the assurances given by Bissell and others had proved false. They had told him that the flights would hardly be detected, let alone tracked.

During long-range training flights from the Ranch, U-2s had flown far to the north and within range of the DEW-line early warning radars, which managed to detect them periodically. A controlled series of flights were then made against Nike Hercules radar sites in southern California. The operators there could not assign accurate altitudes, tracks, or speeds to the high-flying bird, however. The CIA concluded that the PVO could not do any better, even in the western USSR, where Soviet radar coverage was most complete.

The CIA was half-right, but to Eisenhower detection was almost as bad as interception. He knew how seriously the Soviets would react to illegal overflights. After the Soviet protest note of 10 July 1956, Eisenhower would never again give *carte blanche* for a series of U-2 overflights. He examined mission requests on a case-by-case basis, and wanted to know all the details regarding routes, defenses, and so on. More often than not, he withheld permission.

At Project HQ Bissell quickly responded to the setback. He confirmed plans to deploy the second U-2 detachment in Turkey, close to the USSR's southern border, where the PVO's radar coverage was thought to be weaker. He also turned to his trusted scientific advisors again, and asked them to determine whether radar-fooling devices could be added to the U-2 airframe.

Windfall

The "take" from the first U-2 flights was analyzed by Lundahl's team in the Photo Intelligence Division. Bissell and DCI Dulles also reviewed the imagery. They chuckled with amazement at the clarity of the black and

---

THE INTELLIGENCE VALUE OF AQUATONE

After the Soviets detected and protested the first U-2 overflights, and President Eisenhower called a halt, a deep gloom descended over Project HQ. From the photography of those first five flights over the USSR, they knew just how valuable this aircraft was as an intelligence tool. The prospect of not being allowed to conduct further missions caused DPS executive officer Herb Miller to write a long, thoughtful memo. Here are a few extracts:

A full review of the 4 July mission yields results of much greater significance than (even the) highest priority intelligence targets. For the first time, we are really able to say that we have an understanding of much that was going on in the Soviet Union on 4 July 1956....We now have a cross-section of a part of the entire Soviet way of life for that day—their military installations, their farms, their irrigation systems, their factories, their power systems, their housing, their recreation, their railroads and the amount of traffic they carry, their scientific accomplishments at least in the field of electronics, their port activities....

These are but a few examples of the many things which tend to spell out the real intentions, objectives and qualities of the Soviet Union, that we must fully understand and appreciate of we are to be successful in negotiating a lasting peace for the world....

While we must grant that, in the week of operations permitted to Project Aquatone, only a relatively small area of the Soviet Union was examined, the sampling appears to be good....Yet there is a huge area included in the Urals and beyond about which we know even less from other intelligence sources, and which may really hold the key to the understanding of the Soviet Union which we seek.

To bar the United States from reaching this understanding through overflights...could well be tragic. Five operational missions have already proven that many of our guesses on important subjects can be seriously wrong.

- Memo for Project Director, DPS, 17 July 1956

AQUATONE, TALENT, AND CHESS

The photography from the U-2 overflights was of great value, not only to strategic intelligence analysts at the CIA, but also to military planners working out targets and attack routes for U.S. bombers. To disseminate the photography more widely, and yet protect the source, an elaborate security system was set up:

A control system named Talent was created for handling the U-2 overflights and related products. Access to Talent did not give one access to what type of aircraft engaged in the overflight. When Gary Powers was shot down on 1 May 1960, there were people who came into our shop in Germany and remarked, "so that's the aircraft that was flying these missions!" The codeword that went on U-2 products was Top Secret Chess.

The CIA Photo Interpretation Center had related units overseas named OPICs. One was within the USAF's 497th Reconnaissance Technical Squadron (RTS) in Schierstein, West Germany, and another one was within the 67th RTS in Yokota, Japan. Both of these OPICs had a Talent Special Projects section, and every effort was made to keep them at a low profile. These OPIC teams were headed by a CIA employee, and consisted of multi-service personnel. The 497th RTS Special Projects did the initial exploitation of the Middle East U-2 missions in 1956. Later, it received duplicate positives of all missions west of 100 degrees, while the 67th RTS OPIC got copies of all missions east of 100 degrees. The 544th Reconnaissance Technical Group at SAC HQ got copies of all missions worldwide.

- Allen Shumway, Jr, speech to Early Cold War Overflights Symposium, DIA, February 2001

The characteristic herring-bone pattern of an SA-1 surface-to-air missile site is apparent in this U-2 image, taken near Moscow on the only overflight of the Soviet capital. The notations at the edge of the image read "5-7 56 A2014 TOP SECRET TALENT," indicating the date of the flight, the type of camera prefixed to the mission number, and the classification and codename applied to the product (CIA).

U-2s AND UFOs

The CIA's Chief Historian Gerald Haines wrote a long article describing the Agency's role in the study of UFOs. The U-2 was responsible for many sightings in the mid-to-late 1950s, he wrote:

The early U-2s were silver and reflected the rays from the sun, especially at sunrise and sunset. They often appeared as fiery objects to observers below. By checking with the Agency's U-2 Project Staff, Air Force "Blue Book" UFO investigators were able to attribute many UFO sightings to U-2 flights. They were careful, however, not to reveal the true cause of the sighting to the public.

According to later estimates, over half of all UFO reports from the late 1950s through the 1960s were accounted for by manned reconnaissance flights over the U.S.

- Studies in Intelligence, Vol 1, No 1, 1997

white prints. Dulles rushed off to the White House with some samples. The President spread them out on the floor of the Oval Office and "we viewed the photos like two kids running a model train," Dulles later told Bissell.[24]

It soon became clear that the Iron Curtain had been thrust aside, in intelligence terms. To cope with the deluge of film and information PID had to be expanded. More photo-interpreters from the Army and Navy were brought into the Automat project at the Steuart Building, though the USAF refused to assign its men there full-time. In particular, SAC jealously guarded its autonomy in photo-interpretation. The U-2 film contained many likely new Soviet targets for its bombers. SAC headquarters maintained the USAF's largest photo-interpretation shop, and insisted that a duplicate negative and a duplicate positive of the U-2 film be sent to the 544th Reconnaissance Technical Squadron (RTS) at Offutt AFB.[25]

Within the PID, one group of photo-interpreters was assigned the military targets, and another the industrial targets. A third group compiled an index—a vital role given the sheer volume of film. The initial "readout" of target information was compiled into an "OAK" report, for quick circulation to those who were cleared to receive intelligence derived from the U-2 flights. Strict new control procedures were introduced to protect the source, which was classified above Top Secret by means of additional codewords. The U-2 imagery itself was codenamed Chess, and the intelligence derived from it was codenamed Talent.

After the OAK report was done, the PIs settled down for a more considered, second-phase study of the film. At first, they used paper prints derived from the original negative for interpretation, but it was soon realized that the high-quality U-2 imagery could best be interpreted from the

duplicate positives, which gave a better gray scale. Film from the U-2's 70mm tracker camera, which ran continuously throughout the flight, was also examined. It provided positional reference, especially when the aircraft had flown over featureless terrain, and was very valuable to the photogrammetrists within PID.[26]

The big news from the first U-2 overflights was that no massive Soviet bomber build-up was evident. There were plenty of *Badger* medium-range bombers on the film, mostly based in European Russia. They posed a threat to Western Europe, but not to the U.S., unlike the supposedly long-range *Bisons* and *Bears*. But none of these were seen deployed. The CIA concluded by late 1956 that there was no "bomber gap."

The estimates of Soviet long-range bomber strength were formally revised downwards in 1957-58, although the USAF continued to take the bomber gap seriously. The film product of the U-2 missions was so highly compartmented by security that even within the intelligence community, many were not aware of this highly reliable new source of information. For instance, drawings of the important targets revealed by the U-2 flights would be passed to the United States Air Forces in Europe (USAFE), rather than the imagery itself. USAFE target planners would superimpose the new data on their old German wartime imagery. Often there were conflicts, as the target planners protested that famous hunting lodges or hotels were located where the new data indicated runways. Even so, the U-2 imagery represented an intelligence windfall for USAFE, which soon began filling its target folders with the new or revised locations.[27]

Suez

In late August 1956 Detachment A was alerted for more operational missions. This time, though, they were to fly south instead of east. The targets were in the eastern Mediterranean, and were prompted by the Suez Crisis. The increasingly pro-Soviet President Nasser of Egypt had nationalized the Suez Canal in late July.

After a month of tense negotiations, British and French troops set sail for Cyprus on 29 August. On the same day, two U-2s departed Wiesbaden and flew eight-hour missions across the entire area before landing at Incirlik, the USAF base in Turkey where accommodations for Det B were being prepared. The next day, the two aircraft flew similar missions before landing back at Wiesbaden. The imagery showed the military preparations of various parties to the dispute, but it was only made available to one of them. On 7 September Jim Reber from ARC and Art Lundahl from PID flew to London and briefed British intelligence officials. Unbeknownst to President Eisenhower, who did not believe that his closest ally would take military action over Suez, the British subsequently used the U-2 imagery that Reber and Lundahl left behind to identify landing sites, drop zones, and invasion routes.[28]

Soviet radars detected the first U-2 overflights, and MiG fighters rose to challenge them. But these MiG-15s could not come close to the U-2's operational ceiling.

The Suez crisis was deepening, and the CIA decided to use the U-2 on a regular basis to monitor the situation. To speed up the interpretation of imagery, Lundahl made arrangements for the USAFE's 497th Reconnaissance Technical Squadron (RTS) at Wiesbaden to process the U-2 film, and he sent some staff from Automat to do the initial readout there. Fortunately, the CIA's second U-2 group was just now moving into Turkey, and would be close to the area of interest. Following approval for a U-2 base by the Turkish Prime Minister in early May, Leo Geary and the CIA station chief in Turkey surveyed various airfields before recommending Incirlik, near Adana, in the isolated southeast of the country. Det B began moving from the U.S. in late August.

Accidents at the Ranch

The CIA's second U-2 group had not been accident-free during the work-up period at the Ranch. On 15 May, Billy Rose became the first U-2 pilot killed when he stalled the aircraft while turning base leg. Rose had just taken off with a full fuel load, but a pogo had "hung up," and he was returning to try and shake it loose. He let the bank angle increase too far, and the fuel-laden right wing just kept on dropping. Two weeks later, another pilot ran out of fuel on final approach to the lakebed. The aircraft was damaged, but repairable.[29]

The third group arrived at the Ranch for training in August, but one of its pilots was soon killed. During a night takeoff on 31 August, Frank Grace became disoriented, lost control, and stalled in. Det B eventually deployed to Incirlik with eight pilots in early September. A ninth pilot who had trained with them, Howard Carey, was sent to Det A. Shortly after he arrived Carey became the third U-2 fatality. On 17 September he lost control at 35,000 feet during a climbout and crashed. The cause of the accident was never satisfactorily determined.[30]

The U-2 had been built, flight-tested, *and* deployed in an unprecedented 17 months. It was hardly surprising that some things were not right yet. After the fatal accidents some modifications were made. The solenoid release valve for the pogos was replaced by a system that allowed the pogos to drop away automatically upon takeoff; the elevator tab was extended to provide more sensitive trimming; and a gyro-compass was added as another aid to navigation.

Seen here at Wiesbaden in 1956, Carmine Vito (left) and Marty Knutson (right) were two of the pilots from Detachment A who flew the first missions over "denied territory" in the U-2 (via Jim Wood).

Det B over Suez

Det B flew its first operational mission over the eastern Mediterranean on 11 September, and its second on 25 September. Det A also flew nine missions to monitor the Suez Crisis this month, as U.S. Secretary of State John Foster Dulles (the brother of CIA's Allen Dulles) became increasingly suspicious of British, French, and Israeli intentions. One U-2 flew over the French naval base at Toulon during its delivery flight to Det B from Germany to Turkey. The British islands of Cyprus and Malta in the Mediterranean were regularly re-photographed; the CIA's photo-interpreters counted the Hunter fighters and Canberra bombers arriving from the UK as the build-up continued. Det B flew another nine missions in October, and some of these revealed nearly 60 Mystere IV fighter-bombers on Israeli airfields, whereas France had admitted supplying only 24.[31]

Foster Dulles described the Suez invasion, which began on 29 October, as "a collusion and deception" against the U.S. by the UK, France, and Israel. But thanks to the U-2 photography, plus SIGINT intercepts and the diplomatic comings and goings in Europe, the U.S. was not caught unawares. Once the fighting started, U-2 pilots had a grandstand view from 70,000 feet through their driftsights, since flights were mounted from Incirlik every day. The most notable of these was flown by Bill Hall on 1 November, when he passed twice over Almaza airfield, near Cairo. During the first pass, when he was heading west, rows of Egyptian fighters were captured on film. The second pass was only a short time later, after Hall re-

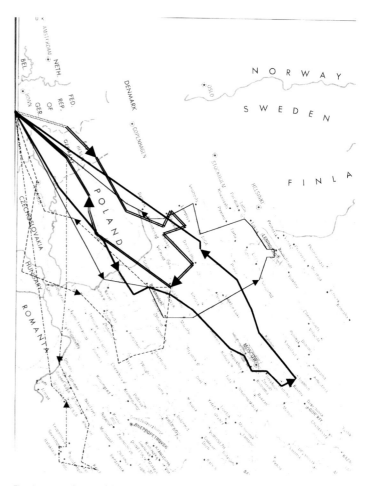

Five long overflights of Soviet territory were accomplished before a Soviet protest caused President Eisenhower to suspend them on 10 July.

versed course to head east again. This time, though, the Egyptian fighters were smoking wrecks. British and French bombers had attacked the base between U-2 passes. President Eisenhower was shown the before-and-after photographs, and is said to have remarked "Twenty-minute reconnaissance—now that's a goal to shoot for!"[32]

Det B continued to fly over the region, although less intensively after the British and French agreed to a cease fire on 7 November. To shorten the intelligence cycle still further, PID set up a film-processing unit at Incirlik itself. In the subsequent three years, Middle East missions became a "milk run" for Det B, since they usually went undetected and unopposed.

Detection - again

But the main intention of basing U-2s in Turkey was to overfly the USSR. U.S. intelligence estimated that the PVO had limited radar coverage along its Central Asian border, and fighter bases were few and far between. If the U-2 could penetrate from this direction undetected, it might not subsequently be "tagged" hostile, even when it approached more heavily-defended areas. President Eisenhower was well aware of this thesis, but despite the combined pleadings for more flights by Bissell and the chairman of the Joint Chiefs of Staff, Admiral Radford, he remained cautious. Eventually, he approved a few overflights of the satellite countries and a flight into the southern USSR, which "should stay as close to the border as possible."[33]

On the morning of 20 November 1956, Det B pilot Frank Powers took off from Incirlik and flew into Syria and Iraq. He passed over Bagdhad and into Iran before turning north towards the Caspian Sea. He crossed the Soviet border and flew over Baku before turning west to overfly Yerevan. The flight was then supposed to head for Tbilisi, but the aircraft's electrical inverter malfunctioned, forcing Powers to make an early return to Incirlik. Mission 4016 was one of the first to use the B-camera, which returned some imagery of the border airfields. But the flight had not gone undetected. Soviet fighters had once again been scrambled, as Powers had seen their contrails.[34]

First SIGINT mission

A month later, Det B flew its first dedicated SIGINT mission along this same border, staying outside Soviet airspace, but extending all along the Soviet coastline from the Black Sea to the Caspian Sea, and beyond to Afghanistan. This was an attempt to determine the Soviet radar "order-of-battle" for the region in greater detail with the dedicated sensor package designed by Ramo-Woolridge. It weighed over 500 lbs and completely replaced the camera sensor in the Q-bay.

Even so, the package was much smaller than the bulky SIGINT equipment previously flown along Soviet borders by converted U.S. bomber and patrol planes. Those systems required a crew of airborne "ferrets" to tune the receivers and direction-finding (DF) equipment and record the intercepted signals. The U-2 packages (designated Systems 4 and 5) could not do DF, but it was a significant advance in automation, so that all the read-out and analysis could be done on the ground after the flight returned. U-2s would continue carrying the smaller and less capable SIGINT Systems 1 and 3 in the nose when photography was the primary mission. System 1 provided electronic intelligence (ELINT), but its crystal video re-

Before-and-after photographs of Almaza airfield, Cairo, taken by a U-2 from 70,000 feet on 1 November 1956. The flight passed over twice; in the interim, British and French bombers attacked the airfield (via Dwayne Day)

ceivers had to be preset to certain radar bands before takeoff, and only Pulse-Repetition Frequency (PRF) and scan rate were recorded. System 3 was a COMINT system using three swept-frequency receivers to record VHF transmissions, such as those between Soviet fighters and their ground controllers.

The D Package

Yet another sensor system was adapted for the U-2. In 1957, Dets A and B each had a single aircraft equipped with the Westinghouse APQ-56 side-looking radar (SLR). This radar had been commissioned by SAC in 1954 as an extra means of identifying and locating airfields behind the Iron Curtain. It used a wide band receiver and a special recorder, and produced mapping images that were higher resolution than the "standard" Plan Position Indicator (PPI) airborne radars. It was first fitted to 10 of SAC's RB-47Es.

Although the APQ-56 antennas were long, they were not heavy, and a time-shared version was soon developed that used only one transmitter and receiver, switching them back and forth between the left and right-looking antennas. This further reduced the weight, and since this SLR operated in the rarely-used Ka-band, using a narrow antenna beamwidth, the danger of its signal being intercepted by Soviet defenses was slight.

According to SAC, these factors made it a practical proposition for the U-2, on which it was called the D Package. The antenna was installed in a faired radome below the U-2's rear fuselage, and a cathode ray tube (CRT) and film recording device was fitted in the cockpit. The pilot had to make occasional adjustments to the radar image, and this proved awkward, since the CRT was located behind his right elbow! He had to use a mirror to see the image. But compared with the U-2's superb photo imagery, the SLR had little to offer. The resolution was no better than 40 feet. The aircraft had to be flown in a straight line to ensure the correct map geometry, and a RADAN navigation system had to be added to help the pilot maintain a precise course.[35]

The RB-57D

On 10 December 1956, Dets A and B flew over Albania, Bulgaria, and Yugoslavia. President Eisenhower had authorized these flights a month earlier. The next day, though, the USAF flew three RB-57Ds straight over Vladivostok at lunchtime on missions that the President claimed he knew nothing about.[36] Six days later, the USSR delivered a strong protest which noted that the violation had occurred in such clear weather as to "exclude the possibility that the pilots were lost." A furious Eisenhower told JCS Chairman Admiral Radford and DCI Dulles to stop all further U.S. reconnaissance flights over Iron Curtain countries.

The RB-57D was one of the aircraft sponsored by the Bald Eagle project. Despite its known deficiencies, compared with the U-2, the USAF had proceeded with the rewinged jet bomber. It entered service with the 4080th Strategic Wing at Turner AFB, GA, which (like the U-2) inherited personnel from SAC's disbanded fighter wings. The flights over Vladivostok were part of the first operational deployment of the "D-model," which could reach 65,000 feet—on a good day. The aircraft were temporarily resident at Yokota, the USAF airbase near Tokyo.

The CIA was planning to base its third U-2 group in Japan. Det C began training at the Ranch in mid-August 1956, and was ready to deploy by year's end, despite losing one aircraft in an accident on 19 December. The deployment was held up by SAC, which was pushing its own over-

NAMING THE DRAGON LADY

For an aircraft that has never officially been named, the U-2 has been given a lot of titles! In the earliest days, Lockheed people called it the "Angel" because it flew so high. For security reasons, the CIA preferred the "Article," which was used in official cables and correspondence.

After the aircraft received its military designation, the Agency pilots and groundcrew began calling it the "Deuce." Once the U-2 became notorious in the wake of the Gary Powers shootdown, the press began calling it the "Shady Lady" or "Black Lady of Espionage."

But the nickname that was assigned by the USAF to denote the military U-2 program in 1957 is the one that really caught on. It was a reference to a mysterious oriental lady who was a key character in the cartoon strip "Terry And The Pirates." Originally drawn by Milton Caniff in 1934, the cartoon featured a young American who tangled with pirates along the coast of mainland China. The series remained popular right through the 1950s, by which time Terry was a fighter pilot, and the Dragon Lady was on the same side, leading an underground group fighting the communist regime in mainland China. But she remained distant and mysterious, sometimes defeated but never conquered, and it ill-behoved anyone to take her for granted. Terry's relationship with the Dragon Lady typified that between a U-2 pilot and his tricky mount.

When the Air Force assigned this very appropriate nickname to its U-2 program, 4080th SRW pilot Cozy Kline got his wife to draw an emblem. She had taken art classes in college. "There were some ground rules, such as nothing to suggest picture-taking. I had her draw a dragon entwined around an astrolabe used by ancient navigators," he recalled. The legend "Toward The Unknown" was added beneath the emblem. The rest is history. – *C.P.*

flight program of the Soviet Far East, using the RB-57D. Det C eventually deployed to the U.S. Naval Air Station at Atsugi, west of Tokyo, in mid-March 1957.[37]

U-2s for the USAF

The 4080th wing was also scheduled to receive the USAF's own U-2s. In January 1956, the service ordered 29 of them for $32 million, through the CIA.[38] In August, the wing's first cadre of maintenance troops was sent for training to the Lockheed factory at Oildale, CA, 90 miles north of Burbank. The USAF U-2s were being built here, rather than in Building 82, which had produced the 20 aircraft for the CIA. The finished articles were disassembled and wheeled onto the adjacent Bakersfield Airport, from where C-124 transports airlifted them to the Ranch. The first USAF aircraft, Article 361, arrived at the still-secret base in September 1956. The first USAF pilot, Colonel Jack Nole of the 4080th, was checked out on 13 November 1956. USAF headquarters assigned the unclassified nickname Dragon Lady to the project.

As the USAF's Dragon Lady project got underway, General LeMay lobbied again for control of the whole U-2 program. Thanks to Eisenhower's ban on overflights of Iron Curtain countries, there was not much activity in the CIA detachments, except for a few flights over Albania and Yugosla-

The USAF ordered 29 U-2s in early 1956, as a follow-on from the CIA order. The Air Force aircraft were not built at Burbank, but instead at a small factory at Oildale, where workers are seen assembling the long wings (Lockheed PR-1039).

Baghdad in 1956, taken from a U-2 flown by Gary Powers on 20 November 1956. This flight also penetrated Soviet territory, but only in the area around Baku (CIA).

The Martin RB-57D was a long-winged version of the B-57 that SAC sponsored, despite the success of Project Aquatone. Three of them overflew Vladivostok on 10 December 1956, sparking another Soviet protest. After that, only the U-2 was allowed to fly over the Soviet Union. (USAF).

via. Bissell wrote a memo to Dulles, justifying the retention of the Agency's U-2 operation...greater security, deeper cover, civilian pilots, and so on. The issue was thrashed out at a White House meeting on 6 May 1957, where the President rejected the USAF takeover bid.[39] LeMay had to be content with a secondary role for "his" U-2s—nuclear fallout sampling in the upper atmosphere.

Eisenhower's decision to keep the CIA in the U-2 business was partially based on the prospect of renewed overflights, which the President's own Board of Consultants on Foreign Intelligence Activities had recently recommended. The Soviet threat was switching from bombers to guided nuclear weapons, and there were huge gaps in Western knowledge. But there was another reason why Eisenhower was prepared to consider more flights. Dick Bissell said he had a new way to prevent the flights being detected.

4

Rethink and Retry

After the original series of U-2 overflights were detected, and therefore stopped by the White House, Dick Bissell consulted his scientific advisors again. Din Land's group repeated their earlier advice, that the U-2 would only be able to out-fly the Soviet air defenses for a couple of years. In August 1956, therefore, Bissell and his military deputy, Colonel Jack Gibbs, began searching for a successor to the Angel. The task would take them to research laboratories and aircraft companies all across the U.S. Gibbs, a Caltech graduate, was amazed at Bissell's ability to master aerodynamic theories without having an academic grounding in the subject. From unlikely beginnings, the DPS was emerging as a new government "sponsor" of leading-edge aerospace technology.[1]

Bissell was indeed a "Renaissance man." Before joining the CIA full-time in 1954, a stint at the Massachusetts Institute of Technology (MIT) brought him into contact with mathematicians, electrical and aeronautical engineers, and physicists. Bissell now tapped these contacts, especially within MIT's Radiation Laboratory (RadLab), and asked them if the U-2 could be modified to make it less vulnerable to radar detection.

In mid-August Kelly Johnson traveled east for a meeting with Bissell and some of the Boston scientists. Ed Purcell, a physics professor at Harvard University and a wartime pioneer of microwave research at the RadLab, was briefed on the U-2's overflight problems, and related his "mirror" theories on radar deception. The RadLab had already designed two types of resonant radar absorber, though their main application had been to reduce electromagnetic interference, rather than radar cross-section. The small group brainstormed into the small hours and reconvened at 7 am. By midday, they had devised a program to apply radar-canceling devices to the U-2. Project Rainbow—the first-ever attempt to make an operational aircraft "stealthy"—was underway.[2]

An Invisible U-2?

It was possible to apply a resonant absorber to the U-2 to fool the USSR's *Token* early warning radars, it was thought, since they operated at microwave frequencies around 3 GHz. The absorbers worked on the quarter-wavelength principle: a thin resistive sheet would be placed one-quarter wavelength from the aircraft's skin, and would reflect some of the incoming radar energy. The remaining energy would strike the U-2's metal skin and be reflected, but these "emergent waves" would cancel out the reflected waves, being 180-degrees out of phase with each other. To defeat the 10-centimeter wavelength of the *Token*, the absorber needed to be "only"

some one inch thick. But it would probably have to be applied to the whole of the lower half of the aircraft—wherever those radar waves might strike.[3]

But the metric-wavelength Soviet radars posed a greater problem! In addition to the *Token* (which the USSR designated the P-20 Periskop), the Soviet early-warning net still relied on numerous P-3, P-8, and P-10 static radars operating in the 65-86 MHz frequency range. These radars, nick-named *Dumbo* and *Knife Rest* by the West, had also detected the U-2, though unlike the *Token* they had no inherent height-finding capability. Defeating their 3-4 meter wavelengths called for a different solution, and one that did not appeal one jot to Kelly Johnson. RadLab proposed that small-gauge wire with precisely-spaced ferrite beads be strung around the aircraft. If they, too, were placed at quarter-wavelength, they might trap and defeat the metric radar waves.

The Soviet early warning radars, such as this Token, were able to detect the early U-2 overflights. This caused the CIA to embark upon Project Rainbow—an attempt to make the U-2 invisible to radar.

Bissell prevailed over Johnson, and both methods of making the U-2 "invisible" were given the go-ahead. The practical work was contracted by the Scientific Engineering Institute (SEI), a "front" company set up by Bissell so that the CIA could write formal contracts with the scientists in Boston. The key scientist who took Purcell's theories and applied them to the U-2 was Dr. Frank Rodgers. He left the MIT RadLab to work full time on Project Rainbow. At the Skunk Works, the effort was led by Luther MacDonald, assisted by Mel George and Ed Lovick. They had to devise a mounting system for the wires, and adapt the laboratory-standard absorbers for the rigors of flight. Eventually two absorbers would be used: the Salisbury Screen grid, consisting of graphite on canvas; and Eccosorb, an elastomeric type that could be tuned to more than one frequency.

Death in the Desert

By mid-December the first U-2 in a Rainbow configuration was being test-flown against radars at Indian Springs AFB, on the Nevada range. These were operated by Edgerton, Germeshausen & Grier (EG&G), another offshoot of the MIT RadLab. The wires were mounted on laminated wood poles attached all along the leading and trailing edges of the wings and horizontal tail. There were further attachment points at the nose, and even above the cockpit, meaning that the last wires had been secured *after* the pilot had climbed in. Not surprisingly, the test pilots hated them. They flapped in the slipstream, and were a potential hazard to flight control if one should break.

Dr Frank Rodgers was the radar scientist at MIT who was tapped by the CIA to work with Lockheed on Project Rainbow. He later advised how to design the A-12 Oxcart to have better radar-absorbing characteristics (via Herb Rodgers).

Throughout the first few months of 1957 the flights proceeded with much trial and error. The wires were cut and spaced to different wavelengths, and assembled in different configurations. The various absorbers were tried out, along with ferrite-based paints. The results were mixed, but some success was achieved against the Indian Springs radars.

However, the weight and drag penalties were significant; they reduced the U-2's maximum altitude by at least 5,000 feet, and range by 20%.

On 2 April 1957, Lockheed test pilot Bob Sieker was flying the prototype U-2 on yet another Rainbow test when the engine quit at 65,000 feet. As his pressure suit inflated the faceplate clasp on Sieker's helmet failed, and the pilot quickly lost consciousness. The aircraft went out of control and entered a descending flat spin. As it reached the lower atmosphere, the hypoxic Sieker recovered enough to realize he must get out of the plane! Struggling against the g-forces, he eventually managed to discard the canopy

BISSELL TAKES AIM AT THE AIR FORCE

In a memo dated 24 January 1957 for his boss DCI Allen Dulles, Project Director Richard Bissell vented his frustration at the Air Force's attitude toward the CIA's U-2 operation. The type of tension described here would endure for years...

The attitude of the Air Force has undergone a marked change since mid-autumn from one of full and open support and partnership toward one of increasing jurisdictional jealousy. The most important manifestation of change has been the long-continued effort to prevent AQUATONE from "competing" with Black Knight in the Far East.

Still another was the time-consuming and counterproductive insistence that any processing of AQUATONE film in the field should be done by units under Air Force command.

Finally, I am convinced that much of the pressure behind the SAC follow-on program involving the U-2 aircraft has, as its purpose, not the creation of a much-needed hot war reconnaissance capability, but the readying of Air Force units having the same capability as AQUATONE so as to undermine any argument for retention of this capability by the CIA.

The increasing Air Force disfavor is particularly hard, of course, on Air Force personnel assigned to this Project. There are several senior officers who already feel that their Air Force careers have been prejudiced by their loyalty to this Project, which has aroused the criticism of Generals Lewis and Everest (and quite possibly of General LeMay).

and climb out. But it was too late. Still in a flat spin, the aircraft hit the ground virtually intact, bounced, and a small fire broke out. It took rescuers nearly four days of searching from the air to find the crash site, in the remote desert about 40 miles north of the Ranch. They found Sieker's body less than 200 feet from the wreckage. His parachute pack was opened, but the chute was only partially deployed.[4]

A post-mortem on Sieker at Tonopah revealed his hypoxia, and since the aircraft was virtually intact, it was not too difficult to work out the root cause of the accident. The radar absorbent coatings had acted as insulation around the engine bay, causing the hydraulic system to overheat and reduce pressure to the fuel boost pump motor. Additional cooling was added to correct the problem. But if his life support system had not failed, Sieker could have still brought the plane home. Kelly Johnson called for a redesign of the faceplate, a dual oxygen regulator, and an ejection seat that could be used on an interchangeable basis with the existing seat. At least two U-2 pilots had strongly recommended a dual oxygen system more than a year earlier, and the accident in which Det C pilot Bob Ericson had lost control and been forced to abandon a U-2 the previous December was also caused by hypoxia, induced by a faulty oxygen feed.[5]

Goodbye to the Ranch

At the time of Sieker's accident, training activity for the USAF's own U-2 operation had reached a peak, with 18 pilots plus maintenance crews at the Ranch. Unfortunately, operations at the secret base were being disrupted by renewed nuclear testing at the AEC range right next door. The Plumbbob

series of atmospheric tests kicked off on 28 May, producing a fireball 900 feet wide. The AEC preferred to set off the tests when the wind would blow the fallout northeast, away from Las Vegas and the populated areas of California. The Groom Lake area was therefore usually directly under the fallout path, and had to be evacuated each time.

With the Plumbbob series scheduled to last for many months, a decision to abandon the Ranch was reluctantly taken. The CIA would establish a test unit to continue development work on the U-2 at Edwards AFB, in a remote location at the northern edge of the Rogers dry lake named North Base. It would be supported by Lockheed flight test and maintenance personnel. The growing fleet of USAF aircraft would move out to the permanent base that SAC had chosen for the U-2. This was another remote location at Laughlin AFB, outside Del Rio, on the border between West Texas and Mexico.

The U-2 was going semi-public, but the USAF was still wrestling over the security classification to apply to its strange-looking new jet. The 4080th wing, which moved to Laughlin in April, where it displaced a pilot training wing, was told that "a positive attempt will be made to release very little information." SAC devised cover names for the U-2's photographic and SIGINT payloads, in an attempt to associate them with the "weather research" mission. Cameras became "Nepho," short for nephograph: an instrument for photographing clouds. SIGINT systems became "Sferics," a shortform of "atmospherics." [6]

No Big Secret

In reality, the true mission of the U-2 was already obvious to anyone with a modicum of intelligence skill. Within a month of Det A's arrival at Lakenheath in May 1956, the UK's Flight magazine ran two sarcastic editorials scoffing at the cover story and the excessive security surrounding the deployment. "Very high weather we're having lately!" remarked another British magazine. Soon the aircraft spotters that gathered around the perimeter of British military bases were taking snatched photographs of U-2s on approach to Lakenheath—and sending them to the aeronautical press. In February 1957, the U.S. government finally released the first official photograph of the U-2—an aircraft in NACA markings. Soon after Det C began operations from Atsugi, a Japanese photographer snapped one of the aircraft on approach, and the result was published in Koku Joho (Aviation News) magazine in May 1957. Security officers from the base allegedly searched his home while he was out.[7]

Then, on 30 May 1957, the CIA's cover story was well and truly blown. The London Daily Express reported that:

"Lockheed U-2 high-altitude aircraft of the U.S. Air Force have been flying at 65,000 feet, out of reach of Soviet interceptors, mapping large areas behind the Iron Curtain with revolutionary new aerial cameras. They are making mathematically precise maps essential to bombardment with missile weapons."

The true nature of U-2 operations also leaked into the U.S. press, but not into the major newspapers, since top editors were persuaded by the government to suppress the story in the national interest. The security for the U-2 project was run by a special CIA team in Project HQ headed by Walt Lloyd. Many workers within the project thought the security team was overzealous, to say the least. But the rigid policy of admitting no connection between the U-2 and airborne reconnaissance continued. Maybe the security team calculated that Soviet intelligence relied upon the U.S. press for all its U-2 information, and never monitored the British or Japanese press!

Death in Texas

On 10 June 1957, the CIA and Lockheed moved from the Ranch to the North Base at Edwards. The next day, Colonel Jack Nole led a formation of four USAF U-2As from Nevada to Laughlin AFB. A further six aircraft arrived at the Texas base over the next two days, to continue the extensive training program that SAC had devised. The 4080th wing had been allocated primary responsibility for the sampling mission, but would also train for photo and SIGINT missions. The 4028th Strategic Reconnaissance Squadron (SRS) was activated to operate the U-2s, with Nole as the commander. The U-2 squadron would operate alongside the RB-57Ds of the 4025th SRS, which had moved from Turner AFB to Laughlin a few months earlier.

After just eighteen days at Laughlin, SAC's "secret" U-2 operation was compromised. The first pilot to be checked out at Laughlin decided to take a trip downtown—*with* his airplane! Lieutenant Ford Lowcock had set up house on the outskirts of Del Rio, near to the small civil airport. Just before nine in the morning on Friday, 28 June, on only his second checkout ride in the U-2, Lowcock flew across town at 1,500 feet. Apparently, he wanted to stage a private airshow for his wife and two small sons. Lowcock made two descending turns to the right over the house, but he was unable to bring the wings back level. The aircraft spiraled into a ceniza-covered hill next to the airport and flipped upside-down. There was no fire, but the 28-year old Lowcock was knocked unconscious and died from asphyxia-

tion. He hadn't realized that, with the U-2's ailerons in gust control, their effectiveness in roll was much reduced.[8]

Only two hours later, First Lieutenant Leo Smith took off from Laughlin for a high-altitude training flight and he, too, did not return. The plane crashed about 45 minutes later, some 30 miles north of Abilene, Texas. The accident investigation determined that an autopilot or trim malfunction might have occurred, leading to loss of control. Another possible cause was fuel imbalance in the wings (a contributory factor in the Lowcock accident). Oxygen problems were also on the list of possible causes. Smith had evidently tried to escape but—just like Sieker two months earlier—he had been pinned back by g-forces, and the bulky pressure suit had not helped. After these two accidents, the USAF agreed with Kelly Johnson that an ejection seat should be provided, and work began to adapt Lockheed's own lightweight T2V seat. But there was no decision to adopt the dual oxygen regulator, another safety item that Lockheed had recommended.

Dirty Birds deploy

After the White House meeting in early May 1957, which gave preliminary approval for more Soviet overflights, Project HQ decided to deploy the U-2s with the radar-evading modifications, even though flight tests were not yet complete. In June, one modified U-2 was sent to each of the CIA detachments. They were not enthusiastically received. "Part of my big paycheck was compensation for high-risk missions in a semi-experimental airplane, but I had never before risked flying an airplane wired like a guitar!" recalled Det B pilot Jim Cherbonneaux.[9] The Skunk Works engineers had named the modified aircraft "Dirty Birds," in an obvious comparison with the aerodynamically very "clean" standard U-2. The detachments called them "Covered Wagons."

A U-2 having radar-absorbent material applied to the lower fuselage at the Ranch in early 1957 (Lockheed).

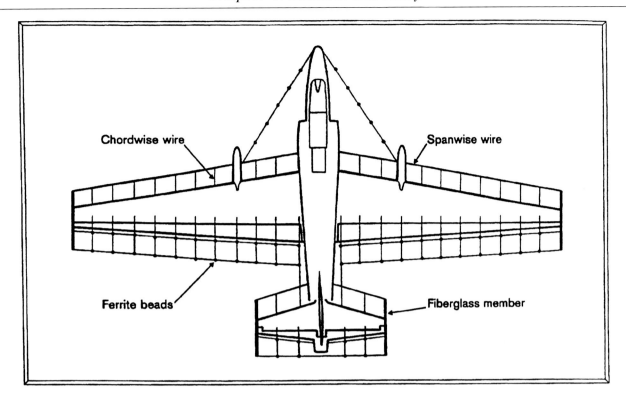

Above and below: In an attempt to fool Soviet radars operating in the metric (VHF) wavebands, wires were strung across the aircraft's surface at carefully-measured distances, and from booms attached to the wings and tail.

Det B's Jim Cherbonneaux flew the first operational tests of a "Covered Wagon" on 21 and 30 July 1957. They were routed along the Soviet border at 12 miles distance, to determine whether the modified aircraft could fool the air defense radars. The first one went east from Incirlik to the Caspian Sea. The second one went north to test Soviet defenses on the other side of the Black Sea.[10]

Cherbonneaux had flown a similar border flight four months earlier, in a conventional U-2. This mission was designed to collect the latest Soviet radar frequencies for use in the Rainbow project, so it used a big SIGINT package in the Q-bay designated System 5. Cherbonneaux had flown all the way across Iran to Afghanistan above a solid undercast, failing all the while to pick up any useful signal for the radio compass, which could help him fix his position. Reversing course, but still relying on dead reckoning, he strayed across the border near Baku. Cherbonneaux had not realized this until he saw the contrails of Soviet interceptors heading his way. The U-2 pilot beat a hasty retreat to the south.[11]

On the second flight with the Covered Wagon, Cherbonneaux flew up and down the Soviet Black Sea coast. Occasionally, his flight plan called for the aircraft to fly towards the coast rather than parallel, to deliberately provoke a radar response. The NSA's ground stations in Turkey would also be listening for a Soviet reaction. The results of the mission were inconclusive. There had been a complication during the flight when the engine bleed valves had opened at random a few times, causing each time a rapid 4-5,000 foot descent through loss of power.

On both test flights System 5 recorded some alerting of Soviet radars, especially when the aircraft was flying directly towards or away from the radar sites. Upon further study, it was realized that most of the radar re-

turns were coming from the U-2's cockpit, engine intakes, and tailpipe, which could not be covered with absorber.[12]

The results were good enough for Bissell, though, as he pressed the case for more overflights. The CIA had contacted the president of Pakistan, who had given permission for U-2 overflights from his country. That was a double bonus. Soviet air defenses were weaker in that area than anywhere else. And many of the highest-priority targets were deep inside the USSR, from the Urals to Siberia. Even with its long range, the U-2 could not reach them from anywhere else.

Operation Soft Touch

At Project HQ there was a flurry of activity, as multiple mission plans were being drawn up for Operation Soft Touch. Each flight was planned around one or two of the highest priority targets on the ARC list. Then as many lower-priority targets as possible were added. At Incirlik, Det B commander Colonel Ed Perry prepared a deployment plan. In late July, C-124 transports lifted all the required fuel and support gear to the airbase at Lahore. It was the CIA's second choice, but the preferred airbase further north at Peshawar was closed for runway repairs. Two U-2s were ferried in, and hidden inside a hangar that had been borrowed from the Pakistan air force.

Early on 4 August, the first mission headed over the Karakorums, over the desert wastes of Sinkiang province in far western China, and onwards towards the border between Mongolia and the Soviet Union. The prime targets were around Lake Baykal, as well as the Soviet cities of Irkutsk and Ulan Ude. But the weather there was much cloudier than forecast, and the pilot turned back before reaching them.[13]

On 5 August 1957 two U-2s were launched. One was another attempt to reach Lake Baykal, but it had to turn back shortly after takeoff with technical problems. The other one was the Covered Wagon, flown by Eugene "Buster" Edens. He went north to enter Soviet territory over the Pamir mountains before turning northwest to Tashkent. Mission 4035 was searching for the very highest-priority target—a suspected new Soviet long-range missile launch base.

By the middle of 1957 the USSR had been testing its new series of ballistic missiles from the Kapustin Yar test range south of Stalingrad for four years. Since mid-June 1955, the U.S. had been monitoring launches from Kapustin Yar with a powerful ground radar at Diyarbakir, in Turkey. Other ground stations in Turkey monitored Soviet down-range communications whenever a launch was planned, and attempted to intercept telemetry from the missile in flight. On 22 June 1957 the big radar observed a missile launch from Kapustin Yar that impacted much further east, in the remote Kazakhstan desert, than usual. Further tests of this 1,100-mile range missile followed in quick succession. Meanwhile, SIGINT and other intelligence suggested that a new test range was being built to handle intercontinental-range missile firings, from a launch site somewhere east of the Aral Sea, and an impact area on the Kamchatka Peninsula, 4,000 miles away.

The CIA had already made two attempts to photograph the Kamchatka area with the U-2. On 8 June, Det C pilot Jim Barnes flew north out of Atsugi in the first attempt to overfly the suspected impact area. But the entire Kamchatka peninsula was covered in cloud. Barnes therefore stayed offshore, and flew the aircraft on to the planned destination at Eielson AFB, Alaska. On 18 June the weather forecast for Kamchatka was better, so Al Rand took off for a second attempt. He completed the mission as briefed,

OPERATION SOFT TOUCH

We borrowed a hangar from the Pakistan Air Force. Our three aircraft almost completely filled it. There was a major outbreak of Asian flu just starting up there, and two of our guys got really sick. Others got diarrhea. I swear, if he could have gotten away with it, (Detachment Commander) Ed Perry would have appointed an official food taster for each pilot.

All of the pilots had at least one long and grueling mission over Russia. The rest of the Det really worked their butts to the bone getting the aircraft and flight plans ready for those missions. The whole of the Lahore operation was done exceedingly well. We did not have any aircraft problems or aborts, despite all odds to the contrary. Every time I think of those days in Pakistan, I raise an imaginary glass in silent toast to all the guys who were there.

- Jim Cherbonneaux unpublished memoir

returning to Eielson. However, there was still a lot of cloud, and a camera malfunction ruined every third frame. Nevertheless, the photo-interpreters were able to discern some preparations for missile tests around Klyuchi.[14]

It was clear that the Soviet missile program was shifting into higher gear. In fact, a huge booster with intercontinental range and designated the R-7 was being developed. It could only be moved by railroad. Construction of a launch site in the desert east of the Aral Sea was already well complete. After two failed attempts, the first R-7 was launched from the new launch site on 15 May 1957, but after only 50 seconds it exploded

Bob Sieker, the Skunk Works test pilot who was killed in the crash of the prototype U-2 on 2 April 1957 (Lockheed 05626).

over the test range. On 12 July 1957, another missile had to be removed from the launch pad after three failed countdowns. None of this was known to the CIA, although SIGINT intercepts told of heightened preparations along the test range.

And so, when Buster Edens flew onwards from Tashkent on 5 August, his route followed the railway that ran northwest from Tashkent, searching for the new launch site. The B-camera, with its option for horizon-to-horizon coverage, proved invaluable on this type of mission. Edens continued northwest along the Syr Darya river valley, all the way to the Aral Sea, before turning north and returning along a parallel track. There was no discernible reaction to the flight, but it was not a real test of the radar-evading modifications, since the Soviet air defense system had only poor radar coverage in the Kazakh SSR at this time.[15]

When the B-camera film from Mission 4035 reached the PID in Washington a few days later, the huge launchpad was visible on one of the high oblique frames. But it was little more than a speck on the horizon, since the launchpad was located at the end of a spur extending some 15 miles into the desert from the main rail line.[16]

PID's all-source analyst Dino Brugioni turned to the best available map of the area, which was still the 1939 map drawn up by the German Wehrmacht. This map also showed a spur leading north from the station at "Tjuro-Tam." Brugioni deduced that the spur had been built to serve a prewar quarry, which had been converted to serve as the flame pit for the large new Soviet missile. The launch site would henceforth be known as Tyuratam in the West. The big booster was given the reporting designation of SS-6. A second U-2 mission was quickly requested to fly directly over the launch pad.[17]

Targets, Cameras, Routes

Meanwhile, in the cramped hangar at Lahore, Det B stayed on alert for more missions. In addition to the two missile launch sites and their downrange installations, the reconnaissance target list was rich with possible nuclear weapons development sites and military industrial complexes. The furthest of these were nearly 2,000 miles from Lahore, in the Kuznetsk Basin, known as "Stalin's second industrial bastion." Many of the targets were "secret cities," completely closed to foreigners. For instance, there was Krasnoyarsk, where a huge new complex of apartment houses, laboratories, warehouses, and machine shops had been revealed in 1956 by one of the few balloon flights to produce any useful intelligence. There was also Tomsk, where returning German prisoners of war had suggested there was a "secret undergound atomic plant." The CIA arranged for the fur hat that one of these Germans had worn to be analyzed by nuclear scientists. The hat contained traces of the U-235 isotope, suggesting that Tomsk was a separation plant.[18]

Other targets listed for the new U-2 missions included uranium concentration plants in the Kirghiz and Tadzhik SSRs; an atomic energy complex and a factory producing fighter-interceptors at Novosibirsk; another aircraft plant in Omsk; and a rocket motor production and test site at Biysk.

Some of the targets could not be located with enough certainty to guarantee that the U-2 would pass overhead, and thus provide the best-quality imagery. This was true of the impact areas for missiles launched from Kapustin Yar, somewhere west of Lake Balkhash, and the nuclear weapons proving ground, which was thought to be near Semipalatinsk. In the latter case, the only intelligence available was seismic data, but none of the 20 nuclear tests that had taken place here in the previous eight years could be fixed closer than within 30 miles. Therefore the mission planners had to orient the flight lines for maximum coverage of the most likely territory, or specify that the U-2 perform some search patterns.

When all the target and camera choices had been made in project HQ, the mission plan was transmitted to the Det, where the pilot maps were drawn up. The flight lines on the map were drawn in color: red for portions of the flight where the course had to be followed exactly so that a particular objective was covered; blue for less important sections; and brown for emergency abort routes back to base. The straight flight lines were linked by "ten-cent turns," so-called because they could be drawn on the map with a dime. Notations on the map instructed the pilot when to turn the camera and SIGINT systems on and off, or select different operating modes for them.

A fourth Soft Touch mission was launched from Lahore on 12 August, flown by Bill McMurry in the Covered Wagon. He was heading north-northeast in almost a straight line, towards Tomsk and Novosibirsk. But when the pilot turned the B-camera on it soon malfunctioned, and he had to abort after flying 1,400 miles along the China-USSR border. The good news was there was very little indication of Soviet tracking, and no protest note.[19]

A third aircraft was flown in from Incirlik and squeezed into the hangar. Then, on 21 and 22 August, as fine weather prevailed across the entire southern USSR, five more missions were flown. It was an enormous effort, and not only for the maintenance crews. Although the mission plans were devised in Project HQ and transmitted to the Det, the waypoints still had to be transcribed onto the pilots' maps and the fuel curves plotted. There were many target objectives for each flight. Under great pressure, the detachment's operations officer Major Harry Cordes did most of this work in the hangar at Lahore. On the 22nd, he had to draw up maps for three overflight missions that took off in quick succession.

On the 21st Sammy Snyder reflew the previous, aborted mission, all the way to Tomsk. Athough U.S. intelligence knew that there was a nuclear reactor here, this was still pretty much uncharted territory. One large city

that Snyder flew over wasn't even marked on his map! Also on the 21st E.K. Jones flew just as far, but further to the west, to cover Omsk and Tatarsk.

Both these missions flew over Lake Balkhash and Semipalatiinsk on their way to or from the targets further north. The analysts were looking for another missile test range known to be located near the lake, and for the nuclear test site at Semipalatinsk. The next day, Mission 4050 was planned to fly west of Semipalatinsk town—and Jim Cherbonneaux returned with near-perfect photography of ground zero! Another mission routed further east was less successful. Tom Birkhead went all the way to Krasnoyarsk, another secret nuclear city, where uranium enrichment and plutonium production was accomplished. But it was cloudy here, and the photography was rated poor overall by the interpreters.[20]

The wreckage of the prototype Article 341 in the Nevada desert. As was often the case when a U-2 crashed after loss of control at high altitude, the aircraft was still substantially complete upon impact. This time, however, a fire broke out and destroyed most of the forward fuselage (CIA).

SEMIPALATINSK

During Operation Soft Touch, as with all other operations during the early days, mission pilots were told as little as possible about the targets they would fly over as a matter of security. On one of the three flights launched from Lahore on 22 August, Det B pilot Jim Cherbonneaux had been flying over Soviet territory for about three hours when he noticed some familiar-looking landmarks beneath him. There were large circular areas of ground that had been cleared and graded, with paved support roads leading outwards towards distant block houses. It was just like flying over the AEC proving grounds in Nevada from the Ranch, the pilot recalled!

When the plan for this mission was transmitted from Washington, Det B had not been told that this flight was designed to find the Soviet nuclear test site. In fact, CIA nuclear analyst Henry Lowenhaupt had calculated the average epicenters of the five largest nuclear detonations in the area. He requested a flight track that passed over this spot, which was 70 miles due west of the inhabited area at Semipalatinsk. So the mission planners at Project HQ routed the flight west-to-east between Karaganda and Semipalatinsk, for maximum coverage. And on U-2 Mission 4050, they hit paydirt!

Cherbonneaux adjusted course slightly to fly over the center of one of the cleared areas. He brought the driftsight up to full ×4 magnification and scanned around the site. There was a large tower at the center, which was completely deserted. But at a large block house in the far distance, a number of vehicles were parked. Suddenly, the U-2 pilot imagined that the tower might be holding a nuclear weapon that was about to be detonated! Even at 400 knots TAS, it seemed an eternity before the aircraft was clear of the area. Cherbonneaux set course for his next targets in the Omsk area and breathed a sigh of relief.

When Cherbonneaux returned to Lahore and told his debriefers about the nuclear test site they didn't believe him. But within 24 hours, Project HQ confirmed that a half-megaton nuclear test had taken place there about five hours after the U-2 flew overhead. When the film was analyzed, it showed a bomber aircraft at Semipalatinsk airfield. This was subsequently determined to be the carrier for the 22 August explosion, which was actually an air-dropped nuclear weapon. But the tower that Cherbonneaux had observed did indeed also contain a nuclear weapon, although this relatively low-yield device was not detonated until 13 September. – C.P.

The third mission on the 22nd did not penetrate the USSR, but flew over Tibet instead. This mission, flown by Bill Hall, was designed to map large parts of this remote country. The CIA had just begun supporting a group of Tibetan exiles in their attempts to expel the communist Chinese who had invaded their homeland in 1950. The U-2 photography helped to identify suitable infiltration routes and paratroop drop zones. These air-drops began two months later, in December 1957.[21]

Lift-Off!

The last overflight from Lahore was launched on 28 August, when E.K. Jones flew the return trip to Tyuratam that the missile analysts had urgently requested. Exactly a week earlier, the huge SS-6 had finally achieved a successful lift-off there. In fact, the 21 August flight of the SS-6 was not a complete success. The re-entry stage carrying a mock-up of the nuclear warhead reached the specified range over Kamchatka, but disintegrated into a few thousand pieces at 30,000 feet.[22]

Nevertheless, on 26 August Moscow announced the successful flight, adding pointedly that "it is now possible to send missiles to any part of the world." But the announcement still did not identify the launch site. Eventually, the USSR misleadingly named it Baikonur, after a town that was located fully 200 miles to the northeast. But on the 28 August flight, Jones obtained excellent vertical photography of the Tyuratam site, which showed just one launch pad. Mission 4058 only just missed photographing the rollout of the next SS-6, which was successfully launched on 7 September in the presence of Khrushchev himself.[23]

But Mission 4058 was a failure in one important respect. Despite being flown with the Covered Wagon, Soviet radars picked it up. The flight was intercepted as it flew towards Stalingrad. With the heavier weight of the radar absorbers and the wires, the aircraft was only at 66,000 feet. Jones estimated that some of the fighters were only 1,000 feet beneath him. He cut the flight short and turned around.[24]

Desperate to get some idea of how accurate the SS-6 missile could be, the CIA tried again for U-2 coverage of the impact area on Kamchatka. The fourth "Dirty Bird" was ferried from Edwards to Eielson, from where Det C pilot Barry Baker flew Mission 6008 and successfully photographed the Klyuchi area on 16 September. But no evidence of any guided missile activities was apparent.[25]

Eighteen days later, yet another SS-6 was launched from Tyuratam. But this particular test flight had a different, and highly public purpose. The guidance system and dummy warhead in the nosecone had been replaced by a small satellite! The firing sequence of the SS-6's core engine and strap-on boosters was modified to push the missile higher into the stratosphere. The successful launch into earth orbit of Sputnik 1 by the SS-6 on 4 October 1957 was a propaganda and technical coup for the USSR. The world sat up and took notice.

If the Soviets could blast a satellite into orbit, they could probably loft a nuclear warhead towards the U.S. The "missile gap" controversy began. But the U-2 was providing some solid information about Soviet missile flight tests. It had soared over Tyuratam and Klyuchi and, in another overflight flown out of Det B's home base at Incirlik on 10 September, also over Kapustin Yar for the first time. One of Yangel's new R-12 missiles was photographed on the launch pad.

Analysis

It took the photo interpreters at PID many months to identify all the significant Soviet nuclear sites from Operation Soft Touch. Some uranium mines were captured on film, but not discovered for a whole year. The "secret underground atomic plant" at Tomsk turned out to be a huge complex covering 40 square miles: not only a U-235 gaseous diffusion separation plant, as expected, but also one plutonium-producing nuclear reactor in operation; two more nuclear reactors under construction; and a plutonium chemical separation facility.

It took the CIA's missile and nuclear analysts even longer to extract maximum intelligence value from this series of flights. Often, collateral information was acquired at a later date that prompted a second, third, or even fourth look at the original imagery. The analysts used every possible means to try and understand what they were seeing on the U-2 film. Scale models were built of important sites, such as Tyuratam. Project HQ was asked to fly U-2 photo missions over the Nevada nuclear test site, in order to compare the imagery with that from Semipalatinsk, in case some ground features were common to both sites.

Lessons about the Soviet nuclear program—such as the plutonium production rate—were still being learned from the Tomsk photography five years later. Analysts eventually realized that they could determine the water flow through the Tomsk reactor and its rise in temperature. From

The USAF began receiving its own U-2s at the Ranch in September 1956. 56-6696 was the third one delivered, and is seen here in an official photo released later in 1957, after SAC moved the U-2 squadron to Laughlin AFB, Texas (Lockheed LA546).

The CIA conspired with Lockheed to convince the Soviets that 55,000 feet really was the maximum altitude. Ernie Joiner and his flight test engineers, Bob Klinger and Mich Yoshi, were instructed to create a fake U-2 flight manual, Klinger recalled. They sketched out a much heavier airframe with more conventional maneuvering load factors, and the same airspeed limits as the T-33. Graphs were invented showing a much poorer rate of climb to the aircraft's officially-acknowledged maximum altitude of 55,000 feet. They even included cockpit photos in the manual, showing instruments whose markings had been altered to correspond with the fake data. The Skunk Works engineers included genuine data on the U-2's weather reconnaissance package—but not on any of the other payloads. Three or four copies of the fake manual were artificially aged with dirt, grease, coffee stains, and cigarette burns. Kelly Johnson turned them over to the Agency's clandestine people in DDP, which presumably attempted to "plant" them in the appropriate Soviet channels.

It is not known whether the manuals reached the intended recipients. There is one tantalizing clue that at least one of them did. Pyotr Popov, a Lt Col in the GRU who had been spying for the CIA since 1952, reported to his U.S. handler in April 1958 that he overheard a drunken Colonel boasting that the KGB had "many technical details about the new high-altitude spycraft." Of course, the KGB might simply have aggregated the considerable amount of information about the U-2 that had been published in the Western press by now! (The USSR discovered Popov's treachery later in 1958 and executed him the following year). – C.P.

The U-2 could carry a dedicated SIGINT package in the Q-bay, instead of the cameras. Designed by Ramo Wooldridge, Systems 4 and 5 were flown along the Soviet border in 1957-58 to determine Soviet radar frequencies and signal characteristics.

that, they could deduce the power output of the reactor and its annual production of plutonium in kilograms. By comparing the techniques used in U.S. nuclear reactors, factoring in the limited technical data available from open Soviet technical literature, and closely studying a cinefilm of "a new Siberian atomic power plant" that Soviet scientists revealed at the 1958 Geneva Conference on the peaceful uses of nuclear energy, the CIA analysts were eventually able to make confident estimates of the USSR's total plutonium production.[26]

The flush-mounted panels apparent in the nose of Article 368 indicate where the antennas for the small SIGINT packages were carried. Systems 1 and 3 were designed to pick up and record enemy air defense activity that was directed against an overflying U-2, for analysis after the mission landed (Lockheed C88-1447-54).

In their tight-fitting MC-3 partial pressure suits, the operational pilots and support officers of Detachment B pose for a rare group photo sometime in 1956-57. This was the group that conducted the most intensive series of Soviet U-2 overflights, in August 1957. Top row, from left: Frank Powers, Sammy Snyder, Tom Birkhead, Col Ed Perry (commander), E.K. Jones Bill McMurry, and Bill Hall. Bottom row, from left (Lt Col Chet Bohart and Lt Col Cy Perkins (operations officers), Buster Edens, Jim Cherbonneaux, and Maj Harry Cordes (mission planner) (via Sue Powers).

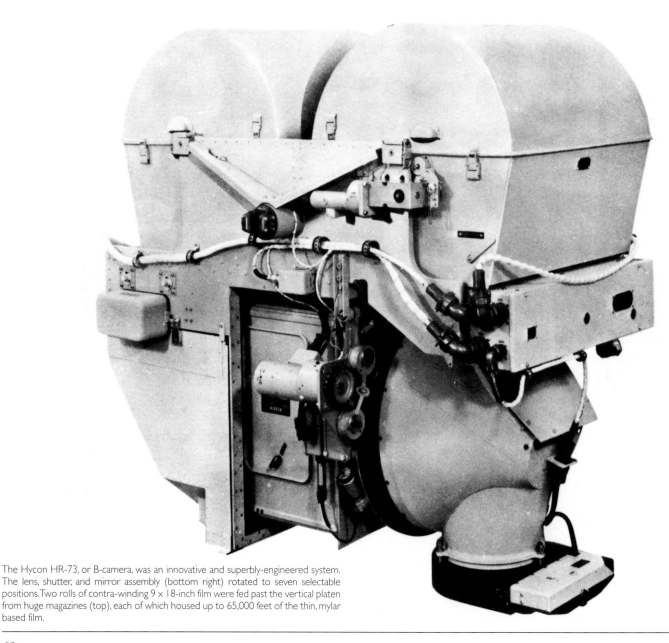

The Hycon HR-73, or B-camera, was an innovative and superbly-engineered system. The lens, shutter, and mirror assembly (bottom right) rotated to seven selectable positions. Two rolls of contra-winding 9 x 18-inch film were fed past the vertical platen from huge magazines (top), each of which housed up to 65,000 feet of the thin, mylar based film.

PVO tracking

The USSR detected only three of the eight overflights staged from Pakistan during August. From the CIA's perspective this was a big improvement, but it wasn't thanks to the radar-evading Covered Wagons. Whenever they had flown over areas where Soviet radar coverage was good, they had been picked up. The Soviets figured out what was going on, and protested to the Pakistan government. Det B was obliged to pack up and go home.[27]

Barry Baker's trip to Klyuchi in September had been detected and trailed by five MiGs. Worse still, Baker had been unable to fly higher than 59,000 feet in Det C's Covered Wagon, partly because of its extra weight, and partly because of warmer temperatures than had been expected in the upper atmosphere there. Looking down through the driftsight, Baker could even make out the bonedome of one Soviet pilot as his interceptor shadowed the U-2 only a few thousand feet below.

Bill Hall's mission to Kapustin Yar on 10 September was flown to get coverage of the missile test range that had been denied to Buster Edens on 28 August, because he cut short the flight after being intercepted. Once again, Det B used its Covered Wagon. But although Hall flew up the west side of the Caspian Sea and across the basin of the Volga River without incident, as soon as he neared Kapustin Yar he saw interceptors rising beneath him. The PVO launched 18 of them that day. Hall turned southwest towards Stavropol, the Black Sea, and safety to avoid them. He therefore missed some targets on the western end of the missile range.[28]

On 27 October, Det B flew another mission along the Soviet Black Sea coast with the Covered Wagon, to test Soviet air defense reactions. It was no good. Again, the radars tagged the aircraft and interceptors were launched.[29]

Within the PVO, development resources were switched to surface-to-air missiles (SAMs). During Operation Soft Touch, U-2s had flown over the test range that stretched 8,000 nautical square miles to the west of Lake Balkhash. The flights photographed a well-planned, modern community of some 20,000 people on the western shore of the lake. The CIA's analysts determined that this was an area for test-launching SAMs, as well as an impact area for medium-range offensive missiles. They named it Saryshagan.

The seven windows of the B-camera hatch are evident here, as well as the extent of the U-2's camera bay. This was designed to take modular payloads, and later became known as the "Q-bay" (author).

The launch site for test flights of the Soviet ICBM was pinpointed by two U-2 overflights of the desert area east of the Aral Sea in August 1957. To disguise the location, the Soviets named it "Tashkent-50," but the CIA named it Tyuratam, after the nearest railway station shown on their old wartime maps of the area (CIA).

Enter the SA-2

In fact, the PVO had its own proving grounds within the Saryshagan complex. It was testing a new surface-to-air missile system here. It had a solid fuel booster below the liquid second stage, and was placed on a single-rail launcher. Its command guidance radar used the track-while-scan technique that had been patented by a U.S. scientist at Bell Laboratories in 1954. This radar was initially nicknamed Fruit Set by Western intelligence, but in the early 1960s it was renamed Fan Song, due to the fan-like sweep of its beam and the chirping sound of its electronic signal.

With the missile on a semi-trailer, and the radar mounted on a four-wheel trailer, the new system was semi-mobile. A newly-developed VHF radar designated Spoon Rest provided initial target acquisition for the system at a range of 125 miles, with its Yagi-type antenna mounted on the roof of a box-bodied mobile trailer. Each missile regiment had one Spoon Rest, and commanded three or more batteries that were spaced some miles apart. Each battery had a Fan Song and six missile launchers, and could salvo-fire three of the missiles at six-second intervals.[30]

The missile for the SA-2 was shown in public for the first time in Red Square on 7 November 1957. Within months, the first operational systems were being deployed around Moscow, Leningrad, and Baku.[31] It was given the designation SA-2 and nicknamed Guideline by the West. Eventually, it would prove to be the U-2's nemesis.

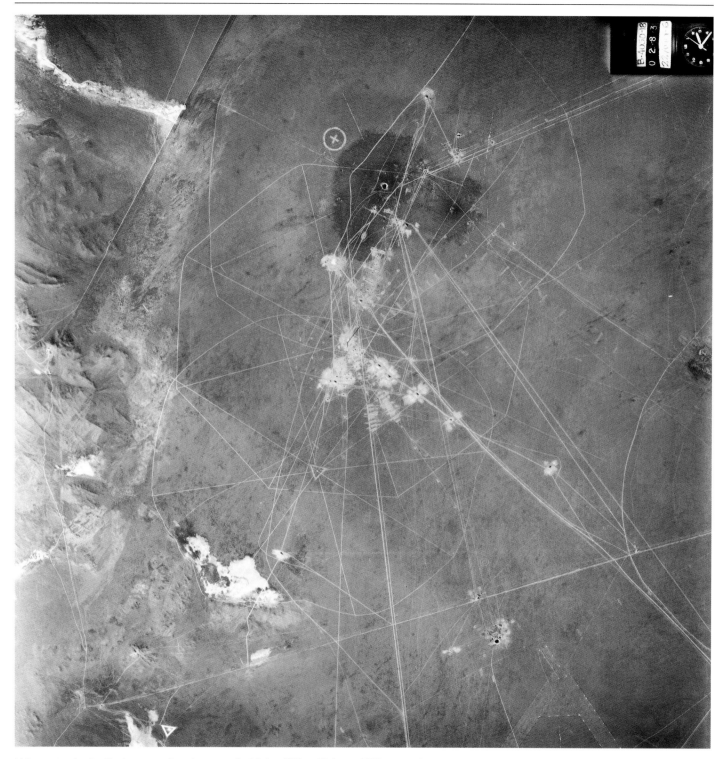

Unknown to pilot Jim Cherbonneaux, the prime target for Mission 4050 on 22 August 1957 was the Soviet nuclear weapons test site at Semipalatinsk. This image shows some of the eight ground zeros and weapons effect test areas that were captured by the B-camera (CIA).

5

High Altitude Sampling

So far in 1957, all the significant action in Project Aquatone had taken place in Detachments B and C. There had been virtually no operational missions for Det A at Giebelstadt. Morale and discipline had suffered accordingly; the pilots had little to do except fly the Det's two T-33s and single L-20 Beaver (for additional "taildragger" landing practice). After a series of incidents that potentially breached security, Det A commander Col Fred McCoy was replaced by Col Hack Mixson from Project HQ. In the fall of 1957, Project HQ made plans to close Giebelstadt. The contracts of the "sheep-dipped" U-2 pilots were coming up for renewal; it was decided to maintain Dets B and C, but reshuffle the personnel.

At the same time, however, a requirement arose to monitor Soviet naval exercises in the Barents Sea. The U.S. Navy—which had representatives on the ARC and in the PID—was keen to discover more about Soviet warship development, particularly the nuclear-powered submarines. Conventional U.S. and British reconnaissance aircraft had been probing the area for years, and the U.S. Navy regularly sent its own submarines to the area, where they would clandestinely monitor Soviet fleet movements. On one such sortie in 1956, a strange modification had been spotted on one Soviet diesel submarine at Severomorsk. U.S. naval intelligence analysts were still pondering its significance. In fact, it was the prototype Soviet ballistic missile-launching submarine.[1]

Det A was alerted for some flights to the north. It was a long way from Giebelstadt to Murmansk and back, but the Det had just received its first U-2 with the Giant Stride modification. This added a pair of external "slipper" fuel tanks to the wings, each carrying 100 gallons. The effect was to restore the range of the standard U-2A model, which had dipped below 4,000 nautical miles as various items of equipment had been added. The slipper tanks were flight-tested at Edwards North Base in the summer of 1957, and the modified aircraft were issued to Dets C, B, and A in turn. On 11 October 1957, while it was still dark, Jake Kratt climbed into Article

Four U-2s within the tight but secure confines of Det C's hangar at Atsugi in late 1957 or early 1958. The aircraft in the foreground carries the new, wing-mounted slipper tanks that carried more fuel for extra range. This aircraft is one of those modified with radar-absorbing materials, which were now painted gray, hence the new nickname "Gray Ghost" (Lockheed PR1033).

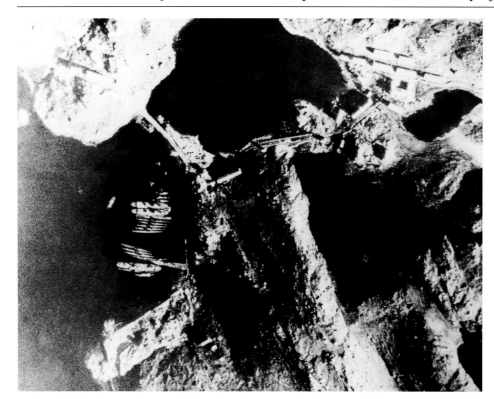

An overflight of Soviet Northern fleet bases on 13 October 1957 by Det A pilot Hervey Stockman yielded good imagery of submarines, cruisers, and their support facilities onshore. (CIA via Rolf Tamnes)

Before it closed in November 1957, Det A staged this unique formation flight over Wiesbaden, Germany.

351 with its new slipper tanks, and took off from Giebelstadt on Mission 2037.

This would be a non-penetrating flight, using the System 4 payload to pick up ELINT transmissions from the Northern Fleet. After two hours flying over solid cloud, Kratt calculated that he had reached Tromso, in northern Norway. He switched the ELINT system on, and turned onto the first leg of a triangular pattern that would take him way out over the Barents Sea and back across northern Norway 3.5 hours later. It was still completely overcast below.

Northern Flights

This was the first time that a U-2 had been sent as far as 70 degrees north. Flying above the Arctic Circle in a single-engine, single-pilot aircraft with only basic navigation aids was a significant challenge. Snow-covered land merged into ice-covered sea, and in any case, polar clouds often prevented a pilot from viewing the earth's surface through the driftsight. The basic standby compass was unreliable so close to magnetic north. The U-2 was also equipped with an MA-1 gyro compass that could be "unslaved" from the magnetic system. This provided an accurate heading signal derived from the gyroscope. But the unavoidable phenomenon of gyroscopic "precession" was a factor, and the rate of precession varied from aircraft to aircraft. The pilot had to perform frequent celestial observations using the sextant; plot the data on his route chart, which was divided into grids; and make the appropriate adjustments to his gyro and his heading.

But even the best exponents of this "celestial grid navigation" technique could still find themselves 10 or more degrees off course by the end of a long flight, when they eventually flew back over a known point. The technique could take no account of crosswinds which—contrary to perceived wisdom—were not always negligible at the U-2's very high altitude. Moreover, in order to use the precomputed star fixes exactly as provided to him by the mission navigator before take-off, the U-2 pilot had to start the celestial-navigated portion of his flight from a precisely-fixed point and time. If his takeoff was delayed for more than a few minutes, all those calculations were thrown out.

On the final leg of his planned route across the Barents Sea, Kratt spotted contrails beneath him through the driftsight. He *thought* that he was still in international airspace, but he could not be sure. (There was, in any case, a difference of interpretation between the U.S. and the USSR

over the definition. The USSR maintained a 12-mile limit, whereas the U.S. was still insisting that sovereign airspace extended only three miles offshore). When he eventually reached the waypoint at Tromso, where the cloud had cleared a little, Kratt determined that he was more than 50 miles south of the planned route. He set course for home and landed back at Giebelstadt fully nine hours and 53 minutes after takeoff. He had travelled more than 3,900 nautical miles.[2]

The same aircraft was now prepared for a photo mission. The clear weather moved east into the Murmansk area. On 13 October, at the same early hour, Article 351 again roared off the Giebelstadt runway, this time in thick fog with Hervey Stockman at the controls. The weather was again overcast on the long flight north, but it began to clear as the U-2 approached the northern tip of Norway. Stockman turned east and flew parallel to the Soviet coast for a while before turning south towards the Kola Fjord. With the three cameras of the A-2 configuration running, Stockman flew across Polyarnyy, Severomorsk, and Murmansk, where many submarines, cruisers, and other vessels were moored.

Heading further south, Stockman spotted two contrails heading his way, and thought for a moment that Soviet fighters had reached his level—more than 70,000 feet! But the U-2 pilot soon realized that this was an optical illusion; the contrails were far below, as usual, but they were reflecting in the curved canopy above his head, in a "fishbowl" effect. Bill Hall had experienced the same illusion over Volgograd a month earlier. Stockman thus flew on unpeturbed, and upon reaching Monechegorsk, he turned back to the northwest and left Soviet territory at its short border with the northernmost part of Norway. It took more than four hours to reach home base, where Mission 2040 landed after more than nine hours. When the film was examined at AUTOMAT, the PIs found a MiG-19 captured neatly inflight, directly below the U-2.[3]

A few days later, the Norwegian government sent a protest note about Stockman's flight to Washington. The CIA had not bothered to ask formal permission from Oslo for the aircraft to overfly Norwegian territory. Norway was, after all, a NATO ally in the fight against communism, and had allowed its bases to be used many times for intelligence-gathering flights. But the savvy Norwegians had worked out what was going on, from their own SIGINT intercepts of the alert messages that passed between Soviet air defense command posts as Stockman flew over the Kola peninsula. When he flew back south across Norway, two Norwegian air force inter-

By mid-1957, the fleet of U-2s operated by SAC's 4080th SRW was growing. They were deliberately based in remote southwest Texas, at Laughlin AFB, Del Rio. (USAF).

Flt Lt Tony Bevacqua was the youngest pilot to check out in the U-2, and was assigned to the 4080th wing. He is seen here eating the regulation preflight meal of steak and eggs. (USAF via Tony Bevacqua)

One of the SAC aircraft that were built with special noses for nuclear fallout sampling. The nose intake door is open, and also the side panels, which provided access to the filter papers. This photo was taken at Ramey AFB, PR, in late 1957, during the 4080th wing's first deployment on Operation Crowflight. (USAF via Tony Bevacqua)

ceptors were scrambled from Gardermoen airbase, near Oslo, but they were unable to make contact. As a form of compensation, Norwegian intelligence chief Vilhelm Evang demanded copies of the U-2 imagery. The CIA finally agreed, but only on the condition that they be made to appear as if the Norwegian air force had taken them! It was another lesson in political reality for Project HQ.[4]

Det A disbanded

The two long flights to the north were Det A's swan song. Within a month, the unit was packed up and returned to the U.S. Henceforth, Giebelstadt was used only as a refueling point when U-2s were ferried to and from Detachment B in Turkey (this practice began in February 1958, as a better alternative to disassembly and transport from Edwards by the lumbering C-124s, followed by re-assembly at the Det). Most of Det A's personnel returned to the USAF, including three of the pilots. Colonel "Hack" Mixson,

who had replaced Fred McCoy as unit commander, moved to the same position at Det C. There he replaced Colonel Stan Beerli, who moved in turn to Det B, where he took over from Colonel Ed Perry. Beerli brought five pilots with him from Japan, and four made the reverse journey. When the reshuffle was over, Project Aquatone had lost a third of its operational personnel.

The pilots and other contractors who renewed their CIA contracts were allowed to bring their families to Turkey and Japan for the first time. It helped relieve the monotony, and the relatives who came to Atsugi found an agreeable lifestyle in the well-provisioned naval base and other U.S. facilities in the Tokyo area. But Incirlik was a less attractive location for accompanied tours. Base facilities were rudimentary, although the married couples were now allowed rent houses off base in Adana. The single men continued to live in the mobile trailers that had been provided for them when the unit first moved in. Beyond the gates lay a barren and sometimes

CROWFLIGHT

The Crowflight logo designed by the 4080th wing.

An airman removes one of the filter papers after a U-2 sampling mission. The minute particles of long-term fallout captured on their cotton fibers were carefully analyzed by government and contract laboratories (NARA 164464AC).

HIGH ALTITUDE SAMPLING PROGRAM (HASP)

The HASP has resulted in a definitive measurement of the stratospheric reservoir of fission products....The development and availability of the Lockheed U-2, using a new filter medium of low resistance to air flow at high velocities, yet with the high collection efficiency under flight conditions...made Project HASP possible.

Based on theoretical work by Dr. Elliot Read of Stanford University, Lockheed designed and built a sampler having the capability of exposing four filter papers consecutively.

Two sampling missions, each of which collects 16 samples from the corridor, are scheduled per week. A single sample consists of the particulate matter filtered from between 5,000 and 20,000 cubic feet of air. To date, over 1,300 samples have been collected.

- AFSWP report dated 1959, in DoE archives

dangerous world where Kurdish tribesmen roamed, and travelling after dark was a dangerous proposition. Drinking and playing poker therefore remained the favorite pastimes at Det B. Large amounts of alcohol were consumed, and substantial amounts of money changed hands.

Fortunately, in addition to the two T-33s assigned for proficiency flying, Det B also had two C-54 transports at its disposal. On some weekends they were available for shopping and sightseeing trips to Athens, Bierut, Rome, or Wiesbaden. This relieved the monotony. Slowly, too, base facilities at Incirlik improved, as more USAF units were assigned there, some permanently, while others were on a rotational basis.

More Mishaps in Texas

Three of the aircraft made redundant by the closure of Det A were transferred to the USAF. They joined SAC's fleet of U-2As at Laughlin AFB, which was now 18 strong and still growing, as the 4080th wing prepared for the far-flung deployments that had been deemed necessary to conduct the sampling mission. After the two accidents shortly after the U-2s first arrived in June, training at the SAC base continued without a major mishap until late September. The aircraft were still mostly powered by the original -37 engines with their suspect fuel controls and oily air conditioning systems. There were many flameouts, some blamed on autopilot and bleed valve problems, and others on "abrupt maneuvers."[5]

SAC's selection criteria for U-2 pilots was rigorous, but the experience level of some was not as great as those selected to join the CIA project. Half of the 4080th U-2 pilots were only First Lieutenants, and the youngest (Tony Bevacqua) was only 24 years old when he was checked out. When the time came to select commanders for the first two sampling deployments, no field grade officers were available, and two Captains were chosen instead (However, they were later replaced by Majors).

On 21 September 1957, Captain Jim Qualls was flying over Nevada on a high-altitude training flight when he flamed out during a 180-degree autopilot turn. He descended to 34,000 feet and managed a relight. Two hours later, Qualls had another flameout and relight over Big Springs, Texas. As the SAC pilot headed for home base, he experienced *another* two flameouts and relights, and was eventually forced to deadstick his U-2 onto a dirt airstrip at a Texas ranch.

The aircraft was recovered to Laughlin and examined. Five days later, U-2 squadron commander Colonel Jack Nole took the same plane up for a test flight. As he climbed through 53,000 feet and deselected the gust control, the nose suddenly pitched down. Nole lost control and had to bail out. The root cause of the accident was determined to be an uncommanded deployment of the flaps, following an electrical short circuit. But Nole's escape also pointed to the need for quick-disconnect fittings for the radio, oxygen, and electrical lines; modification of the parachute, and—once again—an ejection seat.

Crowflight/Sampling

The SAC wing continued to struggle with training and maintenance problems as it prepared for the High Altitude Sampling Program (HASP), or Operation Crowflight, as it became known within the 4080th wing. The HASP requirement, set by the Armed Forces Special Weapons Project (AFSWP), was to determine the quantity of fallout particles from nuclear weapons tests in the stratosphere; the pattern of their dispersal around the globe; and the extent to which the fallout was returning to earth through the troposphere.

By now, the U.S. had conducted over 80 nuclear tests in the atmosphere, and 20 Soviet tests had been announced (sometimes by Moscow, other times only by courtesy of the U.S.). There had also been nine British tests. So there was now a good data base, especially since American sampling and diagnostic techniques had been proven by reference to the country's own nuclear test program. Of course, the patterns of fallout dis-

A U-2A of Det C on approach to Atsugi carries the special hatch with protruding airscoop for the gaseous sampling of nuclear fallout.

persal from nuclear tests varied considerably according to the weather and the winds. The advent of thermonuclear weapons (H-bombs) had made the collection process a little more predictable, provided that high altitude aircraft were available. This was because the fireball from a weapon of megaton yield, being larger and much hotter than that produced by an A-bomb, would inevitably rise into the stratosphere, where winds were negligible and airflow more stable.

During August and September 1957, Lockheed delivered six U-2A-1 models that had been specially modified for Operation Crowflight. They had a small intake door at the tip of the nose that was opened and closed by a cockpit control. The door led into a duct, which gradually widened to slow the airflow down, until it reached a filter paper placed across the airflow in a ring holder. The newly-developed papers were made from cotton fibres with a gauze backing, which were impregnated with an oily substance designed to retain minute particles. Ed Baldwin of the Skunk Works designed an automatic mechanism that could rotate four filters into the airflow in turn from their stowed position in a circular rack, which pivoted at its center above the duct. By means of an electric actuator operated by the U-2 pilot from the cockpit, the papers could be rotated in and out of the duct in sequence. Since the six modified aircraft lacked the fibreglass panels used for the SIGINT and ADF antennas on other U-2s, they were referred to as "hard nose" aircraft. In late October 1957 the 4080th deployed three of them each to Ramey AFB, Puerto Rico, and Plattsburgh AFB, NY, to start the HASP.

The first phase of flying entailed the sampling of a "corridor" along the 70 degree West meridian from roughly 65 degrees North to 10 degrees South, at various altitudes from 45,000 feet to 70,000 feet. It was thought that, over a period of time, most of the earth's stratospheric circulation would pass through this corridor. From each deployment base, the U-2s flew north and south twice each week along the predetermined tracks, usually launching two aircraft at a time to head in opposite directions. A typical flight profile required a level-off at 45,000 feet to collect samples for an hour, then a climb to 55,000 feet and another hour of sampling, then the same from 65,000 feet. Finally, the pilot was required to gain maximum altitude (around 70,000 feet in these profiles) for his final set of samples.

This entailed flying across some quite inhospitable terrain for seven hours or more, over the frozen wastes of northern Canada or the wide open spaces of the western Atlantic Ocean. Three hours before the U-2 was due to take off, therefore, an Air Force search-and-rescue (SAR) C-54 would depart from the Crowflight base and proceed along the flight path. Since the U-2 flew about twice as fast it would eventually overhaul the lumbering transport, but this procedure gave the maximum SAR coverage of the route, since both aircraft would reverse course at about the same time. The C-54 carried a paramedic team to assist the pilot if he went down. Unlike the CIA's U-2s, the USAF aircraft were equipped with a rudimentary Collins KWM high-frequency radio, which had to be preset to a single frequency. The pilot was required to make routine calls to the C-54 and the detachment base every so often; otherwise, the rescue services sprang into action.

The exposed filter papers were sent to Isotopes Inc in Westwood, NJ, for radiochemical analysis. Eventually, the results of the analyses were published, and the findings also went to a United Nations committee set up in 1955 to monitor the effects of nuclear radiation in response to growing worldwide concern. As yet more megaton-yield shots were staged, and long-range radioactive fallout spread around the globe, India and Japan led the protests, but there was also concern in Western scientific communities. Two reports from British and American scientists in 1956 attempted to soothe public concern, but even they were forced to admit "the inadequacy of our present knowledge." The presence in long range fallout of the Strontium-90 isotope caused the greatest concern. This fission product remained radioactive for years, and was known to concentrate in the bone structure once it had penetrated the human body. A heavy dose could theoretically cause bone marrow cancer.

The General Takes Command

After deploying the six HASP aircraft, the SAC wing continued to train U-2 pilots and groundcrew, amidst growing concern about how such a unique reconnaissance system should be managed. The peculiar circumstances in which the U-2 had entered the USAF inventory meant that the normal procedures and paperwork so beloved of the military—and especially of SAC—had been side-stepped. Technical manuals and flight handbooks were

The airscoop of the P-2 hatch sampling system is also visible in this shot of a 4080th SRW aircraft landing at Laughlin AFB. Note Crowflight mascot is carried on the tail (USAF).

CELESTIAL NAVIGATION

Flying the U-2 was a big enough challenge, but navigating it could be an even bigger one. Especially when you were all alone, at night, over featureless terrain or, worse still, over a cold ocean or a solid undercast. In the early days, there was no doppler, no inertial, no computer. Pilots had to become proficient in celestial grid navigation, as these SAC pilots explain:

Jerry McIlmoyle: All of the celestial was preplanned on the ground, so that meant an absolutely on-time takeoff, and a departure point at altitude that was absolutely known. For me, the point was to get stars that were bright enough, and shoot triangular fixes. Then you can drop perpendiculars from most points and find the best estimate for yourself. You plotted the data onto your route chart, which was divided into a grid.

Chuck Kern: The pilot cranked in the preset information and peered into the sextant. The field of view is very small, and if the star to be "shot" is not there, then you sweat. Go back over all the numbers and settings again to make sure they're proper. Still nothing? Look out the canopy and see if there's anything identifiable.

On all the missions to the far north we were in "free gyro" operation—that is, we were "unslaved" from the magnetic compass, because it was so unreliable as a heading indicator the closer you got to the Pole. But all gyros precess to some degree—some more than others. Anytime a turn is made in "free gyro" it aggravates the precession even more.

Jerry McIlmoyle: You had to keep very accurate records of the precession rate, eg one or two degrees every 30 minutes, so that you made the proper correction at each waypoint. Some of our flights around the USSR were over nine hours, after which you could be 10-15 degrees off when you eventually returned to a known position, such as coasting-in over Nome, Alaska.

Dave Ray: Even if everything was correct—precomps, inflight shots, inflight manual computations, accurate autopilot, accurate winds— then that directional gyro could send you way off course. It had an allowable error of +/- four degrees per hour. The one used in the B-47 and the B-52 had no more than one degree per hour error!

non-standard; sometimes the groundcrew worked from handwritten notes they had made in the classroom during U-2 ground school at the Ranch. If they wanted a particular part it came direct from Lockheed, rather than through the usual logistics channels. And there was the constant problem of every plane being *different*—it was axiomatic that, for instance, a canopy or a balance arm from one U-bird would not fit another! The "Article" number had to be specified each time a U-2 part was ordered.

In the small, dedicated, and contractor-maintained world of the CIA's Project Aquatone, these hurdles were easily overcome. In the larger, military-regulated world of SAC's Dragon Lady program, they were not. The 4080th wing was also trying to keep the troublesome RB-57D operational in a second squadron, plus maintain a large fleet of training and support aircraft. A series of incidents focused the attention of higher headquarters

on the Laughlin wing. In addition to the U-2 accidents of June and August 1957, two of the wing's T-33 trainers were lost while in the traffic pattern, one at Laughlin, and one at Offutt AFB. Two pilots died in the crash at SAC Headquarters, and two more when a B-57C trainer crashed at Andrews AFB.

General McConnell of SAC's 2nd Air Force (to which the 4080th reported) decided to make an inspection at Laughlin. On 5 November he flew over from Barksdale in his C-54, but as the staff transport entered the traffic pattern at Laughlin, another B-57C making a touch-and-go landed with the wheels up. The runway was blocked, and the fuming general had to divert back to Barksdale! Within a week McConnell had fired the 4080th wing commander, Colonel "Hub" Zemke, despite the latter's fame and status as a wartime ace. The general decided that the wing needed more standardisation and accountability—not less—so he drafted in Brigadier General Austin J. Russell to replace him. Russell had commanded a SAC bomb wing, and was a dour disciplinarian in the LeMay tradition. The 4080th's U-2s were shoe-horned into the overall SAC war plan, and in consequence, many flying hours were wasted on filling unnecessary training "blocks."

Russell had only been in charge for 10 days when the 4080th suffered another fatal U-2 accident. Captain Benedict Lacombe was returning from a celestial navigation training flight late on 22 November when he crashed on base leg. The accident report concluded that he allowed the aircraft to enter a descending spiral while his attention was diverted. When the warning horn sounded as he exceeded 220 knots, he instinctively applied back pressure on the yoke to reduce speed, but now he exceeded the g-limits and the aircraft broke up. His body was found some way from the wreckage—another U-2 pilot had tried to escape over the side, but failed. By the time Lacombe was clear of the aircraft he was too low for the parachute to deploy. Ironically, the new lightweight ejection seat was cleared for service on the U-2 just a few weeks later.[6]

"Hot" Sampling Begins

A different type of sampling deployment now beckoned for the 4080th: Operation Toy Soldier. Unlike the HASP, this was a more highly classified effort to gather "hot" samples of Soviet nuclear tests for intelligence purposes. The amount of information about a nuclear weapon that could be deduced from a study of the fallout was quite substantial. Indeed, the very first Soviet nuclear test had only been detected when a USAF RB-29 on a sampling mission between Japan and Alaska had encountered high amounts of radioactivity. This was on 3 September 1949, five days after the event, and a long time before any announcement was made by the USSR. Since then, the esoteric science of "weapons diagnostics" had advanced, so that careful analysis of air-gathered samples could reveal precise details about a nuclear bomb's yield, construction, and composition; the nature of the fusion and/or fission reaction; and whether it had been detonated at ground level, underwater, or in the air.[7]

The Air Force Office of Atomic Testing (AFOAT) used a variety of aircraft to collect samples for weapons diagnostics, but the U-2 was potentially the best platform for high-altitude collection. A new hatch for the U-2 equipment bay was developed and flight tested in early 1957. This contained the P-2 Platform (or "ball sampler package"), which collected gaseous samples by a bleed from the engine compressor, and stored them in six spherical shatterproof bottles. The pilot monitored the pressure build-up in these bottles. After about 50 minutes, upon reaching 3,000 psi, a shut-off valve was automatically activated, and the pilot selected the next bottle on his control panel. AFOAT also required particles to be collected as a secondary mission, and the same hatch was also fitted with an airscoop leading to a similar filter paper system as that being used on the "hard-nose" HASP aircraft.

The U-2 "hot sampling" missions had to be flown in the northern latitudes to the east of the Soviet landmass, in order to intercept fallout from the nuclear test sites at Semipalatinsk and Novaya Zemlya, which topped out in the stratosphere and then began drifting in that direction. The first five ball sampler packages were issued to the CIA for use by Det C, which flew the first missions out of Eielson in June 1957. Subsequently, Det C flew sampling missions out of the home base at Atsugi. On one of these, John Shinn made the first "hot" interception of nuclear debris in a U-2, during a flight going northeast along the Kurile Islands.

The next 10 ball samplers were issued to the 4080th wing after it was assigned the primary responsibility for "hot" sampling in late 1957. Operation Toy Soldier—SAC's first deployment to Eielson AFB, Alaska—began on 30 January 1958 with three aircraft. The usual area of collection was way to the north, over Point Barrow, where fallout from Soviet tests on Novaya Zemlya would usually arrive within 24 hours. As in Crowflight, collection was required at various high altitudes, and the missions often lasted eight hours or more; these flights were long and boring for the pilots. They were enlivened only by the demanding task of polar navigation, and the thought of trying to find a frozen lake to land on if a flameout forced a descent and landing in the Arctic wilderness!

All through February and into March 1958, the U-2s flew almost daily from Eielson as the pace of Soviet nuclear testing accelerated. Det C also continued to fly sampling missions on a track running north from Japan. The radiation count of the air entering the sampling duct was measured and presented to the pilot on the B/400 radiation exposure meter in the cockpit. There was also a warning light that could be set to come on if the count got too high. The most harmful radiation present in stratospheric fallout was that from gamma rays, which was known to decay within the first 24 hours. It was therefore not usually a factor during the U-2 flights, but if the dosimeter had registered a "hot" count during a sampling sortie,

the returning aircraft was washed down with soap and water before the groundcrew were allowed to service it. The samples collected on these flights were sent to AFOAT's laboratory at McClellan AFB, CA, for analysis. There, it was said that scientists could determine a nuclear weapon's characteristics "down to what color it was painted" from the minute samples. Eventually a laboratory was set up at Eielson, because the half-life of some radioactive constituents was only a few hours or days, and rapid analysis was mandatory.[8]

More Overflights Requested

The pace of Soviet nuclear and missile testing now alarmed many analysts and politicians in the U.S. Politicans reacted to the launch of Sputnik by orchestrating an anguished national debate about the supposed shortcomings of U.S. missile and space technology. Along the Soviet southern border, the listening stations picked up preparations for another R-7 launch. On 26 October 1957 Dick Bissell went to see General Goodpaster in the White House, and requested another U-2 mission over Tyuratam. Goodpaster told him that the President felt it was best to "lie low in the present tense international circumstances."[9]

Eight days later, an R-7 launched the second Sputnik, and U.S. gloom deepened. The CIA still believed that the USSR was two years away from achieving an operational ICBM, but powerful voices in the Congress and the military disagreed. They constructed and broadcast alarming scenarios: what if SAC's nuclear bombers were caught on the ground by a preemptive Soviet missile strike? The U.S. did not even have an early-warning radar network that could track incoming ICBMs. SAC's bomber dispersal and alert programs were stepped up, and development of the Ballistic Missile Early Warning System (BMEWS) was accelerated.

The CIA estimate that the Soviets were still two years away from deploying an ICBM was based partially on knowledge that there were failures, as well as successes, at the Tyuratam launch site. When the listening stations detected preparations for a launch the CIA's Det B was alerted, and a U-2 configured for SIGINT would be launched for a border flight to the east, in the hope of gathering more data if a missile was actually fired. At the same time, a Boeing RC-135 aircraft codenamed Nancy Rae would

In late 1957, the primary responsibility for "hot" sampling was assumed by SAC, and given the codename Operation Toy Soldier. This U-2A of the 4080th carries a small Toy Soldier cartoon on the tail (Lockheed U291-028).

The polished metal finish on the CIA's U-2s gave way to a very dark blue in 1958, since this made them less visible at high altitudes to enemy pilots attempting to intercept. This U-2A from Det C is landing at Atsugi.

take off from Eielson AFB and orbit off Kamchatka to monitor the impact area. Often, the countdowns were aborted and the spyplanes returned empty handed. Occasionally, the missile was launched but failed to achieve the proper trajectory. After the New York Times inadvertently disclosed on 31 January 1958 that the U.S. was eavesdropping on the countdowns, the Soviets limited the extent of their transmissions to the downrange stations. The U-2 could not get off the starting block in time, and neither could the Nancy Rae. The U.S. had to enlarge the airfield at Shemya, at the westernmost end of the Aleutians, so that the reaction time of the RC-135 could be shortened.[10]

Although the U-2 border flights continued, no further overflights of the USSR were authorised during the winter of 1957-58. However, Project HQ began planning for another high-intensity series like Operation Soft Touch for March or April, when the light and weather over the USSR would be better.[11]

But as it transpired, only one overflight was authorised in the spring of 1958. On 2 March, Det C pilot Tom Crull flew Mission 6011 over the Soviet Far East, opposite Hokkaido. He entered denied territory over Sovietskaya Gavan, passing over the naval aviation base there before heading for Komsomolsk and Khabarovsk, where more airbases and aircraft production facilities were situated. Then the flight followed the Trans-Siberian Railroad southwards, close to the Chinese border. Despite using one of the "Dirty Birds," with new anti-radar treatments, the mission was once again tracked. Soviet interceptors were launched. Shortly after Crull "coasted-out" of denied territory he had a flameout. Luckily, the MiGs were no longer on his tail.

Four days later, the USSR lodged a strong protest about Crull's flight. President Eisenhower discussed the protest with Secretary of State John Foster Dulles the next day. He had come to the conclusion that these flights just weren't worth the political risk. What if the Soviets misinterpreted an

overflight as being an inbound U.S. nuclear bomber? It was all bad news for the CIA's U-2 operation. The Soviet protest proved that they had little difficulty detecting the "Dirty Bird," and the 10,000-foot altitude penalty could have been disastrous on Crull's flight.[12]

Although some work on "stealthing" the U-2 did continue in a series of flight tests codenamred Buckhorn, the Rainbow project was over. The absorbers and the wires worked at some frequencies and aspects, but not at others. Moreover, the foam-based absorber was a maintenance nightmare. In reality, the laws of physics could not be contradicted—the U-2's shape had not been devised with "stealth" in mind.

In a new design study named Gusto, the Skunk Works was now working on a subsonic, swept wing replacement for the U-2 with no tail, which would have a very low radar cross section. But other studies commissioned by the CIA from SEI, the Skunk Works, and elsewhere indicated that the best chance of evading radar detection completely would be through more speed and altitude. Therefore Bissell and his military deputy, Jack Gibbs, asked Lockheed and Convair to submit designs for a supersonic reconnaissance aircraft in early 1958. It would be an ambitious project, with no guarantee of quick results.[13]

For the U-2 meanwhile, altitude was still the best defense, just as Kelly Johnson had always said. As an added precaution against fighter interception, though, the aircraft could be visually camoflaged. In early 1958 a U-2 was painted in dark matt blue for flight trials at North Base. A Lockheed test pilot flying an F-104 in an attempted interception reported that the repainted aircraft was much less conspicuous at high altitude. Some variations of the paint were tried out, but eventually an overall coat of a standard specification known as Sea Blue was chosen. In the summer of 1958, therefore, the CIA's U-2s lost their shiny metal finish, at a weight penalty of 48 pounds. Even Kelly Johnson thought *that* was a price worth paying![14]

6

New Partners

On a dark evening in mid-November 1957, the British Prime Minister (PM), Foreign Secretary, and Minister of Defence gathered for a briefing at the Air Ministry building in Whitehall. The subject was simple but extremely sensitive: should the UK respond to the CIA's invitation to become a fully paid-up member of the U-2 project?[1]

When the first U-2 detachment was effectively expelled from the UK in May 1956 by Prime Minister Eden just a few weeks after it arrived, senior MI6 and RAF intelligence officials were embarrassed. In the early Cold War years they had painstakingly built close relationships with opposite numbers in the U.S. intelligence community. Both sides had valued the "two-way street" of information-sharing. In the mid-1950s, the Brits still held a lead in some airborne reconnaissance technology, such as side-looking radar and ELINT. But the sheer weight of resources that the U.S. could bring to bear on technical intteligence-gathering was beginning to tell. After a visit to the U.S. in fall 1956, a British intelligence official warned his superiors that "if the U.S. thought that we were lagging behind, they would not be so forthcoming in exchanging information."[2]

From time to time the U.S. continued to provide intelligence from Project Aquatone to the UK. Art Lundahl of PID was instructed to prepare special briefings, which would be given to senior RAF intelligence officers in Washington. The British officers were allowed to take the materials back to the UK with them. They made sure that their political masters were made fully aware just how important this U-2 intelligence was. "When fully utilized, it will provide us with up-to-date information on the Soviet Air Force which we could not get in any other way, in present circumstances," the Chief of the Air Staff told the Air Minister in late 1956. The Air Minister asked for more details, and passed them on to the PM.[3]

But the British knew they were only getting part of the story. After the first set of U-2 photos of the Middle East were handed over by Lundahl in September 1956, no more coverage of that area was forthcoming. As the "special" briefings to the UK on the results from Project Aquatone continued in 1957, Bissell sensed the dissatisfaction of the British intelligence establishment. He hatched a scheme to turn this to his advantage. He proposed that the British would join the U-2 project, in return for full sharing of the product.[4]

Bissell reckoned that Whitehall might be more willing to approve overflights of the USSR than the White House, especially now that Sir Anthony Eden had been replaced as Prime Minister (by Harold Macmillan). Bissell took the scheme to the White House in late October 1957, and exactly a month later, it was briefed to the British PM by an enthusiastic

Air Ministry. It involved the induction of a complete British cadre into the CIA's U-2 operation: some pilots and a flight surgeon would join Det B; an operations officer would join Project HQ; and a photo-reconnaissance expert would join Art Lundahl's operation at the PID. Surprisingly enough, Macmillan agreed.[5]

Arrangements were made in the strictest secrecy by the Assistant Chief of the Air Staff (Operations), Air Vice Marshal Ronnie Lees. He established a small project office in the Air Ministry, staffed by a Group Captain and a Wing Commander. Five RAF pilots were carefully selected: they were all in their late twenties, unmarried, and with plenty of experience, including A2 instructor-pilot ratings from the renowned Central Flying School. Upon arriving in the U.S., they were met by Bill Crawford, the same CIA case officer who had escorted all the American pilots through the U-2 induction process. This process was to be no different for the Brits: rigorous medical screening at Wright-Patterson and the Lovelace clinic; then escape and evasion training at Camp Peary, VA. One of the prospective British U-2 pilots backed out at this stage, but the other four made it to Laughlin AFB, where SAC's 4080th wing began checking them out in the U-2 in late April 1958. The arrival of the Brits and the formal designation of the Development Projects Staff (DPS) prompted a change in the cryptonym used to denote the U-2 operation. Aquatone became Chalice on 1 April 1958.

Four British pilots were sent for training at Laughlin AFB in April 1958. From left: Sqn Ldr Chris Walker and Flt Lts John McArthur, Mike Bradley, and Dave Dowling. Walker was killed in a training accident, but the other three graduated and moved on to the CIA's Det B in Turkey (via Pat Halloran).

Covert Operations

On the other side of the world, the U-2 was getting mixed up in a CIA covert operation for the first time. Since late 1957 the Agency's Deputy Directorate for Plans (DDP) under Frank Wisner had been supporting rebel Indonesian army Colonels who were opposed to the regime of President Sukarno. The White House had approved the covert action, having deemed Sukarno to be too pro-communist.[6] But troops loyal to Sukarno attacked the rebel bases on populous Sumatra. The rebels had another stronghold at Manado, on the northern end of the remote Celebes island chain more than a thousand miles to the east. The DDP decided to step up its aid to the rebels by providing them with wartime-vintage P-51 fighters and B-26 bombers, which they could use to attack Sukarno's military bases and shipping.

Dick Bissell was happy to lend support to Wisner's covert action. In fact, he reckoned that after two years, during which the DPS had amassed tremendous air operations experience of its own, it should actually be running a show like this, rather than the DDP's Air Maritime Division! In mid-March, Det C was told to quickly deploy U-2s from Japan to the Naval Air Station at Cubi Point, in the Philippines. Lockheed manager Bob Murphy hurriedly arranged 100-hour inspections on two aircraft, and Det commander Hack Mixson agreed that the ferry flights to Cubi could also serve as the post-inspection functional check flights. Murphy and Mixson flew to the Philippines on a C-47, while 55-gallon drums of the special fuel were loaded and dispatched on a C-124.

Det C began flying missions across the entire Indonesian archipelago on 30 March 1958, looking for the disposition of Sukarno's forces and likely targets for the rebel air force. The DDP wanted the imagery so that it could identify targets for the rebel air force. But it was a huge area to cover; a straight-line roundtrip from Cubi Point to the Indonesian capital at Djakarta was over 3,500 miles. Many of the 30 U-2 missions flown over the next 10 weeks were more than nine hours long. Art Lundahl arranged another field deployment to quickly process and interpret the film. Specially-cleared photo-interpreters and equipment from PACAF's 67th Reconnaissance Technical Squadron (RTS) in Japan were sent to Clark AB. After each mission, the U-2 film was flown over from Cubi Point in a C-47. It was no mean task to develop and process two spools of B-camera film, each over 5,000 feet long, under field conditions. For instance, the processor only worked at seven feet per minute!

While the U-2s flew intensively, Bissell decided that two of "his" U-2 pilots should join the rebel air force. In late April, two of the project U-2 pilots now based at Edwards AFB with the test unit were dispatched to Manado. Carmine Vito and Jim Cherbonneaux would act as advisors to the Filipinos who had been engaged to fly and maintain the P-51s. But the pair had become pawns in the power-play between Bissell and Wisner: they were not exactly welcomed with open arms by the DDP contingent at Clark AB. As it transpired, their stay was short-lived. The Indonesian air force attacked the base at Manado and, a few days later, a rebel air attack on some of Sukarno's airfields led to the shooting-down of one of the B-26s. Its American pilot was captured, and DCI Dulles ordered an end to the operation.

Overflying Mainland China

The last U-2 flight over Indonesia from Cubi Point took place on 14 June, and Det C began packing up for the return to Japan. However, another long flight over denied territory beckoned for the detachment. Mission 6012 was flown on 19 June out of Naha, Okinawa, when Lyle Rudd became the first U-2 pilot to fly over populated regions of the Chinese mainland. After "coasting-in" over Fuzhou, Rudd flew west across Fujian and Jiangxi provinces before turning north and flying all the way to Beijing. Turning back south, he flew through Shandong and Jiangsu provinces before leaving communist airspace close to Shanghai. Rudd's flight lasted nine hours and 25 minutes. Chinese interceptors shadowed him throughout much of it—obviously their radars were also perfectly capable of detecting a high-flying intruder.

The imagery from Mission 6012 would soon prove useful, as tensions between the nationalist Chinese on Taiwan and the mainland communists increased. Two nationalist F-84 fighters were shot down over the Taiwan Straits on 29 July. The U.S. professed its support for the nationalists, and sent them more missiles and fighters. But on 11 August the communists started a bombardment of Matsu and Quemoy, the small offshore islands close to the mainland, which the nationalists still held and had fortified. It seemed for a while that Beijing might be preparing for a full-scale invasion of Taiwan.

Lockheed test pilot Bob Schumacher pulls the oxygen line and faceplate for the MC-2 helmet towards him. Problems with the faceplate clasp and the oxygen system contributed to three fatal U-2 accidents in 1957-58, forcing a redesign of the pilot's vital life support system (Lockheed C88-1447-76).

But U-2 photography told otherwise. Det C deployed again to Okinawa, from where another mission over the Chinese mainland was flown by Lyle Rudd on 20 August. It revealed a big build-up of fighter aircraft on airfields opposite Taiwan, but no corresponding moves by the communists to build up ground or naval strength in the region. Another mission was flown on 10 September, and for the first time Beijing issued a protest. By agreement between the State Department, Pentagon, and the CIA, further flights were suspended. Bissell and DDCI Cabell pressed for another one 12 days later, but State demurred. Eventually, a further U-2 mission over the mainland was flown by E.K. Jones on 22 October, by which time the crisis was receding. When this penetration was discussed in the White House on 30 October, the President said he was unaware that such flights had resumed, and stressed that permission for them must be secured from him on a mission-by-mission basis.[7]

The last few months had again demonstrated that the U-2 could be used as a "tactical," as well as "strategic" intelligence tool. Not only over Indonesia and China, but also during a renewed series over the Middle East by Det B during the Lebanon Crisis, Lundahl's PID arranged another field deployment. They provided timely processing and analysis of the imagery. But was "tactical" photo-reconnaissance a role for the CIA? During a discussion with the President on the CIA budget in September 1958, DCI Allen Dulles made a casual suggestion that the Agency's U-2 opera-

tion could be transferred, in part or whole, to the USAF. Eisenhower thought some savings could be made, perhaps by passing maintenance responsibility to the Air Force. Bissell, who thought he had won this particular battle twice already, hurried to the White House and scotched the suggestion. He told General Goodpaster that the aircraft should remain "in a small autonomous organization, so as to provide security, direct control, and extremely close supervision."[8]

U-2 safety questioned

According to Kelly Johnson, the maintenance performance at the SAC U-2 wing had been so poor, that the Air Force Inspector-General's office had been called in to investigate.[9] The 4080th wing suffered four serious accidents within a month. On the afternoon of 8 July 1958, Squadron Leader Chris Walker was killed when his aircraft went out of control at high altitude and crashed in the Texas panhandle near Amarillo. He was one of the four RAF pilots now in training. The next morning, Captain Alfred Chapin crashed in similar circumstances less than 100 miles away, near Tucumcari, New Mexico.

SAC grounded all its U-2s while accident investigations were carried out. Sabotage was suspected, but when the gaseous oxygen systems of other U-2s were checked, excessive moisture was found. Walker's autopsy revealed that he had become hypoxic; it was soon suggested that both accidents could have been the result of the pilots being starved of oxygen, after the supply was restricted by ice formation at the reducer valve. But there were other indications, and other mysteries. Apparently, Walker had tried to use the ejection seat, but it had not worked. There was also evidence of a fire in Chapin's oxygen supply.[10]

On 25 July a U-2 caught fire on the ramp at Laughlin while the Firewel techrep was checking a new oxygen pressure reducing valve. On 2 August, while investigations continued, the U-2s were cleared to fly again, but only as high as 20,000 feet. Four days later Lt Paul Haughland was killed on his first U-2 flight when the aircraft stalled on final approach, rolled rapidly to the left, and struck the ground in a near-vertical attitude.[11]

"The airplane has been exonerated," wrote Kelly Johnson in his diary, when the dust finally settled on this unfortunate series of accidents. "We're trying hard to get General Flickenger to take more active steps to go to our dual oxygen proposal," he continued dryly. But Lockheed was assigned some of the blame. SAC insisted that the ejection seats be disabled until Lockheed could assure their reliability. As another precaution, the radio leads to the pilot's helmet were re-routed so that they no longer ran alongside the oxygen tubes: a short circuit in that wiring could have caused a fire in Chapin's cockpit.

As a result of Haughland's fatal accident the procedures for training novice U-2 pilots were revised. But the SAC wing complained that the flight manual did not sufficiently highlight the "unusual stall characteristics" of the airplane, and asked Lockheed to check the aircraft's performance in the landing regime. The 4080th was also still concerned about the autopilots, especially the pitch trim. Eventually, the USAF told the Skunk Works to perform a complete re-evaluation of the U-2's stability and control characteristics. Major Dick Miller, an aeronautical engineer from the Edwards Flight Test Center, was assigned to work with the Lockheed flight test team at North Base, and a new series of flight tests with a specially-instrumented U-2A was agreed. The Lockheed report of this re-evaluation reaffirmed the U-2's basic stability, noting that the de-

Sqn Ldr Robbie Robinson was the British replacement for the unfortunate Chris Walker. Robinson was a test pilot who had already flown at high altitude in the rocket-assisted Canberra B.2. That aircraft forms the background to this posed photo, in which Robinson improbably wears a collar and tie with his partial pressure suit! (Paul Lashmar collection).

sign met all the key requirements of the basic Military Specification that covered flying qualities (MIL-F-8785).[12]

Twelve U-2s had now been lost in accidents. The CIA had paid for 20 aircraft, and the USAF had taken delivery of another 30—one more than originally planned. Now Kelly Johnson offered the government a sweet deal to produce another five aircraft, which would be partially built from spare parts left over from the earlier contracts. The USAF took up the offer, and the five additional aircraft were delivered between December 1958 and March 1959.

Sampling Stepped Up

The accidents and groundings at Laughlin disrupted plans for the start of a new phase of sampling under Operation Crowflight. Radiochemical analysis of the filter papers from the first series of flights out of Ramey and

Plattsburgh had confirmed that fall-out was not mixing across the stratosphere as much as had been thought. It was flowing round and round the earth as expected, but was staying at roughly the latitude at which it had been injected. Even though the HASP sampling corridors were half a world away from some of the test sites, debris from individual shots could nevertheless be identified almost every time the U-2 flew along them, and sometimes within a fortnight of the test shot. Often, the aircraft's radiation exposure meter registered "hot." Another, somewhat disturbing conclusion was that strontium-90 and other nuclear debris was falling-out of the stratosphere more rapidly than had been anticipated. It was also becoming clear that higher concentrations of harmful particles were descending to the ground in certain regions than had been anticipated. Now that the U.S. and Britain were staging megaton-range nuclear tests in the Southern Pacific, a further extension of the sampling corridor into the southern hemisphere was deemed necessary.

After some complicated negotiations, Argentina gave permission for HASP flights to be staged from its territory, although the communist opposition protested. Ezeiza airport, near Buenos Aires, was chosen as the base, but the three aircraft that departed Laughlin for there in early July only reached as far as Ramey before being recalled after the 8/9 July accidents. They finally flew direct from Laughlin to Ezeiza on 10 September, and Det 4 remained there for the next eleven months. Flights were staged up and down the 64 degrees west meridian, going as far as Trabajares, Brazil (9 degrees south), in one direction, and the Falkland Islands (57 degrees south) in the other. The sampling gear soon picked up debris from the new American and British tests, which were codenamed Operations Hardtack and Grapple, respectively. Meanwhile, the 4080th wing's Det 3 continued at Ramey, from where monthly deployments were made to Plattsburgh to cover the northern latitudes.

Because there was now clearly a weapons diagnostics value to the Crowflight sorties, the six "hard-nose" U-2s at Ezeiza and Ramey were also equipped with the P-2 platform in the equipment bay. The gas and particle samples obtained from the P-2 went to the AFOAT laboratory at McClellan AFB for analysis. The filter papers exposed in the nose continued to be analyzed in the unclassified laboratory of Isotopes Inc. Also in September, the 4080th wing began a second "hot" sampling deployment, codenamed Toy Soldier, to Eielson AFB. The pace of Soviet nuclear testing quickened, and the deployment was tasked to mount a flight every day throughout October, using the P-2. Since the three aircraft sent to Alaska had the "conventional" nose, with Systems 1 and 3 installed, SAC also took the opportunity to exercise the two SIGINT systems in a few night missions flown closer to Soviet territory than the daytime sampling flights.[13]

The CIA's detachments relied on extensive contractor support, especially by the Lockheed maintenance crews. Bob Murphy was the field service manager at Det C, then Det B, in the late 1950s (via Jim Wood).

Jim Wood was a long-serving Lockheed techrep, typical of those who served the CIA project (Jim Wood).

In early 1958, Ed Martin was appointed as the U-2 project manager for Lockheed by Kelly Johnson. Prior to that, he was a member of the original design team, responsible for payload integration. (Ed Martin)

The RAF selected a replacement for the unfortunate Walker, who had been scheduled to take command of the British detachment within Det B. He was Squadron Leader Robert Robinson, a test pilot who had been flying the rocket-boosted Canberra. Robinson was therefore already familiar with the high-altitude regime. He arrived at Laughlin in early August. The three other British pilots completed their U-2 training in early October, and together with their flight surgeon and navigator, were soon on their way to Turkey. Every effort was made to conceal the presence of these new arrivals from the Turks and other Americans who worked at the base. The British group occupied their own trailers in the detachment's compound. Meanwhile, the RAF sent Wing Commander Norman Mackie to Project HQ in Washington, where he participated fully in mission planning for all flights; not merely those that would be allocated to the British pilots. Wing Commander Bob Abbott joined the staff of Art Lundahl's AUTOMAT operation, performing U-2 image analysis.

When the British team arrived at Incirlik in fall 1958, a large part of Det B was missing. The detachment commander, five pilots, two aircraft, and support personnel had departed for a secret destination. They were away for over two months. According to the usual strict rules of compartmenting that the Project's CIA security officers laid down, no questions were asked by those that stayed behind.

Northern Flight

In fact, the missing group was at the Norwegian air force base in Bodo, Norway. Their mission was all the more sensitive since, although the Norwegian government had given permission for them to be there, the main purpose of the deployment had been carefully finessed. That purpose was to overfly the northern USSR looking for offensive missile sites.

Despite its enormous size, the Soviet SS-6 missile now being tested from Tyuratam did not have sufficient range to reach the whole of the U.S. when launched from that southerly location on a polar trajectory. In mid-July 1957, therefore—two months after the first successful flight of the SS-6—the USSR began constructing its first operational ICBM base in a sparsely-populated forest region south of the Arctic port city of Arkhangelsk. Because of the rail transport imperative for the SS-6, the base was located close to the railway line running north from Moscow to Arkhangelsk. Great secrecy surrounded the site, and it was codenamed Leningrad-300 to disguise the location. The base was actually known to those constructing it as Angara, but the nearest village was named Plesetsk.[14]

U.S. intelligence had realized that the Soviets needed one or more northern launch bases for their ICBMs. By SIGINT or other means, the CIA apparently detected signs of activity in the Plesetsk area by mid-1958.

The analysts in Automat and OSI were desperately keen to get photos of any potential ICBM launch base, especially during the construction phase. That would give them a known "footprint" by which to compare imagery of the site with other sites where subsequent missile bases might be constructed. Right now, the analysts didn't even know for sure whether the operational launch sites would be fixed or mobile, and hardened or not.

But they *did* know that President Eisenhower was reluctant to approve U-2 overflights. Especially after the latest intelligence fiasco with camera-carrying balloons. Two years after the ill-conceived Project Genetrix, the President was persuaded by the USAF to sanction a new project designated WS-461L and codenamed Moby Dick. This time, he was told, a much larger balloon with an improved panoramic type of camera would be launched into the recently-discovered jetstream that ran west-to-east across the USSR at over 100,000 feet. Deputy Secretary of Defense Donald Quarles told Eisenhower that the Soviets would not detect the balloons. These would eventually drop their payloads over Western Europe on command from a timing device. Three of the new balloons were launched from a U.S. aircraft carrier in the Bering Sea on 7 July 1958. Three weeks later, Poland announced that one of the payloads had dropped onto their territory, and a Soviet protest also soon followed. The other payloads were never recovered. Eisenhower was furious.

Despite this, a group of intelligence experts who met with the President at the end of August 1958 recommended that he approve a "northern operation" by the U-2. After checking with Secretary of State Dulles, Eisenhower gave his permission. The flight would enter denied territory from the Barents Sea, and search for Plesetsk and other possible ICBM bases along the railroads of the northern USSR. And now two U-2s were concealed in a hangar at Bodo, the closest possible "friendly" launch base for such a mission.[15]

Only a half-dozen top government officials in Oslo, and two Norwegian air force officers at Bodo, officially knew that the U-2s were there. The advanced guard arrived at Bodo on a C-130 in late August, led by Stan Beerli, the det commander. They set up base in a remote hangar covered in earth and well hidden on the far side of the airfield. The U-2s were ferried in on 15 September. The operation was codenamed Baby Face.[16]

Art Bradley took over from Martin as Lockheed's U-2 Project Manager in the fall of 1959 (via Jim Wood).

To this day, it is not clear whether the Norwegian intelligence chief Colonel Vilhelm Evang discovered the real reason why the U-2s were at Bodo. If he did know, Evang never told his superiors. Instead, he told them:

"It is evident that the Americans have only provided the minimum information necessary in order to obtain clearance. In any future request for similar operations, we must demand more adequate information."

The Norwegians were left with the impression that the deployment was to do only sampling flights related to the new series of Soviet nuclear tests on Novaya Zemlya island, 1,100 miles to the east. (There were a dozen nuclear explosions here in October 1958, followed by a unilateral Soviet moratorium on further tests).

Indeed, Det B had brought the P-2 sampling platform with them, as well as the dedicated SIGINT System 4, which was by now in routine use on border surveillance flights from Incirlik. But the Norwegian government's standing policy was to deny the U.S. (or any other country) permission to use its air bases to launch flights that actually penetrated the USSR.[17]

Waited

In the small hangar at Bodo, the CIA group waited for a mission plan to be transmitted from Project HQ. In Washington, they waited for a break in the weather over the northern USSR. The area of interest was notorious for almost constant cloud cover. Two long weeks passed, with only a few training flights. A mission was finally alerted...but although it was ambitious, it was not a photo overflight. It would be a SIGINT flight all along the Soviet northern coastline, to a landing at Eielson. Jim Barnes was "on the hose" (eg prebreathing) for this mission when it was scrubbed by Project HQ. A

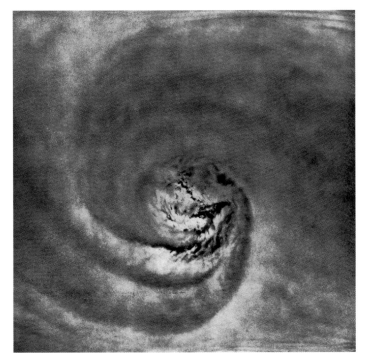

On 25 September 1958 Det C pilot Tom Crull flew a genuine weather reconnaissance mission. From 70,000 feet he brought back a valuable series of photographs of Typhoon Ida, an intense storm that caused major damage in Japan (Weather-wise magazine).

few days later Barnes did fly a mission, this time with the sampling platform as the primary sensor. On 9 October he took off after midnight and flew around the Barents Sea, returning to Bodo after 7 hours 55 minutes. Another two weeks passed before the next alert. This time, it was a SIGINT flight to the same area.

Bob Ericson flew this one on 25 October, but it did not go smoothly. His flight plan was similar to that of Barnes two weeks earlier, with a takeoff before dawn, followed by a transit up the Norwegian coast to the Barents Sea, where the U-2's SIGINT systems were switched on. By flying the U-2 as close as 12 miles to the Soviet coast, the hope was that the newly-upgraded recorders would pick up radar activity, as well as communications, within the air defense system and the Soviet Northern Fleet. As with previous flights to the area, the navigation task facing the pilot was demanding, especially since it was only daylight during the middle portion of the flight. Ericson reached Novaya Zemlya and identified some of the test installations there through the driftsight as he cruised along the coast. But as he headed back west, he realized that his fuel curve was "out"—that is, consumption was exceeding that predicted and plotted by the navigator at Bodo. Ericson decided to abandon that section of the mission that called for him to enter the White Sea inlet. He continued along the coast of the Kola Peninsula instead, but the change of plans meant that his celestial pre-computations were no longer accurate. In fading light, Ericson had to "eyeball" the navigation from hereon.

After flying for eight hours and 25 minutes, the U-2 pilot landed back at Bodo in a crosswind with only 10 gallons remaining. He had made the right decision, although Stan Beerli and mission planners were upset that the White Sea area had gone unmonitored, especially since the postflight read-out of System 4 revealed good SIGINT for the other portions of the flight. Shortly after Ericson landed, another U-2 being ferried into Bodo from Plattsburgh AFB by Tom Birkhead was blown off the runway by the crosswind. Luckily, the aircraft was undamaged, and was quickly recovered into the remote hangar.[18]

Soviet air defense communications on the Kola Peninsula were routinely monitored by Norway's own ground-based SIGINT operators. They were listening as usual on 25 October. From their intercepts of PVO chatter, they suspected that an unwelcome aircraft had penetrated Soviet airspace, or come very close. The Intelligence Staff in Oslo queried the matter with the U.S., which denied performing any such flight![19]

By the end of October the long darkness of the northern winter was descending on the region. The chance to photograph the suspected Soviet missile base was gone, and would not reoccur until the spring. The Americans prepared to depart from Norway. To salvage something more from the deployment, one of the U-2 ferry flights back to Turkey was planned as another SIGINT mission. After two alerts and stand-downs, John Shinn finally departed Bodo at 0200 on 6 November and flew east across Finland to the Soviet border. There he turned south and flew along the coast, past Leningrad and the Baltic States, then across Poland and Romania, and out over the Black Sea. A large number of Soviet fighters were launched against this mission, without success. An even larger number of Soviet radars were identified and located by the American ELINT analysts![20]

Nuclear Ransom

In Washington, the missile gap debate was heating up. The National Intelligence Estimate compiled in August 1958 (NIE 11-5-58) suggested that the USSR might achieve an initial operating capability (IOC) with "ten prototype ICBMs during 1959." The intelligence community had detected only six test firings of the SS-6 from Tyuratam by this time, and none since April 1958. In fact, there had been about a dozen such tests from the end of 1957 to the spring of 1958. Moreover, a third version of the SS-6 had launched the much heavier Sputnik 3 into orbit on 15 May 1958. This satellite weighed over one ton, and therefore clearly indicated that the SS-6 could deliver a nuclear warhead (in fact, Korolyev's missile had a nuclear payload of over five tons).[21]

The uncertainties that were implicit in the CIA's analysis of Soviet missile capabilities were seized upon by Senator Stuart Symington, a Democrat who had been Secretary of the Air Force in the Truman administration. Symington was getting different estimates from retired USAF Colonel Thomas Lanphier. He lobbied on behalf of the Air Force Association, and also worked for Convair, which was building America's first ICBM, the Atlas. The Colonel claimed to have good contacts in the intelligence community, and claimed that there had been no fewer than 80 test firings, including two with nuclear warheads. He claimed that the Soviets were "two or three years ahead," and would therefore be able to hold the U.S. at nuclear ransom. Symington had taken these concerns to President Eisenhower, and the debate had gone public, with articles written by syndicated columnist Joe Alsop, who was also privy to inside information from the intelligence community. Soviet Premier Khrushchev stirred the pot some more by claiming in public that the production of ICBMs "has been successfully set up"[22]

In fact, Symington and Alsop were getting their inside information from hardliners in the USAF who refused to accept the CIA's estimates, and Lanphier was relying on a former CIA analyst who now worked for Convair. This analyst was discredited within the Agency, but Lanphier had taken him to see General Power at SAC headquarters. Here, the analyst had presented two reports on Soviet ballistic missile deployment, one of which alleged that the USSR had colluded with China and was building railroads into the People's Republic, along which to deploy ICBMs.[23]

On such shaky foundations rested the case of the missile gap proponents. But the cause was enthusiastically adopted by the Democratic Party, which then made substantial gains in the mid-term elections in November 1958. Meanwhile, the intelligence community was obliged to re-assess the August NIE on Soviet ICBM capabilities. The CIA established an Ad-Hoc Panel consisting of outside consultants. The guided missile experts on the U.S. Intelligence Board also reviewed the data. Thanks partly to U-2 overflights and sampling flights, these analysts all knew that the USSR had developed powerful thermonuclear warheads to place on top of the missiles. But they found no reason to change the August 1958 NIE in any significant respect.

In late November, the CIA reported that it still had a "high degree of confidence" that no Soviet missile tests had gone undetected. Why, in that case, did they validate the NIE's prediction that the Soviets would never-

The SS-6 Sapwood was the first Soviet ICBM, as well as the launch vehicle for Sputnik and the lunar probes. The Soviets designated this huge booster R-7. By late 1958, the debate in the U.S. over how many such missiles were in the Soviet inventory was heating up (Russian Aviation Research Trust).

theless have an *operational* ICBM in 1959, albeit only with prototypes and in small numbers? Because (the CIA report continued) of "the Soviets' progress in the whole field of missiles...(the) earth satellite and other (medium-range) ballistic missile launchings." The review was classified at the Secret level, and therefore did not mention the Top Secret intelligence that suggested the USSR was constructing at least one operational ICBM base, at Plesetsk. The fact that not a single ICBM test launch from Tyuratam had been observed in the previous six months was also omitted, again probably to protect sensitive sources and methods.[24]

7

More Small Wars

On 5 December 1958, Dick Bissell replaced Frank Wisner as the CIA Deputy Director (Plans), or DDP. Thanks to the U-2 project, Bissell's stature within the Agency had risen rapidly. When it became clear that Wisner was having a mental breakdown, Dulles chose the "golden boy" to take over the CIA Directorate that dealt with spying and covert operations. Richard Helms, who had been in line to replace Wisner, was passed over, and remained number two to Bissell in the DDP.[1]

Bissell made sure that the U-2 operation moved with him. His Development Project Staff (DPS, eg Project HQ) previously reported direct to DCI Allen Dulles' office. But on 18 February 1959 the project HQ was formally re-assigned to the DDP. Bissell created a new Development Projects Division (DPD) to manage the U-2, plus all the covert air operations that Wisner had been running. The DPD was headed by Bill Burke, another USAF Colonel, who had replaced Jack Gibbs as Bissell's military deputy in DPS in May 1958. Jim Reber remained on the DPD staff, and continued to chair the Ad Hoc Requirements Committee (ARC), which prioritized the targets for the U-2 flights.[2]

DPD stayed put in the old DPS headquarters in the Matomic Building at 1717 H Street NW. But the offices were expanded and divided into various secure compartments, and each dealt with a separate project: covert air drops in Tibet, new technical developments, the U-2, and so on.

Meanwhile, Art Lundahl's Photo Intelligence Division (PID) was also reorganized and expanded. The deluge of imagery from Operation Soft Touch in 1957 led Art Lundahl to conclude that the cooperation between the CIA and the military services within Automat should be formalized. Instead of the services nominating representatives who would do temporary duty alongside the CIA staffers, but return to their own outfits to write intelligence reports, Lundahl suggested permanent assignments. The Army and Navy agreed, but (as usual) the USAF guarded its autonomy. The Air Staff insisted on retaining an independent photo-interpretation group in the Pentagon (in addition to the large 544th RTG operation at SAC headquarters). Despite this Lundahl's plan was implemented, and the PID became the PIC (Photo Interpretation Center). Henceforth, Lundahl reported directly to the CIA Deputy Director for Intelligence (DDI), Robert Amory. Despite its new status, however, Automat continued to occupy the obscure Stueart Building in Washington's run-down northeast suburbs.[3]

Ambitious

The elevation of Bissell to become DDP represented a significant victory for technical intelligence over human intelligence within the CIA. In addition to the U-2 and the covert air operations, the expanded DPD was also now in charge of two hugely ambitious aerospace technical developments. The first of these was the continued search for an air-breathing successor to the U-2. The CIA had now rejected some of the more unlikely proposals, such as hydrogen-fueled airplanes, a huge aerostat that could fly above 100,00 feet, and a ramjet-powered vehicle that would be towed to 60,000 feet behind a U-2 before the ramjet was lit. A new panel of scientists, once again chaired by Din Land, was helping Bissell evaluate two competing proposals for Mach 3 air-breathing vehicles from Lockheed and Convair.

The second top-secret development that DPD now managed was Corona—the project to field a photo-reconnaissance satellite as rapidly as possible. In February 1958, President Eisenhower had approved a plan to "hive off" part of the USAF's large and multipurpose WS-117L satellite program and establish it as a CIA-led program. Corona would use a panoramic camera that was scaled up from the one used in the USAF's unsuccessful Moby Dick reconnaissance balloon. The film, which was exposed in space, would be returned to earth unprocessed, in a reentry capsule. The USAF's preferred alternative of scanning the film electronically in space, and sending the results to earth via a datalink, was more technically ambitious. Therefore it was less likely to produce early results.

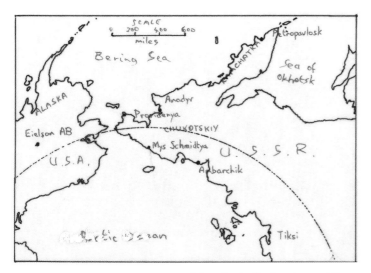

The targets for a series of peripheral photo flights of Soviet Siberia codenamed Congo Maiden and flown by SAC in the spring of 1959.

Bissell and the DPD had responsibility for getting the "interim" Corona satellite system into operation as quickly as possible, to provide an alternative window on Soviet strategic capabilities. This move reunited Dick Bissell and Ozzie Ritland, who was by now a Brigadier-General at Ballistic Missile Division in Los Angeles. Bissell and Ritland became the senior managers for Corona within the CIA and USAF, respectively—just like their partnership in the early U-2 days. In another echo of the U-2 program, a cover story was devised to hide the true purpose of Corona. The planned launches of the satellite on a Thor booster mated to an Agena upper stage were said to be for research purposes, in a series named Discoverer. The first Discoverer launch took place on 28 February 1959, only 12 months after the program go-ahead. It failed.[4]

Congo Maiden

Bissell's empire had grown by leaps and bounds, but he hadn't been able to prevent one particularly sensitive U-2 mission from being claimed by the USAF. The blue-suiters emerged from the renewed discussions in July 1958 over who-does-what with the responsibility for U-2 peripheral photo-reconnaissance. That is, flights which gathered imagery intelligence but were not intended to overfly denied territory. On 20 March 1959, SAC deployed three U-2As of the 4080th wing to Eielson AFB to conduct photo missions codenamed Congo Maiden along the eastern and northern coastline of Siberia. The detachment was led by Colonel Hayden "Buzz" Curry, and used three of the five most recently built U-2s from the supplementary batch.

The main purpose of this operation was to determine the status of Soviet airfields in this frozen region. Many of these had been built along the coast before the Second World War, and six of them were known to have been upgraded in recent years, despite the difficulties of constructing paved runways and buildings in the permafrost. The upgrading of the Arctic airfields, especially those in the Chukotsky Peninsula, suggested that Soviet nuclear bombers might use them as staging posts, on their way to attack prime targets in North America. SAC also wanted to find out more about Soviet air defenses in this region, in case a pre-emptive U.S. strike on the Arctic airfields was ordered.

The mission planners at Offutt set to work on the flight routes, which would be flown 12-15 nautical miles off the coast using the B-camera in Modes 3 and 4, which provided coverage from the vertical out to the right or left horizon respectively. The U.S. still formally insisted on its right to

fly as close as three miles to the Soviet (and any other) coast. But international sentiment now favored 12 miles. The mission planners at SAC headquarters deliberately did not press for three miles, since they did not want the politicians in Washington to sit up and take notice of these flights. In addition to the B-camera, the aircraft would also carry the small ELINT (System One) and COMINT (System Three) receivers in the nose.[5]

SAC deployed three U-2As of the 4080th SRW to Eielson AFB, Alaska, for the peripheral photo flights. (Lockheed LA-1673)

Captain Bobbie Gardiner was one of four pilots from the 4080th that flew the photo missions along the Soviet coastline in 1959. (NARA 164462 AC)

The window of opportunity for mounting such photo flights was limited, not only by the darkness of the northern winter, but by frequent fog and cloud in summer. But in the second half of March 1959 the weather was unusually fine in the area of interest, with only some high cirrus cloud. The SAC detachment quickly prepared for the missions, and on 23 March Major James "Snake" Bedford took off towards the Bering Strait on the first mission. Over the next five days, another six missions were staged, heading southwest down the Chukotsky and Kamchatka peninsulas, and northwest into the Chukchi and East Siberian Seas. The navigation was challenging: through the driftsight, and the pilots had great difficulty distinguishing frozen snow-covered land from frozen, snow-covered sea. There was precious little vegetation on the land. Once again, celestial navigation

was essential. But it would not have been surprising if the 15-mile limit was breached on a few occasions, given the well-known difficulties of navigating in the Arctic North.

The longest mission of this peripheral photo series was flown by "Buzz" Curry himself on 27 March, a nine-hour flight that went to the Kamchatka peninsula and was a 100% success. The other pilots who made these long and lonely flights were Captains Rudy Anderson, Bobbie Gardiner, and "Snake" Bedford. The only snags were with the tracker cameras, which failed on two flights. However, the PVO had radar coverage even in these frozen wastelands, and MiGs were stationed at some of the bigger airfields, such as Anadyr, Mys Shmidta, and Provideniya. It seems likely that at least some of the Congo Maiden flights were detected. After completing the task, the SAC detachment remained at Eielson and conducted a new series of sampling flights from there until mid-May.

More Small Wars
The record for the longest U-2 flight in 1959 went to the CIA's Detachment C, thanks to its involvement in the crisis over Tibet. A rumour that the communists intended to abduct the Dalai Lama, spiritual and temporal leader of the Tibetan people, led to a full scale rebellion in that remote land in March 1959. The CIA had been lending active support to the rebels since fall 1957. But the Red Army was firmly entrenched, and the Dalai Lama and many of his supporters were forced to flee across the border into India when the March rebellion failed.[6]

In early May 1959 the Eisenhower administration authorized a major expansion of U.S. support, including the training of 700 Tibetans at a special operations camp in the mountains of Colorado. After training, the nationalists would be air-dropped into Tibet, with the aim of disrupting Beijing's supply lines to the remote region.

More imagery of Tibet was needed to identify suitable drop zones and targets for sabotage. The U-2 was ideal, since mission planners in project

A typical view through the driftsight. During the Congo Maiden flights the SAC pilots had difficulty navigating, because the frozen Soviet coastline was not clearly defined (via Chuck Wilson).

This U-2 photograph shows the Potala Palace, in Lhasa. The Tibetan crisis of March 1959 prompted a series of overflights by Det C, as the CIA stepped up aid for the Dalai Lama's supporters as they resisted the Chinese communist takeover of Tibet.

HQ had other targets near the Sino-Soviet border to which Jim Reber and ARC had assigned high priority. A portion of Detachment C was redeployed to NAS Cubi Point and flew two long missions north from there, all the way across China and Mongolia. Tom Crull flew the first on 12 May 1959, a nine-hour 10-minute trip across North Vietnam, southern China, and Tibet that landed at Kermitola, a military airbase near Dhaka, in East Pakistan.

Two days later, Lyle Rudd flew for even longer across barren Chinese steppes and deserts. Rudd eventually reached Lhasa, Tibet, and had a superb view through the driftsight of the Potala Palace in the late afternoon sunshine. Like Crull before him, Rudd recovered into the Dhaka airfield in East Pakistan as planned. His low-fuel warning light came on even before he found the airfield. Rudd landed after nine hours 40 minutes in the air, which was probably the longest operational U-2 mission to date. He had covered over 4,200 nautical miles.[7]

The film from these two missions was processed and analyzed by interpreters from PIC, who deployed to Okinawa. The USAF had agreed to provide C-130A transports based there for the airdrops over Tibet. These began in July 1959, staging out of an airbase that DPD had secretly estab-lished at Takhli, in Thailand. The following month, Det C deployed U-2s to the new Thai base, along with pilots Tom Crull, Buster Edens, Lyle Rudd, and Sammy Snyder. Three more U-2 flights over China and Tibet were mounted in early September.[8]

From Takhli, Det C also flew three missions over Laos and North Vietnam in September 1959. The Geneva Agreement, which supposedly guaranteed the neutrality of Laos, was being broken daily by North Vietnam, but also by the U.S., which sent "military advisors" to this small, landlocked kingdom. The "advisors" were apparently controlled by DDP. On 7 September 1959, the pro-western government in Vientiane asked the United Nations to intervene, because rebels trained by the North Vietnamese had invaded frontier areas. Photo-interpreters derived the North Vietnamese order of battle from the imagery, but were unable to determine the extent of infiltration into Laos, due to the thick jungle canopy covering the border areas.[9]

However, everyone in DPD knew that the Soviet Union was still the primary target. Where were the missiles? Could the U-2 find them? Would the President let it fly? Most important of all, could the Soviets shoot it down?

8

The New Model

The Soviet fighter threat to Project Chalice was growing. PVO pilots were practicing the "zoom-climb" technique. After climbing to near maximum altitude, they accelerated in the straight and level, or even a shallow dive, to maximum speed, before pitching up sharply. The interceptor entered a ballistic curve, gaining a few thousand extra feet. The maneuver was risky, since the fighters' control surfaces had little effect at the top of the curve. But in theory, the interceptor pilot might be able to bring weapons to bear on a high-altitude target, if the zoom-climb had been entered at exactly the right spot relative to the target.

Meanwhile, Soviet fighter designers were working on new variants. Codenamed Farmer-B by the West; the MiG-19PM was credited with a ceiling of 60,000 feet, and it also carried an early Soviet airborne search radar and a beam-riding air-air missile. The MiG-19 might now be a threat to the U-2, if the interceptor pilot could get a radar lock-on for the missiles and fire them upwards. Of course, if the U-2 was forced to descend for a relight after flaming-out, the threat would be that much greater.

The new missiles and radar were also fitted to a new interceptor designed by Sukhoi, which used a more reliable and powerful axial turbojet. The Su-9 evolved from Sukhoi's T-3 experimental delta, which had been flown and revealed in May 1956. The T-3 was capable of Mach 2 and could reach 65,000 feet. But Western intelligence knew very little about the Su-9: although it entered production in 1959, the reporting name Fishpot was not even allocated until 1961.

New SIGINT systems

It was obvious, though, that the U-2 was becoming increasingly vulnerable. The more so because each time a new piece of equipment was added the aircraft got heavier, and its maximum altitude declined. The new equipment included an improved SIGINT system that used new antennas designed by HRB Singer under contract to the CIA. System 6 was introduced in 1958 to replace the rudimentary System 1 ELINT package on the Agency's U-2s. It provided continuous coverage of a wider frequency range without the need to preselect certain bands before takeoff. Small spiral and parabolic antennas were installed behind flush-mounted radomes on the equipment bay hatches, which could nevertheless still carry the primary A or B camera payloads. A larger scimitar antenna was added beneath the rear fuselage, enclosed in a rectangular radome. This antenna was shared by System 3, the COMINT system that had previously used a nose-mounted antenna. Responsibility for the overall design and maintenance of the U-

2's SIGINT systems now rested with STL, a subsidiary of Ramo-Wooldridge that had survived the 1958 breakup of that company.

By now, moreover, U-2 mission planners fully realized that the maximum altitude of the U-2 could also be reduced by unexpected variations in the outside air temperature at high altitude. The problem was particularly acute in the northern latitudes. This was because the tropopause was lower towards the pole than it was at the equator—sometimes as low as 25,000 feet. Above the tropopause air temperature rose steadily again, so that by 60,000 feet it could be 5-10 degrees Centigrade warmer than the standard (which was -55 degrees). Under these conditions the U-2 climbed slower, and even failed to climb at all if the temperature was more than 10 degrees warmer than the standard.

Considering that the northern regions of the USSR were prime intelligence targets, this was bad news. Kelly Johnson concluded that a more powerful engine was needed to boost the U-2 back above 70,000 feet. Fortunately, the Pratt & Whitney J75 engine was the solution. This was a scaled-up version of the J57, which had entered production in 1957 to power the USAF's latest fighters, the F-105 and F-106. Although mass airflow was increased by one-third, the J75's dimensions were only 10 percent greater than the J57.

A quick study confirmed that the J75 would just fit in the existing U-2, if the width of some main fuselage rings was reduced. The CIA was offered nine J75P-2 engines which were originally intended for the Martin XP6M Seamaster, a jet flying boat that the Navy was about to cancel. They were converted for high altitude flight by modifying the hot section and

The MiG-19PM (Farmer-B) was thought to pose a greater threat to the U-2 than earlier variants. It carried an air-to-air radar that could guide four beam-riding AA-1 Alkali missiles. (Russian Aviation Research Trust)

fuel controls. In the new J75P-13 configuration they offered 17,300 lbs thrust, which was a huge increase compared to the U-2's existing J57-31A. A few other modifications to the airframe were necessary to accommodate the heavier, more powerful J75. The intake duct had to be widened, and the main landing gear bulkhead was strengthened to cope with the higher gross weight. The modified aircraft would be 1,450 lbs heavier than the U-2A, with the engine itself accounting for 1,100 lbs.[1]

Eisenhower's Doubts

Development of the new U-2 model took place in the spring of 1959. In Washington, though, the prospects for further U-2 overflights of the USSR were very uncertain. Despite persistent prompting by senior intelligence officials, President Eisenhower was as reluctant as ever to approve them. Just before Christmas 1958, Ike told his Board of Consultants on Foreign Intelligence Activities that he doubted whether "the intelligence which we receive from [the U-2 flights] is worth the exacerbation of international tension which results." Moreover, he believed that the previous flights had already provided plenty enough strategic targets for SAC's bombers and missiles.[2]

After a meeting of the National Security Council on 12 February, Defense Secretary Neil McElroy, his assistant Donald Quarles, and Joint Chiefs of Staff chairman General Twining all stayed behind. Just a few days earlier, Premier Khruschev claimed that series production of an ICBM was underway in the USSR. McElroy pressed for more flights, reminding Eisenhower that not a single launch base for operational Soviet ICBMs had been found. Twining backed him up, claiming that the risk of a U-2 being shot down was remote. Top officials in the Pentagon were still disputing the conclusions of the high-level review of the missile intelligence estimating process that had been undertaken the previous fall. According to them, the reason that the Soviets had not test-flown any more ICBMs from Tyuratam for nearly a year was that they were satisfied with the big missile's performance! Ergo, they were now deploying it.

Ike's response was to doubt whether the Soviets could actually build operational launch sites so quickly. "We generally overestimate the capability of the USSR to outperform us," he noted, reminding the meeting of how the threat of a "bomber gap" had been so exaggerated a couple of years earlier. He still thought that the U-2 flights were provocative: "noth-

The runway at Incirlik airbase, Turkey, appears over the left wing tank of a T-33 trainer used by Det B to maintain pilot proficiency. Incirlik was Det B's home base, from which the missions over the Middle East and along the Soviet border were launched.

A BRITISH ATTEMPT AT INTERCEPTION

Pilot Officer Roger Hymans flew Hunter F.6 fighters for the Royal Air Force in Germany during the late 1950s. He recalled intercepting what must have been a CIA U-2 being ferried to the U.S. or the UK:

Nobody ever got scrambled on battle flight. But this early morning was different. GCI told me there was a real bogey coming west. I nervously removed the sticky tape from the safety catch of my guns. I pondered whether, as the most junior pilot in the entire air force, I was now about to initiate World War III.

As I passed 40,000 feet on the climb, I was informed that my target bogey was "12 o'clock high and 20,000" above! As I passed 50,000 feet the aircraft started to feel sloppy, and eventually at 55,000, I was on the edge at high Mach number but very low indicated airspeed.

I was told to turn around. As I staggered around, just on the stall, I looked up into the sky above. There, still way above me, was what looked like a majestic glider, black, with high aspect ratio and—even more amazingly—moving even more slowly than me.

As I passed this information to the controller, he suddenly became very terse and told me to return to base without delay. On landing, the WingCo flying asked me what I had seen, listened to my description, and then immediately told me in no uncertain terms that I was completely mistaken—I had to forget the whole thing.

It was not many months later when Nikita Khrushchev banged his shoe on the table at the UN in a temper tantrum over the exploits of some American civilian chap by the name of Gary Powers. It was then that I knew for certain I had not dreamed up my solitary trip to a mile above our usual max operating height!

J-75 ENGINE FOR THE U-2

3 February 1959

Kelly Johnson called me last evening with information that the conversion of one U-2 aircraft and installation of a J-75 engine, plus four months' flight tests, would come to $481,000...He was most interesting in his estimates of performance. He believed that it would be possible to establish a mission profile with 70,000 feet at start of climb and 72,000 feet at high cone. The worry, however, is some loss in range...I authosied him to start immediately, on a crash basis, the necessary engineering.

- memo by Richard Bissell, DDP

Carmine Vito had to stop flying U-2s in 1958 with a medical problem. He transferred to Washington and flew a desk at Project HQ from 1959 to 1960:

There were six major projects going on when I was there. There were all these rooms, and it was very compartmented. You couldn't talk to anyone outside your cell. We had different color-coded badges. The main briefing room had five or six doors, and all the offices surrounded it. They were all locked, with red and green lights, and only when it was green could you go in. I briefed sometimes from behind a screen—I wasn't supposed to know who I was briefing. Crazy!

I was the TWX reader, after the comms section had unscrambled them. Turkey was 12 hours ahead, so they came in at god-awful hours, and somebody had to get it all together for the morning. I used to sleep in HQ when we were running a mission. The TWXs started coming in at 0100 and 0200. Sometimes they were important and you had to wake someone up.

There was a lot of effort and redundancy. Three guys made the flight plans out independently, and they were cross-checked for accuracy.

I did not go to all the briefings. I was squeamish about learning too much—the A-12, the ELINT, the clandestine flights. The way that headquarters are, you learn too much and then you're useless. You can't go out into the field again.

- interview with author

Compared with the J57, the Pratt & Whitney J75 engine offered a large increase in thrust, although it was 1,000 lbs heavier. It could just be squeezed into the existing fuselage contour of the U-2! (author)

these missiles at any U.S. reconnaissance aircraft. Quarles chipped in, assuring the President that only a few overflights of the USSR would be planned, and each one would be brought to him for clearance. The meeting broke up, with Eisenhower reminding those present that the USSR was ratcheting up the tension over the status of Berlin.[3]

Mission planners once again reviewed the options for the "northern flight" and other high-priority targets. But their efforts were frustrated within days, when the President told General Goodpaster that he had decided to disapprove any additional U-2 flights because of the crisis over Berlin. Still, the U.S. intelligence community, led by Bissell, pressed for a resumption. Their cause was strengthened in March, when the USSR finally resumed ICBM test-flights from Tyuratam. (In the meantime, however, there had been three unsuccessful Soviet attempts to launch a probe to the moon from there, followed by another propaganda coup when the Luna rocket did finally achieve success on 2 January 1959. The Luna was based on the R-7 ICBM, with the addition of a new third stage).[4]

More U-2 flight plans were laid out, reworked, and refined within the secure confines of 1717 H Street. On 3 April, DCI Allen Dulles himself discussed them in the White House. As well as the much-prized "northern flight," there was a proposal for another flight over Tyuratam. Both flights would cover a number of other high-priority targets. President Eisenhower was reluctant to approve them, but said he would consult with Acting Secretary of State Christian Herter. Three days later, Ike did give a go-ahead for the flights, after his trusted advisor General Goodpaster said he favored them taking place. But within 24 hours Eisenhower had changed his mind. On 7 April the President called in Dick Bissell and Secretary of Defense

ing would make me request the authority to declare war more quickly, than violation of *our* airspace by Soviet aircraft," he declared. Ike wanted to wait for the successor airplane to the U-2 that the CIA was striving to develop, with its promise of undetectability. Better still, wait for the reconnaissance satellite, which did not violate Soviet airspace at all.

Ike left open the possibility of approving one or two flights, though. At this point, General Goodpaster reminded him that he had already approved a mission over the northern USSR to find and photograph suspected ICBM bases. It had not been flown because of the unfavorable sun angle and weather. (This was the mission which Det B had attempted to fly out of Bodo during the previous October). This mission was the number one priority, Goodpaster continued, and conditions to fly it should be favorable again from March. Twining emphasized how important this flight was, and Eisenhower reluctantly agreed. "At least we'll then find out whether the Soviets have an adequate surface-to-air missile," he noted drily. Twining quickly reminded Ike that the Soviets had not yet fired one of

This is the U-2C prototype (Article 342) standing on the dry lake near Edwards North Base in summer 1959, marked with its USAF identity 56675. Outwardly, there was no difference from the U-2A, except for the widened intakes needed to feed a greater air mass to the new engine's compressor face (Lockheed Report SP-179).

McElroy and told them that the flights were not worth the political risk. Ike agreed that the missile intelligence was needed, but expressed his concern over "the terrible propaganda impact if a reconnaissance plane were to fail." He thought that the Soviets were ready for a Summit Meeting, which he did not want to jeopardize.

A frustrated Bissell returned to the Matomic Building. He never told the staff there exactly what transpired in any of the White House meetings, but they could guess. Each time a U-2 flight was proposed, they would make up detailed briefing boards with maps of the route and send it to the Executive Office. The maps were accompanied by a cogent, one-page summary justifying the flight. This was crafted by Jim Reber, with help from CIA analysts in specific fields, including Herb Bowers (strategic bombers), Sidney Graybeal (missiles), and Henry Lowenhaupt (nuclear weapons). Usually, DPD's military boss Colonel Bill Burke would take the briefing to the White House Staff Secretary, Colonel Andrew Goodpaster. He would subsequently take it in to the President. But "Speedy Gonzales"—as the DPD staffers called Eisenhower—was obviously not swayed by the briefings. There had not been a single deep penetration overflight of the USSR for 18 months.

U-2C First Flight

On 13 May 1959, at Edwards North Base, Ray Goudey made the first flight of a U-2 re-engined with the J75. Article 342 was the prototype, and the conversion received the new designation U-2C. An intensive series of test flights followed, in which the advantages and disadvantages of the modification were quickly explored. On the plus side, the maximum altitude was raised to more than 75,000 feet, and the new engine had a much greater compressor stall margin. There were no more bleed valves to worry about, either. But range was sacrificed for altitude: a reduction from 4,000 to 3,300 nautical miles when a maximum power cruise profile was flown. This was the favored profile, however, since the U-2C entered the cruise-climb at the higher altitude of 67,000 feet, and nearly two-thirds of the mission was flown above 70,000 feet.[5]

On the minus side, the re-engined aircraft's center of gravity (cg) limits were narrower. On an early test flight, Lockheed pilot Bob Schumacher

The American pilots of Det B in 1959-60. Top (from left), Bob Ericson, Marty Knutson, Al Rand, Frank Powers. Bottom (from left), Jim Barnes, and Barry Baker. Not in picture: John Shinn and Glen Dunaway.

reported that the cg was so far forward that the aircraft might become uncontrollable if the autopilot disconnected before the slipper tanks had emptied. The horizontal tail was modified with a more rounded leading edge and an increased camber to balance the aerodynamic load. Even so, ballast had to be added at the tail for most operational configurations. However, Lockheed did take the opportunity to incorporate three improvements for controllability of the C-model based on earlier experience with the A-models. The elevator trim tab operating speed was doubled, and the down elevator travel was increased from 11.5 to 20 degrees to offset the nose-up pitching tendency during rapid application of power. The speed at which the flaps and ailerons moved to and from gust control position was halved, to decrease the rate of change of elevator stick force.

The Israeli Bomb

In Turkey, Detachment B's only operational flying was occasional SIGINT flights along the Soviet border, and the photo missions over the Middle East and the Mediterranean at roughly monthly intervals. The Lebanon Crisis of mid-1958, and the overthrow of Iraq's pro-Western monarchy, taught U.S. policy makers to keep an eye on the increasingly-volatile region.

The photo-interpreters at Automat began to notice a lot of activity at an Israeli air force bombing range south of Beersheba. Near the small desert town of Dimona, a large barren area was fenced off and a new access road was built. From successive U-2 flights, the PIs noted the arrival of construction machinery, and then the digging of heavy foundations, which were reinforced with concrete. They began to suspect that Israel was secretly building a nuclear reactor. After the latest imagery showed that concrete footings had been poured—surely for a reactor dome—Art Lundahl took the evidence to the White House. There was no immediate reaction: the U.S. was quietly supporting Israel against its pan-Arab, pro-Soviet neighbors.

Throughout 1959 Lundahl continued to report the activity at Dimona to the White House and to the Atomic Energy Commissioner, Lewis Strauss. Construction of a second underground site began nearby, and the CIA analysts concluded that it would be a chemical reprocessing plant to make weapons-grade plutonium. They noticed a striking similarity between Dimona and the French nuclear reactor and processing facility at Marcoule....

The Israelis began reacting to the U-2 overflights. They launched interceptors, but without success. The CIA briefed U.S. military attachés in Tel Aviv, who began snooping around the perimeter of the desert site. By the end of 1959 there was no doubt that Israel was developing a nuclear weapon. But the White House seemed determined to look the other way.[6]

More Soviet Border Flights

With the resumption of missile tests from Tyuratam, the U-2's ability to collect electronic intelligence along the Soviet southern border assumed new importance. Whenever there were indications from the ground stations monitoring Soviet communications that a test was planned, an aircraft and pilot were put on standby at Incirlik.

These "strip alerts" were also endured by another set of crews on the Incirlik flight line. They were from SAC's 55th Reconnaissance Wing, flying a version of the B-47 bomber that was specially configured for the same TELINT (Telemetry Intelligence) mission. Two of these aircraft, codename Tell-Two and designated EB-47TT, were also alerted when the first indications that there might be a missile launch were received. The primary aircraft would depart to the east and set up an orbit over northeastern Iran, providing another means to intercept the countdown. If the countdown was delayed for some reason, the secondary aircraft was available to relieve it.[7] But the Tell-Two could not fly high enough to intercept any telemetry from the vital first-stage burn of Soviet missiles launched from Tyuratam. Nor could it venture beyond Iran's eastern border with Afghanistan. That was where the U-2 came in. If the U-2 was actually launched, it would fly higher and further than the B-47.

Most U-2 missions of this type went as far east as the Afghan-Pakistan border and lasted up to nine hours. Many were unsuccessful, as the Soviets aborted the countdown. On one frustrating occasion, John Shinn loitered as long as he could at the turnaround point before turning for home. Three hours later the countdown resumed, and the missile was launched just after the U-2 landed back at Incirlik. Finally, though, the elaborate preparation and coordination paid off. On 9 June 1959 the first-stage telemetry of the R-7 was intercepted for the first time during U-2 mission 4120.[8]

Operation Touchdown

The renewed activity at Tyuratam may have persuaded President Eisenhower to finally heed the urgings of his advisors and approve a new overflight of the launch site. Or it may have been the hope that the U-2 would not be detected: the plan was to takeoff from Pakistan and penetrate Soviet territory over an area where there was no Soviet early-warning radar coverage. Det B was alerted while Allen Dulles and Bissell brought a plan named Operation Touchdown to the White House on 7 July. After launching from Peshawar, the flight would overfly Tyuratam and then head northwest towards the Urals, where many military-industrial targets were on ARC's list. The flight would then turn back from Sverdlovsk to the south, and depart Soviet territory at the border with Iran and Afghanistan.

For the first time a landing would be made in Iran. The Shah was being supported by the CIA and had no objections. Det B commander Stan Beerli and executive officer John Parangosky had flown over Iran in a C-47, looking for suitable landing sites. They selected an airstrip near Zahedan. It had an old wartime runway, a radio beacon, and little else! It was suitably remote, but there was some concern that the place was not secure from mountain bandits, who operated freely in the area.

Eisenhower liked the idea of entering and leaving Soviet airspace at widely separated points in the south. But he withheld final approval until Secretary of State Herter could be consulted. At a second meeting in the Oval Office to discuss the flight the next day Herter strongly supported Dulles and Bissell. Ike bowed to their combined pressure, but noted that "a complete disavowal" would have to be made if the Soviets protested the flight.[9]

The "QuickMove" procedure swung into action. Colonel Stan Beerli, the Det B commander, had devised this fast and stealthy means of deployment using a couple of C-130s. All the items necessary to support a mission—commo, PSD, and maintenance gear—was packed onto three trailers that could be easily pulled on and off the C-130 by a jeep, which traveled on the transport's loading ramp. Another Hercules carried the drums containing the special U-2 fuel. Under cover of darkness, the C-130s would fly to the deployment base, followed at an appropriate interval by the U-2 itself.[10]

John Parangosky, the Agency's executive officer at Det B, flew to Iran in this C-47 to help secure landing rights for renewed U-2 overflights of the USSR (via Stan Beerli).

The C-130s were loaded and dispatched to Peshawar airbase, in northern Pakistan, arriving there in radio silence during the early evening, when most of the base personnel had left. Under cover of darkness, the U-2A was ferried from Incirlik by Frank Powers, landing just after midnight. The B-camera was loaded in the darkened hangar, while mission pilot Marty Knutson was briefed on the flight and began prebreathing. At six the following morning, before most of the airbase had woken up, Knutson took off on Mission 4125.

It was an almost complete success. The flight was apparently not detected by the PVO. Knutson flew deep into the USSR, departed denied territory to the south as planned, and approached the Iranian base. He was relieved to see the C-130 that had brought the recovery crew parked below. Knutson had half-expected to find them under attack from the mountain bandits, having been told at his preflight briefing that there was some concern over security at the remote airfield! After nine hours 10 minutes in the air the U-2 was virtually running on fumes. After Knutson landed, they found only 20 gallons left in the sump tanks. The aircraft was quickly unloaded, refueled, and flown back to Incirlik by Barry Baker.[11]

The imagery of Tyuratam from Mission 4125 revealed preparations for what turned out to be a second successful Luna rocket launch nine days later. Because of the pace of recent launches from here, the missile analysts had been expecting to see a second or even third launch pad in use already. The imagery *did* reveal a second launch complex 14 miles northeast of the first one, but it was still under construction. The surprised analysts noted that "the single launch facility, coupled with the relatively short periods between several launchings, indicates a highly efficient approach to check-out and launch of large missiles."[12] The upcoming second launch complex was judged by CIA analysts to be a prototype for the sites at which the SS-6 would be deployed.

The analysts still badly wanted some imagery of those operational sites, wherever they had been built or might be under construction. Their best guess was now that the first SS-6 deployment was somewhere in the Polyarnyy Ural area (evidently, no new intelligence pointing to Plesetsk as the first location had been received). But although the USSR did not protest the 9 July flight, Eisenhower was not encouraged enough by its success to allow further flights. Especially after Premier Khrushchev accepted, in mid-July, an invitation to visit the U.S. in late September.[13]

The U-2C Deploys

At North Base, two more of the CIA's U-2A aircraft received the J75 engine and joined the U-2C flight test program. The CIA pilots who were resident with the "headquarters" unit there also began flying the new model. They found the U-2C to be quite a handful, especially at high altitude and heavy weights when slipper tanks were installed. This was because of the aircraft's reduced longitudinal stability, compared with the U-2A. Lockheed conceded that the U-2C could not be flown manually for extended periods of time. Accordingly, the entire autopilot adjustment box was transferred to the cockpit. This allowed the pilot to "tweak" the pitch, roll, and yaw characteristics of the autopilot for better performance while inflight.

For a time, the J75 showed a tendency to engine roughness and flameouts when climbing between 40,000 and 60,000 feet—just like the bad old days of the early J57-P-37 powerplant! The problem was solved on an interim basis by reducing power, and eventually by adjusting the fuel control, but not before CIA pilot Jim Cherbonneaux set a new record of eight flameouts on a single flight!

After 400 hours of flight tests in only 11 weeks, the C-model was declared ready for deployment on 1 August. On 12 August, Articles 351 and 358 departed Edwards, bound for Det B in Turkey. A six-man team from the Skunk Works followed to check out the pilots and maintenance crews at the Det on the re-engined aircraft. Following the by-now regular routine for ferry flights, the aircraft made refueling stops at Plattsburgh AFB, NY, and Giebelstadt. By the end of August, 10 pilots had been checked out at Det B on the re-engined bird: five CIA, four RAF, and the recently-appointed detachment commander, Colonel William Shelton. He was a newcomer to the U-2 operation and a replacement for Stan Beerli, who was posted to Project HQ in Washington as Director of Operations.

In September 1959, another two U-2As were re-engined with the J75, test flown, and ferried to Det C in Japan. On 24 September Tom Crull made a familiarization flight from Atsugi in one of them (Article 360). Having experienced for himself the C-model's improved high-altitude performance, Crull ran short of fuel on his way back. A descent from 75,000 feet in the U-2C would consume 35 gallons and take 20 minutes, but the first 10,000 feet took a long time. The pilot had to ease the throttle to idle and extend the gear and speed brakes. Even then, the Angel hardly seemed inclined to leave the heavens; there was precious little drag created by the gear and brakes at these altitudes, and the engine thrust was still considerable even on minimum power. To cut it back further would invite a flameout. At the same time, care had to be taken to ensure that the speed did not build up so that mach buffet was encountered. In view of all this, and the possibility of encountering strong headwinds during the descent, most pilots did not feel comfortable leaving cruise altitude with less than 100 gallons remaining.

The U-2A configuration used on Operation Touchdown. The slab radome under the rear fuselage housed a scimitar antenna for the new System 6 ELINT receiver.

Deadstick

Crull later said that, on this occasion, the gust control did not work, which slowed his descent even further. Whatever the reason, Article 360 ran out of fuel on approach to Atsugi, 10 miles short of the runway. Fortunately, Crull had enough altitude remaining to deadstick the aircraft onto a small civilian airfield at nearby Fujisawa, although he was unable to lower the landing gear in time. In less than a minute, Crull was surrounded by curious Japanese civilians, some of them carrying cameras. He remained in the cockpit until help arrived from Atsugi, in the form of an L-20 Beaver lightplane carrying the detachment's security officers. They cordoned off the area and ordered the Japanese onlookers away at gunpoint. This only excited their curiosity still further, since the U-2 was flying completely unmarked, save for a minute three-digit serial on the tail. Photographers snapped away, and the story reached the local papers. They asked pointed questions as to why a so-called weather research plane should cause such a security flap, and be flying in an all-black scheme without national insignia or registration marks! Article 360 was dismantled and returned to the U.S. for repair.

Meanwhile, at North Base, the U-2C prototype was now engaged on trials of the "Granger." This was the first item of electronic countermeasures (ECM) equipment to be added to the U-2, and it was designed to combat the new Soviet fighter radar. None of the ECM devices that had been developed for U.S. bomber and attack aircraft would fit on the U-2. The CIA let a contract to a small Palo Alto, California, company named Granger Associates. The task was to build a radar jammer that was small enough to fit in the brake parachute compartment at the base of the tail. (The parachute was rarely used, and was therefore dispensable).

The "Granger Box" used deceptive techniques, repeating the conical scan signal that was generated by an X-band fighter radar, but returning it 180-degrees out-of-phase. The radar jammer weighed only 38 lbs including the radome, but of necessity, its radiated power was small, and it was only effective in the rear quadrant. Still, it was judged to be better than no protection at all. Flight tests were completed in the fall of 1959, and all of the CIA's aircraft were quickly modified to accept the box.

Crowflight Re-organized

In September 1959 the 4080th Strategic Reconnaissance Wing began a new phase of Operation Crowflight. The grinding routine of twice-weekly, eight-hour flights up and down the sampling corridors had continued, although neither the U.S. nor the USSR had conducted a nuclear test in the atmosphere since November 1958, when a mutually-agreed moratorium came into effect. The filter papers of the aircraft's A-Foil (nose) and P-2 (equipment bay) systems were still collecting plenty of debris particles, however. But the Defense Atomic Support Agency (DASA, which replaced the Air Force Special Weapons Project in a 1959 re-organization) wanted to cover the northern latitudes more comprehensively, as nuclear scientists continued their quest to understand the long-term dispersal pattern of nuclear fall-out. In August 1959, therefore, det 4 at Ezeiza was temporarily closed, and so was det 3 at Ramey, and all six "hard-nose" sampling U-2As returned to Laughlin. The following month, three of them were sent to a new det 9 at Minot AFB, ND. The other three formed det 10, which remained at Laughlin, but made a deployment to Ramey every five or six weeks.

SAC was asked to extend the U-2 sampling flights from Minot all the way to the North Pole, but the 4080th was not ready for this yet. Apart from the challenges of grid navigation, and flying a single-engine aircraft over such hostile territory, there were also problems in determining in advance the winds that the flights would encounter in the upper atmosphere. In the lower latitudes, this was accomplished by taking data from radiosonde balloons sent aloft by weather stations. There were none of these stations in the polar regions. DASA eventually arranged three B-52 sampling flights to the North Pole instead.

Meanwhile, the furthest north that SAC's U-2s would venture was about 75 degrees, and this only on the Toy Soldier missions out of Eielson AB. The "customer" for these classified flights, where the primary purpose was to diagnose the nature of Soviet nuclear warheads, was renamed AFTAC (Air Force Technical Applications Center) in September 1959. The 4080th wing mounted its fifth deployment to Alaska in late September for three weeks.

Back at Laughlin AFB, the 4080th continued to train for wartime and other contingencies with the 20 other U-2A models on strength there. SAC

FIGURE 4

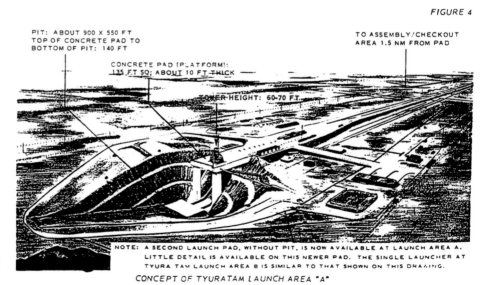

PIT: ABOUT 900 X 550 FT
TOP OF CONCRETE PAD TO
BOTTOM OF PIT: 140 FT

CONCRETE PAD (PLATFORM):
135 FT SQ; ABOUT 10 FT THICK

TOWER HEIGHT: 60-70 FT

TO ASSEMBLY/CHECKOUT
AREA 1.5 NM FROM PAD

NOTE: A SECOND LAUNCH PAD, WITHOUT PIT, IS NOW AVAILABLE AT LAUNCH AREA A. LITTLE DETAIL IS AVAILABLE ON THIS NEWER PAD. THE SINGLE LAUNCHER AT TYURA TAM LAUNCH AREA B IS SIMILAR TO THAT SHOWN ON THIS DRAWING.

CONCEPT OF TYURATAM LAUNCH AREA "A"

This CIA drawing of the first launch pad at Tyuratam is based entirely on analysis of imagery returned by overflying U-2s (CIA).

did not re-engine any of its aircraft, and they did not receive the Granger box or the System 6 ELINT upgrade. The wing did keep four aircraft in a dedicated SIGINT configuration, with Systems 1/3/4 loaded, but they were proving troublesome. The aircraft's rotating anticollision light interfered with System 1, and new filters had to be designed. The mean-time-between failure for System 3 was only eight hours. Moreover, the RADAN/ASN-6 system that had been added to these "ferret" aircraft for more precise navigation never worked properly. In mid-1959, it was replaced by a VOR/ADF installation, but still these SIGINT U-2s flying with SAC had not yet made an operational deployment. SAC was also persevering with the Westinghouse APQ-56 SLAR on three U-2As, though this too had never been used for an intelligence-gathering flight. In September 1959 the 4080th failed its Unit Simulated Combat Mission, a test of operational readiness. [14]

The 4080th wing gave up most of its Martin RB-57Ds to USAFE and ARDC in mid-1959; the twin-engined reconnaissance aircraft that SAC had once championed over the CIA's U-2 had never been a great success. In particular, the Martin company's two main attempts to shave weight from the design had both caused serious problems after the RB-57D entered service. The honeycomb wing panels delaminated from the thin metal skin which covered them, and were a maintenance nightmare. The reduced-thickness wingspar failed on one aircraft as it landed, causing all aircraft to be grounded and then structurally strengthened.

The 4080th retained just six RB-57D2 models, a dedicated ELINT aircraft in which a second crew member was carried to operate a complex, semi-automated "ferret" system designed by Martin. During a deployment to Eielson in mid-1959, one of these aircraft confirmed that latest Soviet early-warning and height-finding radars were capable of detecting aircraft at least 200 nautical miles beyond their Far Eastern borders. [15]

Khrushchev Keeps Quiet

Premier Khrushchev paid his visit to the U.S. in the second half of September as planned. Despite many opportunities to raise the subject in private,

he never mentioned the U.S. spyplane overflights to President Eisenhower. Soon after he had gone, the CIA was back in the Oval Office trying to get permission for the long-mooted U-2 flight over northern Russia. But Ike turned it down. A limited penetration over the Soviet Kurile Islands to the northeast of Japan was flown instead, on 1 November 1959. [16]

In late August the ad-hoc panel that had been advising the CIA on Soviet ICBM progress reminded Allen Dulles that the U-2:

"...possesses altitude capabilities which make it a unique platform for the reliable acquisition of high quality telemetry data prior to first stage burnout on Tyuratam ICBM launchings. Such data is of extreme importance in determining ICBM characteristics." [17]

From July to December 1959 Det B mounted another 14 Operation Hot Shop flights along the Soviet southern border in connection with missile test-launches from Tyuratam. System 7, dedicated to picking up telemetry from the missile tests, was added to the detachment's newly-converted C-models. It featured automatic intercept receivers that were activated when launch control frequencies were used, and high-speed tape recorders. It used an additional pair of antennas that were mounted on the upper fuselage of the U-2, and which were better tuned to receive the L-band telemetry transmissions from Soviet missiles. On some flights, pilots were even given a 16mm handheld Bolex movie camera to film the missile's plume as it ascended from the launch pad if they could. Some of the Soviet missile firings took place at night, and even though the U-2 was flying 500 miles to the south, the pilots witnessed the sky lighting up for hundred of miles. [18]

First "British" Overflight

The pace of missile testing evidently encouraged the President to approve another mission to the launch sites in November, and the overflight fell to a British pilot for the first time. The four RAF pilots had now been atttached to Det B for nearly a year. They took turns flying the SIGINT flights along

When Tom Crull crash-landed Det C's newly-acquired U-2C on a small airfield near Tokyo in September 1959, Japanese photographers were quickly on the scene. Despite the best efforts of project security officers, photographs were taken and soon published in Japanese aviation magazines (Aireview).

MISSION B8005 OVERFLIGHT REPORT

This is the summary by the Photo Interpretation Center (PIC) of the first U-2 mission over the Soviet Union by a British pilot, Sqn Ldr Robbie Robinson. Note the reference to his overflying 20 SAM sites!

Mission B 8005, flown 6 December 1959, coverage included the industrial and military development in the area around Uralsk, Kuybyshev,..Saratov and Stalingrad; and the special weapons storage area at Engels; the Chemical Warfar proving Ground near Volsk; and the Kapustin Yar Guided Missile Test Center with its various components.

The mission also covered 46 airfields of various categories, and 20 surface-to-air missile launching sites. The Volga River, ice-bound for the winter, was covered...and the Volga-Don Canal. With the exception of the Kapustin Yar area, there has been no coverage of this region since the end of World War II.

the border, as well as the continuing photo flights over the Middle East. Another two British pilots had been trained by the SAC wing at Laughlin AFB, but were not deployed to Turkey.

Det B had also made three deployments to the UK in December 1958, and May and October 1959. These deployments were given the oh-so-British codename High Tea, and were conducted as operational tests of Stan Beerli's Quickmove procedure. They also gave the RAF's top brass a chance to look over the aircraft. Each time, a C-130 and a U-2 were flown to RAF Watton, in East Anglia. "Genuine" U-2 weather reconnaissance missions around the UK and out to the Bay of Biscay were flown from Watton by the RAF pilots.[19]

However, Dick Bissell's original scheme, whereby the British would stage their "own" flights over the USSR, had not worked out in practice. Eisenhower had never really been persuaded that the U.S. would somehow be absolved if a U-2 was brought down over the USSR with a British pilot at the controls. So no separate chain of approval to London, bypassing the White House, had ever come into play.[20]

But when the President approved the new November mission, the mission plan was transmitted by secure means to the small office within the Air Ministry in London that managed the RAF's U-2 involvement. From there, Squadron Leader Colin Kunkler took the plan across Whitehall to 10 Downing Street, accompanied by the assistant Chief of the Air Staff (Operations), Air Vice Marshal John Grandy. "The Americans want us to fly here, and here, and here" Kunkler told the British Prime Minister, as he laid out the route map on a table. As sanguine and unruffled as ever, PM Harold Macmillan had no objection. Operation High Wire was on.[21]

Mission B8005 was launched from Peshawar on 6 December 1959 and flown by Squadron Leader Robbie Robinson, the leader of the British group within Det B. Again, the flight was not detected as it crossed into Soviet territory. The targets included a cloud-covered Tyuratam and Kapustin Yar, the IRBM test-launch base on the Volga River that had not been overflown by a U-2 since September 1957. In the intervening period, the big GE radar and the listening posts in Turkey had monitored continuing and frequent missile tests from there. Further up the Volga River, Robinson flew over the bomber production plant at Kuybyshev, and his route was also designed to cover as many railroads in these areas as possible, in the continuing search for an operational Soviet ICBM base.

At the end of the mission, Robinson was due to "coast-out" of denied territory over the Black Sea and recover directly into Det B's home base at Incirlik. But the Det was worried about the reduced range of the U-2C compared with the U-2A. In case the RAF pilot was low on fuel, and thus obliged to land at one of the airbases in northern Turkey, the Det launched a recovery crew in a C-130, complete with ferry pilot Jim Barnes. Robinson was supposed to contact Barnes in the C-130 on a pre-arranged frequency, but they never heard his call. In any case, the British pilot successfully returned to Incirlik.

No operational ICBM bases were found on the imagery from Robinson's flight, but the PIs did discover a line-up of Bison bombers at Engels airfield opposite Saratov, and many developments within the seven missile test launch complexes at Kapustin Yar. Since the USSR also trained its operational missile troops here, there was much to be learned from detailed study of this imagery, especially concerning the mobile medium-

After the British joined Det B in Turkey, three practice deployments were made to the UK. Seen here in front of the supporting C-130 transport at RAF Watton in East Anglia are (from left) Maj Don Scherer (Det B operations officer), Sqn Ldr Robbie Robinson (RAF U-2 detachment commander), Col William Shelton (Det B commander), three members of the C-130 crew, and Dr John Clifford (the RAF flight surgeon at Det B). (Paul Lashmar collection)

Operation Crowflight was reorganized in mid-1959, but the long, regularly-scheduled sampling flights continued. Officers and airmen assigned to the 4080th SRW's home-based sampling "detachment" at Laughlin AFB are shown here, complete with Crow mascot (via Tony Bevacqua).

The Saratov airframe plant was a target on the first British U-2 overflight made by Robbie Robinson on 6 December 1959 (CIA).

range SS-4 nuclear missile. It was not yet operational, but imagery of the trailers, erectors, warhead vans, and other equipment now being tested here would reveal the patterns to look for in future deployments. (Nearly three years later, the USSR would dispatch the SS-4 and the longer-range SS-5 to Cuba, and thus provoke the Missile Crisis of October 1962).

Slow Soviet Progress

On 15 December 1959 the huge SS-6 missile roared off the first launch pad to be completed at Angara (Plesetsk). This was indeed the first Soviet operational ICBM base, although no one in Western intelligence yet knew this for certain. The USSR had taken 30 long and hard months to make the base ready. The long, hard winters, followed by springtime thaws, slowed the pace of construction, especially in the swampy wastelands that had been chosen for the site. Angered at the costly delays, Premier Khrushchev nearly canceled the project in 1958 in favor of other sites. The construction plan for Plesetsk was reduced from 12 launch pads to only four. Two days after the successful launch, Khrushchev announced the formation of the Strategic Missile Forces, a new branch of the armed services.[22]

The first launch of an Atlas D—the U.S. equivalent to the SS-6—had taken place on 9 September 1959 from Vandenberg AFB, in California. Seven weeks after this SAC placed the first Atlas ICBM on alert there. The U.S. and the UK already had Thor and Jupiter IRBMs pointing at the USSR from Europe. But there was still no way of knowing whether the Soviets had deployed enough ICBMs to hold the U.S. at ransom, as the missile gap theorists feared. Also, had the Soviets reached the same decision as the U.S., to curtail production of the first-generation liquid-fueled ICBMs in favor of solid-fueled designs that could be placed in silos to reduce their vulnerability?

On 19 January 1960, the USSR demonstrated an extended range for the SS-6 when a test-launch overflew the usual impact area on Kamchatka and landed near Johnson Island, in the Pacific Ocean. That same month, the latest formal estimate of Soviet ICBM capabilities was finalized in Washington. NIE 11-8-59 admitted that the U.S. still had "no direct evidence of Soviet ICBM deployment concepts, or of the intended nature of operational launch sites." Were they rail-mobile units, hard or soft fixed installations, or some combination of these methods? The analysts simply

On the opposite bank of the Volga river to Saratov was Engels, and a Soviet air force heavy bomber base. Mission B8005 captured a long line-up of Bison bombers on the snow-covered airfield (CIA).

did not know. The NIE tentatively suggested a total of 35 Soviet ICBMs on launchers by mid-1960, and 140-200 by mid-1961.

In a long footnote to the top-secret NIE, the USAF strongly disagreed with this estimate. Influenced by the hawkish views of General Curt LeMay and his successor as SAC commander, General Tommy Power, USAF intelligence reckoned the Soviets were going all out to "force their will on the U.S. through the threat of destruction." Power made a public speech that suggested "the Soviets could virtually wipe out our entire nuclear strike capability within 30 minutes." Senator Symington alleged that "the intelligence books have been juggled so that the budget books can be balanced." He was the main mouthpiece for the missile gap theorists. At the end of January DCI Allen Dulles was obliged to counter their alarm with a public speech of his own.[23]

More Flights Urged

On 2 February 1960, the President's Board of Consultants on Foreign Intelligence Activities (PBCFIA) held another of its periodic meetings with Eisenhower in the White House. General Jimmy Doolittle and the others urged the President to use the U-2 over the USSR "to the maximum degree possible." In reply, Ike told them that this was one of the most soul-searching decisions to come before a President. He had opened a personal dialogue with Premier Khrushchev during their meetings at Camp David the previous September, and now a Summit Meeting of the big four powers (the U.S., UK, France, and USSR) was planned for mid-May. "If one of these aircraft were lost when we are engaged in apparently sincere deliberations, it could be put on display in Moscow and minimize the President's effectiveness," Eisenhower continued.[24]

It was a sentient observation. Nevertheless, by the time that he met the PBCFIA, the President had already approved another U-2 mission into the southern USSR, encouraged perhaps by the knowledge that the British would be sharing the political risk again, with an RAF pilot at the controls. Like the previous overflight, this would depart from Peshawar, Pakistan, and recover into Det B's home base at Incirlik, Turkey. Once again, the flight would search for missile sites along the railroads of the Urals and the Volga River valley. The codename for the operation was Knife Edge.

Det B deployed the fuel, launch crew, and mission pilot (Flight Lieutenant John MacArthur) to Peshawar in the usual manner. But when John Shinn, one of the Det's American pilots, tried to ferry the mission aircraft from Incirlik later that day, it malfunctioned enroute. It was Article 360, the aircraft that had belly-landed in Japan and since been repaired by Lockheed. Since arriving at Det B, 360 had acquired a bad reputation. Each of the hand-built U-2s had their own idiosyncrasies, but 360 was universally disliked by the pilots. For one thing, its autopilot never behaved properly.

There was a 24-hour delay while a substitute U-2C was prepared. Even then, it arrived behind schedule at Peshawar. There was a huge rush in the dark to get it refueled and prepared. Mission B8009 took off late, and there was no time to adjust the celestial precomputations. MacArthur crossed the border and headed northwest. The skies were crystal clear, but most of the ground below was covered in deep snow. Beyond the Aral Sea, the terrain below was virtually featureless, except for the Emba and Ural river valleys. At the flight's most northerly point, MacArthur flew over the Soviet Aircraft Factory No 22 at Kazan. This had been an objective on the previous British U-2 mission, but Robbie Robinson had decided to elimi-

nate that portion of the flight when his aircraft unexpectedly began contrailing.

This time, though, the U-2 flew straight over the snow-covered airfield and captured eight aircraft of a new design with highly swept wings and long pointed noses on film. It was a new supersonic medium bomber that was later given the reporting name Blinder. The CIA checked previous intelligence reports, and found that reliable observers had noted a new type of aircraft there in the summer of 1958. That must have been a prototype of the new bomber, the analysts concluded, and now they were looking at a development or pre-production batch. Kazan had previously produced the Tu-16 Badger, and it was correctly assumed that this was another Tupolev design. (It wasn't until July 1961 that the USSR finally "revealed" the Tu-22 in public, at the Moscow airshow).[25]

From Kazan, MacArthur turned south and flew down the Volga, covering more airfields and following more railroad lines. Crossing the Donetsk basin, his last major target was the city of Dnepropetrovsk. The SS-6 Sapwood missiles were built here, though the CIA did not yet know that for sure.[26] Moreover, this was the location where a new intermediate-range missile was built. It had been observed on a launchpad at Kapustin Yar on the previous U-2 overflight.

MacArthur turned south and eventually left Soviet airspace at Sevastopol, in the Crimea. Only at the very end of the flight did the Soviet radars establish tracking of the intruder. The commo section at Incirlik waited anxiously for his call. The flight had fallen even further behind schedule when MacArthur found himself off course when approaching one of his targets. He made a wide 360-degree turn to ensure that he was properly lined up. Eventually, the British pilot landed at Incirlik, and the film was rushed to the U.S. by courier plane, as usual. When it reached the Stueart Building, Art Lundahl's photo-interpreters scoured the extensive imagery of railroads for any sign of a Soviet ICBM deployment. They found none whatsoever.[27]

Corona and Oxcart Problems

Despite his misgivings, President Eisenhower reviewed DPD's plans for four more U-2 overflights in mid-February.[28] There was no technical alternative. Since the first, unsuccessful launch of the Discoverer/Corona reconnaissance satellite one year earlier, there had been no fewer than nine more failures. There had been problems with the Thor-Agena launch rocket; the ingenious but complicated panoramic camera; and the film capsule ejection and recovery system. Morale within the program was low, and the technical competence of the CIA (eg the Development Projects Division) to manage the project was called into question.[29]

Meanwhile, progress with the stealthy and high supersonic successor to the U-2 had been even slower. A joint DoD, USAF, and CIA selection panel chose Kelly Johnson's A-12 proposal over the rival entry from Convair, labeled Kingfish in August 1959. But the A-12 design needed further refinement, with the CIA's Land Panel and SEI's Frank Rodgers providing advice on the aircraft's radar cross section. The project was given the cryptonym Oxcart. DPD brought John Parangosky back from his job as Detachment B's executive officer to manage it. Finally, on 11 February 1960 the CIA issued a firm contract to the Skunk Works for 12 aircraft. But the first aircraft would not be ready to fly until August 1961. Moreover, Johnson noted in his diary that the Oxcart project was "12 times as hard as anything we have done before."

9

Square Deal and Grand Slam

The Ad-Hoc Requirements Committee (ARC), chaired by Jim Reber, now designated four areas of the northern USSR as the highest-priority targets for U-2 missions. They were the railway lines from Kotlas to Salekhard, Perm to Vologda, Vologda to Archangelsk, and Petrozavodsk to Pechenga. Almost anywhere along these 2,500 miles of rails, they thought that a rail spur leading to an operational ICBM site might be found. At Project HQ, though, the question of how to cover these northern targets had exercised the mission planners time after time. The biggest problem was choosing launch and recovery bases that were within range of the targets. The problem was exacerbated by the political constraints that were imposed on U-2 operations by those foreign countries whose bases were the best situated for takeoffs and landings.[1]

For political reasons, it was now impossible to launch overflight missions out of Norway or Turkey. The UK or West Germany could be persuaded, but their territory was too far from the main areas of interest inside the USSR. In any case, the depth of Soviet radar coverage along its European borders guaranteed that any flight from there would be detected at an early stage. Thanks to Ayub Khan, the military leader of Pakistan whom the CIA had assiduously cultivated, Peshawar was still available. And it seemed that the last three overflights—all launched from Peshawar—had not been detected on entry by Soviet early-warning radars. But there was no way that a U-2 could fly from there to the railways in the northern USSR and back again.[2]

Two different solutions to the problem were proposed by the mission planners of Project Chalice. They were codenamed Operations Time Step and Grand Slam. The former involved launching the U-2 out of the USAF base at Thule, way inside the Arctic Circle on Greenland's western coast. It would then fly across the Arctic Ocean and the Barents Sea, and cross into Soviet airspace over Novaya Zemlya Island. The nuclear test site there would be a bonus target, before the aircraft flew over the southern Kara Sea and crossed the Soviet mainland coast. Then it would turn southwest to begin the search of the railroads, passing over Kotlas before turning north and heading for Plesetsk. From there, the flight would continue to Severodvinsk, where the CIA's clandestine sources suggested that the shipyard was building nuclear submarines. From there, the flight would cross the White Sea, and would follow another railroad north to the Murmansk naval base. By now running short of fuel, the U-2 would then turn west and fly down the Norwegian coastline to a landing at Andoya or Bodo.[3]

Norway would not be explicitly informed that the arriving U-2 had just completed an overflight. There was another political risk attached to this flight. The launch base at Thule in Greenland was theoretically part of Danish territory. There were other disadvantages to Operation Time Step, not least the likelihood that the U-2 would wander off course during the long initial transit across the Arctic Ocean.

Jim Reber chaired the Ad-Hoc Requirements Committee (ARC), which selected the targets for U-2 overflights. By early 1960, ARC had designated four areas of the northern USSR as the highest priority for coverage, since operational ICBM bases would most likely be situated there (CIA).

Mission planners create the maps and boards that were given to U-2 pilots for navigation. The desired coordinates for operational missions were devised in Project HQ, then cabled to the Dets so that the maps could be made up (Lockheed C88-1447-77).

The second proposed overflight was equally ambitious, because it entailed flying all the way across the USSR from south to north. For this reason, no doubt, the mission was codenamed Operation Grand Slam. However, it had some advantages. Firstly, it could be launched from Peshawar with Pakistan's full approval. It could then fly over Tyuratam again, before heading north to that rich complex of targets in the Urals industrial heartland—Magnitogorsk, Chelyabinsk, Kyshtym, and Sverdlvosk. From there, the flight could follow railroad lines northwest to Perm, Kirov, and Kotlas. Then it would follow the same route as the proposed Operation Time Step, to a landing in northern Norway.

Range versus Altitude

Project HQ had been mulling a flight straight across the USSR for many months; Bissell had mentioned the idea to President Eisenhower in July 1959, during the discussions about Operation Touchdown. Now that the re-engined U-2C was available it was a more practical proposition, even though some range was sacrificed when maximum altitude was required. Operation Grand Slam would be a nine-hour flight covering about 3,300 nautical miles. By coincidence, this was exactly the range to zero fuel that Lockheed had calculated for the U-2C's maximum altitude profile. Clearly, this allowed no fuel margin at all, and was not an acceptable option for mission planning.

However, because the new J75 engine could be operated anywhere between minimum fuel flow and maximum power, various reduced power cruise profiles were possible with the U-2C. Each of these profiles would extend the range by improving the fuel consumption. In fact, the aircraft could theoretically fly for as long as 11 and a half hours and 4,600 nautical miles. But this maximum range profile required the pilot to enter a cruise-climb at only 57,000 feet. By so doing, the aircraft's fuel consumption in the second half of the flight would be a miserly 2.7 miles per gallon, but even by the end of it, the U-2 would be no higher than 68,000 feet. By now, the threat from Soviet air defenses was simply too great to risk so low a cruise.

The best compromise between altitude and range was to fly the first 900 nautical miles, then cruise-climb to 70,000 feet and maintain this altitude until starting the descent 75 nautical miles from the recovery base. By flying this "split profile," the range was increased to 3,800 nautical miles, and the endurance to nine hours 55 minutes. Therefore, this was the profile that Project HQ chose for the Grand Slam option.[4]

Meanwhile, though, two less ambitious mission plans were also drawn and briefed inside DPD on 16 February. They covered similar territory to the previous three overflights. Both would launch out of Peshawar. Operation Sun Spot would revisit Tyuratam and Kapustin Yar. Operation Square Deal would fly over the former, but not the latter, ranging instead further to

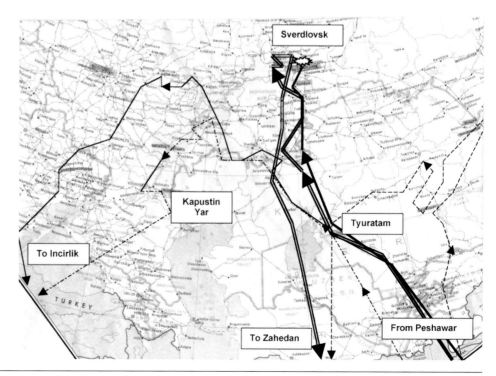

The routes of the last five overflights of the Soviet Union, all launched from Peshawar. Mission 4125 on 9 July 1959 (solid double line) flew to the Urals, then landed in Iran. Missions 8005 on 6 December 1959 (thin dot-dash line) and 8009 on 5 February 1960 (thin solid line) flew to the Volga region after Tyuratam, and landed at Incirlik. Mission 4155 on 9 April 1960 (thin dashed line) covered Saryshagan and Semipalatinsk before Tyuratam, then landed in Iran. Mission 4154 on 1 May 1960 (thick solid line) was shot down over Sverdlovsk.

the east, to get new and more complete coverage of the very large missile test range at Saryshagan and the Semipalatinsk nuclear test site. After Bill Burke and his ops chief Stan Beerli reviewed all four proposed mission plans they were sent to the White House.[5]

White House Meetings

How would the President react to the latest flight plans? Dick Bissell went to the White House again, accompanied by Dr. Herbert York, the Director of Defense Research and Engineering in the Pentagon. York was a nuclear scientist whom Eisenhower had come to know through the President's Scientific Advisory Council (PSAC), where York served alongside Land, Purcell, and the others. Like the PSAC chairman James Killian, York didn't believe in the missile gap. But he did not entirely trust the CIA's estimates either. Unless the intelligence on Soviet missiles could be improved, the U.S. would have to accelerate its strategic weapons programs. York supported the idea of more U-2 flights, especially over the northern USSR. The weight of advice was now irresistible. Eisenhower conceded that one of the four proposed U-2 missions could be flown, with a deadline of 30 March.[6]

Launching from Pakistan was the favorite option. The CIA still believed that missions staged from there had a good chance of evading the Soviet early-warning radar net. This was crucial since, if the PVO did not initially detect the flight, they might not be able to alert radar, missile, and interceptor forces further in the interior, in sufficient time to effect a shootdown. This was especially so, since the U-2 flightpaths often zig-zagged their way across denied territory, with frequent turns and only a few long, straight flight legs. This was done mainly so that multiple intelligence targets could all be overflown on a single flight, but the frequent turns also served to reduce the opposition's chances of tracking and intercepting the aircraft.

The trouble with Operation Grand Slam, in particular, was that by flying all the way across the USSR, the options to zig-zag the U-2's flight path were much reduced. This theoretically made the U-2 more vulnerable, if the Soviet air defenses had now perfected a means of interception.

The SAM Threat

Project HQ had already asked the USAF's Air Technical Intelligence Center (ATIC) for a new assessment of Soviet capabilities against the U-2. Dick Bissell's military deputy, Colonel Bill Burke, reported the findings to his boss on 14 March 1960. "The greatest threat to the U-2 is the Soviet SAM," Burke told Bissell. ATIC had concluded that "the SA-2 Guideline has a high probability of successful intercept at 70,000 feet, providing that detection is made in sufficient time to alert the site."[7]

Since its first appearance in late 1957, the PVO had been steadily deploying the SA-2 surface-to-air missile system to protect the major cities and military-industrial complexes of the USSR. It was capable of detecting and tracking a fighter-size target at about 110 miles, using a surveillance radar. Each S-75 regiment had one of these at the command post, and another at each missile battery[8] under its command. The target's range, altitude, and bearing was initially determined by the regiment, which then passed the data to the nearest individual battery, where another surveillance radar and the dedicated engagement radar would take over. The missiles themselves were improved through further testing at Saryshagan. Each battery consisted of six missile launchers, and it was normal practice to

salvo-fire three missiles at each target, in order to increase the probability-of-kill.[9]

But some Western analysts believed that the missile's control surfaces were not big enough to provide adequate guidance in the thin upper atmosphere inhabited by the U-2. That view was reflected in the latest National Intelligence Estimate on Soviet air defenses. This NIE was being finalized at the very time Bill Burke received the USAF technical assessment that DPD had commissioned. The NIE was approved for release just two weeks later, on 29 March 1960, and credited the SA-2 with less high-altitude capability than the USAF report to DPD. The NIE suggested that the "maximum effective altitude (of the SA-2) is about 60,000 feet, with *some* capability up to about 80,000 feet, especially if employed with a nuclear warhead."[10]

The NIE hedged its bets on whether such a warhead was yet available to the PVO (in fact it was not, and no nuclear warhead was ever planned for the S-75). But the NIE did state unambiguously that the SA-2 had been deployed rapidly and extensively "to defend major centers of population

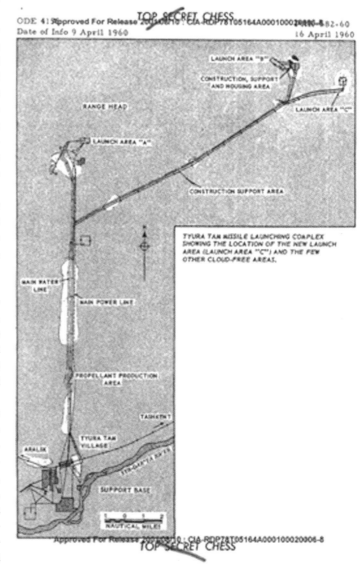

This is the map drawn by CIA photo-interpreters and missile analysts, which showed the new launch complex discovered by the last successful U-2 overflight of Tyuratam on 9 April 1960.

Colonel Bill Burke was the senior military officer assigned to the CIA U-2 project from 1958-60. He recommended the routes for the last overflights, taking into account such factors as whether the Soviet air defense system could detect and intercept them (Bill Burke).

and industry." The NIE listed locations within the USSR where SA-2 sites had been identified, including Baku, Kharkov, Kiev, Moscow, Odessa, Rostov, and Sverdlovsk.[11]

The big city in the heart of the Urals was on the planned flight path of Operation Grand Slam. The SA-2 missiles had been deployed at Sverdlovsk since at least July 1959, when Vice-President Nixon made a goodwill tour of the USSR. Nixon and his party visited Leningrad, Novosibirsk, and Sverdlovsk, as well as Moscow. Before they left Washington, they were briefed by Lundahl's experts in the PIC on potential intelligence targets.[12] As the Soviet airliner carrying the Americans approached Sverdlovsk from the southwest, a young State Department officer noticed an unusual pattern of revetted clearings grouped around a radar trailer and linked by service roads. Ray Garthoff leaned towards the window and surreptitiously photographed the site.[13]

In June 1959, intelligence officers assigned to the British Mission to Soviet Forces in Germany (BRIXMIS) learned that the new Soviet SAM had been deployed at Glau, just south of Berlin. They could not get close enough to photograph it from the ground, so they took to the air, flying the mission's Chipmunk, a two-seat lightplane that was based at RAF Gatow. They trespassed beyond the Berlin Air Safety Zone and flew towards the site, staying at treetop height to evade detection. Wielding his camera, the rear-seat passenger got excellent close-ups of the missile site, including the revetted launchers, the Spoon Rest surveillance radar, and the Fruit Set (Fan Song) missile guidance radar.[14]

BRIXMIS had obtained the best intelligence yet on the new Soviet SAM. Later in the year, ELINT intercepts of the radars at the Glau site were obtained. The missile analysts reviewed some earlier data: previously-unidentified ELINT intercepts; the 1957 U-2 imagery of the Lake Baikal test range; and the Guideline missile's first appearance in Red Square later that same year. All the intelligence pointed to a sustained deployment of the new SAM since 1957.[15]

The U-2 itself brought back more imagery of the SA-2 in December 1959, when Robbie Robinson flew over Kapustin Yar. There were Guideline missiles protecting the missile test complex, and more of them were found in another area, where PVO troops were being trained to fire them.[16]

In sum, therefore, Western analysts had made a slow start on assessing the new Soviet SAM, but they were now catching up with the nature and the extent of the threat posed by the SA-2. But the missile analysts apparently did *not* know one vital piece of information, which might have

caused them to take the SA-2 threat even more seriously. Grushin's S-75 system had *already* shot down a high-flying enemy spyplane!

The Chinese shootdown

However, the action had not taken place over Soviet territory. It was over mainland China instead. On 7 October 1959, Captain Wang Ying Chin of the Chinese Air Force (CAF) on Taiwan flew a Martin RB-57D reconnaissance aircraft deep into communist mainland China. As we have seen, the RB-57D was a poor relation to the U-2 in the spyplane business, but it could reach over 60,000 feet. When SAC decided to phase out the Martin design, two of the 4080th wing's machines were assigned to a joint USAF-CAF project to overfly the People's Republic.

Unknown to the U.S. or Taiwan, communist China had secretly received five SA-2 systems from the Soviet Union in late 1958. After a period of training, which evidently was not affected by the growing Sino-Soviet split, the missiles were declared fully operational in defense of Beijing during late September 1959. But no public announcement was made. Just over a week later, Captain Wang's flight took off from Taiwan. The Fan Song radar from one of the SA-2 batteries identified his aircraft from 70 miles as it flew towards the communist capital. Three missiles were fired at 43 miles range, and the RB-57D was shot down some 18 km south of the capital. Beijing announced that it had intercepted and ended the spyflight, but was careful not to specify the exact means. Wang was listed missing, and believed killed. Neither USAF, nor CAF intelligence was able to determine for certain what had happened. They presumed that fighters had intercepted the RB-57D.

In fact, this incident near Beijing was the world's first downing of an aircraft by a surface-to-air missile. Moreover, Wang had been flying at 63,000 feet when he was shot down.[17]

The SA-2 missile's maximum range against a high-flying B-52 was estimated to be 25 nautical miles. Mission planners in Project HQ had the option of routing the U-2 clear of the engagement zones around SA-2 sites— if they knew where the sites were actually situated. But if the sites were defending prime intelligence targets, such as Tyuratam, that would defeat the object of the flight. In reality, therefore, the U-2 mission planners hoped that the PVO's early warning system was still not good enough to provide adequate data to the missile sites. But if it *was* good enough, they hoped that the aircraft's high cruising altitude would provide a last but vital margin of defense.

The SA-2 surface-to-air missile system was first shown in a Moscow military parade in November 1957. By 1960, the system had been deployed around most major cities and miliary-industrial complexes in the USSR.

More Planning

In view of the now-crucial importance of avoiding detection by the Soviet early warning radars, the mission which was planned to approach the northern USSR across the Arctic Ocean (Operation Time Step) was now rated the least desirable. Burke told Bissell on 14 March that this flight stood a 90 percent chance of being detected on entry. If so, it could then be tracked accurately throughout the four hours that it would spend in denied territory. The flight would evoke "a strong PVO reaction (including) alerting of SAM sites and pre-positioning of missile-equipped fighters in the Murmansk area (point of exit), thus enhancing the possibility of successful intercept." Even if the Soviets did not manage an intercept, Burke continued, they would have enough radar data "to document a diplomatic protest." He recommended Operation Square Deal out of Pakistan for the next overflight, because there was "a reasonable chance of completing (it) without detection."[18]

This was an optimistic assessment, because the USSR had now virtually completed its early-warning net along the southern border. Indeed, the new NIE on Soviet air defenses issued two weeks later warned of the "impressive" extent of the cover provided by the increased numbers of Token and Bar Lock radars, with detection ranges of 190-220 nautical miles and from 70,000 feet (Token) to 220,000 feet (Bar Lock). "Gaps in (Sino-Soviet) peripheral early warning radar coverage now appear only in southwestern China," the NIE also noted.[19]

More SAC photo flights

The steady improvement in Soviet air defenses was bad news for SAC as well. In the event of war, would the nuclear-armed B-47 and B-52 bombers get through? One area of the USSR which was of particular interest to SAC's war planners was the Siberian coastline, since many of the U.S. bombers would fly over the North Pole or across the Bering Sea to attack their assigned targets in the Soviet interior. The Generals in Omaha decided to send their own U-2s to probe the Soviet defenses around Siberia. The 4080th wing was alerted to deploy to Alaska for a second series of peripheral reconnaissance missions codenamed Congo Maiden. Like the first series exactly one year earlier, these would be long, challenging, and potentially dangerous flights over icy and remote waters. But although the aircraft would come within range of Soviet air defenses, SAC did not have to get political authority from Washington for the flights. As long as the pilots managed to fly a few miles off the Soviet coast, they would be legal.[20]

The 4080th pilots practiced for the new deployment by flying 15 miles off the Texas coast. They put a notch in the hand control of the U-2's driftsight to help them maintain the correct distance, and honed their celestial navigation skills. Where they would soon be flying, there were few radio stations to help them navigate by ADF! Major Joe Jackson was selected to command the detachment. On 11 March 1960, three aircraft left Laughlin for Operating Location Five at Eielson AB, ready to fly the photo missions now that the dark northern winter was coming to an end. As in the previous Congo Maiden deployment in 1959, the aircraft were configured with the B-camera, plus System 1 for ELINT and System 3 for COMINT on any reaction from the Soviet air defenses.[21]

On 15 March, Majors "Snake" Bedford and John McElveen both flew successful photo missions from Eielson along the Soviet Bering Sea coastline. A few days later, Major Ed Dixon covered the Chukotsky Peninsula as far as Mys Schmidya and flew around Wrangel Island. Major Dick Leavitt was assigned the next flight, the very long haul across the ice-covered north coast to Tiksi and back. He had flown the mission profile a number of times from Laughlin, to ensure that the U-2A had sufficient range. After waiting some days for a good weather report from SAC HQ, Leavitt took off. He flew a great circle route over the Arctic and intercepted the Siberian coast near Ambarchik. The sun was still very low and straight ahead, making it difficult to identify the pressure ridges, and to distinguish the islands or the coastline in the eternal whiteness below. Eventually, he saw Tiksi off to the right and realized that he had accidentally strayed over the mainland! He quickly turned right, flew past the remote Arctic coastal city, and headed northeast. After rounding the New Siberian Islands, Leavitt headed back to Alaska.[22]

There was no doubt that these Arctic flights by the USAF's bluesuiters were detected by the opposition. The USSR had already sited early warning radars on some of their northern offshore islands, as well as the mainland coast, to defend against SAC's bombers. The PVO could not protect the entire coastline with fighters, but the SAC U-2 pilots saw contrails beneath them occasionally. On one of the flights, the System 3 COMINT recorder brought back an excited conversation between a GCI controller and the pilot of a Yak-28 fighter that was attempting to intercept the U-2. Through such SIGINT, plus imagery of the coastal radars and

The pilots of the last two U-2 overflights of the Soviet Union were Frank Powers (left) and Bob Ericson (right). Ericson was fortunate to return from his 9 April 1960 mission, after repeated Soviet attempts to shoot him down. On 1 May 1960, he strapped Powers into the cockpit for his ill-fated flight (via Jim Wood).

At Project HQ, these three USAF officers played key roles in planning the last few overflight missions. Colonel Stan Beerli (center) was posted to Washington from Det B in August 1959 as the operations chief. He brought with him Majors Ray Sterling (left) and Bill Seward (right). In late April, Beerli flew to Norway to head the recovery team for Operation Grand Slam. A wasted journey, as it transpired! (Stan Beerli).

airfields, however, SAC's intelligence experts could re-assess what chances the bombers would have of penetrating. The USSR did not protest Leavitt's unintentional overflight. SAC planned more U-2 missions in the Arctic.

Deadlines Approach

In Washington, meanwhile, the deadline of 30 March that the President had specified when approving one of the CIA's four proposed overflights was fast-approaching. There had been a delay in gaining permission from Pakistan to use Peshawar, and no deployment had yet been mounted. On 28 March, Eisenhower agreed to extend the deadline to 10 April, and even authorized a second overflight to be performed by 19 April.[23] On 1 April, the CIA station chief in Oslo sent a request to the Norwegian government, requesting permission to use Andoya airbase for two U-2 flights during April. Andoya was a remote island 140 miles further north even than Bodo, and hence that much closer to the Soviet border from which the U-2 would be coming, if either of the two options for a northern overflight were exercised. The CIA told Colonel Wilhelm Evang, Norwegian intelligence chief, that the purpose of the U-2 flights was SIGINT. The Norwegians were preoccupied with a large NATO naval exercise in Northern waters, and suggested a postponement until at least 19 April. They also recommended Bodo instead of Andoya, because it offered greater security.

The northern flight could therefore not now be launched before the President's latest deadline. But weather conditions were improving over the southern USSR. Project HQ decided to launch Operation Square Deal—the flight to Tyuratam, Saryshagan, and Semipalatinsk. Det B was alerted, and on 8 April the usual routine for an overflight deployment swung into action. It was Bob Ericson's turn "in the barrel," but he was accompanied aboard the C-130 on the trip to Pakistan by the next-in-line U-2 pilot, Frank Powers. He would be a backup, in case Ericson fell sick at the last minute. The overflights were now so few and each so critical that no chances were being taken. The backup pilot would attend the preflight briefing and go though the prebreathing process, just in case.

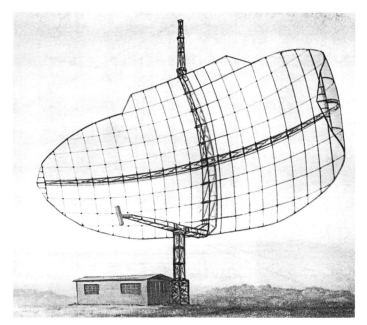

The extent of Soviet early warning radar coverage was a key constraint when the last overflights were planned. The CIA hoped that gaps still existed along the southern border, allowing the U-2 to penetrate without detection. But powerful new search radars, such as this Tall King, were now being deployed.

Operation Square Deal

The deployment to Peshawar went smoothly, and the U-2 was ferried in on schedule later that night. In the early morning sunlight of 9 April, Ericson took off on Mission 4155. He headed north to cross the Soviet border over the Pamir range of mountains. But only 150 miles into Soviet territory, and contrary to the mission planners' best hopes, the PVO detected the flight. The Turkestan Air Defense Corps had radars dotted all over the Pamir range. The U-2 was shielded from the first of these at Khorog by high ground. But stable tracking of the aircraft was accomplished by a second site at Kara-Kul, to the north. Col-Gen Yuri Votinsev had revitalized the poorly-organized Turkestan Corps since being given its command a year earlier. He was in the command post, and ordered four MiG-19 fighters to take off from Andizhan airbase. They were accurately vectored towards the target by ground controllers. But the MiGs could only reach 52,500 feet, and failed to make contact.[24]

System 6, the ELINT detector on the U-2, picked up the Soviet tracking. But there was no real-time display to the pilot of the data, which was all recorded on tape for subsequent analysis on the ground. Ericson pressed on towards his first major target, which was the missile test range at Saryshagan, on the shores of Lake Balkhash.

The next objective was 400 miles to the north: the strategic bomber base at Dolon and Semipalatinsk nuclear test site. Here, the flight plan called for Ericson to fly a search pattern so that maximum coverage of the huge test area was obtained. Unknown to the U-2 pilot, two of the latest Sukhoi Su-9 interceptors were on alert at the nearest PVO base, some distance away. The supersonic tailed-delta fighter had been rushed into service with the PVO before the formal state acceptance process was completed. The powerful Su-9 was equipped with four beam-riding K-5 air-air missiles. But it was short on range.

The Su-9 pilots calculated their fuel and realized that, if they were to reach the U-2's position, they would have to land afterwards at the airfield on the nuclear test site, rather than return to their own base. But that airfield was off limits to anyone without a special top-secret clearance. The correct procedures had to be followed! Frantic messages were passed up the PVO's chain of command from the regiment, to the air defense district, to the headquarters in Moscow. Here, the duty officer woke Marshall Biryuzov, who informed Defense Minister Marshall Malinovsky, who telephoned the Minister of Medium Machine Building who controlled the Semipalatinsk site. Meanwhile, the new Sukhoi jets stayed firmly on the ground. By the time the required clearance was issued, Ericson had completed his search pattern and was headed south out of range.[25]

The U-2 headed back towards Saryshagan to photograph another part of that large air defense site. This was quite a risk, since test and training firings of the SA-2 system were regularly conducted here. In fact, the latest version of the missile's engagement radar was currently being tested. It had a greater ability to hold target track at high altitude. Although no test flights were scheduled for this day, two missiles were ready on one of the launch pads. However, instead of warheads, they had miss-distance indicators fitted for the test flights. As the U-2 flew back over the test range, the test site commanders did contemplate firing the missiles, despite the lack of warheads, but decided against doing so because the chance of a successful interception was virtually nil.[26] Unaware of the commotion below, Ericson set course for Tyuratam and flew blithely on.

Interceptors

A pair of MiG-19s from the 356th Fighter Regiment at Sverdlovsk were assigned to the chase. This was one of the few PVO units whose MiGs were fitted with the new RP-5 search radar. The pilots were kept on alert, in their pressure suits. This regiment had shot down some of the Moby Dick balloons that the U.S. attempted to float across the northern USSR in mid-1958. But the two MiGs had to stop at Omsk for refueling, and they failed to arrive in time.

Another pair of Su-9 interceptors were also available in this area, but they belonged to a new unit that was converting from the MiG-19 and was not yet combat-ready. Missiles from the MiG-19 were hurriedly loaded onto one of the new jets while the other took off. Inexperienced GCI controllers were unable to vector it towards the target. The second Su-9 also took off. Its pilot, Captain Darashenko, did catch a glimpse of the U-2 from 57,000 feet, but he was inexperienced in zoom climb techniques, and couldn't gain the extra 10,000 feet required to bring the missiles to bear. The interceptors returned to base, but one of the MiG-19s crashed on approach to Sverdlovsk, killing the pilot, Vladimir Korchevsky.[27]

From Tyuratam, Ericson turned south and headed for the border. By now, he had been over Soviet territory for nearly six hours. Occasionally, he had seen the fighter contrails below as they vainly tried to intercept. During most of the overflight, Marshall Sergei Biryuzov had maintained a grim, silent vigil at the PVO's Moscow headquarters, while the catalogue of PVO errors unfolded. The U-2 was now back in Col-Gen Votinsev's area of command. As it neared Mary, in the southern Turkmen SSR, Votintsev sent a message to Biryuzov, suggesting that the intruder might start his descent once he had left Soviet airspace. In desperation, two MiG-19s were scrambled from Mary with orders to chase the U-2 over the border, and destroy it by ramming if necessary. Shadowing the Angel above them, the MiGs flew nearly 200 miles into Iran on Ericson's tail. But the U-2's destination was the Iranian airstrip at Zahedan, 500 miles south of the border, and it did not descend yet. The MiGs returned to Mary with their fuel nearly exhausted. The U-2 landed unscathed, and the Lockheed recovery crew soon had it turned round and flown back to Turkey.

Blame

Premier Khrushchev had to be informed, and he was furious at the PVO's failure. The chastened Biryuzov set up an enquiry. It was another exercise in self-denial. Anastas Mikoyan, co-leader of the MiG design bureau, told the enquiry that no aircraft in the world could fly for more than six hours at 20,000 metres. This was despite Andrei Tupolev's continuing assertion that it was indeed possible (the famous bomber designer had sketched out the design of such a plane for Khrushchev three years earlier). In typical Soviet style, most of the blame was placed on the local air defense commanders for their "criminal lack of concern," and the enquiry called for them to be severely punished for failing to bring down the flight. However, Biryuzov was also criticized by his political masters, for failing to anticipate where the spy flights were going, and concentrating his forces there. "Do not lose heart," Biryuzov told Votintsev, "in air defense, one who has been flogged is worth not two, but a dozen who have not. Remember this!"[28] The entire PVO was put on a heightened state of alert.

Ericson's flight was another intelligence bonanza for the CIA's photo-interpreters and analysts. It returned the first useful imagery of Tyuratam since Marty Knutson's mission nine months earlier, and revealed a third launch complex. This consisted of two pads, but they were being constructed in a different manner from those at the first two complexes, from where the SS-6 ICBM and its derivatives for the Sputnik and Luna space projects had been fired.[29] This was the first indication to U.S. intelligence that the USSR might be preparing to test a second-generation Soviet ICBM.

Indeed, engine tests for the new SS-7 ICBM had begun in late 1959, and the prototype missiles were moving off the assembly line at Dnepropetrovsk. Like the SS-6, it was still fueled by kerosene, but was smaller and with no strap-on boosters. Because it used nitric acid as the oxidiser instead of liquid oxygen, the SS-7 could be fueled and remain ready for launch for up to two days. The SS-6, on the other hand, had to be laboriously filled with kerosene, plus the liquid oxygen that acted as the oxidant. This was a 20-hour process, and if the missile was not fired almost immediately, the SS-6 then had to be de-fueled before the super-cold liquid oxygen reverted to its natural gaseous state.[30]

At Saryshagan, Mission 4155's B-camera captured for the first time two new radars that were soon associated with Soviet attempts to create an antiballistic missile system. It was a significant find; the CIA had not estimated that the Soviets were serious about ABM development until two months earlier, when Marshall Konev made a tantalizing reference to the possibility in a speech to Warsaw Pact Defense Ministers. The technical approach that the USSR was taking to ABM was completely unknown. The analysts made a further scrutiny of the buildings surrounding the two radars, which they codenamed Hen House and Hen Roost. They concluded that ABM research and development was a high priority in the USSR, and had probably been going on at Saryshagan since early 1959.[31]

Premier Khrushchev decided not to send a protest note about the 9 April flight. "Why give our enemies the satisfaction?" he told his son Sergei. According to the latter, the Soviet Premier did not want a confrontation. He thought that Eisenhower had not personally authorized the flight, and calculated that when he heard of it, the American President would certainly not approve another. The USSR had not protested the previous overflights in July and December 1959 and February 1960, either.[32]

Captain Roger Cooper of the 4080th SRW made a great save of a SAC U-2A when he landed on frozen lake in Canada after a flameout in March 1960.

This time, though, the CIA had unambiguous evidence that the latest flight had been detected at an early stage. It came from the read-out of System 6, and also possibly from U.S. ground stations along the Soviet border that intercepted the PVO's communications. In his postflight report, Ericson also detailed how he had seen fighter contrails beneath him. [33]

Unfortunately, Bissell and his subordinates in Project Chalice failed to draw the appropriate conclusion from Mission 4155—that time had finally caught up with the U-2. Moreover, while the impressive intelligence gains from the flight were becoming known in mid-April, Project HQ was already in possession of that most rare commodity—Presidential authority for a further overflight!

Temptation

The temptation to use that authority was just too great. It is not clear whether Eisenhower was informed of the flap in the Soviet air defenses that had been caused by the 9 April flight. However, on 19 April DCI Allen Dulles briefed Secretary of State Christian Herter on the three remaining proposed U-2 missions. [34]

Dulles explained that the delay requested by Norway, plus too much cloud over the target areas, had prevented the crucial, northern overflight mission before the President's new deadline of 19 April. He asked for more time. Eisenhower had imposed the deadline because the Paris summit of the Big Four powers was now looming. On 21 April High Cumming, the head of the State Department's Bureau of Intelligence and Research (INR), advised DPD chief Bill Burke that Secretary of State Herter had no objection to any of the three possible U-2 missions. But what did the White House think?

On Monday, 25 April, Goodpaster called Bissell to tell him that President Eisenhower had extended the deadline to 1 May, so that one of the three proposed missions could be executed. "No operation is to be carried out after May 1," Goodpaster emphasized. The summit was due to open on 16 May. [35]

Which operation was it to be? Project HQ had by now discounted Operation Time Step out of Greenland and across the Arctic Ocean because of the air defense threat. Operation Sun Spot out of Pakistan would be less risky, but would only cover the southern and central portions of the USSR. That left Operation Grand Slam out of Pakistan, the one that flew right across the USSR to cover the unknown territory in the north. But on Tuesday, 26 April, Burke warned Bissell that "penetration without detection from the (Pakistan) area may not be as easy in the future as heretofore." Nevertheless, the go-ahead was given. [36]

Burke and his staff knew how delicate the situation would be at the recovery base in Norway. Operations chief Colonel Stan Beerli was dispatched from Washington to take charge of operations there. Beerli had commanded the October 1958 deployment to Bodo, and so already knew the key Norwegians who would have to be involved. At the same time, Det B was alerted to dispatch the launch and recovery crews from Incirlik. On Wednesday morning, 27 April, a C-124 transport was loaded with 55-gallon drums containing the special U-2 fuel and took off for Pakistan. A C-130 Hercules followed carrying Det B commander Colonel William Shelton, the launch crew, the mission pilot, and the backup pilot. The pilots were respectively Frank Powers and Bob Ericson, two of the project's most experienced and well-regarded "drivers." Two more C-130s left Incirlik with the recovery crew, including Marty Knutson, the pilot who had been assigned to fly the U-2 back to Turkey as soon as the mission was over. These C-130s would stopover in Germany until instructed to fly on to Norway. [37]

After a seven-hour flight from Turkey, including a refueling stop in Bahrain, the C-130 carrying the launch crew arrived at Peshawar. The C-124 was already there. The 20-strong party unloaded all the equipment and fuel from the two transports into the hangar, which was some way from the main part of the base. Meanwhile, Stan Beerli arrived in Oslo and renewed his acquaintance with Colonel Wilhelm Evang, the Norwegian intelligence chief. He told Evang that the proposed "SIGINT operation" would take place within the next 24 hours. [38]

Glen Dunaway took off from Incirlik for Peshawar to ferry the U-2C that would fly the mission. It was Article 358, the best plane of the four that Det B possessed. Night fell as Dunaway flew across Iran and Afghanistan. He arrived at the Pakistani base around 2 am. Meanwhile, Powers had been trying to sleep on a camp bed in the hot and noisy hangar, without much success. He had just been woken and was dressing when the commo people got word relayed from Washington that the mission had been postponed 24 hours. There was too much cloud over the target areas.

Shelton told Ericson to fly the U-2 back to Turkey. This was a departure from the previous routine. On recent operational deployments, if a mission was postponed, the spyplane was kept hidden in the hangar. This time, though, it would be sent back to Turkey and flown out again the next night. Ericson took off before daybreak for the five-hour return flight to Incirlik. Glen Dunaway took Ericson's place as the mission backup pilot to Powers. [39]

Weather Factor

In Washington, at 1717 H Street, mission planners scanned the weather reports anxiously. Most of the information on which they based a go or no-go decision was provided by the Global Weather Center at SAC headquarters in Omaha and the USAF weather forecasting group at Andrews AFB. But some of it came from routine Soviet weather forecasts, which were broadcast to all! Operation Grand Slam had particularly demanding weather criteria, since the maximum success would only be achieved if the route all the way across the USSR was cloud-free. The probability of such conditions was not great! In fact, the whole of central and northern Russia was currently covered in cloud. There was even a late spring snowstorm predicted for the Urals. [40]

At Incirlik, John Shinn was assigned to ferry the U-2 back to Pakistan. Towards evening on Thursday, 28 April, he flew off to the east. When he landed in the small hours at Peshawar, the mission was still on. Powers and Dunaway had finished breakfast and were "on the hose" when the word came from Washington: another 24-hour postponement! Dunaway completed his prebreathing and flew the aircraft back to Turkey again. Shinn now took his place as the backup pilot to Powers.

The contingent at Peshawar whiled away the long, tedious hours playing cards and reading. They were not allowed to leave the hangar or its immediate surrounds. They cooked their own food from rations they had brought with them on the C-130. Some slept on camp beds. On Friday afternoon, just before Powers and Shinn were due to go to bed again, a further word was passed from the commo van. No flight on Saturday, either.

Accidents and Incidents

Frank Powers thus had plenty of time to reflect on the unusual nature of his postponed mission. He was probably more aware than most of his colleagues, about what could go wrong. Because he was the safety officer for Det B, Powers received all the accident reports concerning the U-2.

There had been no fatalities or airframe losses in the U-2 program since September 1958. But there had been plenty of incidents, some of them serious. Within the CIA's detachments, Marty Knutson had suffered a complete electrical failure during a border SIGINT flight at night. With his faceplate partly frosted over, Knutson had somehow recovered the aircraft to Incirlik. He flew nearly four hours using a flashlight to illuminate the sextant display, through which he identified the North Star, which indicated roughly which way he should fly! Robbie Robinson had stalled an aircraft and lost 20,000 feet trying to recover, after deploying the gust control without first raising the nose. Sammy Snyder was returning from an overflight of China in 1959 when the bearings froze up. He managed to dead-stick the aircraft into Taoyuan airfield, Taiwan.

The SAC U-2 wing also reported plenty of incidents. Captain Pat Halloran had seen the low-fuel warning light come on during a climbout: the fuel would not feed from the wing tanks due to a maintenance error. Halloran turned back, but the engine flamed out, and he was forced to make a silent return to the runway through heavy overcast. A trainee pilot suffered a broken fuel line during a long-distance navigation leg at night, forcing him to make a deadstick landing at a remote civilian airport in Colorado. A tailpipe adapter collapsed as one aircraft throttled up for take-off, causing an explosion.[41]

Most recently, two U-2s had made forced landings on a frozen lake and in a rice paddy. The frozen lake was in Saskatchewan, Canada, where Captain Roger Cooper of the 4080th wing had been forced down on 15 March 1960 after the aircraft's battery malfunctioned and then blew up. Although the cockpit filled with smoke and the engine quit, Cooper descended through a 10,000 feet overcast to make a textbook deadstick landing. He had been flying a sampling mission out of Minot AFB, ND. The aircraft was later flown off the lakebed.

The rice paddy was in Northern Thailand. CIA pilot Bill McMurry had ended up there on 5 April after running short of fuel during another overflight by Det C of southern China and Tibet. Det C had redeployed to Takhli, and two similar missions had been successfully accomplished seven days earlier by Tom Crull and Lyle Rudd. But unknown to McMurray, his tailwheel doors failed to close after takeoff. On such a long flight, the additional drag took a steady toll of the aircraft's fuel reserves. McMurray apparently didn't pay close enough attention to his green card, a standard takealong on each U-2 flight, on which the mission navigator predicted the fuel remaining against elapsed time. McMurry did not notice the extra fuel consumption until well into the flight. When the low-fuel warning light came on, he was obliged to penetrate the solid overcast and search for a clearing in the jungle below. He managed to crash-land the aircraft. Working up to their waists in water, a recovery crew dismantled it with the help of local villagers.

How long would it be before a technical failure took place during a Soviet overflight? There was no doubt that the CIA detachments enjoyed superior maintenance by the contract Lockheed employees, and every possible technical contingency was covered in preflight planning. But there was such a thing as the Law of Averages! And nine-hour missions really stretched the endurance of both man and machine.[42]

CONGO MAIDEN 1960

Ed Dixon was one of the three SAC U-2 pilots who flew the second series of peripheral photo missions along the Siberian coastlines of the USSR in spring 1960. It took guts, skill—and a little bit of luck—to fly these long, lonely missions. Dixon recalled:

We practiced off the coast of Texas first. We had a notch in the viewfinder to tell us when we were at 15 nautical miles out.

They had about 10 different missions preplanned. (Fellow U-2 pilot) Snake Bedford told me that SAC had looked at the chart in the U-2 handbook that showed you could fly 4,000 nm to fuel exhaustion. They had some missions planned even longer than 3670 nm, but (detachment commander) Buzz Curry called them off.

We could see some problems; it's 20 degrees warmer at altitude in Alaska than in the U.S., so we would be using a little more fuel. Now, when its warmer you need a little more throttle to hold your preplanned airspeed, so you start dropping further and further behind the "howgozit" line on your green card.

Another problem was everything—both sea and land—was snow-covered and frozen. There was no vegetation on the land, nor a big bluff where it met the ocean, to distinguish Soviet land from water.

We cut cards to see who would fly first. Bedford, McElveen, then me, and Leavitt was fourth. Bedford and McElveen flew two missions the first day and got good coverage to the south, probably covered 800-1,000 miles of Soviet coastline. The second day I went further north to Mys Schmidta, and then came back and covered the north side of Wrangel Island. There were a couple of weather days before Leavitt could fly. Leavitt eventually took off, but came back about two hours early. He had got disoriented (around Tiksi) and had to abort.

We stood down for about a month and did some sampling. In April, we resumed the special missions. Now it was my turn to fly to Tiksi. I coasted out at Wainwright and started doing my celestial. It was crystal clear, and you could see forever. After two hours I looked to the left and there was Mys Schmidta.

I was about halfway through my fourth celestial shot when, son-of-a-gun, I'm about to coast-in! I turned to the right and tried to figure out where I was. I was about to do another Leavitt.

I could feel the camera cycling behind me OK. My slave gyro started to precess a bit, and I couldn't use my preset headings on my card, so I flew strictly pilotage. I made my 90 degree turn left into Tiksi Bay. I looked down and saw a flash. A missile? What to do? I turned my autopilot off and hand-flew a 180 to the left, out of the bay. I was flying due North, but the slave gyro said a wierd heading. I was supposed to fly around the north of those islands, but I decided not to take a chance of overflying there, so I would go back out the way I came in.

I headed for Wainright. When I got down to 30K approaching Eielson, my low fuel light was on. So I put it in gust and spiralled on down to the runway. I landed and had 22 gallons left as they put the pogos in.

The U-2 being recovered from the Thai rice paddy after the forced landing on 5 April 1960 (CIA).

Incidents over Siberia

Ed Dixon knew this only too well. On 16 April, SAC had launched him on another of the long flights in the Congo Maiden series along the Soviet Siberian coast. He was repeating Dick Leavitt's flight of three weeks earlier, because SAC wanted better imagery. Above the ice-covered wilderness, Dixon also had difficulty in staying 15 miles offshore. Moreover, as he turned into Tiksi Bay he saw a flash on the ground, as if a missile had fired. Dixon hurriedly turned the autopilot off and hand-flew a 180-degree turn to quickly exit the area. He decided to return the way he had come, through the narrow Laptev Straight, rather than fly around the New Siberian Islands. Even so, he ran short of fuel on the way back to Eielson. The warmer temperatures above the northern tropopause meant that the U-2 went a little faster and used more fuel. Dixon squeaked into Eielson with 22 gallons remaining.[43]

Bill McMurry was the pilot from Det C who ran short of fuel when returning from an overflight of Tibet.

Around the same time, another Congo Maiden flight was passing the coastal town of Anadyr, on the Chukotsky, when an SA-2 was fired at it. The pilot was blissfully unaware at the time, and the attack was not discovered until the imagery from the flight was processed and analyzed. The missile's characteristic shape ("like a long telegraph pole") appeared to rise and then level off some way below the U-2. This seems to have been the first confirmed occasion on which the Soviet air defenses fired an SA-2 at a U-2.[44] The PVO had never fired one at any of the CIA's penetrating overflights. But the PVO was about to get another opportunity.

Still Waiting...

Powers and the launch crew whiled away Friday night and all day Saturday in Pakistan. They didn't have the big picture, of course, to understand why there was such a hold-up. Apart from Shelton and a few key people in Washington, no one did. The Agency's compartmented security procedures took care of that. The commo people had the best understanding, since they sent out all the messages with their top-secret routing slugs and codenamed addressees.

On Saturday morning, 30 April, in Project HQ, the duty team checked the weather reports yet again. It was still cloudy over the southern USSR, but the bad weather had cleared from the north. It was now or never! The White House had stipulated that no mission be flown *after* 1 May. Dick Bissell was away for the weekend. Duty staffers contacted DCI Dulles himself for final authority to launch the flight. After consulting with CIA Deputy Director Pierre Cabell, Dulles gave the go-ahead.[45]

At Incirlik Det B had a problem. Because the mission aircraft had been ferried to Pakistan and back twice it had run out of hours. The 200-hour phase maintenance check was now due, so a different aircraft was substituted. It was Article 360, hardly the pilots' favorite. On Saturday evening Bob Ericson flew it to Peshawar.

He arrived about three am. While the groundcrew readied the aircraft yet again, the pilots went into the makeshift briefing room. Shelton reviewed the mission again. Powers thought it looked a long way. He worried that in case of mechanical trouble, there were no short escape routes out of hostile airspace. Ericson did not believe the plane could go the distance, despite the plan to level-off at 70,000 feet. There was a long discussion between the pilots and Shelton about this. The Det B commander suggested that, if Powers was running short of fuel when he reached Kandalaksha on the Kola Peninsula, he could abandon the remaining targets, turn west, and head straight for Norway across Finland and Sweden. Powers and backup pilot Shinn started suiting-up. Ericson would act as "mobile," helping Powers strap in and taxi out.[46]

Colonel Shelton asked Powers if he wanted to take the poison pin. Since the first overflights in 1956, pilots had been offered a means of committing suicide in case of capture and torture. Until recently, the means had been a small cyanide capsule.[47] After Shelton joined Det B, he pointed out that there would be unforeseen consequences if the capsule should accidentally break or leak in the pocket of the pilot's coveralls. With the help of the Agency's clandestine specialists, Jim Cunningham came up with an alternative. The Administrative Director at Project HQ provided a silver dollar with a tiny hole, into which was placed a needle smeared with a deadly toxin. Powers decided to take the silver dollar along.

Refueling

The ground crew loaded the B-camera and the SIGINT systems. One of them mistakenly put Ericson's emergency seatpack back into the cockpit instead of Powers'. The error wasn't noticed. The refueling process began: a painstaking process of transferring the JP-TS from the 55-gallon drums. It was important that this specially-refined kerosene was allowed to settle, so that each tank could be topped up completely. Three months earlier, an aircraft had been hurriedly refueled for an overflight mission after arriving late at Peshawar. The fuel being transferred from the drums was warm, and some spilled out over the wings when the specified load could not be accomodated within the tanks. British pilot John MacArthur was seriously short of fuel by the end of the flight. Fuel temperature was an important variable. At Det C, they had even suggested that the U-2's fuel be deliberately pre-cooled, in order to increase the aircraft's range. Powers remembered that the fuel system was one of Article 360's idiosyncracies; every now and then, one of the wing tanks failed to feed.

The scheduled takeoff time was 6 am. With 40 minutes to go Powers climbed into the plane, which was still inside the hangar. Ericson helped him strap in and hook up to the radio, oxygen system, and so on. The PSD technician made his final check, and Ericson did the walkaround. As the scheduled takeoff time neared the plane was towed out to the runway. The sun had already been up an hour, and Ericson took off his shirt to use as a makeshift sunshield over the cockpit. Ericson was still worried about the length of the mission. He reviewed the flight maps that Powers was taking, and made sure that the Finnish airfield of Sodankyla was clearly marked. Shelton had briefed this small airstrip as an emergency landing site, in extremis, if Powers was really short of fuel by then.[48]

They were all ready to go. The launch crew packed up the maintenance and PSD trailers and loaded them into the C-130, ready for the re-

This was the communications station on its mobile trailer that Det B used to receive coded operational messages when deployed. At Peshawar on 1 May 1960, the "commo" technicians could not pick up the "go-code" on the pre-assigned frequency. It was eventually received "in the clear," a theoretical breach of security (via Jim Wood).

turn trip to Turkey. The final signal to execute the mission had still not been received. This "go-code" always came all the way from Project HQ in Washington, along the CIA's own secure lines in Morse Code. Usually, it was sent four hours before scheduled launch time. This time, though, six o'clock came and no signal. The commo van was still outside, set up some way from the plane. Inside, the operators hopped from one prearranged frequency to another but heard nothing, although there was a Morse signal on the guard frequency as they swept by it. Eventually, one of them tuned into guard, and realized that it was the transmission they had been seeking. The "go-code" had reached as far as Incirlik, but the Agency's radio operator there had been unable to transmit it onwards on the pre-allocated frequencies, because of the ionospheric interference which sometimes occurs at sunrise in springtime.[49]

Shelton had been standing anxiously behind the operators. As soon as the go-code was recognized, he rushed out of the cabin and ran towards the plane, signaling permission to depart. Powers had been in the hot cockpit for a whole hour, and his long underwear was soaked with perspiration. Ericson closed the canopy, and Powers started up. He pushed the throttle forward for takeoff and, as usual, the U-2 leapt into the air after little more than a thousand feet of runway. Mission 4154 was 26 minutes late taking off on its long trip across the Soviet Union.

10

May Day

Powers climbed skywards from Peshawar in the usual spectacular manner of a U-2. The roar of the J75 in the still morning air startled Pakistani airmen all over the base. Powers made the single-click signal to base on the UHF radio to indicate that he was proceeding. Ericson acknowledged with another click. From now on, there would be no radio contact until he was ready to descend into Bodo over nine hours later. After 30 minutes in the air, the U-2 approached the Soviet border in the same Pamir region as the previous U-2 mission three weeks earlier. Looking ahead, Powers could see a solid undercast stretching from the lee of the mountains on the Soviet side and away into the distance. He cursed the late takeoff. All the celestial computations would be out, and he would have to resort to dead reckoning as the primary navigation aid.

The PVO's early warning radars soon detected the intruder, just as they had the previous overflight. The mission was easily plotted heading north, and the command post at PVO headquarters in Moscow was alerted. In the Soviet capital, the time was one hour behind Pakistan. By 6 am Moscow time, Biryuzov and all the top PVO generals had been awakened and rushed to the command post, which was in the Defense Ministry, on the bank of the Moscow River. Over at the Kremlin, preparations for the MayDay parade were well-advanced. It was due to start at 10 am. The entire political and military hierarchy were supposed to be there, including Biryuzov and his men.[1]

Defense Minister Marshall Malinovsky woke Premier Khrushchev and told him about the new intruder. The Soviet leader ordered that it be destroyed regardless of cost. All air traffic across the entire Soviet Union was grounded so that radar operators could concentrate on the vital target. On the plotting screen in the PVO command post, Powers' plane was moved steadily north. Interceptors were scrambled from Tashkent in pairs. As usual, they could not climb high enough to get near.

Powers had been over denied territory for well over an hour before he saw a break in the clouds. He spotted the Aral Sea off to the left in the distance and realized he was about 30 miles off course. While he was making a correction, he noticed a contrail beneath him for the first time, moving at supersonic speed in the opposite direction. More interceptors had been launched from Tyuratam, which Powers was now approaching. But the pilots here did not even have pressure suits, and they didn't make contact. Powers continued to monitor them through the driftsight, disappointed that the flight had been detected so early, but relieved that the fighters remained so far below. By now, he had levelled off at 70,000 feet.

There were thunderclouds over the launch site. Powers switched on the B-camera as planned, but noted that the intelligence would be less than 100%. There were three S-75 batteries at the missile site, but one was unmanned because of the Mayday holiday, and the U-2 did not fly within the engagement zone of the other two. Now the solid undercast resumed. Powers tried a sextant shot as a cross-check on the compass. It seemed to be accurate.

Pressure in Moscow

The PVO commanders in Moscow now expected the U-2 to turn northeast or northwest, to cover the same objectives as the three previous intrusions, but it headed straight north. Biryuzov was fielding angry phone calls from Malinovsky, and even from the Kremlin. "It's a scandal," Khrushchev berated him. "The country gave all the necessary resources to the Troops of the Air Defense, yet you cannot destroy a subsonic plane!"[2]

This U-2 is in the same configuration as Article 360 when it was shot down on 1 May 1960. There were no exterior identifying markings on the aircraft, and it was painted in the dark sea blue color that appears black on monochrome photographs. The slipper tanks provided precious extra fuel for the nine-hour mission.

It was not that easy, though. The PVO was still learning how to operate the new missiles, and how to properly coordinate all the radars involved. It took nearly a day to dismantle, move, and set up an S-75 battery. Once established, it took up to five hours to bring the battery to combat readiness. Even then, the diesel generators could not be kept running indefinitely. If there was no other source of power, they had to be turned on. That caused another 13-minute delay. If the target aircraft was flying at high subsonic speed, it had to be detected 80 miles away in order to slew the missiles, acquire the target with the engagement radar, and fire. But the surveillance radar that began the search and acquisition sequence had a range of only 110 miles against a fighter-size target. There wasn't much scope for error or delay. Furthermore, each battery could only remain at the highest readiness state for 25 minutes.[3]

By 0800 local time the U-2 had passed Magnitogorsk, and was clearly heading for the central Urals. Here were many nuclear weapons-related facilities that the USSR had taken great trouble to isolate from prying eyes in so-called "secret cities." Unlike further south, the skies over the Urals were fine and clear—great weather for aerial reconnaissance!

Autopilot Problem

Powers saw the clouds thinning below him. He peered through the driftsight, trying without success to relate the emerging ground features to his maps. Fortunately, his flight plan showed a radio beacon in this area, so he tuned the ADF. The specified frequency was correct, though the callsign was wrong. The radio fix helped him re-establish the correct course. He was some way south of Chelyabinsk. But with one problem solved, another one emerged. The autopilot mach sensor malfunctioned, causing the nose to pitch-up. Powers retrimmed, flew manually for a while, then re-engaged the autopilot. The plane flew fine for a while, then pitched up again. Powers repeated the corrective action, with no better result. Faced with the prospect of flying manually for another six hours, he nearly turned back. After all, the U-2C Flight Handbook clearly stated that "proper autopilot operation is mandatory...to satisfactorily accomplish the mission."[4]

"An hour earlier, the decision to turn back would have been automatic," Powers later recalled. "But I was more than 1,300 miles inside Russia, and the visibility ahead looked excellent. I decided to go on and accomplish what I had set out to do."[5]

An SA-2 regiment was located at Chelyabinsk. It was brought to highest alert status. A surveillance radar acquired the U-2, but the "hand-off" (transfer) of target from radar to missile battery went wrong. One of the radar circuits at the battery fused, and the missile control officer searched his screen in vain.[6]

A Sukhoi-9 interceptor was thrown into the hunt. The pilot took off and flew south towards the approaching target. But he had been scrambled too early: running short of fuel, he was obliged to descend and land on the small airfield at Troitsk. This didn't even have a runway—it was the first time anyone had landed a Su-9 on grass!

Powers flew on, crossing unscathed over Chelyabinsk. He was relieved to see no interceptors beneath him. The next target was the USSR's first plutonium production complex, which was located amongst the lakes and forests to the east of Kyshtym. Powers was now flying over the scene of a serious nuclear accident three years earlier that the USSR had managed to hide from the world. High-level nuclear waste, which was kept in solution within an underwater concrete tank, had exploded and released 70-80 metric tons of radioactive debris into the atmosphere. Over 200 towns and villages with a combined population of 270,000 had to be evacuated. Despite the massive scale of this disaster, only the vaguest reports had yet reached Western intelligence (and it would be another 29 years before the full story emerged from behind the Iron Curtain).[7]

More Interceptors Launch

Powers turned onto a northeasterly heading which would take him towards Sverdlovsk.

The PVO had now repositioned two MiG-19s belonging to the 356th Regiment from Perm to Koltsovo airbase, on the military side of Sverdlovsk airport. They were being hurriedly refueled. The same regiment had participated in the chase for Mission 4155 three weeks earlier. Another two Sukhoi Su-9s were also on the ramp. They were on a delivery flight from the factory in Novosibirsk to Belorussia, and had only stopped at Koltsovo to refuel. But the Su-9s had been held up there over the MayDay holiday by the same poor weather that had caused Mission 4154 to be postponed three days running.

The pilot of the second Su-9, Captain Igor Mentyukov, had no pressure suit, and the plane was unarmed. But Gen Yuri Vovk, who commanded the fighter-interceptors in the Sverdlovsk district, knew that the Su-9 had a

The Sukhoi Su-9 was the PVO's best chance of intercepting the U-2 in the air. Unknown to Western intelligence, it had been rushed into service by spring 1960. It could reach 65,000 feet. But the aircraft sent to challenge Powers had no missiles, and was ordered to ram the target (via Yefim Gordon).

better chance of reaching the high-flying target than the MiGs. He ordered Mentyukov to takeoff. As the Su-9 climbed away, Vovk radioed to Mentyukov:

"There is a real target at high altitude. The mission is to destroy the target, to ram it...Dragon has ordered this."

Dragon was the personal codename of Marshall Yevgeny Savitsky, the commander of all PVO fighter units, Vovk reminded Mentyukov.

Without a pressure suit to protect him if the cockpit depressurized, Mentyukov was facing almost certain death if he were to fulfill the mission. Under the usual tight control from the ground, Mentyukov was directed to turn towards the target. He jettisoned his drop tanks and accelerated to Mach 1.9. As he climbed through 65,000 feet, the ground controllers told him that the target was only 25 kilometers away. They could see both the interceptor and the intruder on their radar screens. But in the black sky all around him the pilot could see nothing. Mentyukov switched on his radar, but the screen showed only interference. This was strange—it had worked just fine when he tested it just after takeoff.[8]

The supersonic Su-9 was closing fast on the subsonic U-2, and the controller ordered him to switch off the afterburner. Mentyukov protested that this would cost him altitude, but the controller repeated the instruc-

tion. The pilot complied, and the Su-9 began descending as it passed the still-unseen U-2. The ground controller now told Mentyukov he had overshot. After some mutual recrimination between pilot and controller, Mentyukov reported that he was running short on fuel. The controller told him to return and land, and the two MiG-19s were scrambled instead.[9]

The Missiles Engage

Meanwhile, Powers had reached a point some 35 miles southeast of Sverdlovsk. At the PVO district headquarters, the command post that controlled the missile batteries was on a separate floor to Gen Vovk's command post, which directed the fighter interceptors. And the overall district commander was away on a training course. It was a recipe for confusion.

The missile command post identified the nearest missile battery to the approaching plane and passed its range, altitude, and bearing to the site, with orders to fire. The commander of this battery was also away, and the task fell to his deputy, Major Mikhail Voronov. His three radar operators had to acquire the target by means of the two narrow fan-shaped beams generated by the *Fan Song*. It was a difficult task, since the U-2 was passing close to the edge of the battery's engagement area. Eventually, the operators managed to switch the radar into automatic tracking and missile guidance mode, and a firing solution was obtained. Voronov checked his own screen and ordered the launch, a salvo-fire of three missiles. The launch control officer hesitated, and Voronov yelled at him to fire. The solid fuel booster at the rear of one V-75 missile ignited, and it roared away. Another two missiles should have followed seconds later, but they did not; the target was fast receding, and the fire control system calculated that it had now passed beyond range.[10]

But the first missile was streaking towards the U-2, some 14 miles distant. The command guidance link from Voronov's battery to the missile was properly established, and the missile accelerated past Mach 2. It would take only a minute to reach the target, even though the U-2 was at 70,000 feet. The fire control computer issued the appropriate changes of course as the missile closed on the target from behind. After flying for some 12.5 miles the second-stage would be exhausted, and the missile would then continue on a ballistic trajectory.

Powers had no idea he was under attack. As the missile neared, he made a 90-degree left turn as shown on his flightplan, in order to line up on the next intelligence objectives on the southwestern fringes of Sverdlovsk. He was making routine notes of the time, altitude, speed, and EGT when "there was a dull thump, the aircraft jerked forward, and a tremendous orange flash lit the cockpit and sky," he recalled. It was 0853 local time, and his long ambitious flight had been cut short after only three and a half hours.[11]

Shoot-Down

The missile had exploded some way behind (and probably below) the U-2. The V-75 missile's warhead was designed to explode upon command guidance, or automatically when it reached close proximity to the target. A direct hit was not required, because the 180-kilogram fragmentation warhead broke up into 3,600 shotgun-type pellets, which were projected forward in an expanding cone.[12]

The pellets hit the tail and rear fuselage of the U-2. In the cockpit, Powers was shielded from their forward path by the engine and wings. Maybe the left turn that he had just made also helped the pilot escape the full force of the blast. Powers instinctively grasped the throttle with his left

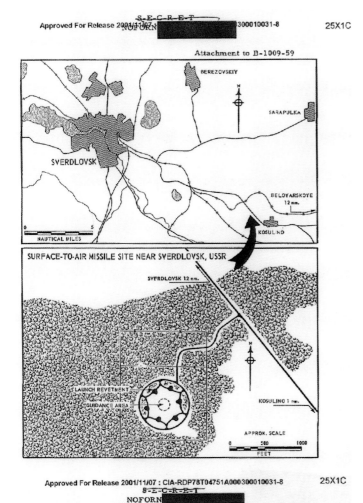

Attachment to B-1009-59

BEREZOVSKIY

SARAPULKA

SVERDLOVSK

BELOYARSKOYE
12 nm.

KOSULINO

NAUTICAL MILES

SURFACE-TO-AIR MISSILE SITE NEAR SVERDLOVSK, USSR

SVERDLOVSK 12 nm.

LAUNCH REVETMENT

GUIDANCE AREA

KOSULINO 1 nm.

APPROX. SCALE

FEET

Photo-interpreters at the PIC in Washington had already identified the SA-2 missile site outside Sverdlovsk that shot down Powers. This map was drawn in late 1959.

hand, and keeping his right hand on the big control yoke, corrected a slight drop in the right wing. But then the nose dropped, and no amount of pulling back on the yoke could bring it back up. Then a violent shaking erupted, flinging the pilot all over the cockpit. He later reckoned the wings had come off. "What was left of the plane started spinning, only upside down," Powers recalled. Experiencing up to 4g, and with his pressure suit now inflated, the pilot had extreme difficulty trying to make his escape. He was being forced forward and up, and could not activate the ejection system for fear that his legs would be chopped off by the canopy rail when the rocket fired and the seat rose up its track.

As the spinning fuselage descended through 34,000 feet, Powers realized that he had an alternative means of escape—to bail out. He pulled the canopy release handle, and the canopy sailed away. He tried to reach the destruct switches on the right canopy rail, then changed his mind, thinking that he ought to ensure that he could escape before he operated them. So he pulled the "green apple" handle, which activated his emergency oxygen supply, and released his seat belt. Immediately, the centrifugal force threw him halfway out of the aircraft, but he was restrained by the oxygen hoses, which he had forgotten to disconnect. His faceplate had now frozen over. He kicked and squirmed blindly, and suddenly he was free.[13]

On the ground, Major Voronov's crew saw the target dissolve into interference on their radar screens. They were not sure whether this represented a successful kill, or whether the intruder had deployed electronic countermeasures against their radar, such as chaff. Voronov reported his uncertainty up the chain of command. The regiment commander, Colonel Pevnyi, ordered the adjacent S-75 battery at Beryozovsk, into whose zone of engagement Powers had now flown, to fire at the target. At this battery, Major Nikolai Sheludko and his crew successfully salvo-fired three missiles. They climbed towards what was now a descending mass of debris, comprising the U-2's fuselage, wings, and tail (all now separated), and the fragments of the single missile from Voronov's battery. Two of Sheludko's missiles either detonated close to the debris, or flew through it and detonated some way further on, as they were automatically programmed to do when no target had been intercepted. (the third had flown off in completely the wrong direction).[14]

By now Powers had made his escape from the spinning, falling cockpit of the U-2. Once again, he was incredibly lucky. Somehow, he was not hit by the two newly-fired missiles headed his way, or by the many pieces of aircraft and missile debris that were now falling from the sky.

PVO Confusion

That debris was now creating an even bigger bloom on the radar screens of the PVO's batteries and command post below. From a third S-75 battery to the north of the city, Major A. Shugayev reported that his crew was tracking targets that appeared to include the enemy aircraft, now descended to 36,000 feet. It was not responding to their IFF ("identification friend or foe") interrogation. There was still no outcome reported from Voronov's battery, or from Sheludko's. Pevnyi, the commander of the missile regiment, suspected that the targets that Shugayev had identified were the PVO's own interceptor fighters.

But the district command in Sverdlovsk didn't even realize that the fighter command post in the same building had some MiGs airborne. Some minutes passed, and still the target was being tracked at 36,000 feet. Pevnyi was ordered to engage the newly-reported target by the most senior PVO man present, deputy district commander Major General Solodovnikov. So Shugayev was cleared to fire, and another three missiles streaked skywards. A short time later, back at the first battery, Voronov finally realized that he had destroyed the intruder with the very first missile. He belatedly reported a confirmed kill.[15]

Major Mikhail Voronov was in charge of the SA-2 battery that shot down the U-2. But his failure to report the successful action in timely fashion led to confusion among PVO commanders, and the order to fire more missiles.

In the confusion surrounding the shootdown, two MiG-19 fighters were misidentified by the Soviet air defense system, and attacked by another SA-2 battery.

So what target had Shugayev's battery just fired at? Captain Boris Ayvazyan was leading the flight of two MiG-19s that had been scrambled from Koltsovo 10 minutes before Powers was shot down. They were directed to fly to the north of the original missile engagement zone, towards Perm. The ground controller told Ayvazyan that the target was ahead of him by 10 kilometers, then only five. The pilot looked around for his wingman and found him some way behind, struggling to keep up. At the same moment, Ayvazyan saw an explosion above and to his right, and turned towards it. Was this his target? The flight leader wasn't sure (in fact, it was probably the first missile from Voronov's battery exploding and downing the U-2). Shortly after, Ayvazyan saw another explosion off to his right (probably one of Sheludko's missiles).

A third MiG-19 joined the pair. It was flown by the 356th Regiment commander Gennady Gustov, who had scrambled from their home base at Perm. He was having difficulty communicating with the ground controller, so Ayvazyan relayed his request for instructions. The answer came back: Gustov to return to Perm, Ayvazyan's pair to land back at Koltsovo and refuel.

Ayvazyan set course for the airfield and decided on a straight-in approach. His wingman was still some distance behind. Ayvazyan saw the runway ahead as he began to descend from 10 kilometers (33,000 feet). Suddenly there was an urgent warning from the controller: "Lose height quickly!" Someone on the ground had realized that fighters and SAMs were now in the same firing zone, although they didn't explicitly warn Ayvazyan to this effect. Nevertheless, the flight leader reacted intuitively by putting his aircraft into a vertical dive, pulling out only 300 meters (1,000 feet) from the ground. His wingman Safronov was instructed to do the same thing, but no more was heard from him.

Ayvazyan did a circuit of the airfield, hoping that his wingman would rejoin. But Senior Lt Sergei Safronov had been hit by one of the missiles fired from Sheludko's battery. He ejected from his stricken aircraft, and the parachute deployed, but the unfortunate pilot was found dead on the ground. The wreckage of the MiG fell into a public park near a village to the west of Sverdlovsk.[16]

According to the most detailed published account of the shootdown, at least one more missile was fired, from a fourth battery. This one was successfully evaded by Igor Mentyukov, the Su-9 pilot who had been ordered to ram Powers' plane, as he descended to land at Koltsovo.[17] It was nearly 40 minutes after the shootdown before the PVO's Sverdlovsk command post finally realized that it had shot down the intruder, and stopped trying to track it![18]

Senior Lt Sergei Safronov was killed when he was unable to evade the SA-2 fired at his MiG-19 over Sverdlovsk.

President Khrushchev was reviewing the May Day parade in Moscow's Red Square when the PVO finally confirmed to him that they had shot down the U-2.

Powers Captured

Powers saw nothing of this. Almost immediately after escaping from the aircraft, his parachute opened automatically. The American realized therefore he was already below 15,000 feet, where the barostat operated. He could not tell for sure, though, since his faceplate was still frosted over. He undid the clasp and removed it. He floated slowly down, just missed some power lines, and landed in a ploughed field near a village. Two farm workers helped him to his feet and removed the parachute. More people arrived. There was no chance of escape.

Confirmation that the spyplane was down was belatedly passed to Marshall Biryuzov in Moscow. He hurried to tell the Soviet leadership, which was already watching the Mayday parade. Western observers noticed a distraction as Khrushchev and others left the Kremlin reviewing stand temporarily to hear Biryuzov's whispered report. A delegation of senior officers from the party, the KGB, the GRU, and the PVO was quickly dispatched to Sverdlovsk. They left Moscow's Vnukovo airport at midday in a Tu-104 airliner—the first aircraft allowed to take off since the nationwide grounding order had been issued. By the time the airliner arrived at Sverdlovsk, Powers had already undergone his first interrogation, at the hands of the local KGB. It was decided to bring him secretly to Moscow. By evening, he was inside the Lubyanka Prison at KGB headquarters in the capital. The Soviet leadership was uncertain whether to publicize the shootdown.[19]

At Bodo airfield, Norway, the recovery crew waited in vain. They had already spent three nights waiting at Rhein-Main airbase, Frankfurt, for clearance from Washington to proceed to Norway. During the fourth night, the clearance had finally come. The two C-130s departed for Bodo early on Sunday morning, 1 May. One of them flew via Oslo to pick up Stan Beerli. Arriving at Bodo, Beerli met the most senior Norwegian officer there, Maj Gen Tufte Johnson. He arranged for the recovery team to set up in the same remote hangar they had used for the long deployment to Bodo in fall 1958.

Powers was due to arrive around midday local time. With an hour to go, Beerli told ferry pilot Marty Knutson to start pre-breathing. That way, the U-2 could be turned around and on its way back to Turkey as fast as possible. Minimum exposure! But the recovery crew listened in vain for the radio callsign "Puppy 68," which Powers was supposed to use as he neared the airfield. They waited five hours before giving up all hope and flying back to Oslo in the C-130. Using the CIA's secure line from the U.S. embassy, Beerli sent word to Washington that the plane was overdue.

At Project HQ they already suspected as much. As usual, the National Security Agency (NSA) had been listening to the PVO's air defense communications. In order to span the huge distances of the Soviet interior, and link the network with Moscow, the PVO was still using high-frequency (HF) radio. These HF signals could be intercepted by the NSA's listening stations ranged all along the Soviet southern border from Karamursel, near Istanbul, to Peshawar itself. Within these top-secret facilities, linguists who were fluent in Russian replayed the tapes, trying to follow and make sense of the major alert that had been called in the Soviet air defense system. Forty minutes after Powers was shot down they intercepted the PVO report from Sverdlovsk which told Moscow headquarters that radar tracking of the unidentified target had been discontinued. Three hours later, in the small hours of Sunday morning in Washington, that news reached the CIA.[20]

Cover Story

Carmine Vito, the former Det A pilot who was operations duty officer in DPD that Sunday, started working the phones. He rang Bob King. King notified Colonel Goodpaster and tried to reach Bissell, who was out of town for the weekend. High-level officials at the other government agencies who were cleared into the U-2 program had to be told: the State Department, the Pentagon, and NASA. Goodpaster called the President at Camp David and told him that the plane was missing. Bissell flew back to Washington and went straight to Project HQ on H Street, where he was met by a grim-faced Bill Burke. Hugh Cumming, head of the Bureau of Intelligence and Research and DPD's main contact at the State Department, was also there. They rehearsed the long-established cover story about a NASA weather reconnaissance mission having gone off course. Cumming requested that they delete all reference to the flight having started from Pakistan. The revised cover story had the plane straying off course—possibly—from a mission that was supposed to be conducted entirely within Turkish airspace.[21]

The next morning, Monday, 2 May, Goodpaster took the cover story to Eisenhower for his approval. But the cover story—especially now that it had been amended—depended on the pilot being dead so that the fiction could not be contradicted. Allen Dulles and Dick Bissell had personally assured the President that a U-2 pilot would not survive a shootdown, so the cover story was approved by the White House.[22]

In the countryside outside Sverdlovsk, the wreckage of the U-2 was slowly collected over the next few days. It was scattered over nine square miles, but the larger pieces were clearly recognizable as an aircraft, indeed as a spyplane. Film from both the tracker and the B-camera film was sal-

vaged and sent for processing. Some of the SIGINT systems were virtually intact. A crane was summoned to recover the engine, which had fallen into a marsh. Some drunken Mayday celebrants from one village had taken their axes to one wing that fell near them. The special fuel spilled out, thus making it more difficult for Soviet military experts to analyze it.[23]

PVO Shortcomings Suppressed

The PVO set up a commission to investigate the shootdown. But Marshall Biryuzov realized that this was no time to advertise the PVO's shortcomings. These included a severe shortage of trained manpower and missiles, and the lack of coordination—even jealousy—between the PVO's fighter interceptor troops, led by General Savitsky, and the missile troops, led by General Kuleshov. This went all the way down the command, and was a major factor in the confusion over Sverdlovsk on 1 May. The commission decided that in the hurry to dispatch the Su-9 and two MiG-19 interceptors, no one remembered to change their transponder codes. These were still set to the mode for April, but it was now the first of May. As a result, Shugayev's missile battery did not receive the proper IFF response when it interrogated the fighters, the commission concluded. That helped Shugayev conclude that he was tracking the intruder at 36,000 feet, rather than the PVO's own interceptors.[24]

It seems that Biryuzov managed to ensure that Premier Khrushchev never heard about the multiple missile firings, or the shooting down of the MiG. But word soon spread within military circles in Moscow that the official version of events was incomplete. Officially, Powers had been shot down by a single missile above 20,000 km (65,000 feet). That was true, of course, but it wasn't the whole story. According to some rumors, the PVO fired as many as 14 missiles over Sverdlovsk that day. The full story related in these pages emerged slowly from 1990, as various participants recounted their part in the action to bring down the U-2.[25]

On Tuesday, 3 May, NASA released the CIA's cover story. It was a detailed fiction, describing how a NASA U-2 research plane "apparently went down" after the pilot "reported he was experiencing oxygen difficulties." A search was being conducted in the area of Lake Van, eastern Turkey. To maintain the fiction, the C-54 transport used by Det B took off from Incirlik, with orders to search the area in question.

Unfortunately, no one had informed Powers before he took off that oxygen difficulties formed part of the cover story. In any case, the U-2 pilot had soon abandoned the fiction of a weather reconnaissance flight which had gone astray. The weight of evidence to the contrary was overwhelming. While he was still in Sverdlovsk, his interrogators had recov-

To satisfy the curiosity of American media in the wake of the Powers' shootdown, this U-2 (Article 378) was towed from North Base to the main area of Edwards AFB for their inspection. First, though, a NASA tail band and fictitious serial number were added—the cover story that the U-2 was engaged on weather research flights had not yet been discredited.

HOW THE "NASA" U-2 WENT PUBLIC

It so happened that, in the same week that Frank Powers was shot down, the Aviation and Space Writers Association was meeting in Los Angeles. NASA had arranged a bus to take the journalists out to their hangar at Edwards, for a first-hand look at the Bell X-15 rocket plane, which was then some 10 months into its record-breaking flight test program. The tour was scheduled for Friday, 6 May, just 24 hours after NASA issued the cover story prepared by the CIA, about one of "their" U-2s being missing on a weather recon flight from Incirlik. Someone evidently hit upon the bright idea of backing up the cover story by showing the aviation writers a suitably-marked U-2 during their visit to the NASA facility.

Early on the morning of the planned tour an unmarked, all-black Agency U-2A model was towed the three miles along the lakebed from North Base to the NASA hangar at the main Edwards base. Here, a bemused NASA mechanic was told to find a stepladder, a paintbrush, and a NASA decal in double-quick time, and to paint on the NASA identity and a tail number. He was given the Air Force serial number of a target drone that had been shot down in operations at Edwards some days earlier, and so it was that when the U-2 was revealed to the pressmen a short while later, it carried a neat yellow tailband containing the letters "NASA" and the numbers 55741 below. What with all the rush, the mechanic's main concern was that the press or someone else would climb up the tail and smudge the paint, which wasn't yet dry! As for the visitors, they climbed off the bus and rushed over to the unfamiliar black U-2, almost completely ignoring the X-15, which was standing some 20 yards away with a deputation of famous test pilots surrounding it. There was no one around the U-2 to answer questions, but the press got its pictures of a "NASA" U-2, which were duly published alongside the cover story.

The whole effort was in vain, of course, since within a week President Eisenhower had gone on record repudiating the cover story and taking full responsibility for the U-2 overflight operation.

– C.P.

'Leaves Little Hope for Summit . . .'

SOVIETS SHOT DOWN U. S. PLANE, SAYS K.

(Page 3)

Inside The News:

It was headline news all round the world when Gary Powers was shot down, and Premier Khrushchev decided to exploit the incident for maximum propaganda value.

ered incriminating evidence from the wreckage and shown it to him: his flight maps over the USSR; his survival pack, which included 7,500 Russian roubles; even the tracker camera with its exposed film. Powers decided that he had little option but to tell the truth to his captors' questions, with some limitations. But he would not volunteer any information they did not ask for.[26]

Soviet Strategy

Throughout Wednesday in Moscow, the Central Committee of the Communist Party debated how to handle the incident. Khrushchev proposed that he reveal only that the plane had been shot down, *not* where, *nor* that the pilot had been captured. He planned to make political capital out of the incident, by forcing the U.S. to elaborate on the cover story, before blowing it apart. It was news management on a grand scale, and it worked. At a scheduled meeting of the Supreme Soviet the next day, Khrushchev revealed that an American spyplane had been shot down and asked rhetorically who had sent it. In Washington, the press demanded a response. In a second statement, NASA added some detail to the cover story. The State Department told reporters that the pilot might have lost consciousness over Turkey, allowing the plane to "continue on automatic pilot for a considerable distance and accidentally violate Soviet airspace."

At a Moscow reception on Thursday evening attended by the U.S. Ambassador, a Soviet diplomat let slip that his government was "still questioning the pilot" who had been shot down. This was the first indication that Powers was still alive. The bad news was immediately cabled to Washington. On Friday, 6 May, the State Department categorically denied that there had been a deliberate violation of Soviet airspace. DPD scrambled to concoct an alternative cover story. Dick Newton, the executive officer at Det B, was nominated as the fall guy. He would confess to exceeding his authority by sending Powers into Soviet airspace. The CIA official was hurriedly flown from Turkey to Germany and hidden in an Agency safe house, where he could not be reached by reporters.[27] Meanwhile, a Moscow newspaper published a photo showing a heap of twisted wreckage, which was identified as "the pirate plane."

The American newspapers had been bawling for a close look at the U-2. On Friday their wish was granted, when a photo call was arranged at Edwards. Not at the top-secret North Base site, though. The gentlemen of the press were taken to a ramp on the main part of the flight test base. The CIA unit towed one of their U-2A models (Article 378) over from North Base. It had been hurriedly painted with a yellow NASA tail band and a fictitious serial number. The photographers clicked away, but the groundcrew remained tight-lipped when quizzed about the plane.

In fact, no one cleared into the project at Edwards was allowed to discuss the shootdown, even amongst themselves within the secure confines of North Base. Project HQ told unit commander Lt Col "Rosy" Rosenfield to clamp all mouths shut. "What was being said on the morning talk shows became classified information the minute it was discussed on the base! We pilots were the only ones in the whole of the Antelope valley that didn't have anything to say about the incident," noted one frustrated U-2 pilot.

The Awful Truth

On Saturday, 7 May, the Soviet Premier returned to the Supreme Soviet to wind up its meeting. He now revealed the awful truth: "We have the remnants of the plane—and we also have the pilot, who is quite alive and kicking!" Khrushchev held up a photograph of an airfield that he claimed was taken by the U-2's camera. Again, he speculated that "American militarists" had ordered the flight, rather than President Eisenhower himself.[28]

Of course, the Soviet Premier caused an immediate sensation. Headlines screamed from the Sunday newspapers around the world. In Washington, Allen Dulles offered to resign and take the rap. On Secretary of State Herter's advice, a statement was issued that admitted the U-2's mission as a border surveillance tool. The aircraft had "probably" flown into Soviet airspace, but this had not been authorized in Washington. The statement did not play well with the American press, let alone in Moscow. Was the White House in charge here, or not?

Finally, at Eisenhower's insistence, the State Department admitted on Monday, 9 May, that the President had authorized the entire U-2 program as a means of gaining adequate knowledge of the Soviet military-industrial complex. But specific missions had not been subject to the President's authorization, the statement lied. There were more sensational headlines around the world.

At Eielson airbase in Alaska, SAC U-2 pilot Dick Leavitt heard about the shootdown of Powers with even more interest than the rest of the 4080th wing contingent deployed there. A few days earlier, Leavitt had flown the 11th and last Congo Maiden flight. He had paralleled the Soviet coastline, photographing airfields and radars all the way to Petropavlovsk, on the Kamchatka Peninsula. Soviet fighters chased him for several hundred miles. He had taken off from Eielson around 11 am on 30 April, and returned at 8 pm—another very long mission. But he had crossed the International Date Line, so it was Sunday, 1 May, in Siberia when the flight took place. Leavitt realized that he had been airborne at the very same time as the CIA's U-2. Powers was not the only U-2 pilot to have stirred up the Soviet air defenses on their national holiday![29]

In Washington Art Lundahl—the master briefer—pulled off one his best performances, as 18 leading Congressmen were privately told the extent of the U-2 program and its accomplishments. In Burbank, Kelly Johnson told reporters that the photo of the wreckage that had been released in Moscow was a fake. But Johnson unaccountably went further:

"I do not believe they shot down the U-2 by either a missile or another aircraft. If they have the U-2, it is because some mechanical or oxygen failure caused it to descend far below its normal cruising altitude."

In Moscow that same day (Monday, 9 May), newspapers published a decree of Supreme Soviet. Honors were awarded to 21 PVO officers who had been involved in the shootdown. Voronov, Sheludko, and Safronov headed the list: they were given the Order of the Red Banner. The fact that the MiG-19 pilot's award was posthumous was carefully omitted from the official record.

Propaganda

The wreckage of the U-2 was brought to Moscow. On Wednesday, 11 May, it was put on display in Gorky Park. Three months earlier, President Eisenhower had foretold exactly this scenario if a U-2 were to be shot down. Trailed by reporters, Premier Khrushchev was one of the first visitors to the unusual exhibition. He was milking the U-2 incident for all it was worth. The U.S. ambassador in Moscow concluded that the Soviet leader would turn the forthcoming Paris summit into a propaganda event.

President Eisenhower faced the press in the White House and talked of "the distasteful but vital necessity" of intelligence gathering.[30]

The Soviets also turned the heat up on those other countries that were clearly associated with the U-2 program. Because of their direct involvement with the 1 May mission, Norway, Pakistan, and Turkey were all in the firing line. The State Department spokesman claimed that those countries knew nothing about U-2 missions into the USSR. "These planes come and visit our country. How do we know where they go after they leave?" declared Ayub Khan, the Pakistani leader (who knew exactly where the spyplane was going). The Shah of Iran denied all knowledge of the U-2 (and the use of the Zahedan airbase to recover two previous overflight missions did remain a secret).[31]

The Norwegian foreign minister cross-examined intelligence chief Wilhelm Evang, and the Bodo-based Norwegian air force commander Tufte Johnson. Both denied that they knew anything about a plan to overfly the USSR with the U-2. Evang was furious with the Americans; the CIA station chief in Oslo had deliberately disappeared, and the Norwegian had to rely on the newspapers to discover what the U.S. was saying about the shootdown, and Norway's involvement. Oslo sent a secret protest note to Washington. The government issued a statement, in which Tufte Johnsen was quoted saying that landing permission for "that airplane" at Bodo had neither been requested nor granted.[32]

In London, Secretary of State for Air George Ward summoned the RAF U-2 pilots to his office. The British fliers had been quickly evacuated from Turkey as soon as news of the shootdown reached London. But the British press was picking up rumors that the RAF was somehow involved in the U-2 overflights. Opposition Members of Parliament (MPs) had tabled some questions in Parliament. The Air Minister wanted to know if Powers would spill the beans to his Soviet captors about the British group. The Minister told the pilots that he was torn between lying to Parliament, or saying nothing.

When the Soviets revealed that they had captured U-2 pilot Powers, DCI Allen Dulles offered to take responsibility for authorizing the flight, and to resign. But President Eisenhower decided to take the rap himself.

British U-2 detachment commander Robbie Robinson described Powers as a pleasant, quiet, and likable American. He told Ward that Powers probably would reveal the RAF involvement, but he could not be sure. Ward told the British fliers to disappear from view for a few months, just in case. In Parliament on 11 May, Ward refused to answer when an MP asked him to confirm the "cooperation between the RAF and the USAF for obtaining photographic information about Russian air and military bases."[33]

In Japan, the U-2 incident threatened to scuttle a new security treaty with the U.S. The treaty was being discussed by the Diet—the Japanese parliament—amidst a growing uproar over the presence of the "mysterious black-painted spyplanes" just outside Tokyo. "There is no truth to reports that a U-2 aircraft conducted intelligence missions from Japan," said the U.S. State Department. Again, this was not true.

Interrogation

In Moscow, Frank Powers was undergoing intensive daily interrogation. But he was not physically abused, and as the questioning continued, Powers realized that he could successfully keep some important details of the U-2 program secret. His task was complicated by the revelations about the program that were now occurring back home. The interrogators could trip him up when he denied something that was then admitted in Washington. Incarcerated in the Lubyanka prison, it wasn't easy to second-guess!

Nevertheless, Powers did manage to withhold significant information. The Soviets never asked about any British pilots, so he did not tell them. They accepted that he had not flown over the USSR before, when he once had. They didn't press him on flights over other countries, such as the wide-ranging Middle East missions that Det B regularly flew. He successfully convinced them that he knew little about the cameras, and nothing about the SIGINT systems. In general, Powers played the role of the poor dumb pilot. His superiors in the detachment only told him what he needed to know for the flight, he explained to the Soviets.

(To some extent, this was true. Officially, only the pilot actually assigned to each overflight mission was briefed. The CIA's security officers encouraged a tacit understanding amongst the pilots that, by and large, they wouldn't inquire of each other's missions in great depth. That way, if one of them did eventually fall prey to Soviet defenses, they would have less to tell. Moreover, the nature of the targets to be overflown were not explained to the pilots in great detail. Nor did they get much feedback on the intelligence results from their flights).

Powers was asked to reveal how high the U-2 could fly. The pilot thought of his colleagues who might, even now, be sent on similar missions. He wanted to deny the Soviet air defenses the possibility of setting their missiles to detonate at the correct altitude. So Powers said that he had been shot down at 68,000 feet, instead of 70,000 feet—a small lie. He claimed that this was the plane's maximum altitude—a bigger lie. The interrogators did not challenge him. After all, the PVO radar tracking was so confused, they had no serious evidence to the contrary.

In Washington, though, the intelligence community jumped to their own conclusions. The NSA's intercepts of the Soviet air defense reporting network were played and replayed. Some of the PVO reporting related the mistaken notion that originated in Shugayev's battery, that the U-2 had descended to 36,000 feet. The State Department weighed in with a report from the U.S. embassy in Moscow, on the exhibition of wreckage in Gorky Park. "The unusually good condition of debris from the crash, and its reported disposition over a nine-mile-wide area, was inconsistent with it having fallen from 68,000 feet," the report said.

Summit Failure

The summit meeting in Paris in mid-May was a disaster. Khrushchev demanded that Eisenhower denounce the U-2 flights over the USSR as provocative. Ike had said as much to Dulles, Bissell, and the others in private, but he refused to apologize for them in public. He did tell the Soviet Premier that there would be no more flights during his administration, which still had nine months to run. This wasn't good enough for Khrushchev. He withdrew an invitation for Eisenhower to visit the USSR and walked out. Art Lundahl and Jim Cunningham played a bit part in the Paris summit. They were summoned from Washington when Eisenhower decided to show General De Gaulle some U-2 imagery. At a briefing in the Elysee Palace, the French leader showed considerable interest in the photographs of Soviet nuclear and missile installations.[34]

(De Gaulle probably didn't know that the U-2 had recently been spying on France's own nuclear weapons program. An aircraft from Det B had flown over the test site at Reggane in Algeria where, on 13 February 1960, the first French nuclear test took place).

66952 was one of three 4080th SRW U-2A models that flew the second series of peripheral photo flights around Soviet Siberia in the spring of 1960. On 1 May 1960, while Gary Powers was flying over the Urals, other PVO units further east were also trying to intercept one of these USAF aircraft as it skirted the Kamchatka Peninsula.

Back in Washington, on 24 May the President called a meeting of the National Security Council (NSC) and reviewed the whole sorry affair. He observed that the previous overflights had been so successful that "we may have become careless." He previewed what information should be made available to the Senate inquiry that was pending. He did not want it made public how many overflights there had been, nor that he had approved specific missions. Most of all, he didn't want anyone to admit that other countries had been party to reconnaissance overflights.[35]

Eisenhower insisted that he had previously been briefed to the effect that, "the pilots on such flights were taught to destroy the plane, rather than let it fall into enemy hands." He would never have approved the cover story if he had not believed this.

Apparently, Powers had not activated the destructor. Why not? It was a legitimate question, but the President had been sorely misled by whoever told him that the plane would be destroyed. The destructor was a 2.5 lb. charge of cyclonite that was placed in the equipment bay behind the cockpit. Its purpose was to destroy the camera—the most incriminating evidence. There was some hope that the explosion might lead to further breakup of the wreckage inflight, but this theory had never been tested. However, it is doubtful whether a 2.5 lb charge could have completely destroyed even the camera, let alone its huge, tightly-wound film magazines.

The control panel for the destructor was mounted on the forward right canopy rail; the pilot threw one switch to activate the system, and a second switch to start the timer, which was usually set for a 60-second delay.[36] The delay was provided so that the pilot could have enough time to escape after setting the timer, since he might otherwise be injured in the blast. Powers would later say that he had considered setting the timer before he tried to escape from the disabled U-2, but then he decided to ensure that he really could get out of the cockpit first. Unfortunately, when he released the seat belt, g-forces threw him half out of the cockpit, and he was unable to reach the switches.

The NSC meeting continued with more ill-tempered remarks and unfounded speculation from the nation's leadership. "Apparently Powers started talking as soon as he hit the ground," the President remarked irritably. Then DCI Allen Dulles chimed in, noting that "we traced the U-2 piloted by Powers down to 30,000 feet." This was from the NSA intercepts, of course. Bullets had been fired at the plane while it was in the air—the pictures of the wreckage in the Moscow exhibition showed this, Dulles asserted.

Eisenhower and Secretary of State Herter told the meeting that they were worried about revealing the "fact" that the U.S. had tracked the U-2. This was a highly secret SIGINT capability—officially the National Security Agency didn't even exist! In reality, though, the NSA had not "tracked" anything. As we have seen, it had intercepted fragments of the PVO's long-range communications. Herter's deputy Douglas Dillon recommended that they use the wreckage photos to make the case that the U-2 had descended before being shot down. But surprisingly enough, the DCI was more willing to reveal the SIGINT capability. Dulles explained that the USSR was claiming that their rockets could shoot a plane down from 60-70,000 feet. It would be reassuring to our allies if we could inform them that the plane had *not* been shot down at this high altitude, he continued.[37]

There was the rub! It was not politically expedient in Washington to admit that the Soviets had a high-altitude SAM that worked. For a start, SAC's subsonic nuclear bombers could be sitting ducks if they attacked the USSR. How could America reassure its allies on the frontline of the Cold War that the nuclear deterrent would hold Soviet aggression in check? On Capitol Hill, moreover, questions might be asked about all the money being spent on the supersonic XB-70. Could it, too, be vulnerable?

One day later, Eisenhower made a television address explaining the summit failure. He displayed a B-camera photograph of NAS North Island, San Diego. "It was taken from more than 70,000 feet...the white lines on the parking strips around the field are clearly visible," he told viewers.

Flameout Story Grows

The next day, 26 May, Congressional leaders took breakfast in the White House. The President told them that he did not believe the Soviets had shot down the U-2 with a rocket. "The plane's engine had flamed out," he believed. It was "obvious" that the bullet holes shown in the photographs "must have been put in the wing at a lower altitude," possibly by Soviet fighters.[38]

On 27 May, the Senate Committee on Foreign Relations began four days of closed-door hearings on the U-2 affair. Herter testified on the first

Wreckage from the downed U-2 was displayed in Moscow 11 days after the shootdown. All of the basic structure was recovered (via Jay Miller).

The display of U-2 wreckage also included the camera and SIGINT systems. The spool for the 70mm tracker camera and various parts of the main B-camera were placed on a table in front of a map depicting the route of the doomed flight.

The National Security Agency (NSA) intercepted long-range Soviet air defense communications from sites like this. But NSA analysts could not appreciate the full picture of what went on over Sverdlovsk, since the Soviets themselves were so confused, and this was reflected in the PVO reporting.

day; among other comments, he confirmed that the U.S. Ambassadors in Turkey and Pakistan knew nothing of the flights (all the liaison went through the CIA station chief's office). On 31 May, a delegation from the CIA briefed the Senators. DCI Dulles did most of the talking, though his deputy Pierre Cabell was also there. So was Art Lundahl and Dick Helms, Bissell's deputy at DDP.

Dulles told the senators that the main intelligence targets for the U-2 flights had been the Soviet bomber force, air defense system, and its missile, atomic energy, and submarine programs. He showed imagery of Kapustin Yar and Tyuratam, noting that the U.S. had learned much about the Soviet doctrine of ICBM deployment, as well as technical characteristics of the missiles themselves. In the atomic energy field, the U-2 coverage had included the production of fissionable materials, weapons development and test activities, and the location, type, and size of many Soviet nuclear stockpiles. The photography had provided the first firm information on the magnitude and location of Soviet domestic uranium ore mining and processing activities, so that its production of fissionable material could be estimated.

The material obtained had been used to correct military maps and aeronautical charts, Dulles continued. Hard information about the nature, extent, and location of Soviet ground-to-air missile development had been obtained. Much had been learned about Soviet air defenses in general, and early warning radar development. Scores of airfields had been photographed. U-2 photography provided new and accurate information to SAC's strike bomber crews, Dulles noted, making it easier for them to identify their targets and plan their navigation. "In the opinion of our military, our scientists, and senior officials responsible for our national security, the results of this program have been invaluable," Dulles concluded.

The questions began. When the sensitive issue of whether the President had personally approved each overflight was raised by the senators, Dulles hedged and dissembled. But he had no such inhibitions about describing the shootdown. The U-2 "was initially forced down to a much lower altitude by some as-yet undetermined mechanical malfunction," he said. "If the plane had been hit by a ground-to-air missile, it would have disintegrated," he added.[39] It seems that no one at CIA headquarters could believe that a SAM might disable a U-2, rather than outright destroy it. Towards the end of his testimony, Dulles did concede that a Soviet SAM "might have had a near miss...(which) caused (the U-2) to lose altitude". But no one seemed to take this theory seriously.

Concerning the destructor, Dulles did make clear to the senators that "no massive device capable of ensuring complete destruction could be carried in this aircraft." He also confirmed that pilots "were not given positive instructions" to take their own lives with the poison pin. Suggestions had already been aired in public that Powers should have jabbed himself with the poison pin to avoid capture, like any self-respecting spy. That was never the intent of providing the pilots with the pin; it was provided only as a means of suicide in the face of unbearable torture.

Rumor and Misinformation

Dulles therefore laid to rest, for the Senators' benefit, a couple of U-2 myths-in-the-making. But this was a closed session of the committee. Only a heavily-censored transcript of the proceedings was issued. The media continued to peddle rumor and misinformation about destructors and poison pins as fact. Moreover, Dulles' inaccurate testimony to the Senators about the circumstances of the actual shootdown soon leaked. Within a week, headlines read "Soviet Radar Defense System Far From Perfect, Ineffec-

Just two months after the U-2 was shot down, one of SAC's RB-47H aircraft was downed by Soviet fighters while flying a SIGINT mission close to the Kola Peninsula. This was a further embarrassment for the Eisenhower Administration, which subsequently moved to exert tighter control of military peripheral reconnaissance missions (USAF).

tive at Altitudes at Which U-2 Flies" and "Despite Boasts, Plane Could Not Have Been Hit at 65,000 feet."[40]

The story grew with the telling. Soon, Powers was said to have had a flameout, and to have made three or four attempts to restart, none of which worked. One version even offered direct quotes from Soviet radar operators as proof: "He's coming down, he's still descending!" Another version held that Powers himself had radioed back to base that he was in trouble. This ignored the fact that the CIA's U-2s were equipped only with a short-range UHF radio, transmissions from which could not possibly be picked up from so deep inside the USSR.

Kelly Johnson wanted to test the flameout theory. At North Base, Lockheed test pilots made four flights in the prototype U-2C to check the restart characteristics of the J75 engine. Skunk Works engineers tested the destructor, analyzed photos of the ejection seat from Moscow, and reviewed the data from previous U-2 accidents. The wreckage as displayed in Moscow showed some similarity with that from a USAF U-2 that had broken up at about 35,000 feet.

On 24 June, Johnson concluded that Powers "did not have enough time to (activate) the destructor switch or even use the ejection seat." This was partially correct. He further concluded that "the airplane was hit at less than normal altitude by a rocket." This was only correct in the sense that, during their descent to the ground, some parts of Powers' plane may have been hit by the second, third, and fourth missiles fired by the PVO. Johnson still discounted the possibility that the aircraft had been disabled by a missile at cruising altitude, even though the technical report by his own engineers on the four new test flights was careful to note that "there is no direct evidence at this time that a high-altitude engine blow-out occurred." (The technical report was signed off by Art Bradley, who had taken over from Ed Martin as U-2 program manager for Lockheed nine months earlier).[41]

No More Overflights
Ed Martin was one of a growing band of ADP engineers whom Kelly Johnson had transferred to the A-12 project, now that the supersonic successor to the U-2 was firmly under contract. But at the highest level, even

General Twining, chairman of the U.S. Joint Chiefs of Staff, joined the chorus of those who were wise after the event. He complained that the CIA "did not know how to handle this type of operation" (USAF).

this project was threatened by the fallout from the U-2 incident. In early June, the President told General Goodpaster that he "did not think the project should now be pushed at top priority." After all, he had already told Khrushchev that there would be no more overflights, at least not on his watch. Maybe the Mach 3 spyplane could go forward "on low priority, as a high performance reconnaissance plane for the Air Force in time of war," he mused.[42]

Now that the U-2 was out in the open, Kelly Johnson didn't see any point in keeping scores of workers out at the isolated North Base site. In mid-June, he moved the IRAN (Inspection and Repair as Necessary) program for the USAF's U-2 fleet to Burbank.

On 1 July 1960, one of SAC's RB-47H reconnaissance aircraft was shot down by Soviet fighters in the Barents Sea while flying parallel to the Kola peninsula on a SIGINT mission. The co-pilot and navigator were picked up from the water by the Soviets. The four other crew members perished. Premier Khrushchev claimed another "gross violation" of Soviet airspace, but the NSA knew otherwise from SIGINT intercepts. The U.S. refuted the charge at the United Nations with a detailed map of the aircraft's offshore route.

The RB-47H had taken off from Brize Norton airbase in the UK. The new incident prompted a fresh round of Parliamentary questions to British ministers about the Anglo-American security relationship in general, and the U-2 in particular. Despite his reputation for unflappability, Prime Minister Harold MacMillan was now quite worried that British participation in the U-2 program would come to light. The USSR had announced its intention to put pilot Powers on trial in Moscow for espionage. Would the UK's biggest intelligence secret be revealed there?

British Minister's Dilemma
Already left-wing MPs had discovered that Squadron Leader Chris Walker was killed during U-2 training at Laughlin two years earlier. The Air Minister George Ward told Parliament that "it is quite customary for RAF aircrew...to fly USAF aircraft, particularly advanced types." In private, Ward was still wrestling with his conscience. "To give information to the House would also...give it to our potential enemies. As a Service Minister...this places me in an awkward dilemma, from which I could only escape at the expense of betraying...the national interest," he wrote.[43]

Still, the British government stuck to the party line. When MacMillan's turn to face MPs came on 12 July, he retreated to the time-honored formula:

"It has never been the practice to discuss (intelligence) matters in the House, and I have come to the conclusion that it would be contrary to the public interest to depart from precedent on this occasion."[44]

President Eisenhower wrote privately to congratulate MacMillan:

"I thought you handled this matter very well indeed. It is clear that we are up against a ruthless Soviet campaign against our free world bases."[45]

Ike admired the British ability to keep their mouths shut, and told colleagues the U.S. should have done likewise after 1 May.

On Sunday, 11 July, 10,000 Japanese demonstrators gathered outside NAS Atsugi, demanding that the U.S. remove the U-2s stationed there. In fact, the Japanese government had already requested their removal. The

U-2 aircraft performed spy missions for a number of years, and that presented a complicated problem for the Soviet Air Defence and Air Force. It also became a permanent pain in the neck for the top military command and political leadership.

I served in the Soviet Air Defence intelligence troops. Initially there were strong doubts regarding the capability of U-2 aircraft to fly at such high altitudes. Many radars at that time were not equipped with altimeters, and were capable of detecting only a target's bearing and range. Enhanced radars were capable of locating targets at an altitude of 20 km or more, but there were few of them, and therefore it was not always possible to lock on to the target without gaps in the coverage.

The Peshawar airfield was not selected as a U-2 base at random. The Air Defence radar network in the Turkestan military district was weak.

The bitter lesson learned on 9 April was given every consideration in every Air Defence unit and was not in vain. The next visitor, Francis Gary Powers, was shot down on 1 May 1960.

- *remarks by Col Aleksandr Orlov, PVO, retd,*
at CIA U-2 Conference 1997

Frank Powers on trial in Moscow. He managed to keep some important secrets about the U-2 program from his interrogators. Still, he was criticized for saying that he was "profoundly sorry" for what had happened.

two aircraft were hastily dismantled and flown out by transport planes. There wasn't even time to send for the proper wing and fuselage transport carts: the Lockheed maintenance crews grabbed some old mattresses to use as protective padding for the disassembled parts. It was an ignominious departure, but the U-2 incident had created an uproar in Japan. The three remaining aircraft in Turkey were grounded. Project Chalice was facing an uncertain future.

The USAF weighed in with some blatant Monday-morning quarterbacking. General Nathan Twining, former USAF CinC and now Chairman of the JCS, asserted that the CIA:

"...got too big for their britches. They did not know how to handle this type of operation...they made a mistake and went in twice from the south. We screamed and yelled, and we insisted that they change the plan and come in over Norway and Sweden and get closer to the target area."

Twining went on to complain that Eisenhower should not have approved the CIA's running the U-2 program in the first place. Bissell was "a smart young man who wanted to take over, and he did."[46]

Twining conveniently ignored the fact that blue-suiters made up a significant proportion of the CIA's U-2 operation. Moreover, by formal agreement Bissell's deputy at DPD was appointed by the USAF. Indeed, USAF vice-commander and former SAC CinC General Curt LeMay had personally selected Colonel Bill Burke to take the job in 1958. He wanted one of "his" people to be at the helm in Washington, to exert as much military influence as possible.[47]

All this time, the U.S. Embassy in Moscow had been requesting access to Powers. He was kept in solitary confinement in the Lubyanka Prison. Except for a few heavily-censored letters, the U-2 pilot had been denied all contact with the outside world. The trial was set for 17 August, and a Soviet lawyer was appointed to defend him. "He specialized in losing state cases," Powers noted dryly.[48] The USSR continued to deny access to the pilot.

Inside Information

Late on the evening of 12 August 1960, two young American tourists were approaching the bridge over the Moscow River, just south of Red Square. A Soviet citizen approached them, began a conversation, and walked on with them. He was Oleg Penkovsky, the Colonel in Soviet military intelligence who was to become the West's most valuable spy in the Soviet military heirarchy. This was his first attempt to make contact with Western intelligence. During his conversation with the students, Penkovsky told them that he knew exactly what had happened to Powers and the U-2. The downed pilot was due to go on trial in Moscow just four days later.

Penkovsky had been the GRU duty officer on 1 May, when Powers was brought to Moscow. But the KGB had kept Soviet military intelligence at arm's length during the U-2 pilot's early interrogations. To the American students, Penkovsky repeated the details that he had learned second-hand from various GRU, KGB, and PVO sources. He confirmed that Powers had been shot down at high altitude, after his aircraft was disabled by a near-miss from a Soviet surface-to-air missile. Penkovsky related the story that a total of 14 missiles had been fired. He revealed that one of the missiles had inadvertently shot down a MiG-19 interceptor.[49]

Show Trial

The show trial of Francis Gary Powers was held in Moscow's impressive Hall of Columns from 17-19 August. The indictment was read out—a litany of propaganda complaints interspersed with occasional "facts." Curiously, the indictment made repeated references to the U-2 having "remained at an altitude of 20,000 meters (65,000 feet) throughout the entire flight"[50] This was even lower than Powers had admitted, but probably more politically acceptable to the Soviet fighter lobby!

During cross-examination, Powers explained about the cruise-climb technique. He also repeated for the benefit of U.S. government representatives in court, that he had been shot down at 68,000 feet, which was the "maximum altitude" for the plane. Most of the information about Operation Chalice that Powers had revealed during his interrogation was repeated in court. It should have been obvious to knowledgeable observers that he had kept plenty of details to himself. The British pilots, the flights over Israel, and the rest of the Middle East, the various deployments in support of CIA covert operations....

But the PVO had also kept some secrets. A short statement from Major Voronov, the battery commander at Sverdlovsk who had first engaged the U-2, was read to the court. It "confirmed" that a single missile had been fired. Of course, nothing was said about the other missiles, or the downed MiG-19.

After Powers had testified, Soviet technical experts described the U-2's B-camera and SIGINT systems. They gave considerable detail on Systems 3 and 6—the frequencies covered, the antennas, the tape recorders. (Forty years later, the U.S. still considers this information to be classified!). More experts told of the destructor and the poison pin. Then came the closing speeches.

Powers declared that he was "deeply repentant and profoundly sorry." They sentenced him to 10 years confinement, with the first three years in prison. Predictably, his apology was not well received by the armchair critics back home. But the State Department announced that Powers had fulfilled the terms of his contract, and would be paid while in prison.

Misunderstanding

The press wouldn't leave the shootdown alone. The New York Times ran a story quoting Powers' father—who had attended the trial—as believing his son had not been shot down. The KGB re-interrogated Powers, and asked him to write a letter of clarification to the paper. "I'm sure my father misunderstood what was said during the trial," Powers wrote. "I hope this letter will clear up any misunderstanding."

Fat chance! In the September issue of True magazine, Drew Pearson and Jack Anderson revealed the "Inside Story of Pilot Powers." This repeated the flameout story in great detail, and added spicy new details. They included how the pilot had made a distress call that was "heard across the Turkish border 1,200 miles away, where a handful of Americans were watching the drama helplessly on radar screens and listening by high-powered radio monitors."[51]

But a small group within the CIA knew better. The details about the shootdown that Oleg Penkovsky had passed to the American tourists were at odds with the information the USSR revealed at the trial. And they were embarrassing to the Soviet regime. This helped the DDP's Soviet Division conclude that Penkovsky's approach was genuine. They laid plans to renew contact with this very promising new source of intelligence.

The Soviet Copy

The remains of the U-2 were removed from Gorky Park and analyzed in detail by Soviet aeronautical engineers. The J75 engine excited particular interest. Its gas generator unit was so good that the Soviets thought it might replace the RD-3M turbojet in the Tu-104 airliner. The OKB-16 design bureau in Kazan was instructed to produce a direct copy of the J75 as the RD-16-75.

Two months later, the Soviet government decided that the structural, technical, and maintenance characteristics of the U-2 made it worth copying the airframe itself. The wreckage of Article 360 was carefully sorted and transported to the Beriev Design Bureau in Taganrog. Beriev's team was ordered to produce five copy aircraft designated S-13, and to have the first ready to fly in early 1962. Dozens of other state enterprises were involved in the effort, including one which would reproduce the B-camera, another the ELINT system.

By April 1961, Beriev had completed a full-scale metal mockup of the S-13 fuselage. But it was a huge task reproducing not only the airframe, but all the avionics, fuel system, life support system, and so on. Not surprisingly, weight control was another problem. The effort continued, however, and test rigs for the hydraulics, autopilot, and many other systems were built. TsAGI (the main Soviet aviation research laboratory) carried out wind tunnel tests, and a Tu-16 bomber was prepared as a testbed for the RD-16-75 engine.

Although the Soviet aircraft industry learned much from the S-13 project, it was never completed. On 12 May 1962 the government in Moscow called a halt.[52] Meanwhile, the Yakovlev Design Bureau had adapted the Yak-25 fighter-bomber for high-altitude reconnaissance with long, straight wings. It could reach 65,000 feet. Many years later, the Myasischev Design Bureau produced the M-17, a specialized high-altitude interceptor. Both aircraft were sometimes characterized in the West as "U-2skis." But there was one huge difference. The Yak and the M-17 were both twin-engine aircraft. There was nothing to match the real U-2—the only single-engined subsonic plane in the world that could reach 70,000 feet and stay there for hours on end.

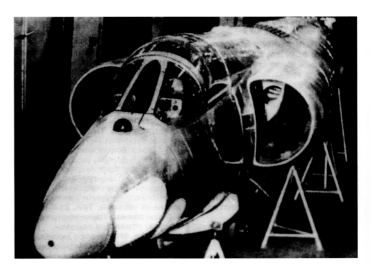

Looking much like the real thing, this mock-up of the U-2 was constructed by the Beriev Design Bureau. But Soviet attempts to fully replicate and fly a "U-2ski" were abandoned in 1961 (Russian Aviation Research Trust).

11

Fallout

On 10 February 1962, Frank Powers walked to freedom across the Glienicker Bridge, which separated Potsdam from West Berlin. Walking in the other direction was Colonel Rudolf Abel, the Soviet spy for whom the U-2 pilot was being exchanged. Before the swap was made Joe Murphy, a CIA security officer from Project HQ, walked to the Potsdam side to make a formal identification of Powers.

Powers underwent a long debrief at Agency "safe" houses near Washington. Then he was taken to see Allen Dulles, who told the pilot "we are proud of what you have done." But Dulles was no longer the DCI. The Kennedy administration had appointed John McCone, a millionaire industrialist, to replace him. And McCone was not at all happy with the way that Powers had behaved. The new DCI set up a Board of Inquiry to formally determine whether Powers had "acted in accordance with the terms of his employment."

The inquiry was chaired by retired Federal Judge E. Barret Prettyman and held in secret. The Board examined 22 witnesses, plus Powers himself. They included Jim Cunningham from Project HQ; the CIA's chief security officer, Col Sheffield Edwards; Col Leo Geary from the USAF liaison office; the Det B commander, Colonel William Shelton; and four of the team from Turkey, including John Shinn, the pilot who was Powers' backup on 1 May 1960. Dr Louis Tordella, Deputy Director of the National Security Agency (NSA), and two of his analysts also testified on the

John McCone, who was the DCI from 1962-65, only reluctantly accepted the verdict of the CIA's own inquiry, which exonerated Powers. He remained hostile to the U-2 pilot.

matter of the SIGINT evidence, which appeared to conflict with Powers' account of the shootdown. The Board also considered written evidence, including some that came (they were told) from "a reliable Soviet source who was in an excellent position to acquire this information."

That source was Oleg Penkovsky, who had become the West's best-ever spy from inside the Soviet military heirarchy. Following his initial approach to the West just days before Powers' trial in August 1960, CIA and MI6 officers were finally able to meet with the GRU Colonel in London and Leeds eight months later. He handed them technical details of the SA-2 missile, and again described his knowledge of the Powers shootdown. "No direct hits were made...but (the U-2) was within the radius of explosion of one of the missiles...the U-2's tail and wing assembly were slightly damaged," he told them. "The damaged parts were not shown at the Moscow exhibition, and your intelligence personnel should have spotted that," he added.[1]

Powers Cleared

The three-member Board of Inquiry worked intensively and completed the investigation within a week. Their report to DCI McCone, dated 27 February 1962, unequivocally cleared the U-2 pilot. They found that he had told the truth about the May Day flight and shootdown, and conducted himself properly throughout his confinement. The only evidence that conflicted with his version of events came from the NSA intercepts, the Board noted. But Tordella and his analysts admitted "the obvious possibility of confusion and error" within the Soviet air defense system. The Board concluded that it could not "make a flat assumption of accuracy" from the SIGINT reports.[2]

McCone was not happy, and neither was the NSA. McCone asked the Board to reconvene on 1 March and reconsider the evidence. Prettyman told the DCI that the NSA's "evidence" was at best unverifiable hearsay once removed. Tordella continued to complain about his treatment. On 24 March he called CIA General Counsel Lawrence Houston about "the markedly hostile nature of much of the questioning." Houston explained that the Board ejected the NSA evidence after weighing all the factors.[3]

McCone reluctantly accepted the Prettyman report. He took it to the White House, where President Kennedy endorsed it. On 6 March 1962 a sanitized version was released to the public, just before Frank Powers testified to an open session of the Senate Armed Services Committee. The public version finessed the references to the SIGINT evidence, which was still highly classified:

"Some information from confidential sources was available...that which was inconsistent (with Powers' own account) was in part contradictory with itself and subject to various interpretations. Some of this information was the basis for...subsequent stories in the press that Powers' plane had descended gradually from its extreme altitude and had been shot down by a Russian fighter at medium altitude. On careful analysis, it appears that the information on which these stories were based was erroneous, or was susceptible of varying interpretations."

Senate Hearing

The Senate hearing was Powers' first chance to explain himself properly in public. He did not fluff it. The exact circumstances of the shootdown, the destructor, the poison pin, the cover story, and all the other controversies became a matter of public record. Powers stayed on the CIA payroll for a while as a training officer, helping to teach recruits about Soviet interrogation methods and the like. In September 1962 he was finally allowed out to North Base. Over a three-day period he flew intensively with Jim Cherbonneaux in one of the CIA unit's T-33s. Cherbonneaux confirmed that Powers had lost none of his flying skills. The visit ended with an alcoholic reunion party with the half dozen other pilots from Operations Aquatone and Chalice who, like Cherbonneaux, were still flying U-2s for the CIA.

Then Powers took up an offer from Kelly Johnson to become an engineering test pilot on the U-2 program. He reported for work at Burbank on 15 October 1962. He clocked up another 1,400 hours on the aircraft from 1962 to 1969, flying from Burbank, Van Nuys, Palmdale, and Edwards. But after the last U-2R was delivered, the work dried up. In February 1970 he was made redundant.

John McCone remained hostile to the returned U-2 pilot. In April 1963 the CIA's Intelligence Medal was awarded to the project U-2 pilots in a secret ceremony. Powers was left out. (He eventually received the 10-oz gold star two years later, when McCone left office).[4]

When the CIA's U-2 pilots received the Intelligence Star in 1963, DCI McCone withheld the one due to Frank Powers. He eventually received it two years later, after McCone left office (via Sue Powers).

SO WHERE WERE THE SOVIET MISSILES?

On 19 August 1960 the first recovery of a film capsule from a U.S. reconnaissance satellite was made. It was the ninth attempt in the CIA's top secret Corona project. The satellite had made eight north-south passes over the USSR. But when the film reached Art Lundahl's men at the PIC in Washington, it got a mixed reception. There were the inevitable clouds—only 25% of the coverage was completely cloud-free. Some of the PIs were disappointed by the resolution of the smaller-scale film exposed by the satellite's panoramic camera. At 20-30 feet it was nowhere near as good as that obtained by the large-format framing cameras carried by the U-2. But the first successful Corona mission covered more Soviet territory than all the previous U-2 overflights combined.

The resolution was good enough for the PIs to identify several new airfields, and 20 new SA-2 missile sites. But there was still no imagery of offensive missile sites in the northern USSR. The Polyarny Ural area, which was rated the likeliest area for deployment, was completely covered by cloud.

More Corona missions were scheduled, but the next three were failures. On 10 December 1960 the second recovery of a capsule with successfully-exposed film was made. This time, the satellite's orbit had taken it directly over Plesetsk, but high cirrus cloud covered the target area, making positive interpretation impossible. The next successful Corona mission was not until June 1961, and it took two more successes in July and early September before the CIA's missile analysts felt confident enough to make a "sharp downward revision" in Soviet ICBM strength.

The analysts concluded that the Soviets had curtailed deployment of the big SS-7 in favor of one, possibly two smaller, more flexible missiles. They corresponded to the U.S. Titan II ICBM in that they were kerosene-fueled and tandem-staged, and used a storable oxidant. The first generation ICBMs, both Soviet and the U.S. Atlas, ignited all stages at launch. There had been a large number of test-launches of the Soviet second-generation missiles in 1961, including many failures. They would probably not be operational until late 1962.

Yur'ya was the operational launch site for these new Soviet missiles. This site was reached by a spur off the railroad leading northwest from Kirov. The analysts concluded that the complex must have been started in the autumn of 1959. Had Frank Powers not been shot down over Sverdlovsk, he would have flown right over Yur'ya during its construction phase, as he followed the railroad from Kirov to Kotlas.

And what of Plesetsk, the primary target for the U-2 mission of 1 May 1960? Good imagery of the remote, cloud-covered site in the northern tundra was still eluding analysts. But they reckoned that the Plesetsk site housed two, four or more launchers for the first-generation ICBM. Making allowance for some yet-to-be discovered sites, the analysts now reckoned there could be 10-25 of these first-generation Soviet ICBM launchers ranged against the U.S. As usual, the USAF disagreed. In a formal dissent to the NIE, the blue-suiters alleged that there were about 50 launchers posing "a serious threat to U.S.-based nuclear striking forces."

In fact, the true number of launchers was...just four, and they were *all* at Plesetsk. Despite all the bombast and the boasts from Premier Khrushchev, the Soviet ICBM program had suffered serious setbacks. The shortcomings of the SS-6 as an operational ICBM had led to the canceling of plans to build other SS-6 launch sites after Plesetsk. Development of the SS-7 was hurriedly advanced. But on 24 October 1960, there had been a terrible accident on the new launch pad at Tyuratam, while the SS-7 was being prepared for its first test flight. A cataclysmic blaze erupted, killing over 200 technicians. They included the head of Khrushchev's much-vaunted new Strategic Missile Troops, and most of the SS-7 design team.[1]

It was a huge setback for the Soviet missile program. The SS-7 did enter flight testing in 1961, as was duly observed by U.S. intelligence. But progress was slow compared with the U.S., which began deploying 60 Titan ICBMs to join a similar number of Atlas ICBMs already on nuclear alert. From 1960 to 1962 there was indeed a substantial missile gap—but it was in favor of the United States, not the Soviet Union! - C.P.

"Operation Overflight"

In the closing pages of his book "Operation Overflight," published in 1970, Frank Powers reviewed some evidence that his May Day flight might have been "betrayed." This was a recurring theme in the growing body of U-2 literature. It was strictly speculation, the U-2 pilot explained.

He referred to the case of two SIGINT analysts from the NSA who defected to the USSR in July 1960. William Martin and Bernon Mitchell both monitored Soviet air defenses during U.S. airborne reconnaissance operations in the late 1950s, notably the SIGINT flights conducted specifically for the NSA along Soviet borders. In the course of their work, Martin and Mitchell may have gained some insight into the U-2 overflights. They undoubtedly did grave damage to the U.S. by passing on many of the NSA's secrets, beginning in 1958. Powers wondered whether they had learned of his flight in advance, during the course of their duties, and had passed the information to their Soviet handlers.

Then Powers raised the problems in communicating the "go-code" to Peshawar on the morning of 1 May 1960. After his return to the U.S. in 1962, said Powers, he had conversed with Det B's communications supervisor at Incirlik on 1 May. The "commo" man told Powers that there had been a problem relaying the go-code from Germany to Turkey, and that it had eventually been relayed "over an open telephone line." The supervisor told Powers that he was off-duty at the time, and learned of the incident later. Had he been on duty himself, the supervisor said he would never have sent the message on to Pakistan, since "the risk of the call having been monitored (was) so great."

Finally, there was Lee Harvey Oswald. The man who assassinated President Kennedy served in the U.S. Marine Corps at NAS Atsugi, Japan, for 14 months in 1957-58 as a radar operator. A year later he "defected" to the USSR, and remained there until 1962. During his tour at Atsugi, Oswald undoubtedly witnessed Det C's U-2 operations at close quarters, and may have learned something of its high-altitude capabilities from the height-finding radar that he helped to operate. Powers suggested that Oswald may have revealed the U-2's altitude to the USSR, six months before he was shot down.[5]

Speculations

As speculations go, these by Powers in his autobiography were reasonable. Others were not. For example, in a 1975 television documentary, Norwegian fisherman and convicted Soviet spy Selmer Nilsen claimed that the U-2 had been downed by a bomb planted in its tail before takeoff. In a 1993 book, former KGB Colonel Victor Sheymov recounted a conversation that took place during the 1970s with a Major in the Russian air force. According to Sheymov, the officer claimed that the USSR "knew the exact flight plan of every U-2 invading Soviet airspace several days in advance." This information was provided by a Soviet source "who was also able to influence" the flight plans. The source had managed to fix things so that Powers "flew within reach of the ground-to-air missiles" on 1 May 1960.[6]

What are we to make of these stories? Nilsen's bomb can be easily dismissed. At least half of the 20-strong launch crew in Peshawar would have to have been party to the planting of any bomb. Sheymov's spy is difficult to disprove: such is the nature of cloak-and-dagger allegations. However, Sheymov was himself a spy, exfiltrated from the USSR in 1980 by the CIA. There is no indication that the CIA took the allegation seriously, if indeed Sheymov even suggested it to the Agency during his debriefings. And the ancilliary detail provided by Sheymov, about the Soviet reaction to U-2 overflights, is far from convincing.

Might the NSA analysts Martin and Mitchell have tipped off the Soviets about impending U-2 flights, as Powers wrote? According to senior U-2 project officers consulted by this author, the NSA was *not* informed in advance of any U-2 overflight plan. In any case, the two NSA analysts were in no position to influence flight routes.[7]

The "Go-Code"

Much has been made of the unusual circumstances in which the "go-code" was relayed to Peshawar. Could the USSR have intercepted the signal, and thus been alerted that the flight was about to take place? The account that Powers gave in his book differs in material fact from that recorded in the CIA's archives, and related in a previous chapter of this book.[8] However, it is true that the correct procedure for transmission was *not* followed at some stage of the message's journey onwards to Pakistan from Germany.

It should be noted that the go-code alone would have told the Soviets nothing about the route of the impending flight. It was only the "execute" signal. The mission plan itself (giving the route co-ordinates and intelligence objectives) was transmitted much earlier (routinely, it was 12 hours before a flight, but in this case, some days earlier since the mission was postponed twice). The mission plan would have been only one of several signals relayed each day from Project HQ to the U-2 detachment. Some of these dealt with routine matters, while others had no purpose at all. This was to ensure that no pattern of communication could be discerned by eavesdroppers, enabling them to make deductions about pending U-2 operations.[9]

Despite this precaution, we now know that some messages to Det B were monitored by the Soviet Union, although they may not have been decoded. Prior to the overflight on 9 April 1960, Soviet communications intercept facilities in the Transcaucasus region did pick up indications that a special operation might be imminent. However, the subsequent Soviet inquiry into the failure to shoot down that flight found that this piece of intelligence was not reported to the command element because of a number of chance happenings.[10]

Moreover, the Soviets might have been alerted to the flight through their own efforts on the ground. Despite the precautions that were taken, it would have been possible for KGB agents to observe the U-2 operation at Peshawar. The taxiway to the runway ran close to the perimeter fence of the airfield. At least one pilot of an earlier overflight mission from the Pakistani base recalled seeing bystanders outside that fence as he taxied out.[11]

Furthermore, the hangar that was used by Det B at Peshawar was not secure during normal working hours, according to one member of the Det B deployment crew. Various Pakistani base workers visited, and there was even a tuition class for schoolchildren held there one day, during the crew's long wait to launch the mission.[12]

Soviets Alerted?

The lack of security at the hangar may have been the reason why it was decided to ferry the U-2 to and from Peshawar, rather than keep it hangared there during the daytime. But that decision itself may have led to a security breach, according to Colonel Stan Beerli, the former Det B commander who was waiting in Bodo for Powers to arrive. Thirty-seven years after the event, Beerli told this author that he knew nothing of the decision to ferry the U-2 to and fro, if the mission should be postponed. He would not have approved such a policy for fear of alerting the Soviets.

Beerli noted that Soviet early warning radars could have picked up the aircraft as it was being ferried across Iran and Afghanistan, and the more such flights there were, the more likely a radar intercept was. Certainly, we know now that the latest PVO early warning radars in this area could "see" more than 200 miles past the Soviet border; even Peshawar itself is inside the 200 mile radius, although the Hindu Kush and Pamir mountain ranges would have obscured the radar line-of-sight at lower altitudes.[13]

The "shuttle" flights, then, might have helped the Soviets deduce that an overflight was imminent. Conversely, though, U-2s had been performing regular, non-penetrating SIGINT flights along the Soviet border. Furthermore, when each of the last four missions over the USSR were launched from Peshawar, another U-2 was launched from Incirlik to fly a mission along the Soviet southern border from Incirlik, in a deliberate attempt to divert the attention of Soviet radar operators.[14]

Kelly Johnson offered Frank Powers a job flying U-2s for Lockheed. In early 1970, though, Powers was made redundant after engineering test work on the U-2 declined. Powers was killed six years later, when the helicopter that he was flying for a Los Angeles TV station crashed (Lockheed LCA 87-1).

DEATH OF FRANK POWERS

After leaving Lockheed and having his book "Operation Overflight" published in 1970, Frank Powers was unemployed for a while. He was understandably upset when his application to join three former colleagues and U-2 pilots flying U-2s under contract to NASA was turned down for political reasons. Then he started flying for a Los Angeles radio station, reporting on traffic conditions from the air in a Cessna lightplane. In late 1976 Powers was hired by television station KNBC and sent on a helicopter flying course. He would be piloting the station's heavily-equipped "telecopter" to provide live pictures of fires, police chases, and other newsworthy events in the L.A. area.

On 1 August 1977 Powers and his cameraman were returning to Burbank after covering a brush fire near Santa Barbara when the engine quit. The helicopter crashed onto a sports field in Encino, killing Powers and his passenger. It carried a TV camera and data-link antennas on unweildy external mounts, which may have contributed to Powers' failure to control the machine's unpowered descent. Some suggested that Powers did not have enough helicopter flying experience to cope with such an emergency.

Whatever the case, it seemed an inappropriate end for the man who had cheated death over the Soviet Union. Moreover, there was a sad irony to come when the official accident report on the helicopter crash was released. Having flown 2,000 hours in the U-2, where fuel management was one of a pilot's highest priorities, Powers had allowed the helicopter's fuel tank to run dry! – C.P.

The Russian sources consulted by this author do not suggest that the PVO was pre-alerted that a U-2 would be penetrating their airspace on or just before 1 May 1960. In the final analysis, indeed, the Soviet air defense system should not have needed such a warning. The PVO had been thoroughly "tipped off" three weeks earlier by the previous U-2 overflight. That mission was easily detected and tracked as soon as it crossed the border. When the PVO failed to intercept the intruder all hell was raised by Premier Khrushchev. The PVO's state of readiness was further improved after the 9 April incident. Ironically, the May Day holiday caused it to be somewhat relaxed again, and this evidence counts against the possibility of a specific tip-off.[15] (Incidentally, it has been suggested that the flight was launched on this very day precisely *because* U-2 mission planners hoped to take advantage of just such a relaxation. As we have seen, however, weather conditions and President Eisenhower's deadline were the two crucial factors governing the launch date).

What is certain, is that the Project HQ was well aware that the 9 April flight had been detected and tracked from an early stage by the PVO. That did not stop Bissell and Dulles from recommending another flight. With the considerable benefit of hindsight, we can judge that they were overconfident and made the wrong call. But so did Premier Khrushchev. If he had swallowed his pride and protested the 9 April flight, all the evidence of his previous reluctance to approve U-2 overflights suggests that President Eisenhower would have canceled Operation Grand Slam. And there would have been no "U-2 incident" at all.

12

Aftermath

On 6 May 1960, the news that Frank Powers had been shot down over Sverdlovsk began reverberating around the world. The noise level was deafening, and it would not die down for many months...the abortive summit meeting in Paris was followed by the Senate hearing, then the show trial in Moscow. Moreover, on 1 July 1960 one of SAC's RB-47Hs was shot down by Soviet fighters in the Barents Sea while collecting SIGINT from the Kola peninsula.

The Soviets were turning up the heat on those countries that had hosted U-2 flights, especially Japan, Norway, Pakistan, and Turkey. The Agency's overseas U-2 operation was grounded, with all personnel under strict instructions to say nothing, and to hide their association with the project if possible.

That was not always easy. For instance, after the Soviets paraded Frank Powers in Moscow, his picture was in all the papers and on all the TV news bulletins. At his school's next show-and-tell session, the son of CIA U-2 pilot Barry Baker proudly told classmates and teachers how the captured pilot had played with him during off-duty sessions at Adana, Turkey.[1]

The Air Force was guilty by association, of course, and people in the SAC U-2 wing were pointed out and questioned wherever they went. The 4080th SRW tried to continue as normal. The next phase of the atmospheric sampling program was getting underway, and it was a complicated exercise. For the first time, U-2 sorties from three separate bases (Ezeiza, Laughlin, and Eielson) would be coordinated. Martin JB-57 Canberras would also be sampling at lower levels at the same time. Three U-2As left Laughlin for Ezeiza, Argentina, on 3 May, but were held at Ramey AFB, Puerto Rico, while higher authority debated whether they should continue. Then the Argentines withdrew permission for the SAC planes to operate from Ezeiza.

Someone in Washington decided that it would be a good idea to make the Agency's U-2 personnel at North Base disappear until the fuss died down. The four pilots needed to keep current in the airplane, so they and their support team were packed off in a C-124 to Ramey, where they took over the 4080th birds and flew them from there on the sampling missions. The detachment continued for a few weeks before the aircraft were flown back to Laughlin AFB by SAC pilots. Sampling flights also continued through late May from Eielson AFB with another three aircraft, conducted by OL-5 of the 4080th. By mid-June, though, all the SAC U-2 fleet was back at home base in Texas.

Carriers and drones

Meanwhile, policy-makers mulled options for the future of the U-2 fleet. How could Soviet overflights continue if foreign bases were denied? Should the CIA get out of the U-2 business? At Project HQ, they dusted off the 1957 Lockheed proposal for operating the Article from aircraft carriers. All but the "upper central third" of the USSR could be covered from carrier-launched missions, but qualifying the pilots would be "troublesome and time-consuming." Another scheme was to convert three aircraft to drone configuration—then there would be no pilot to worry about if another U-2 was shot down.[2]

But when he heard of it, Kelly Johnson did not like this drone idea at all. Because of the light stressing of the aircraft and its narrow performance envelope at altitude, he reckoned that several million dollars and 18 months would be needed to develop an unmanned version. Even then, he predicted the loss rate might well be as high as 50%.[3]

There was another way. If the U-2 could be modified to take on fuel inflight, the ferry range could be stretched, and therefore permit quicker deployment from the U.S. to staging bases overseas. The mission could be flown, recovered, and the aircraft be on its way back to the U.S., hopefully without the Soviets (or whoever) even discovering from where it had been launched. This was the "QuickMove" scheme on a global scale. In fact, the

The SAC U-2 wing was based at out-of-the-way Laughlin AFB, Del Rio, Texas. Still, that did not prevent lots of unwelcome attention in the aftermath of the Gary Powers shootdown (Ed Naylor).

author of that scheme, Col Stan Beerli, was now taking over from Bill Burke as Acting Chief of DPD.

Reorganize

On 23 May, Beerli sent his proposal to reorganize Project Chalice to Dick Bissell. The R & D unit at Edwards North Base would become an operational detachment, with three airplanes capable of mounting operations in the Far East as a substitute for Det C. With protesters at the gates of Yokota AB on a daily basis, it was already clear that the Japanese operation would have to close. But Beerli still believed that Det B in Turkey enjoyed "relative immunity to political pressures." So it would continue to operate four U-2C models converted for aerial refueling. All the Agency's aircraft would also be upgraded with the J75 powerplant, as well as the refueling mod.[4]

Project HQ wanted its U-2s ungrounded so that training flights could resume, at least. On 25 May Secretary of State Herter agreed that "local U-2 weather flights" could resume. Hang on, there, said NASA! Its top officials were really uncomfortable at having been dragged into the U-2 affair because of the cover story. They wanted out. The aircraft remained grounded, officially because Lockheed was studying the whole question of their future airworthiness. Jim Cunningham told NASA officials that in future, the Agency might use the Air Weather Service of the Air Force as cover for a reduced U-2 operation.[5]

While the DDP tinkered with the Chalice reorganization plan, DCI Dulles made his appearance before the closed session of the Senate Foreign Relations Committee, to outline just how valuable the U-2 had been. But the President had already declared that he would not authorize any more overflights of the Soviet Union. That move had been designed to placate Premier Khrushchev and keep him at the Summit table in Paris. It had not worked.

While everyone associated with Chalice had been told to avoid the press like the plague, someone in Washington with inside knowledge of the Project was exploiting the media. On 27 June an article entitled "The U-2 Must Fly Again" appeared in U.S. News & World Report. It took the form of an interview with an anonymous source representing—according to the magazine—important groups of officials in the military services and the State Dept. The interviewee declared that the Soviets would gain a

---

IGNOMINIOUS WITHDRAWALS

The worldwide notoriety of the U-2 in the wake of the Powers shootdown meant that an unwelcome spotlight fell on both of the Agency's overseas detachments. Outside Yokota AB, Japanese protesters gathered. The Japanese government formally requested the removal of the aircraft on 8 July. With tension rising, it was decided to dismantle them for departure. But such was the hurry that not even the proper wing and fuselage carts were available in time. Bob Murphy and his Lockheed techreps scrambled to provide make-do alternatives. The day after the request to leave, the Articles were airlifted out by C-124.

The end of Det B was not quite so traumatic. Project HQ directed an orderly withdrawal starting in mid-September 1960. But Washington didn't want the pullout to be seen as under pressure, or resulting from the show trial in Moscow of Frank Powers in mid-August. The folks at Det B were not even supposed to tell their relatives that they were heading home. "There should be no wholesale stampede to dispose of cars or personal possessions on base or in town, less this be a dead giveaway on unit move," they were told. The rundown was slowed when the CIA's Office of Scientific Intelligence (OSI) pleaded to retain the peripheral SIGINT missions using System 7, whenever a missile launch from Tyuratam was predicted. – C.P.

SAMPLING MISSIONS WERE A BORE

We flew those sampling missions from Ramey while HQ was still figuring out what to do with us after Frank was shot down. We were delighted to have any kind of job to do at the time. I flew four times and man, talk about boring: those flights were the living end! After the first couple, we got to thinking of them as kindergarten exercises, so we were real happy when told we could finish and go home!

- Jim Cherbonneaux, pilot, CIA Test Unit, Edwards AFB 1960

A 4080th SRW U-2A in the early 1960s. 66714 was the second of the six "hard-nose" aircraft built specially for the sampling role (NARA KKE 47588).

major military advantage if U-2 flights did not resume. They would be able to build and camouflage their missile sites without detection; nuclear blackmail could follow, perhaps when the Soviets forced a showdown over Berlin. "A reconnaissance satellite is still years away" from replacing the U-2, the interviewee continued, before revealing the plan to launch U-2 missions from U.S. aircraft carriers!

Bissell finally sent the Chalice reorganization plan to the White House in early July. He noted that in addition to the USSR, the U-2 had also flown over the European satellite countries, the Middle East, Indonesia, and China. There was "an urgent and high priority requirement" for more recon of China, plus possible requirements in Southeast Asia and the Caribbean (by which Bissell meant Cuba). The DDP was bold enough to suggest that the President might change his mind about Soviet overflights "if a drastic change should occur in the world situation." Moreover, there would be a new President eight months' hence, who might take a different view.

Bissell argued that an undercover U-2 operation should be preserved. The old premise still held good. In Bissell's words:

"...to ensure that in the event of compromise, the activity would be identified as a form of civilian espionage, rather than an aggressive military act."

Refueling, SSB radio

What about the U-2's vulnerability? "It was unlikely" that Powers' aircraft had been hit by a SAM at cruising altitude, Bissell mistakenly told the White House. Project HQ was still in denial! Just in case, though, future missions would avoid flying over known or suspected SAM sites. Fighter aircraft still could not catch it. Improved electronic countermeasures could possibly be added to the aircraft, and also a pyrophoric ignition system to relight the engine at high altitude. The inflight refueling would not only enhance mobility in ferry flights, it "would permit operational missions to be launched from bases up to 1,500 miles from the point of penetration of the target area." Carrier launch was another option, Bissell noted.

Another improvement would be Single Side-Band (SSB) radio. Although the SAC U-2 fleet was already equipped with an HF radio so that the pilots could communicate during their long, lonely sampling flights across remote wastelands with no UHF or VHF coverage, the system was a rudimentary, fixed-channel affair. This radio had not been fitted to the

Enroute to Australia in October 1960, the Crowflight U-2s stopped in Nandi, Fiji (Bob Spencer).

CIA aircraft at all, for fear that any HF transmission from an overflying U-2 would give away its position to the unfriendlies on the ground below. Frank Powers and the others had therefore been sent out with only a UHF set providing line-of-sight range. When things started going wrong over a thousand miles from friendly territory, Powers had no way of communicating the problem. With very little idea of what had happened to him, the agency issued the pre-rehearsed cover story, thus setting up Uncle Sam for Khrushchev's carefully-staged propaganda coup. The SSB radio could also be used to recall an overflight mission if, for instance, COMINT revealed that the aircraft was being tracked by air defence systems.

Turkey

When Bissell first sent his plan to the White House, he hoped that Det B could continue for at least a few more months. Training flights from Incirlik could be explained as the final phase of the NASA weather research program, he wrote.

But Turkey would never entertain another illegal overflight from there, Bissell admitted, and the Det would eventually have to redeploy. At this time, the Agency apparently hoped that the British might be persuaded to allow the U-2s to be based on Cyprus and/or in the UK. But that hope nosedived after the RB-47 was shot down: it had taken off from an RAF base in Oxfordshire. By mid-July, it had been decided to withdraw most of the assets from Turkey in the near future.

All future Agency U-2 operations would be staged from the Edwards base, with one exception. Plans were moving forward to establish a joint operation with the nationalist Chinese on Taiwan, Bissell now wrote. This would operate two aircraft on overflights of the mainland. But if all of the U-birds were now turned over to the Air Force, it would take three to six months to reconstitute a civilian, or a non-U.S., operation.[6]

If the President had any reservations about Bissell's plan, they are not on record. He approved it. The Agency was still in the U-2 business! In reality, other than turn the whole operation over to SAC, there was no alternative.

Drivers retained

Project HQ began the CHALICE downsizing. DPD's Security Chief wanted to dump all the current U-2 pilots. He argued that they possessed "intimate knowledge" of Agency operations, and should be replaced by a fresh batch of recruits from SAC. In particular, there was "general knowledgeability among the drivers that the Agency is presently engaged on a successor vehicle to the U-2, with a speed of Mach 2.5 to 3."[7] DPD Assistant Chief Jim Cunningham agreed. So much for the dedication and service of these long-serving pilots!

In fact, Stan Beerli rejected the advice, and 10 of the 15 American U-2 pilots were retained. Jim Cherbonneaux, Barry Baker, and Al Rand stayed on at Edwards, to be joined by Jim Barnes, Glen Dunaway, Jake Kratt, and Marty Knutson from Det B, plus Buster Edens, Bob Ericson, and E.K. Jones from Det C. The others returned to the Air Force. But because of their knowledge of covert U-2 operations, none of these five (Tom Birkhead, Tom Crull, Bill McMurry, Lyle Rudd, and John Shinn) were allowed to serve overseas for the next three years.[8]

Coming in the other direction was a new contingent of operations officers and mission planners assigned to DPD by the Air Force. They included Lt Col Bill Gregory, who became commander of the new operational DPD unit at Edwards North Base. The unit's "cover" designation was Weather Reconnaissance Squadron (Provisional) Four (WRSP-4), but within the Project, it was known as Detachment G. The set-up was more or less the same as the previous, overseas Dets. That is, blue-suiters for operations; Agency civilians for administration and in charge of security, and civilian contractors for airframe maintenance (Lockheed), sensor maintenance (Hycon and STL), and life support (Firewel).

Gregory was previously the boss of SAC's RB-57D squadron, which had been deactivated at Laughlin early in 1960. Some of the Agency's old U-2 hands resented the newcomers, who brought with them the circumscribed, triple-regulated world of SAC. There were new ops policies, and new training squares to be filled out. The veterans also complained about the "blame culture," which they saw as another deficiency imported from SAC.[9]

4080th wing, and Myers accident

In deepest Texas, meanwhile, some of the redundant RB-57D pilots and crew chiefs from the 4025th SRS joined the 4028th and checked out on the U-2. The five Chinese pilots from Taiwan, who had been trained by the 4080th one year earlier, returned for a refresher course. The 4080th wing continued to send U-2A models from its 24-strong fleet back to the Skunk Works at Burbank for the IRAN (Inspect and Repair As Necessary) program.

In the early morning of 14 July 1960, 56-6720 crashed about 30 miles northeast of Laughlin during a training flight. Major Raleigh Myers ejected safely from about 24,000ft. The accident refocused attention on the aircraft's escape system, and prompted changes to the oxygen system. This was ironic: part of the cover story issued when Gary Powers had gone down was that he might have had problems with his oxygen system. Now there were some real problems to resolve.

Myers was on a low-medium altitude training flight, and was therefore not wearing the pressure suit and helmet. Instead, he wore a regular flight suit and helmet with oxygen mask attached. The mask contained the pilots' radio-microphone, which was kept on to enable air-ground communication. According to the investigating team's report, the pilot removed his gloves and mask in order to have a cigarette. That was not a smart thing to do, of course. Before lighting up, however, Myers had taken the precaution of turning off both oxygen reducer valves, and depleting the oxygen supply remaining in the mask. Feeling the need to relieve himself, he stubbed out his cigarette on the right canopy rail and took a pee. Reaching for his gloves, he heard a rifle-like crack and saw a flame coming from the left lower console near the reducer valves. Thick smoke spread in seconds as the flames spread along the console. Myers jettisoned the canopy and punched out.

The Accident Board determined that high-pressure oxygen had begun flowing into the cockpit after the pressure-reducing switch failed (ie the sharp noise that Myers heard and, presumably, reported back to base). This had been ignited by the 24-volt power supply line to the switch—and *not* by Myers' cigarette! After the mid-1958 accidents that killed Chapin and Walker, Lockheed and Firewel, the safety system subcontractor, had considered changing the oxygen system, but concluded that this was not feasible.[10]

Now the U-2 program manager Art Bradley promised a rethink. The system was redesigned so that only low-pressure oxygen would be plumbed into the cockpit. The pressure relief valves and reducers were modified and relocated to the Q-bay. The pilot was provided with new, slow-open-

> ### GETTING USED TO "DUAL CONTROL"
> *Lt Col Don Songer was the operations chief at Project Idealist from 1960-1966. He recalled:*
>
> I was summoned to Washington without any explanation and interviewed by Leo Geary and Jim Cunningham. I don't know why they picked me—I was a deputy group commander from Air Defense Command.
>
> I was there six years, and didn't wear my Air Force uniform once during that time! But the "dual control" aspect of Project HQ was difficult to handle at times—the CIA civilians and us from the Air Force. Dick Helms did not like the blue-suit element within OSA—he couldn't control our careers!
>
> I got used to briefing the senior officials. When the first Chinese U-2 went down, DDCI Carter seemed really nervous about telling the White House, so he took me and (Idealist Branch chief) Bill Seward along with him. When we lost one in training off Taiwan, I had to fly all the way to Manila to brief Carter. Later on I briefed Secretary Rusk on proposed missions. He was very informal.
>
> *- interview with author*

ing manual control valves in a new console assembly.[11] After two brief groundings while the accident investigation took place, SAC's U-2s were flying again in early August.

Sampling again

A new base in the southern hemisphere for the Crowflight sampling missions was needed, if Argentina was now off limits. Australia seemed just about as far away from the Gary Powers fuss as possible. In August, the 4080th sent a survey team there, for the prospective new OL-11 at East Sale, Victoria. They received a warm welcome and so, in mid-October, three of the HASP aircraft left Laughlin for the long transpacific journey, piloted by Captains Bob Powell, Bobby Gardiner, and Deke Hall. The deployment via Hickam AFB, Hawaii, Canton Island, and Nandi took 12 days, and was not without incident. On the first leg, Hall had a complete hydraulic failure, and flamed out while still some 1,000 miles from Ha-

Briefing for a SAC U-2 mission out of Eielson AFB in the early 1960s. The 4080th SRW flew long sampling and SIGINT flights from Alaska, often in complete darkness (via Tony Bevacqua).

It is often said that the American public never got the opportunity to inspect a real, live U-2 until after Gary Powers was shot down. Not so!

But the first public display on the U.S. mainland was not until 1 November 1960, when a SAC U-2A was put on display at the Patrick AFB, FL, open house. The event coincided with a briefing of the National War College, given by Major Pat Halloran of the 4080th SW.

Australians got a good look at the U-2 when the SAC aircraft currently deployed to East Sale for Operation Crowflight was displayed at the base open house on 14 May 1961—one was renamed "City of Sale" in honour of the occasion. Six days later, a base open day was held back home at Laughlin, with a 4080th U-2 forming part of the static display for the very first time –C.P.

FLYING ALONG THE SOVIET BORDER – AT NIGHT

Major Jerry McIlmoyle was a U-2 pilot with the 4080th wing from 1959 to 1964. He recalls the long and difficult SIGINT missions along the Soviet northern borders:

During the photo series in 1959, Dick Leavitt had strayed off course and flown over Petropavlovsk. After that, SAC introduced the new training criteria that we must stay within 15 miles of the flight line for 85% of the time. On training flights, they checked our proficiency at navigation by wiring the radio compass to the local station before takeoff, and plotting us on radar through a two-hour flight over the Gulf of Mexico.

If we passed this test, we were qualified for the deployments. I did some of those night time SIGINT flights along the Soviet border out of Alaska. We were looking for gaps in their early-warning radars. They had to keep them turned on because the U-2 was such a tricky target.

We flew them in winter using celestial navigation, since it was dark nearly all of the time. We stayed 15 miles off the coast, which the U.S. recognized as international airspace. I think the Soviets took a different view. There were two routes, one going nearly all the way to Novaya Zemlya and back. If the engine quit on that one, you were dead! The other one went south through Shemya and their ICBM impact area, then home to Eielson via a circle.

The RB-47 flew below us at the same time, and our flight tracks would cross occasionally. We would coordinate via HF radio calls, and they would pass on any threats to us.

- interview with author

waii. He managed to get a relight and pressed on at lower altitude. This burned more fuel, and the tanks ran dry 35 miles short of the Hickam runway. Hall still made it to a deadstick landing there, guided through an overcast by a T-33 scrambled from the base.

The Aussies were good hosts, but more than curious about the now-notorious "spyplane." A huge crowd of press and onlookers greeted the arrival of the silver birds on 25 October. Commanded by Lt Col Kenneth McAslin, OL-11 was soon in action. The sampling corridor ran from 40 to 45 degrees South latitude, along the 147 degrees 30 minutes line of longitude. The U-2s were joined by four JB-57s from ARDC, which sampled below them at 40,000 feet. As usual, two SC-54s stood by for rescue missions. The entire deployment lasted two months and involved 180 men and 12 C-124 transports to move them and the support gear. This new phase of Crowflight also involved coordinated U-2 and JB-57 sampling over the U.S. from 30 to 35 degrees North. The U-2s flew out of home base at Laughlin, although organized as the separate OL-10.[12]

Ike sees the U-2

On 24 October 1960, in a hangar at Laughlin AFB, President Eisenhower finally came face to face with the spyplane that had caused him so much trouble in the previous few months. He had flown into the base en route for a meeting with the Mexican President, which took place on the bridge linking Del Rio with Cuidad Acuna. There they signed the initial agreements authorizing construction of a huge dam across the Rio Grande, which would provide irrigation control in the lower river and create a 67,000-acre lake in the canyons to the north of the twin border towns. Returning from the bridge to Laughlin by helicopter, Ike and his senior aides were ushered through the 4080th facilities by Col William Wilcox, who had taken over from Col Bratton as wing commander three months earlier. The accompanying party of pressmen was left outside on the deserted flightline—all the U-2s had been hidden from view.

Publicly, sampling and weather research were still the only missions assigned to the 4080th. At a classified level, of course, the wing trained to perform photo-recon missions, and used the B-camera operationally during the Congo Maiden sorties along the Far East borders of the Soviet Union in spring 1959 and 1960.[13] Now, the wing finally got orders to exercise two other sensors on real operations.

A new deployment in the Toy Soldier series to OL-5 at Eielson AFB, Alaska, began on 1 November. Similar to the five previous deployments, it consisted of three U-2As equipped for gas, as well as particle sampling, with the P-2/F-2 system. But a few days later, Major Rudy Anderson flew another aircraft to Alaska, equipped with the big System IV ELINT package and the APQ-56 side-looking radar.

Three long peripheral missions codenamed Venice Lake were then flown, all at night; two of them down the Kamchatka Peninsula, and the third along the northern border. They were planned by OL-5's navigator, Ed Schug, and flown by Anderson and Jim Black. At least one of the missions was coordinated with an RB-47 of SAC's 55th SRW, which could pick up more ELINT at a lower flight level. Unlike the 55th boys, however, the U-2 pilots did not have navigators onboard to help them keep their distance from denied territory!

The JRC and the NSC

Such flights were now more politically sensitive than ever after the U-2 and RB-47 shootdowns. To achieve greater control, President Eisenhower instructed the Joint Chiefs to establish a system to coordinate, justify, and control all U.S. reconnaissance activities. The result was the Joint Reconnaissance Center (JRC), which was established in the Pentagon in late 1960. Knowledgeable personnel from the Air Force, Army, Navy, and Marine Corps were joined by reps from the CIA, NSA, and State Dept. The head of the JRC throughout the 1960s was Colonel (later General) Doug Steakley. The JRC produced a monthly worldwide schedule of all proposed missions in a bound folder nicknamed "The Book." This was forwarded for political approval to a committee of the National Security Council (NSC). If your mission wasn't in The Book it did not get approved.

The NSC committee was known first as the 5412 Committee, and later as the Special Group. All covert actions, not just reconnaissance flights, were supposed to be approved by this body. It usually consisted of the President's National Security advisor, his Military Advisor, the Deputy Secretary of Defense, the Deputy Secretary of State, the DCI, and sometimes the Attorney General. These high officials received The Book and usually approved it by telephone. Sometimes, though, they met to discuss particularly sensitive missions. The really "hot" ones were briefed to the President for his approval. From now on, most operational U-2 missions required approval via this committee. SAC sent its requests to the JRC via the Strategic Reconnaissance Center in Omaha, while the CIA dealt direct.[14]

Cuba covert action

In January 1960 the U.S. government resolved in secret to overthrow the Communist regime of Fidel Castro in Cuba. As DDP, Richard Bissell was directly in charge of the covert action plan. The main responsibility for selecting, training, and equipping the guerrilla force of Cuban exiles that would "liberate" their country was given to the Western Hemisphere 4 section of DDP, the agency's covert action and espionage organization.

But the air support of covert action was a responsibility of DPD, headed by Col Stan Beerli. He would be responsible for organizing the guerrilla's air force of B-26 bombers.

Naturally enough, Beerli also proposed using the U-2s under his control to support the plan. They could provide complete aerial photographic coverage of Cuba to discover the regime's air and ground order of battle, and to identify suitable landing zones for the guerrillas. In late September 1960, the new Det G at Edwards North Base was certified ready for action. To mark the milestone, the cryptonym for the Agency's U-2 program was changed shortly thereafter from Chalice to Idealist. And the appropriate codename Kick Off was given to Det G's first mission—covert overflights of Cuba.

It was decided to stage these out of Laughlin AFB, which was just within launch-and-recover range of a U-2 equipped with the slipper tanks. The 4080th wing could provide appropriate support, but SAC would not be involved in the planning or execution of the missions. The wing's liaison officer was not even supposed to know the purpose of the deployment! Everyone at Del Rio not directly involved in supporting the Agency detachment was supposed to turn a "blind eye" to the arrival of a U-2 contingent from the "dark side."

To facilitate this, the operation would be conducted using the "Quickmove" concept, from a remote apron at the southeast end of the Texan base. The Agency's own C-54 would serve as a support aircraft, and the pilot plus his backup would suit up and pre-breathe inside it, rather than in the 4080th's PSD facility. After the mission, the film would not be unloaded and processed by the 4080th photo shop. Instead, it would remain on the Article for the ferry flight back to Edwards. There, the B-camera "take" would be unloaded, put on the C-54, and transported to Eastman Kodak at Rochester, just like the old pre-May Day overflight days.

No Agency operation would be complete without a cover story, of course, but by now "weather research for NASA" was out! Instead, a new one was worked out with Kelly Johnson's cooperation. The plane and pilot were supposed to be under Lockheed's control, and on a ferry mission

SAC coordinated the SIGINT flights along the Soviet border in Siberia, so that an RB-47H with its more sophisticated equipment could record air defense reactions to the high-flying U-2 (NARA KKE 26323).

STRIPPING THE BLACK LADY

In 1960 SACs U-2s were still unpainted, and looked so smart in that polished metal finish. But the CIA's aircraft were painted very dark blue, in an attempt to make them less easy to spot at high altitude from an intercepting fighter. The trouble was, in the wake of the Powers shootdown, the Press had taken to describing the U-2 as "The Black Lady of Espionage." So when the CIA's continuing use of the U-2 on covert overflights was approved, this posed a problem. "In the public mind at least, the blue-black color has a direct relationship to the U-2s that have been used for the spy flights," DPD chief Stan Beerli told Dick Bissell. "The unpainted aircraft suggests that a different and innocent use is being made of the U-2," he surmised. For a while, apparently, a few Agency airplanes were stripped of their "sinister" dark coat. That was fine, as long as the denied territory over which they flew—Cuba, Vietnam—was not defended by jet interceptors. But the "public relations" argument probably wore thin when Cuba starting getting MiGs. Soon, the blue-black paint was back. At about the same time, SAC decided to paint its aircraft gray, to prevent corrosion. -C.P.

from Burbank to Ramey AFB, Puerto Rico. A large civilian registration in the N3xxX series was painted on the U-2's tail. In fact, the danger of detection and interception was virtually nil. The Cubans were not known to have any early warning or GCI radar, and their air force consisted of World War II vintage P-47s and P-51s.[15]

Kick Off and Green Eyes

Operation Kick Off was not a great success. First, it had to be delayed until the President's visit to Del Rio was over (see above). The U-2C with slipper tanks sneaked into Laughlin after dark the next day, preceded by the C-54. The first mission on 26 October had to be aborted when a warning light illuminated well into the flight. The next day, cloud obscured much of the island by the time the U-2 arrived overhead, three hours after leaving Laughlin.

So the exercise was repeated a month later, as Operation Green Eyes. This fared better, with two successful missions on 27 November and 11 December. In between, though, there were failures on 4 and 5 December when missions had to be aborted due to heavy and persistent contrails. Det G commander Bill Gregory recorded his pleasure with "the initiative and aggressiveness displayed by the Drivers in getting the sorties off under very adverse weather conditions locally."[16] The covert action planners now had "baseline" imagery of most of Cuba.

Between these two Cuban operations, Det G was also tasked with sampling, for the first and only time. From 9-28 November, it deployed to Hawaii with two U-2A models that were hurriedly removed by Lockheed from temporary store. SAC's U-2s were sampling further north and south at the same time (from Alaska and Australia). The CIA pilots flew 1,000 miles south from Hickam to Christmas Island.[17]

For the second time in weeks, though, Hickam-based aircraft had to guide a stricken U-2 into Hawaii. Returning to Hawaii at night and in bad weather, Det G pilot Glen Dunaway had a complete electrical failure. Two F-86D fighter interceptors were launched to assist, but it wasn't until they fired their interceptor rockets that Dunaway spotted them and turned onto the correct track for home.

A U-2C from Project Idealist in the early 1960s. After the May Day shootdown destroyed the cover story of weather research, the CIA turned to Lockheed for help. When flights over Cuba started in October 1960, the aircraft acquired "civilian" registrations to support the new story. (Lockheed LCA 88-2)

By the end of 1960, the Agency's U-2s were flying over "denied territory" again, first Cuba, then southeast Asia. (Lockheed LCA 88-9)

Det B dead

Over in Turkey, Det B was dead but not yet buried. The British government had decided to stay in the U-2 project, and two new RAF pilots had been selected for training. But no permission to move the Det to a new home on British soil had yet been received. The Agency decided to keep one aircraft at Incirlik pending a final decision. It was costing upwards of $150,000 to keep a support team there, including contractors. There had not been a single flight since the Powers shootdown.[18]

By the autumn of 1960, DPD had a new focus for U-2 operations. In mid-November, the White House approved the joint U-2 operation on Taiwan, and preparations to deploy two aircraft, contractors, and a permanent staff were in full swing.[19] Meanwhile, a minor crisis was developing in southeast Asia, as pro-communist forces threatened to take control in Laos. The JCS pressed for reconnaissance flights over that country, North Vietnam DPD, and southern China. The CIA offered the U-2, and in mid-December DPD quickly planned the deployment of two U-2s across the Pacific to Cubi Point, Philippines. For most of the folks at Det G, Christmas was canceled.

13

The Black Cat Squadron

It was a quiet night in early August 1959, and the two remaining workers at the Montezuma County Airport just outside Cortez, Colorado, were preparing to lock up and go home. It was past 11 pm, and all the Cessna and Piper lightplane owners and mechanics had gone home hours ago. Suddenly, there was an urgent knocking at the door. The airport manager and radio operator went to investigate. They found what seemed like a creature from outer space standing there!

Upon closer investigation, the creature appeared to be a pilot, but he was dressed in very unfamiliar gear. Underneath a drab coverall with various zips and toggles attached, he was wearing something that severely restricted his movements. His face was mostly hidden by a large helmet, but he seemed to be of Oriental descent. He was pointing to the darkened airstrip, and kept repeating the words "Come quick! Bring gun! Maximum Security!" at the confounded guard. He did not appear to know much English.

The pilot was Major Mike Hua Hsi Chun[1] from the Republic of China Air Force (CAF) on nationalist Taiwan. The garb which was causing him so much difficulty was his tight-fitting pressure suit. The USAF was teaching him to fly the U-2 at Laughlin AFB, prior to the start of an ambitious program during which the high-flying spyplane would be sent deep into mainland communist China to gather vital information on Peking's military progress. In common with five of his compatriots now being checked out by Air Force instructors at Laughlin AFB, Hua did have a basic command of English. But in the stress of the occasion—an emergency deadstick landing following a flameout at high altitude—Hua forgot nearly all that he had learned of the foreign language.

Word of the strange happening at Montezuma County Airport inevitably leaked out. But the two airport officials and other locals who came into contact with the Chinese pilot that night were told to keep their mouths shut by the posse of serious-looking security men who descended upon the place. In Texas, the 4080th wing commander, Col Andrew Bratton, was authorized to issue a brief statement describing the incident, but it was hoped that the secret of the proposed U-2 flights from Taiwan could be maintained.

Partnership

The USAF had gone into partnership with the Chinese Air Force for high-altitude reconnaissance in 1957, when six pilots were trained to fly a specially stripped-down version of the RB-57A. They subsequently flew four missions over mainland China before one of the aircraft was shot down by communist fighters. The CAF was then provided with two long-winged RB-57Ds, with a ceiling of 65,000 feet—hopefully safe from interception. Three pilots were trained by the 4080th wing prior to the aircraft leaving for Taiwan in September 1958.[2] Air Force officers from PACAF led by Col Phil Robertson helped the CAF to develop an operational capability in the D-model.[3]

But by the time of the first CAF RB-57D mission over mainland China in January 1959, the U.S. Joint Chiefs of Staff had already proposed that SAC train some nationalist Chinese pilots on the U-2.[4] At Laughlin, the codename Carbon Copy was assigned to the task, and Major Joe Jackson was appointed as project officer. In April 1959, Jackson traveled to Taiwan

Major Mike Hua Hsi Chun was on only his seventh flight in the U-2 when his engine quit over the Rockies, and he deadsticked into a small local airport (Mike Hua).

and returned with six pilots selected by the CAF. After passing ground school and chamber training, the Chinese group was surprised to be told that they were going to fly the U-2. They thought they were following their earlier colleagues into RB-57D training![5]

These first six Chinese U-2 pilots were carefully selected. Mike Hua and "Tiger" Wang had combat experience in fighters during the Taiwan Straits Crisis. "Gimo" Yang and Chen Huai had flown recce versions of the early jet fighters on dangerous overflights of the mainland, dicing with the PLAAF's interceptors. Still, they had a tough time adjusting to the rigors of U-2 flight training, and the secrecy surrounding their presence at the remote training base outside Del Rio. "There was no handbook or flight manual, and our handwritten notes could not leave the classroom. There was no two-seater U-2, so every pilot's first flight was solo," Mike Hua recalled.

One of the first group did not make it past first flight. Worried about the strict instruction to get the nose up immediately after takeoff to avoid exceeding the speed limit, Capt Hsu Chung Kuei pulled the yoke too early and sank back onto the runway. He was washed out and transferred to F-100 training at Nellis AFB.[6]

Hua's deadstick

But the other five progressed. Hua's deadstick landing came on his seventh flight, a five-hour nighttime celestial training sortie to northern Utah and back on 3 August 1959. It was an epic save. Hua was at 70,000 feet above the Rocky Mountains when the engine quit. Between 35,000 feet and 17,000 feet, Hua made four unsuccessful attempts to restart. Unknown to the pilot, the servo fuel pressure sensing line had failed due to inflight vibration, dumping fuel overboard instead of feeding the engine.

Hua could see a solid undercast beneath him at 14,000 feet. Just below that, he knew, were the highest tips of the Rockies. His desperate May Day calls went unanswered. Then he saw a hole in the overcast and spiraled down through it. Fortunately, he saw the lights of Cortez and spotted the airport's rotating beacon. To stretch the glide, he retracted the landing gear and speedbrakes until he was on finals. Apparently, the gear did not have time to fully re-extend, and although Hua touched down smoothly, the big wheel collapsed beneath him, and he slid off the runway into a ground loop. But he was down, and safe, and U-2A 66721 was still in one

DEADSTICKING INTO THE ROCKIES

Thirty years after the event, Mike Hua recalled his fantastic save of a crippled U-2 on only his seventh training flight. After four unsuccessful attempts to relight, Hua was drifting slowly but surely into the cloud-covered Rocky Mountains, at night:

What should I do? Bail out? Under normal circumstances, that would be the proper decision. But I was unable to see what kind of terrain stretched below. My prospects for surviving a bailout over rough, remote terrain were low at best.

God Almighty, I reckoned, would be the only one to save me now. So I prayed. I prayed aloud.

Suddenly, I was astonished at what I saw: lights on the ground at the eleven o'clock position. I had come out of the clouds to find that I was clipping along through a narrow valley, flying between tall mountains.

I headed towards the lights. Gradually, I discerned alternating white and blue flashes, which I took to be a rotating beacon that normally identified an airfield. The altimeter showed the U-2 to be at about 7,000 feet. Bereft of information about the true elevation of the surrounding terrain, however, I had no way of knowing the actual altitude of the plane above the ground.

As I drew nearer, I saw some runway lights. How wonderful was that vision!

Though this incident had a fortuitous ending, it was for me a solemn lesson about life. I do not believe that it was mere luck that brought me through the difficult moments. Think of the coincidences: the U-2 breaks out of clouds in a valley, flying in the proper direction; within this valley lies the Cortez airfield, with no others around for 100 miles; the Cortez city council, against its better judgement, decides to leave the airfield lights on at night; and I had just the right altitude—no more, no less—required to land on such a short runway. For me, the conclusion to be drawn from all these "coincidences" is inescapable. My prayer was answered.

- extracted from "A Miracle at Cortez,"
Air Force Magazine, August 1989

Hua's U-2 as it came to rest, minus the landing gear, but otherwise undamaged (Mike Hua).

The U-2 program should be reactivated. There are other assignments which have nothing to do with Russia. When we next take a look at what the Red Army is doing, it will be by a scanning satellite. Peking is growling more menacingly than Moscow. We haven't any pledge to lay off Red Chinese airspace. We should resume casing the place. We should make it our business to see whether the Soviets are giving Mao the missiles and atomic weapons he probably is demanding. We'd also be off our trolley if we didn't put that eye-in-the-sky on comrade Castro every day or two.

- by Bob Considine

piece. The aircraft was dismantled and flown back to Texas in a C-124. Col Bratton recommended Hua for the Distinguished Flying Cross.[7]

Hua and the four remaining Chinese pilots completed their U-2 training at Laughlin AFB and returned to Taiwan in September 1959. But the SAC plan to deploy U-2s to Taiwan for them to fly over the mainland did not proceed. Politicking in Washington saw to that.

CIA takeover

On 8 July 1959, DPD Acting Chief Col Bill Burke wrote to the DDCI, General Cabell, suggesting a CIA takeover of the proposed Chinese overflights. "There are logical reasons for using CIA cover, security, equipment, organization, and management," he argued. Det C was already in place with U-2s in the Far East. The CAF pilots could be assigned to this unit, and training and operational missions could be flown by staging deployments from Japan to Taiwan. The USAF would have to develop a separate cover story for a SAC-controlled U-2 detachment on Taiwan. "CIA is in a better position than USAF to accomplish the desired overflights in a secure and clandestine manner," Burke concluded.[8]

DDP Richard Bissell agreed with him, but cautioned that "a softening up process" would first be required. "I am reluctant at this stage to request the DDCI to go to the Air Force and propose to them a transfer of responsibility that they will undoubtedly regard as grasping on our part," he told Burke. Bissell asked the DPD chief for his suggestions on how to approach selected Air Force officers in the Pentagon who would not be hostile to a CIA takeover of Chinese overflight missions.[9]

RB-57D shot down

While the CIA was working out its takeover strategy, events in the Far East intervened. There were tensions between the U.S. and Chiang Kai-Shek's nationalist government over the approval of reconnaissance missions, and the tactics to be employed. RB-57D flights from over the mainland were halted. Five days after they resumed on 2 October 1959, an RB-57D was shot down near Peking. Meanwhile, Det C had gained some unwelcome publicity when Tom Crull deadsticked Article 360 into a small commercial airfield in Japan. The CAF's newly-trained U-2 pilots were ordered to re-

port to their old squadrons, and heard nothing more about the project for many months.[10]

But the CIA eventually did upstage the Air Force and gain control of the potential U-2 overflights. It was decided to set up a separate detachment on Taiwan after all. In the spring of 1960, new DDCI Marshall Carter led a large group from Washington to Taipei, for talks with senior ROC defense officials on the proposal. Taipei CIA station chief Ray Cline was on very good terms with the nationalist leaders, especially Chiang Ching-Kuo, the son of the President and the de facto head of Taiwan's National Security Bureau. Cline made sure that the Generalissimo himself was briefed. The elder Chiang was shown U-2 photographs of Lhasa, the Tibetan capital, taken on one of Det C's overflight missions. He was very impressed.[11]

The group surveyed the large airbase near Taichung, named for the President's son, where USAF squadrons operated. But they preferred Taoyuan airbase as an operating location for the U-2. It was closer to Taipei, more secure, and had a photo laboratory. The CAF's 4th Squadron was based here, flying RF-101s on low-level missions along and over the mainland coast. It had also flown the RB-57s loaned from the USAF, though the remaining RB-57D was now grounded. The group from Washington recommended an upgrade to the photo lab, and also to the old wooden hangar that they selected to house the U-2s.[12]

In June 1960, the five Chinese U-2 pilots returned to Laughlin AFB for refresher training: four rides with an IP in the T-33, followed by three short and six long U-2 flights. They were soon ready for action. But in the aftermath of the May Day incident, the U-2 was a hot topic in Washington. The question marks over the entire CIA U-2 operation were large. The issue was not resolved for many months.

Ray Cline

From Taipei, meanwhile, Ray Cline lobbied for a decision. "I found that no one disagreed with me about the usefulness of a major reconnaissance program for taking a look in particular at the nuclear weapons and guided missile test sites that the Soviet Union might have in the PRC," he recalled. "One the other hand, there was a widespread reluctance to tackle the ticklish and controversial subject of U-2 overflights."[13]

The nationalists in Taiwan were keen to get the U-2 off the ground, of course. They had been overflying the mainland ever since their defeat by the communists and exile to the offshore island in 1948. The two sides were still technically at war, and Chiang Kai-Shek (CKS) still vowed to reclaim the lost territory. The CAF's 34th Squadron based at Hsinchu inserted and recovered intelligence agents, dropped propaganda leaflets, and flew reconnaissance missions. It was a joint operation with the CIA, just as the new U-2 operation would be. The U.S. supported the political aims of CKS, but was ambiguous about supporting actual paramilitary forays to the mainland by Kuomintang forces. The CIA leaned towards supporting these, unlike the State Department and the White House.

General I Fu-En was the head of intelligence in CAF Headquarters. He created a "Weather Research and Analysis" group as a local disguise for the new operation, and nominated his deputy Gen Huang Wei-King to make detailed arrangements. Col Lu Si Liang was appointed commander of the 35th Squadron, which would fly the U-2s. Lu already knew the high-altitude recon business, having previously commanded the 4th Squadron and its RB-57Ds.

Project Tackle

In Washington, once it became clear that the CIA was still in the U-2 business, planning for the new Detachment H on Taiwan resumed. The cryptonym Tackle was assigned, although the agreement that was drawn up and signed with the ROC referred to the joint U-2 operation as Project Razor. Two of the U-2C aircraft languishing in Turkey were dismantled and airlifted back to Burbank, where they were prepared for the new operation. A cover story was prepared, to the effect that two U-2s had been "sold" to Taiwan by Lockheed, which would support the aircraft in the field.

And indeed, Lockheed was contracted to maintain the aircraft at Det H. In some respects, the new outfit was organized along similar lines to the CIA's previous U-2 detachments. Tech reps were also recruited for Taiwan by the other key U-2 contractors: Pratt & Whitney, Hycon, Ramo Wooldridge, and Firewel. The CIA provided communications, finance, and security specialists. A USAF officer was nominated as detachment commander, with other blue-suiters filling slots in operations, mission planning, materiel, and maintenance control.

But since they weren't supposed to be there, these Air Force officers had to assume a civilian identity complete with "cover" names, just like CIA agents stationed overseas. Together with the contractors, they were officially listed as foreign technical employees of the Chinese Air Force. Lt Col Denny Posten became the first "manager" of Det H, with the cover name of Danny Perling. He led the advance party to Taiwan in October 1960, after which work accelerated on the hangar, the photo lab, and a hostel for the American contingent.

From the Chinese side came the squadron commander, Col Lu. "Gimo" Yang was his deputy, and one of the five operational pilots. The CAF also provided an operations chief (Lt Col Jude Pao Bin Kang), a mission planner, a flight surgeon, two personal equipment technicians, a weather forecaster, and others for supply, transport, and security.[14]

White House approved

On 15 November 1960, the White House approved the activation of Detachment H. The American personnel assembled at Edwards prior to their transpacific journey.[15] Bob Ericson was assigned to the joint operation as a test and instructor pilot, and a U-2C was dismantled for airlift to Taiwan by C-133. There was a hiccup when the big transport landed at the downtown Taipei airport instead of Taoyuan. According to the pilot's calculations, the runway at Taoyuan wasn't strong enough to bear the C-133's weight. Fuel was offloaded, and the C-133 made the short hop to the intended destination.[16]

The aircraft was reassembled. Nationalist insignia—a big 12-point star—and tail numbers were applied. Bob Ericson made functional check flights and began converting the Chinese pilots to the C model. (All of their previous experience had been on SAC's lower-powered U-2A version). All the training flights were routed east from Taoyuan and kept below 40,000 feet until passing Taiwan's east coast—to avoid any possibility of radar detection by the mainland, less than 100 miles away from the CAF airbase.[17]

One of the pilots (Chen) designed and submitted proposed insignia for the new squadron. A fierce tiger and a cunning wolf were rejected in favor of a black cat on a red background. The American side apparently liked the double meaning of this Chinese "pussy."[18] Det H, aka the CAF 35 Squadron, aka the Black Cat Squadron, was declared operational by the end of January, even before the unit's second aircraft arrived. Unlike the first, it was flown from the U.S., via Midway.

But getting U.S. political approval for mainland overflights was another big hurdle yet to be overcome. In early February 1961, DPD prepared a briefing that DDCI General Cabell would make to the President. It emphasized the importance of Chinese Communist targets, and stressed that command and control rested securely on the U.S. side, despite the "joint" nature of the project.[19]

The DDCI got no further than Foggy Bottom. Senior officials at the State Dept were very protective of the new President, who was "feeling his way on the international scene," they told Cabell. In any case, the State Dept was not one of Chiang Kai-Shek's greatest fans. The DDCI was obliged to agree that there were other intelligence-gathering projects with higher priority. Under Secretary of State Chester Bowles said that approval for Idealist/Tackle missions should be put off for three to four months.[20]

The first group of U-2 pilots from the Chinese Air Force in a formal pose. From left to right: Mike Hua, Tiger Wang, Gimo Yang, Chi Yao Hua, and Chen Huai.
Major Yang made the longest-lasting impression on the Americans at Taoyuan. He was a colourful character who had already diced with communist fighters on many reconnaissance missions over the mainland. He had flown P-51s, B-25s, F-84s, F-86s and the RF-100. When he later moved up to take charge of the Black Cat squadron, he became known as "Gimo"—short for Generalissimo, after Chiang Kai-Shek, the famous leader of the nationalists in exile. Colonel Chen, like Yang, had survived previous tangles with the Chicom air defence system, when flying RF-84Fs. A devout Christian, upon his safe return from the first CIA/CAF U-2 overflight of mainland China, he declared "Almighty God gave me the vision to see the vastness of China!" After Chen was shot down and killed on 9 September 1962, he became a national hero on Taiwan.

WHAT'S IN A NAME?

At the Black Cat Squadron on Taiwan, the Americans found it tough getting their heads and tongues around the Chinese names. But spare a thought for the Chinese, who had to cope with the CIA's unrelenting secrecy, including the use of false surnames for "cover" by the American contingent:

Everybody there had trouble getting used to the dual names, so we just used first names. In the beginning, I wasn't careful and called some of the Americans by their true name. I had already worked with three of them before during the RB-57D program.

Day and night, soldiers from the Presidential Guard stood watch at the hangar. Without a special access badge no one was allowed in.

There must be secrecy. Every time that (operations officer) Pao and I talked about China mission plans, we needed to be careful that none of the pilots was nearby. I think the Americans were right about this. If shot down and captured, maybe the communists would make pilots tell a lot of secrets.

Every time something came up in the U-2 program, I had to deal with the high-level people around Chiang Ching Kuo. Everything surrounding the 35th Squadron was very hush-hush and had high priority. It made a lot of people nervous.

- Col Lu Si Liang, from his book "Piercing The Bamboo Curtain," with Liu Wen Shiao

THE AMERICAN PILOT AT TAOYUAN

The Agency always assigned one American U-2 pilot to the Black Cat Squadron. He made sure the Chinese pilots were up to speed, performed functional test flights, and stood by for operational missions—usually to southeast Asia. Bob Ericson pulled that duty for the first 18 months. Thereafter it was done on a rotational basis. Marty Knutson recalls:

I pulled the first 60-day TDY to Taiwan. Our role was to give the Chinese pilots confidence that they could do the mission. There was lots of socializing, and the American pilots always had a place of honor at the dinner table. I met Chiang Ching Kuo numerous times.

Amongst the Chinese pilots, Gimo Yang was the most extroverted. Tiger Wang was the most methodical. But we had our moments. They were good flyers, but if anything abnormal occurred, they could get into trouble. One time, a Chinese pilot on a training flight called in with an emergency—a high EGT reading. I told him not to shut off the engine yet, but he did. "Dash One say so!" he said. Now we did have an emergency! He was gliding towards Taichung, and his radio faded out as the battery failed. We fired up a T-33 and took off for Taichung. I was in the back seat. We entered solid cloud at 300 feet. I looked at the ADI. We were going upside down! I grabbed the controls and rolled the right way up. Halfway through the maneuver, we broke cloud at 100 feet!

- interview with author

Chih crash

On 19 March, Chih Yao Hua returned from a night celestial nav training sortie to practice a touch-and-go at Taoyuan. After a good approach and touchdown, he applied power but somehow lost control. The aircraft veered to the left, crashed, and exploded. Rescue teams rushed to the site, but could do nothing to save the pilot. Although there was nothing in the Razor agreement, the CIA decided to pay death benefits to Chih's family.[21]

The four remaining Chinese pilots continued training flights, though the crashed aircraft was not replaced, pending a decision from Washington on whether to proceed with operational missions. The matter was discussed in the White House in early July, when Ray Cline visited from Taipei and saw McGeorge Bundy, JFK's special assistant for National Security. Still, though, no decision was reached.[22]

The State Dept then suggested that some other aircraft be used to satisfy the recon requirement over mainland China. Anything but that "Black Lady of Espionage!" DPD chief Stan Beerli consulted with various Air Force Colonels at the JRC. They discussed the RF-101 (already being used by the CAF for low-altitude penetrations) and the RB-57D (withdrawn from Taiwan after the 1959 shootdown). All were agreed that the U-2 was the obvious choice, and told the State Dept. so a few days later.[23]

At DPD they were very frustrated. "TACKLE has been on the Special Group agenda and discussed 12 times since January this year," wrote Stan Beerli. "Each time, considerations interposed by (the State Dept) or general political events have precluded a go-ahead." In fact, U.S.-ROC relations were going through a bad patch. Chiang Kai Shek canceled a planned visit to the U.S. by his son, Chiang Ching Kuo.[24]

The Generalissimo

CCK had already been a visitor to the Black Cat Squadron, accompanied by his friend Ray Cline and Gen I Fu En. On 9 November 1961, the Generalissimo himself made an inspection of the U-2 Squadron. Chiang Kai Shek and his party spent 30 minutes touring the hangar and workshops, and watched a brief but spectacular U-2 flight demonstration by Lt Col Chen. The visit was a welcome morale boost for the unit.

The Presidential visit coincided with the departure of Denny Posten after his one-year tour as the American "manager" of Det H. His replacement, Lt Col Bob Tomlinson, was very impressed with the unit's proficiency. "I am convinced that the (Chinese pilots) are operationally ready and capable of performing any assigned mission," he told Project HQ. His only reservation was the pilots' reluctance to use the feeding tubes on long flights.[25]

The nationalists were getting restive. On his annual visit to Washington in early December, ROC Defense Minister Yu Ta Wei apparently argued for use of the U-2. Ray Cline flew to Washington to make the case for Chinese overflights in person. "The CIA let me run interference, with the clear understanding that if a U-2 were shot down, it would be my responsibility rather than anyone else's," he recalled. (In early September, photo-interpreters studying film from the latest CORONA satellite mission had discovered surface-to-air missile sites in China for the first time. In fact, the PRC had received five battalions of SA-2 systems from the Soviet Union in late 1958, well before the Sino-Soviet split. U.S. intelligence did not know they were there, or that these missiles—and not a fighter—had shot down the RB-57D).

Cline talked to the National Security Council, and again to Bundy. He argued that the SA-2s were few and far between. The U.S. needed precise information on China's advanced weapons programs in the remote northwest, and probably had a few years of impunity in which to fly the U-2s. The nationalists on Taiwan were delighted to take full responsibility for any incident, he assured them. Then the CIA man was ushered in to see JFK himself. "To my surprise, President Kennedy seemed to have none of the reservations that nearly everybody else had with regard to this subject. It was a piece of cake getting his approval," Cline wrote.[26]

GRC-100

That was it, then. On 5 January 1962, the Special Group reviewed tracks for the first three proposed overflights, and approved one of them. It was transmitted to Det H, and from there to CCK's office for ROC approval. On 13 January, Lt Col. Chen soared into the stratosphere at the start of mission GRC-100.

By now, the U.S. was aware that relations between the two great communist powers were very strained. But what effect was the Sino-Soviet split having on China's budding strategic weapons programs? It was clear that the PRC was intent on pressing ahead with plans to acquire the bomb, despite propaganda statements to the contrary. Even before the rift with Moscow, Peking had laid plans for self-sufficiency in nuclear weapons production, and in the means to deliver them, namely ballistic missiles. In 1958, the Soviets had commissioned an experimental heavy water reactor for the Chinese at the Institute of Atomic Energy near Peking, having previously supplied a chemical separation plant capable of producing weapons-grade uranium-235 and plutonium. This plant had been set up for the two countries' joint use in the remote Sinkiang autonomous region, where radioactive ore products were to be found. Building on this base, the Chinese used Soviet blueprints to construct their own small research reactor at the Peking Institute, fueled by enriched uranium-238 supplied by the Soviets before they quit the country. Between 1959 and 1961, a further four small reactors were established elsewhere, including one of indigenous design at Nankai.[27]

Could the People's Republic replace the Soviet expertise that had now been withdrawn with its own home-grown talent? A large number of leading scientists led by Professor Chien Hsu Sen now left their posts in Peking and the other major cities. They had been transferred to the remote

Ray Cline (right), the CIA Station Chief in Taiwan, was on very good terms with Chiang Ching Kuo (left), the son of Chiang Kai Shek, who was in charge of Taiwan's intelligence organization in the early 1960s (via Marjorie Cline).

Takla Makan desert in Sinkiang province, where a nuclear weapons testing site was established at Lop Nor. The American-trained Chien was also put in charge of China's ballistic missile development. A launch site and test range for the missiles was set up a few hundred miles to the east in the Gobi Desert, at Shuang Cheng Tzu (SCT).

Shuang Cheng Tzu

Shuang Cheng Tzu was the prime target for the first U-2 overflight. U.S. intelligence analysts already had in their possession CORONA satellite imagery of China's only known missile test site. But its quality and small scale precluded the measurement of many buildings, or identification of missiles. However, two SA-2 launch areas had been identified in the central part of the complex.[28]

On 13 January Major Chen headed straight for them, and Chicom radars saw him coming. There had never been much doubt that they would. There were now an estimated 330 early-warning radar sites on the main-

As head of intelligence for the Chinese Air Force, General I Fu En set up the nationalists' side of the joint U-2 project.

land, concentrated along the long coastline and the Indo-China border. But the number of height-finding radars was relatively small, and this reduced Chicom's ability to vector interceptors against intruding aircraft. Especially if they were at 70,000 feet, of course. The PLAAF had no fighters capable of exceeding 60,000 feet.[29]

The missile range at SCT was over 1,300 naut miles from Taiwan. It was a long haul. Back in Taiwan, the U-2's progress could be monitored, after a fashion, by SIGINT operators listening to the Chicom air defense net. Across Chekiang, Anhwei, Honan, and Shansi provinces, Chen flew steadily northwest. There were scattered to heavy clouds along much of the route. On various occasions J-4 and J-5 interceptors (Chinese version of MiG-15 and MiG-17, respectively) rose through the undercast, trying to intercept. But they never came close. As Chen crossed the Great Wall of China, north of Lanchow, the skies cleared—as forecast. Shuang Cheng Tzu and the surrounding area was in the clear! Chen knew he was at the limit of his range, but he covered the extensive target area as requested. Through the driftsight, he could see the massive framework of a missile

gantry. Then, he turned to begin the long return journey along a slightly more southerly route that left denied territory over the Fukien coast.[30]

Reception Committee

At Taoyuan, the reception committee was led by CCK himself. Chen touched down after eight hours 40 minutes in the air, having covered 3,320 nautical miles. He was elated, and could hardly wait to tell those waiting on the tarmac what he had seen and done. CCK hung a medal round his neck before the pilot was led off to the debriefing room. Chen reported no technical problems during the flight, other than his difficulty in sighting waypoints through the driftsight in the featureless desert terrain.[31]

From Project HQ, Deputy Chief Jim Cunningham cabled his congratulations, and reminded Lt Col Tomlinson that time would be needed to analyze the results, including "the nature and caliber of any unfriendly reaction." The film from the B-camera was unloaded and flown to PACAF's 67th RTS in Japan. There, specially-cleared personnel processed it, labeled it as Church Door imagery, and performed the initial readout. The coverage of SCT was excellent![32]

Group photo shows key personnel in the creation of the Black Cat Squadron on Taiwan in 1961. Standing, left to right: Chen Huai and Gimo Yang (pilots); Johnny Chu (navigator); Jude Pao (operations); Phil Yang (navigator); Mike Hua (pilot). Sitting, left to right: Gen Huang (deputy intelligence chief, CAF); Gen Chen (commander, CAF); Gen Pong (chief of JCS); Bob Tomlinson (manager of Det H); and Col Lu (squadron commander).

The Special Group now gave permission for more Tackle flights over the Chinese mainland. At the same time, repeat coverage of North Vietnam was approved. The Razor agreement allowed the U.S. to use Taiwan-based U-2s for non-mainland missions with an American pilot. Bob Ericson was still serving at Taoyuan as the resident IP for the Chinese pilots. On 1 February he was alerted for a possible flight south to Indo-China while, at the same time, Gimo Yang was alerted for a PRC mission. In the end neither was flown, and the next day, Project HQ was instructed to stand down the unit while Robert Kennedy made a two-week visit to the Far East. That suited the Black Cats fine—it was Chinese New Year! In the meantime, a second U-2C was ferried across the transpacific to Midway by Barry Baker, and then onto Taiwan by Jim Cherbonneaux. The mission to North Vietnam was eventually flown by Bob Ericson on 21 February. His route took him over Hainan Island, where Chinese radars had no difficulty in detecting the high-flyer.[33]

Gimo Yang

Two days later, Gimo Yang took off on the second long penetration to the desert northwest of China. Coverage of some targets in Kansu and Szechwan provinces was achieved, but cloudy conditions prevailed over much of the route. At Lanchou, the facility that was suspected to be producing Uranium-235 via the gaseous diffusion method was seen to be incomplete. Two Badger bombers were captured on film at Wu Kung airfield—the first time this type had been seen in China. Analysts concluded that they had been supplied by the Soviet Union in 1959, before the split. Military formations around the port city of Swatow were also photographed.[34]

During March, the other two CAF pilots got in their first overflights. Mike Hua flew west almost as far as the Burmese border to cover multiple targets in the four southern provinces, including the cities of Kunming, An-ning, and Meng-tzu. Tiger Wang followed a circular route that took him over the major cities of Shanghai, Nanking, Changsha, and Canton and their industries, air defense, and naval facilities. The weather was unusually good throughout Wang's seven-hour mission. Communist radars tracked the flights, and fighters were vectored to intercept, but of course they could never reach the high flyers. With two more sorties to North Vietnam also flown by Bob Ericson, this was Det H's most productive month to date.[35]

"The Badlands"

But technical problems were looming. The pilots at Det H were having difficulty ascending through the "Badlands" without flaming out. Were the fuel controls to blame, or was the fuel contaminated? SAC was also having fuel problems. Two shipments to Det H of over 50,000 gallons of JP-TS were condemned after samples failed the test. Sabotage was suspected, but eventually ruled out. Meanwhile, there were no fewer than seven AC generator failures on the two aircraft assigned to Det H within a few weeks. Without the generator, the camera would not cycle and the autopilot could not function.

The Det was grounded while yet more fuel was flown in. Pilots were advised to throttle back during the climbout. The contamination was ascribed to careless handling of the drums during transport. New fuel controls were introduced, as well as fuel additives.[36]

While all this was going on, the military posture of communist China was causing serious concern in the Washington intelligence community. Mao's regime was clearly bolstering the North Vietnamese with weapons,

---

FERRY FIASCO

Ferrying single-engine jets across the wide expanses of the Pacific is not easy, and not much fun. The U-2 was no exception, especially when there were a series of problems with fuel, fuel controls, and dodgy generators. This is what happened when CIA Project HQ needed to swap U-2s based on Taiwan for the first time, at the end of March 1962.

The staging party left Edwards on the 19th by C-118 for Midway, via Hickam. On arrival at Midway, they found that many of the pre-positioned drums of special JP-TS fuel were unsealed, and therefore unsafe. Replacement fuel drums were airlifted from Hickam by a C-124, but were late arriving. The replacement Article, 378, arrived at Midway from Edwards on the 23rd, and was refueled with a mix of original, safe drums and the newly-shipped fuel. A fresh pilot took off, but the U-2's engine flamed out during the climb, and although it was relit, the aircraft returned to Midway, where the AC generator was found to have failed. A test flight next day with all-new fuel was delayed when the main inverter failed. That was fixed, but there was another flameout on the test flight. The staging group at Midway called for a new fuel control to be shipped, but P&W techrep Ben Koziol advised that a climb out at a lower EGT should work. This worked on two subsequent test hops, so the ferry flight on to Taiwan was finally relaunched on the 30th. Article 378 did arrive safely at Taoyuan, but the fuel pump failed enroute. The AC generator was still not working...and by the way, the ferry flight was accomplished with one hung pogo.

Meanwhile, Article 352 took off from Taoyuan, heading for Midway and then an overhaul at Burbank. After an hour, though, the AC generator also quit, followed an hour and a half later by the engine. Luckily, the small island of Iwo Jima was straight ahead and "only" 100 miles away. Pilot Jim Cherbonneaux managed to relight at the third attempt and diverted into Iwo. The staging crew flew there from Midway in the C-118. They determined that 352's fuel was not as thermally stable as advertised, and had frozen in the pump at high altitude. The pump was replaced, and the aircraft was refueled with ordinary JP-4 so Cherbonneaux could fly it back to Taiwan at medium altitude. After a test hop, he did that, but the engine began running rough halfway through the flight. He landed with a hydraulic boost pump malfunction and...the AC generator was still not working. An engine change was decreed—but there was no spare engine at Taoyuan. There was no alternative but to dismantle 352 and send it back to Burbank on a C-124! - *C.P.*

---

as well as comradely support. And the PRC's forces opposite Taiwan were significantly reinforced, it was thought. Would the communists finally move against the offshore islands, Kinmen and Matsu? Or even invade Taiwan? A Special NIE was rushed out, suggesting that they would.

Although Det H was flying again by mid-June, the weather over the Taiwan Straits and the mainland opposite was cloudy. Instead, the Black Cat Squadron flew to clearer skies further afield. On 16 June, Gimo Yang brought back the first U-2 photography of northeastern China, in a mission which went all the way to Harbin, in Manchuria, and was recovered into Kunsan AB, South Korea. Four days later, Tiger Wang made a return visit

WHOSE MISSION IS IT ANYWAY?

Two 4080th wing pilots described how, in June 1962, they helped fly U-2s all the way across the Pacific in 24 hours, for no real purpose.

Ed Dixon: There was a big fuss to fly three aircraft to Okinawa without overnight stops, just refueling 2-3 hours at Hickam and Wake Island. The KC-135 was loaded with supplies, six pilots, and three navs. Three U-2s took off, one aborted, but we were able to take one of the aircraft from our OL at Hickam on to Wake and Kadena. When we got there we found we were only ferry pilots for the Agency. Al Rand and Buster Edens showed up and a major. We were to do mobile and maintenance only! We were scheduled to go to Clark, Philippines, but that was canceled, and the Agency people cleared off. We sat around for a week, and then most people left in the -135 and two U-2s.

Dave Ray: I don't recall if they told us anything at all. I just reported to the squadron, and in a few hours I was on the KC-135 headed for Hickam. It was damned hot in Del Rio, and that tanker was loaded with our flyaway kits, maintenance, pilots, and navigators. The takeoff roll was so long, they had to lower the crash barrier at the other end so that the wheels wouldn't snag it! We made it into Hickam and had minimum ground time for refueling, food, and suit-up for the next leg to Wake Island. There, the same drill was repeated. I flew one of the U-2s into Kadena, and remember shaking my head at the antics of the tower. We were supposed to be low profile, but they repeatedly advised aircraft to remain clear of the pattern because a "classified" aircraft was about to land!

We were all dead on our feet. We were not alone at Kadena. Several Agency U-2 people were there too. There was quite a lot of "wheel spinning." It was decided to remove the USAF markings. Then it was decided that the Agency pilots needed some landing practice, so the USAF markings were re-applied. Then they were removed again. Then whatever missions were planned were delayed while destruct devices were flown in from somewhere—our USAF birds didn't have them. After a week or so I was flown home.

AT THE ELINT CENTER

One means by which U.S. intelligence tried to discover whether the Chicoms were close to bagging a U-2 was from the aircraft's own SIGINT recorders carried on the overflights. The tapes were sent to the PACAF ELINT Center (PEC) at Fuchu AS, near Tokyo, Japan, where one analyst recalls:

We would receive a phone call that a data package was arriving, and the CIA rep would go to meet the courier at Haneda airport. I would warm up the duplicating machines; the originals were 1/2 mil thick and would not stand up to the constant shuttling of the tape that we did during the analysis process. We had a built-in detection system that sounded an alarm whenever it detected the complex scan of the SA-2 system. We would then go directly to these portions of the tape when the duping was finished. I remember that the collection process included switching back and forth from left to right side of the aircraft and included P-, L-, S-, and X-band channels. All the analysis in those days was done through audio because the bandwidth was limited. We used tone matching and the pattern on the scope. It would wobble as you adjusted the line length, and slowly become stable. That was how we read the PRF. I can remember listening to the hordes of Cross Slots, and trying to separate them out. The P-band was almost as bad. We would break in the new analysts by giving them the X-band, which wasn't nearly so busy. We had 24 hours to process and send reports via message to CIA. I know we did find SA-2 activity. I really never did anything as personally gratifying as in the PEC.

to the distant missile site at Shuang Cheng Tzu. Project HQ decided to reinforce Det H by sending a third U-bird, but this got stuck at Midway for a week after the slipper tanks failed to feed any fuel on the ferry leg from Edwards.[37]

McNamara

Secretary of Defense Robert McNamara didn't think much of all this. There was not enough intelligence to make firm judgements, he complained at a strategy meeting in the White House on 20 June. McNamara suggested augmenting the two CIA U-2s on Taiwan with two from the SAC fleet. Then, if the weather cleared, all four could fly over the crucial areas simultaneously. Why can't these planes fly under the clouds, President Kennedy asked.[38]

Although McNamara's plan was not fully approved at the meeting, he gave marching orders to SAC. Within 24 hours, the 4080th wing at Laughlin was deploying two U-2As across the Pacific to OL-2 Kadena

AB, Okinawa, via Hickam and Wake Island. They were accompanied by a KC-135, which carried maintainers, flyaway kits, and spare pilots to take over the Dragon Ladies at each stop.

At the operating level, no one knew what was really going on. The confusion was evident in Washington, too. Sending two USAF birds to Taiwan would well and truly blow the cover story that pretended the nationalists were mounting a self-sufficient U-2 operation there. An alternative plan was sketched to send the two U-2As to Clark AB, Philippines, for a joint SAC/CIA operation, codenamed Top Cat. This would aim to achieve the new coverage required of North Vietnam and Southern China. While the wheels spun in Washington as to who would actually fly these missions—Agency or SAC pilots—Project HQ rushed pilots Buster Edens and Al Rand to Kadena. Meanwhile, Det G at Edwards was running out of aircraft, at a time when another Cuba mission was imminent. Hurried plans were made to re-qualify a Det G pilot in SAC's U-2A models at Laughlin, in case one of these had to be "borrowed" to fly over Castro's island this month.[39]

Det H managed to mount two missions over China's coastal provinces from existing resources and using the Chinese pilots on 25 and 28 June. Because of cloud cover, they were only partially successful. But the CAF's RF-101s were also flying low level—per President Kennedy's request. And by 9 July, the Black Cats had flown three more missions over the coastal provinces. From all this photography, it was clear that the Chicoms were not planning *any* offensive moves! Operation Top Cat was canceled. From now on, COMOR recommended that a monthly U-2 mission be flown over the Taiwan Straits area, to check on communist force deployments. Tiger Wang flew the next of these on 27 July.[40]

Over Peking

On 11 August 1962, Mike Hua took off from Taoyuan to cover the remaining targets in northeast China that had not been photographed by Gimo Yang two months earlier. After coast-in over Tsingtao, his route took him north to Mukden, in Manchuria, then west along the coast to Tientsin. Then, for the first time, he overflew the Chinese capital, Peking. After more twists and turns to cover the Changchiakou area, he was finally turning for home when yet another AC generator failed. Hua nursed the plane back to Taiwan.[41]

When the film from Hua's flight was analyzed, two SA-2 missile sites were identified around Peking. Although Hua's flight had been tracked by communist radars, like every one of the Black Cat Squadron's penetrations of mainland China to date, no attempt was made to fire the surface-to-air missiles against him.

There was a good reason for that. The PLAAF had just moved some of the launchers and missiles south, to the areas that had recently been overflown by the U-2s! Of the five SA-2 battalions supplied to China,

The generator suddenly quit during the turn over Changchiakou. The autopilot and camera would not work. It made no sense to fly the planned course. I turned to a heading of 165 degrees toward Taiwan and switched off all the unnecessary electrical equipment to save the battery for landing. I had to fly in this condition for nearly three hours until reaching the Taiwan Strait. The weather became overcast over the southern part of Shantung province. I began to worry. The only onboard directional instrument was the magnetic compass. Without high-altitude wind information, the aircraft might drift off course, way out over the Pacific Ocean. After I struggled for over two hours, the clouds started to break. Through the driftsight, I spotted three small islands that looked like the Tachens. I had left the mainland and could now descend to ease the workload of controlling the aircraft. By using ADF, I flew back to Taoyuan. I was exhausted when I climbed out of the cockpit.

three of these were originally set up around Peking; the fourth was used for training at SCT, and the fifth served as a model for Chinese engineers to copy and reverse-engineer. In late June 1962, the PLAAF ordered the 2nd Battalion from Peking to Chongshia, in Honan province, over which Tiger Wang had recently passed on his way to the missile range. The move was carried out in great secrecy, at night, and members of the battalion traveled in civilian clothing. There they waited under harsh weather and living conditions for more than 50 days, but no U-2 came near.[42]

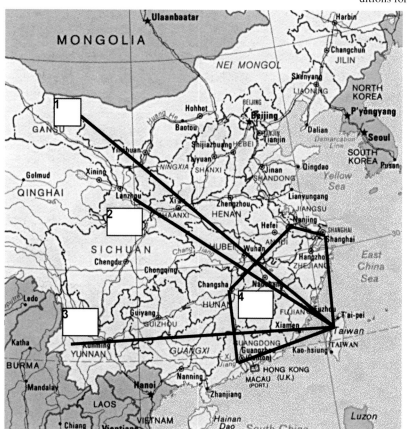

The routes taken by the first four U-2 overflights of mainland China in 1962. The key targets included the missile range at Shuang Cheng Tzu, the nuclear weapons facility being built at Lanchou, the key cities of Canton, Kunming, Nanking, and Shanghai, and numerous airfields and military bases.

The Temple of the Valley of the Spirits, as seen from 70,000 feet during a U-2 overflight of mainland China in March 1962.

As explained above, the focus of U.S. and ROC interest had switched to the provinces opposite Taiwan. So in late August, the 2nd Battalion was ordered to move again, to an airbase near Nanchang that had now been overflown eight times by the U-2s. The new missile site was partially hidden in a valley. There they waited, but the next overflight on 8 September 1962 didn't come close enough.

On that day, Gimo Yang was sent to cover southern China, which had not been overflown since April because of cloud cover. The targets for Yang's mission (GRC-126) were controversial in Washington, because they included seven areas that the nationalists identified as potential drop zones for airborne raids on the mainland. In recent months, Chiang Kai Shek had stepped up plans for military action against the communist regime. With-

The U-2s that were ferried to and from Taiwan carried U.S. markings. For overflights of the mainland by the CAF pilots, they were repainted in the nationalists' insignia (Lockheed LCA 88-4).

out consulting the U.S., the ROC was training and equipping special forces. CIA analysts did not give Chiang much chance of success. But Ray Cline—now back in Washington and promoted to be the CIA's Deputy Director for Intelligence—said that the U.S. should play along with Chiang's plans. The State Dept, and Presidential security advisor McGeorge Bundy, were not so sure.[43]

Yang flew over Canton and the hinterland of Kwangtung and Kiangsi provinces, to the west of the redeployed SA-2 battalion. As well as the potential drop zones, he flew over areas of mining activity, where the communist regime might be extracting uranium for use in making nuclear weapons. But as cloud cover increased, thunderstorms brewed and—yet again—the AC generator failed. So Yang cut short the mission, flew home, and landed after five-and-a-half hours.[44]

Chen Huai downed

The generator was replaced, and the same aircraft was prepared overnight for another mission. Early in the morning, Article 378 took off again for the mainland, with Chen Huai at the controls. Mission GRC-127 was apparently designed to cover the targets that Yang had missed the previous day. The flight coasted-in over Pingtang, in Fukien province, heading northwest. The 2nd Battalion's acquisition radar identified Chen's aircraft when it was 150 miles away. The U-2 drew closer, and the battalion switched on the missile's guidance radar. But the aircraft flew past Nanchang to the east, over the Lake of Poyang and outside missile range! The battalion commander Kueh decided to keep the acquisition radar on. He knew that U-2 flights sometimes made 180-degree turns to return along a parallel course. His patience was rewarded when, after passing JiuJiang and entering Hupei province, Chen turned back towards Nanchang. The U-2 closed to within 18 miles, and the commander launched three missiles. The second and third got their target. After 14 successful missions over the mainland, a Black Cat was downed.[45]

The wreckage fell in a wide area, about 10 miles from Nanchang. Amazingly, Chen was still alive when communist soldiers reached him, but he died later in the hospital. Later on 9 September 1962, the New China News Agency in Peking announced that "a U-2 of the Chiang Kai Shek gang was shot down this morning...when it intruded over eastern China." No mention was made of the pilot's fate. In Peking a few days later, Premier Chou En Lai addressed a rally of 10,000 people called to celebrate the downing of the nationalists' plane.

U.S. officials were instructed to admit that the ROC had acquired two U-2s "in a direct sale by Lockheed," but were otherwise told to disassociate Uncle Sam from the project. Chinese pilots were trained to fly them, just as they had been trained to fly the many other military aircraft that the ROC had acquired from the U.S., the officials said. The PRC knew better, of course, and declared that "the U.S. government is the chief culprit in this aggressive crime." The two American pilots currently at Det H, Jim Cherbonneaux and Marty Knutson, were hurriedly evacuated to the CIA's station on Okinawa.

National Hero

On Taiwan, however, the nationalist government was proud of the Black Cat Squadron's achievements. News of the shootdown was not suppressed by the ROC. On the contrary, 32 year-old Lt Col Chen was elevated to the

After Chen Huai was shot down, President Chiang Kai Shek (seated) summoned the Chinese Air Force pilots and U-2 commanding officer, and asked if they wanted to continue. Standing, left to right: Tiger Wang, Michael Lu, Gimo Yang, and Mike Hua.

status of national hero. The additional forename Sheng, signifying honour, was added to his name by President Chiang Kai-Shek himself. A myth arose that Chen had survived the shootdown, only to kill himself with the hunting knife from his seatpack, rather than be captured. In Taipei, the school attached to the CAF headquarters was renamed the Chen Huai Sheng High School. (It is still there today, with a bust of Chen inside the main entrance). Other monuments to the downed U-2 pilot were erected throughout Taiwan.

A few days after the shootdown, Chiang Kai-Shek invited Col Lu and the three surviving U-2 pilots, Hua, Wang, and Yang, to the Presidential office. He interviewed each of them personally to gauge their morale. He asked about their families. Lu told him that casualties are to be expected on military missions. They all assured Chiang that they were ready to fly again, in the service of the Republic of China.

But flights over the mainland were suspended, as the U.S. and ROC sought to discover exactly what had happened. Only a handful of SA-2 sites had been identified on the mainland and, of course, U.S. intelligence did not know that China had moved one of the active battalions. (Most insiders in the Tackle program actually did not yet know that China had the SA-2. They were not cleared to receive information derived from Keyhole imagery—the Corona satellite—or from Church Door, the codename for U-2 imagery obtained by Det H over China).

In July 1962 the communists had broadcast a message promising the equivalent of $280,000 in gold to any Chinese U-2 pilot who defected with his aircraft. Although this outcome was discounted, there was always the possibility that someone within the unit was spying for the mainland. And there were other issues, such as the maintenance and fuel quality problems that had dogged Detachment H in recent months. Maybe some technical problem had forced Chen to descend before the Chicoms bagged him.

Did some of this sound familiar? Yes, it was a replay of the Gary Powers incident. Despite the addition of the SSB radio, there was still no failsafe method of determining exactly what had gone wrong on a U-2 flight deep into denied territory.

14

Deep Cold War I

From Edwards to Midway is an eight-hour flight in the U-2. On 23 December 1960, pilots Jim Cherbonneaux and Al Rand made the long, lonely trip across the Pacific, as Det G deployed two A-models to Southeast Asia. At Midway, Buster Edens and EK Jones were waiting to take the aircraft on to NAS Cubi Point. Meanwhile, starting four days earlier, two C-124s lifted support gear, fuel, and ferry pilots along the way, stopping also at Hickam, Wake Island, and Guam because of their poor range. A mind-numbing 37 hours 30 minutes flying time for "Old Shakey," in fact, plus 45 hours on the ground at the transit stops! It was late on Christmas Day before the last C-124 transport landed at the Subic Bay airfield.[1]

Now the waiting game began. With the Joint Chiefs being so concerned that North Vietnam was in expansionist mode, COMOR had devised a long list of target requirements across North Vietnam and Laos. But the usual build-up of tropical thunderstorms throughout southeast Asia prevented any missions being launched until the New Year. Then, on 3 and 4 January, missions had to be aborted after crossing the South China Sea because the Articles produced heavy contrails as they coasted-in over Da Nang, in South Vietnam. It was that old problem of extra moisture in the tropical stratosphere. Using the U-2A with its inferior high-altitude performance, compared with the C-model, was proving to be a mistake. The mission duration, and therefore the fuel load, was reduced, so that pilots could climb above the contrail level.[2]

Eventually, five successful missions lasting around seven hours each were accomplished in a 15-day period, despite navigational difficulties caused by inaccurate maps, as well as cloud cover and haze. The flights ranged up the border between Laos and North Vietnam, and across that Communist country, some turning out over the sea beyond Hanoi to confuse radar tracking before re-entering denied territory nearer the DMZ in a southbound direction. A huge number of airfields and military camps were photographed for the first time, together with their contents. Bridges and roads were logged and mapped by type. The first mission also covered the southern end of Hainan Island, belonging to the People's Republic of China.[3]

PIC field deployment

Just as was done in 1958, when Det C flew from Cubi over Indonesia, PIC mounted a field deployment to the Philippines, so that the B-camera "take" could be quickly interpreted. The Laotian government was claiming that North Vietnam had invaded its territory, and was also airdropping supplies to Pathet Lao (communist) troops. But the U-2 photography did not substantiate the Laotian claims, which were in any case dropped by Vientiane

in late January. In early February, Det G began packing for the long redeployment home.

Were the flights as covert as the CIA had hoped? The deployment was made as quickly as possible, using the "Quick Move" concept to keep the Articles shielded from prying eyes. No attempts to intercept the aircraft were made over denied territory, but subsequent analysis of the ELINT gear onboard the U-2 (Systems 3 and 6) did reveal that the flights were detected by various radars operated by the North Vietnamese and China's Southwest Air Defense District. However, there was little evidence of tracking.[4]

Castro regime

In early January 1961, the U.S. government broke off diplomatic relations with Cuba. The CIA's attempts to destabilize the Castro regime in Cuba were not going well. From an airbase in Guatemala, the CIA was airdropping supplies to counter-revolutionaries in Cuba, but the effort was poorly organized, and Castro was rounding up his opponents with ease. The Cuban exile community in Miami was divided into many competing factions. After President Kennedy took office on 20 January, he allowed planning for a U.S.-trained and equipped invasion force to continue, but asked the Joint Chiefs of Staff to assess its viability. JFK wanted as little visibility for the

The British rejoined Project Idealist in 1961, sending two pilots, a mission planner, and a flight surgeon for training. The pilots were Squadron Leaders "Taffy" Taylor (left) and "Chunky" Webster. They flew ferry missions and test flights of new equipment, but the British government never gave permission for them to fly operational missions.

U.S. as possible. Because of this, the landing site was changed to the Bay of Pigs. And there could be no intervention by U.S. armed forces, even in a supporting role.

Against this background, the CIA's U-2 overflights of Castro's island resumed from Laughlin AFB, as Operation Long Green. Now, though, the mission "take" was processed in the 4080th's photo laboratory by Kodak employees sent from Rochester. Then photo-interpreters sent from NPIC to Laughlin would examine the film. If the U-2 landed on schedule, they would have the initial report ready to transmit to Washington by 2 am the next morning.

Two U-2 missions from Laughlin AFB on 19 and 21 March updated the intelligence on Cuba's Order of Battle. The invasion was set for mid-April. At a key meeting in the White House on 4 April, President Kennedy gave the go-ahead. The Special Group gave blanket permission for U-2 flights over the island in the run up to D-day. During Operation Flip Top, 15 U-2 missions were launched from 6-29 April. Det G pilots Barry Baker, Jim Barnes, and Marty Knutson were "in the barrel" nearly every day.[5]

Since Cuba had no means to counter the flights, they ranged up and down the island from west to east and back again. One of them, on 8 April, also took in the neighboring Dominican Republic. But they were no picnic for the drivers. So that the aircraft could arrive over the island before the daily build-up of clouds each morning, the takeoffs from Laughlin were often in the middle of the night. The pilots had to take sleeping pills to cope with the schedule. Sometimes fog would descend on the Texas base in the early hours. The flight could still take off, but it surely could not make a quick return in case of trouble. The normal route was to leave and return to the U.S. mainland at Corpus Christi. Once again, drivers were instructed to abort if they made "heavy and persistent" contrails over denied territory.[6]

Bay of Pigs
The invasion at the Bay of Pigs was set for the early morning of 16-17 April. Two U-2 flights on the 15th, and another on the 16th, were designed to provide post-strike assessment of air strikes mounted by the brigade, which were planned to knock out Cuba's small air force. As history recounts, a nervous President Kennedy scaled these back at the last minute. There was just one strike on the 15th, and none on the 16th. U-2 photography revealed that at only one of the three key Cuban airbases had the runway been damaged. Much of Castro's air force had survived.[7]

Even the one air strike on the 15th raised the political heat—through the United Nations—so much that JFK now canceled the remaining air strike planned for the morning following the overnight landing. As Richard Bissell bitterly reflected, "cutting the airstrikes by 80 percent proved to be the operation's death sentence." The landing was opposed from both the ground and the air. The entire guerilla group was killed or captured.

This was not the end of Cuba missions for Det G, though. Within a few weeks, the Intelligence Community levied a requirement for a monthly overflight, to keep an eye on Castro's forces. It was the same *modus operandi*: deploy from Edwards to Laughlin, takeoff in the early hours, three hours to the island, three hours taking photographs, three hours back to Del Rio. The new flights were codenamed Project Nimbus. The first of them, on 23 May 1961, nearly ended in disaster when the autopilot malfunctioned over Havana. The aircraft pitched up, and pilot Jim Cherbonneaux was unable to prevent it rolling over into a steep, Mach-buffeting dive. Somehow, he regained control despite imposing a 3g-plus

---

THERE I WAS...WITH BLANK MAPS!
On Det G's first transpacific deployment in late December 1960, CIA pilot Jim Cherbonneaux had a problem...

I usually pulled my flight logs and maps out for the first time as I was passing over my first check point. As I was crossing the California coastline, I found to my dismay that they were completely blank. I was really pissed at myself for ever trusting a stupid navigator in the first place. I was considering aborting when I remembered Al Rand, who was 10 minutes ahead of me. I called him, and he told me that all his stuff was complete. "Good," I said, "now slowly read me all of the entries!" Al was always a laconic individual, and he really hated being disturbed when flying. But he finally did give me all the time/heading/distance entries.

As it turned out, Al's flight plan wasn't much good. If we had gone on using the information, we'd have both crashed somewhere in the trackless wastes of the Pacific about 300 nautical miles north of Midway. Fortunately, neither of us trusted navigators. We started getting good signals from Midway's radio beacon about 500 miles out, and our radio compass needle showed a source some 30 degrees left of our course. Because of the dumb navigator, worse-than-forecast winds, and the bad weather in that part of the Pacific (as we let down), we landed short on fuel and even shorter on temper!

PIC BECOMES NPIC

Another big change in the Washington set-up was occurring. After the first successful CORONA satellite film recovery on 19 August 1960, it became obvious that Art Lundahl's Photo Interpretation Center (PIC) would have to be upgraded and expanded. So on 1 January 1961 PIC became NPIC, with the word National prefixed. The Pentagon lobbied for control of the expanding organization. But this was retained by the CIA, which placed NPIC under the control of the DDI.

The Air Force now assigned a full detachment of people to NPIC for the first time, but Gen Power still insisted that a full reconnaissance processing and interpretation capability be retained in the 544th RTS at SAC headquarters.

NPIC remained in the makeshift Steuart building until early 1963, when it moved into purpose-built facilities in the Washington Navy Yard. – *C.P.*

FLYING OVER CUBA

It took us around three hours just to get to Cuba from Del Rio. We would then spend about three hours over the target area, and then it would be three hours more getting back to Laughlin. We would try to coast-in over Cuba between 0800-0900 to get cloud-free photos before the land mass heated up. But it was always a race before the ground became completely obscured by multiple layers of clouds and their shadows. On any given mission, we would consider ourselves lucky to get 70% of the targets.

- Jim Cherbonneaux memoir

SECURITY BREACHES

At Project HQ, the senior Agency civilian Jim Cunningham frequently worried about security breaches. In mid-May 1961, while the CIA was still smarting from the Bay of Pigs debacle, Newsweek published a short item datelined Laughlin AFB that revealed the U-2 had been used to provide photo-intelligence for the operation. Cunningham reckoned that this was "the first indication in the American press that the U.S. government may have continued the use of the U-2 aircraft subsequent to 1 May 1960." He seemed oblivious to the fact that the Air Force maintained a fleet of 20 such aircraft, in more-or-less open view, at the same Texas airbase!

And, indeed, was flying them close to the Soviet Union. A month later, a British newspaper reported that very fact, after its correspondent in Alaska discovered that the SAC U-2 wing was operating periodically from Eielson AFB. Moscow Radio amplified the report, complaining to listeners about "the provocative actions of the U.S. military." A Pentagon spokesman conceded that U-2 aircraft "were still being used as flying laboratories for meteorological studies, high altitude air sampling, and other research programs."

Cunningham's next concern was the number of people around Washington who now required briefing on U-2 missions. The Kennedy Administration had tightened its grip on covert operations, especially after the "Cuban disaster," Cunningham told DPD's Security Chief on 26 July 1961. The 5412 Committee, the Foreign Intelligence Advisory Board, the new Joint Reconnaissance Center (JRC) in the Pentagon, and the State Department were all having to be briefed on "sensitive operational information," he noted. Cunningham fretted about the number of Black Books compiled by DPD containing such information that were now in circulation. "Not only have we literally gone into the publishing business," he continued, "but I feel that we have lost almost complete control of the actual location of the Books once they have left this office. A day does not go by that I don't shudder to think of the repercussions that would follow the loss of one of these books...where knowledge of its contents could pass to some unauthorized personnel, including members of the press." Cunningham's only hope was that as the fuss over the Bay of Pigs failure died down, "confidence in the Agency method of operations (would be) gradually re-established."
– C.P.

load on the airframe. As the pilot headed back to Texas the radio failed, and he diverted from cloud-shrouded Laughlin into Laredo AFB. The aircraft was sent back to Lockheed for investigations: this was not the first time it had exhibited unusual stall characteristics when the cg was moved aft by fuel burn.[8]

Det B rethink
In late March 1961, DPD was still hoping to get Det B flying again in Turkey, by mounting a few training missions "to test the locals' acceptance or rejection" of renewed U-2 operations. In June 1961 it was decided to withdraw completely, but then there was a rethink. The intelligence community was seriously worried about the big new Soviet radar at the Sary Shagan missile test range. Was it designed to intercept incoming ICBMs? ELINT intercepts were needed, but the radar was too far from the Soviet border for intercepts by medium-altitude snoopers like the RB-47. For a time in mid-year, SAC thought that it could provide a high-flying U-2 for this task; after all, the Turks had allowed RB-47 operations to continue from Incirlik.

In August the Special Group considered the matter. But no one seemed able to reach a decision. Aside from politics, there was a technical problem if the Agency was to fly the ELINT missions. DPD was now converting all its U-2s to J75 power, but System 7 did not work with the more powerful U-2C/F models, because of the lower frequency of their AC generator. The system manufacturer, HRB Singer, submitted a quote to modify System 7. But was it worth the cost, especially if U-2 basing rights along the Soviet southern border were not guaranteed? Eventually, in December 1961 it was decided to close Det B and remove Article 355 to the U.S. by C-124. By that time, this aircraft had spent no fewer than 20 months in the hangar at Incirlik![9]

The two new British pilots finished their training at Laughlin and moved on to North Base in June 1961. Project HQ now decided that it could release some of its long-serving American drivers back to the Air Force. Accordingly, in mid-1961 Glen Dunaway and Jake Kratt said goodbye to the U-2. If the security staff at Project HQ had prevailed, all of the original drivers would have been replaced, too. They simply knew too much about previous operations. Project HQ had been debating this question ever since Frank Powers was shot down. But when the difficulties of obtaining and training a half-dozen new pilots was assessed, and getting them through the rigorous medical at the Lovelace Clinic, the idea was dropped.[10]

To house the inflight refueling receptacle and the new SSB radio, the U-2F had a fairing along the top of the fuselage. Lockheed test pilot Bob Schumacher is modeling the high-visibility coveralls that pilots wore over the top of their pressure suits (Lockheed U-2-91-001-K).

RAF contingent

The new RAF contingent comprised a navigator and flight surgeon, as well as the two pilots, Squadron Leaders Charles "Taffy" Taylor and Ivan "Chunky" Webster. Their status in Project Idealist was somewhat hazy, though. For instance, as serving military officers, someone had decided that they could only fly aircraft painted with regular USAF markings. That was an inconvenience at North Base, where aircraft assigned to the Cuban overflights wore U.S. civilian registrations.[11]

The cryptonym Jackson was assigned to British participation in the Agency's U-2 program. In September 1961, Project HQ considered just exactly how the Brits might fit in. It was suggested that the Middle East, southeast Asia (specifically Indo-China), and Indonesia were areas of "mutual interest" to the U.S. and UK. Three categories of participation were sketched out: (a) missions which only U.S. pilots could fly for political reasons, but RAF pilots could help with the ferry flights; (b) *vice-versa*; and (c) joint missions where it was politically acceptable for Jackson and Idealist pilots to be fully integrated.[12]

In any event, very few of the (b) and (c) type of missions were ever approved. The RAF pilots flew HQ-directed missions from Edwards, such as test flights of new sensors and equipment. They also ferried U-2s to Laughlin and Midway on the first stage of operational deployments. Otherwise, they were limited to training flights, and got plenty of stick time on Det G's two T-33 trainers and single U-3 communications aircraft. The Agency still hoped that the British government would allow its overseas bases to be used for U-2 missions The intelligence community especially wanted a permanent base in the Middle East. But there were no guarantees forthcoming from London.

Inflight Refueling

During the first part of 1961, the Skunk Works modified Article 342 to be the first U-2 capable of inflight refueling. Simulated refueling trials had been conducted by Bob Schumacher on 26 October 1960, as he eased Ar-

---

TOWING THE U-2

During the refueling flight tests, the ever-resourceful Skunk Works came up with a couple of supplementary ideas. U-2 program manager Fred Cavanaugh suggested that the aircraft's range could be increased even further if the tanker could actually tow the U-2 along behind it for a distance! This was a variation on a Skunk Works idea from way back in the U-2 design phase, when it was thought that the bird might be towed aloft and released at medium altitude by a B-47. Why not turn the *tanker* into a glider tug instead? Some preliminary flight tests of this towing arrangement were actually conducted by test pilot Bob Schumacher. Once hooked up, the idea was for the fuel coupling to be locked, whereupon the U-2 pilot would slowly ease off the power. The scheme didn't work out in practice. Another idea that never left the drawing board was for one Dragon Lady to refuel another inflight, by means of a wing-mounted drogue, with the U-2 tanker pilot monitoring operations from the cockpit by means of mirrors! – *C.P.*

---

ticle 342 behind a KC-135 flown by Major Jack Thornton and his specially-cleared tanker crew. "It was delightfully easy," noted Kelly Johnson. According to Lockheed, the tests indicated that at 35,000 feet and 220 knots IAS refueling should be no problem. Except, that is, for the pilots, who were now flying an aircraft capable of staying airborne for 16 hours! (In fact, the practical endurance was limited by the aircraft's oxygen supply. A fourth oxygen bottle was now added, enough to supply the pilot for 14 hours). Another problem Kelly did not mention, was that Schumacher was wearing a standard helmet for the trial: when the partial pressure suit and its MA-2 helmet was worn, the visibility for maneuvering to the boom was significantly reduced.[13]

The refueling receptacle on the U-2 was illuminated for night operations, and the boomer in the tanker was given added visual reference for these operations by the placing of white reflective strips on the leading edge of the vertical and horizontal tail surfaces of the agency's all-black airplanes.

Still, the go-ahead came in November 1960, and was confirmed after a conference in Project HQ on 24 January 1961. The first flight test hook-up took place in mid-April 1961. Lockheed designed a neat, retractable receptacle for refueling. It shared a new, pressurized fairing above the mid-fuselage with the SSB radio, also now installed for the first time. This was the Collins Mk 618T unit, a 400 watt system that allowed voice contact at ranges of 3,000 miles or more. There was simply no room in the U-2 airframe to make a fully-internal installation of this radio. The antenna wire was strung from the leading edge of the vertical tail to the top of the new fairing. The rest of the equipment was put in the nose.

The refueling trials took just over a month, and were completed by late May. Two more U-2Cs were sent to Burbank for modification. The refuelable aircraft was redesignated U-2F. Also in mid-1961, DPD sought funds to convert its four remaining U-2A models to J75 power, at the same time that they received the refueling and SSB mods. The contrail problems over southeast Asia and Cuba could only be solved by using J75 airplanes to fly higher, the Agency reckoned. Already, it was SOP to enter denied territory no lower than 70,000 feet.

At North Base, the CIA's pilots were checked out in the refueling procedures during October 1961. The unit had two Lockheed T-33s for proficiency training, and pilots under instruction would first fly in one of these alongside a refueling operation, to see how it was done. But KC-135s were in short supply; only one was available to train Det G's pilots, flown by Major Thornton's crew. By August 1961, Project HQ was already contemplating the KC-97 as an alternative. In this case, refueling would take place lower and slower, at 20,000 feet and 170 knots. By the end of 1961 two more U-2Fs had been delivered, and all of the Project's American pilots had been checked out.

Careful

Despite Lockheed's sunny optimism, the inflight refueling of U-2s called for careful procedures. Usually, the receiver closes on the tanker. But because of the Article's small speed envelope, it was the tanker that had to make the adjustments. With the U-2 stabilized at the right altitude and speed, the tanker was supposed to overtake it about 1/4 of a mile to the right, and at the same altitude. The tanker would then reduce speed, and the U-2 would slide in towards it, while descending about 500 feet. Upon reaching a position directly below and in line with the tanker, the U-2 would rise slowly to the refuelling position. In this fashion, its delicate airframe would not be exposed to jetwash or propwash from the tanker's engines. But if the U-2 pilot were to stray even slightly off center, the bird would begin to roll as it encountered the tanker's downwash.

An alternative method of bringing tanker and U-2 to a rendezvous was sometimes employed when the U-2 was at operating altitude, perhaps having already performed the overflight part of the mission. The two aircraft approached each other from opposite directions. When the U-2 was 50 miles from the tanker, its pilot would start a descent. Upon reaching 35,000 feet he would turn through 180 degrees, which would put him in trail with the KC-135 at (hopefully) the same speed.

The U-bird could take on about 900 gallons from a tanker in about five minutes. The new fuel flowed into the main tanks only, and for maximum efficiency, this meant the aircraft's fuel feed sequence (slippers, then auxiliaries, then mains) had to be reversed. In the refuelable aircraft, the main tanks fed first, so that they could be topped up after, say, two hours of flight. But there were implications for the cg, of course. The ability to cross-transfer fuel between the auxiliary, as well as the main tanks, had to be added.

Through a series of motor and solenoid-operated valves, the ARS system was supposed to operate automatically, but a manual override was provided via a switch on the left console. It was vital that the U-2 pilot kept an eye on the valve operations; if the tanks were filled too quickly by the incoming fuel, the resulting overpressure from displaced air might lead to structural failure of the wing. After refueling, the pilot had to ensure that the U-2's rudimentary fuel counter was reset, there being no other indication of the quantity on board, save for the low fuel warning light.

How, then, could the pilot tell that fuel had indeed been fully transferred from the tanker? The Skunk Works was reluctant to add a fully-fledged system. Instead, it proposed a warning light system—indicating that the main tanks were half-full or full.

The boom operator on the tanker was provided with an illuminated board with which to visually communicate gallons received, together with latitude and longitude information to the U-2 pilot.

The procedure for separating tanker from receiver was for the U-2 to decrease power and descend about 100 feet below the tanker, before sliding away left or right. Once he was 1/4 of a mile abeam the tanker, the U-2 pilot could climb away on a parallel course until he was well clear of any downwash effects

Flexibility

The whole idea was to improve mission planning flexibility. For instance, a U-2 could take off and fly along the periphery of denied territory for up to 1,500 miles at low level, thus avoiding detection by the opposition's early warning radar net. It could then be refueled before climbing rapidly to cruise-climb altitude, and making its penetration from an unexpected direction.

The first operational mission for the refuelable aircraft stemmed from a suggestion by Kelly Johnson. Rather than stage from Edwards to Laughlin for the Cuban overflights, he told Project HQ, why not launch directly out of North Base, and get refueled nearer the target area? This was done for the first time on 26 October 1961, with a rendezvous over Corpus Christi with the KC-135. The mission still recovered into Laughlin, however, since a round-robin flight from Edwards to Cuba would have required a second refueling on the way back, and stretched the mission length to an impossible 14-plus hours![14]

OL-5 of the 4080th SRW flew out of cold and snowy Eielson AFB, Alaska. Freezing fog was only one of the many hazards (Ed Naylor).

Those Cuba missions resulted in high-level concern in Washington. The U-2 imagery revealed that the Soviets were sending arms to Cuba— anti-aircraft guns, artillery, tanks, helicopters, and light transports. Swept-wing fighter aircraft (MiG 15s or MiG-17s) were first identified at San Antonio de los Banos airfield in June 1961. By November there were 20 of them, plus 10 MiG-19s, and more fighters at Camaguey. Soviet early-warning radars were installed along the northern coast.[15]

After the Bay of Pigs, the Kennedy administration—and especially the State Dept—was extremely sensitive to potential screw-ups. Project HQ argued that, in the event of a flameout or similar incident over the island, the U-2 was in gliding distance of friendly bases. But every Nimbus mission had to be approved by the Special Group, and even then, the State Dept sometimes insisted that it be consulted before final mission planning went ahead.[16]

Apart from the monthly Cuba missions, Det G received no other tasking in the second half of 1961, except for a short return to southeast Asia in August. One aircraft was deployed all the way across the Pacific again in Operation Ebony. Only one mission over North Vietnam was flown, two days after the aircraft arrived at Cubi Point.[17]

Toy Soldier

The 4080th wing was much busier. In the first half of 1961 there were two more deployments to OL-5, Eielson AFB, Alaska. The first was for weather research—yes, really! Using the Ivory Tower II instrument package mounted in the Q-bay, two U-2s plus WB-50s and WB-47s from the 55th wing took measurements for the study of cold stratospheric vortexes during a two-week deployment in early February. Ten weeks later, three more U-2s were dispatched to the cold northern base for more gas sampling in the Toy Soldier series. In May, Lt Col "Buzz" Curry led a return by OL-11 to East Sale, Australia, for a month of more Crowflight sampling missions.

Meanwhile, the training of new pilots continued at Laughlin. On some sorties, various photographic surveys for U.S. military and civilian agencies were conducted, such as Dry Wash, Gypsy Fiddle (supporting radar scoring of SAC bomb crews), and Second Scan. The Yellow Moon mis-

sions were more highly classified. They supported development of the Air Force's SAMOS reconnaissance satellite. Using the A-1 or A-2 camera configuration, the SAC U-2s were supposed to photograph the same U.S. territory as the satellite for comparative purposes. The 4080th wing was first alerted to perform this mission in October 1960, but SAMOS launches were repeatedly delayed. The first Yellow Moon mission was not flown until 1 February 1961.[18]

On 20 July, two of the U-2As departed for Hickam AFB at the start of the wing's second deployment for SIGINT flights along Communist coastlines. This time the operating location was Kadena (OL-2), and the deployment was commanded by the new 4028th SRS boss, Lt Col Kenneth McCaslin. But a delay in gaining political clearance to use the base on Okinawa caused a 10-day wait in Hawaii. One aircraft was left there, while 66703 moved on via Wake Island. Here, the U-2 refueled on the ramp directly from the KC-97 that was supporting the deployment. This procedure saved the trouble of pre-positioning the Dragon Lady's special JP-TS fuel by transport airplane.

The SAC U-2A eventually arrived in Kadena on 3 August. Using System IV, these SIGINT missions were conducted at night, and some were again coordinated with RB-47s of the 55th SRW, flying from Yokota AB. On two occasions, though, missions were curtailed when the RB-47s aborted. However, between 22 August and 25 September four eight-hour sorties were flown by Captains Buddy Brown and Jim Qualls into the Yellow Sea and the Sea of Japan against the North Korean and Chinese air defense systems. A fifth SIGINT mission was flown south to Hainan Island and back by Major Ray Haupt.

On 1 September 1961 the USSR resumed nuclear tests in the atmosphere with three blasts in five days at the Siberian site. With OL-2 handily placed already at Kadena, it was also tasked with sampling. Eleven such sorties were accomplished with the F-2/P-2 hatch during the deployment, which ended in late September.

Urgent Call

Meanwhile, the 4080th received an urgent call from AFTAC to resume sampling out of Alaska. Three aircraft were dispatched to OL-5 Eielson AFB on 5 September. The Soviets resumed tests at the Novaya Zemlya site in the Arctic on 10 September. Such was the frequency of the tests, that the

In January 1961 Kelly Johnson paid his first visit to the SAC wing at Laughlin AFB, where he exchanged gifts with 4080th commander Colonel William Wilcox (left) at an officers' dining-in.

At Project HQ, they took security of flight planning extremely seriously. In fact, some people there were obsessive about it. Here's a typical example from mid-1961, when Det G was staging overflights of Cuba from Laughlin AFB:

It is generally recognized within DPD that the operation of IDEALIST missions from Laughlin AFB, Del Rio, is less than desirable. The time has come when such missions must be considered untenable as a covert action. Operational factors are falling into such a definite pattern, that the course of an IDEALIST mission over Cuba could easily be predicted by friendly or unfriendly forces:

- flight lines over Cuba have been oriented in generally the same direction and over the same target areas
- the aircraft arrives over Cuba at approximately the same time of day on successive missions to take advantage of the sun angle/weather combination
- the approach to Cuba is always from the same direction
- while the staging team composition is not always identical to the ones before, there are always some repeats. This tends to identify the operation as one of a series through personal contact
- at least two people who have been on staging teams were previously based at Laughlin AFB and are known to many military and local townspeople
- the same support aircraft (U-3A) arrives at approximately the same time interval before mission take-off
- the U-2 arrives at Laughlin AFB to spend the same amount of time on the ground each trip. It is also conspicuous because of the different marking compared to Laughlin's U-2s
- NORAD has suppressed radar identification for each mission supposedly through the same channels
- on a local clearance filed at Laughlin AFB, the U-2 stays out nine to 10 hours without regular reports to ATC
- at approximately the time the U-2 is nearing Cuba, NAS Key West is advised that we will operate in their area. The conversation is guarded, and also is restricted to one cleared person, however, it is part of the pattern.

Upon examination of the above factors it becomes evident that several of them closely parallel the factors and sequence of events leading up to 1 May 1960. That is, a pattern has been established. In the event of an incident, our position would be difficult to defend.

If we could operate from a base closer to Cuba then we could approach the island from a different quarter every mission, and delay the probability that the Castro forces could present factual information regarding routes and operating bases.

Memo for Acting Chief DPD from Chief, Special Projects Branch, DPD, 19 July 1961. (In fact, Stan Beerli rejected the idea of switching the missions to a new launch base.)

AFTAC wanted two U-2 sorties per day, instead of one. The 4080th sent two more aircraft to Alaska. Forty-nine missions got off the ground in October. This Toy Soldier deployment was the first to use the improved P-3 platform, in which gas samples were taken via the engine bleed air system.

During October half of the SAC U-2 fleet was engaged in the sampling task. While OL-5 was doing most of the "hot" work in Alaska, home-based OL-10 was also in action from Laughlin, and a third deployment to OL-11 in Australia began. For the first time, sampling was carried out during the transpacific ferry flights, from Hickam AFB to Fiji, and on to East Sale. At both operating locations the sorties were coordinated with B-57s flying at lower levels.

After the Soviets set off a mighty 50-megaton blast over Novaya Zemlya on 30 October, the atmospheric disturbance orbited the earth three times. The weapon was dropped by parachute from a Tu-95 bomber and exploded at 13,000 feet. Sampling pilots in their B-57s and U-2s were asked to watch out for odd-colored clouds or haze. In fact, the huge bomb was remarkably "clean," and released a minimum of fission by-products that would increase background radiation levels in the atmosphere.[19]

In response to the Soviet megablast, new equipment was introduced. The 4080th sent 66695 to Burbank in November to have a gamma spectrometer installed, replacing the P-3 system. The aircraft was immediately flown to Eielson, and flown five times at maximum altitude along the Alaska-Canada corridor. It remained at OL-5 with one of the F-2/P-3-equipped aircraft in support, while the others returned home. The three aircraft in Australia were also flown back to Laughlin in late November. The immediate sampling requirements were met, but AFTAC was now proposing permanent, worldwide sampling detachments, including U-2s in Alaska, Australia, and Guam.[20]

President Kennedy

A few weeks after he became President in January 1961, John Kennedy told a press conference that U-2 flights over the Soviet Union remained suspended. "I have ordered that they not be resumed," he added. A few months later, though, events transpired that almost changed his mind.

At an uncomfortable summit meeting in June 1961, Premier Khrushchev renewed his demand for a peace treaty on Berlin, and recognition for East Germany. As the summer wore on the political heat increased. The Soviets announced the resumption of nuclear tests; JFK called for a big increase in military spending. On 13 August, the German border was closed and the Berlin Wall went up. Talk of nuclear war was in the air. But who held the aces?

According to the majority opinion in the U.S. Intelligence Community, the USSR did not have a serious force of ICBMs capable of threatening the U.S. Slowly, the missile gap theorists were falling silent. For the new Administration, Secretary of Defense Robert McNamara had already admitted, in public, that the Democrat's campaign rhetoric on this subject had been way over the top. But SAC was having none of it. CINCSAC Gen Tommy Power and his intelligence chief, Maj Gen Robert Smith, argued that, with U-2 flights banned and imagery from the CORONA satellite only a poor substitute, the U.S. simply could not be sure that the Soviets had not achieved strategic superiority.[21]

Power wanted U-2 flights over the USSR resumed. So did some members of the U.S. Intelligence Board (USIB) at their meeting on 31 August. There had only been three completely successful CORONA missions by this time, out of 21 attempts. The USIB told COMOR to re-examine and review the critical missile targets in the USSR. A flurry of activity ensued. DDCI Cabell told the White House on 7 September that the latest CORONA mission, launched on 30 August, had been successful, and the photography was being processed. Five more missions were scheduled for the next three months that would help harden the estimate of Soviet missile strength.[22]

But the "hardening" was already underway. On 21 September, a new supplement to the most recent National Intelligence Estimate (NIE) on Soviet Strategic Forces was issued. Thanks to recent imagery from CORONA missions, it drastically reduced the estimate of deployed Soviet ICBM launchers to 10-25. The Soviets were curtailing deployment of their first ICBM (the SS-6) in favor of the smaller, more flexible SS-7. But this would not be ready for operational use until the latter part of 1962, the NIE explained.[23]

Power disagreed

Tommy Power profoundly disagreed. A day before the revised NIE was circulated he marched in to see the President. Only 10% of the USSR had been photographed, and the Air Force had identified 20 ICBM pads from that photography alone, he insisted. Gen Lyman Lemnitzer, the JCS chairman, and Gen Maxwell Taylor, the President's military representative, contested Power's data, but the Cold War Warrior from SAC was not to be swayed. Power asked Kennedy to authorize new U-2 flights. The meeting broke up without agreement. The SAC commander was told to put his arguments in writing.[24]

Nevertheless, Power told his subordinates to plan for the U-2 flights forthwith. The next morning, Kelly Johnson was woken at 5:30 am by Col Geary calling from the Pentagon. Geary asked Johnson to go all-out on modifying six J57-powered U-2s to J75, three each from the Air Force and the Agency. Obviously, someone had been thinking about the extra altitude capability of the U-2C model.

In fact, two CIA U-2As were already at Burbank, receiving the more powerful engine at the same time as the refueling mod. "We tore the place up; I discontinued my vacation, and we put full steam on accelerating airplanes 343 and 344," Johnson noted. But no one had told the CIA about the latest instruction to Lockheed. Johnson queried Dick Bissell, who quickly

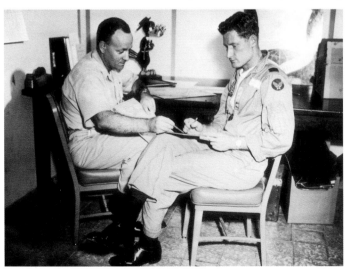

A SAC mission planner briefs U-2 pilot Captain Robert "Deke" Hall. Note the Crowflight mascot of the 4080th SRW in background.

dispatched DPD R&D chief John Parangosky to Burbank. He was accompanied by Geary. They brought Johnson the latest news from Washington, including Powers' meeting with the President. The Skunk Works boss was evidently another hawk in the missile gap debate: "I agreed completely with Powers' analysis rather than that of the CIA," he recalled. "It is amazing to see their preparations, and absolutely vital that we know some details about them. We are going to try low-altitude penetration and a number of other tricks."[25]

But how vulnerable to Soviet air defences would U-2 flights now be? Frank Powers was still languishing in prison, and no one really knew if he had been shot down from 70,000 feet by a SAM or not. Earlier in September, Richard Bissell himself had asked Kelly Johnson to proceed with various ideas to enhance the survivability of the U-2. These included the high-altitude restart (previously, the CIA had baulked at the cost of adding this pyrophoric system); development of a rearward-facing IR countermeasures system to thwart air-launched missiles; reduction of the IR reflection by shielding the tailpipe; weight reduction by removing systems that were not in use; and a "special destructor system."[26]

Moral Problem

This last idea could not have been more controversial, or secret. Johnson was proposing to install a device that would ensure that the U-2 *pilot*, as well as the camera system, was destroyed if the mission should fail. No more propaganda coups for the Soviets! No more show trials of captured pilots! This was "a great technical problem and, of course, a great moral one," Johnson noted. But, he continued, "I have proposed a time-altitude fusing setup for multitude bombs, that looks like it should do the trick."

Was Johnson acting on his own initiative? Certainly, he had suggested a 10 times more powerful destruct mechanism to Project HQ shortly after the May Day shootdown. DPD Assistant Chief Jim Cunningham had not rejected the idea out of hand.[27] But now, as Johnson noted, "(DPD chief Stan) Beerli doesn't want anything to do with this." Nevertheless, the head the targets, and get out again safely. One plan was to fly multiple missions simultaneously. Surely the Soviets would not have the air defense resources to track and engage them all! But in the end, the Recce Branch had to conclude that, as Clancey recalled, "our PKs (probability of kill) were high." No doubt their conclusions reached Power, so he was aware that the chances of a shootdown were high.[29]

On 25 September COMOR reported back to the USIB, endorsing the idea of U-2 flights. "COMOR recognizes that any resumption of overflight operations of the USSR will involve certain risk factors from both an operational and political standpoint," wrote its chairman, Jim Reber. But, he noted, "the U-2 can be operated in optimum weather conditions against specific high priority targets," unlike the satellites. And U-2 photography had "greater interpretability" thanks to stereo and higher resolution.

CORONA imagery had revealed four deployed ICBM complexes that were believed to be intended for the second-generation ICBM. But the question remained, whether the first-generation SS-6 was being deployed there in the interim. As for Plesetsk—a key target on Frank Powers' ill-fated flight—four separate CORONA missions had passed over, but each time clouds had partially obscured the area. Through the openings, the photo-interpreters had discerned highly-secure complexes, defended by SAMs. It was probably an SS-6 launch base, but that was not confirmed.

COMOR recommended U-2 coverage of (in order of priority) Plesetsk, Yurya, Yoshkar-Ola, Verkhnaya Salda, and Kostroma. The Navy pitched in with a footnote: what about the submarine-launched missile threat? It wanted U-2 coverage of Golf, Hotel, and Zulu-class Soviet subs to be given equal priority.[30]

of Skunk Works continued, "we will go ahead and develop it in case someone decides it is necessary."[28]

Was that someone the CINCSAC, Gen Tommy Power?

Overflight Plans

At SAC Headquarters, the Recce Branch was working on U-2 overflight plans. Colonel Ellsworth Powell and Major Orville Clancy tried every which way to devise a scheme that would get the U-2 into Soviet territory, cover

Northern USSR

All of the targets recommended by COMOR were in the northern USSR. The political constraints on launch bases had increased since U-2 mission planners in Project HQ had wrestled with the problem of how to cover the northern USSR, in the months before May Day 1960. Now there was definitely only one option. Launch out of Thule, Greenland, and fly across the Greenland and Barents Seas. The 4080th wing was alerted for a possible deployment to Thule.[31]

While the CIA re-engined all of its U-2s with the higher-powered J75 engine, SAC stuck with the U-2A model powered by the J57.

General Thomas Power, commander of SAC, pressed for the resumption of U-2 flights over the Soviet Union in the fall of 1961.

It was fortunate that a couple of U-2s now had aerial refueling capability, for this would surely be needed. But then, how would the U-2 and tanker rendezvous in the dark, above the Arctic wastelands? The Skunk Works quickly selected the standard military AN/APN-135 rendezvous beacon, and installed one on a U-2F aft of the HF tuner fairing. Using its X-band radar to interrogate the beacon, the tanker could determine range and bearing to the U-2 while maintaining radio silence.

While the State Dept worked up a paper on the political implications, the overflight routes prepared by SAC's Recce Branch were assessed for vulnerability by the Pentagon and the CIA.

Naturally, Project HQ thought it could do better. On 28 September, Stan Beerli sent DPD's own Soviet overflight proposal to the DDP. Bissell subsequently informed DCI Dulles that:

"...we have the equipment and personnel to execute the sortie. The survivability will depend upon reaction time of the enemy...our planning would keep this to the minimum possible. One aspect that is intangible and always present is the operational estimate. This assumes surprise, confusion, equipment malfunction, and command deficiencies will tip the scale towards a successful operation."[32]

In the end, though, the Soviet air defense system was never put to the test. The CIA and HQ USAF agreed with the SAC Recce Branch—U-2 missions over the northern USSR would likely be shot down. The USIB received General Power's written argument against the September NIE, and described it as a "polemic." The Board unanimously rejected the SAC position, reaffirmed the estimate, and recommended against even a limited number of U-2 flights over the USSR.[33]

The tense international situation began to ease, as it became apparent the Soviets would not move against West Berlin. Premier Khrushchev quietly dropped his ultimatum. Successful CORONA missions in September and October further reduced the possibility of a hidden Soviet arsenal of operational ICBMs. Gen Power was not yet ready to give up on the missile gap—but neither was JFK going to approve his U-2 flights. The Dragon Lady never did fly over the USSR again.

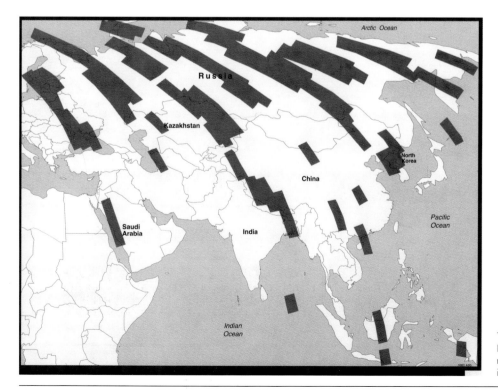

Typical coverage map for a Corona satellite mission. Power and his supporters argued that the satellites could not detect how many missiles the Soviets were pointing at the U.S.

15

Deep Cold War II

The U-2 fleet had all been through a Phase I IRAN (Inspect and Repair As Necessary) at the Skunk Works from 1959-1961. Now a Phase II program was under way. The Angel had not been built to last. How was the structure faring? In the new program, some closed section skins were removed for the first time to check for any corrosion or structural problems. None were found, but for better protection against future corrosion, the Air Force decided to paint its fleet gray during the new IRAN. The Agency aircraft remained dark blue. The Air Force also decided to adopt the more versatile SSB HF radio for all its fleet, and to convert six aircraft for refueling (the number was soon reduced to three, and these aircraft received the designation U-2E).[1]

One of Kelly Johnson's proposals to reduce the U-2's vulnerability to interception was now implemented. The tailpipe shield to reduce IR signature was added—it became known as the "sugar scoop." The continuous ignition system was also given the go-ahead.

The hurried decision to upgrade SAC aircraft with the J75 engine, also taken during the Berlin Crisis, did not stick. The Air Force apparently decided that it could borrow from the Agency fleet, if ever it needed the capability.

Precision ELINT

The first such occasion was in January 1962. SAC's 55th SRW had an RB-47 that carried a precision ELINT measuring system devised by the CIA's Office of ELINT. It could determine the power and radiated pattern of Soviet air defense radars—if they were operating, of course. The trick was to coax them into action, and provide the Soviets with the type of radar target that would cause them to reveal as many of their radar parameters as possible. The U-2 was an ideal target: detectable, but requiring considerable effort on the part of the PVO's radar operators to identify and track.

A deployment to stimulate and measure Soviet radars along the Siberian coast was planned. The RB-47 would fly from Yokota AB, Japan, and the U-2 from Kunsan AB, Korea. For altitude and communications a J75 and SSB-equipped U-2 was needed, but peripheral ELINT was a mission that SAC jealously guarded. Therefore, 4080th wing pilot Major Steve Heyser was sent to North Base for training in the J75-powered model. Det G was then made responsible for ferrying Article 342 (the first U-2F) to Korea, where the Air Force would take over and fly the mission.

The Article was duly delivered to Kunsan and handed over to Colonel Ellsworth Powell, the Director of Reconnaissance at SAC HQ. Steve Heyser

This U-2F has the tailpipe shield, which was nicknamed the "sugar scoop," and was designed to help reduce the aircraft's infrared signature (Lockheed U-2-91-004-3).

was briefed on his role, which was to fly tracks in the Sea of Okhotsk designed to provoke the maximum PVO response. On the night of 12 January 1962 the mission was launched. The RB-47 took off first, but was unexpectedly intercepted by a Soviet fighter on its way to the operating area. In accordance with the SOP for this type of mission, the RB-47 aborted and turned back for Japan.

Screaming

Heyser's U-2 was also recalled, but he failed to acknowledge and pressed on through the mission. "He flew a perfect mission all the way around, and every radar you've ever seen bloomed up and was painting him. And they're screaming at him on the SSB from Yokota to abort," Powell recalled. When Heyser eventually returned to Kunsan, he explained that he had turned the radio off because it was distracting him. Navigating solo at night just miles from a dark Soviet coastline, using only dead reckoning plus celestial navigation, was a full-time task, he explained. Moreover, he added, the charts were drawn up in such a way that "I can go forward, but I can't make a U-turn and come back!" On this unsatisfactory note, the deployment ended and Det G ferried the U-bird all the way back to California![2]

In February 1962, SAC pilots were again snooping along the Soviet Far East borders, as OL-5 was reactivated at Eielson for more SIGINT flights codenamed Venice Lake II. A new version of the big System IV package in the Q-bay was used for the first time. It extended the frequency coverage to the lower VHF spectrum, and included new recorders, scanners, and amplifiers. Captains Jerry McIlmoyle and Bob Powell flew down the Bering Sea to map the Soviet radar order of battle, in conjunction with RB-47s. Marshall Hughes, the Ramo Wooldridge techrep, assured them that System IVA had collected large amounts of SIGINT, especially in the portions of the frequency spectrum not previously covered.[3]

The single SIGINT-configured U-2 was flown back to Laughlin in late February, by which time three sampler-equipped aircraft had arrived. Eielson now became a permanent detachment for this mission. The 4080th also mounted a fourth sampling deployment to Australia in March, and opened a new location for sampling at Howard AB, Panama (OL-18), in April.

Pay Station

In mid-March, meanwhile, two more aircraft were sent to Eielson from Laughlin, this time with the B-camera as the primary sensor. SAC had persuaded the JRC and they, in turn, the Special Group, that more periph-

eral photo missions should be run against Soviet bomber bases along the Siberian coast. Codenamed Pay Station, seven of them were flown by Captains Rex Knaack, Bob Pine, and Ed Purdue. Like the earlier series of flights in spring 1959 and 1960, these were long, risky missions across cold, inhospitable waters. The aircraft also carried a new, experimental

WEATHER CLOUDS

Weather forecasting was always critical to the success of U-2 overflights, as this 1962 memo from the chief of weather staff at DPD makes clear:

These forecasts are provided by the Air Force Global Weather Central at SAC headquarters. A small group there are security-cleared for the DPD projects, and work in a secure area. They are supervised by Lt Col J.J. Allen, who is reputed to be the best practical weather forecaster in the Air Force.

The past record of this group has been phenomenally good. On the missions flown out of Det B prior to May 1960, 92% of the areas forecast to be favorable (eg 2/8 or less cloud cover) were actually found to be favorable.

In the (tropical areas of southeast Asia) we cannot expect the same high degree of forecast reliability. The climatology of this area is such that...favorable conditions can be expected to occur less than two days per month, except during the late fall or early winter, when three to five days can be expected.

In most instances, weather forecast errors are limited to such things as slight displacement of the lines separating favorable from unfavorable weather. In the case of Mission 3069 over Vietnam, we were faced with overcast stratus cloud. If the wind flow pattern, and consequently the moisture content of the lower 6,000 feet of the atmosphere, had changed as the forecaster believed it would, there is little doubt that virtually all of the stratus cloud would have disappeared.

In areas where good weather occurs frequently we can wait until the weather gets good, and the forecaster is certain that it will remain so. In cloudy areas, periods of good weather are of short duration. Therefore, the forecasters must call the long shots, to be certain that a favorable day does not come and go before we can run a mission.

During U-2 deployments, a KC-135 hauled support equipment and carried ferry crews. It also acted as a radio relay, especially on long transpacific flights (NARA 106740).

NUCLEAR CLOUDS

Clouds of a different sort were actively sought by U-2 pilots, especially in 1962. In this year, the renewal of nuclear test shots in the atmosphere caused SAC's U-2s to roam even further afield, in search of gas and particles to sample in the upper atmosphere.

In April, the U.S. began a new series of tests in the Pacific named Dominic. Two U-2As were deployed to OL-18 at Howard AFB, Panama. They flew search patterns at 65,000 ft along the west coast of South America and the east coast of Central America. They exposed the F-2 foils to trap particles throughout the flights, and were additionally told to activate the P-3 gas sampling system whenever they noticed any debris. If the primary aircraft encountered high-intensity radiation, a second U-2 was launched to boost the collection.

In mid-May, two more U-2s were deployed in support of the Dominic tests, this time to OL-9 at Hickam AFB, Hawaii. From here, a new Gross Gama detector was carried alongside the F-2 system.

In July, the Soviets began a new series of tests at Novaya Zemlya. Scientists soon realized that the particles released into the upper atmosphere needed to be sampled along new tracks. One promising area was above the northern North Atlantic. The 4080th wing made hurried preparations to deploy to the UK for the first time. Three U-2As arrived at the USAF base of Upper Heyford, near Oxford, on 19 August as OL-7. Capt Tony Bevacqua flew the first mission two days later. Three routes were flown: one in a straight line to 77 degrees North; one over the Hebrides and all the way up the coast of Greenland to 73 degrees North; and one across the North Sea and up the Norwegian coast to beyond Bear island. Six of the first seven U-2 flights from Upper Heyford were "hot."

Meanwhile, the permanent U-2 deployment at Eielson AFB, Alaska, was told to fly even further north. All the way to the North Pole, in fact. Capt Don Webster made the first such flight on 25 August 1962, a distance of over 3,000 miles requiring celestial navigation all the way. It was the first time a single-engined jet had been over the Pole. Willie Lawson flew the next mission to the North Pole, but other sampling tracks from Eielson were also flown with increased regularity throughout September and October. These were challenging flights in the frozen north, made more so by any technical problems. On 10 October, detachment commander Lt Col Forrest Wilson made an outstanding save of his U-2 after suffering a complete electrical failure at 55,000 feet on climbout. With only battery power to move the flaps and trim, Wilson made an emergency landing in the dark at Elmendorf AFB.

Moreover, 17 of the 36 sampling flights mounted by OL-5 from Alaska in September encountered radioactive material. Were the pilots adequately protected by their pressure suits? Apparently not. The 4080th wing history records that, on his 2 September flight, Dick Bouchard attained 600 milliroentgen. As a result, he was grounded for 12 days. As a further precaution, the pilots of OL-5 in Alaska had blood tests every two weeks. – C.P.

COMINT configuration adding the low-band amplifiers and antennas from System IVA in the nose, alongside the existing Systems 1 and 3.

The CIA did not approve. Deputy Director Research Herb Scoville sniffed:

"The justification for this type of activity is very weak...while the risk may be small, nevertheless it is finite, and some failure could cause another incident like the RB-47 and prevent other operations which have very much greater intelligence potential."[4]

But, Scoville added, he was not opposed to SAC mounting peripheral flights against Kamchatka, which had "a very much higher potential intelligence payoff." At this time, the U.S. intelligence community was very concerned about a possible Soviet Anti-Ballistic Missile (ABM) system. Large radars had first been spotted at Saryshagan by the 9 April 1960 U-2 flight, and the area was now believed to be an ABM test facility. A second such facility was suspected on the upper Kamchatka Peninsula, to where the Soviet ICBM test shots from Tyuratam had long been aimed.

And on 18 April the 4080th deployed another U-2A to fly in this area. But although the deployment was also codenamed Pay Station, it was for SIGINT, not imagery collection. Major Steve Heyser returned to the scene of his night excursion three months earlier, in command of OL-2 at Kunsan AB. The deployment was via Hickam, Wake Island, and Kadena. For the first time, a KC-135 flew below the U-2 during the ferry flights, providing airlift and ground refueling at Wake. Captain Pat Halloran flew the only operational sortie on 8 May—another long nighttime excursion into the Sea of Okhotsk, to provoke Soviet radars while an RB-47 made precision measurements.[5]

To underline just how versatile the U-2 wing now was, the 4080th sent a U-2 to Eglin AFB in late April to form part of a special Air Force static display for President Kennedy. Laid out in front of the Dragon Lady were examples of the A-2, B and C-camera hatches; the P-3 sampling platform; the weather hatch; and the SIGINT Systems 1, III, and IVA. Rudy Anderson stood by his aircraft as JFK drove by—without stopping. But Anderson was able to brief all the good stuff to Kennedy's entourage, including Generals LeMay and Power, and Secretary of the Air Force Zuckert!

In this month, the 4080th also took on yet another mission—the support of U.S. nuclear testing. The three aircraft at newly-opened OL-18, Howard AFB, measured fall-out from the Project Dominic explosions, the airdrops from B-52s. In May, two aircraft went to Hickam so that OL-9 could do weather reconnaissance and sampling for Project Fish Bowl, the high altitude shots from Thor missiles.

Another Accident

On the night of 2 January 1962, Captain Chuck Stratton of the 4080th was at high altitude, flying the second leg of a celestial navigation training flight. Somewhere over the swamplands of Louisiana, 66709 suddenly pitched up and rolled left. The aircraft stalled, the nose fell, and airspeed built up. Despite applying full right aileron and back pressure on the yoke, Stratton was unable to regain control before the mach limit was exceeded. Once again, the tail section came off, and then the wings. The fuselage entered an inverted flat spin. Despite the disorientation, Stratton managed to initiate his escape by pulling the D-ring between his knees to eject.

After the accident, he recalled being ejected from the cockpit, with his arms raised above his head. He then began spinning around wildly in the thin air, unable to control the nauseating motion despite extending his arms and legs in various positions. He began to pass out and so, like Jack Nole had done five years earlier, Stratton decided to take the risk and deploy the parachute while still at high altitude. He too was lucky, and got a good 'chute with no injury. Then came the inevitable long descent, resulting in the emergency oxygen supply running out. Of necessity, he opened the faceplate, and was relieved to discover that he was now low enough to breathe oxygen from the outside air. It was a dark night, and Stratton landed in a tree. The canopy snagged above him in the branches so that he did not fall into the swamp below. He spent the rest of the night in the tree, talking to the rescue parties through his emergency radio. At daybreak they arrived in a boat and helped him aboard.

Later, the rescue party gathered up the wreckage, which was spread over several miles of swampland. When they showed Stratton the cockpit section, he couldn't believe his eyes. *The ejection seat was still in it!* He felt certain he had ejected. During the accident investigation, Stratton agreed to undergo hypnosis in order to try and work out what had really happened. The accident investigators concluded that the seat had failed to rise up the rails because they had been distorted as the aircraft broke up. But the lap belt did release as advertised, four seconds later, and Stratton had been thrown from the aircraft.[6]

But what had caused Stratton's aircraft to pitchup in the first place? The autopilot was suspected again. Other pilots were reporting sudden movements in pitch during high-altitude flight. The Lear Company, who made the model 201, could not figure it out. Lockheed didn't seem to be taking the matter seriously. Writing in his U-2 log about Stratton's accident, Kelly Johnson noted: "We don't have much of an explanation. Many of us believe he went to sleep." The aircraft's main inverter provided power to the autopilot, and was doubled in capacity to 500VA, in case it was overloading.

Two months later another accident cast further doubt on the ejection seat. SAC sent two more pilots to North Base for check out in the Agency's J75 and SSB-equipped models. There were plans to refly the unsuccessful January precision ELINT mission. This time, SAC wanted its own pilots to ferry the aircraft over the Pacific, and so it requested that the pair—Majors Rudy Anderson and John Campbell—be checked out for inflight refueling.

Campbell disaster

Shortly after 2100 on 1 March disaster struck. As he moved in for a night refueling behind a KC-135 at 35,000 feet, Campbell somehow lost control. Article 344 flipped over and fell away, with the SAC pilot desperately trying to assert his authority over the tumbling aircraft. Failing to do so, he attempted to eject, but the seat did not leave the plane. He was apparently still trying to extricate himself from the cockpit when the plane hit the ground; his body was found in the wreckage, halfway out of the cockpit, the canopy having been manually opened.

A formation ferry flight by the SAC wing. These U-2As have recently been through IRAN, emerging with the gray paint scheme designed to protect against corrosion (via Bob Spencer).

Although the accident had taken place virtually overhead Edwards AFB, it took 37 hours to find the wreckage. The search occupied 25 pilots, who flew 57 sorties throughout that day and the following morning. They used T-birds, Cessnas, T-28s, helicopters, and a C-123, which ranged far and wide over Southern California, Nevada, Arizona, and Utah. In the dark, there had been no way for the tanker crew to determine what had happened to Campbell, so they figured he could be anywhere. The crash site was eventually located by Lockheed test pilot Bob Schumacher at 1100 on Saturday morning, while he was flying the faithful Beech Bonanza owned by the Skunk Works Flight Test Department. The wreckage was lying in the Kramers Hills, a section of the Mojave Desert just a few miles east of Edwards! The ejection seat was still in place, and yet the initiators had fired. Something similar had occurred during Chuck Stratton's accident.[7]

Aerial refueling in the U-2 was suspended while Lockheed re-evaluated the loads imposed while maneuvering behind the tanker. If jetwash was the problem, would it be safer to refuel from the slower, prop-driven KC-97 tanker? While Lockheed investigated the ejection seat problem, pilots were told not to use it. If they had to get out in a hurry, bailout was once again the only option.

Cold-soaked

The Skunk Works ran tests, firing some seats containing dummies from a spare fuselage that had been salvaged from a previous U-2 accident. The seat was supposed to fire through the canopy, and duly did so in the tests—until they tried firing it through a canopy that had been cold-soaked to replicate the conditions of prolonged high-altitude flight. Then it rose up the tracks, slammed into the plexiglass, and got no further! When hardened by the coldsoak, the canopy was equal to the force of the seat's rocket thrust.

Now the circumstances surrounding Stratton's escape made sense. He had indeed tried to eject, but the seat had bounced back off the canopy. Then the seat belt had released automatically, as advertised. Somehow, Stratton had managed to pull the canopy release latch—though he could not recall this—and then he was thrown free of the aircraft by the g forces. In Campbell's case, the seat must also have failed to penetrate the canopy, but he did not have enough time (or luck) to recover from the malfunction and make a manual escape.

So the seat had to be modified. Canopy piercers were installed on the protective rail above the pilot's head—three pointed metal spikes that could help shatter the plexiglass. The rocket charge was also increased substantially, and this entailed strengthening the cockpit floor bulkhead. The seat rails were also modified, and the elapsed time between pulling the D-ring, seat firing, and lapbelt release was reduced.

Lockheed also started work on a gas-powered system that would automatically fire the canopy away when the ejection seat sequence was initiated. This was installed on the fleet during 1964. Now the U-2 had a half-decent escape system, but pilots were still aware of its serious limitations. They were advised, for instance, that an ejection from a spinning or diving aircraft should not be attempted below 10,000 feet, and that low-altitude ejections might not be successful unless the aircraft was in a positive climb and doing more than 120 knots.

As for the suspect autopilots, the problems continued. On 23 March, Lt Col Art Leatherwood was climbing out of Laughlin when his autopilot began oscillating in pitch. One problem led to another, and the SAC pilot was eventually forced to make a deadstick landing at Biggs AFB after he flamed out and made six unsuccessful restarts. 4080th wing safety officer Don James concluded that the autopilot should not be used in moderate to heavy turbulence. Meanwhile, Lockheed and the autopilot subcontractor Lear were told to pay more attention to quality control, especially as the aircraft went through Phase II IRAN. Eventually, in August, a conference was held at Laughlin AFB to discuss detailed improvements, such as bonding of the rate gyro, rewiring of the trim indicators, and replacing the diodes in the trim controls with condensers.[8]

Big changes in Washington

Big changes were afoot in Washington. John McCone replaced Allen Dulles as Director of Central Intelligence in November 1961. At one of his first meetings with the PFIAB, the new DCI was told by James Killian and Edwin Land that the Agency's reconnaissance programs should not be controlled by the covert action side of CIA, namely the DDP. Richard Bissell had taken the U-2 and the nascent Corona and Oxcart efforts with him when he took over DDP in 1959. But the PFIAB now believed that high tech overhead spying was becoming a big enterprise, deserving of its own directorate within the CIA. Land was also particularly annoyed that Bissell had used the U-2 so extensively to support the failed Bay of Pigs invasion.

Bissell was opposed to the removal of DPD from his control, even though McCone offered him the job of running it. So he resigned, and the DCI appointed Herbert "Pete" Scoville to run a new Deputy Directorate of Research (DDR). DPD was then transferred to this new organization, minus the Air Support Branch, which remained in DDP to conduct paradrops and resupply of agents, and other covert air activities.

In 1962, three SAC pilots were sent to Edwards so that the CIA unit could teach them how to fly and be refueled in the U-2F model.

Captain John Campbell was killed in March 1962 when his U-2 entered the jetwash behind a KC-135 during air-air refueling practice, and broke up (via Bob Spencer).

A short time later, DPD was renamed the Office of Special Activities (OSA). At about the same time, the organization moved from the increasingly-cramped Matomic Building on 1717 H Street in downtown Washington to the CIA's brand new complex on the other side of the Potomac, at Langley, VA. Col Stan Beerli was nearing the end of his tour, so his tenure as the new Assistant Director for Special Activities (AD), in charge of OSA, was short. He was replaced in early September 1962 by Col Jack Ledford. Jim Cunningham—by now the corporate memory of the Agency U-2 program—stayed on as the senior Agency civilian, i.e. Ledford's Deputy (DAD). Beneath them in the OSA organization were the heads of divisions, notably Col Don Songer at Operations, John McMahon at Administration, and John Parangosky at Development.

JACK LEDFORD – MY BEST ASSIGNMENT

In 1962 Colonel Jack Ledford had already spent four years in Washington, and was being reassigned to a missile wing. He did not like the prospect much, and appealed to his mentor Butch Blanchard, the Air Force Inspector-General. Blanchard told him there was a very good job going—but it would mean staying in Washington. It was Director of OSA—the Office of Special Activities that ran the CIA's Corona, Oxcart, and U-2 reconnaissance programs. Ledford recalled:

I was still only a young Colonel, from a bomber and fighter background, and I didn't know a thing about Recon. But I had a physics degree, and I knew Herb Scoville (CIA Deputy Director Research) from Sandia Labs. So I got the job.

The headquarters group was fabulous. Jim Cunningham was a mine of information, and a brilliant writer. John Parangosky knew everything about the A-12, and had a great rapport with Kelly Johnson. Don Songer was a very good Air Force operations type. I decided on a reorganization to separate ops from admin.

We made our own purchasing decisions, though we had to clear them with the NRO. By comparison, the Air Force procurement rules were a jungle.

I got on well in Washington. Without doubt, it was my best assignment.

- interview with author

A U-2A of the 4080th SRW equipped for sampling on approach in 1962 (Albert Gibb).

HERE THEY COME – THE U-2s

This is how the Daily Express, a British national newspaper, reported the arrival of three 4080th wing birds at Upper Heyford for sampling flights in August 1962. It was front-page news:

Three American U2 "spy" planes flew into Britain yesterday along with a team of five veteran pilots and 50 technicians. And one of the pilots, Tony Bevacqua, said: "Even my dear old mother still thinks I'm a spy!"

The team will fly three of these strange and somewhat sinister aircraft on Atlantic missions to check on weather, cosmic rays and Russian nuclear tests. The U2s will operate from US Strategic Air Command's base at Upper Heyford for six weeks to three months. Their area of operations will include the seas round Greenland and Norway. They carry no guns—and no cameras.

Yesterday the three aircraft flew 3,000-odd miles from New York in seven hours. They have an unconventional undercarriage of "bicycle" wheels fore and aft, so that as they lose speed they heel over until "skids" on the tips of their 80ft glider-like wings set them straight.

Flying alongside Captain Bevacqua, who is 29 and comes from Ohio, is Captain Robert Pine, 33, from Detroit and Captain David Ray, a Texan. Two spare pilots are joining them, and 50 technicians.

Bevacqua and Pine have flown U2 missions from Australia, South America and Alaska—"horrible stints." Their chief, leather-faced Colonel Arthur Leatherwood, said: "We are using very experienced and qualified pilots."

It's a tough job—cramped in pressure suits for long hours. They hope it will be better in England. "I looked at your Chipping Norton from the air," said Bevacqua. "It looked pretty attractive. I'll have to pay a visit there."

Colonel Jack Ledford took over Project Idealist in mid-1962 as Director of the Office of Special Activities (OSA). He stayed four years, during which time he was promoted to Brigadier General (via Jack Ledford).

Parangosky's major task was to oversee upgrades to the Corona satellite system, and to bring the Oxcart project to fruition. The latter was no easy task. The contract for the Lockheed A-12 airplane—a Mach 3 "successor" to the U-2—had been signed in January 1960. Kelly Johnson predicted a first flight in May 1961. But the technical challenges were so great that even the Skunk Works could not make good this promise. Pratt & Whitney also struggled to develop the J58 powerplants. The date slipped to August, then to December 1961. Parangosky hired aeronautical engineer Norm Nelson as Project HQ's man-on-the-spot in Burbank. Unlike the U-2, this thing was too big to simply let Kelly get on with it without supervision.

Oxcart airborne

Eventually, the Oxcart got airborne on 26 April 1962. But this was only thanks to a decision to use two P&W J75s as interim powerplants. The first flight of an A-12 powered by two J58s did not take place until 15 January 1963. The test base was Groom Lake, last used by Project Aquatone in 1957, and now undergoing a costly expansion. Of course, this helped to preserve secrecy, and like the U-2 before it, the Agency's new spyplane remained unknown to the world at large.[9]

In 1962, hopes were still high that the A-12 would be able to penetrate denied airspace without detection. "In addition to reducing the radar cross-section of the vehicle, considerable effort is being placed on detecting and exploiting known weaknesses in the Soviet air defense system," noted an internal CIA document.[10] That effort was the Power and Pattern Measurement System (PPMS), led by Gene Poteat, a CIA engineer now assigned to OSA. U-2s flown by SAC were involved in some of the operations to take measurements of Soviet radars, such as the missions along the Kamchatka Peninsula. Unfortunately, by the end of 1962 it was obvious to Poteat and his colleagues that, despite its speed, the A-12 would still be detected by the USSR's early warning radars, notably the Tall King.

To help the Oxcart flight test program, meanwhile, one of the Agency's U-2s was bailed to Lockheed for development of the new aircraft's ambitious Astro-Inertial navigation system. It was Article 355, the U-2A that had languished so long in Turkey. But this left the Agency short of U-2s. In 1961-62 three aircraft had been lost in accidents. Two Articles were now allocated to the joint operation on Taiwan. That left just three at North Base for development (including an ongoing series of flights over the USA codenamed Red Dot, to test color and infrared films that might prove useful for satellite reconnaissance); training; and operations (such as the ongoing Project Nimbus overflights of Cuba).

The Agency was even planning a return to SIGINT missions with the new System 10 package (although peripheral missions were now supposed to be the preserve of the Air Force). Intelligence analysts were still lobbying for the acquisition of System 10, because they thought it could help them learn more about the large and powerful Soviet radars that might form part of an anti-missile (eg anti-US ICBM) system.[11]

From the Agency's perspective there were plenty of U-2s available at Laughlin AFB. It requested two of them. SAC reluctantly transferred 66683 in April and 66692 in July. Both were subsequently converted to U-2Fs. Meanwhile, Project HQ requested that some of the Det G pilots be requalified on the J57-powered U-2A model by the SAC unit, in case the Edwards-based unit could not muster one of its own J75 models to meet the next Cuban overflight requirement. Then there were moves in June and

At Groom Lake, the A-12 Oxcart finally got airborne in April 1962. But there was still a long way to go before the U-2's supposed successor would be ready for operations.

July to deploy SAC U-2s and pilots to Asia, to augment the coverage that the two U-2s on Taiwan could provide. Things were getting messy.[12]

Consolidated

In fact, the CIA's own Inspector General (IG) now recommended that the nation's U-2 fleet be consolidated into that of SAC. The CIA should retain control of its own crews (eg pilots), the staging of overflights, and of the photo interpretation task, the IG allowed. But the Air Force could "assume responsibility for facilities, staffing, maintenance, research and development, and for operational readiness of the aircraft." The IG explained:

"The loss of the U-2 over Russia in May 1960 indicated a growing vulnerability of the aircraft which now restricts its use against first-class air defense systems to situations of extreme emergency. It may continue to have usefulness against second-rate defense systems for some time to come, but meanwhile superior vehicles are being sought under other programs." The IG was presumably referring to Oxcart.[13]

The transfer never happened. Project HQ jealously guarded its independence and *modus operandi*. Men like Cunningham, McMahon, and Parangosky owed their careers to the U-2. Such was the status of DPD, they did not even have to comply with the CIA's normal administrative rules. Many of the Air Force officers who were assigned to work at DPD supported the need for a separate and distinct "civilian" U-2 capability. Stan Beerli summed up the rationale in February 1962:

"Our experience tends to confirm the desirability of disassociating strategic reconnaissance of the sort accomplished in Idealist...from a strict military context which can be interpreted by the opposition as aggressive."[14]

16

The Cuba Missile Crisis

Beginning in January 1962, Soviet personnel began arriving in Cuba in large numbers. They made every effort to disguise their arrival, and their movements within the island. But word of their presence was carried by the growing stream of refugees to the CIA's debriefing center in Miami. The refugees brought rumours of missile launch pads and all manner of military construction.[1]

The CORONA satellites were not much help in assessing what was really going on. The priority for exposing their precious, finite film supply was over the USSR. In any case, their south-north orbits took them over the island in a couple of minutes. And the elapsed time to expose the film, eject and recover the film-return capsule, and send it for processing was too long.

By comparison, the U-2s of the CIA's Project Nimbus could fly east-west along the island for maximum coverage. The missions could be scheduled at the optimum times for cloud-free photography. And the "take" could be on the photo-interpreters' light tables so much quicker. Typically, it would take only six hours after landing for the B-camera film to be processed at Laughlin and loaded in a military jet for a three-hour flight to Andrews AFB, Washington. Less than four hours later, NPIC would be ready to issue an Initial Photo-Interpretation Report (IPIR).[2]

To check the reports from agents and refugees, DCI John McCone ordered Project HQ to step up U-2 overflights from one to two per month in mid-April. "It was a mammoth undertaking, but where possible we checked every weapon report against U-2 photography, and against other intelligence sources," DDP Richard Helms later recalled. A lot of the refu-

gees' information was inaccurate. "There were reports of underground hangars that could house large numbers of aircraft. I ordered four complete mosaics of all of Cuba, and four U-2 overflights were flown in June 1962. These flights disproved the statements," said DCI McCone.[3]

Task Force W

The U-2 imagery of Cuba served another, less obvious purpose. It was used to assess whether sabotage operations organized by the U.S. against the Castro regime were effective, or not. For although the Bay of Pigs fiasco had harmed the Administration, it did not prevent JFK from sanctioning more covert operations. The CIA's Task Force W organized spies on the ground, propaganda against the Cuban regime, and supplies to anti-Castro forces. It also tried to destroy key infrastructure on the island...oil refineries, railroad bridges, a nickel-mining operation. But when analysts from NPIC checked the film for evidence of success, they had a hard time finding any. Dino Brugioni and other NPIC officials made themselves very unpopular with Task Force W when they pointed this out.[4]

Prior to each mission staged out of Laughlin AFB (or occasionally direct from Edwards when aerial refueling was available), NORAD was given the approximate timings so that it could arrange for the suppression of U.S. radar-tracking reports on the U-2's progress. A waiver was obtained from a new CINCLANT requirement, that all U.S. military aircraft flying in the Caribbean should make hourly reports by HF radio.[5]

But despite the rigorous communications security, the Soviets knew that Cuba was being overflown. First, there had been the press reports after

Intelligence analysts tried to determine what was onboard Soviet merchant ships heading for Cuba in 1962 by studying the crates on open deck. It was subsequently determined that this one was carrying Il-28 Beagle bombers (NARA 167766).

the Bay of Pigs affair. More recently, the KGB had reported on a closed hearing in the U.S. Congress, where CIA officials showed photographs of cargo ships docked at the island's ports. Lately, the KGB spies had found out that U-2 imagery was being used to count the number of MiGs in Cuba. By mid-June, U.S. ELINT-gathering flights near Cuba had recorded signals from up to 13 each of the Soviet-designed Token and Knife Rest early-warning radars. They seemed to be concentrated around Havana and Santa Clara.[6]

Deception

Strangely, though, when Premier Khrushchev took the fateful decision to secretly deploy SS-4 MRBMs and SS-5 IRBMs[7] to Cuba in May 1962, his closest advisors did not take account of the U-2 capability. Yet in order to present the U.S. with a *fait accompli*, the entire plan depended on the most elaborate deception. It was so secret that many high-ranking Soviet military officers knew nothing about it. The operation was codenamed Anadyr, after the river that flows into the Bering Sea in the far north of Siberia. Missile units were led to believe that this was their destination: they were even issued with extra winter clothing. The movement of men and equipment to the six Soviet ports from which the freighters left for Cuba, and their concealment onboard, was a classic example of *maskirovka*—concealment.[8]

In early July, however, Khrushchev ordered that priority be given to deploying air defense missiles ahead of the offensive nuclear missiles. In fact, the Castro regime had requested the SA-2 system more than a year earlier. But the request was not approved until February 1962, and then their supply was delayed because of a bottleneck in the Soviet defense industry. In April, the Soviets decided to divert 12 SA-2 units and 144 launchers intended for Egypt to Cuba. They were on their way by mid-July, accompanied by experienced PVO missile operators from Nikolayev, in the Ukraine. On the ships' manifest they were listed as agricultural engineers.[9]

U.S. intelligence had not discounted the possibility that the SAMs were coming. NIE 85-62, issued on 21 March 1962, described how Cuba's air defenses had been boosted by the supply of 35 MiG-15/17 and 10-12 MiG-19, plus anti-aircraft guns. SAMs and air defense radars could follow, it said, but the Soviets "were unlikely to provide offensive weapons."

There was only one successful U-2 flight over Cuba in July; a second aborted with camera failure. On 5 August, mission 3086 flew along the southern coastline and back along the north, in the usual fashion. Once again, there was no evidence of any missiles, defensive or offensive, on the imagery.[10] By now, though, DCI McCone and some of his analysts did indeed fear that the Soviets might be introducing offensive nuclear missiles to Cuba. But they had no proof.

Some of the Soviet freighters were photographed as they left the Black Sea, a lesser number as they left the Baltic ports. Low-flying U.S. patrol planes attempted to locate and photograph the ships as they crossed the Atlantic. U.S. photo-interpreters honed their recently-acquired skill of "cratology"—trying to determine what was inside the various large crates that could be seen on the decks of the Soviet freighters. They compared them with earlier imagery of Soviet arms shipments enroute to Egypt, Iraq, and Indonesia before they were unpacked.[11]

Project HQ alerted another U-2 mission, but it was repeatedly delayed by bad weather over Cuba. On 29 August, Bob Ericson finally got airborne on mission 3088, crossed the Yucatan Channel, and penetrated Cuba's western edge. Turning half-left, he passed over Havana, then flew down the middle of the island before looping back to cover the southern coastline. Another nine-hour mission for Project Nimbus ended, as usual, at Laughlin AFB, where the film was quickly processed and rushed to NPIC in Washington for examination.

SAM sites in Cuba

Most of the eastern part was cloudy. But there, along the northern coast, was the first evidence of Soviet missiles in Cuba. The Star of David pattern! By the end of the day, NPIC's Earl Shoemaker had identified eight

This was the first SA-2 missile site seen in Cuba, as seen by the camera of Bob Ericson's U-2 on 29 August 1962 (NARA 167783).

THERE I WAS...OVER SAKHALIN

Captain Bob Spencer made his own contribution to the escalating tension just before the Cuban Missile Crisis, when he mistakenly overflew Sakhalin Island on the night of 30 August 1962. Can you blame him, though?

On my first night mission out of Kadena, 7 August, I lost hydraulic pressure, which meant a no-flap landing. This plane was a "chugger," meaning that when the throttle was moved up, for power, it would cough 10-15 times before it would start winding up. So I made a long low approach to keep the power up, but even so I needed more power nearing the end of the runway. But it choked, and I barely made it to the threshold.

We redeployed to Kunsan. After a few days there, waiting for weather or HQ (I don't know what), they gave us another night SIGINT mission. From Kunsan northeast to a point between Sakhalin Island and the Russian mainland. We had a great big heavy tape recorder that put the cg a lot farther forward. As a result, I am sure the fuel consumption was affected. I understand the mission was originally planned for a C-model with slipper tanks, but we were using an A-model. However, we had a fuel cut-off point, and that was my decision.

I got into turbulence and had to take it off autopilot. That impaired my ability to do the celestial. I continued hand-flying it to the fuel cut-off, point where I did the turn and started heading back. There was an undercast. I started getting coded sideband messages from Big Brother that I was off course and to make a correction. But they didn't say which way, and I didn't know whether I was drifting over the Russian mainland or Sakhalin. Since I did not know which way to turn, I didn't. I figured that if things really got exciting they would at least tell me in the clear to turn left or right!

I pressed on, and eventually I could see Hokkaido as the undercast cleared, and I made a correction. Evidently I had been over Sakhalin for about nine minutes, pretty close to an installation. I guess they did everything but launch a missile.

I could see Kunsan well and clear as I approached, but as I turned final the runway lights started disappearing. I figured the canopy was fogged because I didn't have the temperature high enough. So I pulled up and made a go-around, during which I determined it was fog on the outside coming in from the bay. I made the tightest go-around possible because I was running low on fuel. I got the plane down, but by then it was so foggy that I could not taxi in and had to be towed. They later checked the fuel tanks—I could not have done another go-around.

Then everything started hitting the fan. The intel officer asked if I was sure I saw nothing. They thought the Soviets had launched some SA-2s. The next day I was yanked back to Yokota, and the Colonel there was very upset because I was causing him trouble. We hand-carried the tapes back to Offutt and checked into the motel right across from HQ. My escort had the TV on, and Good Morning America was showing where this U-2 had flown into Soviet airspace. I wasn't looking forward to the HQ visit!

But General Power was very friendly. He seemed to understand my explanation as to why I did not turn. They asked me to leave. I waited outside the conference room and could hear Power really shouting at all his staffers....

SA-2 SAM sites in various stages of construction. At least one was occupied. A ninth site was discovered the next day. Shoemaker and his colleagues also noticed another type of missile site on the coast at Banes, and six Komar-class guided missile patrol boats.[12]

Within the CIA, Project HQ prepared to step up the tempo. An augmented staging team was deployed to Laughlin on 4 September, capable of flying onwards from there to a U.S. base in Florida if it seemed better to recover the next U-2 flight there. If the mission did not return to Laughlin, plans were made to fly the B-camera film from Florida by a Navy A3D jet to Eastman Kodak in Rochester for processing.

The mission aircraft set off for Laughlin later the same day, with the pilot practicing hookups with a KC-135 during the ferry leg from Edwards. Inflight refueling gave flight planners greater operational latitude in selecting entry and exit points for U-2 missions over Cuba, and the chance to fly at maximum possible altitude, because a KC-135 tanker could wait off the coast of Florida to refuel the U-2 once it had overflown the island. This was the first time that inflight refueling had been conducted since the accident that killed John Campbell five months earlier. New rendezvous procedures had been devised to bring the U-2 into the correct position for refueling without entering the tanker's slipstream.[13]

Mission 3089 got off on time in the early hours of 5 September. It headed for the western end of the island, which had been cloud-covered on the previous flight. A zig-zag track was then flown up the center of Cuba and over Santa Clara airfield, before coast-out some 60 miles east of Havana. The Banes coastal missile site was overflown, but it was cloudy here.

There was no attempt to revisit the known SAM sites to the west! Nevertheless, this flight identified three more SAM sites, and—for the first time—a MiG-21 at Santa Clara. Alongside were a dozen more crates presumed to contain further Fishbeds.[14]

DCI McCone

What exactly did the SAM deployment mean? Were the Soviets simply protecting Cuban airspace against possible U.S. aggression? After all, most of the sites seemed to be in western Cuba, protecting Havana and the main part of the population. DCI McCone had another explanation. He surmised that the Soviets were deploying SA-2s expressly to stop U-2 surveillance, so they could deploy offensive missiles without detection. Senior Congressional leaders voiced similar fears in public, and on 4 September the Soviet ambassador in Washington was summoned to the White House, where he flatly denied that this was the case.[15]

The U.S. needed more U-2 coverage. But it didn't happen. A combination of bad weather and political and operational caution was to blame. As one CIA official later wrote: "there was always at the back of our minds the knowledge that, in the event of a mishap, we would have to be able to explain, convincingly and in detail, the justification for having undertaken the mission."[16]

Sakhalin overflight

On 4 September 1962 the Soviets protested an overflight of Sakhalin Island by a U-2 five days earlier. It was on a peripheral SIGINT mission, the last of three conducted in August by the 4080th wing's OL-2, based at Kadena AB. Commanded by Lt Col Ed Dixon, OL-2 had retained one of the two U-2As (66719) that was previously deployed in such hurry across the Pacific for possible overflights of China or Vietnam. Using this aircraft, on 7 and 16 August Captains Bob Spencer and Leo Stewart flew seven-hour night missions along the Korean coast and past Vladivistok, returning over the Sea of Japan to Okinawa. The ELINT analysts rated the missions as 90-95% successful, so they decided to try for coverage further north. OL-2 moved up to Kunsan AB, from where Spencer took off after dark on 30 August. His route took him through the gap between the Soviet mainland and Sakhalin Island, to a turnaround in the Sea of Okhotsk, and back. There was a solid undercast and, distracted by turbulence, Spencer miscalculated his position on the way back, and flew for several minutes over southern Sakhalin. The PVO scrambled MiG-19 interceptors, and nearly fired SA-2 missiles as well.[17]

The State Dept was still dealing with the Soviet protest over this incursion when, on 9 September, the Chinese communists downed CAF U-2 pilot Chen over Nanchang. Now, Secretary of State Dean Rusk was *very* nervous about U-2s! He even sought reassurance from the CIA that no one involved in the planning of the Cuban overflights would seek to provoke another U-2 incident.[18]

At a meeting of the Special Group on 10 September, Rusk questioned the utility of further U-2 flights over Cuba. Supported by McGeorge Bundy, he insisted that the Agency modify the routes of the two currently-proposed U-2 missions. They were planned to skirt the coast before crossing into denied territory. Rusk wanted shorter missions, and the peripheral and penetration parts separated. DCI McCone was abroad on his honeymoon, but DDCI Marshall Carter, standing in for him at the meeting, was unhappy. So was Bobby Kennedy. However, to meet Rusk's wishes and reduce the risk the program was recast. There would be two peripheral missions at or near the three-mile limit recognized by the U.S., plus two overflights that would quickly penetrate and exit denied territory, instead of cruising the length of the island as before.[19]

Trophies

Day after day pilots Barry Baker, Jim Barnes, and Marty Knutson stood by at Laughlin. But caution was the watchword.[20] Elaborate plans were laid to prevent any U-2 pilots from ending up as trophies for Castro to show off.

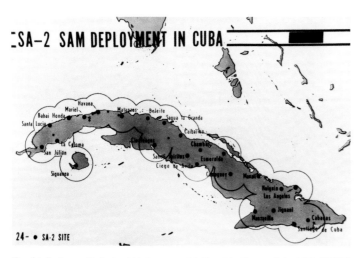

The SA-2 sites multiplied quickly, to pose a big threat to the overflying U-2s (NARA 167782).

The Air Rescue Service was requested to provide SA-16 Albatross amphibians on patrol near the southern and northern coasts of Cuba, ready to pick up a downed U-2 pilot from the water. U.S. Navy fighters from Guantanamo Bay or Key West were on airborne alert to provide cover for any rescue attempt. Of course, it was hoped that a U-2 in difficulties would be able to reach U.S. airbases in southern Florida (drivers were told that Guantanamo—a U.S. enclave on the eastern coast of Cuba itself—was a divert field of last resort!).[21]

Project HQ maintained its standard operating procedure, which was to only launch overflights of denied territory when forecasters predicted 25% or less cloud cover along the planned route. After the first favorable forecast for 10 days, Mission 3091 was launched on 17 September to overfly the Isle of Pines. But the forecasters were wrong. By the time the U-2 reached the island there was a solid undercast.[22]

Two days later, a Special NIE on Cuba was rushed out by the U.S. Intelligence Board. It listed the recent SA-2 and MiG-21 deployments, and suggested that light bombers (Il-28s), short-range Scud SSMs, and submarines might soon follow. But the document still discounted the possibility of MRBMs and/or IRBMs, which would pose "serious command and control problems" for the Soviets. Such missiles had never been deployed outside Soviet territory before, the SNIE noted. (This was wrong: the Soviets had briefly deployed SS-4s to East Germany in 1958-9, but Western intelligence did not detect them).[23]

But underneath the overcast, the Soviets were bringing in the heavy hitters. The first ship carrying offensive missiles docked at the port of Mariel on 8 September. Construction of the first two sites, at San Cristobal (SS-4s) and Remedios (SS-5s), started in mid-September. The first HUMINT report of large truck convoys being transported along narrow Cuban highways reached the CIA's Miami debriefing center on 21 September.

Clouds

By 22 September, Project HQ had positioned all of its three available U-2C/Fs at Laughlin for maximum operational flexibility. The clouds continued to roll over Cuba, however, and it was not until 26 September that Mission 3093 could be launched. It overflew eastern Cuba, discovering three more SAM sites, and confirming that the site at Banes housed a hitherto little-known type of coastal defense missile. On 29 September Mission 3095 tried again for the Isle of Pines, where another SAM site and another coastal missile site were found. There was no sign of larger, offensive missiles on either mission.[24]

When McCone returned to Washington, he was disturbed to find that so little reconnaissance had been accomplished in the past three weeks. At a meeting of the Special Group on 4 October he called for the whole island to be overflown, with particular emphasis on the western end. Around this time, an all-source team at the Defense Intelligence Agency (DIA), led by Col John Wright, also focused on the same area. The concentration of SA-2 sites here suggested some form of "point defense." Were they protecting offensive missiles, Wright wondered?[25]

The Special Group wavered. Instead of acting immediately on McCone's advice it requested the NRO, JCS, and CIA to each study all possible alternate means for conducting aerial reconnaissance of Cuba, and report back five days later.[26]

At the same Special Group meeting, Secretary of Defense Robert McNamara repeated an idea that had first been floated by his deputy, Roswell Gilpatric, some days earlier. The military should now take over the U-2 flights, given the increased risk posed by the SAMs, the threat of conflict, and the likely increase in overflight tempo. In any case, he argued, the CIA's cover story about Lockheed pilots ferrying U-2s to Ramey AFB had worn very thin.[27]

The SecDef had a point. A small air force was now supporting each—supposedly covert—U-2 flight. A KC-135 stood by for inflight refueling. The Navy fighters and ARS rescue aircraft were on patrol. SAC RB-47Hs were also in the air, collecting SIGINT on the SAM sites, and listening for any Cuban and Soviet communications that would indicate an attempt to intercept the U-2. In the Reconnaissance Division at SAC headquarters, Lt Col Joe Jackson was told to start planning U-2 missions over Cuba. A former SAC U-2 pilot himself, Jackson flew to Washington with a preliminary ops plan for McNamara.[28]

Meanwhile, Buster Edens and Jim Cherbonneaux were "in the barrel" at Laughlin for the peripheral missions that had been approved three weeks earlier, but not yet flown. They were to fly close to the island, at or inside the three-mile limit recognized by the U.S. (In the previous days, SAC made some unsuccessful attempts at peripheral photography with RB-47s from 25 miles out—in case the coastal SAM sites were now operational).[29]

Nothing new

On 5 October U-2 mission 3098 skirted the southern coast, from a point east of the known SAM sites in the Cien Fuegos area to the eastern tip of the island. The next day, Mission 3099 took off to skirt the eastern portion of Cuba's northern coast, but had to abort when the aerial refueling system malfunctioned. The next day, though, it was successfully flown as Mission 3100. Apart from yet more SAM sites, nothing new was found on either flight.[30]

Because one of the Agency U-2s at Laughlin had a fuel problem, and the other was due for a periodic inspection, both of them were redeployed back to Edwards on 8 October, together with the supporting KC-135. At the same time, Project HQ finalized plans to switch the staging base to Florida. It was so much nearer the action, and would cut out almost six hours of ferry time. A team from Project HQ surveyed McCoy AFB on 9 October.[31]

On 6 October 1962, COMOR endorsed McCone's call for flights over the western portion of Cuba. The San Cristobal area was rated top priority. COMOR suggested one flight over this area, which would also revisit a nearby SAM site that Bob Ericson had overflown nearly six weeks earlier—the only one then already occupied with launchers, transporters, and the Fruit Set missile guidance radar. If this mission did not provoke an SA-2 reaction, COMOR recommended "maximum coverage of the western end of the island by multiple U-2s simultaneously."[32]

The Special Group met to consider COMOR's recommendation on 9 October. Some of those present were still very nervous about using—and losing—a U-2 over Cuba. Unusually, the chief of Project HQ had been invited to the top-level gathering, to give a briefing on just how vulnerable the U-2 might be. Col. Jack Ledford—who had only just become the CIA's Director of Special Activities—presented an analysis from OSI that concluded there was a one-in-six chance that the U-bird would be shot down. But what were the alternatives? The CIA-sponsored Oxcart had flown in great secrecy at Groom Lake, but was nowhere near proving Mach 3 performance or camera systems integration. The Air Force had adapted a few jet-powered Ryan Firebee target drones for high-altitude reconnaissance within the Big Safari program.

Air Force take over

In the end, the Special Group agreed to make one U-2 flight. As the meeting was breaking up, Gilpatric again pressed for the Air Force to take over the mission. Colonel Doug Steakley, the head of the Joint Reconnaissance Center in the Pentagon, backed him up. DCI McCone asked Jack Ledford for his opinion. The OSA Director raised no objection, but noted that it would be better for the SAC pilots to fly the Agency's U-2F models, with their greater altitude capability and provision for countermeasures against interception by Cuban fighters (eg System 9). He recommended that some of them be checked out immediately.[33]

The question of who should fly the mission was not finally resolved at the meeting. Many in the Agency resented the Air Force taking over. At Project HQ, Jim Cunningham didn't like it at all. But McCone was inclined to cede control, and told Gilpatric so. The word was passed down to SAC Headquarters. The top generals, including Gen Power, were on a trip to Europe. It was left to Col Ellsworth Powell, branch chief in the Recce Division, to make preparations. Two senior pilots in the 4080th wing had already flown the Agency's J75-powered U-2 version: Majors Rudy Anderson and Steve Heyser. They were both at Laughlin, but Anderson had fallen and injured his shoulder, and was not yet fully recovered. 4080th wing maintenance officer Jim Fagan rounded up Heyser and a launch crew, and flew them to Edwards in the wing's C-54 on 10 October.

Amidst much confusion, Det G laid on a refresher training course for Heyser starting the next day. Det G commander Col Bill Gregory sought clarification from Project HQ. Was a military pilot really going to fly the next Cuba mission?

In Washington, DDCI Marshall Carter was resisting the transfer of control from the Agency to the Air Force. At the very least, he argued, there ought to be an orderly transition. What if the weather improved before the SAC pilots were ready to fly? The Agency was also concerned about losing civilian control of the interpretation process to SAC. McGeorge Bundy, the President's Assistant for National Security Affairs, told Carter that the dispute "looks to me like two quarrelling children." Fortunately, the weather over the western end of Cuba remained cloudy while the dithering continued.[34]

On 12 October, control was formally transferred to the Air Force. The same day, Gen Power and his team flew back to Washington from Europe on their KC-135. At meetings in the Pentagon, Power and his Director of Intelligence, Brig Gen Robert Smith, agreed that the B-camera film from military U-2 flights over Cuba would still be sent to NPIC in Washington for initial analysis. The generals reboarded their KC-135 and headed for Offutt.

Brass Knob

When they arrived, Col Powell briefed them on the latest preparations. A new Operations Order codenamed Brass Knob had been sent to Col John Desportes, the 4080th wing commander at Laughlin. Heyser was making his initial requalification flight at Edwards North Base, and Anderson was being flown there to join him. But the staff at Det G had not yet been formally notified that SAC was taking over. Gen Power took care of that, in a short, curt phone call to Bill Gregory.[35]

Col Powell dispatched a team led by Joe Jackson from SAC HQ to Edwards, to plan and launch the first SAC mission. Lt Col Harry Cordes was head of the Penetration Analysis Section at SAC HQ, trying to devise the best routes into Soviet territory for SAC's nuclear bombers. Like Jackson, Cordes was another U-2 veteran, from a tour with Project Aquatone as the navigator at Det B in 1956-58. Cordes suggested that the original flight plan for the vital mission be adjusted so that the U-2 flew between two SA-2 sites, rather than directly over one of them per the original route drawn up in Idealist Project HQ. The change was made. The route still covered the vital area of interest around San Cristobel, where the SS-4 deployment was suspected.[36]

These maps show U-2 flight tracks during the missile build-up in Cuba. The two flights in August took similar paths to those flown previously by Det G of Project Idealist. But after the first SAM site was discovered, mission planners were told not to route any more flights east-west along the island. Because of cloud, only three flights were launched in September. Mission 3101 on 14 October was the first U-2 flight over western Cuba since 29 August. Yet that was where the first offensive missile sites were being set up.

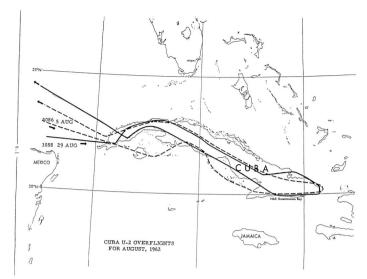

CUBA U-2 OVERFLIGHTS FOR AUGUST, 1962

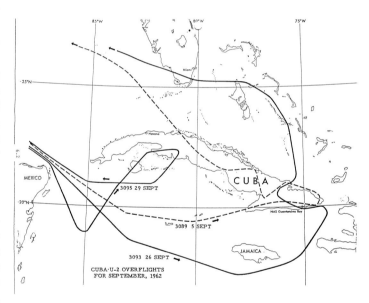

CUBA-U-2 OVERFLIGHTS FOR SEPTEMBER, 1962

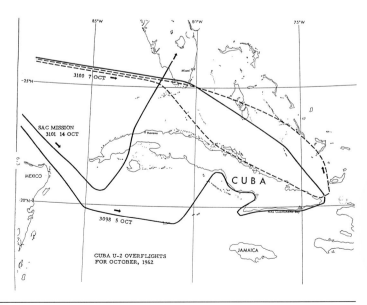

CUBA U-2 OVERFLIGHTS FOR OCTOBER, 1962

ELLSWORTH POWELL

Col Ellsworth Powell was in the Reconnaissance Division at SAC HQ when the Cuban Missile Crisis blew up. He had the task of taking over operational control of U-2 overflights from the CIA to SAC, with a bunch of generals breathing down his neck:

All the staff found out something big was happening, and they congregated at SAC headquarters. So Gen Compton takes off in a T-39, Gen Wilson in a KC-135, and I forget who else, but we have five general officers taking five different airplanes, and they're going to be the fifth hand on the wheel. They didn't know what was going on, hadn't been in on any of the planning or anything.

Heyser took the pictures and landed at Orlando, and then everybody in the world was trying to take credit for the successful mission.

- USAF Oral History interview

HEYSER'S CRUCIAL MISSION

In 1962, Steve Heyser was one of the most experienced pilots in the 4080th wing, and one of wing commander John Desportes' favorites. Here's how he recalled his crucial mission over Cuba on 14 October 1962—the one that discovered the offensive missiles:

My first clue that this would be no ordinary mission was when three SAC generals showed up at the preflight briefing! I was told they wanted to know if Cuba was constructing missile sites or not, and that there were already SAMs there. They didn't know if I would be fired on.

The airplane was unforgiving, but I liked it, and thought I knew what it could do. I had long since passed being nervous about being shot at, and I just didn't think I could get hit up there.

As soon as I hit the Isle of Pines I started my camera. I was at about 72,000 feet. I could see the ground, and I looked in the drift sight, but I never saw anything—not the missile sites or any SAMs or interceptors.

- as quoted in "Alone and Unafraid" by Dino Brugioni, Air & Space, March 2000

Throughout Saturday, 13 October, preparations continued at North Base. The weather forecast for the next day was better. Heyser flew another requalification, took a sleeping pill, and went to bed. Lockheed techreps worked frantically to complete the periodic inspection of Article 343. Meanwhile, Article 342 was the only available aircraft. Both of the dark-painted aircraft had their civilian tail registrations removed and large "U.S. Air Force" markings added.

Three generals from Offutt arrived at Edwards via Laughlin AFB in SAC's VC-97 to observe the preparations. Director of Operations Maj Gen K.K. Compton flew on to McCoy in the VC-97 with 4080th wing commander Col Desportes. Jim Fagan followed in the 4080th C-54, stopping at Laughlin enroute to pick up more men and equipment—and a change of clothes!

Mission 3101

Just after midnight at Edwards, Steve Heyser climbed into Article 342 (hastily painted with its USAF serial number "66675") and took off on Mission

3101. He met the sun over the Gulf of Mexico, and flew over the Yucatan Channel before turning north to penetrate denied territory. The weather was roughly as forecast: 25% cloud cover. He was flying the maximum altitude profile, and by this time the U-2F had reached 72,500 feet. There was no contrail. Heyser switched on the camera and did his stuff. He was over the island for less than seven minutes, but his potential exposure to the two SAM sites was over 12 minutes. Heyser had been briefed to scan the driftsight for Cuban fighters or, worse still, an SA-2 heading his way. If so, he was briefed to turn sharply towards it, and then away from it, in an S-pattern that would hopefully break the missile radar's lock. But there was no opposition from Cuba's air defenses. Heyser coasted-out and headed for McCoy AFB. He landed there at 0920 EST after exactly seven hours in the air.[37]

The reception committee included Brig Gen Smith, who had flown from Edwards in his KC-135, bringing Joe Jackson with him. "It was a milk run—a piece of cake," Heyser told them. The film was quickly unloaded and transferred to Smith's airplane. The general personally couriered it to Washington, and handed it over to the Naval Photographic Intelligence Center (NavPIC) for processing. From there, the first duplicate positive would be trucked across town under armed guard to NPIC, where the PIs were waiting to do the initial read-out.

Also on Sunday, 14 October, Article 343 was test flown at North Base after its periodic inspection. Then Rudy Anderson was hurriedly qualified in the U-2F before it was ferried to McCoy by an Agency pilot. Anderson

Gregory, William J, L/Col
35829A   14 Nov 62

Colonel Bill Gregory was the commander of Det G at Edwards from 1960-65. No stranger to high altitude recon, he was previously the commander of SAC's RB-57D squadron.

was flown to Florida in a KC-135, along with Lockheed techreps assigned to the Agency, who would maintain the U-2F models at McCoy. Now that mission 3101 had successfully returned, two more overflights were authorized for the next day.

Early next morning, Monday, 15 October, Anderson took off on mission 3102 and flew along one entire side of the island. Steve Heyser flew the other U-2F along the other side on mission 3103. Much of central Cuba was cloud-covered, but the west was clear and the east reasonably clear. Again, there was no attempt to intercept the flights. They may have gone undetected, even though the NSA had reported as long ago as 19 September the first intercept of a signal from the Spoon Rest target acquisition radar associated with the SA-2 system. More recently (10 October) the NSA reported the first indication that air defense operators on Cuba were passing tracking reports to higher headquarters, using Soviet procedures.[38]

NPIC analysis

Meanwhile, at the Steuart Building in northwest Washington, NPIC teams led by Earl Shoemaker were examining the film from 3101. There was less of it than usual from a U-2 mission—only eight cans. By noon, they had spotted six long, canvas-covered objects in an area about 50 nautical miles west-southwest of Havana. Through the afternoon the analysis continued. There were trucks and tents in the vicinity. It looked like a convoy had just arrived. Previous U-2 imagery of the area taken on the 29 August flight was reviewed: nothing had been seen or reported here before.[39]

Discounting another SA-2 site, the PIs and all-source analysts led by Dino Brugioni slowly reached their conclusion: the objects were SS-4 missile transporters! They called in NPIC chief Art Lundahl. "If there was ever a time when I want to be right in my life, this is it," he told them. The intelligence community was already under orders to keep Cuban discoveries within a very limited-disclosure security system codenamed Psalm. Lundahl cautioned his staff not to contact anyone outside the building. To confirm the analysis, they worked into the night. They discovered MRBM launcher-erectors at a nearby second site, plus more transporters and tents. A third area came under suspicion.[40]

At 0730 next morning, Tuesday, 16 October, Lundahl briefed top CIA officials at Langley. Most of them were stunned that the Soviet Union could be so audacious. Reached by telephone in Seattle, DCI McCone was not surprised. He had warned about this all along. By midday Lundahl, his boss Ray Cline, and the Agency's offensive missile expert Sid Graybeal were briefing President Kennedy and his senior officials in the White House. The big unknowns, they told JFK, were how long it would take before the missiles were operational, were there any more elsewhere on Cuba, and where were their nuclear warheads? To advise him on how to respond the President set up the Executive Committee (Excom), a crisis group within the National Security Council. He also called for blanket aerial reconnaissance of the island.[41]

SAC was still flying the J57-engine U-2A in 1962, which could not climb as high as the CIA aircraft with their J75s (NARA KKE 12256).

SO WHO FOUND THE MISSILES IN CUBA FIRST?

Although NPIC was supposedly a "national" resource, SAC jealously guarded its independence in photo-interpretation:

The rivalry between the PIs of SAC and NPIC was already well-established when the Cuban Missile Crisis broke. At Offutt, the 544th Recce Tech Group did all-source analysis as well as photo-interpretation. They received the tracker film from the CIA U-2 missions over Cuba long before a copy of the main B-camera "take" reached them. According to then-Col Eugene Tighe, who headed the 544th's Research Center, it was the PIs in his outfit who first deduced that SA-2 missiles were being sent to Cuba, when they noticed the ground scars in that characteristic "Star of David" pattern. This was before the first SAMs actually arrived.

SAC's own history of the Crisis, "*The Missiles in Cuba, 1962: The Role of SAC Intelligence,*" records that the same PIs at Offutt also were the first to discover the offensive missile sites around San Cristobel, from an examination of the 70mm tracker film of Mission G3101. But experts at NPIC told this author that they find this claim incredible.

SAC's history was written in 1984 by a then-member of the 544th (by now a Strategic Intelligence Wing). The author, Captain Saunders Laubenthal, relied heavily on interviews with Lt Gen Tighe. Laubenthal wrote that A1C Michael Davis, a sharp young PI with experience in the exploitation of missile sites, made the initial discovery on the afternoon of Sunday, 14 October. He was examining the tracker film of Heyser's mission, which had been flown direct from McCoy to Offutt. The 544th's role was supposed to be limited to processing and duplicating the tracker film, and sending a copy to NPIC with a report on the overall cloud cover. "NPIC had claimed the right to make the determination, from the main camera film, of what was in Cuba," Laubenthal noted.

No mention of this supposed achievement by SAC is found in Dino Brugioni's "Eyeball to Eyeball: The Inside Story of the Cuba Missile Crisis," published in 1990. Brugioni was a senior all-source analyst at NPIC, and goes into exhaustive detail on how the reconnaissance imagery from Cuba was interpreted and analyzed. NPIC photo-interpreters Bill Crimmins and Earl Shoemaker told this author that the scale of the tracker film would have been 1:240,000. It would be quite impossible to make any positive identification of the offensive missiles from U-2 tracker camera film, they insisted. – *C.P.*

BRIEFING THE PRESIDENT

Here is how NPIC Director Art Lundahl and CIA missile analyst Sid Graybeal briefed President Kennedy on 16 October 1961, after U-2 Mission 3101 discovered the first offensive missiles:

Lundahl: This is a result of the photography taken Sunday, sir...The site that you have there contains at least 8 canvas-covered missile trailers. Four deployed probable missile erector-launchers...In Area II there are at least six canvas-covered missile trailers, about 75 vehicles, about 18 tents...The critical one – do you see what I mean? – is this one...The missile trailer's backing up to it at the moment. It's got to be. And the trailer's here. Those canvas-covered objects were 67 feet long...That looks like the most advanced one. Then the other area's about five miles away. There are no launcher-erectors over there, just missiles....

JFK: How do you know this is a medium-range ballistic missile?

Lundahl: The length, sir...Mr. Graybeal has some pictures of the equivalent Soviet equipment that has been dragged through the streets of Moscow....

JFK: Is this ready to be fired?

Graybeal: No, sir

JFK: How long have we got? We can't tell, I take it.

Graybeal: No, sir

MEMORIES OF CUBA FLIGHTS

I coasted-in on the western end of Cuba and photographed the length of the island, then turned around and photographed all the way back. The scheme was to start taking our pictures as soon as the sun angle reached 20 degrees. On another overflight, I flew over the ocean to the east end of the island and made one sweep from east to west. From there, we would have the shortest possible flight time back to McCoy. When we landed a T-39 would be sitting there, and the film would be whisked out of the U-2 and onto the T-39, almost before the recce pilot could get out of the U-2.

- Jerry McIlmoyle interview with the author

Steve Heyser recalled the routine at McCoy:

About 6pm local time we would get a mission down from SAC to our Operations, and then our navigation section would plan it during the night. We pilots took crew rest. We would get up around 3am, eat breakfast, go down to Operations, and be briefed by navigation, intel, and weather. About two hours prior to takeoff we would start dressing, and start prebreathing oxygen about one hour before takeoff. These were shorter missions than we were used to, some only 2.5 hours. They went off without any hitches— other than the one we lost, of course.

- from SAC oral history interview 27 November 1962

Frantic work

In response, 17 senior officials from the CIA and the Pentagon gathered for a lunchtime meeting in Secretary of Defense Robert McNamara's office. The President had just authorized as many U-2 missions as was necessary to obtain complete coverage of Cuba, on a repeat basis. It was obvious that more pilots and SAC's own U-2As would have to be committed to the effort. McNamara said he was authorizing six flights for the next day. At Offutt, Laughlin, and McCoy, frantic work continued on the new Ops Order for the 4080th wing. But could the film processing facilities cope with the additional volume? NavPIC was already backlogged, as it struggled to produce more duplicate positives and negatives from the three recent missions. It was agreed to use additional sites: Eastman-Kodak's facility in Rochester, and the Air Force photo labs at Laughlin and Westover AFBs. The Navy's F8U-1P Crusader squadron was alerted for low-level overflights. More film processing sites were prepared.[42]

At NPIC, the film from the previous day's two U-2 missions was being examined. It confirmed the suspicions of a third SS-4 deployment in the San Cristobal area. There were tents here now, where none were seen on Heyser's first mission. The tents covered the missiles until they were ready to be mounted on their launchers. Worse still, the PIs identified two sites near Guanajay that looked like they were being prepared to house the SS-5—the newest of the Soviet IRBMs. A SAM site at Bahia Honda had SA-2 missiles visible on every other launcher. Crates that were known to contain Il-28 Beagle bombers were lined up at San Julian airfield.[43]

The 4080th was facing its biggest test, at a time when it had never been busier, thanks to the resumption of nuclear tests in the atmosphere. The previous month, it had a record number of U-2s deployed on sampling duties. There were five at OL-5 in Alaska, three at the home-based OL-10, two at OL-11 in Australia, two at OL-14 on Guam, and three each at two new locations. These were OL-7 at Upper Heyford, in the UK, and OL-9 at Hickam. The aircraft in Hawaii were flying in support of the U.S. nuclear test shots above Johnston Island. With one aircraft loaned to the CIA and another three going through IRAN, this left just two available for training!

Crews and aircraft were hurriedly recalled from OL-5 and OL-10. On Wednesday afternoon, the 4080th was alerted for multiple missions the next day. The number would depend on the weather conditions over Cuba. If it was good, just two aircraft could cover the entire island. In deepest southwest Texas, the weather forecast could not have been worse! Thunderstorms were moving in. In the early hours of Thursday, 17 October, at Laughlin AFB, Captains George Bull and Roger Herman, and Major Jim Qualls suited up, prebreathed, and strapped into the silver U-2As. At 4am they taxied out and took off in a blinding rainstorm and strong crosswinds. Visibility was so poor that they only found the end of the runway thanks to the lights on the mobile van that led them out! But they needed to get airborne straightaway if they were to fly over Cuba in the calm, clear morning air. SAC RB-47s were flying weather reconnaissance missions around Cuba. With the tropical climate being so dynamic, these aircraft provided the real-time reporting that alerted mission planners to gaps in the often-daily build-ups of cloud.

Roundtrip missions

The trio of U-2As flew roundtrip missions, landing back at Laughlin, where the tracker film was immediately transferred to a T-39 and flown to Offutt. The B-camera film was processed by the 4080th Recce Tech laboratory

and then flown to Washington. Shortly after noon, Major Buddy Brown also left Laughlin to fly over Cuba, but he recovered into McCoy. Meanwhile, Majors Anderson and Heyser flew two more Cuban sorties out of McCoy in the U-2Fs.

No less than 200,000 feet of film was processed from missions 3104-3109 on this day. It showed that the Soviets were moving fast! Two more SS-4 sites were under construction near Sagua La Grande; the first Il-28 was out of its crate at San Julian; and there were many more MiG-21s assembled at Santa Clara. Repeat coverage of the Guanajay area suggested that the fixed-site SS-5 IRBMs could be operational within a month. Those missiles could reach the whole of the U.S., barring the Pacific Northwest! Two sites of the mobile, but shorter-range SS-4 MRBMs would soon be ready to fire, it was thought. All four of the missile erectors were in place, and cables led to the launch control facility.[44]

At the planning meeting in McNamara's office on the 16th, Pentagon officials declared that they would henceforth only use the "civilian" U-2 pilots over Cuba in extreme circumstances, and after they had been recommissioned into the Air Force! Still, Project HQ sent some Idealist personnel to McCoy, including pilots Buster Edens and Jim Cherbonneaux, ready to support the SAC operation. To give SAC pilots Anderson and Heyser a rest, Col Desportes planned to use one of the Agency pilots for the next mission on Thursday, 18 October. The plan was rejected in Washington by Under-Secretary of the Air Force Joe Charyk, who was the NRO Director. The two Agency pilots were never used, and spent most of their time on the golf course at McCoy. The Agency presence provoked some tension in the uniformed U-2 contingent there, especially when OSA Deputy Director Jim Cunningham paid a visit and made critical comments about the 4080th's *modus operandi*.[45]

HOW CAN YOU TELL THEY ARE MISSILES?

In his book "Thirteen Days," Robert Kennedy admitted that senior policy makers had to trust what the intelligence experts from NPIC and elsewhere were telling them:

Photographs were shown to us. Experts arrived with their charts and pointers, and told us if we looked carefully we could see there was a missile base being constructed in a field near San Cristobal, Cuba. I, for one, had to take their word for it. I examined the pictures carefully, and what I saw appeared to be no more than the clearing of a field for a farm or the basement of a home. I was relieved to hear later that this was the reaction of virtually everyone at the meeting, including President Kennedy.

Major Steve Heyser was one of the most experienced U-2 pilots in the 4080th SRW. He flew the vital mission on 14 October which discovered the offensive missiles.

Different

Of course, the way that SAC was running the set-up was different. The requirement was different. Instead of launching covert flights to gain strategic intelligence on a timetable that could wait for the most favorable conditions, the military was under pressure to produce the maximum coverage on a tactical basis, day-to-day. Although the existence of "Operating Location X" at McCoy was supposed to be secret, the operations tempo was hardly conducive to secrecy. By mid-October the 4080th had deployed five aircraft, 11 pilots, four navigators, and 68 airmen to McCoy. Wing commander Col Desportes was in charge, assisted by operations officer Lt Col Tony Martinez and maintenance officer Lt Col Frank Shipley. But they had plenty of top brass peering over their shoulders. SAC Director of Operations Maj Gen K.K. Compton was frequently at McCoy, and so was SAC's intelligence chief, Bg Gen Robert Smith (when he wasn't shuttling film to Offutt and Washington!).[46]

On Friday, 19 October, two more U-2 missions were launched. Captain Jerry McIlmoyle flew from Laughlin over Cuba and landed at McCoy. On Saturday, 20 October, there were another three overflights of the island. The President was briefed at least once a day with U-2 photos by Art Lundahl. By now, U-2 imagery had covered 95 percent of Cuba, and it revealed six MRBM and three IRBM sites; at least one nuclear weapons storage facility; 22 Il-28 nuclear-capable bombers; and three coastal defense missile sites. There were 24 SAM sites and 39 MiG-21s, one of which was captured on film taking off.[47]

Excom approved a blockade of Cuba on Friday. Military units were called to alert. Offensive and defensive forces began moving to Florida. Still, though, no announcement had been made about the missiles, though speculation was rife. Radio Moscow accused Washington of preparing to invade Cuba. Indeed, that was an option under active consideration. So were air strikes against the missile sites.

The President decided to brief Canada and the major European allies before going public. Senior emissaries and CIA officials flew to London, Paris, and Bonn. On Monday, 22 October, while the European leaders were being shown the tell-tale imagery, three more U-2 missions took off.

When the Cuban overflights were transferred to SAC in mid-October, Colonel Ledford of OSA recommended that the military pilots use the better-equipped U-2s of Project Idealist, like this U-2F (Lockheed U2-91-005-H).

U-2F models

At about this time Col Desportes realized that more of his pilots would have to be converted onto the two U-2F models to relieve Anderson and Heyser. He was told that Jim Barnes was the Agency's best instructor pilot, and requested that he be sent to McCoy immediately. Assisted by Buster Edens, Barnes began checking out Major Buddy Brown and Captain Jerry McIlmoyle in the higher-powered model the next day.[48]

At 7pm on Monday JFK addressed the nation. He denounced the Soviet Union's deception and demanded that the offensive missiles be withdrawn. He announced a "strict quarantine" on all offensive military equipment being shipped to Cuba. The U.S. military assumed the Defcon 3 alert posture. SAC bombers were dispersed and loaded with their nuclear weapons.

The next morning there were three more U-2 missions, and the first five low-level sorties by the U.S. Navy F8U Crusaders flying from NAS Jacksonville. Their imagery was spectacular, and provided a valuable new dimension to the PIs at NPIC. Policymakers in Excom and elsewhere could now see clearly what was often only apparent to experts from the U-2 photography. On Wednesday, 24 October, a selection of the reconnaissance imagery was released to the media, and was shown at the United Nations Security Council two days later.

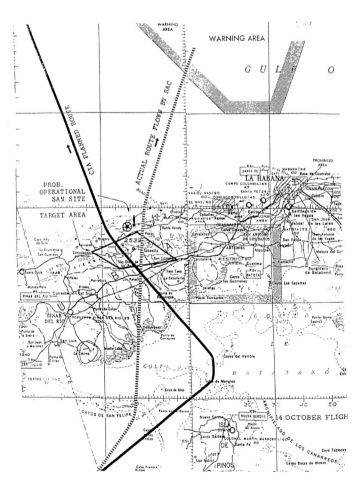

From collateral intelligence reports, analysts calculated that offensive missiles might be found within a "trapezoid" area in western Cuba. SAC mission planner Lt Col Harry Cordes changed the route of Mission 3101 slightly to reduce the threat from SA-2 sites.

SS-5 missiles had not actually been seen yet in Cuba, but were thought to be on one of the ships still heading for the island. During Wednesday, some of these ships stopped or changed course. It was the first indication that the Soviets might have blinked.

One of the many questions for U.S. intelligence was, why had the Soviets not brought the SAM sites to maximum readiness to threaten the U-2s snooping overhead *before* they deployed the first offensive missiles in the field in early October? And since then, there had been a further 21 U-2 missions, starting with Heyser's flight on the 14th. All 24 SAM sites were thought to be operational. Yet none of them had apparently fired at a U-2. But that was about to change.

PVO commander

In fact, until mid-October the Soviets considered their SAMs in Cuba to be a defense against attacking aircraft supporting an invasion, rather than against overhead reconnaissance. The senior Soviet commander on Cuba, General Issa Pliyev, told his PVO commander Lt Gen Stepan Grechko not to fire the SAMs, nor even to activate their acquisition radars to track the U-2s. The MiG-21 regiment—a crack unit from Kubinka airbase, near Moscow—was under similar orders not to challenge the U-2s.

The U-2 flights were, however, detected by early-warning radars on Cuba, and when an inspection team from the Soviet General Staff arrived in Cuba on 18 October, they were very concerned to hear Pliyev's report of multiple U-2 flights over the island since the 14th. Since Pliyev also told

AN AIR FORCE REPLY

Lt Col Tony Martinez was the operations officer for OL-X, 4080th SRW at McCoy during the crisis, and Captain Jerry McIlmoyle was a pilot. They saw it this way:

Martinez: (OSA Deputy Director) Cunningham and others were hanging around at McCoy, making remarks to discredit the job that we were doing. They were very resentful that we had "taken over" their mission, and made no bones about hiding it. They criticized our mission planning, and said we were flying directly over the SAM sites. The fact is, the routes were prepared at the JRC in coordination with the staff at SAC HQ.

McIlmoyle: Those CIA guys were not happy campers. Jim Barnes, Barry Baker, and I were really good friends at Great Falls, as we were all F-84 flight commanders in SAC. We played bridge and partied together. But they looked at Buddy Brown and me like we were from Mars when we met them. No friendly chit-chat, nothing except hello and a handshake.

ANDERSON VOLUNTEERED FOR FATAL FLIGHT

For Rudy Anderson, flying was a passion. He was a highly-rated officer, patriotic, dedicated, and intensely competitive. According to fellow U-2 pilot Jerry McIlmoyle, Rudy Anderson grabbed the chance to fly an extra mission over Cuba—which turned out to be his last.

On the night of 26 October, a pilot's meeting was held in quarters by our operations officer, Tony Martinez. Rudy Anderson complained about being one mission short of Heyser. I recall Martinez saying that he wasn't going to change the schedule, but that Anderson could hang around Ops in case an unscheduled mission was laid on. The next day Heyser and I were playing golf when we saw a U-2 takeoff around 10 or 11am. I remarked to

Heyser that it looks like Andy has caught up with you. Heyser retorted that he couldn't care less about who had the most missions.

Anyway, that flight was Andy's last. He was shot down near where I was fired on—maybe even from the same site.

- correspondence with author

I SAW THE U-2 FALL OVER CUBA

This account of the downing of Major Anderson was given to Virginia resident J.T. Skelly by a Cuban exile that he identified only as "Jose":

I was having a soft drink in a little open-air cafe on the Banes-Holguin highway. Suddenly, two loud blasts pierced the air like the first two bursts of thunder of an unexpected summer storm. A young boy who was passing shouted "look up there!"

I can still see the U-2 slowly descending, at times going out of sight in the clouds, then coming into view again. No one said a word. We just watched. I remember clearly that the left wing fell off. The rest of the U-2 with Major Anderson's body fell into a cane field next to the highway. Although most of the fuselage was intact, there were splinters and many parts thrown around the area. Several persons kept souvenirs. One person I know brought his souvenir into exile to Miami with him.

A crowd gathered at the cafe. About an hour later, a jeep with Major Anderson's body strapped over the fender sped along the highway into Banes. The body was displayed there for a little over two hours. A truck with a loudspeaker went around the town, calling on the residents to "come see the mercenary Yanqui." Then it was removed to the city hospital. Several days later the body was sent to Havana, where Fidel Castro announced that for "humanitarian" reasons he would allow the Secretary General of the United Nations to take it back to the U.S. for burial.

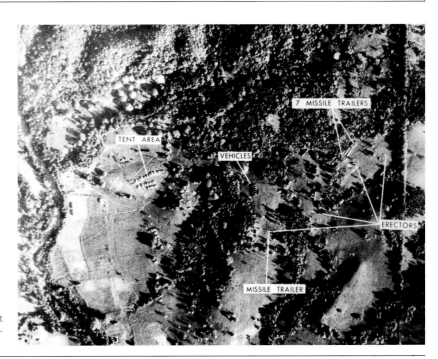

Imagery from Mission 3101 was analyzed throughout 15 October at NPIC in Washington. By the end of the day they had identified an SS-4 IRBM site in the making (NARA 167185).

them that the process of setting up and camouflaging the offensive missile sites had fallen well behind schedule, the visitors from Moscow had no doubt that the U.S. must have discovered them.[49]

On 22 October Moscow cabled new orders to Pliyev. These re-affirmed that only the Kremlin could order the nuclear weapons to be loaded and the offensive missiles to be fired. But in view of the now-obvious U.S. preparations to invade, they also urged Pliyev to "take immediate steps to raise combat readiness and to repulse the enemy." Pliyev therefore gave new instructions to the PVO's Grechko: begin tracking all enemy aircraft, but do not fire without my permission. But it was not until early on Friday, 26 October, that U.S. intelligence detected the change. Signals from two radar-tracking locations were intercepted.[50]

A day earlier, Captain Jerry McIlmoyle flew the only U-2 mission for Thursday, 25 October. He was now qualified in the U-2F model, and its higher-altitude capability may have saved him this day. Halfway through his flight, McIlmoyle was coasting-out over the eastern end of Cuba when he glanced in the rear-view mirror. He saw missile contrails dissolving into vapor clouds above and behind him. He set course for Florida and landed safely. McIlmoyle reported the apparent attack by SAMs, but the intel people at the briefing discounted it. They did not yet have any SIGINT to confirm that the SA-2 sites were operational. (A three-star SAC general told McIlmoyle he definitely had not been attacked. But nearly 20 years later McIlmoyle—by now a Bg Gen—finally received confirmation that he had indeed been fired on. After a briefing he was attending at the CIA,

he asked DCI Stansfield Turner if the records for mission 3125 could be checked. Sure enough, the tracker film had captured the missile contrails topped by their detonation clouds.)[51]

That same day, the U.S. Navy and Marine Corps Crusaders flew no fewer than nine low-level missions. The next day, Friday, 26 October, was too cloudy for U-2 overflights. But Tactical Air Command joined the action, as the RF-101s of the 363rd TRW flew five times over the island. The Castro regime was furious at this very obvious violation of Cuban airspace. Fidel Castro had no control over the Soviet SAMs, but he ordered his anti-aircraft gunners to open fire on the fast and low-flying jets.[52]

Decisive phase

In Washington, President Kennedy was resisting the advice of his generals and admirals, who believed that an invasion was the only sure way to eliminate the missiles. The first ship heading for Cuba was boarded in the mid-Atlantic. The Soviets were rushing to bring the last of the 24 SS-4 launch pads to operational status. The White House went public with this news. Premier Khrushchev sent a conciliatory but ambiguous message to JFK—his second in three days. The crisis had entered its most decisive, dangerous phase.

On Saturday, 27 October, more potential U-2 missions were scheduled. Although it was not his turn to fly, Rudy Anderson had shown up at the briefing room, seeking an extra mission. Ops officer Tony Martinez told him he could wait around, in case additional tasking came in. Buddy

Art Lundahl was the director of NPIC who briefed President Kennedy and senior government officials throughout the Cuba Missile Crisis (CIA).

The first SS-5 missile site in Cuba to be photographed by the U-2 was Guanajay, on 15 October (NARA 167200).

After the first missile sites were discovered, the 4080th SRW scrambled to launch as many flights as possible. Aircraft and pilots were recalled from sampling locations, and a special detachment was set up at McCoy AFB (NARA KKE 47597).

Brown was allocated to the priority mission this day. Anderson was briefed on a possible secondary set of targets. Then Brown's mission was canceled due to cloud in the target area, so it was Anderson that climbed into U-2F 66676 and took off that morning.[53]

His route was supposed to keep him clear of the known SA-2 sites by 30 nautical miles. As another precaution against attack, the flight lines were drawn so that the U-2 would fly straight and level for no longer than 30 seconds before making a turn. The pilot needed those 30 seconds to acquire target through the driftsight and line up correctly, but the missile operators on the ground were thought to need at least as long to track, acquire, and fire their SAMs at the overflying aircraft.[54]

At 9am, air defense radars detected a U-2 entering central Cuba from the north. It passed over Ciego de Avila and headed southeast down the middle of the island, before turning south to pass over Manzanillo, on the southern coast. It then turned east and flew over Guantanamo before heading north towards Antillo and the northern coast. On Cuba, the day had begun with a mighty tropical downpour. At the SA-2 missile site at Los Angeles, near Banes, which was operated by the 507th Antiaircraft Missile Regiment, radar operators feared that the deluge of water would enter their cabin. Around 10am the target was passed to them. The battery's Spoon Rest radar picked it up almost immediately. It was now flying at 72,000 feet. Tracking progressed from manual to auto, and the aircraft entered the battery's kill zone. Despite the rain, everything was working perfectly. Battery commander Lt Col Ivan Gerchenko requested permission to fire. After a short delay the word came back: salvo-fire three missiles.[55]

Anderson shot down

Major Anderson may not have seen them coming through the cloud. Possibly he was a little closer to the SAM site than he should have been: the radar operators measured their target's distance as only six nautical miles away when they launched the missiles. The U-2 was disabled by the first missile and destroyed when the second hit it, according to Soviet accounts. The forward fuselage and cockpit landed near Banes, with the dead pilot still inside. The aft fuselage and tail fell into the bay just offshore.

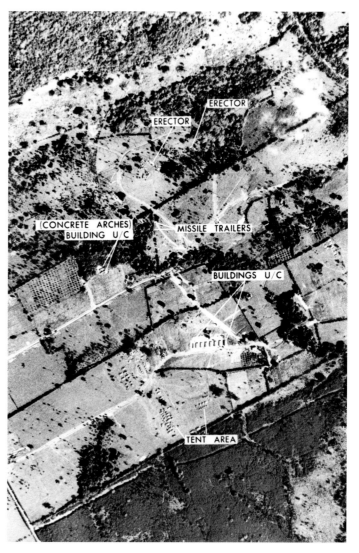

Intensive activity at one of the San Cristobel SS-4 sites was captured on U-2 film, 17 October (NARA 167190).

Lt Col Tony Martinez was the 4080th SRW operations officer of OL-X at McCoy AFB during the missile crisis (via Tony Martinez).

Based on an examination of Rudy Anderson's body after it was returned by the Cubans, U.S. intelligence concluded that one or more missiles had exploded above and behind the U-2. It was a similar story to the Powers shootdown, except that Anderson was not as lucky as Powers. A fragment of shrapnel had penetrated the cockpit and passed through his body. This probably killed him. If not, his life was surely ended as the cockpit depressurized and his punctured pressure suit no longer gave him any high-altitude protection.[56]

When he heard about the shootdown, Gen Pliyev was furious that he had not been contacted for permission to fire. From the PVO command post, Lt Gen Grechko explained that he had tried twice to contact the head of Soviet forces in Cuba, without success. So with the U-2 about to head out of Cuban airspace, he acted on his own authority. Pliyev's mood was not improved when, two days later, a message arrived from Defense Minister Malinovsky in Moscow: "We believe that you were too hasty in shooting down the U.S. U-2 reconnaissance plane; at that time an agreement was emerging to avert, by peaceful means, an attack on Cuba." (Premier Khrushchev mistakenly believed that Fidel Castro controlled the SA-2 missiles, and sent a scolding message to the Cuban leader that same day).[57]

At McCoy they waited in vain for Anderson to return. Soon, though, word reached them that Havana Radio had announced that "Cuban armed forces" had downed a U-2. Col Desportes broke the bad news to the mobile, Capt Roger Herman, and the rest of the recovery crew. Gloom descended upon the outfit. At about the same time, the NSA was reporting that Spoon Rest radars were active on the island again that morning. But no SIGINT aircraft had been patrolling off shore, listening in and ready to warn of PVO tracking activity while Anderson was flying over the island.[58]

Escalation

At the morning Excom meeting in Washington, JFK and his advisers were discussing the ground fire that was being encountered by the low-level recce flights, and whether to provide them with fighter cover. SecDef McNamara was still under the impression that the SAM sites were not yet operational. But then the news that a U-2 had been shot down reached the meeting. "This is much of an escalation by them, isn't it?" Kennedy asked. The meeting puzzled over the contradictory signs: Khrushchev was suggesting a compromise, but aircraft were being shot at over Cuba. "How can we put a U-2 fellow over there tomorrow unless we take out all the SAM sites," JFK asked. "I don't think we can," McNamara replied.

Discussion continued on the feasibility of attacking the SAM sites. "If we're going to continue reconnaissance each day, we must be prepared to fire each day," McNamara said. "I think we can forget the U-2 for the moment," he continued gloomily. JFK veered towards attacking the specific SAM site that had shot Anderson down. In fact, the Air Force had already been given that authority some days earlier. The meeting agreed to continue the low-level recce flights, with fighter escorts armed to strike any anti-aircraft site that opened fire.

JFK eventually decided to hold back from attacking any SAM sites for 24 hours, in case there was another message from Moscow. Khrushchev was proposing to trade a withdrawal of the missiles from Cuba, if the U.S. withdrew its Jupiter SSMs from Turkey and Italy. A frantic message went out to Gen LeMay to cancel the SAM strike. "He chickened out again!" LeMay exclaimed angrily, referring to the President.[59]

Captain Jerry McIlmoyle flew his first Cuba overflight mission on 19 October. Six days later, he was lucky to escape an SA-2 attack over the island (via Jerry McIlmoyle).

ALONE, UNARMED, AND RATHER AFRAID

Chuck Maultsby had a walk-on part in the Cuban Missile Crisis, and he didn't enjoy it. When tensions were at their height, the U-2 pilot strayed into Soviet territory unintentionally, as he returned from a long, lonely sampling mission all the way to the North Pole and back. Here are some extracts from his unpublished memoir:

I asked one of the pararescue jumpers what he would do if he had to bail out over the North Pole. "I wouldn't pull the ripcord" he said. I was sorry I asked!

Over the Barter Island radio beacon I set course for the Pole and took my first star fix. Right on the button: those navigators were masters of their trade! All went to plan until streaks of light started dancing through the sky. This was my first experience with the Northern Lights. I held my heading. I just hoped that the star that I thought I saw was the right one. The last few fixes before reaching the Pole—if in fact I did reach it—were highly suspect....

I had never flown over a land mass where you could not see a single light from horizon to horizon. After leaving the Pole, I began to realize that something was terribly wrong. When I was supposed to be back over Barter Island, but couldn't see the flares that Duck Butt was firing, it was all I could do to fight off a panic attack.... When I picked up the Russian radio station, the suppressed panic set in. I knew one thing, though. I was not going to be another Gary Powers!

With what little fuel I had left, I decided to get away from that radio station. I turned left until it was directly behind me... Twelve minutes of fuel left now...a sense of despair set in as I shut the engine down. When the suit inflated I neglected to pull the lanyard that keeps the helmet from rising, and had a helluva time seeing the instrument panel. The windshield fogged up immediately, and the faceplate followed. I wanted to conserve the battery so I could

make one more May Day call before I punched out. The silence was deafening. All I could hear was my labored breathing. At least 10 minutes went by before the aircraft started to descend. I thought the altimeter had stuck.

Twenty minutes later, damned if I didn't see a faint glow on the horizon directly in front of me. I decided to hold this heading and rate of descent. As I descended through 25,000 feet the pressure suit started deflating. Thank God, now I could look around. There wasn't any cloud, and it was light enough now to see the terrain, which was blanketed with snow. I saw the two F-102s, one on each wing. I actuated the battery switch and gave them a call. They welcomed me home....

When the U-2 came to a complete stop at Kotzebue, I was completely drained both physically and emotionally...the radar site commander let me use a secure phone in his office. I called "Whip" Wilson at Eielson. He said that my little excursion had the White House and SAC headquarters shook up. I'll bet!

The radar commander asked if I would like to see where I had been. It looked like I turned 300 or 310 degrees over the Pole instead of 270, and headed for Siberia. His map also showed my subsequent minor course adjustments, and then my sharp left turn to get out of Soviet airspace.

At Eielson, there was a KC-135 waiting to fly me to SAC headquarters. The underground command post was a hive of activity. When Gen Power entered the room, eight other generals who looked like they had not been out of their uniforms for days followed him. He asked me to describe the flight. Afterwards, he said, "too bad you weren't configured to gather electromagnetic radiation. The Russians probably had every radar on maximum alert." He left the room with the other generals following. One of them told me: "You're a lucky little devil. I've seen him chew up and spit out people for doing a helluva lot less!"

Meanwhile, U-2 flights over Cuba were suspended. Before darkness fell, a low-level recce mission was tasked to fly over the SAM site in an attempt to locate the downed aircraft. A SAR effort was also mounted off the northern coast. But the NSA had already intercepted Cuban military messages indicating that they had located the wreckage and the body of the pilot. The Pentagon declared Major Anderson missing in action.

U.S. Ultimatum

That same Saturday evening, Bobby Kennedy reinforced the earlier U.S. ultimatum to withdraw the missiles in a meeting with the Soviet ambassador. Overnight, preparations for air strikes against the offensive nuclear missile sites on Cuba, as well as an invasion, continued. The crisis had reached boiling point.

And then, finally, Premier Khrushchev climbed down. He knew that more than a thousand SAC bombers, plus ICBMs, were poised to strike the motherland. He also knew that a U.S. invasion of Cuba could be imminent. He decided that a Soviet-controlled Cuba without missiles was of more advantage than a U.S.-occupied Cuba. Early on Sunday afternoon, Moscow time, a broadcast on Moscow radio relayed his decision to dismantle and return the missiles from Cuba.

While all this was going on, another U-2 and its pilot made a unique and potentially dangerous contribution to the crisis. He was Major Charles Maultsby, and he was flying a sampling mission from the 4080th's OL-5 in Alaska, when he accidentally strayed into Soviet airspace.

All through the tense days of fall 1962, the Soviet Union continued to test nuclear weapons in the atmosphere above Novaya Zemlya island in the Arctic. (The U.S. also continued its series of nuclear test shots over the Pacific). At Eielson AFB, OL-5 had three U-2As, and was tasked to fly nearly every day, sometimes twice a day. On the evening of 26 October, Maultsby prepared for the most challenging of these flights: an eight-hour-plus trip all the way to the North Pole and back, in the dark. It had been done at least twice before in the preceding month by Captains Don Webster and Willie Lawson. But no one underestimated the difficulty. The last radio beacon was at Barter Island, way south of the Pole. After that, the only means of navigation was the grid celestial technique. That's why the 4080th deployed three navigators to OL-5, to pre-compute the star shots (Captains Billie Bye and Bob Yates, and 1Lt Fred Okimoto).

Maultsby took off from Eielson at midnight. All went well until he was halfway between Barter Island and the Pole. Then he encountered the Aurora Borealis for the first time. The further North he flew, the more

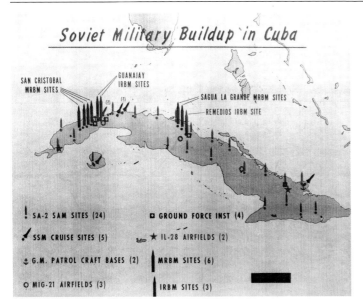

A briefing chart from late 1962 shows the maximum extent of the Soviet military build-up on Cuba.

intense the streaks of lighting became. Maultsby found it almost impossible to take star fixes. He continued to what he hoped was the North Pole, and then turned back using the standard procedure: first a 90-degree turn to the left, then a 270-degree turn to the right. This was designed to place the U-2 on exactly the reverse course, back to Barter Island.

Maultsby off course

However, as Maultsby proceeded south, he suspected that he was off course. But it was not until he was clear of the Aurora Borealis effect that his suspicion was confirmed. His star fixes did not compute. But was he off course to the east, or to the west? If the latter, then he was heading for the Chukotsky Peninsula—Soviet territory! He decided to continue flying time and distance, and hope for the best.

An SC-54 transport of the Air Rescue Service was orbiting over Barter Island, awaiting the U-2's return. This was a standard precaution, often

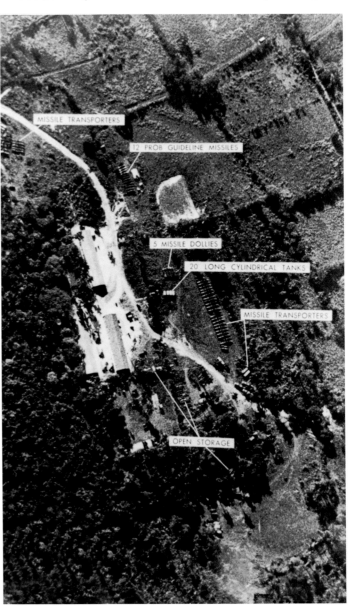

President Kennedy resisted advice from his military commanders to attack Cuba, preferring the blockade strategy. He later told the 4080th wing pilots: "Gentlemen, you take good pictures!"

The PVO retained control of the SAM sites in Cuba throughout the crisis, and did not turn them over to the Cubans for another year. This is an assembly area for the SA-2 missiles (NARA 167170).

THE MAULTSBY INCIDENT: UNANSWERED QUESTIONS

1. As soon as Chuck Maultsby saw the comprehensive plots of his flight in the radar station at Kotzebue after he landed, he wondered "Why in the hell hadn't I been given a steer?" It seemed like everyone knew he was headed into Soviet airspace. No one would tell him. In fact, the U.S. intelligence on Soviet air defense communications was so good that the National Security Agency made sure that the capability remained classified at the Top Secret-plus-Codeword level. Mere U-2 pilots could not be told. There may also have been a remote, very secret site off the Siberian coast to facilitate the listening, and the U.S. also did not want to reveal the capability provided by over-the-horizon backscatter radar techniques, which were still in their infancy.

2. While Maultsby was talking to the navigator in the rescue aircraft, trying to get course corrections, he heard two other calls in English from an unknown source, telling him to turn 30 degrees right. That would have taken him even further into Soviet territory. The pilot challenged the caller, using a code known only to U.S. operators. There was no response. It is quite possible that the Soviets were trying to lure the U-2 into denied territory. This practice was sufficiently commonplace, that the Enroute Supplements issued to peripheral reconnaissance pilots listed the procedures for reporting such attempts.

3. Some of Maultsby's fellow U-2 pilots questioned whether he forgot to disconnect his heading indicator from his magnetic compass. The latter instrument does not provide reliable headings in the high polar regions. Presuming that Maultsby *did* disconnect the compass, so that the aircraft was "running in free gyro," he would have to be careful. Although they were thought to be quite reliable, the gyros on some aircraft "precessed" more than others, especially in a turn. As one pilot noted, doing a 90 + 270 turn to reverse course at the Pole "was a receipe for trouble—the forces of precession could easily have caused a significant heading anomaly on rollout."

4. Finally, author Scott Sagan featured this U-2 incident in his study of U.S. nuclear weapons incidents, "*The Limits of Safety*" (Princeton University Press, 1993). He noted that the F-102s that flew to assist Maultsby were carrying nuclear-tipped Falcon air-to-air missiles, because of the U.S. alert posture at the height of the Cuban Missile Crisis. Sagan judged that the potential for an unintended nuclear incident was high, because the F-102s might have encountered the Soviet MiGs that were trying to intercept the U-2. Because of the rules of engagement posted by Alaskan Air Command, he concluded, "the only nuclear control mechanism was the discipline of the individual pilots in the single-seat interceptors." –C.P.

taken when U-2 sampling missions took remote routes. Maultsby established radio contact with the "Duck Butt" (as the C-54 was colloquially known). But he could not pick up the radio beacon at Barter Island. The Duck Butt confirmed that the beacon was still on the air, and started firing flares. Maultsby could not see them, yet by this time he should have been over the island!

The navigator onboard the SC-54 asked Maultsby to identify a star. He did so. Several minutes later, the navigator told him to steer 10 degrees left. But transmissions from the Duck Butt were getting weaker all the time. With the help of mobile pilot Don Webster sitting in OL-5's command post at Eielson, messages were relayed to the anxious U-2 pilot by HF. He was asked if he could see the glow of the rising sun on the eastern horizon. He could not! As contact with the rescue aircraft was lost, Maultsby realized that he was way off course and had no chance of reaching Eielson. He had already been airborne for nine hours 10 minutes. That meant he only had 30 minutes fuel left. He selected the emergency radio channel and broadcast a May Day call.

Suddenly, he picked up a radio station loud and clear. It was directly ahead—and broadcasting Russian music! Maultsby now knew he had to turn left—and fast! With the sump tank running dry, he shut the engine down and set up a glide. He was at 75,000 feet—could he stretch it to reach friendly territory? After 20 minutes of very gradual descent, it seemed possible—the pilot could now see the sunrise on the horizon. As he descended through 25,000 feet, his pressure suit deflated and he was able to peer sideways. There was a reassuring sight in the dawn light—an F-102 interceptor on each wing!

Major Rudy Anderson was America's only combat casualty during the Cuba Missile Crisis. Shot down on 27 October, the U-2 pilot's body was returned to the US on 4 November and buried with full military honors in his home town of Greenville, SC two days later. He posthumously became the first-ever recipient of the Air Force Cross.

Flamed-out landing

They had been launched from Galena AFS in western Alaska, in response to his May Day call. Maultsby established contact with them on the emergency frequency, and the F-102s guided him to the nearby airfield at the Kotzebue radar tracking station on the coast. He made a safe, flamed-out landing. The flight had lasted 10 hours 25 minutes, including about 45 minutes of glide time. Maultsby was flown back to Eielson, and then onto SAC headquarters at Offutt, where he became the second U-2 pilot within a month who was obliged to explain an unintended overflight to General Power![60]

The Soviet air defense system had detected and reacted to the incursion. From Wrangel Island, the PVO launched a total of six interceptors. What exactly went through the minds of the regional PVO commanders directing the operation? Had they heard and understood Maultsby's emergency calls? Did they know it was a U-2? If so, did they surmise that the spyplane was on some last-minute pre-strike reconnaissance, before SAC's patrolling nuclear bombers flew in? Did the interceptors have orders to shoot the intruder down?

As Maultsby strayed into Soviet airspace, it was lunchtime on the 27th in Washington. Rudy Anderson had been shot down less than three hours earlier, and EXCOM was discussing how to respond. In Moscow it was 9pm, and Khrushchev was agonizing over whether to withdraw. Maybe the report from the PVO in Siberia of Maultsby's incursion helped the Soviet Premier to make up his mind!

(In a formal complaint the next day, Khrushchev asked Kennedy: "What is this, a provocation? One of your planes violates our frontier during this anxious time we are both experiencing, when everything has been

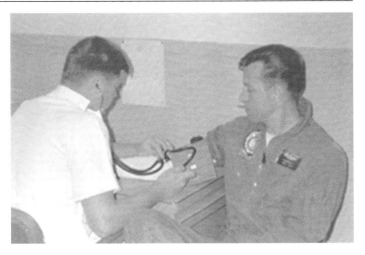

Major Buddy Brown (right, undergoing a preflight medical check) was also due to fly on the same day as Anderson, but his targets were cloud-covered and the mission was cancelled (via Buddy Brown).

put into combat readiness. Is it not a fact that an intruding American plane could easily be taken for a nuclear bomber, which might push us to a fateful step?")[61]

When news of the incident reached the White House, JFK exclaimed "there's always some sonofabitch that doesn't get the word!" It is not clear whether he was referring to Maultsby himself, or to the SAC commanders who let him fly at such a crucial moment. SecDef MacNamara immediately canceled all further U-2 sampling missions worldwide. OL-5 had already launched its next mission from Eielson, which had to be recalled.[62]

17

Vindication

During the Excom meeting on the morning of Sunday, 28 October, officials drafted a long reply to Premier Krushchev's dramatic capitulation. Of necessity, it included an apology for a navigational error made by a nuclear sampling aircraft, eg Chuck Maultsby's U-2. The atmosphere of euphoria in the White House was tempered by DCI McCone. He knew that the crisis was not yet over. The U.S. had to be satisfied that the missiles really were all withdrawn. By evening, the photography from more low-level flights over Cuba was being examined. There were no signs yet of any change on the ground.[1]

On Monday, 29 October, JFK decided to meet some of the key persons involved with the aerial reconnaissance effort. Steve Heyser was summoned from Florida, along with RF-101 squadron commander Lt Col Joe O'Grady. Accompanied by Gen LeMay and Col Doug Steakley, head of the JRC, they spent 20 minutes in the Oval Office as JFK thanked them and their units for all of their efforts. LeMay did most of the talking.

Meanwhile, the RF-8s and RF-101s again flew over the missile sites. Again, there was no sign that they were being dismantled. The next day, flights were suspended while UN Secretary-General U-Thant visited Havana to discuss a possible United Nations role in monitoring the withdrawal. He found Fidel Castro in a foul mood, and nothing was agreed. But senior Soviet officials told the UN delegation that they had received the order to withdraw two days earlier, and the process was underway.

DCI McCone was adamant that the U-2s would not play any part in a UN aerial inspection force. Gen LeMay was against the whole idea, but was overruled by the JCS, which offered TAC's RB-66s instead. But the UN scheme never got off the ground. The next day, 1 November, the U.S. resumed low-level flights. They were not fired upon, and they brought back the first photographs showing that the missile sites were indeed being dismantled.

The big picture

But these were snapshots. U.S. intelligence needed the U-2 to get the big picture: to track the movement of missiles and supporting equipment back to the ports and onto the ships, including the nuclear warheads, and all the other actions that would constitute a complete withdrawal. The CIA urged the resumption of U-2 flights, and NRO Director Joe Charyk agreed. But the Special Group deferred a decision.[2]

The Santa Clara airfield with MiG-21s on alert, seen on U-2 photography of 10 November 1962. In the tense days following the Soviet climb-down, the Castro regime threatened to fire on the overflying U-2s, and MiGs were frequently scrambled on intercept attempts.

There was considerable confusion over what opposition such flights would meet, if any. Khrushchev had warned the U.S. against violating Cuban airspace. Castro had implied publicly that his forces would open fire. The UN delegation got the impression that Cuban forces were making the policy, if not actively controlling all the anti-aircraft and SAM sites. With respect to the SAM sites, at least, U.S. intelligence knew that this could not be true. The SIGINT intercepts revealed only Russian-speaking operators. Besides, there could not possibly have been enough time yet to train the Cubans how to operate the complex SA-2 system. The NSA also intercepted Cuban military messages confirming a ceasefire at the anti-aircraft sites—despite Castro's rhetoric.[3]

At McCoy, the SAC U-2 crews trooped into briefings every day. On Friday, 2 November, five pilots were in their cockpits, ready to go, when the missions were scrubbed. The next day, SAC HQ gave the go-ahead for a single "exploratory" sortie along the coast and past the port of Havana. Captain Bob Spencer took off. When he returned to McCoy without incident, planning began for multiple U-2 sorties starting the next day.[4]

General Power himself attended the briefing of the 4080th pilots the next morning. "I wish I could give you all some encouragement," he said, referring to the SAM threat, "but I can't!" From now on, SAC arranged for an RB-47H SIGINT aircraft to fly offshore whenever a U-2 was over the island, to detect any activity from the SA-2 sites. If they "came up hot," the word would be relayed to the U-2 pilots via an RC-121 AEW and communications aircraft, which was also airborne off Cuba, looking for any MiG fighter activity. Upon receipt of the coded warning, the U-2 pilots were told to break off the mission and get out of Cuban airspace.[5]

Avoid collisions

Unknown to U.S. intelligence, however, the operators at those SAM sites were under instructions *not* to open fire. The order had been sent by Marshall Malinovsky in Moscow to General Pliyev, on the same day that the Soviet Defense Minister first relayed. Khrushchev's decision to withdraw the offensive missiles, eg 28 October. "In addition to the order not to use S-75s, you are ordered not to dispatch fighter aircraft in order to avoid collisions with U.S. reconnaissance planes," Malinovsky added.[6]

5 DECEMBER 1962
MARIEL PORT

KRASNOGRAD

5 FUSELAGES
10 BEAGLE/MASCOT CRATES

As the missile crisis wound down, one of the objectives of the continuing U-2 overflights of Cuba was to monitor the Soviet withdrawal of the offensive missiles. This is a B-camera image of Mariel port.

FLYING OVER THOSE SAM SITES

Captain Chuck Kern was one of the pilots who risked their necks over Cuba during the fall of 1962:

The tactic of skirting around the 25-naut mile lethal radius of the SAM sites was used in Vietnam, but damned little during the Cuban crisis, or I wouldn't have sweated quite so much! The ultimate result had to be that we obtain the photographic evidence, whether or not we kept the other side's air defense guessing. But we did try. Sometimes we would penetrate and turn, maybe twice, and run short tracks, and turn again. Sometimes we would penetrate north to south, feint, and then cut directly across the island, or vice versa.

I got several pictures of two MiG-21s on takeoff as I went over Jose Marte airfield. I saw them through the driftsight and reported them to our RC-121. Seconds later my autopilot surged, and I flamed out. As I began to descend, the two MiGs were climbing fast! My canopy frosted over, but through the driftsight I could see the fighters smoking heavily as they passed through the contrail level. I thought about making for Mexico, but changed my mind and, skirting the western end of the mainland, turned north towards Florida. The battery was losing strength, so another U-2 that had been flying ahead of me relayed my anxious calls to the RC-121 for U.S. fighter support. I was now below 40,000 feet and had to concentrate on trying to get a relight. I was successful, and climbed out of danger just as every U.S. fighter that was airborne in that part of the world converged on the area to try and splash the MiGs!

- correspondence with author

On this Sunday five U-2s were sent over the island, and attempted to make a photographic clean sweep of the island, flying a 5-minute separation and 10 nautical miles apart on east-to-west parallel tracks. But this apparently provoked the air defense system into significant activity; signals from the Fruit Set radars at multiple SA-2 sites were intercepted. The RC-121 transmitted the abort codeword "Green Arrow," and the U-2s scattered in different directions before setting course back to McCoy.[7]

At the Monday briefing, Gen Power frankly told his U-2 pilots they could not have electronic countermeasures (ECM) installed, because of the possibility that the equipment might fall into enemy hands.[8]

That philosophy was not shared by the CIA. After CAF pilot Chen was shot down over China in early September, the Agency investigated ways to give U-2 pilots greater protection against air defense threats. Within the CIA, Don Jackson became the project officer, charged with developing new warning and jamming systems for the U-2. Jackson liaised with the Pentagon, particularly the Director of Defense Research and Engineering, Dr Eugene Fubini. But it was clear that the type of ECM carried by SAC's bombers was impractical for the U-2. These were noise jammers that worked by "brute force," and their weight and power requirements were too great.

System 12

In Palo Alto, California, the company that had provided the first-ever ECM system for the U-2 in 1959 (Granger Associates) was now named Applied Technology Inc (ATI). The Granger system was a simple deceptive repeater to defeat the fire control radars of Soviet fighter interceptors. By now, it was designated System 9 by the CIA. But there were doubts about its practical value against air-air threats. So ATI proposed an improved version. ATI also proposed a radar homing and warning system that would indicate when the U-2 was being tracked by Fruit Set radars associated with the SA-2 SAM. By early October ATI was told to proceed with both. The radar warner was designated System 12 by the Agency.[9]

Meanwhile, Jackson and his team looked at the new deception jammers that the U.S. Navy was acquiring for its A3D Skywarrior carrier-based bombers. They were built by Nashua, NH, based Sanders Associ-

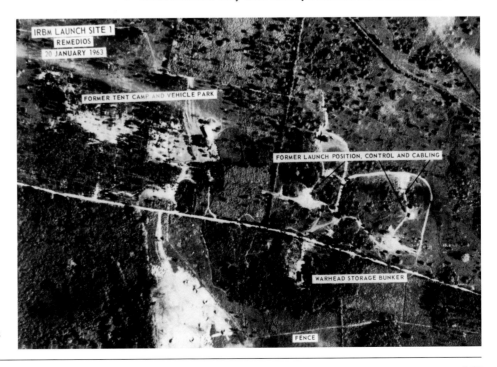

The SS-5 MRBM site at Remedios was confirmed as vacated by a U-2 mission on 20 January 1963.

ates, and covered a range of frequencies. They were still too big to fit inside the U-2, but could be repackaged to fit in the Article's wing-mounted slipper tanks. Engineers from Sanders and the Skunk Works worked round the clock to adapt the Navy systems, a task that was given even greater urgency after Rudy Anderson was shot down. Of particular interest, the ALQ-49 covered frequencies from 4-8 GHz. By now, ELINT analysts had realized that the Fruit Set radars deployed to Cuba were an advanced type operating at these higher frequencies.[10]

By the end of October, Lockheed was ready to install System 12 and the Sanders ECM gear on the first Article. But in the press of the Cuban crisis, there was much confusion between the Agency, Air Force, and the Joint Chiefs over whether and when to proceed. "HQ is in a shambles," wrote Kelly Johnson. "Geary and Scoville have a considerable problem to know who is running the ship." On 1 November the Agency finally got permission to withdraw its remaining U-2F model (article 342) from McCoy, and sent it to Burbank so that installation could begin. The NRO approved the modification of all the Agency's U-2s, and two of SAC's three newly-delivered U-2E models. When General Power got heard of this, he insisted that nothing be done to the SAC aircraft until his people had studied the implications.[11]

As far as the Agency was concerned, the implications were obvious. "SAM sites under Soviet operational control could successfully shield Cuba from reconnaissance by U-2s without ECM," the CIA Daily Summary reported on 6 November. It also noted that the MiG-21s could reach 70,000 feet, but only stay there for a couple of minutes. "Even with the best GCI control, the MiG pilot would have little chance of locating the U-2 and maneuvering into firing position." However, the MiGs could make low-level U.S. reconnaissance "hazardous and difficult." The report went on to warn that the Soviets might clandestinely retain some offensive missiles in Cuba.

System 12 was designed to detect track-while-scan (TWS) radars from 2 to 12 GHz. The antenna array was behind the existing fiberglass radome below the nose of the U-2. If a low-Pulse Repetition Frequency (PRF) signal from a Fruit Set radar was detected, a small yellow light illuminated in the cockpit. If a hi-PRF signal was detected, meaning that the SA-2 site was refining its tracking of the aircraft prior to missile launch, a red light shone. A very small cathode-ray-tube displayed the direction of the threat. An audio warning was fed to the pilot's headset. It was time for him to get out of the area—fast!

ECM pods

System 12 was passive, whereas the new Sanders systems actively radiated a deceptive repeater signal. U-2 slipper tanks were modified with a fiberglass bottom to become ECM pods. A new inverter to power them went into the left slipper tank, while the jamming equipment was carried in the right tank. This could be either the ALQ-49 or ALQ-51, depending on the frequency coverage required. The ALQ-19, an older, less sophisticated Sanders system covering the lower frequencies, could be substituted for the ALQ-51. This was an attempt to meet the concerns that had been expressed over the possible loss of state-of-the-art ECM equipment in another U-2 shootdown. As an added precaution, a destructor charge was also carried in the right pod. The OEL allocated the System numbers 13, 14, and 15 to the ALQ-19, 49, and 51, respectively.

Flight tests of Article 342 with the new defensive gear began on 5 November. Article 342 was flown against various radars at Groom Lake.

System 12 from ATI was rapidly cleared for service, and Lockheed began installing it on the other six U-2s in the Agency's fleet on 20 November. A total of 15 sets were ordered, but it was not until late January that the first SAC aircraft was modified. Until then, the Air Force pilots flying over Cuba had to rely on warnings relayed from ELINT aircraft offshore for their SAM protection. Meanwhile, ATI began building the System 9A kits, to provide improved protection against air-air threats.[12]

The ECM gear was problematical, though. Of course, there were significant disadvantages. A new, more powerful DC generator was required. The entire installation added 670 lbs to the empty weight, and together with the loss of slipper tank fuel, reduced the U-2's endurance to only seven hours. In theory, that did not matter on the Cuba missions, provided they were launched out of Florida or nearby, but the Air Force's reluctance to expose Systems 13/14/15 to potential loss postponed their introduction well into 1963.[13]

In November 1962 the 4080th wing flew a total of 69 missions over Cuba from OL-X, monitoring the Soviet withdrawal. On only two days were there no flights at all. Some days there were five flights, but after the simultaneous penetrations and aborts on 4 November, only one U-2 flight at a time crossed the island. If the SIGINT suggested that the U-2 was being targeted by a Fruit Set radar, the aircraft was recalled.

Low-level flights terminated

After mid-month the U-2s were the only show in town: the low-level flights were terminated after it became clear that the Cubans controlled the anti-aircraft guns, and were preparing to fire again. The Soviets also protested the U-2 flights on a regular basis. The question of what to do if they actually shot one down was frequently discussed in Excom.

So what was the reconnaissance task? The Soviets had sent to Cuba, in total, three regiments with a total of 24 SS-4 launchers (fully deployed); two regiments with a total of 16 SS-5 launchers (partially deployed); the missiles themselves, and their nuclear warheads. There were also a small number of Frog battlefield nuclear missiles. The withdrawal of all these from the sites to the ports and on to the ships had to be monitored. (Not

The ceremony at SAC headquarters on 28 November 1962, when General Power awarded the Distinguished Flying Cross to the 10 surviving Air Force pilots who flew U-2s over Cuba between 14 and 26 October. (via Jerry McIlmoyle)

Not all those U-2 pilots who flew over Cuba got the DFC from General Power. But most of the early SAC U-2 pilots received awards and honors at some time during their tour. In a typical ceremony, 4080th SRW wing commander Colonel John DesPortes pins an award on (from left right): Major Harold Melbratten, and Captains Tony Bevacqua, Dick Bouchard and Bob Spencer (via Tony Bevacqua).

realizing that the tactical cruise missiles were nuclear-capable, the U.S. did not seek to monitor their departure with such care).

Then there were the Il-28 bombers. Much discussion of these ensued. Uncrating of the Il-28s at San Julian continued, while no effort was made to uncrate or assemble the smaller number at Holguin. Why? It was not until the end of the Cold War that it became clear that the Beagles sent to Holguin were nuclear-capable, whereas the ones sent to San Julian were from a Soviet Navy unit, and equipped only for anti-ship missions with mines and torpedoes. The Soviets intended to pass the ones at San Julian to the Cubans.[14]

By the time of his news conference on 20 November, President Kennedy was able to report that the missile sites had all been dismantled, that the missiles themselves had departed on Soviet ships, and that these had been inspected at sea by the U.S. Navy. Moreover, Premier Khrushchev had now promised to remove all the Il-28s. Nothing was said about the SAMs or the MiGs, however. They were defensive weapons, and were clearly staying. It was not clear when or if the Soviets would hand control of them to the Cubans. Meanwhile, Castro was still refusing to admit UN inspectors.

Five days later, U-2 imagery confirmed that the bombers at San Julian airfield were being dismantled, and on 27 November a mission over Holguin revealed that all the crated bombers there had been removed.

Good pictures
On 26 November , President Kennedy reviewed some of the U.S. armed forces that had been involved in the crisis. At Homestead AFB, he pre-

sented Outstanding Unit Citations to the RF-101 unit based there (the 363rd TRW), and also to the 4080th SRW. Colonel DesPortes and his group stood to attention while the President remarked: "I must say, gentlemen, that you take good pictures, and I have seen a good many of them...."

Two days later, there was another ceremony in General Power's office at SAC headquarters, Offutt AFB, when the 10 surviving 4080th pilots who had flown over Cuba during October were each awarded the Distinguished Flying Cross. In addition to Richard Heyser, those decorated were Majors Buddy Brown, Ed Emerling, Gerald McIlmoyle, Robert Primrose, and Jim Qualls; and Captains George Bull, Roger Herman, Charles Kern, and Dan Schmarr.

By then, another eight SAC U-2 pilots had started flying over Cuba. Strangely, though, they were not honored. Yet they faced the same perceived risk of attack over the island as the 11 who had flown in October, one of whom (Anderson) had not returned. The other eight were Jack Carr, Chuck Maultsby, Bob Spencer, Leo Stewart, Chuck Stratton, Roy St Martin, John Wall, and Robert Wilke.

Also not honored in public were the pilots of the CIA's Detachment G, aka WRSP-IV. But during a secret ceremony at Edwards North Base in early December, they were each given the CIA Intelligence Star. To some of them, it seemed strange that it took the Cuban Crisis to prompt their first formal award from the Agency. After all, they had put their lives on the line for four years flying over the Soviet Union itself, from 1956 to 1960! (It seemed even stranger when, as soon as the ceremony was over, a CIA security officer reclaimed the medals for safe keeping. The spooks were worried that the pilot might show them off to "unauthorized persons!")

18

Vulnerabilities

Training flights by the CIA's Detachment H, also known as the Chinese Air Force 35th Squadron, resumed in mid-October 1962 with the remaining Article at Taoyuan (355). Chen's shootdown was still on everyone's mind, however, and when the three remaining CAF pilots experienced a series of flameouts, high-level action was prompted. OSA maintenance chief Lt Col Jim McArthy arrived with Kelly Johnson and Lockheed test pilot Bob Schumacher. After Schumacher flew some test hops, small strips were added to the leading edge of the wings, with the aim of providing a better indication of onset of stall buffet. Lockheed also recommended a new climb schedule, with the EGT reduced to 485 degrees.[1]

Flights over mainland China were not resumed until the new System 12 SAM warner was installed. However, the CAF pilots were not particularly impressed with the new device. "The whole instrument seemed very primitive. The pilot had no way to decide the best maneuver to evade," Major Mike Hua recalled, noting that the small directional display gave no indication of range to the SAM site. Hua took the first operational mission since Chen's loss on 6 December. His task was to fly over North Korea—the first time that this had been done by the Black Cat Squadron. Just before he reached the 38th parallel heading south, System 12 lit up. But the strobe pointed in the six o'clock position, so Hua concluded that if there was any threat, it was behind him! He coasted-out for the long overwater flight back to Taiwan. No SA-2 sites were seen on the mission "take," but the first MiG-21s in North Korea were discovered.[2]

The U.S. Intelligence Board had requested Tackle coverage of the Szechwan Basin as a priority, to search for a possible large water-cooled nuclear reactor. So the next mission over China on 21 December headed there. But it only penetrated 85 miles before a B-camera failure forced Gimo Yang to return home. On 24 December Tiger Wang tried again, but not only was the weather worse than forecast, but the camera failed again before the primary target area was reached! Furthermore, the SAM warning lights came on as soon as he activated System 12 before coast-in.[3]

The lights came on again three days later when Mike Hua took off on a mission designed to detect any Chinese military preparations in support of the communist expansion in southeast Asia. He aborted and returned to base. Unusually, Hua was scheduled for the repeat of this near eight-hour mission again the next day. He reluctantly agreed to fly again, and gained coverage of Kunming, Mengtzu, and northeastern North Vietnam. The camera failed again, fortunately after the main targets had been covered.[4]

Takhli

While the Black Cat Squadron was flying along the Chinese border with Southeast Asia for the first time, an all-American group from Project Idealist was deployed to Takhli, the airbase in Thailand that had already become a covert base for the CIA's support of anti-communist forces in the region. This would be the first of many visits by U-2s to the Thai base over the next few years. This deployment was also tasked to fly over the Sino-southeast Asia border areas. Indeed, if Hua's first flight to this area had proceeded as planned on 27 December, he would have been working the area at the same time as a Det G mission out of Takhli. This flew via Laos, then photographed a very large Chinese military barracks at Ssumao, just 50 miles from the Laotian border. The PIs calculated that it could house at least 35,000 troops, and speculated that it could serve as a base camp for extended forays by the People's Liberation Army into southeast Asia.[5]

But southeast Asia was a secondary objective for this deployment by Det G to Takhli. The primary objective was Tibet, and the Sino-Indian border area, which the U-2 had last flown over in March/April 1960, and on which the U.S. intelligence community wanted renewed coverage.

Air Force Chief of Staff General Curtiss LeMay with Dr. Joe Charyk (right). Charyk was the first Director of the National Reconnaissance Office (NRO), which fought for control of programs that the CIA had developed, such as the U-2, A-12, and Corona satellite (NARA 163483).

WATER-SOLUBLE MAPS

So you've just been shot down over enemy territory and survived. The Agency has given you a cover story, but the U-2 cockpit has landed more or less intact, and the bad guys are just recovering all the maps showing your route over their homeland. Some awkward questions are pending....

To prevent this Gary Powers scenario from reoccurring, Project HQ experimented in late 1962 with water-soluble maps! In a memo to HQ USAF, OSA Director Col Jack Ledford noted that General Jimmy Doolittle, a member of the President's Foreign Intelligence Advisory Board, was insisting on a map destruction capability for overflying spyplanes. The Technical Director of the Aeronautical Chart and Information Center (ACIC) at St. Louis was granted a clearance, and appraised of the problem. He came up with a watertight map container that would be flooded upon command. If the maps were printed on a special type of paper, they would be reduced to an unreadable slurry within 60 seconds.

ACIC was asked to print a batch of 33 JN and 6 GNC series maps on the special paper, for an operational trial. It is not known whether the system was ever used over "denied" territory. - C.P.

NOTHING DOWN THERE!

Jim Cherbonneaux flew one of the many missions along the Sino-Indian border and over Tibet in 1963-64. The Agency was looking for Chinese troop deployments. But as he peered through the driftsight, Jim Cherbonneaux could not see what was worth fighting over!

Turning north from Lhasa, other than the dirt road, there was *nothing* down there. That area is high desert, not unlike western Colorado, only much higher. After turning back to the border areas, I began flying over the most rugged mountainous terrain in the whole world—the Himalayas. While looking down at all that awesome scenery, I was unable to figure out how anyone could live there—much less do any fighting. I decided that if there were actually people engaged in warfare in that area, they were welcome to whatever part they captured.

The CIA was still supporting the Tibetan guerrillas who opposed communist rule from Peking with training, infiltration, and airdrops. The Kennedy Administration was courting India in 1962 as part of a strategy to woo the non-aligned countries away from communism. Senior officials believed that New Delhi could play a critical role in containing China's power and influence. JFK appointed his personal friend, J.K. Galbraith, as the new U.S. ambassador to India.

Then, in mid-October 1962 long-simmering tensions between India and China boiled over. Chinese forces launched major attacks against Indian positions in Kashmir, and in the area of the eastern Himalayas then known as the "North East Frontier Agency" (NEFA). As Indian forces retreated, a senior official on the U.S. National Security Council noted "we may have a golden opportunity for a major gain in our relations with India." Indeed, Indian Prime Minister Nehru was shaken by the Chinese advance, and asked for U.S. military assistance.[6]

The President's National Security Advisor, McGeorge Bundy, called OSA Director Jack Ledford to the White House. He asked if the U-2 could fly over the disputed area. Ledford told him it was possible, using refueled airplanes and with Indian cooperation. Bundy cleared the idea with JFK, and Ambassador Galbraith was cleared to make the offer.[7]

To India

India gave permission for the U-2s to overfly its territory—as long as the whole operation was kept secret. Project HQ dispatched Lt Col Joe Giraudo (the Oxcart branch chief) and John McMahon (the executive officer) to Delhi to make the arrangements "because we looked a bit like Indians," Giraudo recalled. They organized radar suppression, and a flight track northwest of Delhi where the Article could be refueled from a KC-135.[8]

In mid-November, Det G sent U-2F Article 342 to Takhli airbase, Thailand, inside a C-124 . It was reassembled in a small hangar there, and joined by a KC-135 and an SA-16 rescue aircraft. There were two weeks of waiting around for final political approvals. The first U-2 mission to the Sino-Indian border area eventually took place on 5 December. Meanwhile, the Chinese declared a unilateral ceasefire.

With the SA-16 orbiting below in case of emergencies, the U-2 flew north up the Bay of Bengal and over Calcutta. The route continued over the narrow strip of Indian territory between Nepal and East Pakistan, but then violated the airspace of Bhutan before heading into Tibet. Three hours later, the U-2 returned the same way and descended to meet the tanker at 35,000 feet. The hook-up went well, using the new procedures first used

The missions by the CIA's Project Idealist over the Sino-Indian border and Tibet in 1963-64 were flown by refuelable U-2F models (Lockheed U-2-91-0004-2).

over Florida in September during the Cuba missions. Then it was back to Takhli, where the Article landed after 12 hours in the air. A C-130 took the camera film to Yokota AB, Japan, for processing and read-out by PACAF's 67th RTS. The weather was cloudier than forecast over Tibet, so virtually the same route was flown again five days later. These U-2 missions probably helped to confirm that the Chinese troops were being pulled back from the border areas.[9]

Tibet, NEFA, Kashmir

Operating conditions at Takhli were primitive, but Det G's deployment was extended. There were three more missions to Tibet, the NEFA, and (for the first time) Kashmir. The U.S. had offered to act as mediator between India and Pakistan over the disputed territory. Now the U.S. was taking a look for itself, from 70,000 feet. This was politically dangerous, however. Pakistan was already upset about the possibility of U.S. military assistance to India. And while the May Day affair had made further U-2 deployments to Peshawar politically impossible, that airbase still housed a U.S. SIGINT site that was vital to the monitoring of Soviet missile developments at Tyuratam and Saryshagan.

On 19 January U-2 pilot Jim Cherbonneaux was returning from the second flight over Kashmir when a low fuel warning light came on during his refuelling hook-up over India. That meant he had less than 50 gallons remaining, instead of the 160 or so that were supposed to remain prior to the refueling. Although the tanker reported a full offload, the warning light stayed on. From the KC-135, deployment commander Col Bill Gregory ordered him to make a precautionary landing at Kalikunda airbase, near Calcutta. The Indian Air Force was less than thrilled to have the black spyplane drop in, followed by a KC-135! The fuel problem was quickly diagnosed as a false indication, and the two U.S. aircraft were soon on their way back to Takhli.

At Project HQ, OSA's operations chief Lt Col Don Songer had already recommended that U-2s actually be based in India to accomplish the Sino-Indian border missions. "The forward operating base (will) eliminate the need for inflight refueling and airborne search and rescue support. In addition, it will eliminate the requirement for distribution of highly sensitive mission data to other than the host country," he wrote. But the State Department was fearful of the political implications, and then the Indians baulked at the idea. B.N. Malik, the director of the Indian Intelligence Bureau (IB), told PM Nehru to insist on a precondition: all the U-2 film must be processed in India, and the IB must retain a copy. The negotiations on U-2 basing apparently stalled.[10]

Meanwhile, Det G flew an unrefueled mission from Takhli over eastern Tibet, along the Burma/China border, and eastwards as far as Kunming. Two days earlier, Gimo Yang had covered the same area on a Det H mission from Taiwan, after making the Det's third attempt to cover the suspected nuclear facilities in the Szechwan Basin. But there were yet more B-camera problems on this flight: the image quality was poor. Hycon engineers traced the problem to the vacuum solenoid, but advised that some failures were bound to occur. After all, the "B" design was now seven years old, and the cameras had each been cycled several hundred thousand times.[11]

Stand-down

In late January, Project HQ ordered an operational stand-down at both Takhli and Taoyuan, and called a conference to discuss the camera and other re-

HIMALAYAN UNKNOWNS
Still, the folks in Washington made good use of the imagery. Chet Cooper was a CIA liaison officer to the National Security Council in 1963-64:

The Himalayas was an area that very few people knew about. Not many people could find on a map where these (Chinese) operations were taking place, the problems they might be having, the urgency of the threat to the Indians, or whatever. There was an amazing degree of ignorance about the depth of the snow, and whether the wind was blowing in one direction or another, and whether this was good or bad for the Chinese or the Indians. I was able to turn the Agency's cartographers, meteorologists, and geographers loose on the problem. In the course of one day, they came up with a pretty useful assessment on the urgency of India's problems.

- Chester Cooper, Oral History 1966 in the JFK Library

WHAT COULD GO WRONG?
After various technical failures in early 1963, Project HQ issued new codes so that a U-2 pilot on an overflight of denied territory could radio his predicament via the SSB radio, without telling the bad guys below what was wrong. Identified by a single number, the categories were:

- low on fuel, less than 100 gals
- I am lost and require assistance
- returning early
- landing at alternate
- DC generator out
- AC generator out
- complete electrical failure
- oxygen failure
- EGT fluctuation
- pressurization out
- hydraulic failure
- main inverter failure
- autopilot out
- "D" light on
- System 12 out
- Flameout

Within a year of this instruction being issued, however, it was no longer necessary. The Birdwatcher telemetry system was introduced, so that overflight-followers in the command post would know by coded, burst transmission exactly what was wrong. – C.P.

Chapter 18: Vulnerabilities

RECONNAISSANCE WARS IN WASHINGTON

In late 1962, tensions between the CIA and the Pentagon over the control of U.S. satellite and airborne reconnaissance escalated. The National Reconnaissance Office (NRO) had been established in September 1961 to oversee the technical management of ever-more expensive and ambitious U.S. overhead programs. Its existence was top secret; the NRO's Director, Dr Joe Charyk, was publicly identified as an "Under Secretary of the Air Force."

But there were a series of disputes between the NRO and the CIA over "roles and responsibilities," even after a supposed clarification in July 1962. This created three programs within the NRO as follows:

- Program A: satellite systems developed by the Air Force, such as SAMOS
- Program B: satellite and aircraft systems developed by the CIA, such as Corona, Oxcart, and Idealist (eg the U-2)
- Program C: satellite systems developed by the Navy, such as GRAB, the first SIGINT system in space

After the Pentagon gave the go-ahead for an Air Force version of the Oxcart in January 1963, Program D was added to manage what became the SR-71 Blackbird. Within the CIA, the Office of Special Activities (OSA) was responsible for all of the Agency's overhead reconnaissance systems. The CIA nominated Col Jack Ledford, the newly-appointed Director of the Office of Special Activities, to also serve as Director, Program B. Col Leo Geary, who was in his seventh year as the head of AFCIG-5—the liaison office in the Pentagon that supported CIA covert activities—was nominated to also serve as Director, Program D.

At the operating level, blue-suiters like Ledford and Geary got along fine. But Ledford's CIA boss, Deputy Director for Research (DDR) Herb Scoville, viewed the NRO as an Air Force plot to completely take over successful programs, such as Corona and Idealist. His permanent officials, such as OSA Deputy Director Jim Cunningham, supported Scoville's bitter arguments with Charyk.

Another bone of contention was the Joint Reconnaissance Center (JRC) in the Pentagon. The JRC's charter was to manage the operations of sensitive military reconnaissance flights by all three services. The CIA resisted moves to have the JRC also control the covert overflights by OSA's U-2s.

There were also tensions over film processing. Ever since the U-2 went into service in 1956, the CIA had contracted with the film supplier, Eastman Kodak (EK), in Rochester, NY, for most of the processing. Top OSA officials resented the NRO's attempt to control the EK budget, and redirect the company's priorities.

As the tension worsened in 1963, DDR Scoville did not feel that DCI John McCone was fully supporting his power struggle with the Pentagon. Scoville was also unhappy that DDR did not control enough of the Agency's own scientific intelligence effort, which still resided in the other two CIA Directorates. Scoville therefore resigned from the Agency in mid-1963.

DCI McCone asked the OSI's young but talented missile expert, Albert "Bud" Wheelon, to replace Scoville. Wheelon refused, unless the DDR was strengthened. McCone belatedly agreed to expand and rename DDR as the Directorate of Science and Technology (DST).

As Deputy Director (eg the head) of DST, Wheelon renewed the struggle to prevent the Air Force takeover with new NRO Director Brockway McMillan with even greater vigor. In October 1963, he reminded DCI McCone that the U-2 and Corona had produced the majority of raw U.S. intelligence on the Sino-Soviet bloc—and they had both been developed by the CIA. "Intelligence will always rank fourth or fifth on the Air Force priority list," Wheelon continued. "OSA represents a unique national asset: an experienced, integrated organization with a demonstrated capability for developing and operating reconnaissance systems that produce intelligence on which this country has come to rely."

The "NRO Wars" continued throughout 1964 and into 1965. Within the CIA, the management of its satellite activities was transferred from OSA to a new Office of Special Projects (OSP). Also in 1965, an Executive Committee (ExCom) was set up in the NRO to make the key decisions on what strategic reconnaissance programs should be funded. It comprised the DCI, the Under-Secretary of Defense, and the President's Science Advisor. This helped reduce the tension between the NRO and the CIA. – C.P.

cent technical issues. These included EGT fluctuations, cabin and Q-bay pressure variations, inverter and alternator failures, and—an old favorite—autopilot problems.[12]

The stand-down was lifted in late February so that the Black Cat Squadron could fly two important missions over China that had already been approved by the Special Group. The U-2 would return to Lanchow and the SCT missile range, and a large facility midway between the two at Koko Nor, which might also be associated with nuclear weapons R&D. Another target was Paotow, the city in Inner Mongolia where U.S. intelligence suspected a nuclear reactor was being built. To gain more range, the mission planners in Project HQ lobbied for them to be staged out of South Korea. This idea was approved by the politicians, and on 26 February the Article at Det H (355) was ferried to Kunsan AB. But a hydraulic leak was discovered during the postflight inspection. It was sent back to Taiwan, but on the return ferry flight there was a complete electrical failure.

At Takhli, the Det G deployment had also experienced technical problems, but did manage to fly two more successful missions over North Vietnam and Laos on 1 and 2 March. Thanks largely to the U-2, U.S. intelligence now had a better knowledge of the disposition of Chinese forces in the areas bordering Southeast Asia, and of new road networks leading from there into Laos and North Vietnam. The next day, the group packed up and returned to the U.S. OSA Director Jack Ledford resisted pressure to keep them deployed for more coverage over Laos and, for the first time since 1958, Indonesia. Article 342 was ferried to Taoyuan as a back-up for the troublesome 355.[13]

Kelly Johnson blamed overhaul procedures at his subcontractors for most of the technical problems. He recommended another grounding. "There were screams from (DCI) McCone down, but we just went ahead," he recalled. He praised his subordinates Lou Sakala and Fred Cavanaugh for sorting out the problems, but castigated Lear Siegler's "terrible performance in making their generators work." A new DC generator from Bendix was selected and installed within a few months. A new alternator—already selected but delayed in flight testing—was expedited. Johnson ordered tighter quality control at the vendors.[14]

Meanwhile, Project HQ reviewed its own maintenance oversight. "I think we must tighten up our relationship with (Kelly Johnson)...we need to press harder on the new generator/alternator and inverter problems," wrote OSA Deputy Director Jim Cunningham. "From time to time, everyone agrees that the autopilot is in need of support and redesign, but these conclusions are never reflected into action," he complained. Overall, though, as OSA Director Jack Ledford noted, "the majority of LAC and Hycon technicians have been with the Project since its inception. They are all highly skilled, very motivated, and extremely loyal. It was agreed that no higher caliber personnel could be obtained."[15]

SAC U-2E models

SAC was also having generator problems, but was able to continue both training and operational activities. The 4080th wing received its three U-2E models during fall 1962, and checked out five pilots by the end of the year. As the Cuban crisis wound down, OL-X moved from McCoy to the 4080th's home base at Laughlin in late November. But with no prospect of on-site inspections in Cuba, the requirements to overfly levied on the wing from Washington were still heavy. COMOR wanted the U-2s to cover the 20 highest priority targets at least once per week, and all other priority targets at least twice per month. DCI McCone thought that two flights per week would do it—but that was before weather conditions were considered. In fact, SAC flew 39 U-2 missions over Cuba in December.

On 11 January 1963, Major Pat Halloran flew the first and only SAC refueled mission to Cuba, routing east as far as Puerto Rico, before turning to coast-in over southeastern Cuba. His total flight time was nearly 13 hours—the longest U-2 mission to date. By the end of January, the SAC wing had flown 1,370 hours on Cuba missions, and the tempo increased in February and March, when no fewer than 58 and 68 missions, respectively, went over the island. From defectors' reports, there was a scare about offensive missiles being hidden in caves. Belatedly, the intel analysts were getting concerned about the coastal defense missile sites.

U-2 overflights of China by the Black Cat Squadron were routinely detected and challenged by Chicom interceptors, usually J-6s (MiG –19) like the one shown here. But the J-6 interceptor could not reach the U-2's altitude, and never posed a serious threat.

The SAC wing was also still heavily tasked with sampling flights. In January, OL-5 at Eielson flew 251 hours, OL-10 at Laughlin 165 hours, OL-11 at Laverton, Australia, 68 hours, and OL-18 at Albrook, Panama, 79 hours. OL-18 was the latest location, replacing Anderson AFB on Guam, where Typhoon Karen had damaged the OL-14 hangar and the two Dragon Ladies sheltering inside in November 1963.

There was also another deployment to fly SIGINT missions along the Soviet Siberian border with System 4A, this time out of Eielson. An RB-47H flew coordinated sorties. But after the previous fall's accidental U-2 overflights, SAC could not afford any more screw-ups! It set a new navigation standard: 10 nautical miles error or less after a 1,500 nautical mile straight line The pilots' celestial fixes were closely monitored. They were required to check in frequently on SSB radio. The peripheral displacement was increased. Radar stations on the Alaskan coast plotted the U-2's course as it coasted-out. The first mission by Jerry McIlmoyle was aborted when one of these stations wrongly computed his position. The next, by Buddy Brown, supposedly violated the ADIZ upon its return. McIlmoyle flew

In the early 1960s, SAC used the so-called "Ram's Horns" antennas on the upper rear fuselage of the U-2A in conjunction with System 4, the big SIGINT package that was flown along Soviet borders.

two more sorties before the aircraft was redeployed to Laughlin in mid-February.[16]

Transfer tussle

By the end of March, the Agency's U-2s were ready for operational missions again, with modified generators. But there simply were not enough of them. Two USAF U-2s had been transferred to the CIA in late 1962, and were being converted to U-2F configuration. This maintained the Agency fleet at its authorized level of seven. But one of Det G's U-2s remained dedicated to test flights, often in connection with the OXCART development. Two more equipped with the new ECM Systems 14 and 15 remained on standby at Edwards, in case they were needed by SAC over Cuba. Both the CIA and the nationalist government wanted a second U-2 to be permanently assigned to Det H, replacing the shot down one. To meet other COMOR requirements, the CIA was considering a permanent detachment with two more aircraft at Takhli or, better still, in India. So the Agency requested the transfer of two more U-2s from the Air Force. A long bureaucratic tussle ensued with the NRO and the Pentagon, before Articles 348 and 362 became the property of the OSA in summer 1963.[17]

On 28 March, Tiger Wang took off from Kunsan AB to fly the long-scheduled mission to northwestern China. The weather in the north was

Major Pat Halloran flew the first refueled mission by SAC over Cuba in early 1963, using the U-2E model (via Pat Halloran).

Seen here in 1963, this U-2A was the second aircraft to be allocated to the Air Force (serial number 66690). It was Article 390, the 30th and last aircraft of the original production batch for the USAF. The previous aircraft was Article 357, one of the first batch of 20 that was built for the CIA. It crashed in December 1956. 390 also crashed, in October 1966 (via Arthur Pearcy).

good, and the vital targets were covered, including the suspected nuclear facility at Paotow. But when he reached the vicinity of the SCT missile range Wang's System 12 came to life. The strobe pointed in the one o'clock direction, so he made a left turn. The warning ceased, so he continued the turn through 360 degrees to resume course. But the warning system now displayed a strobe pointing to 11 o'clock. This time, Wang turned right through almost another 360 degrees as he decided to set course for Taiwan.

On the ground, the PLAAF's 4th Battalion had set up an SA-2 site, and were cursing their luck as the U-2 twice stayed out of their firing range. System 12 had worked! But as he fled southeastwards, the CAF U-2 pilot got hopelessly lost. Soon, he was flying over a solid undercast. It extended all the way to the coast and beyond. Wang had almost given up hope of finding his way back to Taoyuan when the cloud began to clear, and he spotted, through the driftsight, the shallow reef surrounding the East Sand islands. It was a familiar sight, and he was able to reset course for home base from here.[18]

Two days later, Mike Hua finally flew the Schechwan Basin mission. No nuclear installations were discovered here. Gimo Yang also got another overflight, to southern China on 3 April. About this time, the Chinese Air Force decided that these pilots should "graduate" from the U-2 program when they had each done 10 overflight missions. It was hazardous duty—but they did not get combat pay! Two replacements were selected for training and were sent to the U.S.

In April 1963, Lockheed "sold" another U-2 to Taiwan. In reality, two aircraft had been at Taoyuan for over a month, but Det H was under strict instructions not to have more than one of them outside the hangar at any one time. Through third parties, the PRC had already made its displeasure known to the U.S. about the supply to the nationalists of "new U-2 planes," as well as F-104s.[19]

Cloud-covered

The Black Cat Squadron made another five overflights in May and June. They ranged widely over Manchuria, central and northwest China, and North Korea. By now, CORONA photography covered 90% of the PRC. But nearly half of the satellite imagery was cloud-covered, and it seemed that the intel analysts in Washington could not get enough of the large-scale U-2 imagery.[20]

In July, the USIB issued a Special NIE on Communist China's advanced weapons programs. They were "more ambitious..than we had earlier thought," the analysts noted. The nuclear facility at Paotow appeared to be a plutonium reactor. There might be another one somewhere, in which case the Chinese might already have enough to detonate a bomb. The gaseous diffusion plant at Lanchow was designed to produce weapons-grade Uranium-235, but probably not before 1965 because of the technical difficulties inherent in this process.

As for the means of delivery, the missile test range at SCT appeared to be conducting test firings of MRBMs, though none had been seen yet. Substantial construction had taken place at Chang Hsintien, a missile R&D facility near Peking. The PLAAF had two Tu-16 Badger jet bombers that might be operational.[21]

The U.S. analysts also noted that China had at least 10 SA-2 sites, "not all of which are occupied." In fact, the Chicoms were doing all they could to shoot another U-2 down.

The 4th Battalion had moved from Peking to a new site 130 miles northeast of Lanchow. Mike Hua had flown near it on his 3 June mission

When three 4080th wing U-2As were deployed to the UK for sampling flights in August 1962, the Royal Air Force soon suggested a secret program involving the powerful Lightning interceptor. A pair of Lightning Mk. 1As from the Air Fighting Development Squadron (AFDS) flew from RAF Middleton St. George in eastern England against the U-2s heading north on their outbound course at 60,000 feet, and again when they returned at 65,000 feet. The U-2 pilots were briefed to maintain their course, if they saw the interceptors approaching. The Lightning pilots were briefed to approach no closer than 5,000 feet astern, and to break off if they had no visual contact at five nautical miles range to target.

The RAF pilots and their ground controllers did very well. The Lightnings would climb to 36,000 feet on cold power, then turn to the crossing vector provided by GCI, and accelerate to Mach 1.5. Then they would climb to 50,000 feet, turn onto the target's heading, and perform a 10-degree snap-up to 60,000 feet. This height could be held for about 80 seconds, as the speed decayed from an initial Mach 1.2. For the 65,000 feet interceptions, the initial acceleration was increased to Mach 1.7 and the snap-up to 20 degrees. But the Lightning could only stay at 65K for about 30 seconds before its minimum control speed was reached. There were no flameouts, however.

Visual IDs of the U-2s were made on most occasions, and the seeker heads of the dummy Firestreak air-air missiles acquired their targets at two-three miles range. But the closing speeds were very high, and the Lightnings invariably overtook their quarry. However, the Brit pilots took care not to upset the U-2 with their shock wave. – C.P.

When SAC deployed the Dragon Lady to far-flung operating locations, C-124 transports often provided the logistics support. This scene is at Nandi, Fiji, during a sampling deployment to Australia (via Bob Spencer).

FALL OUT

By 1963, concern over the atmospheric testing of nuclear weapons was reaching a peak. Soviet tests in 1962 were estimated to have injected 60 megatons of fission yield into the atmosphere. Most of the U.S. tests were lower-yielding, but the net result of the U.S., Soviet, UK, and French test shots over time was a measurable increase in long-range fallout. The U-2 High-Altitude Sampling Program (HASP) flights for the Defense Atomic Support Agency (DASA) made a major contribution to these measurements. The other "customer" for U-2 sampling was the secret Air Force Tactical Applications Center (AFTAC), which estimated the design, yield, and rate of production of Soviet nuclear weapons from gas and particle sampling.

By the time the Partial Test Ban Treaty (PTBT) was agreed in July 1963, the U.S. had done 212 nuclear tests in the atmosphere, the USSR 161, the UK 21, and France (which was not a signatory) four.

The 4080th wing continued to fly sampling missions after the PTBT went into effect, but the tasking was reduced. In early 1964, the number of aircraft in Alaska (now designated OL-3 at Eielson) and Panama (OL-18 at Albrook) was reduced to one each. As the number of U-2s dwindled through accidents and the deployment to Vietnam began, the high-altitude sampling mission was reallocated by the Pentagon to the RB-57Fs of the 9th WRW. The 4080th closed OL-10 at Davis-Monthan in October 1964, followed by OL-3 at Eielson the following month. On their last missions, these two locations helped to collect debris from the first Chinese nuclear test. The last two U-2 sampling detachments to close were OL-18 at Albrook in January 1965 and OL-11 at Laverton, in Australia, in February 1965. -CP

THE CHINESE AND THE AUTOPILOTS – WHO'S TO BLAME?

In the early 1960s, the U-2 autopilot was under constant scrutiny. There were technical failures, but were the pilots also to blame? The nationalist Chinese pilots might have been, according to both SAC and the OSA.

When Major Yeh was being trained by the 4080th wing at Laughlin in April 1963 he had a flameout at high altitude. He managed to relight at 35,000 feet on the second attempt. Back on the ground, Yeh reported that the autopilot caused the aircraft to pitch up 70 degrees, and roll. According to maintainers, however, the autopilot worked fine when they checked it.

The following month, Project HQ sent a team to Taiwan after Det H reported autopilot problems on Article 355. The team discovered that the amplifiers had been improperly wired by the Lear Siegler techrep. But, they also noted, "pilot techniques may also be involved." The American pilots assigned to Det H said that the aircraft flew very well at two-three knots above the recommended speed at extreme altitudes. One of the team from OSA reckoned that the Chinese pilots were flying the aircraft in the buffet zone and attributing the difficulties to autopilot jitters.

- from 4080th wing history April 1963 and OSA memo 24 May 1963

---

enroute from Lanchow to Paotow, and had made two S-turns when System 12 indicated a Fan Song (formerly Fruit Set) missile guidance radar. The U.S. analysts could not figure out why this site was in such an isolated area: there was no important facility to protect. They did not realize that the Chicoms were specifically targeting the U-2 flights. As for the 4th Battalion, its commanders now realized that the U-2s were now carrying some form of warning system. They revised their tactics. From now on, they would try to shorten the radar acquisition cycle, so that the U-2 could not escape so easily.[22]

In early April, COMOR called for more coverage of the Sino-Indian border area, and the Special Group approved four missions. Once again, Det G made the long transpacific trek with a single U-2 to Takhli, via NAS Barbers Point, Hawaii, and Anderson AFB, Guam, supported by a KC-135 and a C-133. But at the same time, the U.S. Intelligence Board issued a memorandum that described the Chinese military deployments in Tibet in detail. The memo concluded that Peking would have to deploy many more troops to the region before it could pose a serious military threat to India. The Chicoms were probably more concerned about boosting their forces in southeast Asia, the USIB concluded. This intelligence was presumably shared with India. At any rate, New Delhi withheld permission for any more U-2 flights at this time. Instead, the deployment to Takhli flew six

more missions (codenamed Low Note) over Laos, North Vietnam, and their borders with China, before heading home in late May.[23]

General Power bans advanced ECM

In early May, the Air Force changed its mind about installing System 12 on SAC's U-2As, and removed it from those airplanes already equipped with the SAM warner. There had been some teething problems with System 12. But the Agency was convinced of its effectiveness, and OSA now ruled that if it was not in working order, no penetrations of denied territory could take place. However, the Air Force noted that installation of System 12 precluded the use of the U-2's COMINT System 3, since the antennas were located in the same apertures. General Power had already reaffirmed his ban on allowing the advanced ECM Systems 13/14/15 to be used on missions over Cuba. It seems that the safety and survival of U-2 pilots did not rate high on the list of his priorities.[24]

Recent U-2 overflights had discovered new SA-2 equipment and activity at San Julian. This was not the first time that SAM sites on the island had been shifted, but the new site was suspected to be a training center for Cubans to take over the operation. Would they show the same restraint as the Soviet operators, who had not opened fire against SAC's U-2 overflights, which were still running at about one per day? Hardly, judging by

Castro's attitude. Then, in mid-June, the MiG-21s on Cuba suddenly became more active. Three times in six days they tried to intercept U-2s using the zoom-climb technique. The U-2 missions were aborted, in accordance with the standing instructions to break off if any Cuban interceptor approached within 40 miles at an altitude above 40,000 feet. The U.S. was taking no chances but, if the intercepts continued, the U.S. would not get much reconnaissance of Cuba![25]

By now, most of the Agency's U-2s had received the upgraded System 9A, which was designed to counter enemy interceptors by deceiving their radars. In the cockpit, a three-light control panel warned the pilot when the system was activated, and whether the threat was a range-only gunsight-type radar (RO), or a more sophisticated conical scan missile fire control radar (CS). As an additional precaution, the CIA U-2s had also been given an extension to their lower tail pipes. This so-called "sugar scoop" was supposed to shield the J75's exhaust from heat-seeking missiles fired upwards from an intercepting fighter.

SAC had agreed to install System 9A, but deliveries to the 4080th wing had not yet commenced. The Pentagon came to its senses. SecDef Macnamara and DCI McCone agreed that the better-equipped U-2s of Project Idealist were needed over Cuba again. In late June 1963, three U-2F models were loaned to SAC for overflights of Cuba with immediate effect. Det G was also instructed to provide logistics support.[26]

4080th wing move
The decision coincided with a long-planned move of the 4080th wing from Laughlin AFB to Davis-Monthan AFB, Arizona. At the same time, SAC allocated the fledgling reconnaissance drone operation codenamed Lightning Bug to the wing. Testing of the Ryan drones and their DC-130 launch aircraft continued, mostly at Eglin and Holloman AFBs.

But D-M was even further from Cuba than Laughlin. SAC decided to conduct the Cuba missions from a new Operating Location at Barksdale

AFB, Louisiana (OL-19). Captain Jerry McIlmoyle picked up the first U-2F at Edwards on 25 June and flew it over Cuba before landing at Barksdale. Det G pilots Jim Barnes and Al Rand ferried the other two to OL-19. Barnes stayed on to help check more SAC pilots in the F-models. The ECM pods were removed—SAC was still resisting their use over Cuba. Col Ledford of OSA told General Power: "this operation offers exceptional opportunity to further evaluate improved System 12 and tactics, which have recently shown considerable promise in other operational areas."[27]

In the second half of 1963, SAC flew the Cuba missions from Barksdale at a rate of 25-30 per month. They were usually seven-hour flights.

In early August, the System 1 on a U-2 flying over Cuba brought back indications that an S-band Fan Song A radar was in operation. But System 1 could not actually determine frequency, only PRF and scan rate. The frequency was confirmed a week later by a peripheral RB-47H sortie. Since the Fan Song A radar was being supplied to Soviet allies, whereas only the Soviets had been using the later, C-band Fan Song radars, this was interpreted as more evidence that Cuba was going to take over the SA-2 sites.

QRC-192
The new intelligence spurred SAC into testing some experimental ELINT gear for the U-2 designed by Dr Doug Royal. He worked for Space Technology Laboratory (STL), which was now supporting the U-2 ELINT systems designed originally by STL's parent company, Ramo Wooldridge. Royal's new design was designated QRC (Quick Reaction Capability)-192. It combined an open channel receiver from the dedicated System 4A already in use with a rotating spiral interferometer system, to get direction-finding on the intercepted signal via antennas located in each wingtip. The prototype QRC-192 was nearly lost on its first trial against Cuban radars in mid-August, codenamed Operation Egg Roll. Captain Dan Schmarr took off from Davis-Monthan in a U-2A to fly a peripheral mission along the

The view through the driftsight provided pilots of U-2s on overflight missions with a means of navigation, an indication of whether the terrain below was cloudier than forecast when they set off—and a bird's eye view of fighters and missiles that tried to intercept them from below! (Lockheed AC77-1028-9).

As if a U-2 pilot did not have enough to do flying the airplane, navigating, and working the sensors, the CAF pilots flying over mainland China had to dice with the SAM threat on every other mission. Here are some extracts from the intel briefing for a deep penetration mission in mid-1963:

Radar will keep the aircraft under constant surveillance during almost the entire mission. Both EW and GCI coverage will be heavy and accurate near the coast and less as the mission enters the interior.

The critical target is Shuang Cheng Tzu (SCT) missile test range. Approaching from the southwest, the O-Chi-Na-Ho river and the main railroad should be kept on the left side of the aircraft. Pass the SCT airfield on your left, turning left and crossing the river at 4048M 10002E. The pilot must then keep the missile test range (MTR) on his right side staying around 21 to 22 NM from the SA-2 site at 4107N 10020E. The main support base and the launch area are the critical targets. There are no landmarks for the pilot to overfly west of the MTR but a stream bed which may be dry at this time of year. He should again cross the I-Ching-Ho river north of the MTR.

Request pilot be briefed that the SA-2 sites known in the MTR area will be off to his right. He should reconfirm any System 12 lock-on from the left side of the aircraft after his turn at Point M, before using evasive action in the latest recommended procedure.

- cable from Project HQ 16 August 1963

And here is a post-mission report from Major Terry Lee's overflight on 25 September 1963, when he was nearly ambushed by the Chicoms over Xian. (Nine months later, this brave Chinese pilot would be shot down by an SA-2 near the mainland coast).

Faint System 12 strobes appeared near Point P, cause unknown. System 12 activation at Point R. Initial indication audio followed by strobe at 020 degrees relative bearing, and green light. Red Light came on almost immediately. Driver turned left to 240 degrees with strobe coming around to wing tip. As strobe moved toward 180 degree position all indications disappeared. Driver then turned back toward airfield. Six minutes later strobe appeared at 330 degree relative bearing with almost simultaneous green and red light activations. Driver then turned right and put strobe on wingtip. As strobe again moved toward 180 degree position driver turned back to parallel course. Deviations were approximately six miles to either side of proper course. Both lights remained on for approximately seven minutes in the second activation then all indications disappeared simultaneously.

- OSA cable 25 September 1963

island. He had to fly precise, constant headings, and make very accurate position fixes so that the analysts could cross-check the indications on the new ELINT system. The main mission was accomplished, and Schmarr was recovering to Barksdale when bad weather forced a diversion to Little Rock AFB. The U-2 flamed out through fuel starvation 10 minutes short of the field, but Schmarr successfully deadsticked into the Arkansas base![28]

In hindsight, maybe Schmarr should have been flying one of the inflight refuelable birds. The 4080th continued to train for this capability, which was codenamed Muscle Magic, using its three U-2E models. SAC determined that the practical endurance for the pilots was 12.5 hours—and set about proving it by means of a training deployment all the way across the Pacific! On 14 September a U-2E was flown to Hickam, trailed by a KC-135 carrying spare pilots, ground crew, and the deployment kits. A second pilot flew the U-2 on to Anderson AFB with a refueling over Wake Island. Then a third took over for the leg to Kadena AB, Okinawa. Then it was turn around and back the same way—there were no operational missions during the deployment. It took nearly two weeks, thanks to two generator failures and one complete hydraulic failure on the Dragon Lady. The exercise was repeated in mid-October with another set of pilots and groundcrew. The elapsed time for roundtrip was 11 days. Yet another transpacific deployment test was flown in mid-November, and this time the U-2 and KC-135 went around the circuit in nine days![29]

High Altitude Combat

During July and early August, Det H was ordered to stand down while U.S. envoys were in Moscow and other Communist capitals. On 23 August 1963, Major Terry Lee Nan Ping took off on his first operational U-2 mission over mainland China. He was one of the two new CAF pilots fresh out of training at D-M. It was a seven-and-a-half hour trip around Manchuria, departing from and returning to Kunsan AB, Korea. Ominously, U.S. COMINT sources reported that the Chicom air defenses went on alert for "high altitude combat" as soon as the U-2 was ferried from Taoyuan to the Korean base, even though this was flown at medium altitude in an attempt to keep the U-2 hidden from early warning radars along the Chinese coast. However, although subsequent analysis of Lee's electronic take revealed a strong, high-PRF Fan Song signal, he returned safely.[30]

Had the tight security surrounding the planning and alerting of the Agency's U-2 overflights been breached? A subsequent investigation by the OSA Security office was inconclusive. But it did find, coincidentally, that the mission plan was being distributed too widely: for instance, the JRC was sending its copy on to the DIA.[31]

A week later, Major Robin Yeh Chang Ti flew his first mission, over Hainan Island and along the China-Vietnam border. It was not an auspicious start. Halfway through the mission, the pilot realized from his green card that fuel consumption was higher than normal. He was recalled, but ran seriously short of fuel before reaching Taiwan. He shut the engine off and glided some of the way back. CAF F-104s were scrambled to escort him home. Upon landing, his brakes failed and the aircraft ran off the runway.

Marty Knutson, who was the American TDY pilot at the time, suspected that Yeh had flown the mission with the gear down. When it was developed, the tracker film confirmed it. That had caused the high fuel consumption—and also ensured that the brakes were so cold-soaked that they failed upon landing.[32]

In late September and early October, during a period of good weather over the Chinese mainland, the Black Cat Squadron accomplished five more overflights. But the Chicoms were beginning to figure things out. The main three targets for the spyplanes formed a triangle in northwestern China: the SCT missile range, Lanchow, and Paotow. The PLAAF moved four of its SA-2 battalions to the area around Xian, calculating that the next U-2 mission would fly that way.

On his second overflight, Terry Lee did indeed pass nearby. Somehow he managed to evade an attack, despite flying through both the 2nd and 4th Battalion's coverage areas. The Chicoms made no fewer than seven Fan Song radar acquisitions, but forewarned by System 12, Lee made repeated turns and came no closer than 35 miles to the missile sites. But they were clearly visible to the PIs who examined the "take" from mission GRC-176. On his second mission the next day—another sortie to the northwest—Robin Yeh got SAM warnings over Paotow.[33]

Air Force veto
To help protect the Tackle missions over China and their pilots from the ever-increasing missile threat, OSA wanted to install the ECM pods containing System 14 or 15 on the two Articles at Det H. But the NRO, representing the Air Force, vetoed the Agency's request. Again, the reason was the Pentagon's fear of this advanced equipment falling into Communist hands.[34]

Meanwhile, ATI was trying to improve the System 12 SAM warner by adding an indication to the U-2 pilot of how far away the SA-2 site actually was, in addition to the bearing. A small motorized antenna was added in a small fairing beneath the nose of the U-2. But range indication proved impossible to achieve, given the state-of-the-art in 1963. System 12A was tested on the Nellis range, but never went into service. As an extra precaution against attack, U-2 overflight mission planners were told to increase the "no fly" circle that they drew around known SA-2 sites from 21 to 25 nautical miles radius.[35]

In late September, the Agency reclaimed one of the U-2Fs on loan to SAC at Barksdale, so that it could deploy Det G to Takhli again. The requirements were the same as before: coverage of the Sino-Indian border and Tibet, and Laos/North Vietnam. The Indian government had not yet been persuaded to allow U-2s to use an Indian airbase, so there was no alternative to more long refueled sorties. Indeed, the first mission on this deployment (29 September 1963) was the Agency's longest operational U-2 mission to date—12 and a half hours. Det G flew four more missions to the area in October/November. But there was not much new to be seen on the resulting photography.[36]

The Chicoms tracked these U-2 incursions on their western borders with their early-warning radars, just as they did the approaches from Taiwan and Korea by the Black Cat Squadron. Despite working without any recourse to Soviet expertise—long ago withdrawn—the PLAAF further refined their SA-2 intercept techniques. They deployed the fire control radar from one of their anti-aircraft guns alongside the SA-2 missiles and used it to track the target down to 22 miles (missile firing range) *before* handing over the target to the Fan Song operators. This AA radar had a different PRF that could not be detected by System 12. Once the target was handed over, the SA-2 missile operators needed only eight seconds to acquire the target and fire![37]

Having failed to trap a U-2 around Xian, the PLAAF redeployed its missiles yet again. From 22-29 October 1963 they installed the four SA-2

CHINESE SHOOTDOWN – JUMPING TO CONCLUSIONS

When Frank Powers was shot down over the Soviet Union in 1960, there were plenty of people back in Washington who didn't want to believe that an SA-2 missile had bagged him at cruising altitude. Fast forward to 1963, and the shootdown on 1 November of Major Robin Yeh over China. In Project HQ, they reviewed the available evidence—which wasn't much, since the Birdwatcher telemetry system had not yet been introduced. From the flimsiest of evidence, false conclusions were reached. Jim Cherbonneaux, a former CIA U-2 pilot who had recently been transferred to the Idealist Branch at OSA, thought that the autopilot had malfunctioned. Yeh had then struggled for a long time to hand-fly the aircraft at altitude, before losing control. Cherbonneaux's conclusion was no doubt partly based on analysis of the Chicom's air defense reactions, intercepted as COMINT. As we know now, this analysis was wrong. The same happened after Frank Powers went missing. – *C.P.*

ITEK JOINS THE U-2 PROGRAM
The Itek company was founded in 1957 by Richard Leghorn, who was perhaps the main conceptual "father" of the U-2. Leghorn's company provided the innovative panoramic cameras for the first spy satellites, under contract to the CIA. But it was not until 1963 that Itek became part of the U-2 program, as this company history relates:

The Agency contracted Itek to modify the engineering model of the Corona camera to fit into the U-2. The security requirements allowed only four people, plus management access to the program, so the entire crew consisted of Gary Nelson, project manager, plus Bill Anderson, Rick Manent, and Bill Poe.

A full-size wooden mockup of the Q-bay was built to aid this "cut and paste" project. We discovered that, although the system would fit in the Q-bay, it would not pass through the hatch opening. In order to load the camera into the aircraft it had to be disassembled. It was then inserted through the hatch opening with the widest dimension "fore and aft," and then rotated *in situ*. It was then secured to the frame.

After the first mission, the pilot complained that he could not tell if the camera was working because it was too quiet, unlike the Hycon B-system. We installed a micro-switch that was actuated every time the scan drum oscillated back and forth. This caused a lamp in the cockpit to blink. After a subsequent mission, we discovered that the take-up spool was empty and the supply spool was full. The Kodak film splice had parted upon camera start-up. The pilot was adamant that the light was blinking throughout the whole mission. We had to inform him that the light indicated only that the lens was rotating, not that the film was passing through the camera!

- from an internal Itek history

BREAKING THE BAD NEWS

Colonel Michael Lu Si Liang was the first commander of the CAF's 35th Squadron, also known as the "Black Cats":

Whenever a pilot in my squadron died, I had to see the family and offer my condolences. I was the commander of the RB-57 squadron, then the U-2 squadron, and they lost more pilots than other squadrons. Sometimes I had to tell white lies to the families.

We all thought Yeh must have died (shot down on 1 November 1963), but I told his parents he was still alive, and someday he would come back to Taiwan.

Author's note: In fact, Yeh did indeed survive his interception by SA-2 missiles, but would spend the next 19 years as an enforced guest of the People's Republic of China.

OPERATION SEAFOAM

Just about the most obscure deployment ever made by the Agency's Det G in the 1960s was in December 1963, to overfly Trinidad and Tobago, and coastal areas of Venezuela, plus that country's border with British Guyana. Pro-Castro communist guerrillas were active in the area. The Special Group was persuaded to let the U-2 take a closer look, but no permission for the overflights was sought from either government. Six missions were flown out of Ramey AFB, Puerto Rico, during Operation Seafoam, looking for jungle airstrips and other signs of communist insurgency. But "the results of the effort were inconclusive" according to the CIA's U-2 history. – C.P.

A 4080th SRW U-2A on the ramp at Davis-Monthan AFB. The SAC wing moved to here from Laughlin AFB in mid-1963.

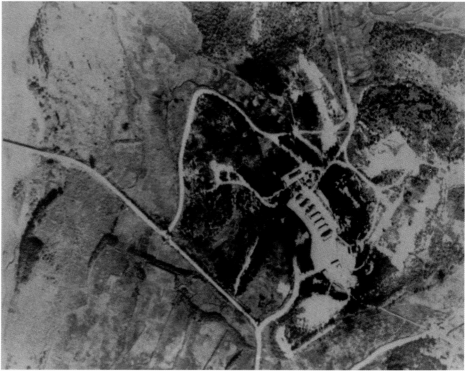

In 1963, the CIA began staging overflights of mainland China out of South Korea. This image from a mission in October 1963 shows Panmunjon, the site on the DMZ where ceasefire talks were conducted between the North and the South.

battalions further south in Kiangsi province, in a broad line that would be sure to form a barrier—as long as the U-2 flew from Taiwan. And sure enough, two days later it did!

Major Robin Yeh's main target on 1 November 1963 was the SCT missile range. China's first ballistic missile had been test-flown here a few days earlier. Yeh took off at 7am, entered denied territory over Wenzhou at 0743, and headed northwest. The 4th Battalion was located the furthermost east, but Yeh's track took him safely past the site, out of firing range. But there were plenty of contrails below, as Chicom GCI vainly tried to vector their fighters to an intercept position.

Three and a half hours later Yeh reached the SCT area. If the mission had been planned to recover in Korea, he would have turned east, and been safe. But his route required a 180-degree turn, so that the U-2 could return to home base at Taoyuan along a close parallel course to the outbound leg. This was Yeh's undoing.

Salvo fired

At 1400 he approached the missile line in Kiangsi. PLAAF commanders ordered two of the three closest batteries to turn on their Fan Song radars at 28 miles. If the U-2 turned to avoid them, it would hopefully still be within the third battalion's lethal range. And this third battalion was ordered to operate only its AA radar, until the target was only 22 miles away. The tactic worked perfectly. No 2 Battalion salvo-fired three missiles, and the U-2 was hit at 1418.[38]

Yeh could see the coastline. So near, yet so far! His warning system chirped into action, but it was too late. He evaded the first missile, but the second one tore off his right wing. There was an explosion. Shrapnel pierced the cockpit and wounded Yeh in the legs. But he managed to escape the aircraft. Like Gary Powers he did not eject, but was flung clear after loosening his shoulder harness, as the aircraft broke up around him. Only half-conscious, he managed to deploy his parachute as he neared the ground, but hit hard and passed out. A search party found Yeh and took him to hospital. There, surgeons removed multiple metal fragments from Yeh's legs.

Two days later, the Chicoms transferred him to Peking and put him under house arrest. Unlike Premier Khrushchev in 1960, Chairman Mao refrained from making a show out of a captured U-2 pilot. Peking's announcement of the latest shootdown merely noted that the people's defenders could shoot down intruders "at any altitude, and whether they come by day or night." Once again, those monitoring the U-2 overflight from the command post and SIGINT stations were none the wiser about whether a shot-down pilot had survived.

Throughout 1963, HRB Singer had been working on a telemetry system nicknamed Birdwatcher. This could relay data on various U-2 operating parameters by the aircraft's HF SSB to a ground station, as a mission progressed. To avoid giving the aircraft's position away to the bad guys below, the data could be sent in burst transmissions, and only when a malfunction was detected. If the Article was intercepted, the volume of relayed information should be enough to provide a good idea of what had happened. But Birdwatcher was not yet ready.[39]

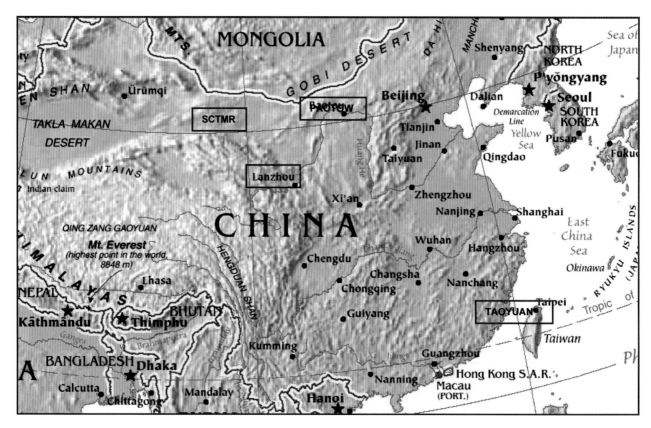

The Chicom nuclear weapons development sites at Lanchou and Paotow, as well as the missile range to the west of Shuang Cheng Tzu (SCTMR), were frequent targets for the nationalist-flown U-2s of Project Tackle flown from Taoyuan.

The Delta camera for the U-2 was developed by Itek from the panoramic design flown in the Corona reconnaissance satellite (author).

New camera

Back in the U.S., the U-2 had a new camera. The A-camera rigs and the remarkable Hycon B had done sterling service. But they were eight years old and beginning to show their age. In early 1963, the Land Panel called for higher resolution photography over Cuba, especially since the low-level missions by tac recon jets were being terminated. OSA tried using a finer-grain film (SO-130) in the B-camera, with reasonable results. Three new B-cameras with improved lenses were ordered from Hycon.

But camera technology had moved on, especially in the Corona satellite program, where the latest version of Itek's 24-inch panoramic camera was producing excellent results, in stereo. Itek was asked whether this so-called "C Triple Prime" camera could be reconfigured to fit in the U-2's Q-bay. The answer: it wasn't easy, but it could be done. Ground resolution of about 13 inches was predicted—a 100 percent improvement on recent results with the B-cameras, even using their new lenses.[40]

Flights tests of the modified Itek camera began in Article 342 (the U-2 testbed) from Burbank in September 1963. This was not the latest Corona system, which had stereo overlap. And the quick mod provided only enough enough film for linear coverage of 1,100 miles. But that was enough for the short missions of Cuba, and the flight test results were spectacular: resolution of less than a foot across a 17-mile swath. In October 1963 the C Triple Prime (also known as System 112A) was sent to OL-19 at Barksdale. SAC pilots flew two successful missions over Cuba before an inverter failure caused possible damage to the camera, and it was withdrawn. But the photo interpreters liked what they saw, and Itek was given a contract for a further four panoramic U-2 cameras derived from the Corona system.[41]

Hyde crash

On 20 November 1963, Capt Joe Hyde crashed into the Gulf of Mexico on his way back from a Brass Knob mission over Cuba. His autopilot had failed just prior to coast-out, so he was hand-flying the aircraft back to Barksdale at 69,000 feet. It was Article 350, one of the Agency's U-2F models. After passing Key West, the aircraft entered a flat spin and fell into the sea. That much was determined from analyzing radar traces. The wreckage was recovered from shallow water off the Florida coast, but there was no sign of Hyde. The ejection seat, seat pack, and parachute were missing.

Had Hyde lost control because he was hand-flying the aircraft, and was not so familiar with the critical cg characteristics of the re-engined aircraft? (He had arrived at OL-19 and been checked out in the U-2F four weeks earlier). Had a faulty flow regulator caused a loss of oxygen to the pilot? The SAC Accident Investigation Board could not make a firm conclusion over the cause of the accident. But there was yet another review of the U-2 escape system. OSA came to the conclusion that the current system of ejecting through the canopy was simply not good enough. It suggested that Lockheed install explosive bolts so that the canopy would be forcibly removed at the start of the ejection sequence.[42]

At the same time, the Agency was about to reclaim its F-models. It had been pressing for their return for months. SAC had finally agreed to make provision for the ECM pods on some of its own U-2A models, for protection against an SA-2 attack. Meanwhile, the interception threat over Cuba from MiG-21s had not really materialized. At least one SAC U-2 pilot reported that a MiG-21 had passed right over him at altitude. But intel now reckoned they could not be effectively employed above 66,000 feet. On the short missions out of Barksdale, with lighter fuel and camera film loads, SAC's own Dragon Ladies could fly higher than that. Two days after Hyde went down, SAC resumed using the lower-powered U-2A models over Cuba. The mission was renamed Golden Tree.[43]

19

The Carrier Capability

On the night of 4 August 1963, one of the CIA's black U-2 models was flown into North Island Naval Air Station at San Diego and craned onto the flight deck of the USS *Kitty Hawk* using a specially-designed sling. Under cover of darkness, the big aircraft carrier headed out of the harbor. It was the start of Project Whale Tale, an ambitious project to "navalize" the Article. Over the next 10 years, more than 17 CIA U-2 pilots would land on aircraft carriers during a dozen deployments. But only one of the deployments would be for real, rather than for training.

Bold and enterprising it was. But the idea of operating U-2s from an aircraft carrier was not new. The fertile mind of Kelly Johnson had first thought of it six years earlier. In 1957, his ideas for the essential modifications included JATO (Jet-Assisted Take Off) bottles and retractable pogos. The Navy was "greatly interested," Kelly wrote. The proposal was even briefed to President Eisenhower. The CIA was happy to go along with the idea, but did not consider a U-2 carrier capability to be essential: "the availability of alternate land bases provides a fair degree of insurance against political evictions," DDCI Charles Cabell told the Navy. In the end, it was the USAF that vetoed the idea.[1]

By 1963, though, times had changed. Thanks to May Day 1960, the U-2 was now a notorious spyplane. It was getting increasingly difficult to persuade foreign governments to allow basing and overflight rights. The idea of using those floating chunks of U.S. real estate, the big aircraft carriers, resurfaced. During an informal meeting at Edwards in March 1963 with DDCI Marshall Carter and OSA Director Jack Ledford, Kelly Johnson pitched the idea again. Over a bottle of Scotch, Carter and Ledford asked him to make a formal proposal.[2]

Carrier conversions

By the end of April, Johnson had quoted for up to three U-2 carrier conversions: a strengthened landing gear; a tail hook; cable deflectors for the landing gear; and a fuel dump system. "This latter change is desirable in order to get back on a carrier, in case of aborting a mission shortly after takeoff," Johnson explained to DDR Peter Scoville.[3]

OSA Deputy Director Jim Cunningham loved the idea. He was a former Marine Corps pilot anyway. And he had been at the center of the recent protracted and so-far unsuccessful negotiations for U-2 staging bases in the Middle East and India. In May 1963 Cunningham toured two aircraft carriers and NAS Pensacola with Fred Cavanaugh from the Skunk Works and Captain Martin "Red" Carmody from the Chief of Naval Operations. This three-man study group concluded that the project was feasible.[4]

The first carrier trials were in August 1963, when a U-2A was placed onboard the *USS Kitty Hawk* at NAS North Island. After the ship left port, Bob Schumacher took off and made four practice approaches before heading back to dry land (CIA).

STAFF STUDY
In these extracts from the OSA Staff Study, Jim Cunningham discussed the whys and wherefores of operating the U-2 from aircraft carriers.

Advantages: ...Carrier operations would permit a wide choice of operating locations for the launch of IDEALIST U-2 overflights. In theory, at least, the oceans of the world are available as launch and/or retrieval areas. This flexibility and mobility can deny enemy radar the advantage of monitoring activities and known or probable IDEALIST bases.... Carrier operations would be entirely under the control of the U.S. government.... The most feasible CVAs for U-2 operations are the *Saratoga, Ranger,* and *Independence,* all of which offer a physically segregated operating facility known as the Airborne Systems Support Center (ASSC). This offers adequate space for the complete processing and initial flash read-out of both "B" camera and tracker film....

Disadvantages: ...The exposure of the U-2 capability to a large group of uncleared individuals on a CVA with its air group aboard...the net weight penalty of about 300 pounds for the U-2 carrier modification...carrier conversion and repeated requalification for all IDEALIST pilots...the handling, launching, and retrieval will always be a special operation, requiring considerable technical skill from both ground support personnel and pilots....

Discussion: ...To direct a large carrier to support a U-2 sortie or series of sorties requires approval by the highest levels of the Department of Defense. A clear plan for execution which requires carrier support for the shortest possible time span will go far toward getting a carrier when it is requested....

KELLY ON THE CARRIER
Here's how Kelly Johnson described the first outing to the carrier in his diary.

4 August 1963: To San Diego to go out on the *Kitty Hawk*. We worked all night hoisting the aircraft aboard and getting it under deck. I don't think more than 2,000 or 3,000 people saw the aircraft go aboard, as they kept coming back all night from a carnival that was held adjacent to the loading docks!

5 August 1963: Steamed out of San Diego to a point south of San Clemente Island. I briefed about 20 Navy people on what we wanted to do, but it seems the Captain on the bridge didn't get word, so we had several instances of going too fast, or too slow in the wrong direction. With all of this, the aircraft took off in 321 feet, with no difficulty whatsoever. Schumacher made three approaches, flying through turbulence aft of the carrier, which was no problem. But on the third approach, Schu bounced, hit hard on the right wing tip, and picked the thing up just before coming to the end of the angled deck. After one more flyby to see that all the parts were on, he flew home.

What was in it for the Navy? In theory, the U-2 had the potential to provide real-time surveillance of surface targets in excess of 600 miles from the carrier task force, and to relay ship-to-ship UHF communications for similar distances. Ten years later, the Navy would seriously consider the U-2 for such tasks. But in 1963, the main rationale was reconnaissance for national objectives. The sponsorship of the Office of Naval Research (ONR) would be the "cover story."[5]

The study group had listed various issues. Above all, how would the U-2 be safely brought to a stop on the flat top, given its difficult landing characteristics? There was also the question of wingspan: how to move the Article to the hangar deck, when even the largest carrier's elevators were not 80 feet wide! The Skunk Works quickly solved that problem, by designing a special fuselage cart with castoring wheels, so that the U-2 could be moved sideways onto the elevator, and into the hangar deck. To test this cart, nicknamed the "LowBoy," and to explore the approach conditions, it was decided to put an unmodified U-2 aboard a carrier first, fly it off, and make some practice approaches. Kelly Johnson assigned experienced test pilot Bob Schumacher for this task.

And so it was that the USS *Kitty Hawk* left San Diego harbor with Article 352 painted as "N315X," a U-2 supposedly assigned to the ONR. The carrier sailed far enough offshore to be out of sight of land. The ships' crew were told not to discuss the strange goings-on with anyone ashore. While still in harbor, the U-2 had already been successfully maneuvered to the hangar deck, using the LowBoy. Now it was brought up and towed along the angled deck and back, to ensure that there was ample clearance for takeoffs and landings. With a 30-knot wind across the deck, the maintenance crew had difficulty holding the aircraft down!

Airborne
Schumacher climbed aboard. Because the pogos might be a hazard to the carrier's island or other deck structures as they dropped away on takeoff, crewmen held the wings level as the test pilot applied power and released the brake. He was airborne in only one third of the available deck length, thanks to the powerful J75 and that strong headwind. Schumacher made three low approaches at speeds between 75 and 78 knots to explore controllability. After one last approach, in which he touched down briefly but rather too firmly, Schumacher set course for Burbank. Johnson and his Skunk Works engineers now set about designing the modifications necessary for full U-2 carrier capability.

There were still many unanswered questions, especially concerning landing aboard. Johnson was having second thoughts about tail hooks. Just how much "beefing-up" of the structure would be needed? Would repeated arrested landings overstress the tail mounting bolts? Would the twisting moments eventually cause wing fatigue, or at the very least, fuel leaks? What about the shock effects of a carrier landing on the U-2's delicately-tuned SIGINT systems, or the camera optics, or the sextant, or the driftsight? Johnson thought that speed brakes plus a parachute might be required. Still, could the landing gear cope with the much higher decelerations? Johnson reckoned that it could be modified to cope with 10 feet per second, but true carrier aircraft were designed for 15-20 feet per second.

To save money, OSA adopted Kelly Johnson's idea of doing the carrier conversions on two U-2As that were being transferred from USAF at this time (Articles 348 and 362). They were already slated for an IRAN, and the J75 engine conversion.

While the modification work proceeded at the Skunk Works, Captain Carmody selected one of the Navy's most experienced Landing Signals Officers (LSOs), LCDR John Huber, to supervise the training program. This carrier-qualified pilot became a full-time member of Det G at Edwards. Four pilots from Det G were sent to NAS Monterey in mid-November for initial check-out in the Navy's T-2A tandem jet trainers. The initial group moved on to NAS Pensacola and, when Huber declared them ready, to their first real "traps" aboard the USS *Lexington* in the Gulf of Mexico. The remaining four Det G pilots, together with Det G commander Bill Gregory and test pilot Bob Schumacher, did their carrier qualifications in the first six weeks of 1964.

By that time, the first modified aircraft was out of the shop at Burbank, redesignated as a U-2G. Instead of a brake parachute, Johnson had opted for a tail hook after all. It was mounted ahead of the tail wheel, attached to the strong framing that formed the engine mounts and wing attachment points. The pilot released it from the stowed position by pulling a T-handle in the cockpit. Small fairings were added in front, behind, and on both sides of the hook. These reduced aerodynamic drag, and coincidentally provided an anchor for a small radome that could be fitted over the modification when not in use, so that the hook would remain hidden from view to preserve the security of this top-secret program.

The tail was beefed up to cope with the additional structural loads imposed by an arrested landing, by extending the three longerons in the main fuselage into the tail section. To deflect the carrier's arresting cable from the tail wheel in the event that the hook failed to connect, a metal tubing structure was added to the gear assembly and doors. The fuel dump system consisted of a dump valve and float switch in each of the four wing tanks, and an overboard chute on the trailing edge of each wing between the flap and the aileron. (This innovation was subsequently extended to the rest of the U-2 fleet, and was much appreciated—if a mission was aborted shortly after take-off, it eliminated the long, boring hours of droning around while burning off enough fuel to bring the bird down to landing weight). The total weight penalty for the carrier mods was about 350 pounds.

Experimented

From the approach trials on the *Kittyhawk*, it was obvious that the U-2's tremendous wing lift would have to be dumped more efficiently, if the aircraft was to be put down precisely where the arresting cables were situated on deck. Kelly Johnson experimented with various schemes in the low-speed wind tunnel at Burbank to reduce the lift and the landing speed. First he tried adding fixed slots in the flap, a design that Lockheed had used on the Lodestar light transport. But this required too great an angle of attack as the U-2 approached the carrier deck. Then he proposed a leading-edge slat extending for nearly the complete wingspan, as on the Lockheed JetStar. But the slat actuation mechanism stole fuel space in the wing, and resulted in a loss of 400 naut miles in range. Eventually, Johnson settled for wing spoilers, plus an increase in the flap travel (to 45 degrees instead of 30).[6]

During February 1964, Field Carrier Landing Practice (FCLP) was conducted on the U-2G at Edwards, where mock arrestor cables were painted on the runway at North Base. It took a while to get the spoilers working properly. Bob Schumacher experienced airframe buffeting, roll-off at the stall, and horizontal tail vibration. Once the Lockheed test pilot had sorted out these problems, the Det G pilots did their FCLPs, under the careful eye of LSO John Huber. They all debated carrier landing techniques.

Bob Schumacher, seen here with Kelly Johnson, was the Skunk Works test pilot assigned to the U-2 carrier trials in 1963-64 (Lockheed).

Jim Cunningham pushed the hardest to turn the U-2 carrier concept into reality. A former Marine Corps pilot before joining the CIA, Cunningham spent 10 years from 1956-66 as the deputy director at Project HQ. He was a fierce defender of the U-2 from its various critics inside the government, and much-admired by the senior Air Force officers involved with the project. "He was a mental pack rat, and absolute mine of information," said Colonel Leo Geary. "He knew more about how the Agency was run than anybody I came into contact with, including some of the top brass," recalled Colonel Jack Ledford. (via Jack Ledford)

Col Bill Gregory was commander of Det G at Edwards during the development of the U-2 carrier capability. He attributed the successful carrier qualification of himself and his operational pilots to the skills of John Huber, the LSO assigned to the Det G for Project Whale Tale:

I gained an increased respect for Navy carrier pilots. Our Navy LSO, John Huber, expected the very best from all of us, and spent hour after hour drilling us in the techniques of making carrier landings. It was a thrilling experience flying out to the USS *Lexington*. John was in the LSO's position on the aft flight deck when we arrived. His calm, authoritative voice on the radio was very reassuring. Thanks to his intensive training, we all completed six landings that day without difficulty. - *correspondence with author*

TRUSTING THE LSO

Flying a U-2 onto an aircraft called for precise flying tactics, and a great deal of faith in the instructions from the Landing Signals Officer (LSO). Det G pilot Marty Knutson learned to place his trust in Det G's very own, very capable LSO, John Huber:

The U-2 was not designed for carrier landings, and had way too much "float" in the landing flare. The LSO had to call "cut"—meaning pull the throttle to idle—when the aircraft was still some distance from the fantail. At this point the U-2 pilot was committed, as the engine had a very slow "spool-up" capability. If the "cut" was made too early, the aircraft would be short and could strike the fantail (not too desirable). If the "cut" was too late, the aircraft would overshoot and would have to go around—if the engine power could be increased in time. John Huber made the call, based on his experience. We pilots learned to trust him to the hilt.

The consensus was that about 40 knots of wind across deck would be required. Since the U-2 normally landed at 70 knots, this would reduce the actual landing speed to 30 knots.

From Project HQ, former Det G U-2 pilot Jim Cherbonneaux coordinated with Red Carmody to get carrier time for the U-2G. On 29 February, Bob Schumacher flew from Edwards to the USS *Ranger*, located off San Diego. Schu flew the touch-and-goes, but reported turbulence as he approached the deck. He was having to make undesirable throttle adjustments. It was the same as he approached for a fourth time, with the hook down this time for a trap. As the test pilot crossed the fantail, he was too fast and a little high. The aircraft hit the deck hard, bounced nose up, and the hook caught the third arrestor cable. It then slammed nose first into the deck. After minor repairs, Schu was able to fly it off the carrier the next day and back to Burbank for more serious attention.

Turbulence
The Navy reckoned that the accident was due to the tension of the arrester cables being too tight. But the U-2 group aboard the *Ranger* realized that turbulence during the Article's flat approach was the big problem. With their higher sink rates and more forgiving landing gear, the Navy's own carrier planes avoided the updraft in the carrier's wake with their steeper

approach. The solution was to reduce the carrier's speed, and therefore the wind over deck to about 25 knots. The updraft then flattened out below the approaching U-2.[7]

The Skunk Works wasn't taking any chances—they modified a landing pogo and fixed it under the nose as protection in case the same thing happened again. Three days later, Schumacher flew back to the carrier. This time he made five successful arrested landings.

Now it was the turn of the Det G pilots. Bob Ericson had just started his touch-and-goes when a Norwegian freighter approached the operating area. It would not go away, so the U-2 was waved off and flew to NAS North Island for the night.

The next day Jim Barnes flew out to the boat. On his first touch-and-go, his approach speed was too slow and he stalled just over the fantail. He jerked the throttle forward, but it was too late. The aircraft hit the deck with the right wing low. The skid was torn off by one of the arresting cables. As the engine spooled up, the U-2 became airborne again and just missed the island at mid-deck! Barnes somehow managed to clear the ship and climb away. The right aileron had been partially jammed upwards by the impact. Fighting to keep control, Barnes struggled back to North Base.

It was another setback, but the carrier effort continued. To prevent a similar accident in the future, the Skunk Works added a reinforcing metal plate to the front of the wingtip skids, and springs were added to their base. At North Base there was more animated discussion. Ivan "Chunky" Webster, one of the two RAF pilots at Det G, now made a significant contribution. This former British test pilot came up with a scheme to ensure that the U-

LCDR John Huber was selected by the U.S. Navy as the Landing Signals Officer (LSO) for Project Whale Tail, the development of a U-2 carrier capability. During a four-year tour with Det G from 1963-67, Huber helped to devise the approach and landing procedures, and supervised the training of the CIA's U-2 pilots. (via Matt Huber)

2 arrived at the carrier's fantail at the correct speed and attitude. While the U-2 was still on approach, the scheme required the LSO to call "Cut One!"— a signal for the pilot to reduce the power to idle. As the Article arrived over the fantail, the LSO would call "Cut Two!," which signalled the pilot to deploy the spoilers. The Article would quickly settle into a more tail-down attitude, hit the deck, and engage the cables. (Of course, regular naval aviators would throw a fit if asked to cut the power *before* engaging a cable!).

Operation Fishawk

After the damaged U-2G was repaired, most of the CIA pilots managed to qualify on 9 and 10 March. The USS *Ranger* returned to port. At Project HQ, Jim Cunningham was already planning Operation Fishawk—to over-fly the new French nuclear test site in the middle of the Pacific Ocean. A year earlier, France had selected a remote site in French Polynesia to replace the site in Algeria that had been lost after that country fought for and won independence from Paris. Mururoa Atoll was thousands of miles from anywhere—an ideal target for a carrier-launched sortie.

Surprisingly to most of those in Project HQ, Cunningham got the Intelligence Community's approval for this plan. But so remote was the target, that the carrier would have to sail over three thousand miles into the Pacific Ocean, even to reach a position from where the U-2 mission could be launched! The Navy insisted that the movement of the USS *Ranger* and its destroyer escort be completely secret. That meant radio silence for nearly three weeks! OSA was obliged to come up with a covert radio system that could handle the ship's minimum requirements for ship-to-shore communications, as well as the deployed U-2 group's communications with Project HQ. The Commo section of OSA designed a scheme that used a clandestine relay station in Panama.[8]

With everything finally settled, a U-2 staging kit and support personnel were loaded aboard the big carrier in San Diego. She and her escort slipped anchor in San Diego and headed into the wide ocean. On 12 May, Det G pilots Jim Barnes and Al Rand flew the two U-2G models out to the deck via Hawaii. Buster Edens was the third pilot on the trip. In the greatest possible secrecy, the *Ranger* continued southwestwards and crossed the equator. On 19 May, when the Ranger was about 800 nautical miles from the target area, a U-2G took off on a maximum range profile mission that would cover 1,000 miles of Pacific Ocean and atolls. Upon its safe return to the big boat, a Navy COD couriered the camera "take" to Hawaii, from where it was rushed by jet to Eastman Kodak's processing facility in Rochester, NY. Meanwhile, NPIC had an interpreter on the carrier, who processed and examined the tracker film to see if all the targets had been covered. It was determined that further coverage was required. A second mission was planned at Project HQ, and launched from the *Ranger* on 22 May.[9]

Project HQ later told Det G commander Bill Gregory and his team that the results of this extraordinary excursion were highly successful. In late September, Jim Cunningham was presented with a medal by DCI Marshall Carter for his pivotal role in creating the U-2 carrier capability. But not everyone was happy. Grumbling was heard from mid-level Navy personnel aboard the USS *Ranger* over the inconvenience. "We will do all this ourselves next time," one remarked. When the next potential carrier mission was suggested in late October, two Admirals in the Pentagon protested. It would unacceptably delay the USS *Saratoga* from arriving on station with the Sixth Fleet in the Mediterranean, they said. Upon further

---

JIM BARNES AT THE CARRIER

There was much debate amongst the CIA U-2 pilots on the best technique to get a U-2 down safely on a carrier deck. And pilots can be opinionated—especially when they've flown an aircraft for quite a few years. By 1964, Jim Barnes and Jim Cherbonneaux were both eight-year veterans of the U-2 business. Here's how Cherbonneaux recalled Barnes' first carrier approach in the U-2G:

Jim B came up with his own ideas on how to land aboard. He decided to fly his approach at between six and 10 knots slower than what Huber and Schu had established to be correct. He was 10 feet above the deck when the Deuce stalled out. He almost got away with having only a big bounce. But the wing touched the deck, and the cable tore the skid right off. Fortunately the engine spooled up, and the aircraft jumped back into the air. After struggling somewhat, Jim managed to get it flying. To hear him tell it, he had control of the aircraft at all times. In any event, he was really lucky that day. If he had hit the island, we would have had to use a blotter to collect his body parts. I will give Jim B this—he did manage to get the severely damaged bird back to Edwards.

BAD IMAGE

Even before the first carrier trials of a U-2 in August 1963, the CIA was considering an operational deployment. COMOR had identified some "high-priority" targets in the Middle East—possibly Egypt or Israel. But no country in the region was prepared to permit a U-2 landing or takeoff. So the plan was for the U-2 to take off from a Sixth Fleet carrier in the Mediterranean, and recover into the U.S.-controlled Wheelus AFB, Libya. But Chief of Naval Operations Admiral Anderson did not like the idea. He feared that the operation would be revealed and reflect badly on the image that the Navy was trying to portray in the Med, namely that of an impartial force for peace on behalf of the Western powers. While OSA was digesting this setback, and scheming to overcome it, the requirement went away. Good coverage of the region was obtained by the latest Corona satellite instead. – C.P.

SCHUMACHER'S BONUS

After the initial carrier capability was proved, Kelly Johnson found himself having to justify the payment of a bonus to Skunk Works test pilot Bob Schumacher. This was accepted practice in the test flying business, by the way. Johnson wrote:

Bob Schumacher made all the carrier development landings, bouncing in one condition and bashing in the nose of the aircraft, and flying it back to land for repairs. Both the landings and takeoffs were considerably hazardous until we learned the proper procedures. The aircraft is so lightly loaded that on several takeoffs the turbulence around the main island drew the aircraft within 10 feet of the metal structure. Bob did an outstanding job on the U-2G program, as well as others he has done for us.

- letter to CIA, 2 October 1964

The first carrier landing of a U-2G was on the *USS Ranger* in late February 1964. The aircraft slammed nose-first into the deck. (Bob Schumacher via Matt Huber)

A few days later, the second attempt to land aboard was more successful. (Bob Schumacher via Matt Huber)

To help protect the nose of the U-2, a "pogo" was modified to provide a sprung steel skid beneath the cockpit. But as the landing technique was improved, this mod was deemed unnecessary and was removed. (Bob Schumacher via Matt Huber)

discussion within the U.S. Intelligence Board and the Joint Chiefs of Staff, the mission was canceled.[10]

Over the following years, OSA would have plenty of problems getting carrier time, even for training purposes. "There were many people in the U.S. Navy that did not want anything to do with the CIA, and more particularly its U-2s," recalled Jim Cherbonneaux, whose job it was to coordinate between Project HQ and the Admirals. However, the Navy did provide the basic carqual course on the T-2A and the USS *Lexington* for new U-2 pilots, such as the four who joined Det G in mid-1964. They were Deke Hall and Dan Schmarr, the pair of U-2 pilots who transferred from the SAC wing; and Squadron Leaders Martin Bee and Basil Dodd, the two latest RAF pilots. Hall and Schmarr replaced Jim Cherbonneaux, who went to Project HQ at Langley. Bee and Dodd replaced "Taffy" Taylor and "Chunky" Webster.

(Webster did not actually leave North Base for long. His expertise was so prized by OSA, that they asked the British government if he could remain in their employ, as the Project's own test pilot. Webster resigned his RAF commission and stayed on at Det G. He wrote all the pilots' notes and flew acceptance tests of new equipment. He later became a U.S. citizen).

One-and-only U-2H

When one of the original U-2G conversions (362) was lost in a shootdown over China in July 1964 it was immediately replaced. The new aircraft (349) was a transfer from the USAF, and received not only the J75 engine plus the carrier capability, but also the inflight refueling mod. It thus became the one-and-only U-2H model. In theory, it offered the ultimate in flexible mission planning: take off from an aircraft carrier, fly a mission, refuel in mid-air, and land at a friendly base thousands of miles away! The trouble was, the weight of all the modifications reduced 349's maximum altitude at a time when the SA-2 and MiG-21 threat was increasing. So the inflight refueling mod was removed after less than a year.

Fully anticipating more carrier missions, Project HQ decided that it needed four U-2Gs in the fleet. When two more aircraft were transferred from the USAF in mid-1964, they too received the structural beef-up, landing gear mods, and provision for the hook.

Once they were trained by the U.S. Navy to fly T-2s onto a carrier, the pilots of Det G flew practice carrier landings at North Base in the U-2G model. A mirror deck landing system was set up there, which replicated that found on carriers such as the *Kitty Hawk* and *Ranger*. On 26 April 1965, two pilots were scheduled for Mirror Landing Practice (MLP). Although the first of these two completed seven MLPs, the left wing dropped during the landings. Each U-2 had its individual flying characteristics—everyone knew that by now. "Buster" Edens took over for his MLPs. Before climbing in to Article 382 he was briefed on the left wing drop.[11]

Edens was one of the original U-2 pilots, now in his ninth year of flying for the Agency. Like all the long- serving agency drivers, he had

Carrier landings were captured on video for subsequent analysis. (Lockheed)

T-BIRDS AND BLUE CANOES

Det G had quite a support fleet: three Lockheed T-33 tandem-seat jets and two Cessna U-3 twin-props. The T-33s were provided so that the U-2 pilots, the Det commander, and flight-rated operations officers could maintain their flying proficiency. The U-3s were supposed to be for communications, crew ferry to the Skunk Works, etc. In fact, these airplanes often provided the means for Det G's flight-rated personnel to escape the high Mojave Desert for more hospitable climes. The justification? Training, of course!

Jerry Losey was a mission planner at Det G from 1963 to 1967. He often hitched a ride to San Diego with John Huber, the Navy LSO who was permanently assigned to Project Idealist. "He would invite me on the pretense that it was a navigation training flight. This gave us *carte blanche* for going just about anywhere we wished," Losey recalled. Oh what fun they had, in those T-33s! Taking off from NAS Alameda one day, Huber elected to fly *under* the Oakland Bay Bridge!

The British pilots attached to Det G relied heavily on the T-33s to maintain proficiency. They were often denied U-2 time because Project HQ had higher priorities. Sqn Ldr Martin Bee recalled the time that he flew Frank Powers to Washington. "One of our T-33s was painted all white. We called it Caspar, after the ghost in Shakespeare's Hamlet. I was flying back to California with Frank when we picked up some ice on the engine intakes, started to get a little low on fuel, and had to divert into a National Guard base halfway across the USA. The duty staff could barely believe seeing a white-painted USAF T-33 arrive in a snowstorm. Then from the aircraft emerged a famous civilian Lockheed test pilot and an RAF officer. By now they did not know what to believe...."

Caspar was eventually written off by Lt Cdr Lonnie McClung, Huber's successor, as the resident LSO at Det G. McClung stalled it on approach to Richards-Gebaur AFB during a cross-country in late December 1968. He walked away from the wreckage.

Det G crashed another two T-33s. In June 1970 new U-2 pilot recruit Dave Young was doing his initial training, supervised by British IP Dick Cloke. During flameout patterns at Palmdale, the aircraft stalled onto the runway after someone forgot to lower the flaps. Young applied power and went around, raising the gear. It would not come down again. He landed on the lakebed back at Edwards, where the aircraft slid across the lakebed. Neither Young

nor Cloke were injured, but the T-bird's main spar was broken. In August 1971 a T-33 lost power during takeoff from North Base and ran off the runway. The gear collapsed, and the aircraft was written off. – C.P

THE COVER STORY: INSTRUCTING THE WIVES

Here are the instructions handed out to the wives of the CIA pilots flying with Det G at Edwards North Base in the mid-sixties. It was a "covert" squadron on an "overt" base. (The "USAF civilian employees" mentioned below were, in fact, the CIA staffers who handled administration, communications, and security.)

Your husband is a member of the Weather Reconnaissance Squadron Provisional IV (WRSP-IV), assigned to North Base at Edwards AFB, California. This unit is composed of USAF military personnel, USAF civilian employees, and employees of the Lockheed Aircraft Corporation. WRSP-IV conducts high-altitude research involving such fields as general weather patterns, upper atmospheric conditions, general climatic conditions, and terrestrial and celestial navigation. In addition, classified research and development studies are conducted for the Department of Defense. A variety of aircraft are utilized by the squadron, including the U-2 aircraft famed for its ability to climb to high altitudes. The squadron must frequently travel to various parts of the world in order to test equipment under various climatic conditions.

Because a large portion of our work is of a classified nature, we must be careful to reveal no information concerning our work to persons who have no need for such information. We should *never volunteer* any information. For instance, when you are asked about your husband's employment, simply state that he is an officer or enlisted man in the USAF; or a civilian with the USAF; or an employee of Lockheed, as the case may be. If questioned as to specific location, simply say EDWARDS AIR FORCE BASE. Should a person wish a more specific answer, it is permissable to state that he is assigned to WRSP-IV at North Base. Answers concerning the type of work done by the squadron should be along the lines stated above, and if more information is asked for, simply answer to the effect that the remainder of the mission is classified, and that your husband never discusses this with you. Further discussions at this point should not be forthcoming, and any strong attempts to continue such questions should be reported to the Security Office through your husband.

---

needed a share of luck to get this far. Three years earlier he had survived a serious U-2 landing accident at Edwards. Today, his luck ran out.

Edens killed

Edens took off and climbed to 13,000 feet to check the stall characteristics. They seemed normal. He returned to the pattern and made an approach. The aircraft touched down left wing low again. Edens immediately applied power, dragged the skid for about 50 feet, leveled the wings, and became airborne. He turned left as if to go downwind, but was advised by

mobile to check the wing balance again. He acknowledged, and began a climb. But at about 3,000 feet, the aircraft entered a spiraling left descent from which it never recovered. Edens extended the speed brakes in a vain attempt to arrest the spin. He ejected at 400 feet—too low! The chute only partially deployed, and Edens was killed as he hit the ground.

The accident investigators recommended that a new effort be made to ensure that the wing stalled symmetrically, and that fuel did not move from one wing to another when the pump was not operating. They also called for a safe altitude to be established for control checks, that would ensure a survivable ejection if the aircraft should go out of control.[12]

Al Rand (left) and Jim Barnes enjoy a British pint during the deployment of Det G to RAF Upper Heyford in 1967. The call to fly an operational mission over the Middle East never came (Martin Bee).

The accident prompted Kelly Johnson to make a frank entry in his diary: "Having terrible time with stall and trim characteristics of the bird at altitude. Every one must be hand-tailored on the wing stall strips. We are caught by the high cruising lift coefficient at altitude. If we put the stall strips where they give us good landing and takeoff characteristics, then we run into buffeting and pitching at altitude. We must rush the installation of retractable stall strips, which I sketched up last week."[13]

At Taoyuan, Det H also had an aircraft with asymmetric stall tendencies. Bob Schumacher was urgently flown to Taiwan to evaluate it. After a couple of test flights, Schumacher recommended that 385 be shipped back to the Skunk Works for attention! This was one of Schumacher's last contributions to U-2 flight testing. After nearly 10 years of continuous service, he was transferred later in 1965 to Lockheed's new Tristar airliner program.[14]

The retractable stall strips were duly installed in the summer of 1965, midway along the wing leading edge. To extend them, the pilot pulled a T-handle down by his right knee. Henceforth, landings were just a little easier. To stop fuel sloshing around when the transfer pump was not being operated, a solenoid-operated shut-off valve was added.

Quid-pro-quo

The Navy pressed to have one of its pilots assigned to Det G, as a quid-pro-quo for providing carrier landing training and (perhaps!) agreeing to more carrier-launched U-2 missions. Fresh out of test pilot's school, LCdr Tom McMurtry joined the CIA outfit at North Base in late 1964.

But the months dragged on without another carrier operation. A plan to revisit the French nuclear test area in May 1965 was canceled. John Huber was under-employed as an LSO, so he augmented the operations staff at Det G. (Huber left the Project in May 1967 to join RVAH-12, an RA-5C Vigilante squadron, as Operations Officer. He was subsequently promoted to command the squadron, but was killed when one of these aircraft crashed in 1970.)

Tom McMurtry took his place on the regular pilots' roster at North Base.

Det G flew only two operational missions in 1965. These were over Cambodia in late October and early November, during a deployment to Takhli. This deployment began in early September, with the purpose of getting new coverage of the Sino-Indian border. Article 384 was ferried from Det H at Taoyuan, and 383 was ferried all the way from the U.S. But the missions to Tibet never happened, presumably because the Indian government withheld permission to overfly.

In 1966 there were no operational missions at all for Det G. But North Base was kept busy with test flights of the many upgrades to the U-2, and the development of new defensive tactics. There were also many long flights over the U.S. codenamed Red Dot, which tested new films, filters, and processing techniques, some of them in support of satellite photography.

Squadron Leader Martin Bee was one of two RAF pilots assigned to Project Idealist in the mid-1960s. (Martin Bee)

One of the tasks was to fly over agricultural areas to determine whether forthcoming crop yields could be predicted. That could be useful to farmers—and also to intelligence analysts trying to assess the economic condition of potential adversaries.

Det G also supported Det H on Taiwan in many ways. It supplied pilots, ops officers, and mission planners, and from mid-1966 took on the training of new ROCAF pilots, which the SAC U-2 wing had previously undertaken. Det G was also responsible for the transpacific ferry flights of newly-overhauled Articles going to Taoyuan. These flights were still organized on a "covert" basis; the cover story was weather reconnaissance, and in the mid-1960s the aircraft wore the tail markings of the USAF "Air Weather Service." (The aircraft were not usually ferried back from Taiwan, since they would be going straight into depot maintenance at Lockheed. Instead, they were disassembled and flown home in a MATS transport as classified cargo).

The pilots still practiced aerial refueling, as well as carrier landings. On 25 February 1966, Deke Hall completed tanking from a KC-135 over Edwards. As he pulled up and away in a rolling maneuver, he over-stressed the wing of Article 342. The aircraft broke up spectacularly, and Hall ejected successfully. Kelly Johnson was not impressed: "The pilot was showing off to the KC-135 crew. The wings broke off exactly like in static test," he wrote. The accident was certainly a graphic reminder: the U-2's g-limits were such that the aircraft could not be mistreated.[15]

Upper Heyford 1967

In an operation codenamed Blue Gull II, the pilots of Det G requalified for carrier missions in February 1967 on the USS *Constellation*, sailing off San Diego. Three months later the Det was alerted for its first operational deployment in 18 months. A U-2G (348) was hurriedly prepared, and a ferry support team boarded a KC-135. In the early hours of 29 May, the pair of aircraft took off from Edwards for Loring AFB, ME. At Loring, the Article was refueled on the ground from the KC-135, and the duo flew on to the U.S. airbase at Upper Heyford, in southern England. The U-2 landed after dark and was quickly hangared to shield it from prying eyes.[16]

The operation was initially codenamed Scope Panic. Since that moniker was too close to the truth, it was subsequently changed to Scope Safe! The plan was to fly over the Middle East, where Israel and its neighbors were at the brink of war. By deploying the carrier-capable G-model Project HQ was keeping its options open. If necessary, the aircraft could be flown to and/or from a Sixth Fleet carrier in the Mediterranean. Of course, a land base would be preferable, and Project HQ was apparently hoping that the Brits would finally come through and allow the use of their sovereign base at Akrotiri, on the island of Cyprus.[17]

There was even some thought that one of the RAF pilots might fly missions. Squadron Leader Martin Bee was one of the Det G pilots standing by at Upper Heyford, along with Jim Barnes and Al Rand, as the next move was discussed at the highest levels in Washington and London. Meanwhile, two C-141s arrived at the British base with support equipment, including spare B and H cameras. On 31 May, Project HQ instructed Det G and deployment commander Col Miles Doyle to install the carrier hook. It looked like France was going to refuse permission for the U-2 to overfly, and the mission would have to be recovered on the USS *Saratoga* in the Med. The Navy was asked to transfer sufficient A-4s to the other nearby U.S. carrier (the *America*) to provide deck space for the U-2.[18]

Meanwhile, the tension in the Middle East reached boiling point. U.S. intelligence was short of information: the last Corona mission had been early May, and the next one could not be launched until mid-June. Of course, even a U-2 mission would not produce timely results, unless the "take" was quickly processed and interpreted. There was much discussion over where that could be done. The possible options were in the UK (by the RAF), in Germany (by USAFE), or back in the U.S.[19]

Second thoughts

British Foreign Secretary George Brown went to inspect the Article at Upper Heyford. The British government approved a U-2 mission on 2 June, to be flown by the RAF pilot. But the 303 Committee in Washington had second thoughts. On 5 June the Israeli Air Force launched a devastating attack on Egyptian and Syrian airfields, and Israeli armor raced across the Sinai Desert. With the U-2 still hidden in the hangar, the support team waited...and waited. Project HQ cabled them from Washington: "Many meetings underway here but nothing firm yet."

The Article needed a shake-down flight. Then the Brits grew nervous about having such a notorious spyplane on their soil, and insisted that it be flown after dark. The word that the U-2 was at Upper Heyford leaked out. On 7 June the UK regretfully requested that the U-2 be withdrawn. The shakedown flight took place that night, and the Article was flown back to the U.S. two nights later. Israel completed a decisive victory in the Six-Day War, unobserved by the U-2.[20]

20

To Vietnam

When Det G returned to Takhli in September 1963 the situation in Vietnam was uneasy, to say the least. The North was stepping up its resupply of the Viet Cong (VC) guerrillas in the South via the Ho Chi Minh trails through Laos and Cambodia. Nearly 20,000 U.S. military "advisors" were helping to sustain the corrupt and unpopular Diem regime in Saigon. On 1 November, the U.S. condoned a military coup that removed Diem and his brother, who were murdered by the ARVN (Army of the Republic of Vietnam). Three weeks later, President Kennedy was assassinated in Dallas.

Before it returned to the U.S. in mid-November, Det G flew six missions over North Vietnam and Laos. At the end of the year, two more missions were flown out of Taoyuan by the American pilots attached to Det H. All were designed to map the VC's infiltration routes. The late December flights used the new Itek panoramic camera derived from the Corona, designated System 112A, but soon to be relabeled as the Delta 1. Although it covered a swath of only 13 miles, the image quality was excellent, and could be enlarged 100 times!

But no amount of technical excellence could defeat thick jungle canopies and the monsoon weather that frequently obscured even the tree tops. In its prelimary evaluation of the latest U-2 missions, NPIC noted: "The small amount of significant intelligence acquired by these missions seems to confirm our previous experience with high-altitude photography over Laos and North Vietnam. As long as the Viet Cong remain a lightly-equipped guerrilla force operating from jungle-covered bases and supplied over water or by an obscure system of overland trails, we believe that it will be virtually impossible to monitor their activities through the use of overhead photography."[1]

SAC wing alerted

Despite this advice, the National Security Council in Washington decided to step up U-2 reconnaissance of Southeast Asia in early 1964. Complete coverage of South Vietnam was requested, a task that Project HQ assigned to the American pilots at Det H, beginning on 7 January. But in the Pentagon, it was becoming obvious that a few missions by the Agency's U-2s would not meet the increased requirement. At Davis-Monthan, the SAC U-2 wing was alerted for an urgent, transpacific deployment. President Johnson personally approved Ops Plan 34A, an escalation of the U.S. commitment to fight communism in Southeast Asia, which included stepped-up U-2 flights.

On 11 February, the 4080th's three refuelable U-2E models took off from DM for Hickam AFB, accompanied by a KC-135. Using the rapid deployment procedures developed in the three previous training exercises codenamed Muscle Magic, the ground time on Hawaii was minimal, as three pilots took over, who had slept on the tanker enroute. Thanks to fuel top-ups from the KC-135 over Wake Island and Guam, they took the three Dragon Ladies all the way to Clark AB, Philippines—a 13 hour 30 minutes flight![2]

The next day, SAC flew the first of its Vietnam missions, which were codenamed Lucky Dragon. But the Philippine government was not happy about the arrival of U-2s in its territory. After some days of inaction while the political wheels spun, the 4080th team was obliged to withdraw to Anderson AFB, Guam—in a hurry!

In Washington, meanwhile, the Special Group debated where to base the aircraft, and how to mesh coverage between the SAC and the CIA U-2 operations. The basing was soon decided: the "overt" SAC aircraft would

In March 1964, the 4080th SRW hurriedly deployed three U-2E models to Vietnam with the aid of inflight refueling. 66703 is seen at Bien Hoa airbase with pilots and groundcrew (via Tony Bevacqua).

The deployment by SAC of three U-2s to Vietnam was codenamed Lucky Dragon. Two of the 4080th senior pilots recall that urgent transpacific journey:

Chuck Stratton: Steve Heyser, Jerry McIlmoyle, and myself slept on mattresses in the rear of the KC-135 from D-M to Hickam. After a quick breakfast and suit-up, we departed Hickam for Clark on 12 February.

Jerry McIlmoyle: We were about five hours late getting off Hickam because of a delayed execution. We dead-reckoned the whole way because our celestial was too old to use! It had been recomputed once, then it ran out, and we were ready to abort when the execution came through! We went with 30 minutes between each bird. Heyser first off, then me, then Stratton. The flight was from Hickam to Wake to Guam, refueling over there, with Anderson as the landing base if we missed the tanker.

Chuck Stratton: We got to Clark well after dark. The next morning, Jim Qualls flew the only operational mission out of Clark. The Philippine government said: "NO MORE!" After several days of nothing, we slipped out one night to Anderson AFB. Same story there, stand around! After about two weeks Col DesPortes arrived, and said we are going to Bien Hoa. We took the three aircraft there on 5 March.

Conditions at OL-20, Bien Hoa airbase, South Vietnam, were far from ideal, as this description reveals:

A lack of adequate facilities affected every facet of the U-2 program at Bien Hoa, and taxed the ingenuity of both support personnel and crewmembers. Ramp space was very limited. Heavy vehicle traffic made taxi and towing operations hazardous. Buildings used by OL-20 were either substandard or overcrowded, or both. The concrete floor of the U-2 hangar cracked and buckled from the weight of the main gear. As an interim measure, it had to be covered with half-inch steel plates. Controlled temperature storage for film was also a problem. However, the housing situation was probably the greatest irritant. There were no quarters in the OL-20 compound for officers, and the airmen housing was extremely crowded.

- from "A Study of the Use of the RB-57 and U-2 Aircraft in Southeast Asia 1965-1967," Air War College, April 1968

fly Lucky Dragon missions out of Bien Hoa airbase, northeast of Saigon. Meanwhile, the CIA would send one of its "covert" U-2s back to Takhli, in an operation codenamed Lazy Daisy. But the division of responsibility was curious.

By its memo of 3 March, the Special Group allocated to SAC the whole of South Vietnam; North Vietnam within 30 miles of the coastline; all of Laos south of Paksane; and Cambodia, within 30 miles of South Vietnam. The Agency would cover the rest of Laos and North Vietnam. The rationale appeared to be that a "military" aircraft should not be "caught" over North Vietnam, Laos, and Cambodia. It was the same type of rationale that had denied for years the presence of U.S. "troops" (as opposed to advisors) in South Vietnam.[3]

Bien Hoa

In early March, the three SAC U-2Es were flown into Bien Hoa, and the single Agency U-2F into Takhli. Near-daily missions were flown from both locations, even when weather forecasts indicated that only a small portion of the target areas could be cloud-free. The new "customer" for the missions—Military Assistance Command Vietnam (MACV)—wanted "baseline" and repetitive coverage.

Using a single U-2, Det G flew intensively from Takhli—15 missions in five weeks. But by mid-April, OSA Deputy Director Jim Cunningham was tired of all this. There were other, more "strategic" priorities for the Agency's fleet of only six U-2s—especially over China. Cunningham proposed that the "artificial restrictions" on the utilization of SAC's U-2 be lifted. He argued that there was "no active air opposition" in any of the three countries to require a "wholly covert" U-2 operation. Within a week the idea was accepted, and SAC took responsibility for all flights over Cambodia, Laos, and the two Vietnams. Having moved from Takhli to Cubi Point, Det G flew its last mission over the area from Takhli on 24 April.[4]

From now on, the SAC wing always kept two or three U-2s at Bien Hoa. There was one mission nearly every day, lasting up to five hours, although bad weather over the target areas frequently resulted in cancellations or recalls. Operating from less-than-ideal facilities, OL-20 was manned by about 50 personnel, all on TDY from the 4080th wing at D-M. There were usually four pilots on 60-day tours, while the support troops pulled 120-day tours. OL-20 was commanded by a Colonel, who took his orders

Flightline scene at Bien Hoa in late 1964, after SAC directed that the U-2s be painted black to help avoid interception by North Vietnam's newly-acquired MiGs.

direct from SAC HQ at Offutt, although he also coordinated with MACV to determine local requirements. After early attempts to process film at Bien Hoa, SAC set up a Photographic Processing Center at Tan Son Nhut airbase, Saigon, to where the U-2 camera "take" had to be flown after each mission. But the SIGINT tapes were sent all the way back to the 544th ARTW at Offutt for analysis and reporting, as they always had been.[5]

As 1964 wore on, the U-2s ranged far and wide over North and South Vietnam, Laos, and Cambodia. A watershed was reached in early August when the USS *Maddox* was attacked by North Vietnamese patrol boats. Congress passed the Tonkin Gulf Resolution, and carrier-based U.S. fighter-bombers struck targets in North Vietnam. The USAF moved B-57s from the Philippines to join the U-2s at Bien Hoa, and deployed fighters to Da Nang. Within a couple of days, the North Vietnamese air force received its first fighters, quickly flown in from southern China. A U-2 photographed 34 MiG-15/17s at the newly-built Phuc Yen airfield. Hitherto, some of OL-20's missions over North Vietnam had been flown at medium levels, due to the lack of fighter opposition, and to defeat the cloud cover. That was no longer an option, however.

Cuba propaganda

In 1964, the fears of a SAC U-2 being intercepted were not confined to Southeast Asia. On 2 May, the U.S. Intelligence Board issued a special estimate on the likelihood of a U-2 being shot down over Cuba. The Golden Tree flights from OL-19, Barksdale AFB, were continuing at a near-daily rate. But Cubans were now being trained to operate the SA-2 system, and were expected to gain complete control within a few weeks. President Castro stepped up his propaganda campaign at the United Nations and elsewhere to have the flights stopped. But would he actually open fire? The intel analysts thought the chances were high.[6]

The Special Group considered alternatives. First, in May SAC's Lightning Bug recce drones, which were now operational at Eglin AFB. Then, in August, the A-12 Oxcart, which was still under protracted development at Groom Lake.

But in the end, the U-2 soldiered on. At last, SAC directed that the podded ECM gear designed to defeat an SA-2 attack be added to the U-2As overflying Cuba. Systems 14 and 15 were sent to OL-19 during May. At the same time, the Delta 1 camera was returned to OL-19 so that its superior resolution could again be employed over Cuba.

Test flights of the experimental QRC-192 ELINT system continued, including another against Cuban radars on 1 June 1964.

The threat from the Cuban MiG-21s was also reassessed. In September, a special trial codenamed Boulder Creek was run from OL-19 to test the chances of survival against IR missile-equipped fighters of the Air

---

MORE INTERCEPTS BY THE FRIENDLIES

Give any hot-rod fighter pilot the challenge of intercepting a U-2, and he's liable to take it! Especially if he is flying that other Lockheed product designed to go very high, but very fast—the F-104. Walt Bjorneby was one such pilot, serving with the 319th FIS at Homestead AFB, FL, from 1964-67:

We intercepted the U-2 fairly often on their training flights, usually above 60,000 feet. Of course, we had to wear pressure suits. Fuel was our limitation: we couldn't afford to wait more than about five minutes if he was behind on his ETA. I was fortunate to fly the first mission against the U-2. During the prebrief, I asked the controller to be rolled out 35 miles behind at 35,000 feet, 0.9 Mach. He did just that. I selected afterburner and started accelerating. As the bird passed Mach 1.4, I started a gentle climb. At something like 18 miles—on a 20-mile scope—I saw his blip on my ASG-14. I was Mach 1.8, passing 58,000 feet! Completed the intercept and peeled off for home with about 2,400 lbs of fuel left!

We were afraid of booming them, not knowing what the shockwave might do. Our tactic was a climbing stern AIM-9B pass followed by a straight-on gun pass. We had a sight that would range to 4,000 feet, so we would put the .7 mil pipper on him and "shoot" down to about 2,000, where an enthusiastic bunt would send us under him. One of our pilots actually made a high-side gun re-attack on a U-2 at 64,000 feet! The U-2 pilot spoke up and said, "I don't believe it!" For sure, a MiG-21 couldn't do that....

- correspondence with author

GOING BLACK

Once the 4080th was committed to the Vietnam conflict, pilots expressed fears that the bright gray paint scheme rendered them too visible and easily subject to hostile fire. In the fall of 1964, the first of the glossy gray paint jobs gave way to flat black. Major Ed Smart and company ferried aircraft 680 to Anderson AFB to get it done. But the local logistics folks refused the job. Undaunted, Major Smart proceeded to the salvage area, found a spray gun, and accomplished the face-lifting in the ARS area. With the paint barely dried, he flew it back to Bien Hoa.

- from the 4080th/100th 20-Year History

U-2A 66953 on the ramp at D-M in 1965, after repainting.

The Lightning Bug reconnaissance drones were deployed to southeast Asia in August 1964. They offered an unmanned alternative to risking U-2s and their pilots over heavily-defended areas (NARA 113171).

Defense Command (ADC). F-100 and F-104 fighters flew against the U-2 over the Florida Test Range. Although the U-2 pilot activated his System 9A and took evasive action, the interceptions were successful. A drone replicating the U-2's IR signature was downed by an AIM-9 fired from an F-104.[7]

During the trials, the CIA sent a black-painted U-2 from Det G to rendezvous with one of SAC's gray-painted Dragon Ladies high over Texas. An F-104 was directed to intercept. The pilot reported that he could easily see the SAC bird, whereas the black aircraft went undetected. SAC decided to paint its U-2s black, with some urgency. It also authorized a con-

tinuation of U-2 intercepts by ADC fighters, as the aircraft from OL-19 returned to U.S. airspace from their Cuba missions.

Although the Lightning Bugs did not get their chance over Cuba, their call to deploy finally came in August 1964, following the Tonkin Gulf Resolution. The recce drones were first sent to Kadena AB for missions over southern China. In early October, though, they moved to join the U-2s of OL-20 at Bien Hoa, together with their DC-130 launch aircraft. In the ensuing years, SAC operated drones of increasing sophistication and versatility over North Vietnam and southern China, from low to high altitude, from photo reconnaissance to ELINT.

F-104 pilots from the Air Defense Command flew practice interceptions against the U-2 at various times in the mid-1960s (Lockheed LN2760).

21

Black Cat-and-Mouse

It was nearly six months after Robin Yeh was shot down before overflights of the Chinese mainland restarted. First, a political clearance was needed from the White House, especially since Taiwan had only "bought" two U-2s, and both had now been shot down. The cover story had to be modified. A replacement Article was ferried to Det H at Taoyuan.

But as 1964 opened, Terry Lee was the only CAF pilot cleared for operational missions. Mike Hua and Tiger Wang had both completed their tours and been reassigned, while Gimo Yang was promoted to Lt Col and soon took command of the Black Cat Squadron, which disqualified him from further overflights. Even before Yeh was shot down, two more pilots had been selected and sent to D-M for training. Major "Johnny" Wang Chen Wen and Captain "Sonny" Liang Teh Pei completed the course in mid-December 1963, although the 4080th reported that Wang's command of the English language was inadequate.[1]

The two new pilots reported to Taoyuan, and training flights resumed to convert them to the higher-powered J75 model. But now there was another rash of flameouts, especially as the U-2 climbed above 40,000 feet. To the U-2 pilots, this portion of airspace became known as the "Badlands." Part of the problem was atmospheric—the tropopause was lower in this part of Asia than elsewhere, and the new fuel control that had recently been fitted to the J75 could not cope with the sudden temperature variation, as the outside air temperature dipped from -35 degrees to -60 degrees, and back to -35 again at around 65,000 feet. The standard climb schedule, which required the pilot to retard the throttle so that an EGT of 485 degrees was maintained throughout the Badlands, no longer seemed to work. Kelly Johnson described the Badlands as a "very involved problem," but he also blamed Pratt & Whitney for failing to take the issue seriously enough.[2]

One or more of the Agency's American pilots were always present at Det H on a rotational basis. They lent their experience and encouragement to the Chinese flyers. Still, though, when Terry Lee took off on 16 March on the first operational mission since 1 November, the route was specially selected to reinstill confidence in the pilot on an actual overflight. It was a shallow penetration over Hainan Island and Kwangtung province.[3]

Birdwatcher

Lee's aircraft had the new Birdwatcher telemetry system installed. This consisted of 40 on/off inputs from flight and engine instruments, and sensors placed throughout the aircraft. Birdwatcher automatically monitored parameters such as altitude, airspeed, engine RPM and EGT, System 9 and

12 defensive warning system activity, G-forces, and seat ejection. If anything should go wrong, a brief burst of data was sent via the aircraft's SSB radio to the command post, which was monitoring the mission back on Taiwan.

But the CAF pilots still did not have ECM protection. The Pentagon refused to let the CIA run the risk of losing such advanced technology over communist China. However, the fear of loss did not extend to the new panoramic cameras derived from the Corona satellite, even though these were also Top Secret. In April 1964, Itek delivered the first of four Delta II units, also known as System 112B. Unlike the single Delta I prototype (System 112A), the new devices were twin cameras mounted at a 30-degree angle to provide stereo convergence. The film spools nested between two honeycomb plates. Lockheed's new U-2 program manager, Fred Cavanaugh, protested that this installation could never fit in the Q-bay! He was right. The Skunk Works had to build a new hatch with a large rectangular window that extended several inches below the fuselage.[4]

Lee returned safely to Taoyuan from his 16 March mission after 7 hours 25 minutes. But if this flight did help boost morale in the Black Cat Squadron, it was not for long. Exactly a week later, Sonny Liang was killed when—according to the Birdwatcher transmissions—he lost control due to overspeed at high altitude. He was flying along the mainland coast on a training flight that also served as a peripheral SIGINT mission. The air-

Major Mike Hua, seen here with President Chiang Kai Shek, was the first CAF pilot to complete 10 overflights of mainland China (via Mike Hua).

THE VOODOOS AND THE BATS

The U-2s of the 35th Squadron were not the only spyplanes supplied by the U.S. to the nationalists, to fly over mainland China. Also based at Taoyuan were the RF-101 Voodoos of the CAF's 4th Squadron. They flew at low-level over the coastal provinces opposite Taiwan, dodging intense AA fire from the Chicom gunners. Three of them were shot down. Then there was the 34th Squadron, another joint CIA-CAF operation based at Hsinchu. This was a special operations outfit that dropped nationalist agents on the mainland and performed electronic reconnaissance. In the 1950s, the "Bats" flew ancient B-17, B-26, and PB4Y converted bombers. Then the CIA provided five specially-modified P2V-7 patrol planes. Four of these were shot down by the Chicoms before the overflight operation was terminated in 1967. – C.P.

FLYING OVER THE HIMALAYAS

It may have been spectacular, but it could also be treacherous, even for a high-flying U-2. In various 1964 messages to and from Project HQ, the following observations were made:

Over the southern slope of the Himalayas from the western border of Nepal eastwards, and northwards to about 150 nm beyond the southern slopes of the Tibetan plateau, there is wholly unacceptable severe turbulence associated with major cumulus buildups to 50,000 feet and more. This condition is persistent throughout the monsoon period and incompatible with the structural limitations of the U-2 aircraft....

Navigation is unquestionably the toughest of any area we have covered. The area looks different to the pilot from one year to the next, due to the difference in size of rivers, amount of snow, and overall appearance....

craft crashed into the South China Sea. The pilot's body was recovered by a fishing boast, half eaten by sharks. His death was a bit of a mystery. Liang had evidently ejected, and his parachute had deployed. He appeared to have drowned, so perhaps he had hit the water unconscious. But there were no bruises to suggest, for example, that he had collided with part of the aircraft on his way out. Someone came up with the idea that he had drowned because he was too small to negotiate the steep side of the inflatable life raft that formed part of the emergency kit in the seat pack. The life raft was therefore modified to make it easier for the Chinese pilots—who were physically smaller than their American counterparts—to clamber in.

The climbout problems continued. The pilots would call out instrument readings as they ascended. On 22 April, another overflight of southern China had to be aborted after a flameout at 63,000 feet. The two Articles at Taoyuan (358 and 359) were grounded to await a trouble shooting team from the U.S.

Fortunately Article 342, which was being used by the Det G deployment at Takhli at this time, was unaffected. In between the Lazy Daisy missions over Laos and Vietnam, the deployment managed to fly a single mission up the China/Burma border and into the NEFA area and eastern Tibet on 31 March 1964. The return route passed to the west of Kunming.

Charbatia

In late April, the task of covering southeast Asia was passed completely to the SAC U-2s now based at Bien Hoa. This freed Article 342 for a new adventure. In New Delhi, Ambassador Galbraith was close to persuading the Indian government to accept a U-2 deployment. Charbatia, an old wartime airbase on the outskirts of Cuttack, close to the Bay of Bengal, would be provided by the Indians. But it was a bare base, which required the U.S. side to fly in most of the support equipment.

This deployment was trouble all the way. The advance party was flown from the U.S. to meet Article 342 at Cubi Point, Philippines. There was a long wait for final approval from Delhi. Then there was a communications snafu, and their C-124 arrived at Charbatia unannounced and with radio problems. It was met by Indian soldiers with raised rifles! When the American group was finally allowed to disembark, it found the base facilities to be decidedly sub-standard. The runway was pot-holed and had a hump in the middle. The hot wind howled, and storm rains blew through the open-ended hangar. The navaids were nonexistent: a portable VOR had to be flown in. There was no proper drinking water: within days, half of the team had developed diarrhea.[5]

There were some delicate security issues to be overcome. Indian Air Force and intelligence officers expected full access to flight planning, briefing and debriefing, flight following in the command post, and the processing and viewing of the "take." One of their biggest concerns was that the U-2 would overfly their aircraft factory at Nasik, where the MiG-21 was produced under license. After some negotiations compromises were made. But there was no way for the Indians to inspect the main camera film. As was often the case with Idealist deployments, the plan was to fly it back to the U.S. for processing at Eastman Kodak, followed by readout at NPIC in Washington. The Indians had to be content with viewing the tracker film.[6]

On 19 May the U-2 was flown in from Cubi Point. The first mission was alerted for 24 May. It was a six-hour flight into Tibet, covering the

Flying over the Himalayas during the Sino-Indian border missions was spectacular, but could also be dangerous. Severe turbulence could be encountered at certain times of the year, even at the U-2's operating altitude (via Marty Knutson).

Sino-Indian border, but also venturing well north of Lhasa. Bob Ericson was the pilot, and all went well until the loss of pressurization in the Q-bay forced him to turn the B-camera off two-thirds of the way through the mission. Worse was to follow. During the landing back at Charbatia—which could not be accomplished from the optimum end because that entailed flying over a populated area, and thus exposing the U-2 to curious onlookers—the brakes failed. The Article gathered speed after it crested the hump in mid-runway. Ericson tried to drag one wing, then the other, to no avail. 342 ran off the end of the runway and the landing gear collapsed.[7]

Fortunately, the camera and film were undamaged. When it was eventually analyzed, the photography was excellent. U.S. intelligence analysts concluded that India's fears about Chicom military preparations along the border were exaggerated. But the flight itself may have raised tensions between the two countries. The New China News Agency reported that, "as on several occasions in the past, an intruding Indian Air Force aircraft made prolonged reconnoitering and harassing activities!" (The previous occasions were obviously also U-2 flights over Tibet).

Having waited so long for Indian basing rights, the U.S. side had planned more flights. They wanted to search the possible downrange impact sites from the SCT missile launch base at the western end of the Takla Makan desert. They wanted to overfly Lop Nor, the remote site in Sinkiang that had recently been identified in Corona satellite imagery as a possible location for China's expected nuclear test.

But Article 342 would have to be airlifted out by C-124, and Project HQ had no replacement to offer. The CIA U-2 fleet had been depleted by one shootdown (Yeh) and two other fatal accidents within six months (Hyde and Liang). The two aircraft at Taoyuan were grounded; two more were committed to the carrier operation against the French nuclear test site in the mid-Pacific; and two more were recent transfers from the USAF, which were being overhauled and converted to J75 power at Burbank. In any case, the Indians had imposed a seven day deadline for the deployment, and the monsoon season was approaching. Project HQ requested that the detachment commander at Charbatia devise a graceful exit, but "leave the door open for a return visit." Det G packed up and flew back to Cubi Point. They were glad to go.[8]

THE NEW HANGAR AT TAOYUAN

For the first three years of U-2 operations, the Black Cat Squadron's home on Taoyuan airbase was a shabby, wooden Second World War hangar. It was 78 feet wide—two feet less than the U-2 wingspan! Maneuvering the two Articles in and out was a pain, involving several back and forth movements. In 1964, the 35th Squadron moved into a purpose-built new hangar, capable of holding four U-2s.

But for the senior Chinese Air Force General in charge of the Razor/Tackle project, the new hangar contributed to his fall from favor. After a 30-year career as one of the CAF's most trusted officers, Lt Gen I Fu En was suddenly put under house arrest, which lasted three years. The American side of the joint project believed that the General made illegal profits from the hangar work. "Everyone in CIA knew that he was on the take," one senior officer at Project HQ recalled. In his memoirs, however, the CAF general speculated that his downfall was caused by politics. His views on the impossibility of retaking the mainland without full U.S. support had riled Chiang Ching Kuo, or his father, the Generalissimo. General I continued:

I met the prosecutor in charge of my case. He asked me a few questions concerning the construction of the U-2 hangars at Taoyuan. I told him all I knew and asserted that the funds had all come from the U.S. CAF headquarters had signed the contract in order to cover U.S. participation in this highly classified operation. When the legal Department could not show that I personally had done anything wrong, they accused me of "illegal action of benefiting others." Those who knew me well were all surprised by my case, and many of them tried to help....

The whole thing was like a bad joke. I went into confinement confused, and got out equally confused. It was totally in violation of military law. Chiang Ching Kuo's son Alan came to see me and said, "Uncle I, the Chiang family wronged you!"

The new hangar built at Taoyuan airbase for the Chinese Air Force's 35th Squadron is seen here. Access to the Black Cat Squadron area was tightly restricted at all times (via Gimo Yang).

WAS THE U-2 ESCAPE SYSTEM RIGGED TO FAIL?

Was the escape system ever rigged to ensure that a U-2 pilot would not survive a shootdown? Unthinkable as it may seem, the idea was seriously considered in 1961, as an earlier chapter relates. Then the Chinese communists stirred the pot in 1964. Some time after Terry Lee was shot down in July, the Chicoms reported that he had been found dead in the cockpit, and that there was no explosive charge in his ejection seat. This was either propagandist mischief-making, or a misunderstanding of the U-2 escape system. The *canopy* did not have an automatic ejection system in 1964—the charged thrusters were not added until the following year. But the rumors did play on the minds of the CAF pilots. Many years later, one of them told this author that he believed that *his* seat had no charge in it. – *C.P.*

CHARBATIA – INDIAN HELL HOLE
Well, that's how the deployed party from Det G saw it, anyway! Here are some extracts from cables and trip reports on the top secret May-June 1964 excursion to this poorly-equipped airbase:

This location, except for the quarters, is about as bad as a deployment site can be. Living standards of the surrounding country are among the poorest, and health standards are among the lowest in the world. People fail to observe even the most basic sanitary procedures.... The water must be classified as "not fit for human consumption." Food and paper waste was dumped locally without landfill, attracting wild dogs and rats. Time will tell what chronic disease will develop in detachment personnel as a result of this deployment.... Just about everyone had gastro-enteritis to some degree.... No outside activity was possible from 1000-1600 because of the extreme heat.... Something must be done about the central air conditioner in the admin building...the 100KW, 60CPS generator was completely out of order...power fluctuations were drastic...the new fire truck almost burned up because it was defective when shipped...the fuel truck was in terrible condition...commo was very slow...the hangars are not really adequate as long as the ends are open, because of the drenching rains driven by high winds.... Urgently recommend resurface runway with black top, patch all pot holes.

Climb schedules

Norm Nelson led the trouble shooting team to Det H that would try to solve the "Badlands" problem. He was an aeronautical engineer who had been employed by Project HQ and assigned to Burbank to keep tabs on the Skunk Works. Bob Schumacher was the Lockheed test pilot, now nearing the end of a nine-year stint on the U-2 program. Special instrumentation was added to Article 348, and it was ferried from Edwards to Det H so that Schumacher could test fly yet more climb schedules. Meanwhile, it was decided to replace the fuel controls on the two aircraft assigned to Det H.[9]

Meanwhile, the COMOR requirements for U-2 coverage of China were going unsatisfied. Project HQ rang the changes. One of the U-2Gs

that had just finished the carrier deployment (362) was ferried to Cubi Point, from where the Det G party flew it on a test mission through the Badlands without any problem. Terry Lee was sent to the Philippines, and flew the next China mission directly out of Cubi Point on 26 June. He flew over Hainan Island again and west along the mainland coast, and then the Chinese border with North Vietnam before returning to Cubi.

Back at Det H, the two Articles had their fuel controls changed during periodic inspections, and were cleared to fly again, using the new climb schedules. Terry Lee flew another mission to southern China on 2 July from Cubi. On 7 July, an ambitious attempt to confuse the Chicom air defenses with three simultaneous overflights was planned. Lee would launch out of Cubi Point in 362 for another trip around southern China. At the same time, Johnny Wang would fly a round-robin mission from Taoyuan over the two mainland provinces opposite Taiwan, to check on the Chicom order of battle facing the nationalists. The third intrusion would be a low-level mission along the coast of Kwangtung by one of the CAF's RF-101s.

The Chicoms were still moving their precious few SA-2 assets around. Knowing that Paotow was a prime target, they sent three battalions to that city in March. But the flameout problems and bad weather prevented any U-2 mission to Inner Mongolia for many months. So the PLAAF moved the 2nd battalion all the way south to the Chanchow area, in Fukien prov-

An SA-2 missile attack on a U-2 over mainland China, as seen from the target. The Chicoms only possessed a few SA-2 batteries, but they moved them around and placed them below the anticipated routes of the next overflights. (via Mike Hua)

ince, opposite Taiwan. Both U-2 missions planned for 7 July would fly over that province! Only one would return.

Nervous

The two flights were both launched at 8 am. A nervous Johnny Wang coasted-in over Shanghai and photographed ports along the Yangtze river all the way to Nanking, before turning back to the coast as if to leave the mainland. But then his route took him over Wenchow and back inland on a big loop through Fukien to cover the many airfields.

Meanwhile, Terry Lee had crossed the South China Sea from the Philippines and entered denied territory over Yangjiang. For more than two hours, he zig-zagged over targets in three southern provinces before coasting out near Swatow. His route, too, was drawn to persuade the Chicoms that he was heading home. But their early warning radars were not to be fooled. They followed Johnny Wang's re-entry over Wenchow, and all the way to his second coast-out south of Foochow just after midday. The 2nd Battalion was alerted, but Wang never came close enough to the missile site. As he set a safe course for home the Chicoms picked up the RF-101 running in low-level across the coastal islands off Swatow—and Terry Lee high overhead as his route took him back to the mainland.

Lee flew directly towards the 2nd Battalion's SA-2 site. The Chicoms used the same tactic they had against Yeh—an AA gun radar colocated with the missiles tracked the target until it was less than 20 miles away. Then they switched rapidly to the Fan Song and salvo-fired. Lee's warning system lit up, and he made one short, anxious transmission on SSB: "high light on 12." But it was too late to take evasive action. Although one missile blew up soon after launch, and another flew by the target and self-destructed, the third blew poor Terry Lee out of the sky.[10]

Dumbfounded

At the command post on Taiwan they were dumbfounded. No SA-2 site had been reported anywhere near Chanchow. Birdwatcher relayed the System 12 activation, then went silent. The COMINT station in Taiwan that intercepted the Chicom's air defense net reported a possible shoot-down. A ground radar site at the southern tip of Taiwan tracked a descending target inland from Swatow—it was obviously Lee's crippled U-2. An air and sea search was mounted as close to the mainland coast as the nationalists dared, in case the pilot had managed to get out of the stricken plane and had been blown out to sea.

But the Chicoms found Lee dead in the cockpit, seven miles west of the SAM site. That evening, Peking Radio announced that "a heroic PLAAF unit" had shot down a U-2 over eastern China. From Project HQ, OSA Director Jack Ledford cabled to Det H his "shock and distress" at the incident. The only slight consolation was that the Chicoms apparently did not realize that Lee's flight had originated in the Philippines. After the flap over the SAC U-2s flying out of Clark AB earlier in 1964, the Agency was hoping to hide the presence of a U-2 detachment at Cubi Point from the Filipino government.[11]

Once again, the Black Cat Squadron was grounded as the implications of the third shootdown were digested. In Burbank, Kelly Johnson had his own view. "Many people in Washington did not believe the aircraft was shot down, because there weren't supposed to be any SA-2s in the area. A month later, the SAC airplanes near Hanoi saw definite missile bursts within 1/4 mile of them, and again there were not supposed to be any SA-2s there.

CARBON COPIES

Between 1959 and 1974, a total of 28 pilots from the CAF completed training on the U-2. SAC had the task until 1967, when it was reassigned to the CIA's own Det G at Edwards. SAC allocated the codename CARBON COPY to the training of nationalist Chinese U-2 pilots by the 4080th wing. Inevitably, these gentlemen became known as the "Carbons" to their American hosts. Their training did not go smoothly, often because of language difficulties. But cultural misunderstanding—and maybe even downright prejudice—also played a part. "There's not enough generations between these guys and the Water Buffalo...they just can't hack it!" one exasperated IP from the SAC wing was heard to exclaim.

None of the training material was translated into Chinese. When the CAF pilots were airborne a Chinese interpreter would standby on the mission frequency, but misunderstandings occurred nevertheless. In the classrooms and on the flightline, instructors would ask the Chinese if they understood the point being made. The answer was always "yes." It took time for the Americans to realize that there was a cultural difference here: the Chinese did not like to say no, because it might represent a loss of "face." It didn't help when the 4080th would assign an IP to a Chinese student, the two would become familiar with each other's ways, and then a second instructor would have to take over halfway through the course because the first had been sent on an overseas deployment.

When 28-year old Captain Steve Sheng lost control and ejected from a U-2A during training in August 1964, the accident report concluded that he allowed the wing fuel to become unbalanced. "This pilot is highly intelligent, and eager to comply" the report noted. But language difficulties reduced his understanding, in this case of the recovery procedures, the report continued.

When Sheng destroyed a second U-2 four months later, the 4080th investigators were less forgiving. He crashed on approach to D-M as a big storm moved in. Sheng bailed out and landed painfully in a cactus patch. "He flew into a Cumulonimbus cloud during its building phase, contrary to the mission briefing," was the verdict. Sheng argued that he was only following Approach Control's guidance. He was transferred to an F-104 training course and graduated successfully. But after returning to Taiwan, he crashed his CAF Starfighter and was killed.

After Sheng's first crash, the Chinese Air Force made sure that one of its U-2 veterans accompanied the new trainees to D-M. First came Lt Col Jude Bao, who as operations officer had helped form the Black Cat Squadron in 1961. Later, Major Johnny Wang was sent, the survivor of 10 missions over the mainland.

On 22 March 1966, Captain Andy Fan Huang Ti wrote off another U-2 at D-M. He ejected on his very first flight after entering a spin at 20,000 feet. The initial accident verdict was that he used improper procedures when recovering from a practice stall. But then it was discovered that a flap actuator had malfunctioned, causing an asymmetric condition. Fan was allowed to continue his training, and spent three years as an operational U-2 pilot. After his accident, a recommendation that a two-seat training version of the U-2 be provided was forwarded to higher headquarters. Six years later, the U-2CT was finally built! – C.P.

I don't understand why they can't get it through their heads that it should not be difficult to make the SA-2 a portable missile."[12]

If the U-2 was grounded, how could the U.S. acquire high-resolution aerial reconnaissance of southern China, to track Peking's support of the communist expansion in southeast Asia? In early August this requirement became urgent after the Tonkin Gulf incident, and the U.S. airstrikes against North Vietnam that followed. Det H was alerted for a possible mission to southern China, to be flown by the U.S.-pilot-in-residence at Taoyuan. This flight was discussed at great length in the 303 Committee (the new name for the subcommittee of the National Security Council that approved or disapproved covert operations). But it was never approved.

Lightning Bug drones

Instead, the 303 Committee sanctioned the first operational deployment of the Lightning Bug drones. The SAC-operated RPVs arrived at Kadena AB in August. The GC-130 launch aircraft flew southwest from there to release the drones over the South China Sea. They flew over the mainland in a northwesterly arc towards Taiwan. The CH-3 helicopters that retrieved them in mid-air were based on the island. The drones carried the nationalists' insignia, even though the CAF had no part in the operation. In October, both the launch and recovery bases were relocated to South Vietnam.[13]

More Chinese U-2 pilots were in the pipeline. In his new post at CAF HQ, former 35th Squadron commander Colonel Lu selected the new recruits. Major Jack Chang Li Yi completed the U-2A course at D-M in August, followed by Major Pete Wang Chen Wen in September. In July, Captains Steve Sheng Shi Hi and Charlie Wu Tsai Shi entered training. But on 14 August, Sheng lost control of a U-2A over Idaho during a high-altitude navigation training flight. He made a successful ejection and was allowed to continue training. The CAF selected yet another four pilots for U-2 training; they arrived at D-M in November. On 18 December, Sheng wrote off his second U-2A on approach to D-M when he flew into a heavy thunderstorm. The horizontal stabilizer failed in a gust that exceeded the design limits. The unfortunate pilot elected to bail out this time. He was now scrubbed from the program.[14]

In September, Det H was deployed to Takhli for the first time. An ambitious plan was being discussed in Washington to fly U-2 missions all the way to Lop Nor. The suspected Chinese nuclear test site in the deserts of remote Sinkiang had always been just beyond the range of U-2 flights from Taoyuan. But the latest Corona satellite imagery revealed that preparations for a test shot there were now well advanced. The B-camera could bring back finer detail, perhaps allowing the analysts to estimate the date of the forthcoming test with greater accuracy. On 15 September, the proposed flight was discussed at two meetings between DCI McCone, Secretary of Defense McNamara, and Secretary of State Rusk. McGeorge Bundy, the National Security Advisor in the White House, was also present, and recorded: "we agreed it would be much preferable to conduct any overflight in a plane with China markings and a Chinat pilot." Later that day, President Johnson approved the idea.[15]

A Project Idealist U-2C on a test flight. Flameouts plagued the Black Cat Squadron in Taiwan during 1964, as new fuel controls failed to cope with the sudden temperature variations in the tropopause over that part of Asia (Lockheed LN 2768).

Second Thoughts

The planning continued, but McCone had second thoughts. On 5 October, the subject was discussed again in the White House. McCone now told LBJ that unless he or Secretary Rusk really needed a more accurate prediction of the Chinese test date, he could not recommend the flight. It was a deep penetration extending the U-2 to the full limit of its range, during which time no other important targets could be covered. Rusk said he was not that bothered about the test date. But he *was* worried that the U-2 mission would have to cross Burma and India, which was undesirable. The plan was dropped.[16]

While the political wheels were turning Johnny Wang mapped Thailand on training missions, while the newly-assigned Jack Chang was checked out in the J75-powered Article. To maintain "cover" at Takhli, the Det's security officers told Gimo Yang and his Chinese U-2 pilots to masquerade as Hawaiian Americans flying for Air America (an airline owned by the CIA and used for covert operations, which kept some aircraft at Takhli). But with the missions to Lop Nor canceled, Det H returned to Taoyuan in October.

Project HQ renewed its effort to clear the use of ECM pods for the Tackle operation. The Pentagon finally agreed in early October. System 13 was airlifted to Det H immediately and installed in the Articles there, replacing the slipper tanks. Now, the Black Cat Squadron might stand a better chance against those frequently-moving Chinese SA-2 missiles. The downside was the added weight and reduced fuel load, which reduced the maximum altitude and cut the endurance to seven hours.

China nuclear test

On 16 October 1964, the People's Republic of China did indeed conduct its first nuclear test. The big surprise was the analysis of fallout particles from the blast collected by a large number of sampling flights, including some by SAC U-2s. The fissile material was Uranium-235, not plutonium. How had the Chinese acquired enough of this highly-enriched material to

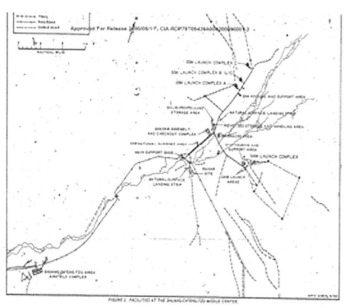

The communist regime tested all new missile developments at the Shuang Cheng Tzu range in northern China. This map of the facilities there was drawn by analysts at NPIC, from photography obtained by overflying U-2s and Corona satellites.

create the explosion? Had they stockpiled the isotope from the days of Sino-Soviet cooperation, or had the gaseous diffusion plant at Lanchow gone into top gear with the difficult process of separating the isotope from the naturally-occurring uranium ore?

On 31 October, the CIA began trying to piece together this puzzle, with the first U-2 mission over mainland China since the loss of Terry Lee in early July. It was also Jack Chang's first overflight. He took off from Takhli and flew along the Burma-Laos border before passing west of Kunming as he headed more or less straight for Lanchow and the gaseous diffusion plant. Then he turned south to pass over Xian, on a straight line taking him home to Taiwan via Wuhan and Nanchang. He landed at Taoyuan after 6 hours 40 minutes in the air. There had been only a few fighters trailing below, and no encounters with SAM sites. The reason was simple, but unknown to the U-2 mission planners. Anticipating U-2 flights over Lop Nor in the wake of the first nuclear test, the Chicoms had moved three SA-2 battalions there![17]

A week later, Johnny Wang flew over North Korea and Manchuria, photographing airfields and ports. A week after that, Jack Chang flew over southern China and landed at Takhli. The next day, 15 November, Johnny Wang was over Kwangtung. The Black Cat Squadron was back in business! Not only that, they moved into a newly-constructed hangar at Taoyuan. It was a vast improvement on the old one. The Photo Laboratory was also expanded, so that film from the U-2's main camera could be processed in Taiwan, rather than being sent to the 67th RTS in Japan, or even all the way back to the U.S.[18]

IR scanner

New infrared (IR) sensor technology now aided the task of assessing the productive capacity of China's nuclear facilities at Lanchow and Paotow. An IR scanner that could record radiation at 8 to 14 microns was designed by Texas Instruments using CIA funds. Operating at this much shorter wavelength, the scanner was nicely suited to capturing not only the peak radiation emitted by most terrestrial backgrounds, but also any hotter objects on the terrain. It was the first IR scanner developed specifically for use from high altitude.

The new scanner was adapted to the U-2's Q-bay and test-flown from Edwards during September and October 1964. The results were excellent! The major road networks and airports in the New York and Los Angeles metropolitan areas were readily identifiable by the scanner's output, which was converted onto film via a modulated light source. More significantly, the power plants and oil refineries showed up very well. The scanner was then flown at night over U.S. nuclear plants whose production levels were known. By extrapolating from this data, the results that the IR scanner might obtain over China could be predicted.[19]

The IR scanner, designated FFD-2, was airlifted to Taoyuan in November 1964. The design only provided for a few minutes of film exposure, but that would be enough to cover the two locations of greatest interest to the U.S. analysts of China's progress in nuclear weapons.

An extraordinary series of flights followed. On 22 November, Jack Chang took off after dark for the long, lonely night journey across mainland China to the Paotow nuclear plant. A similar mission to Lanchow was planned for the following night, weather permitting. At the preflight briefing, Chang was told to expect continuous tracking by the Chicom air defenses, and that there were eight known SA-2 sites not far from his flight path. Now that the U-2 was weighed down with System 13 ECM pods,

The two deployments of CIA U-2s to India in 1964 were very politically sensitive and hush-hush. At the political level, there were tortuous negotiations before they were approved. At the operating level, there were many tensions between the deployed Americans, seeking to preserve maximum security, and their Indian hosts. Here is an extract from the deployment commander's cables, and his report to Project HQ, written after the second deployment in December 1964:

Coordination with the Indians is considerably more exacting than we have ever experienced before. Initially, the insistence that they be allowed to view the route prior to the mission created a problem, and resulted in at least half a dozen meetings. Ultimately, our perseverance won out....The entry and exit points and times, and a clear definition of the target area, was passed at the time we were alerted for the mission. The flight tracks were not passed...until the aircraft was safely back. These people are very sensitive...and are suspicious by nature until they gain confidence and are being given fair treatment. The coordination at the local level must be handled with the utmost care.

The CIA had high hopes of staging more U-2 deployments to Charbatia in 1965, because it was the best possible location to launch missions over the wild and remote Takla Makan desert in China's Sinkiang province. Here lay the Lop Nor nuclear test site, and the downrange impact sites for missiles launched from the Sheng Cheng Tsu test site. But there were no further deployments. According to rumors circulating within the Idealist project, the Indians held out for the supply of 50 F-104s as the price for renewed U-2 landing rights. However, the Indians did permit the CIA to install a remotely-operated listening device on a Himalayan summit in 1965 that could pick up signals from the Chinese test sites.

mission planners had little alternative but to draw a more-or-less direct route to the target and back. Major Chang was over Wuhan—nearly half-way there—when he had to abort because of electrical problems that would affect the IR scanner's operation. The next night Johnny Wang took off for Lanchow, but had to abort before entering denied territory when his System 13 failed the routine pre-penetration self-test.[20]

The Chicoms had tracked Chang's flight, and seen it turn around at Wuhan. Now they knew that the U-2 had some type of night vision. Somehow, they guessed (or knew) that the nuclear plants were the target. The 2nd Battalion, which had shot down all three CAF U-2s to date, was moved yet again—to Lanchow.[21]

Missiles roaring up

Techreps from Lockheed, Sanders, and Texas Instruments fixed the malfunctions. Johnny Wang took off from Taoyuan at 2am on 26 November. The target: Lanchow again. After more than three hours flying across four provinces he was approaching the city. With just 30 miles to go, Wang's SAM warner came alive, showing a missile site almost directly ahead. Simultaneously, System 13 began to jam a Fan Song radar. As briefed, Wang began a descending turn to evade the threat. Only seconds into the turn, Wang saw the first of three SA-2 missiles roaring upwards, with its sustainer motor still burning.

On the ground, the missile operators in their cabin at the center of the SA-2 site had salvo-fired three missiles, as usual. But then they saw the steering dot on their radarscope suddenly distort in shape. Without the correct guidance signals, the missiles self-destructed. Temporarily blinded by the light of the explosions, Wang completed his turn. He had escaped! When his night vision returned, Wang re-engaged the autopilot and set course for Taoyuan. He landed at dawn after a fruitless, 6 hour 40 minutes in the air.[22]

Both sides of this epic struggle assessed the situation. The good news on the U.S. side was, System 13 worked! The bad news was another U-2

The locations prepared for most SA-2 batteries could be spotted, even on small-scale overhead photography, by the distinctive "footprint," as in this U-2 imagery of a site in Cuba. But the PLAAF modified the site plan for their missile sites, and camouflaged the deployments. Every time a U-2 was shot down over the mainland, an inquest was held over why the attacking site had not been previously identified (NARA 167785).

had been routed too close to an SA-2 site. The what-went-wrong analysis suffered from the lack of SIGINT from the U-2's own onboard systems. All of System 3 and half of System 6 had been removed to save weight. The S-band pre-amps and recorder were quickly re-installed. In Washington, there was yet another debate about NPIC's ability to locate and report SA-2 sites. From the available Corona imagery, the PIs had assessed that the known site at Lanchow was unoccupied. But a new Corona mission, launched the day after Johnny Wang's aborted mission, revealed the new site established by the 2nd Battalion so recently.[23]

As for the Chicom air defense troops, they realized that the U-2 had been equipped with some sort of jamming system, and began thinking how to counter it.[24]

U.S. intelligence did not know how many SA-2 missile systems China possessed, and whether the Soviets were still supplying them, despite the political chill between Moscow and Peking. It now seemed obvious that the number of units was considerably smaller than the number of sites. The Chinese air defense troops were playing a shell game! The big question was, had the Chinese learned to reverse-engineer the system, and started to produce it themselves? There was no firm photographic evidence to support this...yet.[25]

There were no known SA-2 sites in northeast China. On 9 December Pete Wang flew his first operational mission, a successful daylight sortie over the Yellow Sea, into Manchuria, and down the North Korean border and western coastline.

Back to India
Neither were there any known SA-2 sites in Tibet, and reconnaissance of the Sino-Indian border was still a regular requirement. The Indians gave permission for a second U-2 deployment to Charbatia. Since the first excursion to there six months earlier the airbase had been improved, using CIA funds. The runway had been resurfaced, the apron extended, and the hangar improved. As part of the support equipment, a water purification plant was airlifted in!

In early December, Article 359 was ferried to Charbatia from Taoyuan. Three missions were flown by pilots from Det G in a five-day period from 16-20 December, covering most of India's long border with Tibet, from the Karakorums in the far west to the NEFA area, which adjoined Assam in the east. The terrain was as wild as ever. "Eyeball" navigation through the driftsight was not an easy proposition for the pilots Marty Knutson, Tom McMurtry, and Dan Schmarr, due to the varying snowfall and river courses. Still, the weather was excellent, and good coverage was obtained. The deployment was over by Christmas.[26]

Paotow and Lanchow
Project HQ came up with a new plan to get the much-desired infrared imagery of Paotow and Lanchow. Both could be overflown on the same mission, if the launch was made from Korea. On 19 December, Det H sent a staging crew and two of the three Chinese pilots to Kunsan AB. The U-2 followed after dark, ferried in by an American pilot who flew all the way from Taoyuan at 40,000 feet, so that if the Chicoms tracked the flight, it would not be identified as a high-flyer.

Just before midnight, Johnny Wang took off into the dark night. But after only 20 minutes, he had to abort the mission when System 13 failed its self-test again. Wang set course for Taoyuan via the offshore route, while the support crew packed up and reboarded their C-130 to follow him home.[27]

ESTIMATING CHINA'S NUCLEAR WEAPONS
...was a tough call. Three months after China's first nuclear test, the latest U.S. Intelligence Estimate was issued. Per the usual practice, no explicit reference was made to the contribution to the estimate that was made by the U-2 flights over the mainland. But it was substantial, as these extracts suggest:

There is a large facility on the Yellow River near Lanchou. We have good quality photography obtained over several years, but there are major limitations on what can be learned from such photography. The facility has elaborate physical security protection, including anti-aircraft defenses...an analysis of the buildings, physical layout, and power available at Lanchou suggests that the Chinese could have both gaseous diffusion and electromagnetic equipment there.

There is a small air-cooled reactor located at Paotow that we believe is now producing plutonium. Details of this reactor's progress, as seen in photography, indicate that it probably began production in late 1963 or early 1964....

We believe the Chinese Communists are developing a medium-range ballistic missile. The Shuang Cheng Tzu missile test range is designed to permit the testing of surface-to-surface missiles up to a range of about 1,000 nautical miles...We believe that operations at the range began in 1961 with some kind of SSM tests, and that there were further firings in 1962, 1963, and 1964.

BAD NEWS IN THE COMMAND POST
Every U-2 overflight of mainland China was "followed" to some extent from the command post on Taiwan. In the first two years, there were only the COMINT intercepts of the Chicom air defense system to go on. These were provided by the nationalist's listening post at Ta-Hsi. Birdwatcher, the secure and stealthy telemetry system which relayed critical data direct from the U-2 on HF, came later—if it worked. A Commo technician recalled the night when Jack Chang was shot down:

At 6.30 that Sunday evening Jack took off. His radio callsign was "Bar Girl." At 8pm his scheduled Birdwatcher transmission could barely be heard. The Communications Officer had selected two frequencies for the mission based on distance and time of day. Jack should have been on the second of these frequencies by now, but the manager had made a last-minute decision—based on recent antenna tuner difficulties—to keep him on one frequency for the whole flight. Jack penetrated the mainland just down the coast from Tsingtao, but the frequency was only good for about 500 miles at that time of night.

At 9.20pm the Chicoms canceled their air defense alert. We learned of this almost immediately from Chinese nationalist intelligence sources. Listening posts in Seoul and Okinawa maintained a tape recorded watch on Jack's radio frequency during the mission. We put in long hours listening to the tapes, searching for an explanation, longing for some further contact with Jack. But we learned nothing. Only (*Black Cat squadron commander*) Gimo Yang's anxious pleas punctuated the static in our headsets as we heard him calling in vain: "Bar Girl, A switch. Bar Girl, A switch."

After Jack Chiang was shot down in January 1965, the Chicoms put on a big display in Peking of the four U-2s that they had bagged to date (Lockheed PR1812).

The weather did not permit another try for the night mission until early January. Meanwhile, on 30 December Jack Chang flew a daylight mission to the Szechwan Basin, the area east of Chungking on the Yangtze River, where analysts had identified four suspect sites where China might have located another nuclear reactor. The airframe and engine plants at Chengtu were also overflown. It was another near-maximum endurance flight, and for the brave Chinese pilots the tensions were increasing all the time. Although Chang was briefed that there were no SAM sites along his route, another worry developed during the mission. He found the high-altitude winds were greater than forecast, and diverted at one enroute point to save fuel. He landed at Taoyuan after 6 hours 50 minutes with 93 gallons remaining.[28]

On the evening of 8 January, Det H tried again for Lanchow. It was the fourth time lucky. Johnny Wang launched from Taoyuan and got the required coverage, despite overshooting a crucial turn point. He recognized the lights of the city to one side and corrected in time to fly a good course over the gaseous diffusion plant. This was critical to the success of the mission; the FFD-2 scanner had a much narrower scan width than the B-camera. (When the "take" was analyzed back in the U.S., it proved that the Lanchow gaseous diffusion plant was indeed operational, and there-fore the probable source of the U-235 used in China's first nuclear test). The mission was continuously tracked by the Chicoms, but their two SA-2 sites at Lanchow were not currently occupied.[29]

Two days later, with the weather still clear in northern China, Project HQ decided to go for Paotow; it was Jack Chang's turn. Before the waypoints for the overflight were transmitted to the Det, Project HQ asked NPIC to check previous photography for any SAM sites within 50 miles of the planned route. There were none, came the reply.[30]

Fireball

Chang took off from Taoyuan at 6pm, flew across the Yellow Sea, and coasted-in near Tsingtao at 65,000 feet. The route was straight, but it kept him south of the known SA-2 sites around Peking. Everything was going smoothly, except that unknown to the pilot, transmissions from his Birdwatcher system were not reaching the command post. After three hours flying Chang rose to 68,000 feet as he approached Paotow. Suddenly and without warning, a fireball erupted around the U-2. Chang felt a sharp pain in his right shoulder, but managed to pull his D-ring, and the ejection seat fired.[31]

Far below him, the PLAAF's 1st Battalion was reporting its first kill. The unit had moved to Paotow in mid-October, and had been working with China's Electronic Research Center to counter the System 13's jamming of the SA-2 Fan Song guidance radar. A solution had been devised: by installing another, more powerful radar transmitter at the SA-2 site, which used a different Pulse Repetition Frequency (PRF), the Fan Song's signal would be masked from detection by the U-2. The scheme worked! Neither System 12 nor System 13 was activated. Poor Jack Chang had no warning of attack until a few seconds before the explosion. The battalion fired three missiles at 21 miles range: two of them hit and crippled the target.[32]

Chang was unconscious as he plummeted earthwards in the ejection seat. But for once, the escape system worked as advertised. He came to as the seat separated, and his parachute opened at 15,000 feet. It was a dark night, and the pilot could not see the ground approaching. He hit hard, broke one ankle, and sprained another. His shoulder had been pierced by fragments from the missiles. The temperature was way below zero, and he could not move. Trying to keep warm, he wrapped himself in the para-chute. He crawled in the snow towards the nearest sign of life. The stricken pilot was eventually found after daybreak by local villagers and turned over to a military search party.[33]

Radio Peking claimed another victory for "Mao Tse Tung Thought." Again, the Chicoms gave no detail on the shootdown, nor of the pilot's fate. Three months later, though, a big display was mounted at the People's Revolution Museum in Peking. It consisted of the wreckage from all four U-2s shot down over the mainland plus, for good measure, three Lightning Bug drones bagged over southern China by AA guns.

Another loss. Another enquiry in Washington. NPIC rechecked the Corona imagery. They found not one, but two sites around Paotow. The U-2's route flew between them, but within lethal distance of both (unknown to U.S. intelligence, of course, only one site was occupied).

OSA Director Jack Ledford tried to keep a sense of proportion. In a long cable to Det H commander Lt Col Walt Meyler he wrote:

"The two sites were difficult to identify because of the scale of coverage, and they did not follow the traditional signature. The job of search and identification with the KH (*eg Keyhole satellite*) systems over a country as large as mainland China is a difficult one. The unfortunate circumstance of not having found these key installations is painfully evident to everyone."

Close-ups of U-2C wreckage on display in Peking. Most of the pieces assembled here are from Article 358, the aircraft shot down on 10 January 1965 (S. Wright/R. Waxman).

Declining Asset

By early 1965 more than half of the U-2 fleet had been lost. Six of them had been shot down. Another 24 had been destroyed in accidents. Kelly Johnson explored the options for a new production run in Washington. And yet, although the U-2 was still in demand over China, Cuba, and Vietnam, the purse-holders were unwilling to commit. After all, a huge amount of money was being spent on the A-12 Oxcart and its new Air Force sister, the SR-71 Blackbird. And these Mach 3 spyplanes had been conceived as a replacement for the U-2!

But something had to be done to keep the remaining U-2s viable over denied territory. In 1963, OSA began discussions with three contractors on a new electronics package to replace the piecemeal additions of the past few years. For a while, the plan was to carry the new ELINT and ECM gear in a detachable ventral fairing located aft of the main landing gear and close to the cg. That idea was dropped in favor of extending and enlarging the fairing on top of the fuselage that housed the ARS receiver and the SSB radio tuner. The new upper fairing extended all the way to the tail and was nicknamed the "canoe." During 1964 ATI, Sanders, and HRB Singer received "black" contracts for upgraded electronic systems that would provide enhanced warning and jamming of threats to the U-2, and yet fit neatly in the available fuselage space.[1]

The first upgraded aircraft (Article 385) was flying by early 1965. System 9B from ATI provided all-aspect jamming of fighter radars for the first time, and with much greater power. It was integrated with the company's System 12B, an improved warning of Fan Song radar activity. A larger (3-inch) scope was provided on the upper right instrument panel, showing the direction of SAM threats as a solid green line, and fighter threats as a dotted line. The five previous warning lights already associated with Systems 9 and 12 were retained in a vertical line to the left of the scope. So was the aural warning fed through the pilot's headset.

But now there was also a sixth, red light above the threat scope, labeled "OS." This was the indicator of a very sensitive new warning receiver that was conceived by a team in the Agency's Office of ELINT, led by Alex Carson. It was designed to detect the command guidance transmitter of the SA-2 system. Just before the missiles were launched, this L-band transmitter was operated into what was known as "dummy load" as a self-test. A small, saucer-shaped antenna on the U-2's lower Q-bay hatch could pick up the faint leakage of radiation out of dummy load, at an advertised range of up to 90 miles! If that happened, the red light above the threat scope in the U-2 cockpit would illuminate steadily. If the light then began blinking, it meant that the detected signal strength had increased, because the transmitter had been switched from dummy load to the SA-2 guidance antenna, eg. the missiles were being launched.. At the same time, a "beep-beep" warning was transmitted through the pilot's headset.

Oscar Sierra

Officially, "OS" stood for Oscar Sierra. Unofficially, it stood for "Oh Shit!" For if that red light came on, it signified to the U-2 pilot that he was under attack, and should start taking evasive action. That was easier said than done in a U-2 cruising at high altitude, close to "coffin corner." The pilot had to control his airspeed carefully as he banked the U-2 into a maximum 30-degree turn. If he maintained the turn through 180 degrees he would lose several thousand feet of altitude. But the maneuver was designed to complicate the intercept equation for the SA-2 guidance computer.

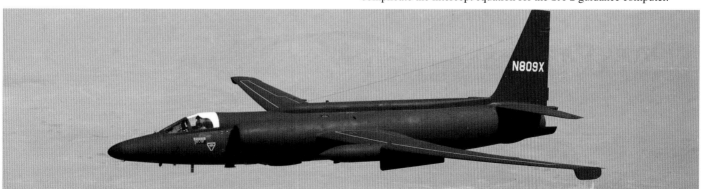

A major upgrade to the defensive systems on the U-2 in 1964-65 resulted in the long dorsal "canoe" above the fuselage. This contained parts of System 9B and 12B, designed to counter air-to-air and surface-to-air threats, respectively. (Lockheed U2-91-012-96)

The beauty of Oscar Sierra was that, although it was a last-minute warning, it was unequivocal. Also, since the guidance transmitter operated at a different frequency to the Fan Song acquisition radar, it was a counter to the countermeasures that the Chicoms had so cleverly implemented against the U-2 penetrations from Taiwan.

The last element of the defensive upgrade was System 13A, a lighter and smaller redesign by Sanders of the automatic, deception ECM device that had already thwarted at least one SA-2 attack on the U-2. The big disadvantage of the original Systems 13/14/15 were that they were housed in pods that replaced the slipper (fuel) tanks on the wings. Part of the space in the pods was taken up by an explosive charge that could destroy this highly sensitive technology if the U-2 was about to fall into enemy hands. The new version eventually combined most of the frequency coverage from the previous Systems 13/14/15, yet was repackaged to mostly fit in a new pressurised box that was added to the fuselage, just forward of the U-2's tail wheel. The technology was still highly sensitive, but was now protected by small incendiary panels that were mounted against the circuit boards. These would destroy the boards, but not the aircraft.

The H-camera
Another new U-2 camera system was test-flown at Edwards in the first half of 1965, sponsored this time by the USAF. The HR-329, otherwise known as the "H-camera," was designed by Hycon. It was a 66-inch folding focal length system designed primarily to take long-range oblique frames of spot targets, on a 4.5-inch square negative. It could provide coverage up to 50 nautical miles to the side of the U-2's flight path, at the maximum oblique angle of 70 degrees. But the big telescope of the "H" needed careful pointing by the pilot, who used the driftsight to identify the preplanned targets. It was also very heavy (660 lbs) and very temperamental.

Like the Delta II camera, the "H" was too large to fit in the Q-bay, until a larger hatch that extended below the fuselage was provided. OSA was not keen on the "H," despite its promise of six-inch resolution. The Agency was having its own problems with the weight and drag penalty of the Delta II, although the 12-inch resolution and panoramic coverage was excellent. In 1965, Itek rebuilt the four Delta II cameras into the Delta III configuration. This provided a light-tight casing (previously, the *hatch* had to be light-tight), and reduced both weight and size, so that a flush-fitting hatch could be used.[2]

A new tracker camera was also flight tested towards the end of 1965. It was a 35mm system produced by Perkin Elmer, which weighed a lot less than the old 70mm tracker that PE had provided since the very start of the

Another view of the upgraded aircraft. This shows the large slab antenna fairing for ELINT System 6; the small fairing under the tail containing the ECM System 13A, and the shield to the tailpipe, extended from 90 to 150 degrees (Lockheed U2-91-012-13).

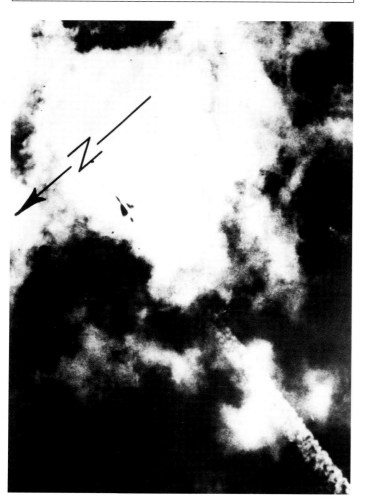

MiG-21s began to challenge the U-2 flights over China and North Vietnam during 1965. This one was captured on a frame of B-camera photography (via Bob Spencer).

U-2 program. It went into service in 1966. A lighter-weight version of the faithful Hycon HR-73 B-camera was also introduced.

The USAF was persevering with the QRC-192 ELINT system, with its advanced direction-finding (DF) techniques. SAC wanted to fly it at the same time as the cameras. Now that the System 14 and 15 ECM pods were cleared for use on operational missions, elements of the 192 system were relocated to the pods. Meanwhile, the CIA Office of ELINT (OEL) was developing a rival system for the Agency U-2s. System 17 was a wide-frequency coverage SIGINT system covering frequencies all the way from VHF to X-band, with antennas in the wingtips and horizontal tails for DF. Flight tests began in October 1965.

The list of improvements extended to the navigation system. For 10 years, U-2 pilots had been obliged to rely on a combination of dead reckoning; tuning in on unreliable radio stations with the ADF, star shots with the sextant; and peering through the driftsight. Now, they were finally provided with a navigation computer (ASN-66) and a Doppler radar (APN-153). There was also a new HF radio and an IFF transponder. These were tested in late 1965 and introduced during 1966.

China flights resume

The first Article with the upgraded EW systems was ferried to Det H in early April 1965. Even before it arrived, the Black Cat Squadron had resumed overflights of mainland China, following the loss of Jack Chang on the night mission in January. As the Vietnam War escalated, the need to know whether China was planning to intervene was crucial. The U.S. did not want a repeat of the surprise in 1950, when the PLAAF swarmed into Korea to push back the advancing UN troops.

In February and March 1965 the Chinese Air Force pilots flew five missions over southwest China, monitoring troop movements and Chinese logistical support for the Ho Chi Minh regime in Hanoi. Det G sent a support crew to Takhli, so that these flights could recover into the Thai base, or be launched from there, with a recovery back at Taoyuan.[3]

The most worrying intelligence brought back from these missions was that China had reinforced its fighter force at airfields along the border with North Vietnam. The new arrivals included some Soviet-supplied MiG-21s, capable of reaching 60,000 feet. They had occasionally been captured on film at airfields further north by overflying U-2s. But now the PLAAF had apparently spread its limited fleet of Fishbeds to six airbases in the south.

On 14 March, Captain Charlie Wu was halfway between Kunming and Mengtsu when he was attacked by one of the MiG-21s. He saw two black puffs of smoke ahead of him, and then a delta-winged interceptor suddenly zoomed up from beneath his right wing, less than 300 feet away. It dropped below the nose of Wu's U-2 just as quickly. Apparently, the MiG-21 had zoom-climbed to his altitude and fired a couple of missiles that failed to home, and detonated instead at the end of their runs. When the camera film was interpreted, it showed the silver MiG-21 below the U-2. An earlier frame showed possibly the same aircraft taking off from Kunming airfield as Wu passed overhead.[4]

Scary

"Things are getting very scary," noted Kelly Johnson when he heard about this intercept. The ROC side of the joint U-2 operation on Taiwan was reluctant to fly further missions over the area until MiG-avoiding tactics were refined. But Johnny Wang was sent over Hainan Island three days later. There was some thought given to providing him with an F-4 fighter escort from a U.S. Navy carrier located south of the island. Det H stood down again during April. The Black Cat Squadron commander, Gimo Yang, traveled to the U.S. with General Yang Shao Lien, who now headed the Razor project in CAF headquarters. They discussed tactics, and were briefed on the new EW systems.[5]

In early May 1965, another series of U-2 intercept trials was conducted over Edwards AFB. The Air Defense Command flew century-series fighters against a U-2, to see if further refinements to tactics were required. The U-2's System 9B was no protection against IR-guided missiles. And the sharp turn away from danger that was recommended against an SA-2 threat was not necessarily a good move against an intercepting fighter, since the U-2 lost altitude in the turn. In the end, it was again decided that the MiG-21 had little or no maneuverability above 65,000 feet. To shoot down a U-2, the Chicoms would have to demonstrate superb GCI control, coupled with lots of luck. But they were working on it. It seemed that they were vectoring one interceptor to fly below the U-2 on the same course, at contrail level. Then a second interceptor would zoom-climb through the contrail in the hope of bringing guns or missiles to bear.[6]

So a few added precautions were taken. The radius of the "sugar scoop" extension beneath the U-2's tailpipe was extended to 150 degrees, so that the hot exhaust would be better shielded from below. Pilots were briefed that when a fighter intercept was suspected, they should maintain altitude and make a small alteration of course. This would probably be sufficient to foil the floundering MiGs.

Black Velvet

In October 1965 another round of experimentation in U-2 camouflage took place. It resulted in the adoption of the "Black Velvet" paint scheme. This very matt black coating, devised by the Pittsburgh Paint and Glass Co., soaked up the light and provided the best reduction yet in visual signature. It also supposedly made a small contribution towards reducing the aircraft's radar return. Microscopic particles of ferrous material weakened the electromagnetic currents on the aircraft's skin, and hence helped to suppress sidelobes.

To accompany "Black Velvet," the cockpit sunshade was repainted from white to black, the speedbrake and landing gear wells from silver to black, and the canopy was treated to reduce its reflective qualities. Heeding the lessons from aerial combat in earlier conflicts, the Skunk Works did all it could to reduce the possibility of a stray burst of reflected sunlight reaching a pair of unfriendly airborne eyes. This effort complemented precautions that were already employed by the Agency's U-2 operation. It had, for instance, been the practice for some years to pull the circuit-breaker from the aircraft's top and bottom anti-collision beacons before an overflight mission, and to stick masking tape over the lenses so that they could not serve as a reflector.

The Black Cat Squadron resumed operations on 14 May, and flew over China 20 more times in 1965 without a serious incident. But there were no more long missions to the deep northwest—and no more night missions with the IR scanner. This was only partially due to the SA-2 threat. The other main reason was that the U.S. now had a second satellite reconnaissance system capable of taking a closer look at China's nuclear weapons development sites than Corona. The Kodak strip camera in the KH-7 Gambit system achieved 2-4 foot resolution. While that was not as good as the B or Delta cameras in the U-2, it was good enough. That is, when weather conditions were favorable.

As a further measure to prevent interception by fighters, all operational U-2s received a very dark matt black paint scheme nicknamed "Black Velvet" in 1965-66 (via Jay Miller).

Nearly all the overflights conducted by Det H in 1965 were of the three southern provinces (Kwangsi, Kwangtung, and Yunnan) closest to Vietnam. The Chinese were boosting their fighter numbers and building new airfields to defend the southern border. The airfields also served as a refuge for Hanoi's newly-supplied jet fighters, where training, repair, and maintenance took place. Hainan Island was another target for U-2 reconnaissance, because of the threat that its air defense facilities posed to U.S. Seventh Fleet warships operating against North Vietnam. As the U.S. air war against North Vietnam escalated, the U-2 missions were stepped up.[7]

ROC grew restive

The ROC side grew restive, as the U.S. made the protection of its own forces in Vietnam the number one priority for the joint Tackle/Razor project. The nationalist regime was more interested in the Chicom military disposition conditions closer to home, across the Taiwan Straits. In May 1965 President Chiang Kai-Shek (CKS) took a personal interest in Det H mission planning, and Project HQ felt obliged to make an overflight of the Fukien coast, opposite Taiwan, the number one priority. This was flown in

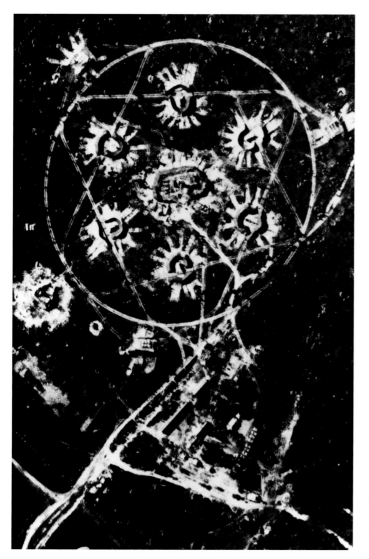

In 1965, North Vietnam rapidly fielded SA-2 missiles supplied by the Soviet Union. By the end of the year, the SAM rings were so extensive that Hanoi and Haiphong were becoming "no-go areas" for the U-2.

late May by Charlie Wu. Three similar missions were flown later in the year.

The Black Cat Squadron mounted three other overflights of mainland China during 1965. One was a five-hour sortie in late August over Kiangsi and Chekiang provinces, coasting out at Hangchow. There was also a mission to the coastal cities of Shanghai and Tsingtao, and one flight over North Korea.[8]

On 25 August 1965 Johnny Wang flew a circuit around Hainan Island to complete his tenth overflight. Because of the obvious dangers, and the four tragic losses already, the CAF now decreed that 10 would be the maximum number of operational missions that a U-2 pilot should perform. By the time Wang "graduated," however, three new pilots had joined the Black Cat Squadron. Lt Col Terry Liu Jai Chung, Major Mickey Yu Ching Chang, and Lt "Spike" Chuang Jen Liang all completed their training at D-M without major incident.

But one of their predecessors, Major Pete Wang, never got the chance to "graduate." He was killed on 22 October 1965 when he lost control during a high altitude training flight off Taiwan's northern coast. Neither pilot nor Article was recovered. Once again a misbehaving autopilot was suspected, especially pitch oscillations. After a Det G U-2 flying from Edwards experienced a sharp wing roll-off at altitude, Project HQ restricted its Articles to training flights that did not use the autopilot while a fix was investigated.[9]

The stand-down at Det H continued into 1966 for political reasons. The Johnson Administration was now deeply mired in the Vietnam conflict, with thousands of U.S. troops committed and major battles occurring. The President called a Christmas halt to the Rolling Thunder bombing campaign in the North. SecDef McNamara also requested a halt to U-2 missions over China. But the Taiwan government was told that the renewed stand-down was due to bad weather over southern China.[10]

U-2s over North Vietnam

While the Agency's Chinese-flown U-2s operated mainly on the Chinese side of the border, SAC's U-2s flew over North Vietnam itself. The mission codename changed from Lucky Dragon to Trojan Horse, but in the first half of 1965 the routine was much the same. With two or (occasionally) three aircraft assigned, and four TDY pilots, OL-20 aimed to launch an average of one U-2 mission per day. Below them now were U.S. fighter-bombers; the Rolling Thunder air campaign began in earnest in early March.

OL-20 also operated the Lightning Bug reconnaissance RPVs, with the DC-130s flying out of Bien Hoa to launch their "chicks" over the South China Sea, and the drone recovery choppers flying out of Da Nang. The operation was codenamed Blue Springs, and in the first half of 1965 it was still focused on southern China.

As well as OL-20, the 4080th wing at D-M continued to support OL-19 at Barksdale, and the missions over Cuba codenamed Golden Tree. But the number of U-2s available was declining all the time. In June 1965, the Agency raided SAC's U-2 fleet for replacement Articles yet again. The last two "hard-nosed" aircraft from the now-abandoned High Altitude Sampling program (HASP) were chosen (66714 and 66716). This left SAC with just 11 aircraft—and half of those were undergoing modification by Lockheed.

China and the Soviet Union both responded to the U.S. bombing of North Vietnam by stepping up their military assistance to Hanoi. On 1 May 1965 the first SA-2 regiment was formed, and the USSR provided an accelerated training program. Although U.S. intelligence identified a single SAM site at Hanoi on overhead photography as early as April 1965, frequent cloud cover meant that it was hard to monitor further developments. By early July there were four sites identified around Hanoi. But it was not until 24 July 1965 that a SAC U-2 mission photographed any of them. By then they were already operational, thanks to Soviet personnel that helped man the SA-2 system until the North Vietnamese were fully trained.

On the same day, the USAF lost its first F-4 in combat to the Soviet-supplied SAM. During that night the North Vietnamese moved the battalion to another site. Two days later they shot down another fighter, and a Lightning Bug drone. From then on the North Vietnamese SAM force expanded rapidly. And just like the Chinese, they played the shell game with their missile sites, building many and moving the hardware between them overnight.[11]

The viability of the U-2 over North Vietnam had to be reassessed. Missions to the Hanoi/Haiphong area continued, and were routed around the known SAM sites. But the Communists learned to camouflage their deployments. They also developed dummy missiles and decoy sites. In an attempt to counter the camouflage, and generally to improve the interpretability of the B-camera photography over the jungle-covered areas of Indo-China, color film was trialed.

The Chicom air defense net was very efficient, and invariably detected the U-2s from Taiwan whenever they overflew. They also cleverly adapted technology that they received from abroad, such as this SCR-270 antenna with four extra elements (Historical Electronics Museum).

Lethal envelope

SAC sent the H-camera to OL-20 in August 1965. In theory, it offered a means for the U-2 to get imagery of areas protected by an SA-2 site, because it could image obliquely at ranges beyond the lethal envelope of the missiles. But it was a difficult and temperamental sensor to introduce, especially to a tropical climate and an airbase now operating under wartime conditions.

The drones were a low-risk means of getting continued photo coverage of North Vietnam, although the resolution of their cameras did not match that of the U-2. At the SAC Reconnaissance Center, Col Ellsworth Powell had long been an enthusiast for the unmanned solution. But his was a rare voice amongst the pilot-oriented SAC hierarchy. Nonetheless, the frequency of Lightning Bug flights over the North was increased; a second

FIGHTERS ESCORTING U-2s

In an attempt to protect Trojan Horse missions over North Vietnam from fighter intercepts, PACAF provided fighter escorts, as recalled by U-2 pilot Ward Graham:

Those who covered our missions by radar noticed that the MiGs were vectored so as to start their dynamic zoom just after we rolled out on a new heading, and would be wings level for several minutes. To counter this threat, the 555th TFS "Triple Nickel" was tasked to provide air "cover"—from several thousands of feet below! We made contact with our fighters on a discrete frequency. The EC-121 was to call out the location of the MiGs by a specially concocted grid reference given to us and the F-4 crews. If we were attacked, the F-4s were supposed to intercept the MiGs before they released missiles at us. We enjoyed the company of the Triple Nickel crews on a normally very lonely mission.

U-2s ESCORTING DRONES

There may have been rivalry between the U-2 and RPV operations at OL-20, but at least by having them operated by the same outfit there was easier coordination. Major John Dale was a C-130 pilot and Lightning Bug specialist in Vietnam. He recalls:

I took off out of Bien Hoa with a Ryan 147G model fitted with a new contrail suppression kit. I had a U-2 on my wing that followed the drone during climb and reported on the Nocon system's effectiveness through a code that had me asking if we were "smoking." We were trying to keep the test covert. It did not work very well. We found that the extra weight of the system kept the drone down in the contrail area. Without the extra weight it climbed high enough to be out of the conning level! The U-2 pilot also had a tough time staying with the drone due to the difference in airspeeds at altitude.

U-2s HELPING DRONES

When the Ryan 147G model came along, with its ELINT-gathering capability, a joint mission was set up with one of the Agency's U-2s flying out of Det H, on Taiwan. It was part of Operation United Effort, to get the proximity fusing data for the SA-2 missile. The target was the SAM site at Kuang Chow (Canton), and the plan was for the U-2 (flown by a Chinese pilot) to take off from Taoyuan at night, and simulate a penetration mission in order to alert the Chicom air defense system. Then the drone would sneak in as a substitute, and draw the SAM unit's fire. Before meeting a fiery end, the drone would relay the fusing data to an RB-47H flying offshore.

In the small hours of 12 January 1967 the U-2 took off from Taiwan. But the drone failed its airborne mating check with its carrier aircraft (a DC-130). The operation was postponed for 48 hours. During that time the U.S. State Department and the nationalist government on Taiwan got wind of the operation. One or both of them got it called off. – C.P.

launch area from the DC-130s was established over Laos. More and better RPVs were ordered from the Ryan company. Powell pushed for a low-altitude drone capability to fly under the tropical weather, as well as the SA-2 envelope. It was introduced in October 1965.[12]

That same month, Captain Ed Purdue was flying over Haiphong Harbor when an SA-2 flew by his left wing. He was just rolling into a right turn. Otherwise, he reckoned, the missile would have nailed him. The SAC U-2s now deployed to Bien Hoa were all equipped with the Sanders ECM pods, as well as the System 12 SAM warner. But they had not alerted Purdue to any danger.[13]

The SAM rings were fast-expanding. By the end of 1965 North Vietnam had already fired 180 SA-2s, and shot down 11 U.S. warplanes. In an attempt to keep the U-2 viable over the North, the maximum length of flight lines and the minimum degrees for turns were specified within the SAC Ops Order for various hostile areas. SAM sites were to be avoided, of course. So were contrails—and these were the cause of many aborted missions. Gradually, U-2 missions were confined to the northwestern portion of North Vietnam, plus Laos and Cambodia, all of which remained unprotected by SAMs.

U-2Cs for SAC

SAC finally realized it needed the extra altitude of the J75 version as an extra margin of safety against the SAMs, and to eliminate the tell-tale contrails that the U-2As were leaving on every mission. The Skunk Works began converting the 11 aircraft remaining in the SAC fleet, starting in October 1965. During the conversion to U-2C, the SAC aircraft also received the dorsal canoe and the upgraded EW Systems 9B/12B/13A. The conversion program left SAC seriously short of aircraft. To compensate, two of the Agency's U-2G models were sent to OL-20 in early 1966, until the first of SAC's own U-2Cs became available in April. OSA also lent SAC one of its high-resolution Delta III cameras for use over Vietnam.[14]

The drones also did ELINT. The signals that they picked up could be relayed to an RB-47H orbiting in the Gulf of Tonkin. To capture "live" signals from an SA-2 launch, a traveling wave tube was added to some of the ELINT drones to augment their radar return and make them look like U-2s. They were then flown over the SAM sites in North Vietnam as "bait." The operation was codenamed United Effort, and after some initial failures, in February 1966 it succeeded in capturing the proximity fusing data for the SA-2. This was vital in designing further ECM to protect U.S. fighters, bombers, and reconnaissance aircraft like the U-2.[15]

On 6 February 1966, the North Vietnamese unequivocally confirmed that their new MiG-21s were operational—a pair of them tried to intercept a SAC U-2. The pilot of the Dragon Lady managed to evade the attack.

Henceforth, fighter escorts were provided for the Trojan Horse missions heading north. At preflight intelligence briefings, U-2 pilots were told that North Vietnam had dedicated a small number of MiG-21s to shoot down the high-flyers. The pilots might be Russian. The trouble was, the F-4 escorts usually got within firing range of the MiGs *after* they had tried to intercept the U-2![16]

The drones were also having problems. In 24 high-altitude missions 16 of them were lost, either to MiGs and SAMs or to technical malfunctions. To improve the survival rate OL-20 started launching a second, decoy drone at the same time.

On 17 March there was a long discussion in the U.S. Intelligence Board (USIB) on whether to deploy the A-12 Oxcart over North Vietnam and/or southern China, to replace the U-2s and supplement the drones. The Mach 3 spyplane had passed an operational test at Groom Lake four months earlier, and in anticipation of the requirement, OSA had already sent support equipment to Kadena AB. Despite a consensus at USIB in favor of deployment, the 303 Committee deferred a decision. There were worries about Japanese political reaction to basing the Oxcart on Okinawa, and fears that Communist China would interpret its use over their territory as an escalation.[17]

Back to action

So SAC's U-2 flights from Bien Hoa continued, and the Black Cat Squadron was called back to action, after nearly four months of inactivity. On 28 March Major Spike Chuang took off from Takhli on what proved to be a long and difficult mission over Yunnan province. After following the Burma/Laos border northwards, he got lost on the way to Kunming as the weather below deteriorated. Then Chicom MiGs tried to intercept him.[18]

When Spike Chuang next flew over Kunming the reception was even hotter. On 14 May he was ambushed by a new SA-2 site. At least two missiles were fired, possibly more. He was first warned when his System 13 started jamming, and then by his System 12 and OS receivers. As he took evasive action to the right, he looked through the driftsight and saw two of the missiles coming up! His careful, 30-degree bank to the right, coupled with the jamming, did the trick. The missiles failed to close and passed behind him. It was the first SAM attack on a U-2 over China for 16 months—since Jack Chiang was shot down.[19]

According to the standard paperwork prepared by OSA to justify missions over China at this time, "defensive systems installed in the U-2 should prevent a successful intercept by an unknown SAM site." The CAF pilots were now testing this theory in the field! A week prior to Spike's escape over Kunming, Terry Liu flew a mission along the mainland coast from Taoyuan in which he took repeated evasive action, as his System 13A ECM activated every time he went closer than 20 nautical miles offshore.[20]

In fact, China was now producing its own version of the SA-2 missile system, named Red Flag. U.S. intelligence believed that although Peking was "working hard on a SAM program," no production facilities had been identified by either U-2 or satellite photography. The analysts had seen a

In 1966, the PLAAF began to receive the Red Flag SAM, a Chinese copy of the SA-2 system.

large facility at Taiyuan, in northern China, which they believed to be producing the solid propellants. But they missed the first successful test of the indigenous SAM on the SCT missile range in June 1965. By June 1967 the PLAAF had built up a force of 21 combat-ready Red Flag battalions.[21]

A CIA intelligence memorandum issued two months later titled "Improvements in Communist China's Air Defense System" had nothing to say about new SAMs. But it did tell how China had built nine new airfields close to its border with Vietnam. It also noted that production of the high-performance MiG-19 (Chinese designation Jian-6) had been resumed at Shenyang. This piece of intelligence probably came from another recent U-2 mission: on 19 April 1966 Mickey Yu flew over this factory during a short penetration of Manchuria.[22]

After the SAM attack over Kunming in May 1966, Det H did not fly over China again for nearly three months. An improved version of the Sanders protective system was being rushed into service to protect the Agency's U-2s. This was System 13C, which could be automatically activated by the OS receiver, as well as System 12B. It also had improved antennas. The OS receiver was also improved in sensitivity and directional indication.[23]

This painting by Shigeo Koike depicts the attack on Spike Chuang over Kunming in May 1966 by multiple surface-to-air missiles. The aircraft has entered the evasive "OS" turn, started by the pilot when his defensive systems warned of imminent ambush. (via Gene Monihan)

For years, the CIA wondered whether the joint operation with the nationalists on Taiwan had been penetrated by an enemy agent. Every time a U-2 from Det H flew over the mainland, the Chicoms seemed to see it coming. Was it "sheer deductive reasoning by which they could predict the targets of interest and flight timing based on available weather data and their prior knowledge of previous missions?" the Chief of Security for OSA wrote in October 1966. Or was there a spy somewhere?

In a previous review of security, he continued, it was noted that no fewer than 12 organizations received a pre-alert of each mission. In addition to the ROC government, and the U.S. Embassy in Taipei, they included the JRC, NRO, NPIC, and the White House in Washington; the NSA; SAC Weather Central at Omaha (which provided the forecasts of cloud cover); Eastman Kodak in Rochester, NY (which stood by to process the film); and Air Force and Navy operations centers in the Pacific (to ensure radar suppression). Of course, the amount of detail in the pre-alerts varied depending on the recipient: only a few addressees would receive the mission plan with actual routings. But the number of people within all those organizations that actually got to hear that a new mission was imminent, could not be estimated, and was "a genuine cause for concern," the Security Chief continued. Secure means were used to transmit the data, but the security chief reckoned that there was subsequently some loose talk over unsecure telephone lines. No spy was ever found. – C.P.

Fatal hesitation

Meanwhile, the Black Cat Squadron suffered its third fatal accident in eight months. On 21 June Major Mickey Yu was halfway between Okinawa and Taiwan on a high-altitude training flight when his engine seized after a first-stage disc failed. The CAF pilot first thought he was close enough to stretch the glide to Taiwan. Then he changed his mind and turned back towards Okinawa. The hesitation proved fatal. He no longer had sufficent altitude to make it as far as Naha. His last desperate option to save the plane was to deadstick onto a small island that was visible in the ocean below, but as he neared the ground, he realized that the terrain was unsuitable. He ejected at 300 feet, but the plane was too low for him to survive. The final moments of the drama were witnessed by the crews of three fishing boats in the vicinity of the island.[24]

The previous loss was on 19 February, when Captain Charlie Wu was killed when he overshot the short runway at Taichung while trying to make a deadstick landing. He had shut down the engine after an overtemp warning, which was subsequently found to be false.[25]

Det H resumed overflight missions from Taiwan in early August 1966 with the two surviving pilots. Spike Chuang flew a Taiwan Straits mission, and Terry Liu flew over Hainan Island. On 24 August it was Spike's turn again. Only 13 minutes after he penetrated southern China, south of Canton, his warning systems lit up again. The System 12B strobe pointed directly ahead. What to do? "Since I turned right the last time—over Kunming—I turned left this time!" Chuang later recalled. Once again, he saw two SA-2 missiles rise towards him. Once again they failed to close on the U-2. The Chinese pilot aborted the mission and returned to Taoyuan.[26]

At Project HQ, Gen Paul Bacalis had just taken over from Gen Jack Ledford as the Director of OSA. "Please relay to Spike my heartiest congratulations for a job well-done on mission C176C," Bacalis cabled to Det H. "The manner in which he executed the prescribed evasive maneuvers, while remaining calm in a very critical situation, was very impressive."[27]

Bacalis called for a thorough review of the U-2's future chances of survival against Chicom SAMs. He asked the Agency's Office of Scientific Intelligence (OSI) to report on the number of SAM sites, new signatures, the time required to move a SAM site, and whether there was any significant COMINT to give away their position. The Office of ELINT (OEL) was asked to review the SIGINT tapes from selected U-2 missions, compare them with SIGINT supplied by the NSA, USAF, and U.S. Navy, and consider more modifications to the airborne equipment. OSA itself would review tactics and mission planning. The review concluded that the U-2 *was* still viable over China.[28]

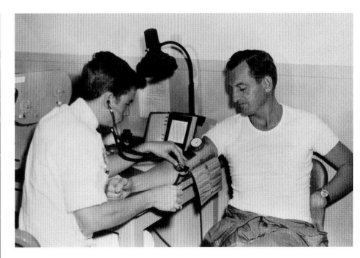

Bien Hoa airbase—the home of OL-20 and its U-2s—was periodically attacked by Vietcong guerillas. Dragon Lady pilot Bob Spencer is seen during a spell of defensive duty (via Bob Spencer).

Captain Bob Birkett gets a preflight medical. He flew Vietnam missions for SAC out of OL-20 in 1966-68 (via Bob Birkett).

Chinese Air Force Chief of Staff General Yang Shao Lien (centre) and Black Cat Squadron commander Colonel Gimo Yang (right), discuss U-2 business with Colonel Don Songer, who was the head of operations at OSA from 1960-66 (via Gimo Yang).

OSA staff changes

Bacalis was not the only new blue-suiter assigned to OSA that summer. Col William Shelton became the new Deputy for Operations, replacing Col Don Songer, who had served at Project HQ for nearly five years (during which time his title had been Deputy for Field Activities. His replacement was not the same Bill Shelton as the one who was commanding Det B when Frank Powers was shot down in 1960!). There were other staff changes within OSA, too. After nearly 10 years as the number two, the CIA's Jim Cunningham moved on to run Air America in southeast Asia. He was succeeded as Deputy Director by John Parangosky, who had been managing the tremendous effort to bring the Oxcart to readiness.

Ready it was, but the majority of the 303 Committee still refused to deploy the A-12 in Asia (or over Cuba, which was also discussed). SAC's U-2s continued to fly over Castro's island, and over the areas of North Vietnam that were deemed safe. The 4080th wing was redesignated the 100th SRW in late June 1966. Home base was still D-M, where the 349th SRS (previously the 4028th SRS) continued to train new U-2 pilots and provide combat-ready crews for the two remaining OLs.

On 8 October 1966 SAC lost its first U-2 in Vietnam—but it was not to enemy action. Major Leo Stewart was returning to Bien Hoa when he became distracted and allowed the aircraft to overspeed. He disconnected the autopilot, but could not bring the nose up. He ejected at 46,000 feet, landed safely, and was picked up by a rescue helicopter. But the aircraft was in a Vietcong-controlled area. Special forces were sent in to blow it up.[29]

This latest accident reduced the operational U-2 fleet to only 14 aircraft: eight with SAC and six with the Agency. It was hardly enough to meet the continuing requirements. Fortunately, a decision had been taken only a few weeks earlier to build a new version of the U-2.

MEMORIES OF VIETNAM
Captain Bob Birkett flew out of OL-20 on frequent TDYs from 1966 to 1968. He recalled:

At Christmas 1966 there was a ceasefire. Apparently no one told SAC, because I was tasked for a mission up north that went all the way to the Chinese border. It was a lovely day, but very strange to be flying with no chatter at all from other planes on the guard frequency. I was told that the ELINT system picked up lots of intel this day—the North's radars had nothing else to do!

We were supposed to be routed around SAM sites by at least 50 miles. One day, I found myself directly over one of them: the warning scope was all over the place. Afterwards, they could not find the site on the film. They concluded that the North Vietnamese had put the transmitter on a truck, and deployed the missiles elsewhere. They were always moving them around.

I flew the H-camera five or six times running, and it malfunctioned every time. Things would happen to it in cold conditions at altitude that they could not reproduce on the ground, where it was so warm and moist....

Letting down into Bien Hoa during the frequent thunderstorms was no joke. The only VOR was an old, weak one at Tan Son Nhut that the French must have left behind. There were plenty of TACANs, but we didn't have TACAN—or ILS. One time, I had to divert to Tan Son Nhut very low on fuel, and make a downwind landing because yet another storm was approaching the other end of the runway. I landed OK, taxied off the runway, and shut down with seven gallons remaining....

- interview with author

In 1966, Colonel William Shelton took over from Don Songer as Deputy for Operations at OSA. (via Gimo Yang)

THE SEARCH FOR SYSTEM 13

When Leo Stewart ejected from 66690 on his way back to Bien Hoa in October 1966, SAC lost its first U-2 in Southeast Asia. But worse still, System 13A was lost in VC-held territory! The newly-upgraded aircraft was carrying the latest airborne ECM technology in a small box in the base of the tail. If it fell into Chinese or Russian hands, electronics experts would probably analyze the system and develop counter-countermeasures. That was why a battery-powered destruct device had been included in System 13, to burn up the system's logic circuits. The trouble was, Stewart's plane *had been sent out without the destruct system onboard!*

Because the proper technical data had not yet been issued, no one in the electronics shop at OL-20 had wanted to take responsibility for wiring it up, in case something went wrong and they were blamed for writing off such a valuable piece of equipment.

When the wreckage was located, two officers from OL-20 accompanied Army special forces to the area by helicopter and supervised the blowing up of the remains. Unfortunately, the tail section had separated inflight and could not be found!

In an attempt to find it, a U-2 was quickly despatched from Bien Hoa on a low-level photo mission over the area where Stewart had ejected. The film revealed nothing. Some RF-101s were sent to cover the same area with their low-level oblique cameras, but again nothing was apparent on film. Eventually, eight U.S. special forces soldiers and 120 Vietnamese soldiers were inserted into an area that OL-20 reckoned the tail might have fallen. After combing the dense jungle for three days the Green Berets found the tail—and the missing ECM system. –C.P.

Author's note: In his book "A Soldier Reports," Gen William Westmoreland had an even more exciting version of this story, to the effect that when the tail was found the black box was missing, and Special Forces had to attack a VC camp to recover it.

THE LITTLE U-2 THAT KEPT ON GOING

U-2 missions over Cuba continued all through the 1960s. Castro huffed and puffed, but never did shoot one down. But the U.S. Navy nearly did. On 28 July 1966, Captain Robert Hickman took off from Barksdale AFB in 66719, but failed to make a scheduled turn over Florida. The aircraft continued southeast on the same course, while the OL-19 command post and the Joint Aerial Reconnaissance Control Center (JARCC) at Key West made vain attempts to contact the pilot by radio.

A Navy F-4 interceptor was launched from Key West—two were kept armed and on alert there, in case a recon mission over or around Cuba got into trouble. According to one of the pilots, John Randolph, the JARCC controller cleared him to fire on the U-2 after his RIO made radar contact. But the F-4 pilot reported that he was struggling to climb and close on the target, and would not be within Sparrow radar-guided missile range before he crossed into Cuban airspace.

Nothing more was heard from Hickman, as the plane crossed Cuba and continued serenely southeast along a constant track on autopilot. It eventually crashed on a mountainside in southern Bolivia, more than 3,500 miles away, when the fuel ran out! Oxygen problems were suspected. But Hickman had been getting headaches and was taking aspirin. He is believed to have had a stroke or a hemorrhage. – C.P.

Another paint scheme to help the U-2 defeat fighter intercepts. "Polka Dot" was tested at North base in 1965-66, but not deployed in operations (Lockheed).

23

Reinvention

The idea that the U-2 might be put back into production first surfaced in 1963. In March of that year, Kelly Johnson noted in his diary that the U-2 was "in great use all around the world. We haven't got nearly enough of them.' Twenty-one out of the original 55 had been lost by now, mostly to accidents. But Kelly was wary of pushing for more U-2s in Washington.

His dilemma was that the U.S. government was spending huge sums on its "successor," the A-12 Oxcart. Moreover, the USAF had hitched a ride on the CIA's bandwagon. The Skunk Works already had a contract for three AF-12 interceptor versions. In March 1963 Johnson also secured a contract for six R-12s, a reconnaissance version for SAC, with the promise of more to come.

Moreover, the USAF was also now sponsoring the RB-57F, a bizarrely-modified B-57 that could theoretically haul a much greater payload to altitude than the U-2. Kelly was sceptical. "It will be interesting to see what Convair can do. I understand that they are already three months late on a ten-month program," he wrote in December 1962. The RB-57F made its first flight in May 1963.

But Johnson well understood the continuing requirement for "a good 75,000 foot airplane," despite the ongoing A-12 development. The original U-2 models were now struggling to reach such altitudes, having been weighed down by heavier payloads, ECM, and more sophisticated navigation systems.

U-2L

Johnson set a team of Skunk Works engineers led by Merv Heal to work on a U-2 upgrade. They came up with the U-2L, a minimal modification except for two 30-inch fuselage plugs, one aft of the Q-bay and the other aft of the wing. The lengthened fuselage could better accommodate such items as the inflight refueling and tail hook for carrier landings. In September 1963, Johnson briefed the U-2 enthusiasts in Washington: Jim Cunningham and John Parangosky at OSA; Col Leo Geary representing the USAF; and Captain Red Carmody of the U.S. Navy, who was pushing the U-2 carrier capability. Johnson suggested building a new batch of 25 aircraft, costing around $1 million each.

The project was given a boost by a new CIA requirement. The scientists at DS&T believed that an optical sensor could be designed so that U.S. intelligence could determine the type and purpose of Soviet satellites that were now passing overhead. A high-flying aircraft could carry the big telescope above the dust and haze of the lower atmosphere for a better view. Johnson liked the idea, and asked Itek to study a 240-inch focal length

camera that could fit in the U-2's nose, looking upward. He then proposed the U-2M, with the same airframe as the U-2L. Later, the U-2M was refined with a rotating nose so that the big telescope could also take pictures of the ground, if required![1]

DS&T director Bud Wheelon liked the U-2M proposal, and enlisted DCI John McCone's support. In the Pentagon, Leo Geary was enthusiastic about the "basic" U-2L version. "Interest is building up," noted Johnson optimistically.[2]

But the days when one of Kelly's proposals would be approved and funded by a small circle of insiders at the CIA and rubber-stamped by the White House were over. The National Reconnaissance Office (NRO) now held the purse strings for all "black" programs. It was theoretically a joint organization between the military services and the CIA. But there were huge bureaucratic battles between the Agency and the NRO. Wheelon and his senior managers at DS&T considered the NRO nothing but a thinly-disguised vehicle to ensure a complete Pentagon takeover of overhead reconnaissance.

Bg Gen Leo Geary chats with Kelly Johnson during an official function in 1966. By now, Geary had spent 10 years in "black" programs, and was Director of Program D at the NRO. But despite his support, Johnson was unable to raise much Air Force interest in his proposals to build new and improved U-2s (via Leo Geary).

TWEAKING THE POWER TO BEAT THE "BADLANDS"

Some idea of the delicate relationship between engine and airframe, and the implications for high altitude flight, are evident from this report on the early tests of the improved J75-P-13B engine in 1965-66:

Wing buffeting was encountered during the heavy cruise climb when the engine was operated at 665 degrees centigrade EGT on standard climb schedule. The buffet was moderate to heavy from 67,000ft through 71,200ft. The preselect autopilot turns could not be made using 665 EGT. Reducing climb speed was not effective in avoiding buffet, and an EGT reduction to 610 degrees was required to obtain standard characteristics.

The weight/altitude performance of Article 349 with the "13B" engine at 610 degrees EGT is equivalent to the standard configuration with a "13A" engine at 640 degrees. Increasing the EGT reduces the speed margin between the operating conditions and the buffet boundaries, and considerably reduces the maneuvering capability. On Article 349, increasing EGT from 610 to 665 will increase the cruise altitude 500 feet and result in buffet at the new cruise climb altitude. The buffet intensity is increased considerably if the aircraft is put into a turn. Speed changes above schedule result in an increase of buffet. Tuck or reductions in speed do not appreciably reduce buffet. The wing leading edge modifications improve the low speed stall characteristics, but do not change them at cruise Mach number.

- OSA Idealist Summary 4 April 1966. It was soon realized that the new powerplant would work much better if the aircraft inlet was enlarged. The new "Coke Bottle" design provided a high critical Mach 0.8 inlet with 99% recovery, yet still with low drag. It was introduced on the U-2C/F/G airplanes, as well as the U-2R, in 1966-67.

GETTING THE U-2R OFF THE GROUND

In 1966, former Agency U-2 pilot Jim Cherbonneaux was serving as an Idealist operations officer at CIA Project HQ, Langley. He was a member of the team that evaluated Lockheed's U-2R proposal and helped it through the procurement bureaucracy. He recalled:

I have a hard time remembering how we did manage to get the U-2R program slipped through. Maybe it was because of the relatively small cost...just under one million each. Hell, at one of our operational briefings, I remarked that in just one week, the A-12 program spent more money than we'd ever need for the U-2Rs!

It might also have been because of Kelly's promise to have the aircraft flying in only 14 months from go-ahead.

It took three months of hard work before going to contract. In late March, four of us led by John Parangosky went to Burbank to complete the negotiations. We were finished by lunchtime. Our contracting officers and the Lockheed bean counters spent the afternoon drawing up the final version. Then John and Kelly signed the final document. Today, it takes between eight months and a year to do what we did in less than eight hours that day.

Mismanagement

"There is a noticeable change in management from the days of Dick Bissell," complained Kelly Johnson. "Wheelon wants to do a good job and is highly competent, but their whole organization back there is subject to a great deal of mismanagement."[3]

The NRO continued to pour money into the AF-12 and the R-12 programs—the latter became the SR-71. That was the good news for the Skunk Works. But on 1 September 1964 the NRO rejected Lockheed's U-2L proposal in favor of less costly modifications to the existing U-2 fleet. As for the U-2M, Convair was invited to submit a competitive bid for the satellite inspection requirement (and the NRO eventually killed the idea).

Yet the existing U-2 fleet was dwindling almost by the month, thanks to accidents and the shoot-downs over China. And although the RB-57F was approved for production, it could never match the U-2's altitude, or its reliability. On 22 March 1965 the NRO Director Brockway McMillan told the CIA and the USAF to study the future needs for U-2 aircraft. He wanted a comparison of the U-2 collection capability versus the A-12/SR-71 and new satellite systems, and whether there was a role for the aircraft in the face of increasing air defenses. Three months later, in their roles as head of NRO Program B and Program D, respectively, Bg Gens Ledford and Geary recommended more U-2s.[4]

At this time Kelly Johnson's attention had switched to the U-2 wing, which had remained virtually unchanged in the U-2L design. He investigated new high-lift wing designs from NASA, a swept wing, and a simpler change to the aspect ratio. Then came the U-2N proposal, which Kelly pitched in Washington during mid-July. But in mid-August, NRO Director McMillan deferred the recommended purchase of 27 U-2N models. "Although a new version would have somewhat improved performance, it would still be highly vulnerable to both ground and air missiles," he noted. For the time being, he approved only the updating of SAC's U-2s, including re-engining with the J75.[5]

Undaunted, the Skunk Works continued to investigate how to improve the U-2. But the idea of a radical new wing had to be abandoned. In his diary Johnson wrote: "We have spent $250,000 in design and wind tunnel tests of a new U-2 incorporating a new NASA flap designed to increase the critical Mach number. In spite of repeated tests the net result is zero, because while we were able to increase the onset of the drag rise, the profile drag of the aircraft went up 30%. When we combined this with the extremely heavy weight of the new wing and its controls we obtained a very discouraging outcome."[6]

P-13B engine

Then Pratt & Whitney saved the day. The engine maker came up with an improved version of the high-altitude J75-P-13. By improving the disks, blades, and turbine vanes, and redesigning the compressor inlet case to provide increased airflow, P&W was able to boost the thrust from 15,800 lbs to 17,000 lbs. The effort was primarily directed at solving the climb problems of the existing U-2 models that had never really been solved, despite numerous changes to the schedule. The first P-13B engine completed high altitude chamber testing in October, and was flying in Article 349 at Edwards by the end of November. The initial test flights were encouraging, but it became clear that the engine air intake would have to be widened to produce optimum performance. The NRO confirmed an order for 24 of the new engines to re-equip the entire fleet.[7]

Johnson realized that this power increase could be the key to a better U-2. In October 1965 he instructed Merv Heal to start a new study on the U-2, retaining the basic principles of the original design, but scaling up to take advantage of the increased power. "It's extremely difficult to beat the original U-2," he noted.[8]

It was the birth of the U-2R, and all that has since followed. Kelly Johnson noted: "We made a complete circle and ended up merely enlarging the present U-2...going back to the original concept, where we can fly with a lift coefficient of .6 to .7, gives us an airplane with a 7,000 mile range unrefueled and a few thousand feet more altitude. However, it includes much better installation for equipment, a detachable nose, and the satellite upward-looker if required."[9]

Johnson took the U-2R proposal to Washington and briefed Bud Wheelon and others on 18 January 1966. He knew that money was tight, and offered to build two aircraft for $12.5 million "to get the program started." At OSA, Gen Ledford assigned John Parangosky and Col Don Songer to head the preliminary evaluation team. The USAF, however, was not very interested, and did not take part. To them, the SR-71 was a much higher priority.[10]

Ed Baldwin

An OSA team led by John Parangosky wrote a specification and thrashed out the detailed requirement with the Skunk Works. By mid-May, the CIA issued a three-month study contract to Lockheed for the basic engineering. "We put in almost an equivalent sum of Lockheed money to build a wind tunnel test model," Kelly Johnson recalled. Johnson assigned Ed Baldwin as U-2R program manager. Fred Cavanaugh, who was running the existing U-2 program, was his deputy. "Will make sure that we get better maintainability, electrical systems, and service provisions in this airplane," Johnson resolved.[11]

At the same time, OSA commissioned studies on the U-2's vulnerability to air defense systems. Hughes worked on fighter interception, and a team from E-Systems and General Dynamics (GD) worked on the SAM threat. Apparently, Parangosky realized that the NRO was not going to provide serious money for a new U-2 until the CIA produced some technical evidence that the R-model was not a sitting duck. The studies took

Ed Baldwin thumbs his nose for the camera. He was one of the most talented engineers in the Skunk Works, and was chosen to lead the U-2R project by Kelly Johnson. (via Bob Baldwin)

advantage of the latest advances in simulation and automation. For instance, E-Systems and GD built a simulated SA-2 control van that could reproduce all the aerodynamics of the missile in flight, and the warhead explosion pattern. They then "flew" a simulated U-2 with and without defensive systems. The results not only helped justify the U-2R, but also helped OEL and industry to further develop Oscar Sierra and the other threat warning and jamming systems. (In a separate program named Phoenix, OSA began development of an automated mission planning tool that could take account of the opposition's radar coverage and threat envelopes when drawing up routes over denied territory).[12]

ORD and OSA wrote their final evaluation report on the U-2R at the end of July, and the CIA Director of Reconnaissance, Carl Duckett, sought approval to buy eight aircraft. These eight would all be for the Agency's Project Idealist; the USAF was still noncommittal. The NRO Executive Committee approved the purchase on 17 August 1966, and told the OSA that it would consider whether to buy more aircraft later. At the beginning of 1967 Kelly Johnson was told that a further four would be ordered. He was hoping for 25. By the time the contract was signed the U-2 fleet was down to 15 aircraft, nine with SAC and six with the Agency.[13]

In the black

The Skunk Works set to work. Johnson gave his team a full year to get the new bird airborne. "I expected nine months at maximum," Ed Baldwin recalled. Johnson wanted higher-quality tooling than on the earlier models. There was also one static test article. An unclassified codename was allocated to the U-2R development—Combat Shack—although the effort remained wholly "in the black."[14]

The U-2R (for Revised or Reconnaissance) was about one-third bigger than the original model, and the improvements in range and payload that Kelly promised were impressive. At the maximum gross weight of 37,780 lbs the ferry range was over 6,000 nautical miles, some 2,000 miles better than the U-2C, and fully twice that of the RB-57F. The range for a cruise-climb to the maximum altitude of 75,000 feet was 5,610 nautical miles. By now, the original Articles could only reach 72,000 feet. In practice, though, these brochure values for the U-2R were not quite achieved.[15]

Bob Weile led the wing design. He retained the same cross-section and taper, but wingspan was increased by 23 feet to 103 feet, and the overall wing area by 400 sq ft to 1,000 sq ft. As a result, the wing loading was reduced to original U-2A values, and the Lift/Drag ratio returned to 25:1. Lift coefficient was 0.6 to 0.7, and the aspect ratio 10.667.

The wing fuel tanks were rearranged, compared with the earlier models. These were running out of pitch trim, and their forward main and aft auxiliary tank configuration meant that the cg shifted considerably during a mission as fuel burned off. To eliminate the problem, the U-2R tanks were reconfigured as main inboard and auxiliary outboard. Fuel stored in the larger (1,169 gallon capacity) inboard tanks would be used first during a mission, so that the weight of the remaining fuel in the smaller (239 gallon capacity) outboard tanks would help dampen wing bending and torsional loads. With another 99 gallons of fuel in the sump tank, this brought the total U-2R fuel capacity to 2,915 gallons, or nearly 18,500 lb—enough to keep airborne for 15 hours. (When some former pilots attached to Project HQ at OSA first saw these numbers, they complained that no pilot should be expected to fly solo in a pressure suit for so long!).[16]

SECURITY AT THE SKUNK WORKS

The development of the U-2R attracted much more government oversight than did the original U-2 12 years earlier. Still, though, the Skunk Works wrote most of the rules. For instance on security, as U-2R program manager Ed Baldwin recalled:

We did our own policing of all documentation and work done. We marked our documents "Special Handling Required" in lieu of official categories, such as Confidential, Secret, Top Secret, etc. This placed the responsibility on the recipient of each copy to protect the security and need-to-know basis. We did not stamp security classifications on our drawings and reports because, if they somehow fell into the hands of the "man on the street," he would not think that he had a really important document.

- letter to author

DESIGNING THE U-2R

Bob Anderson was a member of the Skunk Works team that designed the U-2R in 1966-67. He later became the U-2 program manager. He recalls:

We called Kelly Johnson the benevolent dictator. It was tough to convince him that something ought to be changed. We did four or five studies to try and get the lightest empennage. I liked the idea of the long, interchangeable noses, but Kelly did not like the vertical line and the extra structure. I called Dick Boehme, told him the advantages, and asked him to persuade Johnson. A while later, Kelly came by my bench with his carpenters' pencil, and drew the line for me—just like I had designed....

After the CIA gave the go-ahead, Boehme told me, "you stuff the turkey!" My group of three made sure that all the ships' equipment was allocated to dedicated areas forward of the pressure bulkhead and in a new "E-bay." Learning from the U-2A/C experience, we did not allow any mixing of ships' and mission equipment, which went in the Q-bay and the big nose section.

After it flew I became the engineering manager, working for Fred Cavanaugh, who was brought back from Van Nuys to be the U-2R project engineer. Ed Baldwin actually did that job first, and saw the 12 planes off the line. But he was not big on charm, and the customer didn't like him, so Kelly brought Cavanaugh in.

The Agency and the Air Force had disagreements over technical matters, and we would be in the middle. Fred wanted to please the customer, but we did not exercise the design control that we should have. Suppliers would show up at the door with a new black box, and instructions on where we should fit it.

- interview with author

Kelly Johnson tail

After various studies, the group led by Herb Nystrom that designed the empennage opted for the all-moving tailplane that had first been employed on the Lockheed Jetstar. The so-called Kelly Johnson tail effectively distributed the pitch forces to the entire horizontal tail, and the whole slab trimmed. The design helped widen the aircraft's cg limits, and eliminated the need for ballast as well as trim tabs.

Ed Baldwin led a complete redesign of the fuselage, which was wider and 25 percent longer than the earlier birds. Systems that had been "bolted on" to the exterior U-2C as an afterthought—such as an engine oil cooler, HF radio, and ECM System 9—were accommodated within its confines. Other systems variously added to specific U-2Cs, such as ILS, TACAN, and Doppler, were now included as a standard fit. There were new avionics for flight reference and flight direction. The longer tailpipe helped mask the engine's infrared signature: another bonus. The payload was 1,050 lbs, distributed between the nose and the Q-bay.

The 45 percent increase in cockpit area allowed pilots to wear the bulkier (but much more comfortable) full pressure suit. It was also now possible to install a "proper" zero-zero ejection seat, copied from the Blackbird series. The characteristic driftsight was retained, but not the sextant.

In the original U-2 models, cameras, SIGINT, and sampling packages could be interchangeably uploaded to the "Q-bay" behind the cockpit—an area spanning the entire width and height of the fuselage. That modular concept was retained, and additionally applied to the U-2R's nose, which was also interchangeable. The SIGINT antennas were very elaborate, flush-mounted designs. Payload specialist Bob Anderson kept ships' equipment segregated from payload, in the area immediately forward of the front pressure bulkhead, and in a large "E-bay" aft of the Q-bay.

As the wind tunnel tests proceeded a problem developed. The roll rate was lower than expected. This was important. The survivability of the U-2R was being "sold" to the sceptics on the basis that its increased turning rate at altitude (coupled with effective ECM) could defeat the SAMs and the interceptors. The roll rate was improved by adding a second pair of hydraulically-actuated spoilers outboard on the wing. An inboard pair dumped lift during descent and landing.[17]

Mock-up review

The mock-up review was held in late November 1966. A significant input to the cockpit design was made by seven experienced U-2 pilots: three from Det G; two from SAC's 100th SRW; and Frank Powers, now working for Lockheed. They were each fitted with full pressure suits to check the visibility and operation of dials, switches, etc. The pilots' main suggestion was to group all the basic flight and navigation instruments on the left side of the panel, and the engine and high-altitude mission instruments on the right.[18]

The old-fashioned round dials were retained. Bill Park, the Skunk Works test pilot who would make the first flight, preferred the contemporary strip instruments that were going into the Blackbird. Park got his way for the prototype—only. In January, the NRO authorized procurement of another four aircraft.

At Burbank, Lockheed began cutting metal. "I am constantly amazed at the size of the airplane as the various pieces begin to come through," noted Kelly Johnson. In March the static test program was started. By April the prototype was recognizable as an airplane. The weight was about 800 lbs over design goal, but half of that was due to added customer equip-

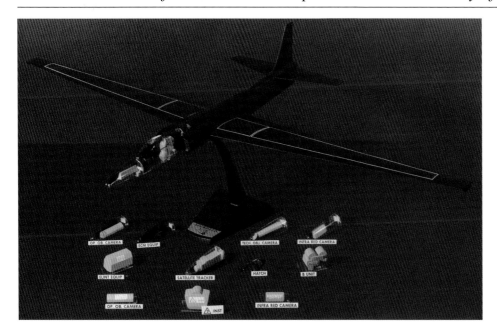

The U-2R design featured a detachable nose, as well as interchangeable Q-bay hatches, to house a variety of alternative payloads. This model display includes the satellite tracker that was never built, and the technical objective camera that would not be added for many years yet (Lockheed C245-1).

ment. "We have the first team on the airplane, and they are doing a really professional job," noted Johnson with approval. Nevertheless, he added, "it will be a struggle to meet our first flight date, as always." He had promised the end of August.[19]

Out at Edwards, some features of the U-2R were already being flight-tested on the original Articles. 359 had flown with the inboard-outboard fuel tank arrangement in the wings. The same aircraft was flight-testing the big new H-camera. Meanwhile, 349 was testing a new warning device against air-air attack. System 20 was an infrared sensor that could detect the exhaust plume of a fighter as it climbed towards the U-2. It faced rearwards from a small pod faired into the trailing edge of the right wing. Extensive flight tests were needed through 1967 to make it work properly,

but once its warning indication was integrated with the other defensive systems it was a valuable alert of zoom-climbing MiG-21s. (It was also added to the remaining original Articles).

First flight

Final assembly of the U-2R was accomplished in Building 309/310 at Burbank, with the aircraft trucked to North Base at Edwards for first flight. Bill Park took Article 051 (68-10329) up for its first flight on 28 August 1967. Johnson was in the Skunk Works chase aircraft, a Beech Bonanza flown by Bob Schumacher. On the ground was a crowd from CIA headquarters and the Pentagon. Kelly had kept his promise; it was almost one year since the contract was let.[20]

The U-2R cockpit mockup. Seven experienced U-2 pilots made their inputs during the design process—including Frank Powers (Lockheed).

Flight testing began. Art Peterson was the second test pilot to fly. In November, F-104s from ADC flew practice intercepts against several high-altitude aircraft, probably including the U-2R.

The larger control surfaces and higher critical Mach number made the U-2R somewhat easier to fly than the earlier models. Above 60,000 feet the improved margins between stall and buffet allowed more reliable autopilot control, and the longitudinal pitch trim was better. Still, the big-winged bird was a handful to fly. The unboosted controls, worked by cables, push rods, and bell cranks from a huge yoke in the cockpit, were unchanged. So was the U-2's most distinctive external feature: the bicycle landing gear and drop-out pogos. There was no doubt that pilots for the new U-2 would still have to be selected and trained with care!

The second U-2R made its first flight on 29 December 1967. It was allocated to flight testing of the mission equipment. In January, two of Det G's operational pilots flew three sorties in the new model. But a serious problem was emerging: the aircraft was veering to the left during the take-off roll. It was because of unaxisymmetric thrust. The flight test program was delayed two months while the Skunk Works investigated the aerodynamics of the ejector-type exhaust nozzle. A five-inch extension was made to the tailpipe, but this resulted in unusually high, audible vibrations that "made the U-2R sound like an F-104 in afterburner," according to Kelly Johnson. The tailpipe was extended a further seven inches, and bypass doors were added at the engine face. These closed to prevent the compressor from drawing air away from the ejector on the ground (when the nacelle pressure was higher than that at the engine face). The doors opened inflight now that the pressure at the engine face was higher. The doors provided cooling airflow to the nacelle and secondary airflow to the ejector.[21]

Inevitably, as in any flight test program, there were some other problems...air conditioning, engine oil cooling, fuel feed, and tail vibration. But none of these were show-stoppers. The range/altitude performance figures were looking good. A typical U-2R operational mission could consist of a 3,000 lb payload as part of a 22,500 lb zero fuel weight. By adding 12,250 lb of fuel, a 3,000 nautical mile mission lasting 7 1/2 hours could be flown, most of it above 70,000 feet. The maximum achievable altitude remained subject to a host of variables, such as gross takeoff weight and outside air temperature, but with the J75 red-lined at 665 degrees Centigrade, it was usually in the mid-seventy thousands of feet.

New pressure suits

From the very first test flight with the B-Camera the R-model proved to be more stable, and its window glass better than its predecessor. But the Q-bay needed insulation to reduce the temperature variations. The new S1010 pilot's pressure suits arrived from the David Clark Company. After some initial problems were fixed they were accepted. The third airplane flew in mid-February, the fourth in late March, and the fifth in early May. By the end of May 1968 two Articles had been handed over to Det G so that operational pilot training could begin.[22]

Kelly Johnson called for an updated report on the U-2R flight test program, so that he could brief progress in Washington. He wanted to keep the production line open: although this was a low-cost program, if only 12 were built it would hardly amortize the tooling. He was scouting for new "customers," and was already talking to the U.S. Navy about using the R-model as a communications relay.

The briefing stressed reliability and flexibility. The new model was improving a breed that had already amassed 135,000 hours of flight. The J75 was a well-proven engine that would only need overhauling every 1,200 hours. Maintenance was much easier, thanks to built-in access panels. The navigation and communication system was comprehensive: Doppler, TACAN, X-band beacon, Flight Director, HF, UHF, etc., etc. The Birdwatcher system had 50 channels, 20 more than the U-2C. The power system had multiple backups, and the two batteries ensured that HF communication could be retained in a power-off glide.

The intelligence sensors had nearly all been proven on the U-2C: the A-1, A-2, B, Delta III and H-cameras, plus the 35mm tracker; the FFD-3 infrared mapper; the gas and particle samplers; and System 6B for ELINT. The only new item was System 21, a compact COMINT receiver from TRW designed to pick up the opposition's air defense communications. The antennas faired neatly into the leading edge of the engine inlet duct, along with those for System 6B.

The U-2R under construction (Lockheed CC6091-03).

Optimistically, the briefing charts displayed long-duration U-2R missions over the USSR launched from the UK, Pakistan, or Alaska. More realistically, they illustrated a mission from the UK to the Mediterranean, orbit on station for six hours, and return.

The last eight slides in the briefing were devoted to electronic warfare systems. Apart from the new System 20 infrared warner, these were the latest versions of existing U-2 systems: 9, 12, Oscar Sierra, and 13. (The latest upgrades to keep abreast of the threats had just been qualified on U-2C Article 385, prior to its dispatch to Det H). According to the studies commissioned by OSA, the U-2R had a 92.5% chance of surviving a SAM attack, even if it flew directly over the site. The chances of escaping a MiG-21 attack were put at 99.6%.[23]

Control

This was all very impressive. Having stood back while the CIA sponsored the U-2R development, the USAF now decided that it wanted the new model after all! It was a repeat of the early-model U-2 history from 12 years earlier, when SAC belatedly realized that this plane was something special. This time, though, the SAC Generals did not want to buy their own—they wanted to take all 12 that were already allocated to the CIA! Recently-appointed DCI Richard Helms found himself fighting Secretary of Defense Robert McNamara for control of the U-2R.[24]

The obvious answer would have been to buy a lot more. Unfortunately, the U-2R did not convince enough influential people in Washington. A high-level committee set up under the chairmanship of Paul Nitze to analyze Reconnaissance Force Needs still concluded that the U-2R was not suited to operation over the priority areas of North Vietnam, South China, North Korea, or the Middle East "because of a combination of political and vulnerability factors." No doubt they were influenced by the latest National Intelligence Estimates, which looked forward to an ever-improving air defense system in the Soviet bloc. Not only was the SA-2 being improved all the time, but the new SA-5 was judged to have significant capabilities against even the Mach 3 SR-71. Moreover, the MiG-25 Foxbat interceptor, with a ceiling of 70-75,000 feet, was expected in ser-

Once we got "higher authority" approvals, we were told to coordinate every step of our progress with the air staff and SAC. From the very start the SAC staff were very uncooperative, and said they were happy with their old U-2s. We were even told it was a waste of taxpayers' money to be purchasing an aircraft that was virtually obsolescent.

But when the top people in SAC were briefed on the greatly enhanced flight envelope of the U-2R, they decided that they had to have them—and I mean ALL of them. I don't know why it took so long for the performance specs to filter up to them. The U-2R had twice the range of their U-2As, could fly almost 5,000 ft higher, and its most important feature (by far) was its greatly enhanced survivability.

At the ceremony to mark the first flight a mass of Air Staff weenies stood around, beaming with pride at their accomplishment. An ancient saying came to mind: "Success has many fathers, failure has but one!"

FRANK POWERS AND THE U-2R

Shortly after he returned to the U.S. from a Soviet prison in 1962, Kelly Johnson offered Frank Powers a job as an engineering test pilot on the U-2 at Burbank. Powers accepted the offer, and from 1963 through 1967 worked happily as one of the small Skunk Works flight test team. He would ferry aircraft from Edwards to Burbank or Van Nuys for overhaul, perform functional check flights after the overhauls, and fly some of the numerous development sorties needed to qualify new sensors, defensive systems, etc. But when Lockheed got the contract to build the U-2R, Kelly Johnson chose Bill Park to make the first flight.

Frank did not hide his disappointment about that. He contacted John Parangosky, now the No 2 at Project HQ in Washington, asking for a job there instead. John P checked with Kelly Johnson, then wrote: "Mr. Johnson has a high regard for Frank Powers and would like to see him continue his work at Lockheed. He stressed, however, that long experience in flight test convinces him that he must use the most qualified and experienced pilots/engineers in the initial phases of flight test of a new vehicle."

Powers decided to stay with Lockheed, and did get to fly the U-2R. But in October 1969 he was informed by Kelly Johnson that since U-2 test work was running down, his services would no longer be required. – C.P.

Article 051, the prototype U-2R, in final assembly at Burbank (Lockheed U2-91-033).

NAMING THE U-2R

When the U-2R came along, someone in Project HQ began thinking about what to call it. Officially, that is. Of course, there were plenty of nicknames already in use. To the Agency, it was the "Deuce." To the Air Force, it was the Dragon Lady. To just about everyone associated with the U-2, it was also the "Article." That appellation was suitably nondescript for a top-secret spyplane. The trouble was, ever since 1 May 1960 the U-2 had been famous. According to the person in Project HQ, if the U-2 was going to be effective in the future as a covert reconnaissance aircraft, it needed a name that would help reinforce the "cover story":

We suggest the familiar Lockheed Angel—so that the press (with PR assistance) can indeed dub it the "Homesick Angel." A few spiral takeoffs at airshows would soon bring public acclaim for this name. "Angel" may sound a little corny at first, but it does give the impression of operating at great heights and doing good deeds.

The present U-2 project is backed into a corner politically by adverse world opinion, which unfortunately worries our leaders. Some USAF bureaucrats are seizing upon these factors to place disfavor on the U-2 in order to enhance their pet projects.

The U-2 capability is viable and useful—it needs air to breathe in order to be useful and fulfill its mission. We believe this is possible providing it has a cover role...research, cartographic, humane purposes...a role that will allow us to appear on a worldwide basis without undue speculation.

In 1970, Project HQ was still mulling the question of the U-2's image:

A new designation would be more diplomatically palatable...(but) a change may give credence to a new, improved vehicle and arouse undue interest by technical intelligence people on the red side of the fence. Communist countries may use the change for propaganda purposes by noting it is the same old aircraft, but we are changing the name to try and dupe the world into thinking it is something else. A name change could suggest that money was being spent for development of a new weapons system without public knowledge. It is likely that the world press would identify the aircraft as a "spy plane" in spite of the name change. A great deal of money and effort would be expended in changing manuals, tech orders, etc.

For these reasons, recommend that no change be effected. If redesignation is considered essential, recommend using YR-7. The "Y" for experimental, the "R" for reconnaissance, and the "7" or any other number desired.

Author's note: the Air Force side of the U-2 business used "Dragon Lady" to refer to the U-2, of course. However, there was a time when the pilots at the 4080th SRW in Del Rio, Texas, wanted to rename it the "Lonestar." They figured this would bring in some sponsorship from the Texas brewery that produced the beer with the same name!

First flight of the new Article, as seen from the chase plane that contained Kelly Johnson (Lockheed PR-1023).

The CIA sponsored the U-2R development. With no apparent interest from the Air Force, Kelly Johnson looked elsewhere for support. Hence, the markings painted on the prototype Article in 1968 (Lockheed U2-91-021).

vice by 1971. However, there was no way to tell whether the Soviets would "export" these advanced weapons to client states.[25]

In November 1968 Helms and McNamara agreed to split the R-models 50-50 between the CIA and USAF. The NRO Executive Committee confirmed that no more would be ordered beyond the first dozen. Instead, it directed the CIA and the USAF to keep the remaining U-2C/G models in flyable storage so that they could replace (at least for training purposes) any R-models lost through attrition.[26]

At North Base, meanwhile, all the remaining new Articles were flown by the end of the year, and the initial U-2R flight test program was wrapped up. In mid-September high humidity testing was accomplished at McCoy AFB, as part of a first U-2R deployment test for Det G. The hosts at this Florida base were SAC's OL-19 detachment, recently transferred from Barksdale AFB. The new model was still on the secret list. OL-19 commander Major Dave Patton told his troops not to discuss the presence of "a modified U-2" with anyone outside the detachment.[27]

Some tweaking of the performance was still required. The maximum promised altitude of 75,000 feet was being missed by up to 1,400 feet because of extra weight. A less conservative EPR schedule was devised by P&W. "It may be possible to operate the engine to 665 degrees EGT under

Another view of the U-2R on the lakebed also shows the "Howdah," or wheeled sunshade that was used to protect the cockpit from hot sun. Program manager Ed Baldwin is at center, with Bill Park on the left and Dick Boehme, who was Kelly Johnson's long-serving assistant at the Skunk Works, to the right (via Bob Baldwin).

all conditions, if no instabilities occur at the coldest known altitude temperatures," Project HQ hoped. The range was 10% down on expectations, and a study was started on how to reduce the induced drag over the big wing. The study did not lead anywhere, and the effort was abandoned after a year.[28]

Itek IRIS

The most significant event in the latter stages of the initial U-2R flight test program was in late August. Article 054 was fitted with a new panoramic camera from Itek named IRIS. It was a 24-inch folded focal length stereo design that offered a scan angle of 140 degrees—twice that of the Delta III. Moreover, it was an optical bar system in which the entire mirror-lens assembly rotated continuously. This eliminated the vibration problems that could reduce the resolution of camera systems with reciprocating shutters and lenses. The IRIS was first designed for a new high-altitude Ryan reconnaissance drone, the Model 154 Compass Arrow. But Itek pitched it to OSA as a replacement for the Delta camera in the U-2, and secured a contract for 13 units to go in both CIA and SAC U-2Rs.[29]

The camera flown at Edwards in August 1968 was an IRIS I (or KA-80A) borrowed from the Compass Arrow program. By the end of the year, the version for the U-2R designated IRIS II, and with a much larger (10,500ft) film capacity, was delivered. After some initial problems matching camera to platform the results were outstanding, in terms of both resolution and coverage—a 65-mile swath from 70,000 ft. The IRIS II immediately replaced the Delta, and also eventually the long-serving B-camera.

Bill Park (center) discusses flight test plans with Kelly Johnson (left) on the lakebed at Edwards (via Jim Wood).

A line-up of the enlarged and improved Articles at North Base, with the prototype in the foreground (Lockheed).

24

The Epic Missions to Lop Nor

On 7 May 1967, Major Chuang Jen Liang took off from Takhli at the start of one of the most extraordinary of all U-2 missions. The black U-2C aircraft carried the Chinese Air Force tail number 3517. This would be the 93rd time that a U-2 from the joint U.S.-ROC operation based in Taiwan had penetrated mainland China. For "Spike" Chuang, it would be his seventh flight over denied territory. Already on two previous missions he had survived attacks by SA-2 missiles.

What was so unusual about this flight? First, the destination. It was Lop Nor, the Chinese nuclear test site that was 1,800 miles away to the north. A U-2 had never before flown so far into the remote northwestern deserts of mainland China. Second, the payload. Attached to pylons beneath each wing the U-2 was carrying thin, 10-foot long pods that Spike would drop from high altitude over the test site. Their purpose was to clandestinely record and transmit data from the Chicoms' nuclear tests.

The classified cryptonym for this daring operation was Tabasco. The unclassified codename was Purple Flash. Yet the outcome of mission C167C was far from certain. It was 3,100 nautical miles roundtrip, and at the limit of the U-2's range. Since the pods each weighed 285lbs, Spike would have to fly the maximum range profile. That meant entering hostile airspace at only 60,000 feet—well below the usual altitude, and making the U-2 even more vulnerable to Chicom air defenses. There were no known SAM sites enroute, and there was a chance that the flight northwards across Burma and eastern Tibet might go undetected. Chicom early-warning radar coverage of these remote areas was far from complete.[1]

But over Lop Nor itself, the U-2 would surely be detected by the radars associated with the Shuang Cheng Tzu (SCT) missile test rangehead, 500 miles to the east. Six months earlier the Chicoms had launched a ballistic missile westwards from SCT and exploded its nuclear warhead over Lop Nor. The People's Republic proudly announced that unprecedented test, which U.S. intelligence interpreted as a prelude to development of an ICBM system.[2]

SAM battalions

The Chicoms knew that U.S.-controlled spyplanes might come snooping. In mid-April they sent SAM battalions to Lop Nor for the first time. The Corona satellite system provided nearly all of the overhead photographic intelligence of the nuclear test site. By specific request from Project HQ, NPIC searched their Corona archive for SA-2 deployments along the route of every planned U-2 overflight. But the Chicoms' SA-2 deployment to Lop Nor occurred after the last Corona satellite mission in early April.[3]

Mission C167C would have to avoid the newly-installed SAMs. It would then have to drop the precious pods accurately. The parachute that slowed each pod would have to deploy properly, so that they hit the ground with the correct amount of force to half-bury themselves in the soft sand. Then—and only *if* the sensor and long-range, low-power transmitter/antenna were undamaged—the pods would begin sending the data that they acquired to a listening post far away. Meanwhile, Major Chuang would have to make the long, lonely return journey to Takhli—if he had enough fuel left to make it back!

A lot could go wrong. But the Tabasco operation had been painstakingly planned for well over a year. The go-ahead was given by Bud Wheelon, the head of DS&T, a few months before he left the CIA. The pods were designed by the Sandia Laboratories in Albuquerque, the national laboratory managed by Western Electric that specialized in nuclear weapons development. Sandia began working for the CIA in the early 1960s, adapting the instrumentation that was used to measure U.S. nuclear tests for the purpose of gathering intelligence on Soviet and Chinese test shots. The scientists and engineers at Sandia had experience in terradynamics, as well as aerodynamics, and the CIA supplied the best detail it could on the sand and soil characteristics of the Takla Makan desert. In conditions of great secrecy, three small groups at Sandia were assigned to work separately on the pods, on a light-detecting sensor, and on a communications system that would convert the sensor data and broadcast it via a 10-foot telescopic antenna.[4]

Provision for drop tanks was added to the CIA's U-2C/F/G models in 1965-66. The hardpoints later came in handy for carrying the sensor pods that were dropped over Lop Nor during the Tabasco mission (via Tom Bowen).

<table>
<tr><td>

DROP TANKS

The idea of adding droppable fuel tanks to restore the range of the U-2 was first mooted in spring 1964. The early consensus at Project HQ was against the idea:

(a) The political implications of two U-2 drop tanks landing on someone, or something, coupled with all the implied overt acts of war of an airplane dropping bombs, germs, etc.
(b) the cost versus the limited range gained by these tanks
(c) the increased possibility of a tank hanging, which would be cause for an abort of an operational mission
(d) some doubt as to whether the pylon stub will cost as much in fuel consumption as empty slipper tanks

But such was the need to restore the U-2's range that the scheme was approved. The Skunk Works designed the wing hardpoints; the pylons; and an engine bleed air system to transfer the 100 gallons of fuel from the tank first. The tank itself was modified from a fire bomb manufactured by Sargent Fletcher. The permanent weight increase was 100 lbs, with the fully-fueled tanks adding another 150 lbs. If they were dropped early in the mission, their weight and drag were an acceptable trade against range/payload. They were added to the Agency's U-2s starting in late 1965, but apparently were only used on one operational mission—the return trip to Lop Nor by the Black Cat Squadron in August 1967. *–C.P.*

</td></tr>
</table>

Test drops

The first pods were ready for test drops by late April 1966. Only a few months earlier, Project HQ had begun adding wing pylons to the Articles, outboard of the slipper tank installation. The pylons and the necessary strengthening of the wing had been designed by the Skunk Works for another purpose—to carry droppable fuel tanks. The idea was to restore the fuel capacity lost when the U-2 slipper tanks were replaced by ECM pods. But by the time the drop tanks were cleared for use, the U-2's ECM protection had been reduced in size and moved into the fuselage, and the slipper tanks were once more available for fuel to boost the aircraft's range. So why not adapt the pylons to carry new intelligence-gathering payloads?

Shortly before he quit as the CIA's Deputy Director of Science and Technology in 1966, Bud Wheelon approved the development of the U-2 sensor pods by Sandia Labs. Wheelon was young, talented, and acerbic. During his three-year tenure as DDS&T, he nurtured the CIA's development of advanced reconnaissance platforms and technology. (CIA)

On 29 April 1966 the prototype pod designed by Sandia was dropped by Marty Knutson of Det G from a U-2 over a suitable area of the White Sands Missile Range. This first test had mixed results. The device cleared the aircraft satisfactorily, although Knutson noticed some pitch motion. He could not see the parachute deploy, but evidently it did, since the pod inserted into the ground at a 35-degree angle, and within 800 feet of the desired impact point. But the top antenna mounting failed and the optics were damaged.[5]

The Sandia team reworked their design. There were more test flights in October, including maximum-endurance sorties to test the fuel consumption with the podded configuration. In November there were three Tabasco test missions, two of which dropped dummy pods over the Tonopah Test Range. Good ballistic data was obtained to help calculate where the pods should be released, relative to the desired impact area.[6]

Also in November, Det G flew with the slipper-plus-drop tanks configuration to get fuel consumption data for the maximum possible 1,720-gallon load. Project HQ wanted to demonstrate that both Lop Nor and Shuang Cheng Tzu were within photographic range for a U-2 sortie launched out of Takhli. OSA Director Gen Paul Bacalis briefed senior intelligence officials about the capability. Some of them thought that satellites could adequately do the job. But the new DDS&T Carl Duckett saw some value in the U-2 flying east-west along the Chinese missile test range, down which the Chicoms had just fired that nuclear-tipped ballistic missile. The satellite orbits took them south-north over the area, and could therefore only provide limited downrange coverage.[7]

Looking for business

In effect, OSA was looking for more "business" for its two U-2 detachments. Satellite photography was getting better all the time, and the U-2 was becoming a serious risk when flown over defended areas. In the whole of 1966 there were only nine U-2 overflights. All of them were by Det H over China; Det G did not fly a single operational mission.

Furthermore, the U-2 partnership with Taiwan was going through another difficult period. Chiang Ching Kuo reacted badly to the CIA's request to terminate the joint P2V squadron at Hsinchu in mid-1966. He saw the move as another example of U.S. "disengagement" from the nationalist regime, at a time when the chaos in the People's Republic induced by the Cultural Revolution had revived his fathers' hope of retaking the mainland. In a fit of pique, perhaps, Taipei even suggested closing down the Black Cat Squadron.[8]

Towards the end of 1966, the ROC withheld or delayed approval for five U-2 missions suggested by the U.S. side. The only one that got airborne included seven targets of particular interest to the nationalists. These targets were invariably in the provinces facing Taiwan. On 26 November, Terry Liu flew northwards along the mainland coast to Shanghai, then inland to Nanchang. He was hassled by MiG-21s for much of the flight, including one that got close after a full-frontal zoom-climb approach to the U-2. Two-thirds through the overflight his System 13C overheated. Liu aborted the mission and returned to Taoyuan by the most direct route.[9]

In January 1967 the nationalists continued to demonstrate their displeasure with the U.S. They approved only one out of five proposed U-2 missions, over Kwangtung province. Project HQ contemplated running a parallel program of peripheral U-2 flights along the China coast with its own American pilots. They would utilize the newly-delivered H-camera, with its big telescope capable of pointing at least 50 miles into denied territory from a safe, stand-off position.[10]

Utmost secrecy

In the meantime, preparations for the Tabasco flight to Lop Nor continued in the U.S. Since it would be staged from Thailand, the all-American Det G could fly the mission, if Taiwan was still proving awkward. In Washington, OSA lobbied for approval by the intelligence community of the requirement to drop the pods. The head of the Joint Atomic Energy Intelligence Committee (JAEIC), Dr. Donald Chamberlain, signed off on it. To preserve the utmost secrecy he suggested bypassing COMOR and USIB and going direct to the 303 Committee for political approval.[11]

The Sandia technicians returned to North Base with what they hoped would be the final version of the pods. Amongst other improvements there was a new parachute. But a drop test from Article 383 on 4 February did not go well, with a dangerous condition noted during the separation. The team from Albuquerque went home mid-month to engineer more changes. They were soon back, though, and on 1 March another test flight lasting nearly eight hours was entirely successful. An operational pod was dropped from the left pylon, and a ballistic test vehicle from the right pylon.[12]

In Taipei, meanwhile, the ROC government decided to press the U.S. for a new formal agreement covering the joint U-2 operation, before it would approve any further missions. The negotiations were conducted through CIA Station Chief Hal Ford. Surprisingly to the U.S. side, they were quickly concluded.[13]

New agreement

The new "Project Razor" agreement was signed in mid-March 1967. According to the first paragraph, it "clarified the relationship" between the two sides. In reality, the four-page agreement changed none of the basics. The U.S. would still supply the "special articles" (eg the U-2 aircraft), and could withdraw them for "other commitments" when necessary. The U.S. would pay for any upgrades to the U-2 base facilities on Taiwan, but in return, could use the site "for operations of interest solely to the U.S. side" as long as the Chinese Air Force agreed. The CAF would normally process the photography before providing the U.S. side with the original negative. Under special circumstances, though, the U.S. could process the "take" elsewhere and provide the CAF with a duplicate negative.

But the ROC now insisted that a "joint target list" be mutually agreed, although the U.S. would still do the mission planning. The CIA also promised to provide incentive pay and subsistence for the CAF personnel assigned to the joint operation, as well as death benefits for any Chinese pilot killed on operational duty. (In fact, Project HQ had informally paid out compensation to the families of most, if not all, the nine Chinese U-2 pilots already killed or missing in action).[14]

Det H, aka the CAF 35th Squadron, aka the Black Cat Squadron, resumed operations from Taoyuan. Captain Andy Fan flew his first mission along the mainland coast opposite Taiwan. Major Terry Liu flew his tenth and last mission to Hainan Island, returning via the Pearl River Delta and a long excursion into Kwangtung province. Andy Fan flew his second mission all the way up the Yellow Sea to photograph Chinese naval activity at the ports of Darien, Tsingtao, and Shanghai.[15]

This U-2F is just becoming airborne during a test flight from the Lockheed depot at Van Nuys in 1966-67. It carries the drop tanks as well as the slipper tanks (via Jay Miller).

Meanwhile, two other Chinese U-2 pilots were sent back to the U.S. to train especially for the Tabasco mission. This op was too important to leave to chance! The most experienced Black Cat pilot was Spike Chuang, and he was designated the primary pilot. The recently-qualified but highly-rated Billy Chang was to be the backup. They reached Edwards in late March. After two night flights in the T-33 they were each given three U-2 flights that introduced them to the new Doppler navigation system. Then they each flew a simulated operational Tabasco mission, which was designed to match the actual flight profile to be used over China as closely as possible.[16]

The two pilots flew their simulated missions from Edwards in mid-April. Then Article 383 was ferried across the transpacific to Takhli, sensor pods and all. The two Chinese pilots and the deployment team rode on the accompanying KC-135. Article 373 was ferried from Det H at Taoyuan to the Thai base to serve as backup aircraft. Black Cat Squadron commander Gimo Yang also made the trip to Thailand.[17]

Everything in place

By 30 April everything was in place at Takhli. The weather was fine all the way up the route, but not over the drop area. Although this was not a photo mission, the aircraft was fitted with the 35mm tracker camera, which was supposed to record whether Spike had navigated accurately to the two drop locations. Project HQ waited for the best possible weather forecast over Lop Nor, but the cloud did not begin clearing over the test site until 5 May.

The delay was helpful in one respect. A Corona satellite launch was imminent, and the weather satellite that always preceded it was already in orbit. Early on 6 May that satellite flew right over Lop Nor and transmitted an up-to-date image of cloud conditions. When the "Go-No-Go" briefing was held in Project HQ at 9am that morning, the forecasters were able to assure OSA Director Col Paul Bacalis that the weather would be clear over the target area.

Bacalis sent the go message to Takhli. "We are expecting a large crowd in the control center during the mission, and will appreciate any info that you can provide as the mission progresses," he cabled.[18]

The launch time had been precisely calculated. First, the mission planners wanted to ensure that the U-2 had climbed as high as possible before dawn broke over the high desert plateaus south of Lop Nor. This was especially important since, with the U-2 weighed down by the heavy sensor pods, and having to fly the maximum range profile, it would not be above the contrail level when it first entered Chinese airspace. But they also wanted Spike to arrive over the first drop point when the sun was high enough to illuminate the pod as it fell away from the aircraft. The hope was that the U-2's tracker camera would capture the deployment and jettison of the parachute (or not!). (The parachute was supposed to jettison as the pod neared the ground, so that the correct impact velocity was achieved).[19]

On course

At 0220 local time on 7 May, the hot tropical night reverberated as Spike took off from Takhli in Article 383. His route was northwest to Chiang Mai, and then into Burma. Forty minutes after takeoff a Birdwatcher transmission to the command post revealed that Spike had left his IFF on. He was contacted by HF radio and told to switch it off. He flew on towards his next waypoint, over Myitkina. Then he made a slight eastward adjustment to avoid Indian airspace before the U-2 entered China at the base of the Himalayas. Spike had been given celestial navigation computations to help

him stay on course until the sun rose about three hours into the mission. He was on course as he entered Chinese territory.

Spike had been warned to expect clear-air turbulence as he flew across the eastern end of the Himalayas. But the ride was fairly smooth as he flew over the high mountain ranges, where two great rivers—the Mekong and the Yangtze—began their long journeys to the sea. Spike's journey was just as long—and he was now just over halfway there.

Dawn was now breaking. Spike glanced in his rear-view mirror and was disturbed to see his aircraft making thick contrails. They persisted for far longer than predicted. The CAF pilot made repeated small turns left and then right, to try and see if enemy fighters were following him. But there was no indication from System 9B that the bad guys were on his trail. As he cruise-climbed some more the contrail eventually evaporated. Then a new problem arose. Spike rechecked the fuel consumption against his green card. It was 50 gallons below the curve—he reckoned that the winds at altitude were greater than forecast. Risking a tell-tale transmission, he reported the bad news to the command post by HF.

Lop Nor

Now he was approaching the northern edge of the plateau, where the ground below him fell away steeply into the eastern end of the great Takla Makan depression. The large dry lake of Lop Nor was ahead and to his left. As planned, he made a large 180-degree turn to take him over the southern half of the lake. As he flew back towards the south, both pods were to be dropped within 60 seconds of each other, so that they fell into the rising terrain at the appropriate angle and location. Spike released one, then the other 50 seconds later. They fell away as advertised.

Now he started the long journey home. To save fuel, he decided to set course directly for Myitkina, which meant bypassing a couple of waypoints and flying over the eastern edge of Assam. This was Indian territory—but what the hell! The U-2 left Chinese airspace at about 9am. Not once had Spike's warning systems been activated to signify that fighter or SAM radars were turned on him.

Now all he had to worry about was getting back to Takhli. Two hours before he was due to land a C-130 took off from there with a recovery crew, waiting to hear whether Spike would divert into Myitkina on his way home, due to diminishing fuel reserves. The CIA had arranged this unusual alternate airfield by bribing a Burmese General to ignore the arrival of a long-winged spyplane and a C-130 transport! To make sure he was famil-

The two Chinese pilots who flew the epic U-2 missions to Lop Nor in 1967. Spike Chuang (right) dropped the sensor pods. Bill Chang (left) returned to the remote nuclear test site in an attempt to interrogate them from the air (via Al Pinkham).

iar with the approach the C-130 had flown over the Burmese airbase a few days earlier, with Spike in the cockpit.[20]

Approaching Myitkina Spike decided to press on. He was well into the descent before the fuel low-level light came on. Article 383 landed at Takhli after eight hours and 45 minutes, just 15 minutes longer than scheduled. There were hearty congratulations all around. But when the ground crew unloaded the tracker camera, they found that it had malfunctioned.[21]

No response

The CIA's Office of Research and Development (ORD) had a group standing by at the U.S.-operated Shu Linkou SIGINT site in northern Taiwan. They would interrogate the pods by HF radio signal. The reception group turned on their interrogator, hoping to hear a test signal. There was no response.[22]

The inquest began. Had Spike really dropped the pods in the correct location? Although there was no tracker film to prove it, the pilot was sure that he had. Maybe the transmitter had failed? But on both pods? To guard against failure, the Sandia engineers had built the transmitter in one pod to run on solar power, and the other to run on battery power. Surely the pods had not been discovered in that remote location? The CIA had anticipated that problem, and tried to counter it. In case anyone should come across them, the pods bore the legend: "China Science Institute – Do Not Touch" in Chinese characters![23]

The ORD team suggested doing an interrogation test from another location. Again, though, there was no response from the pods. Meanwhile, Corona mission 1041 detected preparations for a new nuclear test at Lop Nor. On 17 June the Chicoms exploded their first H-bomb. It was dropped over Lop Nor by a Tu-16 Badger bomber, one of only two supplied years earlier by the Soviet Union. The Tabasco pods were still silent, but the information that they *should* have provided would have helped U.S. intelligence analyze China's progress in thermonuclear technology.[24]

After the Tabasco mission Spike Chuang was flown back to Taiwan while his backup, Billy Chang, stayed at Takhli. Chang took off from there on his first overflight on 16 May. It was yet another trip along the China/Vietnam border. These U-2 missions by Det H helped U.S. intelligence assess that, although China was helping North Vietnam in the "struggle against imperialist aggression," there were limits to Chairman Mao's support for Uncle Ho. The Chinese did send troops, but they operated mainly in the border areas, building roads and defending the airspace with AA artillery units.

Salvage

Within the CIA, China's H-bomb test spurred ORD and OSA to try and salvage the Tabasco project. Perhaps the pods *were* transmitting, but only a weak signal that could not be heard so far away! In late June a plan was hatched to send a U-2 back to Lop Nor with an airborne interrogator/recorder and a high-gain trailing wire antenna. Within days the equipment was rushed to Burbank, where the Skunk Works engineered it into the Q-bay. The trailing wire would be deployed over the target area, and a cutting device was provided in case the wire did not retract.[25]

The equipment was test-flown over California in mid-July. At first it did not work. There were problems with the transmitter, and the antenna was shorting to ground at the cutter. The problems were solved in short order, though. On 9 August the interrogation system was airlifted to Tai-

wan for installation on Article 383. It would be deployed from there to Tahkli to fly the long interrogation mission.

August was a very busy month for Det H. With only two U-2s on hand, they were tasked with two overflights of the mainland provinces opposite Taiwan, as well as the first operational mission with the H-camera. Then came the rush instruction from Washington to fly simulated Tabasco mission sorties from Taoyuan to test the fuel consumption. Project HQ wanted to use the drop tanks on the return to Lop Nor, instead of the slippers.[26]

Having been backup for the first Tabasco mission, Billy Chang was selected for the return flight. But on his simulated mission from Taoyuan one of the drop tanks hung up, and he had to make an awkward landing with it still attached. Water had frozen around the tank release bolt at high altitude. Det H advised that slipper tanks be used for the Lop Nor mission instead. Three more simulated sorties were flown before the deployment to Takhli on 27 August. This was timed to ensure that the Article arrived after dark. The less visibility, the better![27]

100th mission

In the early hours of 31 August Billy Chang took off on the return flight to Lop Nor. It was the 100th mission over mainland China by the Black Cat Squadron. After an hour Chang entered Chinese airspace at 60,000 feet. There was a solid undercast nearly all the way. On only his second operational mission, Billy was relying for navigation on the new (and not entirely reliable) Doppler system, backed up by star shots until it was daylight. It was the same route as the drop mission four months earlier.

All went well until Billy was about half-an-hour south of the test site. Suddenly, his warning systems activated! He began the "Oh Shit!" turn and peered through the driftsight. At least two missiles streaked out of the cloud level way below, heading his way. Now all he could do was hope

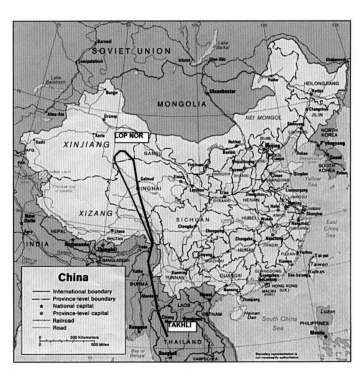

The route taken by both missions to Lop Nor. It was a long roundtrip with a heavy airplane, and a possibility that the fuel would run out before reaching Takhli, Thailand, on the way back!

that System 13 worked as advertised. And it did! The missiles failed to home. Two of them exploded 2-3,000 feet below the U-2, one in front, one behind.

Billy had nearly been ambushed in the middle of nowhere. The thought that more SAMs awaited him when he reached the test site must have weighed heavily in the Chinese pilot's mind. Turn for home, then? Billy

Bg Gen Paul Bacalis was Director of OSA from 1966 to 1968. He cabled congratulations to the CAF pilots from Project HQ (NARA).

decided to press on instead. It was a brave decision. Soon he reached the waypoint where he must extend the antenna. As instructed, he leveled off and threw the switch on the specially-installed control panel. Just behind him in the Q-bay the wire unrolled OK. Next, he switched the interrogator to active and entered the slow left turn over the test site—which was hardly visible through the clouds. Billy glanced nervously at his warning panel, half-expecting those dreaded SAM warning lights to start flashing again. But all was quiet.

On the special control panel a green light came on. But this was good news! It signified that the interrogation system was picking up signals from the Tabasco pods lying far below. Billy continued the turn, rolling out southbound. The green light soon went out, but the pilot waited until the designated waypoint before switching the system off and retracting the trailing wire antenna. Now came the long journey back to Thailand. He resumed the cruise-climb for a maximum range mission. Since he had burned extra fuel during the SAM-evading turns, Billy could only hope that the mission planners had correctly calculated his range against payload.[28]

Congratulations

They had. The fuel low-level light came on only just before touchdown. Billy returned to Takhli at lunchtime, after nine hours and six minutes in the air. It was congratulations all around! "Billy demonstrated truly remarkable ability in navigating to and from the target area without reference to ground checkpoints, and in safely recovering the aircraft with minimum fuel reserve" enthused OSA Director Gen Paul Bacalis in a cable from Project HQ.[29]

Bacalis took comfort from the fact that the flight had also survived an encounter with a previously-unknown SAM site. Two missiles were visible on the tracker film, but Billy thought he had seen more. The site was thought to be at an airfield and Army supply depot along one of the few roads that traversed the high Tibetan plateau. (Why the Chicoms had placed missiles in the middle of remote Tsinghai province was apparently never determined by U.S. intelligence. Either they figured out that a U-2 would eventually head that way enroute to Lop Nor from Thailand, or they were forewarned. Whatever the truth, it is now known that both the 6th and 15th Battalions of the PLAAF's anti-aircraft forces were lying in wait. The flight was detected by early-warning radars to the east, not long after it entered Chinese territory. The two battalions fired a total of six missiles against Mission C287C that day.)[30]

Now came the bad news. The ORD commo specialists examined the interrogation data that had been recorded during the flight. They found only a morse transmission, on the same frequency as the expected pod response. Someone in the Lop Nor area had been manually tapping out morse code as the U-2 flew over. This caused Billy's green light to illuminate. From the precious pods, absolutely nothing was heard! The commo people cabled Project HQ with their finding. They didn't spoil the party by telling the deployment team at Takhli.[31]

Failure

After so much effort, and two epic flights, the Tabasco project was a complete failure. The Chicoms continued nuclear testing at Lop Nor, though the effort was disrupted by the Cultural Revolution. In May 1969 the CIA tried again to emplace the podded sensors. This time they used a C-130 flown from Takhli by CAF pilots belonging to the 34th Squadron, which had for years flown low over China while the U-2s flew high.[32]

As for the Black Cat Squadron, the second long excursion to Lop Nor was a swansong for the entire six-year project to overfly mainland China. OSA's optimism that the U-2 could be protected from Chinese SAMs received a temporary boost from Billy's escape over Tibet. But just eight days later, a fifth CAF U-2 was shot down about 50 miles southwest of Shanghai. It was Major Tom Huang Jung Bei's first operational mission. He did not survive it.

As usual, Project HQ had asked NPIC to do a SAM search of the planned route, which started near Shanghai and covered seven airfields on the way past Hangchow, Nanchang, and to a coast-out near Foochow. NPIC reported two SA-2 sites at Shanghai, so the mission planners made sure that the route kept at least 25 miles west of them, after coast-in north of the big city. Huang's first photo target was the airfield at Chia Hsing, one of seven to be overflown during the five-hour flight.

Red Flag SAM

If the photo-interpreters had examined their most recent Corona imagery more carefully, they would have noticed some unidentified equipment amongst the aircraft revetments at one end of Chia Hsing airfield. It was a Red Flag SAM site belonging to the 14th Battalion. China's own version of the SA-2 was now being deployed in increasing numbers. Moreover, the new radars had special anti-jamming circuits expressly designed to counter System 13 on the U-2!

After Jack Chang was shot down in January 1965, technical experts from the PLAAF recovered the Sanders ECM system from the wreckage. They took it apart, studied the components, re-assembled them, and tested it. They learned that the jammer was a deceptive type, designed to repeat the missile radar's signal 180 degrees out of phase. They designed a counter-countermeasure![33]

The Chicom's ECCM had not quite worked against the Tabasco interrogation mission to Lop Nor.[34] But over Kiangsu eight days later, there was no escape for Tom Hwang. His System 13 sprang into action as soon as he coasted-in. It jammed constantly for the next half-hour as he skirted the SAM sites around Shanghai. When he was 20 miles from Chia Hsing airfield the 14th Battalion turned on their missile guidance radar. In the U-2 cockpit the "OS" light illuminated, and Hwang began an evading turn. But the radar operators below activated their anti-jamming "Circuit No 28" and launched three missiles. Thirty seconds later the U-2 was blown out of the sky when one of the missiles scored a direct hit.[35]

The Chicoms were now clearly winning the SAM battle. It was different over North Vietnam, where the U.S. was having some success in

In September 1967, the Chicoms shot down a fifth U-2 near Shanghai. Overflights of the mainland were suspended a few months later—and never resumed.

countering the SA-2. But in the Rolling Thunder air campaign, U.S. fighter-bombers were going in low on multi-plane attacks, and the SAM battalions also had to guard against attack by anti-radiation missiles, as well as electronic countermeasures. By contrast, a single U-2 in the high sky over China was considerably more vulnerable.

Safe distance

After a three-month standdown, the Black Cat Squadron resumed reconnaissance operations against mainland China in December 1967—but only from a safe distance. Using the H-camera, which pointed inland to a distance of more than 50 miles, U-2 missions stayed 15-25 nautical miles offshore all the way. But the trouble with looking sideways from 70,000 feet rather than straight down, was that even less cloud cover was required to obtain usable imagery. In the first nine months that it was available at Taoyuan, only three operational peripheral missions with the H-Cam were accomplished. There were a number of reasons for that, but weather was an important factor.

There was one last mission over the mainland in March 1968, flown by Andy Fan from Takhli over Yunnan province and the China/Vietnam border. It was no great success. The cloud cover was worse than expected; Fan made some navigational errors, and a MiG-21 zoom-climbed *over* the U-2!

The U.S. intelligence community kept pressing for more U-2 overflights, but they were never approved by the political heirarchy. After the Tet Offensive President Johnson called a halt to U.S. bombing of North Vietnam above 20 degrees North. Preliminary peace talks followed in Paris. From May-September 1968 the CIA could not even get permission from the 303 Committee to fly peripheral missions along the China coast.

In March 1969 the Committee on Imagery Requirements and Exploitation (COMIREX) tried again for an overflight: "Stated simply, our case is that, while we have given top priority to satellite coverage of Chinese Communist targets, we have not been able to obtain the level of coverage desirable. The only way we can see that such coverage can be obtained is by a continuing low-key program for overflight of China by manned aircraft or drones to supplement satellite coverage."[36]

But it was not to be. The Black Cat Squadron's days of dicing with SAMs and MiGs over China were over. Although missions by the SR-71 Blackbird were approved over North Korea as well as North Vietnam, not even the Mach 3 spyplane got to fly over the Middle Kingdom.

By the time that the U-2R was declared operationally ready in January 1969 it was sorely needed. From 1966 to mid-1968 a further 10 early-model Articles were lost. Those that remained were in bad shape. "The airplane is now so heavy that the margin between stall buffet and compressibility is only 6 knots at high altitude," Kelly Johnson noted.[1]

In September 1966 the first signs of corrosion and metal fatigue showed up. In mid-October 1967, fuel leaked out of a SAC airplane on the ground at Bien Hoa. An 11-inch crack was discovered in the lower wing surface. It had flown 4,000 hours. The U-2C/F/G fleet was grounded for ultrasonic inspections. A wing beef-up and partial reskinning was required. Until each aircraft could be repaired, 25-hour inspections were ordered.[2]

SAC's 100th SRW struggled to keep its two operating locations supplied with trained pilots and fresh aircraft. In late 1967 COMIREX required 90% coverage of Cuba every 56 days by the U-2s of OL-19 from Barksdale. However, the requirements levied on OL-20 at Bien Hoa had been relaxed, after the A-12 Oxcart was finally deployed to Kadena in May 1967. Henceforth, the Agency's "Ox" performed most of the North Vietnam coverage.

In April 1968, after SAC's SR-71 replaced the A-12, the Giant Nail U-2 flights were restricted to below 20 degrees North. Six months later SAC ended all U-2 flights over North Vietnam. The pilots of OL-20 did not object—by now, the North had fired SA-2 missiles at four or five U-2 missions. But OL-20 was still tasked to fly over Laos and Cambodia, to try and cover the Ho Chi Minh trail.[3]

One of the 100th SRW's U-2C models after receiving the "Black Velvet" paint scheme. By 1968, accidents and structural problems had reduced the aircraft's availability to critical levels.

Justify

As for the Agency's U-2s, they flew only 12 operational missions in 1968. Ten of these were flown by the Chinese pilots of Det H based in Taiwan, and two by Det G's American drivers (over Cambodia in March/April). By the end of the year, Project HQ was having to justify the continuation of Project Idealist. OSA had already suffered a grievous blow when the A-12s were returned from Kadena and put into storage. Now, the Pentagon formed an alliance with the bean counters in the Bureau of the Budget to close down the Agency's U-2R operation as well, and have the aircraft transferred to SAC.

The new Director of OSA, Bg Gen Gene Ross, although a blue-suiter himself, went into battle for the Agency. "The Agency and DOD U-2 Programs are complementary and not competitive," he wrote. "There is mutual procurement, development, training, and support. In certain situations, such as Cuba and Southeast Asia, it is logical that the mission can and should transition to the military whenever other overt military actions dictate." But, he insisted, the U.S. government should continue to have the option for covert reconnaissance of denied territory. Project Idealist survived this skirmish, but faced a more serious battle for survival one year later.[4]

He might have added that the U-2, U-2R, and SR-71 would not even have been built, had it not been for the CIA!

In happy ignorance of the political machinations back east, Det G continued to train on both the old and new U-2 models at North Base. To answer its detractors, OSA needed to demonstrate that Project Idealist was still an effective, quick-response tool. A new series of practice deployments to do just that had already begun. They were codenamed Scope Saint, and the staging base was provided by the "sleeping partner" in Project Idealist, namely the British.

Scope Saint

Although the RAF was still allocated two pilot positions at Det G (accompanied by a mission planner and a flight surgeon), the Brits had never committed to a formal agreement allowing the use of their bases for U-2 deployments. So the proposed new operation had to be carefully coordinated. "Essential that all arrangements be conducted in slow time to ensure feelings by politicians that exercise will be orderly," noted Project HQ. The first Scope Saint deployment to the UK was in October 1968, and used one of the old Articles (348). After one local training sortie it was flown all the way back to Edwards a week later.[5]

Despite a gradual cooling of relations between the U.S. and the ROC, the nationalist Chinese remained the other active participant in the CIA U-2 project. The first landing accident involving a U-2R occurred on 13 November 1968 when Chinese pilot David Lee ground-looped Article 057 at North Base. He had returned to the U.S. for checkout in the new model, prior to it being transferred to Det H. Fortunately, there was little damage.

A month later there was another incident when Flt Lt Dick Cloke was climbing out on an IRIS II camera test flight. At 15,000 feet the canopy flew open. The British pilot recovered the aircraft on the Edwards lakebed.

In January-February 1969, two brand new U-2Rs were ferried to Det H on Taiwan to continue the Tackle project. Sadly, Det H had only one original U-2 model to send back to the U.S. in return. The other one was lost on 5 January 1969, when Billy Chang crashed into the East China Sea during a peripheral mission. For three days a fleet of warships and aircraft searched for the pilot without success. Some time later a Korean fisherman found his remains, half-eaten by sharks.

Billy had ejected, but the cause of the accident was never established. From the Birdwatcher readout it was known that the airplane exceeded the Mach buffet, after the autopilot was disconnected. But Billy was a highly-rated pilot. There must have been a good reason why he lost control.[6]

Peripheral

Overflights of the Chinese mainland were no longer being approved. That left the Black Cat Squadron with only two missions. The main one was the peripheral imaging of the China coast, using the formidable but temperamental H-camera.

Typical routes were from Tsingtao south to Matsu, or Hong Kong north to Shanghai, or from Hainan Island north to the Taiwan Straits. After a three-month standdown following Billy Chang's crash, the first operational H-camera mission from Taoyuan using a U-2R took place on 8 April 1969.

The secondary mission from Taiwan was SIGINT, using System 17. This was a sophisticated receiver covering a wide range of frequencies and with direction-finding capability. The CIA had sponsored its development from 1964. On the original Articles, it fitted in the Q-bay, with flush antennas mounted in the U-2's wing skids, and in both horizontal tails. Det H flew a few missions with this configuration during 1968. The main target was to capture signals from China's own Red Flag version of the SA-2. In the larger U-2R model, System 17 was housed in a special, interchangeable nose section. This kept the Q-bay free for an imaging sensor, so that combined photo/SIGINT missions could be flown.[7]

Although the Black Cats were now flying 20 nautical miles offshore, the Chicoms did not give up trying to intercept. PLAAF fighters were seen below on most missions, vainly trying to intercept. As a precaution, the U-2 flight tracks were drawn to include a turn every five minutes, to complicate the task of interception. But on 16 October 1969, Major Johnny Shen was flying off the Shantung peninsula when he felt the shock wave as an F-7 (Chinese MiG-21) passed 500 feet below him. Since there was a MiG-21 base on the coast, Shen had been briefed to expect trouble.[8]

But mission planners reckoned that a MiG-21 had little chance of downing a U-2. In the zoom-climb, the MiG pilot would lose most of his energy, arriving at 69,000 feet only Mach 0.18 above the stall. He would have about one minute to acquire his target and fire before having to descend. Meanwhile, the U-2 would be turning to evade, having been warned by his electronic and infrared systems of the approaching hostile.

Group photo at Det H, Taiwan, in the late 1960s. Back row, left to right: CAF U-2 pilots Major David Lee, Colonel Terry Liu, Major Johnny Shen, Major 'Spike' Chuang, Captain Denny Huang. Front row, left to right: Vern Hayward (TRW tech rep), Major Andy Fan (CAF pilot), Bob Ericson (TDY pilot from Det G), and Col Tiger Wang (CAF squadron commander). (via Gimo Yang)

The philosophy behind this training exercise for Det G was to make a quick deployment to a staging base in the UK, and then fly one or two simulated operational missions. The first such exercise took place in October 1968 and passed off without incident.

In April 1969 Det G staged the second Scope Saint deployment, this time with a U-2R. The destination was RAF St. Mawgan, in the far west of England. The Article was flown direct from Edwards in 12 hours 20 minutes. The U.S. Navy had a hangar at St. Mawgan, which was used during the deployment. Unfortunately, on the night before the simulated operational mission was due to be launched, a Navy forklift truck driver drove into the Article's wing. The mission had to be canceled. After it was repaired, Dick Cloke flew the U-2R back to Edwards in 13 hours 5 minutes— a distance of 4,885 nautical miles, and the longest unrefueled operational U-2 mission yet.

Cloke was also the ferry pilot for Scope Saint III, when a U-2R was ferried direct from Edwards to RAF Kinloss, in northern Scotland. Halfway through the 12-hour flight, a ball bearing failed in the ring of his pressure-suit helmet. The RAF pilot was looking half-left at the time—and had to fly like this for the rest of the way!

During this deployment, two simulated missions were flown by Cloke and his fellow RAF pilot attached to Det G, Harry Drew. They flew around the UK using the lightweight B2 camera to photograph London and other landmarks from 70,000 feet. Senior RAF officers were most interested in the upgraded version of Hycon's workhorse sensor. They subsequently acquired this camera for their own Canberra PR.9 high-altitude reconnaissance aircraft.

Project HQ was happy with the outcome of the Kinloss deployment. It concluded that the exercise demonstrated "the feasibility of conducting U-2 operations from UK bases without undue public interest or adverse publicity." And the experience in rapid-reaction capability thus gained was put to good use in the following year, when Det G deployed to the UK and on to the Middle East in double-quick time. – *C.P.*

USAF U-2R pilots

The first operational USAF pilots to fly the U-2R model were Bob Birkett and Jack Fenimore in July 1968. They were sent from the 100th SRW at D-M to be checked out at North Base by Chunky Webster of Det G. The conversion course from the C-model was 20 hours.[9]

The 100th SRW deployed its first U-2R to OL-19 at McCoy in March 1969, and began flying over Cuba in the big-winged bird. Within weeks, however, it was grounded. On 18 April North Korean MiGs shot down a Navy EC-121M gathering SIGINT in international waters. Immediately, all sensitive U.S. reconnaissance missions were suspended. SAC C-in-C Gen Bruce Holloway recommended that the Dragon Lady flying the Glass Lamp mission over Cuba be replaced by his shiny new SR-71s.[10]

Holloway's request raised the hackles of some staffers at the NRO, who maintained that such a decision was their prerogative. SAC was merely the "operator," as delegated by the JCS. A debate ensued—and the NRO won the argument. The U-2 kept the Cuba mission.[11]

SAC deployed its second U-2R to OL-20 at Bien Hoa in July 1969. The mission codename was changed to Giant Dragon, but was essentially unchanged: coverage of Cambodia and Laos only, while the SR-71 out-ran the SAMs over North Vietnam.

That did not mean the U-2 flights were out of danger. They were accompanied by F-4s on combat air patrol, and by F-105 Wild Weasels, whose pilots were primed to take out any SAM site that fired across the border at the U-2 flying over the Plain of Jars.[12]

Later in 1969 SAC accepted the IRIS II panoramic camera. It quickly became the sensor of choice, with its 12-inch resolution and 60-mile swath. SAC retained the A-1 and A-2 camera rigs for mapping sorties in the U-2R, and consigned the B-camera to history.

But SAC no longer wanted to use Hycon's troublesome H-camera. In mid-1968, OL-19 used the "H" for a few missions over Cuba, when intel analysts wanted a good sideways-look at the entrance to a hardened bunker at Santiago. They suspected—wrongly—that it was concealing some newly-received offensive missiles. But pilots found it hard to keep within the strict roll, pitch, and yaw limits that the gyro-stabilized "H" required. Then there was the careful boresighting and aiming that such a big telescope required, not to mention the environmental constraints. If the temperature in the Q-bay varied by more than five degrees the lenses would not stay in focus. SAC transferred its single H-camera to OSA, which persevered with the design, and tried new filters and different f-stops. For the peripheral mission flown by Det H there really was no alternative.[13]

1130th ATTG

In mid-1969, OSA changed the "cover" designation of Det G at North Base from WRSP-IV to the 1130th Air Tactical Training Group (ATTG). The pretence that the outfit did "weather reconnaissance" was effectively dropped. (The totally bogus instrumentation package that supported this cover story was retained, however!).

The philosophy now seemed to be one of "hiding in plain sight.' In other words, Det G was just another USAF U-2 unit, if anybody asked. In fact, the Articles usually carried the Star and Bar insignia on their intakes and USAF serial numbers on the tail (ironically, SAC chose to dispense with the star and bar on its own U-2Rs!).

Still, there were some secret things going on at the northern end of the Edwards lakebed. The Fortune Cookie project was one of them. This was an effort to marry the long range and high-altitude of the U-2R with the survivability and deniability of a supersonic drone. It was started in early 1968 when OSA responded to a proposal by Kelly Johnson to build a small, rocket-powered vehicle that could be launched from under the wing of the U-2.[14]

Perhaps Project HQ seized on the idea as a good alternative to the increasing use of the USAF-sponsored Ryan drones over southern China. At any rate, OSA Deputy Director John Parangosky pursued the concept, but decided that Kelly's quote to build and test 25 of these drones was too expensive. He found an alternative supplier: Beech Aircraft Corp in Wichita. They built the AQM-37 air-launched supersonic target drone that was used by all three U.S. armed services. It was heavier than Kelly's proposed drone, but could be adapted for much lower cost.[15]

During 1968 the drone concept changed from a recoverable vehicle equipped with a camera to a disposable vehicle, whose primary purpose would be to stimulate enemy air defense systems so that ELINT could be collected and relayed to the U-2R or other airborne platforms within range.

THE "MAKE-WORK" PROJECTS AT NORTH BASE?

In 1968-69, after the U-2R entered service, a number of unusual and ambitious test programs were started by the CIA. According to one contractor working at North Base during this period, they were essentially "make-work" projects to overcome a shortage of operational missions for the Agency's U-2s, and to justify the large staff still employed at Project HQ despite the death of the Oxcart program. That may be a harsh judgement. What do you think? (None of them worked, by the way).

1. Magic Paint, aka "Chameleon" Not to be confused with the 1965 idea to camouflage a U-2 as viewed from *above* with polka dots, this was an attempt to develop a paint that would camouflage as viewed from below—at whatever altitude the U-bird was flying. In other words, light blue in the lower atmosphere to very dark blue at high altitude. The NCR company was the supplier, having promised that some of its paints could change color according to the temperature. U-2C Article 383 was used for the flight tests, which went on for six months in 1969. Thermocouples had to be installed to measure the exact skin temperatures. T-33 flights had to be laid on to rendezvous with the Article at 30,000 feet and film the results.

2. Low Altitude, Quiet aka "Wailing Wall" To determine whether the U-2R could fly a low altitude mission without detection. Lockheed was paid to study background noise over jungles, deserts, oceans, and "industrial environments," and then judge whether linings in the intake duct and different shapes in the nozzle would make the aircraft inaudible at 500 feet or less. Of course, flying low level would burn up fuel at an alarming rate, so this idea was linked to:

3. Probe-and-Drogue Buddy Refueling for U-2R The ultimate in self-sufficiency, for the U-2 unit that wants to go everywhere, without bothering those reluctant Admirals for a carrier to land on!

4. Day-Night Driftsights A proposal from ORD to allow a pilot to navigate from high altitude by terrain features after the sun had gone down.

5. High Altitude Bullshit Bomber To persuade the Commies to give up and join the good guys, leaflets would be dropped from 70,000 feet. This was not a new idea. A special hatch had been designed for the early models as long ago as 1957. Someone in the Skunk Works—who probably did not take the project seriously anyway—designated them the "U.S. Mule" hatch. This was a reference to the Li'l Abner comic strip, where a cartoon character delivers the mail by mule.

6. High Altitude Restart Probably the most sensible of the 1968-69 projects, this was a revival of the 1960 plan to avoid descending for an engine relight to the MiG level. Two additional igniters were provided in the combustion chamber, and oxygen was injected to all four. Sealed crossover tubes were added to the burner can. The latter mod alone worked quite well at 50,000 feet. The oxygen igniters worked occasionally at 56-58,000 feet. The normal relight altitude for the J75-P-13B in the U-2R was 40,000 feet.

The new and the old lined up at North Base. The U-2R (foreground) was about one-third bigger. Wingspan was 104 feet, increased from 80 feet (Lockheed C-0471-09).

This scheme was being tried over North Vietnam at the time, using Ryan drones launched from DC-130s in a program named United Effort. In November 1968 the NRO Executive Committee approved R&D funding for the Fortune Cookie project.[16]

Beech worked on adapting the AQM-37 for high-altitude launch, and a new nose that would enhance the drone's radar signature. The ELINT receivers were provided by ESL. The Skunk Works designed a wing pylon with a trapeze to extend the drone clear of the Article before its rocket engine was lit. By mid-March 1969, inert versions of the modified drone were ready for flight tests on the U-2R. This was an interesting proposition: the basic AQM-37 weighed over 600 lbs![17]

Launch tests

The Beech drone's minimum speed of Mach 0.7 almost exactly matched the U-2R's cruising speed. The U-2R pilot was provided with a small launch control panel. Launch tests started on the Pacific Missile Range (PMR), with Det G pilots flying the U-2R. Meanwhile, Project HQ conferred with OEL and OSI on a suitable target for the first mission. They selected the Red Flag SAM that China had developed from the Soviet SA-2, which had already shot down at least one U-2 and some of the Ryan drones. In early April 1969 two CAF U-2 pilots (Andy Fan and Denny Hwang) were recalled from Taiwan to train for the operational phase of the program. At least one AQM-37 was launched on the PMR by Andy Fan.[18]

If all went according to plan, the two drones would be fired from the U-2 at up to 12 minute intervals. They would simulate an attack by much larger fighter-bombers. The SAM site would respond by launching missiles, and various signals of interest would be recorded and relayed—such as the missile's beacon frequency and the fuzing data. A "Black Book" was prepared for the 303 Committee to approve in early June. The Chicom SAM sites near the coast at Changchow (Canton), Luta, and Shanghai were all potential targets for the mission.[19]

Apparently, it was the 303 Committee that shot down the Fortune Cookie drone, rather than the Chicoms. By OSA's own admission, gaining political approval would be difficult because of the "provocative nature in operational application" of the system. The timing of the request was also

Brig Gen Gene Ross was the Director of OSA from 1968 to 1970. He fought the first attempt to have the Agency's U-2 operation closed down (NARA).

British U-2 contingent at Edwards in 1968. From left to right: Flt Lt Andy Cummings (flight surgeon), Flt Lt Harry Drew and Sqn Ldr Dick Cloke (pilots), and Flt Lt Rod Booth (navigator). (via Dick Cloke)

unfortunate. The Navy EC-121M had been shot down off North Korea a few weeks earlier. The fallout from that loss was that even the standard U-2R peripheral missions along the China coast from Taiwan were stood down for two months. Fortune Cookie missions with the U-2R were never approved. The hardware was stored unused until the summer of September 1972, when the ELINT receivers were fitted on SAC's Ryan drones instead. Four missions codenamed Compass Cookie were then flown against North Vietnamese SA-2s, ahead of the Linebacker B-52 raids.[20]

U-2R to sea

In August 1969, preparations began to take the U-2R to sea. A capability to operate the new model from "Kittyhawk-class" carriers had been built-in at the design stage. The outer six feet of each wing could be hinged upwards, to reduce the wingspan sufficiently to accommodate the Article on a carrier's elevator. The removable tailhook design was the same as on the U-2G. The hook was fitted and tested during a two-day visit to the mock carrier deck at NAS Lakehurst, NJ, in early September. The carrier landing characteristics of the U-2R seemed to be much better than the U-2G, thanks to the new model's option to set the flaps at 50 degrees. Also, the J75-P-13B engine had a higher RPM, which allowed a faster response to waveoffs.[21]

Then four pilots from Det G were sent to NAS Pensacola for carrier landing qualification on the U.S. Navy's T-2B. They were Ben Higgins and Dave Wright, recently recruited from the USAF, plus Dick Cloke and Harry Drew, the two RAF pilots currently assigned to the project. Their chaperone was Lt Cdr Lonnie McClung, a rated Navy pilot who was now serving as Det G's resident LSO. Lockheed test pilot Bill Park also took the Navy carqual. All five pilots returned to North Base, where they flew mirror landing practices in the U-2R.[22]

The team then migrated to the East Coast, where the new carrier USS *America* had been made available during its shakedown trials. Two U-2Rs were ferried to Wallops Island, the NASA airfield in Virginia. The assigned day of 21 November 1969 dawned clear, although the sea state was fairly rough. Park flew out to the carrier and began his first approach. He had

BLUE GULL V

This was the codename for the first carrier landings of the U-2R, on the USS America *off the east Coast in November 1969. Vic Milam, who had flown U-2s in the SAC wing, was now the operations officer for Det G. He recalled:*

First trap didn't work, as they forgot to take the pin out of the tail hook. Bill Park returned to Wallops Island, they pulled the pin, and he then made several touch and gos and traps, and "qualified" the aircraft. Our guys at North Base had been practicing on our little 3,000 ft strip with a marked-off carrier deck. We had a Navy LSO assigned—Lonnie McClung. He basically ran the show.

The R was standard, with the exception of the tail hook and the flaps modified to 50 degrees. Talk about barn doors! When they pulled off power, it settled. It really hurt to watch the bird hit the deck on some of the tries.

We only used one wire. One of our pilots thought he had missed it and started around. In fact he had hooked the wire. Then he realized it, and pulled the power. One wing was hanging over the side. They pulled it back. After my heart attack had subsided he launched for home.

It was quite an operation. The idea was great, but the cost was too much to sell. The Navy had to commit a carrier for probably only one operational mission.

HOW DR. KISSINGER RESCUED PROJECT IDEALIST

In December 1969 Henry Kissinger, National Security Advisor, persuaded President Nixon to retain a separate U-2 program within CIA. Kissinger wrote:

The program provides a flexible overhead reconnaissance system with unique capabilities for high resolution photography, ELINT collection, and sensor airdrop. It can react rapidly to worldwide crisis situations cheaply, effectively, and at little political risk to the U.S. government.

Agreements for joint operations exist with the Republic of China and the United Kingdom, enabling effective covert U-2 operations unattributable to U.S. government sponsorship. This new U-2R capability can be utilized with a reaction time of approximately 50 hours anywhere in the world.

During noncrisis periods this asset is used to collect intelligence on communist China, which is made available to the ROC. Removal of the U-2 detachment from Taiwan would have serious political consequences, and might adversely affect other important joint intelligence projects.

The SAC U-2s do not now have adequate sensors for all types of missions, lack the defensive equipment to operate in a hostile environment, and of course do not afford the U.S. government the option of non-attributability.

decided upon an approach speed of 72 knots with a wind-over-deck of 20 knots. Like the earlier G-model pilots, Park had to rely on the airspeed needle—he had no angle-of-attack indicator in the cockpit. As Park neared the ship he pulled the lever to lower the hook, but nothing happened. Someone had forgotten to remove the locking pin before he took off! He returned to shore for a quick fix, and was soon out at the boat again. He completed two traps, plus a lightweight and heavyweight takeoff. In Park's opinion, you hardly needed the hook at all.

After the test pilot had proved the concept, the four Agency pilots each qualified by flying two waveoffs, four touch-and-gos, and four traps. The Article was moved to and from the hangar deck, to prove that it would

fit. Det G was certified ready to perform operational carrier-based missions.[23]

Valuable deck space

The question was whether they would ever get the chance. Some Admirals wanted nothing to do with Project Idealist. They opposed the U-2 taking up valuable deck space on their precious aircraft carriers. However, other officers in Naval Aviation were showing increased interest in the U-2 as a data relay platform operating high over a carrier group. When Det G went to sea again in July 1970—a quick requalification visit to the USS *Kitty Hawk* off San Diego—a delegation of top Navy brass flew out from Washington to observe.[24]

A CIA U-2 on the compass rose in the late 1960s, just before the early models were replaced by the U-2R (Lockheed).

After the Cuban Missile Crisis, the U-2 continued flying over Cuba—for the next 12 years! From time to time, politicians and generals worried that the Dragon Lady was too vulnerable. The last thing they wanted was another downed pilot for Fidel Castro to show off as a trophy—dead or alive! But despite the Cuban leader's frequent threats to shoot down an overflying U-2, U.S. intelligence had a pretty good idea that this was all bluster—thanks to SIGINT. Here are some extracts from an intelligence assessment in August 1967:

Since mid-March 1967 there have been 24 U-2 overflights of Cuba. Mig-21 fighter aircraft have five times been scrambled from San Antonio de los Banos Airbase, southwest of Havana, for the purpose of intercepting a U-2 flight. In the first case, it is not clear that Cuban air defense personnel realized that the overflying plane was a U-2; in the four subsequent cases it is quite clear that they did. No order or instruction was communicated to a MiG-21 suggesting that it was to try to shoot down the U-2. And in no case, as far as we can determine, did a MiG-21 reach a high enough altitude to intercept the U-2....

In only one case was an element of the SAM system ordered to improve its state of readiness. On 11 July the Campo Florido SAM site was informed by its regional command that by order of those higher up it should proceed to a state of personnel readiness without turning on its equipment. Although this communication sounded ominous, it contained no specific indication of hostile threat. No attempt was actually made by this site to fire a missile at the U-2, nor even to track it with the fan Song guidance radar....

It is possible that the Cubans have sent up the MiG-21s—and even indulged in some mild chicanery at a SAM site—to harass the overflying U-2 and induce it to abort....

Whether or not the Cubans try further harassment of U-2 overflights, we believe that the same basic factors that have in the past deterred the Castro government from attempting an actual shootdown will remain operative in the foreseeable future...We cannot, however, entirely rule out the possibility of an irrational act, particularly in some crisis situation.

- Special National Intelligence Estimate 85-1-67, 31 August 1967

This was all good stuff, but it did not impress the bean counters in Washington. The Bureau of the Budget (BOB) wanted the U-2R fleet cut to eight, and the CIA out of the high-altitude recce business. Of course, the Pentagon supported the latter idea. But the NRO Executive Committee had already rejected this, not least because it meant ripping up the Razor/Tackle agreement with nationalist China. However, on 19 December 1969 BOB Director Mayo sneaked the subject into his meeting with President Nixon on the Fiscal 1971 budget. Nixon agreed to the BOB plan.

Fortunately, the Agency's U-2 program had a powerful supporter in the White House. At a meeting of the 303 Committee the next day, the National Security Advisor, Dr. Henry Kissinger, strongly supported the retention of Project Idealist. The other members of the committee agreed with him (Deputy Secretary of Defense David Packard, who supported the BOB, could not attend the meeting). Four days later Dr. K persuaded Nixon to reverse his decision. It was a nice Christmas present for OSA, whose Director Bg Gen Donald Ross lost no time in distributing the news within the Project.[25]

U-Tapao

In June 1970, SAC said goodbye to Bien Hoa after six years, and relocated OL-20 to U-Tapao, Thailand, as OL-RU. It consisted of a single U-2R flying photo missions over Cambodia and Laos now codenamed Giant Nail, and the much larger drone operation codenamed Buffalo Hunter, which was providing the coverage of North Vietnam, in conjunction with the SR-71.

At the same time the photo mission over Cuba was renamed Old Head, and OL-19 at McCoy was redesignated OL-RD. From April 1970 the coverage requirement was relaxed to 90% of the island every 90 days, or one sortie per month. On a clear day, a U-2R equipped with the IRIS II camera could image the whole Cuba on a single sortie, if required.

On 26 August 1970, an Old Head mission returned with imagery of new construction at the port of Cienfuegos, on the southern coast of Cuba. U.S. intelligence quickly linked this activity to a new Soviet flotilla that was in the Atlantic, and apparently heading for the island. Soviet military activity on Cuba was already on the increase. The 303 Committee approved daily U-2 flights, but clouds prevented any missions until 14 September. On that day, MiG-21s made serious attempts to intercept the overflight, as well as a separate peripheral mission. The flights were aborted. Two days later OL-RD tried again, and brought back conclusive evidence that the Soviets were building a naval base at Cienfuegos, to possibly include support for nuclear submarines with ballistic missiles.[26]

10340 was the last of the 12 U-2R models to be built, and was delivered to the 100th SRW. It is seen here taxiing out at Bien Hoa airbase in 1969-70 (William Clarke).

The Beech AQM-37 supersonic target drone was adapted to the U-2R in the Fortune Cookie project. (via TD Barnes)

It was another Cuban Missile Crisis in the making. The U.S. demanded that construction of the base be halted. The Soviets complied. But subsequent U-2 flights showed that a submarine tender and a salvage tug remained in Cuban waters. All through the remainder of 1970 and early months of 1971, U-2 missions from McCoy tracked Soviet naval activity around Cuba. President Nixon issued a public warning to the Soviets against them servicing missile-carrying submarines at Cuban ports. The USSR continued to send naval task forces to the island, but only one "boomer" showed up, and that was not until April 1972.[27]

Middle East flare-up

The showdown over Cienfuegos came as another East-West crisis unfolded in the Middle East. There was a renewed flare-up in the Arab-Israeli conflict. Egypt had pledged to retake Israeli-occupied Sinai by force, and the

Flt Lt Harry Drew prepares for a low flight from North Base in the late 1960s. His U-2R is in an experimental gray color scheme (via Harry Drew).

U-2 Pilot group at Det G in 1970. Ben Higgins (left) and Dave Young (center) were new recruits, soon to replace veterans such as Bob Ericson (right). (via Arne Ericson)

The U-2R went to sea for the first time in November 1969 when five pilots flew from the USS *America* during Operation Blue Gull V (Lockheed C645-6567).

Although the R-model was bigger, folding wingtips made it fit on the carrier's elevators. Senior Naval officers resented the disruption that U-2 operations could cause, and no operational missions were ever flown (Lockheed PI3088).

Article 383/N805X at Edwards in 1969 during the "Chameleon" trials. The NCR company provided paints that could change color according to temperature—and therefore altitude (Lockheed 6136).

A U-2R of Project Idealist takes off from North Base. Using the "Fast Move" concept, the CIA promised to have the airplane over any world trouble spot within 50 hours of the request (via Arne Ericson).

two sides were slugging it out in a war of attrition across the Suez Canal. To stop the Israeli air force from attacking targets deep inside Egyptian territory, the Soviet Union sent a complete Air Defense Division to Cairo's aid in late February 1970. It consisted of early warning radars, MiG-21M fighter regiments, and SA-2 and SA-3 SAM batteries. After first being set up in rear areas, the mobile missile batteries began rolling east in June, threatening Israel's hitherto unchallenged air superiority over the canal itself. Two of Israel's F-4s were shot down, and a big dogfight followed over the Gulf of Suez on 30 July.

Dr. Kissinger led a U.S. diplomatic effort to mediate between the two sides. They agreed to a 30-day ceasefire, and to withdraw their troops 32 miles back from the Canal. Dr. K promised that the U.S. would monitor the withdrawal using overhead reconnaissance.[28]

The ceasefire was due to take effect on 7 August. Washington's idea was that the U-2R could fly down the Canal and photograph the 64-mile strip of territory within which the two sides had agreed not to make any further deployments. Both the SAC and CIA U-2 units were alerted for a possible deployment. There was a two-horse race to see who could respond fastest. The CIA promised to get there in 48 hours. Det G got the job and was tasked for a "Fast Move." It was codenamed Even Steven.[29]

But would the British cooperate? After about 10 years of trying, there were signs that they would finally give permission to operate out of RAF Akrotiri, the airbase with the UK sovereign area on Cyprus. At Edwards, two aircraft were quickly prepared for a two-stage ferry to Akrotiri via RAF Upper Heyford. The two British pilots at Det G would fly them from North Base to the UK. Then, at the last minute, the British government decided it would rather not have its pilots fly, thank you very much![30]

Caffeine pills

Only two of Det G's American pilots were at North Base that day—the others were already on their way to the UK by commercial airline. Marty Knutson was airborne on a camera cold-soak test flight lasting five-and-a-half hours. Bob Ericson was his mobile. When Knutson landed, he received the unwelcome news that the British pilots were precluded from flying the U-2Rs to the UK that evening. The regulations on crew rest were torn up, and Knutson was given a liberal supply of caffeine pills. The two veteran CIA U-2 pilots took off and crossed the Atlantic in 12 hours 30 minutes, with Ericson calling Knutson behind him every few minutes on HF to make sure that he stayed awake! Permission to land in the UK was

not formally received at Project HQ until the aircraft were halfway across the Atlantic.[31]

USAF C-141 transports were following with staging crews. The plan was to fly across Europe from Upper Heyford and over the Suez Canal before landing at Akrotiri. But France and Italy both refused to let the U-2 transit through their airspace. The missions had to be routed around Europe, through the Straits of Gibraltar, and into the Mediterranean. More long flights! Jim Barnes took off from Upper Heyford on 9 August and flew down the Canal as planned, before eventually landing at the airbase on Cyprus. He noticed no threats, but intercepts of the Israeli air defense net indicated that one of their F-4s nearly opened fire on him! Dan Wright followed in the second U-2R a day later. He flew directly to Akrotiri after the operational part of the flight was canceled by Washington.[32]

The monitoring flights from Akrotiri began on 11 August, and they were a twitchy affair indeed for the pilots that flew them. For starters Egypt had not consented to them, and when the U.S. informed the Soviet Union about them, they too objected. Even the Israelis were suspicious of U.S. motives. Extreme care had to be taken to fly precisely along the allotted track, which was 10 miles inside Israeli-held territory.[33]

Then there was the SAM threat. The Egyptians moved some SA-2 batteries into the zone after the ceasefire took effect; they were definitely close enough to threaten the high-flying spyplanes. The Soviet-manned SA-3 batteries were only just outside the zone. *Both* sides tracked the overflying U.S. spyplanes with their missile radars: the low-PRF light in the U-2 cockpit was almost constantly illuminated! Sometimes the hi-light illuminated, and the aircraft's active jammer went into action.

Detailed coverage

The U-2 flights continued for nearly three months. The ceasefire held, but the provision that neither side would move fresh military equipment into the Canal Zone broke down. That much was evident from the U-2 photography. Detailed coverage of the 64-mile wide zone was achieved on 18 flights using the B-camera, supplemented by 12 H-camera missions for high-oblique coverage. Additionally, the flights carried the latest U-2 ELINT

Upon his retirement in 1970 after 15 years as a U-2 pilot, Bob Ericson was presented with a CIA Intelligence Star by Deputy Director for Science & Technology Carl Duckett (via Arne Ericson).

Whitehall, Westminster Bridge, and the British House of Parliament as seen by the B2-camera of a U-2R during the Scope Saint III practice deployment to the UK in 1969. (Dick Cloke)

systems. The CIA could not resist the opportunity to collect valuable intelligence on the two sides' air defense systems—especially the Soviet SA-3 SAM.[34]

Egypt's objections to the U-2 flights became more vocal as time wore on, and they were halted after the 30th mission on 10 November. It was flown by Marty Knutson—his last operation after 15 years as a U-2 pilot.

This Middle East deployment also saw the last flights of Jim Barnes and Bob Ericson, the other two survivors from the CIA's class of 1956.[35]

The two aircraft were withdrawn from Cyprus in mid-December, and staged through Upper Heyford again on the way home. As a *mea culpa*, perhaps, the British government gave permission for the RAF U-2 pilots to fly the onward ferry legs. Fog delayed the takeoffs on the morning of 14 December. Dick Cloke eventually departed first, followed by Harry Drew. They flew all day to reach Edwards, with the sun overtaking them and shining directly into their eyes as they neared their destination. Cloke landed after just under 14 hours in the air. Drew took 15 minutes longer. They were in the pressure suits for over 16 hours.[36]

As a demonstration of quick-reaction capability and professional airmanship, Operation Even Steven could not be faulted. And it may have saved Project Idealist from extinction in the forthcoming Fiscal Year, for the knives were out again in Washington. NRO Director John McLucas now favored a U-2 fleet consolidation under SAC. On 17 August 1970 he wrote a memo in preparation for a meeting next day of the White House group that made all the big decisions about intelligence-gathering. It was now known as the 40 Committee (previously, the 303 Committee). "In today's environment the ability to conduct a covert reconnaissance flight in a crisis area is becoming very questionable" the NRO head noted. "Modern radar and SIGINT techniques provide the principal nations with the capability to know that we are coming and, in some instances, what we are doing."

This was just one week after the CIA had deployed the U-2 to the Sinai Desert at only 48 hours notice. Dr. Kissinger and the fellow members of the 40 Committee were very impressed with that. At their 18 August meeting they rejected the NRO's advice, and decided to retain a split U-2 fleet through Fiscal 1972.[37]

<h1 style="text-align:center">26</h1>

The Origins of Real-Time Reconnaissance

On 13 August 1971 a SAC U-2R took off from U-Tapao and headed east across Indo-China, before taking up an orbit in the Gulf of Tonkin (GOT). There were no cameras onboard. Instead, a new pallet in the Q-bay housed communications intelligence (COMINT) receivers and recorders, and a new fairing under the tail of the Dragon Lady contained a datalink. From high over the GOT, the U-2 began test transmissions to a secret ground station on the northern Thai border with Laos.

It was the start of real-time airborne manned reconnaissance. The event had profound significance for the future of not only the U-2, but of many other collection systems. Three days after the first test over the GOT a second was flown. Over the next month there were a further 10 evaluation flights. Then, on 1 October, the first operational Senior Book mission was flown. For the next three-and-a-half years, the U-2 would provide almost daily SIGINT coverage of North Vietnam and southern China.[1]

The Senior Book system was derived from a rush effort to put SIGINT receivers into some Ryan high-altitude drones. They would be a substitute for manned collection platforms like the Navy EC-121M that had been shot down by the North Koreans in April 1969. The idea was fast-tracked through the USAF bureaucracy via the Big Safari program. Ryan took a small receiver package built by the Melpar Division of E-Systems, and added a wideband datalink that it had recently developed in-house. The first modified drone was test-flown only seven months after the EC-121 went down. In February 1970 the drone system, including ground receiver vans, was airlifted to Osan AB, Korea, for two months of operational testing. In October 1970 the production version was deployed, and regular COMINT missions codenamed Combat Dawn began over the Yellow Sea.[2]

Candidate

The U-2 was also a candidate platform for Combat Dawn. Col Frank Hartley, the director of Program D in the NRO, realised the possibilities of adding the Melpar package to the Dragon Lady. Especially now that the U-2R model with improved endurance was in service. As the SIGINT drone program proceeded in 1970, the NRO funded development of a similar system on the U-2.

To test the drone system, Ryan had set up a datalink ground station at NAS Point Mugu. But when the U-2 flew over, two-way communications could not be established.

A rival datalink was under development by Sperry, the company that provided the Microwave Command Guidance System (MCGS) for the drones. After ten failed U-2 test flights with the Ryan datalink, the Skunk

Works invited Sperry to the party. The Salt Lake City-based company installed its L-2 downlink on the test U-2. It worked! After more tests, Sperry was contracted to build a deployable datalink system, and Melpar adapted the HARC (High-Altitude Recon COMINT) collection system to the U-2. The Skunk Works did the integration.[3]

With the help of Melpar and Sperry, the USAF Security Service (AFSS) set up a ground station at Nakhon Phanom airfield. AFSS provided the linguists who listened to and translated the opposition's air defense communications. The Senior Book system provided them with eight VHF and two HF channels of multiplexed COMINT. They controlled the receivers remotely via the uplink to the U-2R. At 70,000 feet, the Dragon Lady could be 300 miles away and still be in line-of-sight to the ground station. The antennas carried on the U-2's fuselage and Q-bay could pick up communications to a similar distance.[4]

Senior Book

Straight away, Senior Book became the major activity for OL-UA at U-Tapao. In the first year the SAC unit flew a COMINT mission nearly every day. The U-2R flew a circular orbit over the GOT lasting eight hours, so when transit to and from the Thai base was added, these were 10-hour missions. At first, the link could easily be lost every time the U-2 turned. But in 1972 Sperry provided an improved L-5 system that included a dual axis antenna.

There were now three U-2Rs based at U-Tapao, with the pilots and maintenance crews rotating every 90 days. About once a week, one aircraft would have to be reconfigured from COMINT for a photo mission over Cambodia or Laos. North Vietnam made full-scale military deployments

The Senior Book configuration was added to the U-2R for use in southeast Asia in 1971. For the first time, a data-link relayed SIGINT to a ground station in real-time (via Arthur Pearcey).

EARLY U-2 SIGINT

Bruce Bailey was a "Raven," or SIGINT systems operator, on RB-47s and RC-135s. Here's his view of the development of SIGINT on the U-2.

The early SIGINT configurations consisted of pre-set receivers that could monitor only one or two frequencies; scanning receivers with limited capability; and wide-open receivers that intercepted everything within a pre-set band. The shortcomings of such a system were obvious, and much effort went into improving it. Here the U-2 benefited from its rivals, the drones. Both U-2s and drones soon routinely performed their tasks utilizing intercept systems that were remotely monitored and controlled by specialists in other aircraft or ground sites. This system enabled the specialists to select the signals of most interest, search for suspect emitters, operate the equipment themselves just as if they were onboard the U-2, and relay their intelligence to users around the world via satellites and other communications.

- from "The View From The Top," Warplane, Vol 6, Issue 69

DRYING OUT THE "PACKAGE"

Bob Anderson of Lockheed was charged with integrating the Senior Book system into the U-2R. He recalls:

"When we were first asked to fit the Melpar COMINT system on the U-2R we flew an aircraft to Point Mugu, where they were doing the tests with the drone system off the Pacific Coast. They handed over the package—it was wet! They had just fished it out of a drone that went down over the range. Now we understood why they were bringing us in. We fitted it, dried it out on the plane, and flew it that evening. And the HF channels picked up an F-4 flying over Vietnam! *- interview with author*

THE FLIGHT OF MARSHALL LIN PIAO

According to unconfirmed reports, the brand new U-2 Senior Book system scored a major intelligence coup just weeks after it went operational in August 1971. Early on the morning of 13 September, all air traffic in mainland China was grounded...airliners, fighters, everything. The COMINT receivers on a U-2R orbiting over the Gulf of Tonkin picked up signs of the commotion, probably from the Chicom air defense net on Hainan Island.

The intercepts were analyzed in the ground station at Nakhon Phanom. The intel was passed to U-Tapao, where more AFSS linguists were based. Strict security rules were broken as word leaked out. "You would not believe what we've just found out!" one of them told a couple of the U-2 pilots.

An amazing story began to unfold. Chinese Defense Minister Lin Piao had apparently launched a coup against Mao Tse Tung, but it had failed! He had then attempted to flee the country in a Trident airliner used by top officials as a VIP transport. AFPLA interceptors had pursued the plane, and it had been shot down over Mongolia.

The coup was hushed up, to such an extent that Lin Piao remained officially listed as Minister of Defense for almost an entire further year, despite having perished along with his wife and son, and the six other people onboard the downed airliner. During Dr Kissinger's second round of talks in Peking in October 1971, Premier Chou En Lai made only the most enigmatic of references to the coup attempt and its aftermath. – C.P.

A VIEW FROM THE GROUND

The 6908th Security Squadron operated the ground station that controlled the U-2R SIGINT mission in Southeast Asia. One of the operators recalled:

The Senior Book van was a huge thing, about 10 feet wide and more than 40 feet long. Outside, there was a small datalink control van about the size of a pick-up truck. Beside it was a 40 foot permanent tower with the up/downlink antenna mounted. When the U-bird got on station and we established contact and link, the pilot took naps, read books, ate lunch, played music, or anything else exciting he could find to do. We spent many long hours talking with the pilots about girls, baseball, lousy beer, girls, going home, girls—or anything to pass the time of day.

Regarding North Vietnam tactical air ops, we knew who was on strip alert, the type aircraft, and the scramble data. We listened to their vectoring against our birds. We even knew when they were turned loose to fire. Seventh Air Force initially had difficulty using the Teaball system, with their people listening to our intercepts and plots, and then plotting it all backwards for the on-scene commander. We loaned them a tac air analyst who was a Vietnamese linguist and things took off with a bang. Ultimately, they took over and it worked as designed—to save lives and kill Charlie.

via those countries, as part of the 1972 spring offensive. The Army divisions must have been easier for the PIs to spot, from the U-2 Giant Nail mission photography, than the elusive guerrilla supply movements down the Ho Chi Minh trail!

In April 1972 SAC HQ changed the U-2R COMINT mission codename to Olympic Torch. The following month, the U.S. launched the first of the two Linebacker air campaigns. Olympic Torch provided invaluable, near-real time warning of North Vietnam air defense activity. At the end of July the 6908th Security Squadron implemented the Teaball Weapons Control Center. AFSS combined the COMINT from Olympic Torch with plots from an over-the-horizon radar at Nakhon Phanom to warn of the scrambling and vectoring of North Vietnamese interceptors, and the alerting of SAM sites. The intelligence was relayed via a dedicated KC-135 radio relay aircraft to U.S. fighters and bombers, alerting them to close with or avoid the defenders, as appropriate. Teaball dramatically reversed the air combat exchange ratio in the skies over North Vietnam.[5]

99th SRS

On 1 November 1972 SAC converted the U-2R operation at U-Tapao into a fully-fledged squadron, the 99th SRS. Its first commander was Col Buddy Brown, a U-2 veteran who had flown over Cuba during the missile crisis.

The squadron also controlled the photo drone operations, by now almost exclusively going low-level across North Vietnam.

Following the failure of yet another round of peace negotiations, the U.S. began Linebacker II in mid-December. The massive night bombing of Hanoi and Haiphong was observed from high over the GOT by the U-2R pilots. Their COMINT collection helped to warn against the activation of SAM systems by the North Vietnamese, and the U-2R also acted as a UHF communications relay to the U.S. warplanes for Teaball information. A second air-ground link was established to the U.S. Navy Red Crown control ship operating in the GOT.[6]

For the duration of the campaign a second daily Olympic Torch mission was flown, to provide 16-18-hour coverage. With only three aircraft and five pilots, this stretched the 99th SRS to the limit. Normal crew duty day and rest requirements were waived. But there was only one U-2R abort during Linebacker II—and that aircraft was quickly replaced by another. The squadron provided a total of 344 hours on station time during the 11-day campaign, and through to the end of January 1973. That month, the 99th SRS flew a record 518 hours.[7]

U-2R pilots were also tasked to "eyeball" the SAMs fired at U.S. B-52 bombers, and call out warnings via UHF radio to the air control stations. It was quite a fireworks display. On 26 December Capt "Fuzzy" Furr observed no fewer than 84 SAM firings from his grandstand view of the action. The next day, Major Ray Samay counted 72 more.[8]

It was probably from Olympic Torch that Linebacker mission planners learned that the North Vietnamese SAM sites were running out of missiles. Nearly a thousand SA-2 missiles had been fired, and 15 B-52s downed. The planners switched B-52 raids to SAM storage facilities, preventing a resupply to the sites. By the tenth day of the campaign the North Vietnamese air defense system had nearly collapsed. Linebacker II ended on 29 December, and a peace agreement was reached in January.[9]

Award

The 100th SRW wing was awarded the General Paul T. Cullen Memorial Award for its "outstanding record in support of SE Asia requirements and

unique contributions to Linebacker II operations." In those days, that was just about all that could be said about the Top Secret COMINT mission.

During 1973, the GOT missions continued at a reduced tempo—that is, one per day. The emphasis was now on monitoring North Vietnam's adherence to the peace agreement. A new collection orbit was established over Laos. On some missions the IRIS II camera was also carried, allowing the U-2R to be diverted from the COMINT task to take pictures, if cloud conditions permitted.[10]

In January 1974 SAC began worrying about the safety of the RC-135M aircraft, which also collected COMINT over the Gulf of Tonkin, as well as the South China Sea. The 99th SRS received additional tasking, and sometimes flew double-daily missions to supplement the reduced coverage by the RC-135s.[11]

Melpar improved its COMINT system. The HARC IV version offered more channels—24 of them—and broader frequency coverage. It needed more operators in the ground station, and more space in the airborne platform. The Skunk Works dusted off the design work it had done on equipment pods during the U-2R development. The pods faired into the leading edge of the U-2R wing, rather like the slipper tanks of the early

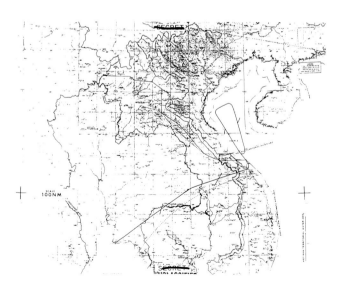

Map shows the transit route from U-Tapao and an orbit over the Gulf of Tonkin, used by the 100th SRW in the early 1970s.

The flying hours soon racked up during the SIGINT missions. From left to right, pilots Ray Samay, Jim Wrenn, Willie Horton, Mike Banks, Doyle Krumrey, and Jim Terry of the 99th SRS celebrate their latest achievement.

Rear view of 10329 shows the datalink fairing, antenna farm, and wing-mounted pods of the Senior Spear configuration, introduced in 1974 (Lockheed C76-1128-01).

A U-2R lands at U-Tapao after another long SIGINT orbit.

10336 on the ramp at U-Tapao during the bitter end of the Vietnam conflict, April 1975. The 99th SRS stayed on at the Thai base for another year (NARA KE66080).

models—only larger. Ed Lovick designed longer blade antennas to go below the right pod. TRW provided direction-finding and Sperry provided the up and downlink again. The Senior Spear program was launched. The system was operational in Thailand by December 1974.

As the Saigon regime faltered under continued pressure from the Viet Cong and their North Vietnamese allies in late 1974, the JRC requested that the U-2R COMINT coverage be increased again. A fourth U-2R was deployed from D-M to U-Tapao so that two sorties could be mounted every day. From November 1974 through to the fall of Saigon at the end of April 1975, the 99th SRS flew 352 Olympic Torch sorties.

Bitter conclusion

The Vietnam War had reached a bitter conclusion, from the U.S. perspective. The 25 remaining Buffalo Hunter drones were immediately withdrawn, returned to D-M, and placed in storage. SAC was full of praise for the drones' achievements—2,982 sorties with 24 different models over 10 years. But the Tactical Air Command (TAC) had been fighting to take them over for years. Within a year it assumed the mission—and proceeded to neglect it.[12]

The following month, May 1975, the U-2R demonstrated its utility as a communications relay during the Mayaguez incident. Cambodian Khmer Rouge communists captured a U.S. cargo ship and imprisoned the crew. Since a vital defense communications satellite was out of commission, the 99th SRS was tasked to provide relay support to the U.S. rescue force. U-2Rs flew at altitude for 27 hours over a three day period to relay messages to and from the rescue force, which succeeded in recovering the boat and its crew intact.

The 99th SRS hung on at U-Tapao for another year. COMINT missions continued at a reduced frequency. There were some photo flights along the Thai border to monitor clashes between Thai troops and the Pathet Lao. SAC hoped to keep the unit there indefinitely. But the Thai government had other ideas. Under pressure from neighboring countries, it requested that the U-2s be withdrawn. The last Olympic Torch mission was flown on 15 March 1976. Having been one of the first USAF units to arrive in Southeast Asia in 1964, the U-2 unit was one of the last to depart, in April 1976.[13]

High-altitude Ryan drones performed the Combat Dawn mission in Korea from 1970-75, sometimes from a captive position beneath the DC-130 launch aircraft. In 1976, the U-2R took over this COMINT operation (NARA KE51279).

Osan, Korea

By then, though, new horizons beckoned. The 99th SRS was not returning stateside. Instead, squadron commander Dave Young was instructed to move most of the assets directly to Osan AB, Korea, to where the 100th SRW had already staged two U-2R deployments for sampling missions. Osan now became OL-OA of the 100th SRW. The U-2R was taking over the airborne collection of COMINT against North Korea.

For nearly five years (1970-1975) the drones had performed this mission in the operation codenamed Combat Dawn. They flew two orbits: a free flight over the Yellow Sea after launch from the DC-130 mothership, and a captive flight along the Demilitarized Zone (DMZ). But Combat Dawn was a mixed success, according to the USAF verdict, because of low reliability and high mission costs, once you took into account all the support equipment...the DC-130s, and the recovery helicopters and boats. Ryan and the drone lobby disagreed, citing the almost 500 flights made during Combat Dawn, and the return rate of 96.8% that was achieved in 1974-75.

Still, the last drone mission was flown on 3 June 1975. Until the U-2 arrived RC-135s took over, but SAC did not consider this a satisfactory solution. The U-2R could provide a higher-listening platform, and a routine eight hours on station. By now, the Dragon Lady had proved its worth as a COMINT collector, not only in Southeast Asia, but also in the Mediterranean, in the new Olive Tree mission now being flown from Akrotiri.[14]

At Osan, OL-OA swung into action, in conjunction with the COMINT analysts of the AFSS 6903rd Security Squadron in a ground station on the Korean airbase. The first Olympic Game mission was flown on 26 February 1976. A dozen were flown each month until a second aircraft was ready for operations in late July, when the sortie rate was doubled. The U-2 has been based in Korea ever since.

ALSS

While the U-2R was out in the field doing COMINT collection, back in the U.S. an ambitious new ELINT program was launched. The Advanced Location and Strike System (ALSS) was designed to rapidly and accurately fix the position of SAM radars so that they could be attacked from the air and silenced. By orbiting a trio (or "triad") of aircraft at high altitude, and datalinking their ELINT sensors to a ground station, the accurate positions of the threat emitters could be quickly calculated by triangulation. This overcame the problem of "traditional" airborne ELINT, where the emitter was required to stay on air long enough for the aircraft to move along track, so that the direction-finding process could be completed.

In the air war over Southeast Asia, the North Vietnamese had failed to cooperate in this endeavor. Just as the Chicoms had done against the U-2 over mainland China, they used other radars for tracking U.S. warplanes, and only turned on the Fan Song radar at the SA-2 site at the last minute. Or, to foil the missiles launched at them by U.S. Wild Weasel aircraft, which homed on the Fan Song transmitter, they quickly shut the radar down. Then they would move the whole site to another location.

IBM Federal Systems was the contractor for ALSS, which was part of a wider project codenamed Pave Onyx, to measure the time of arrival (TOA) of individual radar pulses. TAC was in charge—but SAC owned the U-2s, which were judged the best candidates to form the triad. From 65,000 feet the Dragon Lady could theoretically pick up emissions as far as 250 nautical miles away.

The U-2C models got a new lease of life—and a new paint scheme—for the ALSS mission. This is a post-flight scene from RAF Wethersfield during the 1975 deployment for flights of the triad over Europe (author).

The U-2Rs were very busy, but six of the surviving 12 early models were in storage. In March 1972 the Skunk Works was asked to quote on adapting five of them for the ALSS program. Six weeks later the go-ahead was given. The codename Senior Ball was allocated for the U-2 involvement in ALSS.[15]

The U-2 conversions were done at Palmdale; no fewer than 75 service bulletins were required to strip all the old equipment out of the air-

One of the ALSS aircraft (66700) came to grief over Germany during the deployment. After making a successful ejection, Captain Terry Rendleman (right) surveys the wreckage.

planes, bring them to a common U-2C standard, and install the ALSS equipment. The ELINT system was mounted on a pallet that fit into the Q-bay. The receivers were behind a bulged lower hatch; nine facing left, and another nine facing right. The datalink was housed in a fairing under the tail. The aircraft also received the System 20 IR-warner and the latest defensive aids—System 12F for warning and System 13C for jamming. (The triad was supposed to operate in friendly airspace, but evidently SAC was taking no chances!).[16]

Technical problems

Optimistically, TAC envisaged a quick test program over the White Sands Missile Range (WSMR), followed by a deployment to Southeast Asia in January 1973. In the first phase, only E and F-band radar frequencies would be covered. But the first conversion was not ready until October, with two more by the end of the year. To save time, the first development flights over the White Sands Missile Range (WSMR), in New Mexico, were flown from Palmdale. Technical problems soon became apparent with the receivers, datalinks, and also the airframes. After all, these Articles were 25 years old! Three aircraft had to be launched each time to form the triad, but a series of hydraulic, pneumatic, and oxygen system problems prevented that happening all too often.[17]

The ALSS aircraft were moved to Davis-Monthan. More development flights followed. But the air action was now over in Vietnam, and USAF fighter-bombers were pulling out of Southeast Asia. The scheme obviously had application to other theaters, however, so testing continued. An Operational Test and Evaluation (OT&E) was held from May to September 1973.

The ALSS equipment on the WSMR included the ground station, two ground relay beacon stations, and a number of remote beacon stations. These served as accurate reference points to fix the position in space of the U-2 triad and the strike aircraft by distance measuring techniques. Eight emitters representative of Soviet Bloc radars were used. Between May and September 1973, 42 ALSS test missions were scheduled, with the U-2s launching from D-M to fly designated triad orbits at various ranges from the emitters. A number of F-4 Phantoms would operate from Holloman AFB, NM, as the strike aircraft.

Twice-weekly tests were scheduled over the WSMR. But the U-2 fleet was grounded twice in May for accident investigations, causing the loss of 10 scheduled ALSS missions. On another six occasions, the 100th were unable to get three aircraft launched. Of the 26 missions actually flown, the U-2s were late arriving on station 12 times, despite the use of spare aircraft kept on standby status whenever a mission was scheduled. A sixth U-2C was converted.

66692 was the last U-2 converted for the ALSS mission, in late 1974 (Lockheed C75-1051-23).

Mixed success

The IOT&E was a mixed success. Six of the eight target radars were located to within 75 feet (and the other two to within 100 feet), but the system really only worked well when detecting S-band emissions. Rockwell Mk 84 glide bombs with DME guidance were launched towards the targets by the F-4 Phantoms. An average miss distance of 74 feet was recorded: ALSS seemed promising, but the overall reliability of the system was low. There were many sophisticated components making up the ALSS, and they all had to work properly all of the time—they did not.[18]

Despite this, the Air Force thought that the concept was worth pursuing. ALSS became part of the overall Pave Strike program for precision air-ground strikes. Some tests were flown to determine how well ALSS could direct DME-equipped RPVs to a target. It was decided to conduct a demonstration/evaluation in Europe, flying along the Inner German border to work in a "dense threat emitter environment." In addition to exercising ALSS against the real thing—Soviet emitters in East Germany and Czechoslovakia—it could also be tested for integration into USAFE's command and control network.

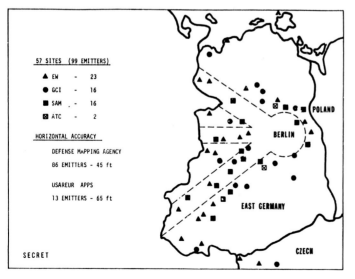

A target-rich environment! The map shows Soviet and East German emitters that were the target of the ALSS trial deployment (ALSS Dem/Val Final Report).

For a flavor of what works, and what doesn't, in the ELINT business, here are some extracts from Olympic Game mission summaries. The operation took place over West Germany in 1975 as part of the ALSS trials:

Mission 1: Difficulty was encountered by the GCI radar controllers in establishing orbits. A software problem caused the system to "hang up" in band 2. One U-2 reported the failure of a high-band preamplifier and was replaced with the spare aircraft.

Mission 3: The D-8 orbit, which incorporated 180-degree turns instead of 90/270 turns, was used to reduce turn times and provide more collection data. All-band emitter location data was collected for three hours.

Mission 6: Upon arrival of the U-2 aircraft at the Initial Point (IP), the ground control station was unable to track one aircraft because of a receiver failure in the ALSS pallet. A spare U-2 was substituted and experienced DME calibration problems.

Mission 8: The U-2s concentrated on locating Berlin radars for 40 minutes—the GCA was located with four fixes. The maximum range from the triad to the ground control station (GCS) was tested. Good track and location data were maintained when two U-2s remained within 200 nautical miles.

Mission 9: Upon arrival at the IP, one U-2 experienced DME calibration value jumps and a poor quality datalink to the GCS. This aircraft was replaced with the spare, but the spare had no direct datalink with the beacon ground stations because of false decoding of ground signals. The fifth U-2 (ground spare) was launched. Upon arrival at station, this aircraft also displayed poor datalink quality.

Mission 18: Approximately three hours of emitter location data were collected from the D-2 orbit. The U-2s were shifted to the D-8 orbit and data was collected for 1.5 hours, in both the all-band mode and by using filter guidelines.

- Advanced Location Strike System Dem/Val Final Report, USAF Tactical Air Warfare Center, February 1976

The exercise was codenamed Exercise Constant Treat, and the U-2 part of it was tagged Olympic Jump. Five aircraft would make the 90-day deployment. As was often the case with overseas deployments of the Dragon Lady, negotiations for basing and overflight rights took longer than expected. The British agreed to house them, but were unhappy at the speculation that would surely follow the arrival of five black spyplanes all at once! To satisfy this concern, the ALSS aircraft were repainted in a two-tone gray "camouflage!"

THE ORIGINS OF "REACHBACK" - OLIVE TREE AND SENIOR STRETCH

In April 1975, nine months after SAC took over the photo mission to monitor the Arab-Israeli ceasefire following the Yom Kippur War, it added a second mission from RAF Akrotiri. The Senior Spear COMINT system was deployed, and the Cyprus detachment flew its first Olive Tree sortie on 15 April 1975.

The unique aspect of the new mission was that a full-up ground station was not deployed. Instead, the "take" was downlinked to a relay van at Akrotiri, and from there uplinked to a Defense Systems Communications Satellite (DSCS). From its geostationary orbit high above the Atlantic, the "Discus" transmitted the COMINT data down to a satellite terminal in Maryland, so that it could be translated and analyzed by the linguists at the National Security Agency (NSA). Via a return link, the folks at NSA also switched and tuned the receivers onboard the orbiting U-2. Ten missions were scheduled each month, during which 80 hours of downlink time was regularly achieved.

- *from SAC Reconnaissance Histories, FY 1975 and FY 1977*

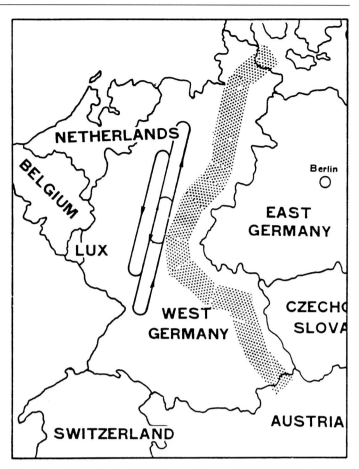

One of the orbits used by the U-2 triads over Germany in 1975 (ALSS Dem/Val Final Report).

RAF Wethersfield

In early May 1975 the 100th SRW flew five of the six brightly-painted C-models via Pease AFB, NH, to RAF Wethersfield, in Eastern England. It was a U.S. airbase that a USAFE fighter wing had vacated, leaving plenty of room. The ground station was set up at Sembach airbase in West Germany, with five remote beacon sites scattered from Bremerhaven in the north, to Neu-Ulm in the south. From mid-May until early July, 18 ALSS missions were flown. The U-2 triad would launch at 10-minute intervals from the rural English base and set course for Germany, followed by an airborne spare. If it was serviceable, the fifth aircraft would be preflighted and ready to go in case one or more of the others aborted. These precautions proved necessary; thanks to various malfunctions, the spare aircraft had to be called forward into the triad on 10 out of 18 missions, and the fifth aircraft was launched five times!

The U-birds generally flew for five hours parallel to the buffer zone, on a racetrack pattern that stretched from the North Sea to the Swiss border. Although special test transmitters had been set up on West German territory below, the aircraft also tuned in to the real stuff coming from the other side of the German border. F-4 Phantoms were again used as the strike aircraft (from the 36th TFW at Bitburg AB), but only unguided ordnance was dropped this time, on two bombing ranges in West Germany. The Phantoms picked up the ALSS data by means of a DME system housed in a converted fuel tank below the right wing.

Official British nervousness over the ALSS deployment was increased on 29 May, when one of the U-2s crashed during the fourth test mission. Captain Robert Rendleman ejected to safety, and the U-bird pancaked onto a track in the forest-covered hills of the Hunsruck, near Winterberg in West Germany. Air Force spokesmen stressed that the plane was unarmed and carrying no cameras; it was one of five engaged on tests of "a precision high altitude navigational system"—which was an approximation of the truth! The sixth ALSS was hurriedly ferried over as a replacement.

Unreliable

A total of 18 test missions were run. The verdict was much the same as before: ALSS was too unreliable. Data links failed, receivers and transmitters went off line, and connectors failed to connect. Even during an English summer, crosswinds at Wethersfield were above U-2C limits on four occasions, forcing two missions to be delayed and another two postponed overnight. When everything was up and running it could work. Unguided bombs struck within 150 feet of their emitting targets on the German ranges. However, a smaller number of Warsaw Pact emitters were located than expected. Their positions were fixed to within 175 feet on average, which was very good in those days. But few of the emitters could be positively identified by type.

The U-2 went home in mid-July. TAC decided not to accept the ALSS system, for a variety of reasons. It reported that the U-2s could only manage five hours coverage every two days; only pulsed, non-agile emitters could be detected; the frequency coverage was not wide enough; and the datalink was vulnerable to jamming. There was no capability against some important emitters, such as the mobile SA-6 SAM with its continuous-wave Straight Flush radar. However, a new program named PELSS (Precision Emitter Location and Strike System) was already being planned. It was decided to keep the ALSS system as a test bed and risk reduction tool.[19]

27

The End of an Era

All through 1970 and into 1971, the Black Cat Squadron continued flying 4-5 hour-long peripheral missions up and down the China coast from Taoyuan. Looking up to 50 miles to the side of the U-2R's flightpath, the H-camera provided some stunning imagery—when it worked! The technical problems continued, compounded by cloud cover and pilot error. On an early 1971 sortie, only seven of the 60 planned targets were covered after the pilot made the wrong selection on the control panel. On the next mission, 22 of the 50 planned targets were missed due to cloud and haze.[1]

The pilot was required to identify the target and keep it in the crosshairs of his viewsight. If the H-cam had been properly boresighted to the hand control of the viewsight, it would photograph the target when the U-2 was 90 degrees abeam. In an attempt to improve reliability, Hycon started work on a new, lighter-weight gyroscopic mount, and new lenses.

But were the missions worth the risk? They were photographing ports, naval bases, shipyards, and coastal defenses, including nine SAM sites. On 1 December 1969, Tom Wang was flying over a small island 40 miles off the mainland coast when his warning systems all came on. He made the "OS" turn and saw three missiles explode off his right wing. The Chicoms had apparently shipped a Red Flag SAM site out to the island in a deliberate attempt to shoot down a peripheral U-2 flight. Within weeks, OSA fought off a request from the 303 Committee that the offshore islands be included in the restriction that the flights approach no closer than 20 nautical miles to Chinese territory. Mission planners at Project HQ were appalled. It would cause a 37-52% reduction in photo coverage, they calculated.[2]

Dr Kissinger

The geopolitical sands were shifting. As the Nixon Administration sought ways to extricate the U.S. from Southeast Asia, the National Security Advisor, Dr. Kissinger, explored channels of communication with Peking. Part of the strategy was to exploit the Sino-Soviet split, which had festered all through the 1960s before degenerating into open conflict along the border of the two communist giants in 1969. In Peking, four of Chairman Mao's top generals advised him to make overtures to the U.S., as a counter to the Soviets. Secret meetings between U.S. and Chinese officials began in Warsaw.

In March 1970 the CIA's Assistant Deputy Director for Intelligence, Edward Procter, advised DCI Richard Helms that "the peripheral (U-2) missions are difficult to justify on intelligence grounds, particularly during the Warsaw talks." But Helms continued to forward requests for Project

Idealist/Tackle missions to the 303 Committee, and a total of 14 were flown in 1970.[3]

As New Year 1971 opened, they continued...along the Taiwan Straits, or up to Port Arthur and the Shantung Peninsula, and (less frequently) along the south China coast to Hainan Island and back. Then, in May 1971 a new COMINT sensor developed by OSA became available for the U-2R. Until now, the photo missions had also carried the wide-frequency-range System 17B intercept system in the nose, plus the smaller System 21 specifically designed to pick up air defense communications. But the new sensor had a special purpose.

It was codenamed Long Shaft, and it was designed to intercept microwave communications. In the China of the early 1970s, these were likely to be generated only by government officials. And now the U.S. wanted to know what was really going on in the People's Republic. The first Americans to visit China since the Cultural Revolution six years earlier had just returned from—of all things—a table tennis tournament in Peking! They had been personally invited by Chairman Mao.

The new intercept system was added to the nose of the U-2. It weighed nearly 600 lbs, thus precluding the simultaneous carriage of the heavy H-camera. The first Long Shaft mission was flown along the coast of central China on 7 May 1971 by Major Tom Wang. The route included figure-eight patterns so that the airplane was pointed towards the mainland, the

The Black Cat Squadron flew peripheral missions up and down the coast of mainland China with the U-2R. This aircraft at Taoyuan carries a small Chinese Air Force insignia on the rear fuselage, and the serial number 3925 on the tail (Al Pinkham).

FLYING ALONG THE CHINA COAST

The Black Cat Squadron flew "only" peripheral missions from 1969 until it was closed down. But while these flights may have seemed less stressful from the safety of a mission planner's desk in Washington, they were still a significant test of piloting skill and courage.

For example, the targets for Mission C111C on 29 April 1971 included three known SAM sites. Major Johnny Shen duly covered them all with the H-camera from the regulation distance offshore. No SAMs were fired—the Chicoms knew he was outside their range. But the PLAAF always launched interceptors against the offshore missions, and since the routes were as close as 20 nautical miles to the mainland, they reckoned they had a chance. It did not seem to matter to them that the U-bird was officially in international airspace. The PLAAF's main force of F-6 (MiG-19) interceptors could not get close. But on this mission, Johnny Shen twice had to take evasive action against F-7s (MiG-21s), after getting warnings from the System 20 IR-detector. One of them passed within 500 feet, Shen estimated.

The navigation had to be spot-on, too, especially with those SAM sites being located close to the coast. On C111C a new SAM site was discovered near Port Arthur. "Quality of photography is excellent," enthused the PIs in their initial report. "Site has six launchers with missiles in place and in firing position. Control is located in center of site, and acquisition radar and missile assembly area clearly evident. Site is fronted on coastal approach by coastal defense site." – C.P.

The Black Cat Squadron received the U-2R in 1969, and flew over 100 peripheral missions in the next five years. This group of the Chinese pilots in their full pressure suits was photographed in 1969. Colonel "Gimo" Yang (fourth from left) was paying a return visit to the squadron, which was now commanded by Colonel "Tiger" Wang (fourth from right).

Hong Kong as seen by the H-camera on a passing U-2R.

better to intercept the narrow beams of microwave signals. Another four Long Shaft flights were conducted during the next two months. Two of them also carried the lighter-weight B-camera, but SIGINT was the primary purpose. The recordings were flown to Washington for analysis by the National Security Agency at Fort Meade.[4]

Secret trip

On 14 July there was a routine H-cam mission to Shanghai. The next day, President Nixon revealed the astonishing news that Dr. Kissinger had just spent two days in Peking talking to Chinese Foreign Minister Chou En Lai. The trip was so secret, not even U.S. Secretary of State William Rogers knew about it! The public reaction from the nationalist regime in Taipei was measured. But the U-2 operation from Taoyuan was an immediate casualty. Flights from Det H were suspended.

When they resumed on 2 October, the 303 Committee had moved them out to 25 nautical miles from the mainland, and 12 miles from any offshore island. The Nixon Administration did not want any incidents, with Dr. K about to visit China for a second time. His visit took place later that month, just days before the United Nations voted to expel Taiwan in favor of the People's Republic. From now on, the Idealist/Tackle operation was living on borrowed time. In his very first meeting with Premier Chou in July, Dr. Kissinger had agreed that "Taiwan was part of China," and pledged to withdraw U.S. military forces.[5]

Det H flew another seven photo and four SIGINT missions before the next stand-down in mid-January 1972. This was caused by President Nixon's historic visit to China, which took place in late February. Nixon and Kissinger certainly did not want the nationalist-flown U-2s patrolling the Chinese border during the visit. To forestall the ROC asking for their early resumption, Det H received word from Washington to tear both U-2Rs down for a three-month maintenance period. The ROC was told that there was a backlog of Service Bulletins to be incorporated.[6]

"Our common old friend, Generalissimo Chiang Kai-Shek, does not approve of this," Chairman Mao told Nixon of their meeting. But the Gimo was an old man, and his son was now running the nationalist show on Taiwan. In May 1972 Chiang Ching-Kuo formally became Premier of the ROC. CCK no longer visited the Black Cat Squadron, but his government now saw the joint operation as a means of prolonging a meaningful relationship with the U.S.

New Det G pilots

At Edwards, Det G trained replacement U-2 pilots selected by the CAF for the Black Cat Squadron. Three new American pilots—Dave Young in 1970, followed by Tom Lesan and Jerry Shilt in 1971—were trained to replace the last of the originals from the very earliest U-2 days (Marty Knutson, Jim Barnes, and Bob Ericson). The RAF also sent two replacement British pilots for training plus, as before, a flight planner and a doctor. A lot of hours were spent flying over the U.S. on surveys for various U.S. government agencies, especially the Red Dot series, which tested films and filters that were candidates for satellite reconnaissance. A new Itek camera with an apochromatic lens was used. It was the first fully color-corrected lens system.[7]

Det G maintained readiness to deploy again to the Middle East, or anywhere else that "higher authority" specified. There was a single 12-hour mission flown from Eielson and recovering back at Edwards, in November 1971, and some photo flights over the Caribbean from McCoy AFB in search of drug runners. There were two more Scope Saint practice deployments to the UK, in October 1971 to RAF St Mawgan, and October 1972 to RAF Wattisham. In both cases the Articles were airlifted inside C-141s, rather than ferried across the Atlantic.

From an original six received, Project Idealist was now down to four U-2R models. One had been destroyed in a landing accident at Taoyuan in November 1970 that killed CAF Major Denny Huang. Another had been loaned in mid-August 1971 to SAC, which was hard-pressed to meet its all its commitments with its own six aircraft.

Folly

The folly of only funding 12 U-2Rs was becoming apparent. There were endless discussions within the NRO, and between the NRO, CIA, and JCS, over how to allocate the precious R-models. In 1972 NRO Director John McLucas started another push to consolidate the aircraft under Air Force management. But he recognized that this would not be possible, until the 40 Committee agreed to end the joint U-2 project with Taiwan.[8]

After President Nixon returned from China, the 40 Committee met to discuss whether to do just that. But the CIA was worried about upsetting

Chinese U-2 pilot group towards the end of the joint U-2 operation from Taiwan. From left to right: Simon Chien; Johnny Shen; Terry Lee; Tom Wang; and Mike Chiu.

SEGREGATING THE CHINESE PILOTS

At Edwards, the CIA security people insisted that measures be implemented to ensure that the British pilots did not meet the Chinese U-2 pilots under training. The Chinese drew the short straw, being housed in remote California City, while the Brits stayed in Lancaster. That took care of after-work hours, but what about during the day? This was awkward in practice, since the Brits were assigned to Det G full-time. Here is an extract from a 1972 SOP:

Chinese will use the main gate for entry and exit from North Base. The guard will notify the Security and Operations sections of their arrival each day. Every effort will be made to avoid Chinese exposure to "Red Badge" or assigned British drivers. Chinese movement in the administration building will be restricted to the Operations Section, Command, and the Chinese training area. Visits to any other areas of the administration building will require escort. Use of the British Flight Surgeon in support of the flying training program of for backup medical assistance will be as approved by the Director of Security.

- "Training of CAF U-2 Pilots," 1130th ATTG, 14 April 1972

MISSION PLANNERS VERSUS IMAGERY ANALYSTS

Every U-2 mission over potentially hostile airspace had to be a compromise. The planners wanted to cover as many targets as possible, but they also wanted the safe return of pilot and plane. In March 1973, the CIA's top imagery analyst criticised the planning of SAC's Olympic Meet photo missions over Laos and Cambodia as follows:

We can only assume that these missions are being programmed against known point targets or against specific segments of the lines of communications (LOCs). They are not providing frequent, comprehensive, near-vertical photography, which is what the U-2R is admirably suited to do.

The aircraft flew short, irregular patterns with frequent turns. Although these flight tracks might help to confuse the enemy, they also reduce the amount of intelligence that can be obtained from a mission, and certainly make exploitation of the imagery more difficult.

Because the aircraft is spending so much time in turns, there are numerous gaps in coverage, and much of the film is oblique, non-stereo, and virtually useless. The imagery analyst cannot follow the LOC or study an area of enemy activity on consecutive frames of a single pass, but must use small portions of three or more legs of the flight track. This is time-consuming, and greatly increases the possibility that something of intelligence significance may be overlooked.

- memo for COMIREX by George Allen, Director, Imagery Analysis Service, 13 March 1973

Haiphong

After the Paris peace agreement in late January 1973, the U.S. wanted to monitor North Vietnamese compliance, including shipping movements to and from Haiphong. But under the terms of the accord, U.S. reconnaissance aircraft could no longer operate over North Vietnam. SAC tasked the 99th SRS at U-Tapao to fly along the coast at high altitude, banking slightly so that the IRIS II panoramic camera could get the maximum coverage. Evidently, it was decided in Washington that the H-camera could do a better job. Since SAC pilots no longer trained to use it, Det G borrowed a U-2R from Det H on Taiwan for the task.

In order to avoid the Chinese radars, Dave Young flew the first Scope Shield mission out of Taoyuan on 30 March at low-altitude (500 feet!) until one hour south of Taiwan. Due to cloud cover, the mission was aborted after three flight lines, all 12 nautical miles offshore. On another try the next day, the weather closed in again. The monsoon season prevented another attempt until 21 July, when the H-camera provided "the best peripheral coverage to date of the Vietnamese coastal areas," according to Project HQ. Still, it was not enough. The 40 Committee eventually approved new SR-71 flights over North Vietnam. (One further Scope Shield mission was flown along the Vietnam coast on 6 January 1974).[11]

Meanwhile, the 99th SRS continued to fly its own photo missions, now codenamed Olympic Meet, using the Iris II. They continued at an average rate of one per month through 1974. Of course, there were many more missions alerted, but not flown, due to cloudy weather over the target areas in Cambodia and Laos.

Olympic Fire

SAC's other U-2 photo mission was still Cuba. When a Soviet naval deployment to Cuba was detected in mid-Atlantic, the frequency of U-2 missions was increased to monitor its arrival and departure from Cuban ports. There was a flurry of activity in April-May 1972 when a Golf-class ballistic missile submarine moored at a Cuban port. Once that flap was over, in August 1972 SAC allowed the 100th SRW to remove the photo aircraft from McCoy and fly the mission (now codenamed Olympic Fire) direct from home base at Davis-Monthan AFB.

This decision made another precious U-2R available for training at D-M—but it also meant some long round-robin flights for the SAC pilots, when the monthly missions were scheduled. SAC waived the standard 12-hour duty day for these flights. Major Carl Larue flew the first Olympic Fire mission out of D-M on 12 August 1972. He was airborne for 12 hours. Some of these flights stretched to over 13 hours.

the nationalist government. Even if the U-2 operation was dispensable, some other joint intelligence projects were not—particularly the ground intercept station at Shu Linkou! The offshore U-2 flights resumed, with a renewed emphasis on SIGINT. Still, Project HQ was under no illusions about the future. "I see the entire Idealist program, as well as the Tackle portion, in serious jeopardy," wrote OSA Director Bg Gen Wendell Bevan. He was right. The new DCI, James Schlesinger, was not a U-2 fan.[9]

Fifteen of the 28 missions flown by Det H from Taoyuan by the end of 1972 were Long Shaft sorties. In March 1973 the agreement with Taiwan for the joint operation was due for renewal. Some delicate negotiations ensued. It was renewed indefinitely, but with a three-months' notice clause. By mutual agreement, neither the U.S. nor the ROC actually signed the document.[10]

An aircraft from Det H/CAF 35th Squadron, inflight during the early 1970s. Although they were flown offshore, the missions were frequently challenged by the PLAAF's MiG-21s—without success (via Jay Miller).

During President Nixon's historic visit to mainland China in 1972, Det H on Taiwan was stood down for three months. In order to forestall nationalist demands for an early resumption, both aircraft were hangared for some "politically correct" major maintenance (via Al Pinkham).

The last U-2R mission over Cuba was flown in late May 1974. The U-2s were needed elsewhere. Overflights of Cuba resumed in fall 1974, using the SR-71.

In July 1973 the NRO again recommended consolidation of the U-2 fleet under SAC. A senior Defense Department official wrote: "Indications are that the CIA aircraft have not been productive in the recent past, and that the program's political risk will continue to grow." DCI Schlesinger was not inclined to disagree. At a meeting of the 40 Committee on 30 August 1973, he concurred with a decision to terminate Project Idealist at the end of the fiscal year, eg 30 June 1974.[12]

No one from Washington told the nationalist government in Taiwan that the end of Project Tackle was coming. But Dr. Kissinger did tell the Chicoms. During his fourth visit to Peking in November 1973, Dr. K promised Chou En Lai that the U-2s would be withdrawn by the end of 1974.[13]

The two CIA detachments carried on as normal. Det H flew 22 peripheral missions in 1973. Det G laid plans to qualify its new pilots for carrier landings in November, and make another practice deployment to the UK in mid-October. But Scope Saint VI was overtaken by events.

The U-2R was designed to fit inside the USAF's C-141 airlifters. In 1971 and 1972, Det G used this mode of transport for practice deployments to the UK (Lockheed U2-91-013-81).

OLIVE HARVEST

The U.S. operation to monitor the ceasefire in the Middle East was approved by the United Nations, and the British government allowed the U-2R to operate out of RAF Akrotiri, on Cyprus. The airbase was within a supposedly "sovereign area," controlled by the Brits. But this was still a very sensitive operation, at least as far as the British government was concerned. It was worried about the Cypriot reaction to one of those sinister black spyplanes flying out of the island. The political situation on Cyprus was volatile enough already, with the island divided between Greek and Turkish Cypriots, as well as strong left-wing elements.

To keep the Brits happy the missions were supposed to be scheduled on weekends, with a takeoff at sunrise, when there were fewer Cypriot workers on the airbase. The same went for any pilot proficiency flights. Even after SAC took over the mission from the "civilians" of Det G no military uniforms were worn. The State Department wanted a "low-profile operation." No one from OL-OH was allowed off base overnight.

The detachment commander was in virtually daily contact with the U.S. ambassador and local British intelligence officials. The British also wanted no suggestion to leak out that the deployment could become permanent. Thirty years later, the U-2 is still there!

– C.P.

Yom Kippur War

On 6 October 1973 fighting flared up again in the Middle East, as Egypt and Syria attacked Israel in an attempt to regain the territory they had lost in previous conflicts. In the Yom Kippur War, Egypt surprised Israel and raced across the Sinai Desert. Israel counter-attacked and crossed the Canal. Both the U.S. and the USSR began major airlifts of military equipment to their respective clients. But the superpowers were also trying to mediate, notably Dr. Kissinger on the U.S. side.

In Operation Forward Pass, Det G deployed a U-2R to Upper Heyford in semi-covert fashion on 7 October. Plans were laid to fly an H-camera mission over the Middle East, with a recovery at Akrotiri. It would have to be another long one: the French would not grant overflight rights. At the same time SAC prepared to deploy an SR-71 to RAF Mildenhall to cover the crisis. But the British government refused to allow the high-profile Blackbird to fly in, and dithered over permission for the U-2 to use Akrotiri. Project HQ replanned the flight to land on an aircraft carrier in the Med.

Meanwhile, SAC successfully replanned the SR-71 flights as 10-hour round-robin missions out of Griffiss AFB, NY, with the aid of multiple inflight refuelings. The first one was flown on 11 October. Det G pilots Jerry Shilt and Dave Young stood by at Upper Heyford, awaiting a mission in vain. On 22 October a United Nations ceasefire resolution was agreed by all the parties except Syria. After a month in the hangar at Upper Heyford, the U-2R was flown back to Edwards in early November.[14]

Akrotiri

In April 1974, however, Dr. Kissinger engaged in his Middle East shuttle diplomacy, and arranged for permanent monitoring of the ceasefire, with the agreement of the warring parties. Once again, Det G headed for the Middle East, this time with British permission to fly out of Akrotiri. The

10334 on the ramp at D-M. This aircraft was lost in August 1975 at the start of a return ferry trip from U-Tapao to the U.S.

PROJECT IDEALIST – A RETROSPECTIVE

Dave Young joined Project Idealist as a U-2R pilot in 1970. He went on to become the 9th SRW commander at Beale AFB. His verdict on the project:

In my judgement this was the most capable, responsive, and thoroughly professional flying organization that ever existed. Having subsequently spent many years associated with the USAF side of the U-2 program, I can say, by way of comparison, that while the Air Force did a good job, the Agency—blessed by having access to highly experienced people and very generous funding—did a truly extraordinary job. - *correspondence with author*

WHO GIVES THE ORDERS AROUND HERE?

When SAC took over the Middle East UN monitoring fights in August 1974, it soon objected to the politicians dictating the fine details of the routes to be flown. But the State Department insisted that they had been agreed at the highest level by Dr. Kissinger himself, and could not be changed. Unfortunately, in the opinion of the Strategic Reconnaissance Center (SRC) at Offutt, they did not take sufficient account of the U-2's navigational shortcomings. They argued that the Doppler system was not sophisticated enough, and that dead-reckoning was tricky over the featureless terrain of the Golan Heights.

The SRC made repeated requests to redraw the tracks to insure the best possible accuracy, without success. One mission in December 1974 strayed over Syria, prompting a diplomatic protest. We told you so, said the SRC! It was the pilot's first mission, and winds in the area were higher than forecast. After that, the SRC provided the 100th SRW with photo-mosaics of the Golan heights for pre-mission study. Before a pilot went TDY to Cyprus, he flew several special training sorties over the Arizona desert, designed to simulate the operating conditions of an Olive Harvest mission.

In mid-1975 the problems were eased when the Litton LN-33 inertial navigation system was added to the U-2R. – *C.P.*

U-2R was deployed there via Pease AFB in mid-April. On 12 May Jerry Shilt began Project Idealist's last operation by flying a two-and-half-hour mission down the Suez Canal and back. Two days later, OSA Director Gen Bevan cabled the Det on Akrotiri: "Am attempting to find out from NPIC if they consider the film and coverage better than SR-71. If affirmative, I'll show it around town for you."[15]

The State Department negotiated two standard routes for the U-2 flights. They covered the Suez/Sinai disengagement zone and the Golan Heights. Egypt, Israel, and Syrian officials were informed 24 or 48 hours before the takeoff of each U-2 monitoring mission. All three had to grant diplomatic clearances each time. After takeoff, it was up to the pilot to abort at the designated "entry point" for each route, if the weather ahead was too cloudy. U-2 mission planners had very little say in the routings, which caused problems for the pilots, especially over the Golan Heights. Obtaining imagery over there was tricky, since Syria would not fully cooperate. The missions had to be routed over Israeli-held territory, and at least 30 nautical miles from Syrian SAM sites. A second track put the U-2R 12 miles off the Syrian coast, to monitor the ports. The Syrians interpreted

10332 at RAF Wattisham during the deployment by Det G in October 1972 (Peter Cowie).

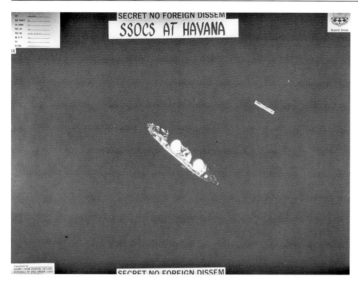

U-2 missions over and around Cuba continued until 1974. This Soviet space operations control ship was photographed in 1972. (USAF)

Davis-Monthan AFB, home of the Air Force U-2 fleet from 1963 to 1976, seen in a 1975 high-altitude oblique image courtesy of the H-camera.

virtually any deviation from tracks as evidence of American spying for Israel.[16]

It was now less than three months before the planned end of CIA U-2 operations. Gen Bevan found himself in a difficult position, since neither the British nor the Taiwan governments had yet been officially informed. It did not seem an appropriate way to treat such long-term partners, especially since it was pretty obvious what was happening, via the rumor mill. Finally the State Department bit the bullet, and the word was formally passed to London and Taipei. In late June, the ROC formally agreed to the closure, to take effect a month later.[17]

Closure

Although Det H continued on alert for three more weeks, it turned out that the Black Cat Squadron had already flown its last operational mission. It was a photo flight on 24 May over the Yellow Sea to the Port Arthur area, flown by Major Mike Chiu Sung Chou. On 23 July the U.S. "manager" at Taoyuan, Lt Col Warren Boyd, officially announced the closure. A few

days later Det G pilots Tom Lesan and Jerry Shilt flew the two Articles away from Taiwan. The U.S. donated the Cessna U-3A that had been used for training chase and crew ferry flights, and most of the equipment in the Photo Lab.

The Idealist/Tackle joint venture had lasted 14 years. From 1962 to 1968 there were 102 overflights of mainland China. From 1968 to 1974 there were 118 more peripheral missions. Of the 28 CAF pilots who had qualified to fly the U-2, five had been shot down, and another seven killed in accidents.

When the two Articles from Taiwan arrived back at North Base, they were immediately turned over to the 100th SRW, together with the other U-2R still there.

The fourth and last Agency U-2R was at Akrotiri, where Det G had now flown another eight ceasefire-monitoring missions over the Middle East. The 100th SRW sent a small team to take over. They arrived just as civil war between the Greek and Turkish Cypriots erupted! They also arrived in time to see Dan Nesbitt return from the latest flight over the Suez

U-2R of Project Idealist at North Base. From 1969, the "cover" designation of Det G here was the 1130th ATTG, and the aircraft wore the USAF star-and-bar. Ironically, this distinguished them from the "real" USAF U-2Rs, which carried no national insignia! (Lockheed U2-091-023-7).

AMERICANS FLY SPY PLANES FROM RAF BASE IN CYPRUS

By our Nicosia correspondent: The RAF base of Akrotiri, in south Cyprus, is used by American spy planes to monitor troop movements and concentrations along the Arab-Israeli ceasefire line, it was admitted in an oblique way in Nicosia yesterday.

The admission was made after two days of evasions by both the Cyprus government and the American embassy in Nicosia. Local press reports had said the high-flying American spy planes flew over the Middle East frontline as part of a peacekeeping effort of Dr. Kissinger, American Secretary of State, with the approval of both Israel and the Arab States.

The operation was kept secret to avoid embarrassing these governments, and President Makarios' government, who had also consented to the stationing of the American planes at Akrotiri.

Britain confirmed yesterday that the USAF has been given temporary use of the British sovereign base. Neither British nor American sources would reveal what type of aircraft was being used, but they are believed to be more modern than the U-2 formerly used over Russia.

- The Daily Telegraph, London, 1 March 1975

A SENIOR LOOK AT SOMALIA

In April 1975 the 99th SRS deployed a U-2R from U-Tapao to the British-owned island of Diego Garcia, in the Indian Ocean. Six photo missions were flown across the Indian Ocean to Somalia, which had recently allowed the Soviets to build a military base. The operation was codenamed Senior Look, and was a significant feat of navigation by the mission pilots. Some fine pictures of the port, airfield, and missile-handling facility at Berbera were obtained from an offshore track. One of the reasons for tasking the U-2 was that, although satellites had already photographed the area, there was no way the NRO was going to allow the release of overhead imagery. But the U-2 imagery *was* released—at a Senate hearing. Besides embarrassing the Somalis, this also served to boost the Pentagon's case for funding a big expansion of the base at Diego Garcia. – *C.P.*

Brig Gen Wendell Bevan was the last Director of OSA. He presided over the end of U-2 operations by Project Idealist in 1974 (NARA).

A U-2R returns to Taoyuan from a peripheral flight mission along the Chinese coast in 1974. The last such mission was flown on 24 May 1974 (via Bob Birkett).

Warren Boyd (center) was the last "manager" of Det H. He looks on, together with CAF squadron commander Tom Wang (left) and pilot "Mory" Tsai (right), while operations officer Bob Birkett offers congratulations to a pressure-suited pilot.

Bob Birkett (left) and Det H maintenance officer Glede Vaughan enjoy one last Chinese meal on Taiwan with David Lee, who flew for the Black Cat Squadron from 1968 to 1971 (via Al Pinkham).

Canal. On final approach he forgot to lower the flaps, floated halfway down the runway, and ran off the other end. No serious damage was done, but it was an unfortunate end to Project Idealist.[18]

SAC formally assumed control at Akrotiri on 1 August 1974, and renamed the operation Olive Harvest OL-OH. The civilian maintenance crews were kept on, with the expectation that blue-suiters would take over by the end of the year. This never happened, and Lockheed tech reps were still employed at Akrotiri in 2004, after 30 years of continuous U-2 operations at the island base.

GUATEMALAN EARTHQUAKE – IRIS GOES PUBLIC

On 4 February 1976 a huge earthquake rocked Guatemala. U.S. Aid asked for aerial photography. The task was assigned to the U-2R and its Iris II panoramic camera. Two 11-hour missions were flown in mid-February by Captain Robert Henderson and Major Tom Doubek. After the first flight, five enlargements were released to the media—the first time that Iris II photography had been released. The pictures grabbed the public's attention all right: Walter Cronkite put them on CBS News. Television crews were invited into D-M to film the launch and recovery of the second mission to Guatemala. "The publicity generated by the U-2 in Guatemala left a lasting and favorable impression of the aircraft," a JCS general told the SRC. – *C.P.*

28

Imaging Radar Takes Off

The U-2 took great pictures—when weather conditions allowed. But even Itek's wonderful new IRIS camera could not defeat cloud cover and haze. The alternative was radar imaging, but in the early 1970s it was a poor alternative. Side-looking radars had been around for a long time—in the late 1950s, some of the original U-2s carried the "D" system produced by Westinghouse (aka the APQ-56). In the 1960s synthetic aperture techniques improved the product, but the resolution still left a lot to be desired.

Phoenix-based Goodyear Aerospace was a leader in the field of radar imaging. When the SR-71 went into service it carried the company's PIP system, which scanned a 15-nautical mile swath beneath the aircraft. The video output was displayed to the back-seat RSO, who used it to cross-check his navigation. The output was also recorded for analysis on the ground, after the Blackbird had landed. But the resolution was six feet at the very best—only good enough for large fixed targets and ships in port, for instance.

Then came a technical breakthrough. The advent of high-speed integrated solid-state circuits made it possible to process the radar video signals digitally in real-time. The advantages over the previous optical processing technique were significant. The range of the area being mapped could be changed by an order of magnitude, detailed large-scale maps could be made, and resolution could be increased dramatically.[1]

Senior Lance

In 1970 the NRO provided funds for development and flight-testing of prototype radars using the new technology. The program was codenamed Senior Lance, and designated UPD-X. The U-2R was chosen as the platform. The payoff was significant. If carried by a high-flying platform, such a radar could peer 100 miles into enemy territory and identify targets in all weather conditions. Moreover, the short wavelengths (eg X-band, around 10 GHz) enabled the sensor to detect targets concealed by camouflage, such as foliage or man-made screening. And this could be a 24-hour operation, unconstrained by visible light!

One of the SAC aircraft (68-10339) was allocated full time to the task. A prototype Goodyear radar was installed in the nose. In April 1971 the Senior Lance test flights began. Most of them were flown from D-M, but the aircraft was also detached to McCoy AFB. The U.S. Navy was interested, as well as the Air Force. A number of test fights were made over the Atlantic and Pacific Oceans as Project Rice. The imagery looked good: you could see the wakes of individual ships. The aircraft also flew along the coast of Cuba, imaging the island from stand-off range.[2]

In this first phase the radar imagery was recorded onboard. In March 1972, 10339 was grounded for the addition of a datalink. There were a number of advantages to be gained from processing the radar returns on

In Project Highboy, the U.S. Navy evaluated the U-2R as an ocean surveillance platform that would operate from land bases. The aircraft is carrying a radar in the nose, plus an ELINT receiver and video camera in the wing pods (Lockheed U2-91-024-11).

In an attempt to keep the Navy interested, Kelly Johnson proposed equipping the U-2R with long-range Condor anti-ship missiles (Lockheed PR1024).

SYNTHETIC APERTURE RADARS

The early side-looking radars were large, and their antennas could not easily be installed on smaller airplanes like the U-2. In the early 1960s synthetic apertures solved this problem. A relatively small antenna was made to function as a very large one by recording the successive returns from the ground in the radar's waveguide network as the aircraft flew along track. The returns would subsequently be combined by a data processing system to offer much better resolution, and the length of the "synthetic" antenna (or "aperture") was limited only by the distance along track for which a given target was within the illumination beam of the actual (or "real") antenna. The data processor was the key element in a SAR; it had to provide the proper amplitude and phase weights to the stored returned pulses, and sum them to obtain a correct image of the scene. Goodyear provided one of these systems for the RF-4 Phantom, and another for the SR-71, on which it was known as the HRR (High-Resolution Radar) and, in an improved version from 1972, the CAPRE (Capability Reconnaissance radar).

– C.P.

the ground. The weight and power requirement for the airborne portion of the sensor could be kept down, and sophisticated computers could be employed to process and present a high-quality finished product. This could then be quickly transmitted to air and ground force commanders, giving them vital, up-to-the-minute intelligence on the disposition of the other side's forces.

Test flights resumed in July 1972 using the codename Senior Dagger, and were moved to McCoy in August. During the next three months the U-2R downlinked imagery to a ground station situated at the Rome Air Development Center (RADC) in New York.[3]

Navy evaluation

When this series of flights ended in November, the trials U-2R was bailed full time to the Navy for six months. Kelly Johnson still had high hopes of a separate Navy production contract. Moreover, the Navy's greatest U-2 fan was now in command of the service's Operational Test and Evaluation Force (COMOPTEVFOR). This was Rear Admiral "Red" Carmody, who had arranged the very first U-2 carrier landings in 1963-64. Carmody still thought the U-2 would make an excellent platform for ocean surveillance. But there were other potential solutions, such as satellites. They were being explored by an evaluation unit (FO-265) at NAS Moffet Field, Califor-

nia, located alongside the Lockheed Missile and Space Company (LMSC) facility at Sunnyvale, which was a prime contractor for the highly-classified reconnaissance satellites.[4]

Carmody apparently preferred the U-2. He gained $5.5 million funding for an Electronics Patrol Experimental (EP-X) program, and placed a contract with Lockheed. It was called Project Highboy. The Skunk Works modified 10339 to the EP-X configuration. A heavily-modified RCA X-band weather radar was mounted in the nose. Wing slipper pods were developed to house more sensors. The left pod contained an RCA return beam vidicon camera, while the right one housed a cut-down version of the UTL ALQ-110 ELINT receiver. An astro-inertial system "borrowed" from the SR-71 was carried in the Q-bay, and a data-link system in the E-bay, with the antenna beneath the tail. The standard T-35 tracker camera was displaced from the nose to the right pod.[5]

In the EP-X flight tests during early 1973 the U-2R flew from Palmdale, and the sensor data was downlinked to a ground station at Sunnyvale. All

10339 carries the inflatable radome that was used for trials of the new imaging radars in the mid-1970s (Lockheed C75-1023-1).

the sensors were controlled from the ground. Real or near-real time information on shipping off the West Coast was obtained. FO-265 saw the U-2's potential as an extension of a Naval task force's radar horizon. The threat to the fleet from long-range Soviet cruise missiles had increased, and the long endurance of the EP-X offered the prospect of round-the-clock cover. The U-2 would not necessarily have to operate from the carrier deck, thanks to the R-model's long endurance. In the Mediterranean, for instance, it could fly out of NAS Sigonella, in Sicily, and still cover all the required ocean space.[6]

In Washington the Admirals were not so sure. Carmody recommended spending $18 million for a follow-on EP-X test program. This would pay for two new-build aircraft—U-2R time was in short supply on the existing fleet, and the NRO wanted 10339 back for more Senior Lance development. There would also be a deployment to NAS Sigonella to demonstrate the system performance in a dense shipping environment; downlinking to a ship-based sensor control and analysis station, and the integration of a higher-resolution radar, such as the Senior Lance, or the Texas Instruments APS-116, which was already flying on the Navy's Lockheed S-3A maritime patrol planes.[7]

Promise

The Navy mulled its options, comparing the U-2 against the lower-flying P-3 and S-3. Meanwhile, a new series of flights with the advanced radar imaging sensor began. The first one took off from D-M on 2 May 1973 and flew over designated targets in Arizona and California before moving offshore to get some shipping imagery for the Navy. To provide a comparison, another 100th SRW U-2R flew over the same targets with the IRIS II camera. The new radar sensor was showing promise, but there were still development problems, including image motion compensation, and correlation with the Northrop NAS-21 astro-tracker. If radar imaging was to fulfill its true potential, the aircraft's position would have to be known very precisely.[8]

In 1973-74, the NRO used the Navy's ocean surveillance requirement to support the consolidation of the U-2R fleet. If the CIA Projects Idealist and Tackle were terminated four aircraft would be available, and the Navy could then borrow two of them for more EP-X trials. Then the U-2R production line would not have to be re-opened, it argued. That was too ex-

pensive an option, argued the NRO—which was spending billions on satellites at the time![9]

Lockheed lobbied hard, but to no avail. "No one in the Navy is willing to take a decision," wrote Kelly Johnson. The Navy interest in the U-2 waned, in favor of satellites. Red Carmody's tour at COMOPTEVFOR came to an end. The U.S. Ambassador to Italy reported that there was no way the Italians were going to let a U-2 spyplane fly out of Sigonella! Despite Johnson's formidable lobbying skills, it seemed that the U-2's future prospects would always be damaged by this image problem.[10]

Bad time

Johnson sketched new ideas. A U-2C armed with laser-guided bombs. The U-2RL, with a longer Q-bay, and a refueling probe protruding from the tip of the fin. And a version armed with Condor anti-ship missiles, to keep the Navy interested. But this was a bad time for the Skunk Works in particular, and for Lockheed in general. The L-1011 Tristar airliner had nearly bankrupted the company. The corporate management was embroiled in a series of bribery scandals, and defense spending was in free-fall as the Vietnam War ended. In 1974 Kelly Johnson had a heart bypass operation and, upon reaching the mandatory age of 65, retired. His deputy Ben Rich took over as the head of Advanced Development Projects. He was under no illusions. It was a tough pair of shoes to fill at a tough time.[11]

Rich would shortly lead the Skunk Works in a new, fascinating, and highly classified direction, leading to the Stealth Fighter. For now, though, Burbank needed new work quickly. Rich offered a "good price" to re-open the U-2R line. The aircraft was clearly a candidate for PLSS, the follow-on project to ALSS, which required a triad of high-altitude platforms in an orbit close to enemy airspace. Then there was Senior Lance, the advanced radar imaging program.

A radar map of Los Angeles produced by early trials of the Hughes Advanced Synthetic Aperture Radar System (ASARS). (Hughes via Jacques Naviaux)

Another view of the U-2R with the inflatable radome.

There were important reasons for choosing a high-altitude platform for what soon became known as the Advanced Synthetic Aperture Radar System (ASARS). The radar returns from a SAR were processed to present a plane, rather than oblique, view of the imaged terrain. At first glance, such a SAR image reproduced on ordinary film could look just like one taken by an ordinary camera from directly over the target. There were significant differences, however, such as those caused by terrain masking when the side-looking sensor painted a hill. The far side of the hill would receive no radar illumination, and would thus appear as a black shadow.

For this reason, unless the SAR platform was a high-flyer, a large proportion of the image would be in shadow, or "masked." A high-flying platform would also provide the stability necessary to achieve good results, since it flew above the tropospheric region of atmospheric disturbance (although even the slightest deviation from a perfectly straight, constant-speed course would still have to be measured, and a compensatory phase correction made to the received signals. Hence the star-tracker on the Senior Lance U-2R).

Hughes Radar

The Radar Systems Group of Hughes Aircraft, in El Segundo, California, was best known for fire control sets carried in the F-4 and F-14 fighters. But it was developing its own imaging radar techniques to challenge Goodyear, Westinghouse, and others. Hughes engineers developed the "squintable antenna" feature to further reduce the terrain masking.

By training the beam of the real antenna forwards (or backwards) and making an appropriate focusing correction and coordinate rotation, the synthetic array could be squinted well ahead of (or behind) the aircraft.

The radar could thus be made to "anticipate" terrain that would become masked, and look around it to eliminate the potential gap in coverage. The "spotlight mode" was another advanced feature. By gradually changing the look angle of the real antenna as the aircraft advanced, and making appropriate phase corrections, the radar could be made to repeatedly map an area of particular interest. By doing this an even better image could be obtained.

Hughes was aiming for images equivalent to infrared photo quality at 100 miles range. Resolutions of a few feet were on the cards, *irrespective* of the distance off the target from the aircraft. This was because SAR technology allowed the resolution to be made independent of range, simply by increasing the length of the synthetic array in direct proportion to the area to be mapped.

Test flights with the Senior Lance U-2R continued. Since the latest radar antenna was too large to fit inside the Q-bay, the Skunk Works designed a radome made from three layers of Kevlar, which was inflated and stabilized by engine bleed air. The radar was mounted beneath the Q-bay, inside this unique radome. Access was by means of two zip fasteners taken from U-2 partial pressure suits! The whole radome assembly weighed only 40 lbs. This was just as well: the new radar itself was only 65 lbs below the Q-bay weight limit.[12]

In 1976 Hughes made its proposal to the USAF for ASARS. At the same time Goodyear proposed a similar system. This became ASARS-1, and was eventually installed on the SR-71, without a datalink. Meanwhile, in September 1977 Hughes was awarded a development contract for ASARS-2, which would be carried by a subsonic, high-altitude platform. The question was, which one?

29

Consolidation

In March 1976, 100th SRW wing commander Colonel Chuck Stratton gathered his troops in a hangar at Davis-Monthan AFB. He told them that the U-2s would be moving to Beale AFB in California, to join the SR-71s. The drone operation—what was left of it—would stay at D-M under the control of TAC. The wing was 20 years old, if you counted the first 10 years of the old 4080th. The 100th number would be preserved in the move by re-assigning it to the wing of KC-135s that also flew from Beale.

The U-2 and the SR-71, dissimilar in almost every respect except that they both performed strategic reconnaissance, were going to become stablemates. It would be an interesting "merger." The SR-71 was exotic, state-of-the-art technology, and now very high profile, thanks to a headline-grabbing trip to the Farnborough airshow in 1974, during which various world speed records were broken. The U-2 was....well, wasn't it the spyplane in which Gary Powers was shot down all those years ago?

The Blackbird had flown over Cuba, North Korea, North Vietnam, and the Middle East with impunity. Who knows where else it might have been? The answer was nowhere else, actually. Since it could be easily tracked by the opposition's radars, the U.S. government had never dared fly the SR-71 (or the predecessor A-12) over the Soviet Union, or even China.

Low-profile

The Dragon Lady was still low-profile. Given its lingering bad press, and the new highly-classified SIGINT mission, that was deliberate policy by the USAF. The latest U-2R model was not even officially acknowledged. In *Jane's All The World's Aircraft*, the reference bible of the aerospace industry, the U-2 no longer rated an entry. The SR-71 got two whole pages to itself.

But the bean counters saw another important difference between the two aircraft. The cost of a single U-2 mission was only one-sixth that of an SR-71 mission. It was already obvious that while the Blackbird was a precious "national asset," it was not a routine, day-in-day-out collection platform.

The U-2/SR-71 consolidation became official on 1 July 1976. Twelve days later, the first U-2 was flown from D-M to Beale, and by 1 October all the aircraft and equipment had been transferred to the 9th SRW. There were 10 U-2R models assigned—the 11th was on long-term loan to AFLC for the Senior Lance and other test programs. There were also the five remaining original U-2C models, still flying triads in the ALSS follow-on phase. Plus the two U-2CT trainers. The Beale-based U-2 squadron was renumbered the 99th SRS, while the operating location at Osan became Det 2. (The SR-71 operation at Kadena AB on Okinawa was Det 1).

Sampling missions using the Dragon Lady resumed in 1973. This U-2R is carrying the special hatch, which included a protruding airscoop for the F-4 foil system (NARA KKE 67046).

Akrotiri officially remained Operating Location OH until September 1980, when it was finally redesignated Det 3. This was to soothe local political concerns that it was becoming a permanent feature—in reality, of course, it was. Unfortunately, the low profile of the U-2R on Cyprus was destroyed on 7 December 1977 when Captain Robert Henderson crashed into the Met Office next to the control tower on takeoff. He was killed, along with one British and four Cypriot civilians. Another 14 persons were injured in the terrible accident. Fires burned for three hours in the devastated area.

Poor discipline

Strong crosswinds blew frequently across the runway at Akrotiri. Henderson was a five-year veteran of the U-2 program. But the Accident Board concluded that no amount of experience could compensate for the aircraft's sharp bank immediately after takeoff, causing the wingtip to touch the ground and the aircraft to cartwheel into the building. The Board members included RAF Squadron Leader Harry Drew, who had flown U-2s in Project Idealist for three years. A separate RAF inquiry was chaired by Gp Capt Bunny Warren. His report slammed the U-2 Det for poor flying discipline.[1]

The crash also destroyed the only U-2R fitted to date with mounts for the Optical Bar Camera (OBC), the latest Itek panoramic camera, which had a 30-inch, fully color-corrected lens. Another aircraft with an Iris III camera was soon flown in as a replacement, so that the Olive Harvest missions, which monitored the Middle East ceasefire, could continue.

The OH flights continued at a regular pace throughout the rest of the decade. If both the Suez and the Golan heights were covered on the same flight, these were five-hour flights. If they were covered separately, they were much shorter. The State Department continued to distribute the Olive Harvest photography to Egypt, Israel, and Syria.

In March 1979 Egypt and Israel signed a peace treaty, which included continued provision for the flights. In mid-1980 the approved flight tracks were modified to provide greater flexibility. Meanwhile, the SIGINT missions codenamed Olive Tree continued at a rate of 8-10 sorties every month, except for a six-week period after 24 April 1980. On that date the OL's sole aircraft was badly damaged in a landing accident, and had to be airfreighted back to the U.S. for repair.[2]

THE BLACKBIRD AND THE DRAGON LADY I

When the U-2s moved to Beale in 1976 and joined the SR-71s in the 9th SRW, the contrast between the two aircraft was thrown into sharp focus. And not only the aircraft, but also their crews. Here's how renowned novelist Ernest K. Gann saw that contrast a few years later:

Flying the fastest and most mysterious aircraft in the world inevitably persuades a man that he matches his equipment. He is a unique, extraordinarily gifted aviator, and an all-around wonderful guy. Hence there is often a certain condescension in the manner of SR-71 pilots and their "backseaters." They are inclined to regard the U-2 as a work mule, with a speed to match that animal.

The reaction of the U-2 people is hardly surprising...they refer to the SR-71 as the "sled," and since the sled drivers seem to make a more romantic impression on the public, they are said to deliberately fly towards thunderstorms because they mistake them for camera flashbulbs...The SR crews claim that they are the wine-and-cheese set of the aviators, and fly a "cerebral" aircraft.

If a sled driver seeks to defend his flying machine with reference to its operating expense and consequent gift of employment to countless citizens, the U-2 drivers agree. They suggest that the Chrysler company was saved from bankruptcy, just by the number of ground-based vehicles required to launch an SR-71. They say that, indeed, if the actual cost of flying an SR-71 is "classified," isn't that because it is the most expensive project ever conceived by man, other than the Alaska Pipeline? Which, of course, was built specifically to support the SR-71.

As for the SR's vaunted ability to survey more than 100,000 square miles of the earth's surface in an hour's time, the U-2 pilots concede that may be so, if there is a tanker squadron on both ends.

- Ernest K. Gann, "The Black Watch,"
Random House, New York, 1989

10336 at RAF Mildenhall in 1976 during the first deployment to Europe of the Senior Book SIGINT system (Peter R. Foster).

OSCAR, THE BLACK CAT

The mascot of Det 2, the new Black Cat Squadron, spent most of his time on the leather couch in the commander's office. Like most living creatures, there were highs and lows in Oscar's life. The lows included the day that he was taken to the vet to be neutered, after one too many nights on the prowl. The "highs" included that notable day in March 1978 when Oscar got his check ride in a U-2R flown by Det commander Lt Col Willie Horton. A special cage was built so that Oscar could take up his position in the Q-bay as Deputy Glock, for a low-altitude functional test flight. After that experience, Oscar would run off in the opposite direction every time he heard a U-2 engine start!

Oscar remained a true friend and faithful supporter to all Osan-assigned U-2R personnel until the sad day in 1990 when he went Missing In Action (MIA). Thereafter, Oscar, Jr., who was acquired in 1985, assumed the duties of Squadron Mascot. – C.P.

OLIVE HARVEST

I was approaching the border of the country I was going to overfly. I needed to orbit there for 15 minutes to make sure I made the IP on time, and to scan the weather inland. If the weather looked bad, I'd go home. Once I crossed the border, we could not go in again for another three weeks: that was part of the agreement. Radio silence was adhered to. Only to send a few mission codes or in case of emergency would I transmit. One last check of the engine, fuel, and camera systems, and I was ready to go.

I got a few "hits" on my radar warning gear, but that was not unusual. It was all low pulse rate stuff, indicating that they were just searching, not tracking.

The frame counter started clicking as some 800 pounds of glass in the plane's belly began rolling and twisting and photographing the ground horizon to horizon. From then on it was just navigate, record data, and make sure the camera kept clicking. Believe it or not, one guy actually flew this mission and forgot to turn the camera on! Hard to explain that to the State Department....

- Lt Col Michael Danielle, taken from
www.southernoregonwarbirds.org, 2000

New Black Cats

At Osan in May 1976, temporary commander Lt Col Dave Young was well aware of the long and notable history of the Chinese Air Force Black Cat Squadron. As a pilot in the CIA's Project Idealist from 1970 until the closure of Det H in 1974, Young had done TDY duty at Taoyuan as the American U-2 driver-on-call. He preserved the tradition by assigning the name "Blackcats" to the new U-2 operation at Osan. Someone acquired a real, and very black, tomcat as a mascot for the detachment, and named it Oscar. In 1977 Det 2 commander Lt Col Willie Horton made sure that Oscar got a check ride in the U-2!

The new Blackcats had two U-2R's assigned. In early 1977 the H-camera was sent to Osan, and on 3 February 1977 Captain Robert Gaskin flew Det 2's first oblique photography mission along the Demilitarized Zone (DMZ). To fully exploit the sensor's capabilities, a new flight track only 10 miles from the DMZ was established. Despite the frequent cloudy weather, the new capability was a hit with regional commanders. Det 2 was tasked to fly four photo missions a month from Osan, in addition to 24 SIGINT missions, which were flown on a standard track 26 nautical miles from the DMZ.[3]

For the rest of the decade Det 2 flew Olympic Game missions on a daily basis, to provide 240 hours of orbit time each month. Since the Senior Spear collection system was housed in the wing slipper pods, the dual photo-SIGINT mission was always possible. During daytime flights the H-camera went along for the ride, in case the weather proved suitable. The only blemish on a smooth-running operation was the crash on 5 October 1980 of 10340. Captain Cleve Wallace survived an ejection. The wreckage was scattered in the mountains 90 miles east of Seoul, and it took three months to recover all the sensitive hardware.[4]

Sampling

Photo and SIGINT were not the only missions assigned to the U-2 in the 1970s. From 1973 the U-2 was back in the sampling business. The RB-57F had taken over the role in the mid-1960s, but the bizarrely-modified aircraft proved difficult to maintain. In June 1973 the 100th wing flew test and training missions with a U-2R hatch, on which was mounted the latest F-4/P-5 filter and gas sampling system. The B-400 rate count meter in the cockpit, together with a sensitive directional receiver system with a maximum range of about 5,000 feet, enabled the pilot to locate and monitor the nuclear debris.

The call was not long in coming. China made its 15th nuclear test at Lop Nor on 27 June 1973. A U-2R deployed from D-M via Pease AFB to Torrejon airbase in Spain and flew two missions back-to-back on 14 July. The next Chinese test came almost exactly a year later. The U.S. had just received permission to fly the Olympic Race sampling mission from Osan airbase, Korea—a more favorable area for intercepting the debris. The 100th SRW sent one U-2R from D-M and another from U-Tapao, and eight missions were flown, including one round-robin trip from the Thai base after the scientists determined that some debris was heading that way.

The sampling missions were codenamed Olympic Race. Tipped off by AFTAC, the U-2R was back in Korea in January 1976 when the Chinese made another test. Only the first of five sampling sorties from Osan picked up any debris, however. The next Chinese test on 17 November was a big one. Det 2 flew four missions from Osan, and the 9th SRW deployed two U-2R's from Beale to Eielson AFB, Alaska, for another four flights. Another aircraft flew from Pease AFB, NH, and there were two round-robin flights from Beale. Altogether, the 9th SRW flew 17 sampling flights in late November 1976 and logged 143 hours on the task. Nuclear debris was picked up on six of the flights. The next alert was not until October 1980, when another big Chinese test generated another seven U-2R missions: three each from Osan and Eielson, and one from Beale. On one of the sampling sorties, the pilot's pressure suit had to be discarded after the flight, because the bleed air passing through it was "hot" with radioactivity.[5]

NATO

In late August 1976, the 9th SRW deployed an SR-71 and a U-2R to RAF Mildenhall so that they could participate in two NATO training exercises, Cold Fire and Teamwork. The U-2R was in the Senior Book configuration,

E-Systems developed the Senior Ruby ELINT sensor for the U-2R in the mid-1970s. It is seen here on testbed 10339 during the dem/val deployment to Mildenhall in mid-1978 (author).

SAMPLING MISSIONS AND THAT "CRAPPY" DOPPLER
Jim Terry flew the U-2R in the 100th SRW from 1970-74. During that time the wing resumed sampling flights, as he recalls:

We would fly a W-shape pattern, 400 miles out for an hour, 180-degree turn, then back for an hour, and on to the next leg. You watched the needle on the graph paper, and if it moved, that was your signal to operate the gas ball samplers. They took in compressed air from the engine, whereas the filter papers were exposed to ambient air.

Now these were over-water flights, navigating by dead-reckoning and with the "help" of that crappy Doppler. There was no sextant in the R-model. The theory was that the TACAN plus Doppler would give us everything we needed....

We did not have weather radar either, of course. That was a big problem, flying out of U-Tapao, with all the thunderstorms. And the base weather radar was frequently unserviceable. When you were letting down at night after a SIGINT fight, you just steered clear of the lightning flashes and hoped for the best.

- interview with author

but also carried the Iris camera. During the month-long deployment, 10336 flew the first U-2R SIGINT mission along the central front against Warsaw Pact communications. The analysts back home must have been pleased with the results. By the end of the year, they were calling for a permanent U-2R detachment in Europe.

Responding to the call, a U-2R was sent back to Mildenhall for four months in 1977 for a demonstration/validation of the concept. On 10 June Capt James Madsen flew the first Olympic Flame SIGINT collection mission, downlinking to an ESC ground station near Hahn, codenamed Metro Tango. A total of 34 missions were performed during the deployment, using a single long track over West Germany that allowed for four complete eight-hour orbits. Some of the sorties were coordinated with flights of the U.S. Army's U-21F Guard Rail turboprop. This also collected SIGINT, but at a much lower altitude, and the U-2 was used as a relay for some Guard Rail missions.

HQ USAFE was enthusiastic about the Olympic Flare missions. It reported: "The demonstration has provided far more extensive and timely intelligence coverage than is usually available. Our interim evaluation reveals several unique intercepts of (Warsaw Pact) tactical flight activity, and more timely reporting on activity that was intercepted by other collectors. The large geographical area covered by this high altitude platform...significantly increases our readiness posture."[6]

As a result, SAC began making plans for a permanent U-2R detachment at Mildenhall. Especially since the SIGINT-collecting capability of a U-2R flying high along the border with the Warsaw Pact was about to be doubled; the Senior Ruby ELINT sensor was in development.

E-Systems

E-Systems was already the prime contractor for SIGINT systems on SAC's RC-135 Rivet Joint aircraft. The company was developing an automatic ELINT system for the RC-135 that was not working very well yet. Nevertheless, in September 1976 E-Systems' Garland Division, in Texas, received a separate contract to develop a datalinked and semi-automatic ELINT system for the U-2R. Like the company's Senior Book and Spear SIGINT systems, the receivers would be remotely-controlled by operators seated in front of consoles in a ground station.

DIA...NSA...JRC...JCS...SRC...SAC

The Defense Intelligence Agency (DIA) validated both the photo and SIGINT requests of U.S. intelligence users. The National Security Agency (NSA) determined the type of collector that could best satisfy the DIA-validated SIGINT requirements. Then, well in advance of the time when the missions were to be flown, the Joint Reconnaissance Center (JRC) in the Joint Chiefs of Staff (JCS) sent the Strategic Reconnaissance Center (SRC) a monthly schedule that included the number of sorties approved for each SAC reconnaissance program. Within this framework, the SRC determined the precise day and time that the intelligence-collecting sorties would be launched, taking into account such variables as weather, maintenance, tanker logistics, and other support requirements. The C-in-C SAC and his senior staff reviewed the monthly and daily reconnaissance schedules, and approved each mission prior to execution, a practice which emphasized both the importance and sensitivity of strategic reconnaissance operations.

- History of SAC Reconnaissance Operations, 1 January-31 December 1977

The plan was to integrate the Ruby system with Spear. But this would need more space for antennas and black boxes on the aircraft. Since SAC did not want to preclude flying photo missions with the same airplane, most of the Q-bay was reserved for a camera. The Skunk Works had a solution—the "superpods."

The superpods were 2 ft 8 in wide and nearly 24 feet long—three times larger than the Spear pods that were mounted at the same wing station. They extended aft as well as forward of the wing, and therefore interrupted the flap surface when fitted. The fore and aft sections of the new pods could be easily removed from the midbody, so that different antenna shapes tailored to specific missions could be carried. To the same end, there was also provision for a belly radome to be attached to the pod forebody, and cooling inlets and outlets could be fitted to maintain the delicate electronics they contained at the correct temperature. Equipment weighing as much as 800lbs could be carried in each superpod.

The new sensor and the superpods were test-flown on 10339 at Palmdale in early 1978. By mid-year, the Senior Ruby system was ready for a demonstration in Europe. It was certainly a dense signal environment—especially on the other side of the border. Flat Face, Squat Eye, Rock Cake, Long Talk, Fan Song, Low Blow...the list of Warsaw Pact emitters was endless. There were well over 700 of them in the radar bands alone. Moreover, the Group of Soviet Forces in Germany was invariably the first to receive the latest Soviet military hardware. This was a target-rich environment!

Senior Ruby

On 3 June 1978 the 9th SRW deployed 10339 to Mildenhall, and a Senior Ruby ground control/processor van was added at the Metro Tango site in Germany. Three checkout and 16 demonstration flights were accomplished during the seven-week deployment. More than 2,500 ELINT reports were generated by the ground station. On two of the sorties some panoramic photo collection was also performed, but this was an unusually rainy summer in Europe, so the opportunities were limited.

Once again, U.S. commanders in Europe waxed lyrical about a new U-2R capability. EUCOM said: "The system appears extremely well-suited to the tactical situation in Europe." The ELINT specialists at NATO's European Defense Analysis Center (EUDAC) found that Senior Ruby "exceeded all our expectations for a new system...the downlinked data experiences very little delay in processing...the accuracy of the system is sufficient for following troop and equipment movement in a battle area."[7]

10339 was returned to Palmdale, and over the next year was the testbed for combining the Spear and Ruby sensors on the same airplane. It was flown against emitters located at various test sites in the western U.S., with the receivers being downlinked to the ground station in Sunnyvale. LMSC was the contractor for the ground station, a development from the one that it had provided to "fuse" the take from various sensors in the EP-X program. Sperry was again responsible for the datalink. By now, the company had developed the improved L52 datalink with a two-axis antenna, and using fiberoptics to carry the signal from sensor. It was probably the first use of fiberoptics on an aircraft.[8]

In the new tests, the task of the Transportable Ground Intercept Facility (TGIF) was to combine the different types of SIGINT collection from the U-2R into a single intelligence report. Meanwhile, the 9th SRW sent 10338, configured with the Senior Book system, to Mildenhall from September-October 1978. It returned to the British base on 30 March 1979, and Det 4 was created as a permanent feature of the East Anglian landscape. The mission was codenamed Olympic Torch, just as it had been out of U-Tapao in 1974-76. Up to 10 nine-hour flights were accomplished each month with the single airplane.

After the Senior Spear COMINT and Senior Ruby ELINT sensors were combined, and a ground station set up in Germany, a U-2R of the 9th SRW began flying permanently from Det 4 at Mildenhall. (author)

A TARGET-RICH ENVIRONMENT!

When the Senior Ruby ELINT collection system was first deployed to Europe, there was plenty of "trade" to pick up. Here is an intelligence summary of the emitters in East Germany alone in the mid-1970s:

Three early-warning networks (57 confirmed sites), two ground-controlled intercept networks (38 sites), SAM and AA radars, and miscellaneous emitters such as ATC, battlefield surveillance and counter-battery radars...EW/GCI: at least 74 Squat Eye and 159 Flat Face low-level radars, 78 Bar Locks for medium-altitude search, and nine high-altitude, long-range Tall Kings. Plus 129 Spoon Rests, 86 Thin Skins, 25 Sponge Cake and 16 Rock/Stone Cake. SAM: As many as 50 SA-2 Fan Song, 24 SA-3 Low Blow, 82 SA-4 Pat Hand and 26 SA-6 Straight Flush. AAA: as many as 107 Gun Dish, 69 Flap Wheel, 43 Fire Can, and at least two Whiff radars.

- *Advanced Location Strike System Dem/Val Final Report, USAF Tactical Air Warfare Center, February 1976, Appendix 1*

MORNING LIGHT – THE COSMOS CRASH

On 24 January 1978 a Soviet ocean surveillance satellite crashed into Canada's remote Northwest Territory. Cosmos 954 was known to have a nuclear power source for its radar—highly enriched uranium. Had this all been burned up during the re-entry? The scientists thought so, but just in case they were wrong, the 9th SRW flew 11 sampling missions from Beale in 1978 to check. The first was flown over northwestern Canada on the evening that the satellite disintegrated, a 10-hour flight. Six more were flown by end-March, and another four during the rest of the year. No radioactive debris was intercepted. – *C.P*

TELINT MISSION?

In 1979, a new U-2 capability was mooted during the great debate over ratification of the SALT 2 treaty between the superpowers. Many U.S. observers were worried that the Soviets would cheat on the treaty, and demanded assurances about Uncle Sam's ability to verify that its provisions were being followed. With the recent overthrow of the Shah of Iran, the U.S. had lost the use of its SIGINT intercept stations in the mountains north of Tehran and Mashhad. These played a vital role in watching for signs of an imminent Soviet ballistic missile test from Kapustin Yar or Tyuratam, and in picking up telemetry relayed back from the missiles once launched. Their loss cast further doubts on the verifiability of SALT 2.

The Carter administration suggested that Cyprus-based U-2s could help close the intelligence gap, by flying over Turkey and the Black Sea. They could be equipped with TELINT sensors that would pick up data from the missiles once they had climbed to an altitude of about 90 miles (just as the U-2 had, in fact, done in 1959-60 in the CIA days!).

SALT sceptics in Congress were briefed on the plan in early April, and details were leaked to the newspapers. A request for overflight rights was sent to the Turkish government. Istanbul, still smarting from a three-year cutoff in U.S. military assistance following its invasion of Northern Cyprus, reacted coolly, and told Washington that it would consider the matter, but only if the USSR raised no objections! A high-level delegation from the Pentagon flew to Istanbul and persuaded the Turks to grant unconditional overflight rights for U.S. spyplanes, but the U-2 scheme was never implemented. Instead, the U.S. deployed a new TELINT satellite, and was able to open two new ground stations in Sinkiang to monitor Soviet missile tests in Xinjiang, thanks to the Chinese government. – *C.P.*

In the last days of December 1979, 10339 was deployed to Mildenhall for the Initial Operational Test & Evaluation (IOT&E) of the combined SIGINT capability. This would eventually be codenamed Senior Glass, but it was also known as the Remote Tactical Airborne SIGINT System (RTASS). Det 4 flew the first RTASS mission on 8 January 1980, downlinking to the TGIF that had been installed at Metro Tango. From the very start the E-Systems/LMSC RTASS was an unqualified success. The early flights went so well that SAC was able to withdraw the Senior Book-configured U-2R 10338 from Det 4 in mid-February. What began as an IOT&E turned into an extended operational deployment.[9]

Moreover, the new RTASS aircraft was soon spreading its wings to the seas surrounding northern Europe. In April 1980, 16 missions codenamed Olympic Fire were flown by 10339 from new orbits over the Norwegian and Barents Seas, downlinking SIGINT intercepts of shipping to a Senior Book ground station placed on a U.S. Navy reconnaissance ship. In September 1980 another 10 missions were flown, this time during a big NATO naval exercise. The ground station was onboard the aircraft carrier USS Nimitz. The missions proved that a high-flying U-2 could indeed provide useful over-the-horizon intelligence on potential adversary ships to a Naval Task Force.[10]

OTHER PLACES, 1980

Yemen: In late January 1980 OL-OH flew one photo mission over North and South Yemen at the request of the Saudi government. The two Yemens had been fighting each other; the South was a Soviet client. The mission was codenamed Senior Look '80, and lasted eight-and-a-half hours. The Saudis got some of the photos, taken by the Optical Bar Camera OBC).

El Salvador: To help determine whether Marxist guerillas were being supplied with weapons from Cuba by boat, an OBC-equipped U-2R was flown over the area on 2 July 1980. The single Olympic Champ mission took off from Beale and landed at Barksdale.

Italy: On 10 December 1980 the Mildenhall-based U-2R flew across France (for a change!) to photograph the earthquake in southern Italy.

30

The TR-1

When the Pentagon revealed its Fiscal Year 1979 budget request to Congress in the early months of 1978, there was one major surprise. Listed among the requests for Air Force aircraft was one for "the TR-1, a new version of the Lockheed U-2, updated for tactical reconnaissance." The military was planning a fleet of at least 25 TR-1s, at a cost of about $550m, including engines, sensors, and ground support equipment. This first-year request was for $10.2m "to prepare for production."

Behind the scenes, the Dragon Lady had come out tops in a quick but influential Pentagon study of future reconnaissance needs. Led by General Alton Slay, the USAF deputy chief of staff for R&D, the Reconnaissance Steering Group brought Army and Air Force officers together in September and October 1977 to kibbutz on whether the recent advances in sensor technology could play a part in redressing the military balance in Europe.

The Warsaw Pact was deploying troops, tanks, missiles, and aircraft in numbers far greater than NATO could afford. The USSR and its communist allies now had the military might to pose a "blitzkrieg" threat to NATO's outgunned and outnumbered divisions. They might be able to advance hundreds of miles in a surprise attack before the West had time to react properly.

The U.S. intelligence community was still haunted by the 1968 Czechoslovakia fiasco, when there had been little warning when the Soviets turned a military exercise into a move to depose the liberalising government of Alexander Dubceck. All the satellite photography in the world could not reveal a sudden movement of massed armour across a cloud-covered continent.

ASARS and PELSS

Imaging radar and SIGINT sensors could defeat cloud cover, and also the USSR's growing ability to camouflage its military deployments. By the time that Slay's group met, the USAF had already issued development contracts for the Advanced Synthetic Aperture Radar System (ASARS) and the Precision Emitter Location and Strike System (PELSS). The study examined how these and other advanced systems could be best deployed, and their data best distributed to those who really needed it.

"It is possible to fight outnumbered and win, provided you know when and where to employ your forces, and if they are employed against those elements of the threat which, if destroyed or degraded, reduced drastically the overall combat capability of the enemy," said Brig Gen Charles Canedy, U.S. Army. These were "critical nodes," and they were "command posts, communications centers, weapons, prime movers, and jammers," he added.[1]

Since the Warsaw Pact would have to funnel its forces for a surprise attack through certain chokepoints, the sensors could pinpoint the most profitable areas some way behind the front line for NATO to target with its medium-range bomber and missile forces. Using this counter-attack doctrine, which came to be known as the FOFA (Follow-On Forces Attack) concept, NATO commanders hoped to blunt any Warsaw Pact advance by denying their front-line troops the supplies and reinforcements they would surely need in order to successfully pursue the "blitzkrieg" strategy.

Compass Arrow

The Steering Group's most important task was to evaluate rival reconnaissance platforms. New Remotely-Piloted Vehicles (RPVs) were contenders. Ryan's Model 154 "Compass Arrow" had been the first of the new-breed RPVs to fly, in 1969. It could carry the 24-inch Itek panoramic camera and ELINT sensors to beyond 70,000 feet, by virtue of a 48-feet wingspan and a GE J97 turbojet. It incorporated stealth principles in its design, such as a flattened undersurface, inward-canted vertical stabilizers, and an engine mounted in an above-fuselage position. Built to fly over China as a replacement for the U-2, it was never deployed.

One major drawback of Compass Arrow was that it still required a C-130 Hercules "mother ship" for launch, and recovery crews plus helicopters to retrieve it after a mission. So the development effort turned towards RPVs that could be launched and recovered autonomously. For the "Compass Dwell" program, E-Systems and Martin-Marietta produced rival designs with conventional undercarriages that could take off and land under their own power. But they were powered by piston or turboprop engines, and could not rise much above 45,000 feet.

The Compass Cope program produced unmanned vehicles that could take off and land like real airplanes, such as this Boeing YQM-94A. But USAF leaders decided that the technology was not mature enough to commit to production. They bought more U-2s instead, re-christened as the TR-1 (NARA 112095).

The rollout ceremony for the TR-1 was held on 15 July 1981 (Lockheed P1247)

Compass Cope

The Compass Cope program was therefore born in June 1971, when Boeing was asked to produce an autonomous, low-observable machine capable of reaching 70,000 feet on the 5,000 lb thrust provided by the J97 turbojet. Almost a year later, Ryan was asked to develop a rival Compass Cope RPV, this time using a Garrett ATF-3 turbofan. Both companies made extensive use of composite materials in their designs, in an effort to reduce weight as well as the vehicle's radar reflectivity.

Boeing won a fly-off, and a $77 million contract for three pre-production YQM-94A vehicles was issued in mid-1976. The company realized that a drone could not be operated over the densely-populated areas of Central Europe unless there was absolute confidence in the system's integrity. Redundancy was built in, including a backup, get-me-home powerplant. But key USAF leaders were not convinced. Undoubtedly, there was some built in prejudice against drones by the former pilots who now ran the major operating commands. General Dixon of TAC spoke for them all when he said: "RPV technology and development has not matured to the point where they can effectively perform all portions of the time-sensitive reconnaissance mission."[2]

Crucially, Slay's group had another set of concerns. "I was never able...to make what I considered a real compelling case for our analysis on the cost-effectiveness of the Compass Cope," Slay recalled. It was cheaper to build, but the savings gained from eliminating the pilot and his support provisions went instead on the expensive remote control system. Slay also mistrusted the automatic flight control on the drones. He talked of the "insuperable problem (of) expected attrition...on landing and takeoff."[3]

Ben Rich's proposal for new-production U-2s at 'a good price" now looked very attractive. It was obvious that there were not enough of them for current missions, let alone new ones using sensors like ASARS and PLSS. Then there was that old Skunk Works reputation and mystique, which still counted for something, evidently.

The Steering Group recommended reopening the U-2R production line for a buy of 25 U-2s, and a total of 15 sensor suites, including ASARS and the Senior Spear/Ruby systems. The study group strongly recommended that control and tasking of reconnaissance aircraft be vested in theater commanders. In the past, they noted, most U-2 missions had been directed from the JRC in Washington and executed by the SRC in Omaha.

DRONES vs. U-2s IN 1977

All through the late nineties, the debate about whether a UAV (eg the Global Hawk) could replace the U-2 was ongoing. But it was *deja vu* to those who had been involved in a similar debate in the mid-seventies. Then, it was Compass Cope versus the U-2.

For a start, there was the payload. The maximum offered by the TR-1 was at least one-third greater than in Boeing's latest Compass Cope design. This was a useful margin of safety if the forthcoming sensors turned out to be heavier than expected, which had often been the case in the past.

Boeing said that their Cope UAV would demonstrate "a significant reduction in operating costs over existing alternatives." They were quoting 10-year lifecycle costs of around $100m, with direct operating costs in the order of $650m (in 1974 prices). They reckoned these to be half those of the current SAC U-2R operation, and fuel burn by the turbofan-powered Cope vehicle would be only 10% of the Dragon Lady, with its old-technology J75 powerplant. The vehicles themselves would cost no more than $2 million, compared with $10m for a new U-2. General Slay's Study Group did not accept these calculations, and deemed the Compass Cope to not be cost effective. The proven performance of the Dragon Lady also weighed heavily in the decision.

At an RPV industry association meeting in mid-1977, TAC's Lieutenant General James D. Hughes admonished his audience, telling them that "the drone community has oversold its product," and that "demonstration capability has been sold as real operational capability."

In the final analysis, it was the presence of that man in the cockpit that was to prove decisive, and this was not just "flyboy" prejudice. There was the unresolved question of whether the NATO allies would approve such an extensive RPV operation above their airways and cities. Most crucially of all, there was the nagging worry about a drone going out of control and heading across the border. The U.S. would be putting some of its most sensitive, state-of-the-art intelligence-gathering sensors onboard this vehicle. An errant drone might hand all this stuff to the Soviets on a plate! – *C.P.*

TR-1 production got underway at Palmdale in 1979 (Lockheed P11695).

ASARS EXTRAS

It wasn't just the range, resolution, and the timely downlink that made ASARS such a neat system. It was the nifty extras that modern computing power could provide in the ground station. The extras included a variety of ways in which the radar image could be manipulated to suit the particular purposes of detection or interpretation. Since metallic objects, such as tanks or other vehicles, were better radar reflectors than surrounding natural materials, returns from the latter could be filtered out in a process known as "thresholding," thus immediately highlighting the real objects of interest in the image.

In another useful process known as "change detection," a newly-received image could be electronically compared with a previous one retained as a reference. And since SAR imagery was processed to show targets in an overhead view, a computer could more easily classify them based on their outlines. This move towards automated target recognition was long overdue; interpreters had frequently been overwhelmed in the past by the sheer weight of data brought back by the proliferating reconnaissance sensors. Now, instead of waiting for great chunks of raw material to land on his desk for analysis, the interpreter could sit comfortably in front of a screen in a facility near the front line and have his attention drawn automatically to changes, such as the appearance of enemy armor in a particular area. – *C.P.*

There was some support in the Pentagon for converting the unloved fleet of F-111D strike aircraft for reconnaissance. But Secretary of the Air Force Dr. Hans Mark favored the U-2 option. So did the Army and USAF hierarchy. In early December, the study's recommendations were approved by the chairman of the JCS, General David Jones, in time for the FY79 budget submission. Compass Cope was canceled.

The TR-1 spyplane

Congress approved the funding. And so the Dragon Lady went back into production—for the third time. Only it was not called the U-2R anymore. "We've got to get this spyplane label off the aircraft!" General Jones declared. TR-1 was the new designation. Ben Rich told him that the public would simply call it the TR-1 spyplane instead! Rich was equally disarming when he briefed Aviation Week magazine. "I'm improving the aircraft using the experience we have had with the U-2," he said. 'But overall, it's still the U-2R. We're not changing the tooling."[4]

The only visible difference between the U-2R and the TR-1 turned out to be in the horizontal tail. During U-2R operations it had been discovered that sonic vibrations from the engine were causing fatigue stress in the internal ribbing, because of the way these were spaced. The fix was to add stiffeners that showed up externally on the stabilizer; on the TR-1 this addition was not necessary, since the spacing of the internal ribs was adjusted to offset the resonance.

There was no change to the powerplant. Retired F-105 and F-106 fighters were stripped of their J75 engines, which were sent back to Pratt & Whitney for modification into the -P-13B high-altitude version.

There were not many changes in the cockpit. But a new threat warning panel signified the upgrading of the U-2's electronic warfare systems.

Kelly Johnson at the TR-1 ceremony with his successor as head of the Skunk Works, Ben Rich (Lockheed).

Just about the only visible difference between the U-2R and the TR-1 was this wingtip housing for a new radar warning receiver (subsequently retro-fitted to all U-2Rs). (author)

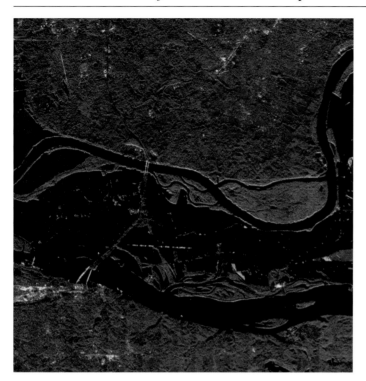

ASARS produced radar maps irrespective of cloud, and in plan view to the limit of the sensor's range. These were big advantages, especially for the TR-1's stand-off mission over central Europe (Hughes).

System 27 was a digital radar warning receiver supplied by Dalmo Victor (later to become Litton). Fore-and-aft-looking antennas were housed in the wingtips. System 29 was an active jammer, a replacement by Sanders of the old System 13.

Rocky start

The Skunk Works set up the TR-1 line at Site 7, Palmdale, with Dick Hesselgrave as production manager. Things got off to a rocky start. Experienced labor was in short supply in the Antelope Valley. Some U-2 production veterans were persuaded out of retirement to help the effort. The learning curve was steeper than it should have been. There were delays in subcontracting.

Military bureaucracy did not help. First, there was a power struggle between two Air Force commands as to who should run the TR-1 development. Aeronautical Systems Division (ASD) was in charge of new projects,

10336 was the testbed for the ASARS radar imaging sensor. The new nose was nearly three feet longer than the original (Lockheed CC2263).

but Air Force Logistics Command (AFLC) claimed this one as a continuation of an existing project—the U-2R. AFLC won.

Next came a debate over documentation. The U-2 had been born and bred as a "black-world" aircraft, sponsored by the CIA. Many aspects of the design did not correspond to laid-down military specifications

Unusual view of the long ASARS antenna about to be matched to the TR-1 radome (Hughes).

(milspecs). For instance, a bolt in the U-2 airframe might have so many threads less than the milspec in order to save weight. Now that the production line was to be reopened, the Air Force wanted everything to conform with the rules. Eventually a compromise was reached, whereby the Skunk Works was allowed to work to the *intention*, rather than the letter, of milspecs. Even so, volumes of new technical data had to be produced so that airmen maintainers with only basic skills could figure out how everything worked.

Then the operational four-star commanders scrapped over who should "own" the TR-1s. "There is absolutely no reason why SAC cannot continue to support the tasking requested by theater commanders," said CINCSAC General Ellis. General Creech of TAC replied that Congress would be confused, and the advocacy for funding the new aircraft less effective, unless it was unambiguously presented as a "tactical" asset. General Evans of USAFE supported Creech. SAC won the ownership argument for the aircraft, but targeting, tasking, and execution, plus ownership of the ground stations, was all assigned to USAFE.[5]

Within a year the USAF upped the total requirement to 35. The increase was supposedly driven by the PELSS program, which was reconfirmed in July 1979. However, the funding for the extra 10 aircraft came out of the NRO's "black budget." Essentially, they were top-ups for the existing U-2R fleet. And these 10 aircraft were never designated TR-1.

First flight

The first new aircraft was supposed to be delivered in July 1981. But it wasn't until the 15th of that month that 80-1066, the first TR-1A, was rolled out at Site 7 of the sprawling Palmdale airfield. This was a public occasion, unlike 1967 and 1955! The onlookers, ranging from Pentagon brass to the local Press, saw a smart black aircraft complete with the superpods. The TR-1A made its first flight on 1 August 1981, with Lockheed test pilot Ken Weir at the controls. It was delivered to Beale a month later.

By this time the Hughes ASARS-2 radar was already flying, on U-2R 10336. A new, extended nose had been designed to house the long antenna, transmitter, and receiver/exciter. It was 32 inches longer than the original, "slick" U-2R nose. The remaining black boxes for the radar were housed in the Q-bay, while the datalink stayed in the same place as the SIGINT-equipped aircraft: in a pressurized cavity aft of the tail gear. The star tracker radome was visible on the top of the fuselage aft of the Q-bay. Fiberoptic cables linked the various components.

Inevitably, perhaps, Hughes had encountered some development delays. But the early flight test results confirmed the radar's promise. "It provides pictures of near-photo quality at remarkable stand-off ranges," declared Gen Thomas McMullen. "The combined increase in range, resolution, and area coverage represents a quantum jump over currently operational systems." Hughes was cleared to put ASARS-2 into production. (ASARS-1 was the parallel program at Goodyear for an advanced imaging radar on the SR-71).

PELSS trouble

And what of PELSS (Precision Emitter Location & Strike System), the other new equipment that featured prominently in the TR-1 acquisition plan? By the time the new aircraft rolled out, PLSS development (the E for Emitter had been dropped) had been underway for four years. But it was in deep trouble. The systems integration contract was held by Lockheed Missiles and Space Company (LMSC) at Sunnyvale. The key subcontractors

The PLSS nose looked even more peculiar than the ASARS nose, with its slab-sided apertures for ELINT antennas.

included E-Systems (for the ELINT sensors) and Sperry (datalink). These latter two companies were also teamed on the Senior Ruby—but that was a less demanding requirement that did not provide targeting-accuracy information.

Compared with the predecessor ALSS, the new PLSS was being designed to detect the pulse width and scan rates of enemy radars, as well as their frequency and PRI. It was supposed to cover the entire frequency spectrum from 50MHz to 18GHz, to detect pulsed and continuous wave radars, and to fix the locations of emitters to within 50 feet, even if they were only on air for five seconds. Then there was the strike side of the system. PLSS was supposed to direct up to 30 weapons against targets at a time, with 30-foot accuracy. This was triple the capacity of the computers and datalinks used in ALSS! There were also stiff targets for system reliability.[6]

That included the triad platform, of course now confirmed as the TR-1. But as prime contractor for PLSS, LMSC had no formal relationship with the Skunk Works; it was dealing with one set of Air Force people at Wright-Patterson AFB, while Burbank dealt with another group in AFLC at Robins AFB. Structural complications such as this bedeviled the PLSS program almost from the start.

Despite what they had learned from ALSS, both the Pentagon and LMSC badly underestimated the difficulty of integrating the various PLSS subsystems. LMSC had 13 different subcontractors working for it at various times during the development. Coordinating all the black box requirements and interfaces became a nightmare. A year-long cutback in funding during 1980-81 didn't help, and neither did LMSC's decision in August 1981 to uproot its PLSS workers and move them to a new division in Austin, Texas.

The hardware was three years late entering flight test. A single TR-1 (01074) flew with the PLSS system in December 1983. It could be distinguished by yet another U-2R nose, this one having flat sides to house the ELINT antennas. The superpods housed the DME antennas. Another 18 months passed before the 9th SRW was finally able to launch a PLSS triad for weekly test missions over the China Lake weapons range.

Eventually, however, the Air Force top brass lost patience, and the Wild Weasel community were openly hostile. PLSS lingered on as the Signal Location and Targeting System (SLATS), and was tested in a two-aircraft (dual) configuration during 1987. The PLSS team claimed success during a Green Flag exercise that year. But now there were other ways to accomplish the mission, including further improvements to Senior Ruby and other single-platform ELINT sensors. SLATS never did make it to Europe in 1988 as planned, and the whole project was abandoned that same year.

Only one aircraft in this "triad" of TR-1s at Beale AFB is carrying the PLSS nose. This precision system for locating enemy emitters spent many years in development, and was never deployed (Lockheed CC3894K).

31

Routinely Useful

The TR-1s were to be operated in Europe by a new wing. In October 1979 RAF Alconbury was selected as the airbase. It was already home to a USAFE wing of RF-4C Phantoms. The UK took a year to approve the choice, but proved to be a willing host, as usual by now. In 1982 SAC reactivated its dormant 17th and 95th unit numbers as the 17th Reconnaissance Wing and the 95th Reconnaissance Squadron.

The plan was to operate 18 TR-1As at Alconbury, with another five held in reserve at Beale. The other two aircraft in the TR-1 order would be twin-cockpit, dual-control trainers—the TR-1B. Many new pilots would be needed for the expanded operation, so a separate U-2/TR-1 training squadron was activated by the 9th SRW in August 1981. The 4029th SRTS was appropriately known as the "Dragon Tamers." It did not receive its first TR-1B until March 1983.

Since ASARS was behind schedule, and the PLSS even more so, it was decided to deploy only three aircraft to Alconbury initially. These would take over the nine-hour SIGINT flights now being performed on a routine basis by the single U-2R of the 9th SRW's Det 4 at Mildenhall. They were given the codename Creek Spectre by USAFE. But USAFE did not "control" their own missions. SAC apparently backtracked on the modus operandi that was agreed in 1979, after the debate over "ownership" of the TR-1. European Command (EUCOM) had to send their tasking requests to the DIA in Washington for validation, from where they went via the JRC to the SRC, and on to the 17th Wing for execution.[1]

First TR-1 deployed

On 12 February 1983 the first TR-1 to be deployed overseas (01068) landed at Alconbury, and was followed six days later by 01070. Det 4 at Mildenhall waved goodbye to its U-2R, but remained active, since the SR-71 Blackbird was now in permanent residence there.

Throughout its first two years, the 17th wing had only three aircraft and eight or nine pilots assigned. Even so, it was a struggle to build a viable new organization from scratch, using makeshift facilities while purpose-built accommodations were being built. In 1983-84, there was only one hangar available for the aircraft, and mission birds had to be preflighted in the open. In the cold and frequently wet atmosphere of a British winter this was no joke for the maintenance people, especially those trying to keep delicate SIGINT and avionics equipment serviceable. It could even represent a hazard to the airplane—one U-2 was nearly lost when water entered the elevator section while the bird was parked on an exposed apron, and subsequently froze when it ascended to high altitude. Eventually, in late 1985, the first of five weather shelters were commissioned at Alconbury, and in 1987 construction of large-span semi-hardened shelters for the TR-1 fleet began.

RAF Alconbury was chosen as the TR-1 base. It was already home to a squadron of USAFE RF-4C Phantoms (author).

The first TR-1A for the 17th RW at Alconbury was 01068, seen here at dawn on a cold winter's morning (author).

In the early 1980s, Lockheed had hopes of selling the TR-1 to selected U.S. allies. The Skunk Works was cleared in 1982 to make presentations to the British and West German governments. In September of that year, the third production TR-1A (01068) was exhibited at the Farnborough Air Show.

It was a rare chance for the Skunk Works to feature on the international aerospace scene. Ben Rich was much more of a showman than Kelly Johnson, and enjoyed the chance to talk with European officials and journalists (this author included).

The sales effort came to naught, however. The Brits didn't have any money, and the Germans were happy for the time being with the converted Atlantic maritime patrol planes that they used for SIGINT missions. – C.P.

CREEK SPECTRE: A VIEW FROM THE GROUND

The 6911th Security Squadron of the Air Force Electronic Security Command (formerly AFSS) operated the ground station to which SIGINT from the TR-1 was piped down the datalink. MSgt Ted Brown served there:

We picked up the TR-1s as they came in over the North Sea, then locked our system onto their equipment and checked it out. By the time they closed to the inner German border, we would be ready. We had tasking from headquarters, telling us what they wanted to know on a particular day.

The pilot didn't do anything with the plane's receivers; he didn't even need a clearance to know what they picked up. We controlled the receivers from the ground. If there was something of interest in a particular area, we could ask the pilot through the datalink to move to a new orbit.

- from The History of US Electronic Warfare,
Vol III, by Alfred Price

ESCAPE AT OSAN

Major Dave Bonsi was the first of three U-2R pilots to fall victim to tailpipe failures in 1984:

It was my second tour at Osan, so I was a little cocky by now. The initial climbout was going well, 3,000 feet, just making the 15-degree left turn. Then a huge bang from behind! The horn sounded and the lights lit. The EGT dial was spinning down, and there was a distinct loss of thrust. Mobile called "Recover!" on the radio. I pushed the nose down and increased my bank angle to check my position relative to the runway. Then I began rolling level and tried bringing the nose up—no response.

Now I knew that I was hardly flying. The roll continued past level flight and to the right. I think the tailpipe separated about now, because the mobile called "Eject!" I had already pulled the handle. I probably pulled it at 60 degrees and ejected at 90 degrees.

I closed my eyes. I felt the parachute deploy. Some debris hit me, not badly. I opened my eyes and thought about where to land. The Koreans irrigated their rice paddies with waste from the latrines! Fortunately, I spotted a dry field....

The British weather posed another serious problem at Alconbury. The base had only a single runway, aligned roughly southeast-northwest. The trouble was, this frequently did not match the wind direction. The cross-wind limit for the Dragon Lady was only 20 knots (later reduced to 15 knots). The first three operational missions out of Alconbury all had to divert upon their return to Mildenhall, due to crosswinds at Alconbury! The mobile and recovery crew raced through the East Anglian countryside to reach the divert base, over 30 miles away.[2]

The wing lobbied to have an old wartime cross-runway reopened, but various buildings had gone up within the obstacle clearance limits for this strip in the meantime. The 17th also explored dispersed operations out of two nearby airbases that had different runway alignments, but both had poorly-maintained aprons and taxiways that caused damage to the aircraft's delicate tailgear.

ESC role

The USAF Electronic Security Command (ESC) was responsible for maintaining the TR-1 SIGINT systems at Alconbury, and for operating the Tactical Ground Intercept Facility (eg the ground station) in Germany. The activity was highly classified, because of the SIGINT aspect. Clearly, though, the advantage of high-flying collection was demonstrated nearly every day. The TR-1 could collect SIGINT at ranges of up to 350 miles, and at distances of up to 250 miles from the TGIF.

In 1984 a series of three serious accidents eventually resulted in the grounding of the entire TR-1/U2 fleet worldwide. On 22 May 1984 Captain David Bonsi had just taken off from Osan when there was an explosion behind him, and the entire tail section separated. He ejected safely. The accident investigators suggested that a small fuel leak had caused the explosion.

Less than two months later, a similar incident occurred at Beale AFB. The tail section crumpled immediately after takeoff. Captain Todd Hubbard survived a low ejection, despite floating through the fireball. U-2 operations were allowed to continue. This time, the accident investigators suspected a hydraulic leak. But on 8 October yet another aircraft was lost, when it broke up at 1,500 feet in mid-flight over Korea. A third pilot (Captain Tom Dettmer) was saved by the ejection seat. Only now was the U-2 fleet grounded.

The U-2 has a long tailpipe. Three serious accidents in 1984 were all caused by tailpipe clamps coming loose. This image shows the new tailpipe that was fitted a decade later, when the aircraft were re-engined (Lockheed).

At Alconbury, 17th RW pilots John Swanson and Larry Faber discuss tactics—or perhaps they are swopping notes on which nearby English pub is worth a visit! (author).

Tailpipe crumpled

The cause of all three accidents was pinned down shortly thereafter. The long exhaust duct on the U-2R and TR-1 was made up of two parts; a forward adaptor section of approximately four feet that was bolted to the J75 engine, and to which the long tailpipe fixed in turn. This adaptor/tailpipe link, consisting of a U-shaped clamp and two 1/4-inch bolts, had come loose and caused the tailpipe to move out of alignment. As the jet blast increased the tailpipe crumpled, and the trapped exhaust blew the tail off at its mounting points just aft of the speedbrake. The fix was relatively simple: a new type of clamp was devised, and more bolts were added.

As for why this problem had occurred after so many years of trouble-free operations, there were various theories. Some thought that the various attempts to tweak the J75 for better fuel consumption had led to more compressor surges, putting a strain on the tailpipe connection. Others thought that the wrong torque was applied to the tailpipe bolts during the manufacture of the TR-1. Inadequate maintenance procedures were also blamed.[3]

The seven-week grounding served to remind senior commanders how routinely useful the Dragon Lady SIGINT missions had become—not only in central Europe, but over the Korean peninsula (Det 2 Olympic Torch from Osan), the Mediterranean (Det 3 Olive Tree from Akrotiri), and the Caribbean (Det5 Olympic Fire from Patrick AFB, FL). Referring to the grounding, and to the U-2's stablemate at Beale, General Charles Gabriel later told Congress that "the TR-1 gives a pretty good picture along the front line more continuously than the SR-71 aircraft...."

COMINT COLLECTION

Of all the intelligence-gathering activities, COMINT can provide the greatest payoff. Even when communications are encrypted—as they most likely will be for any items of particular sensitivity—the analyst can make significant deductions from the type of transmission, its addressees and signatures, the number of messages sent, their length, the type of transmitters used, their powers, ranges, type of modulation, type of code, and so on. If a COMINT analyst can track the relative frequency of multiple address messages to a group of users, he may establish their common interest. Later, information acquired from another source about one of that group may indicate the interests and missions of the others. Order of battle information can be built up, and the other side's intentions deduced.

Of course, the analysts have other sources of COMINT available, from other aircraft, satellites, and ground intercept stations. But the U-2's sensitive receivers, operating at great height, help hoover up a lot of transmissions that might otherwise escape into the ether unheard, particularly from the shorter wavebands. – *C.P.*

Major Thom Evans on mobile duty at Alconbury. Note the selection of reading material. (author)

The ASARS sensor arrived at Alconbury in 1985. Here, a 17th RW TR-1A is taxiing for takeoff in the standard configuration for radar imaging plus SIGINT. (Peter R. Foster)

THE TROUBLE WITH 069...

Even when the new-production TR-1s came along, every Dragon Lady still had its idiosyncrasies. Typically, pilots would report differing trim characteristics, or fuel-balancing behavior. 01069 was a particular problem—especially after it was hit by a security police bus at Alconbury one dark night in 1983! The aircraft was returned to Lockheed at Palmdale inside a C-141 for repair. Three months later it was back at Alconbury, but the 17th RW reported that it did not fly right. In mid-1985 it went back to the U.S. for more attention, returning to Alconbury a year later. It still didn't fly right, according to the Air Force. In 1987 the service gave up on 069 and transferred it to NASA on loan. At Moffet Field, the Lockheed contract maintenance crews carefully rerigged the flying surfaces, and said that it now flew fine...- *C.P.*

CANDIDATE FOR JSTARS

For a while in the mid-1980s, it seemed that TR-1 production might be extended for the JSTARS (Joint Surveillance and Target Attack Radar System) program. This was another new airborne battlefield surveillance sensor. Unlike ASARS-II, however, the JSTARS radar would be multi-mode, featuring, in addition to SAR mapping, a Moving Target Indicator (MTI) mode to pinpoint enemy armour and mobile missiles on the move.

As a platform for JSARS, the Army suggested using its existing low-level reconnaissance plane (the OV-1 Mohawk). Congress favored the TR-1. Then the Air Force proposed using converted Boeing 707s, designated E-18. It argued that the larger plane would be able to process, analyze, and disseminate the radar data onboard, and perform airborne command and control.

Congressmen continued to champion the TR-1 for JSTARS, charging that the lower-flying C-18 was too vulnerable to enemy air defenses. The Air Force countered that the C-18 "lends itself to some self-defense capability, whereas providing the TR-1 with a measure of self-defense would not be possible with the present state of technology." Since the TR-1 already had an electronic warfare suite, it was not entirely clear what was meant.

Eventually, a team led by Grumman was selected and received a $657m contract to put JSTARS on the E-18. – *C.P.*

TREDS

In 1984, the imaging radar was still awaited. The Hughes ASARS underwent three further years of testing in California before it was deemed ready for deployment overseas. Part of the delay was caused by a lag in development of the ground station, contracted to Ford Aerospace. The TREDS, or TR-1 Exploitation Demonstration System, was supposed to combine the new radar processing and exploitation systems with the SIGINT data from the TGIF, which was already in service. One advantage would be that the radar's spotlight mode could be "cued" by the SIGINT. For instance, if a mobile missile site or command post came on the air and was detected, the radar could be "told" where to look to provide confirmation and additional intelligence. The combination of the TR-1, the ground station, and these passive and active methods of target detection was named the Tactical Reconnaissance System (TRS).

In March 1985, the size of the 17th RW fleet at Alconbury doubled to six aircraft with the arrival of three more TR-1As. Within days the wing also received the first of the long-awaited ASARS sensors. Lt Col John Sander, commanding officer of the 95th RS, flew the first operational ASARS-II sortie on 9 July 1985. A week later, the first TR-1 to carry both ASARS and SIGINT sensors was airborne and heading for the orbit over Germany.[4]

It was the start of what proved to be a protracted Initial Operational Test and Evaluation (IOT&E). Meanwhile, the Pentagon requested $94 million for TRIGS, the ultimate TR-1 Ground Station. The money would fund further improvements to the analysis and dissemination process, and put all the vans and cabins at Metro Tango into a hardened shelter.

NATO ground force commanders were excited by the new capabilities, but demanded more flexible methods of distributing the data. The U.S. Army ordered a mobile ground station from Westinghouse named the TRAC (Tactical RAdar Correlator). This was housed in a 40-foot container, and could deploy to the field and operate independently from the TREDS/TRIGS. The UK and U.S. jointly funded a program to process and disseminate ASARS data to NATO. The TADMS (TR-1 ASARS Data Manipulation System) was built by GE and Ferranti in 1989, and was manned by RAF personnel.

Magic Mountain

The 17th RW received more TR-1As direct from the production line, and was eventually assigned 12 aircraft. Although the PLSS had been canceled, the wing needed enough aircraft for its wartime task of providing two TR-1 orbits across Central Europe on a 24-hour basis. That would mean launching six aircraft each day. Expensive new facilities were built at Alconbury,

In 1989 it was Bye Bye Blackbird, as the SR-71 fell victim to budget cuts. Thereafter, the 9th SRW continued at Beale with the aircraft that it had been designed to replace—the U-2 (Lockheed).

SKUNK WORKS NOT-SO-SECRET

In 1986 the Lockheed-California Company was accused by the government of slack security in the safeguarding and classification of top-secret documents. Hundreds had gone "missing." Progress payments on the SR-71 and TR-1, as well as the F-117 Stealth Fighter, were held up. Thousands of documents had to be reviewed. Many of them—especially the older ones—bore no classification marks at all. This was in accord with the old Skunk Works principle of "perimeter security"—strictly control the number of people with access to a program, but do not burden them with excessive paper bureaucracy inside the controlled area.

Two years earlier, Lockheed Chairman Roy Anderson had criticised the increased interference by government and legislature. "In the Skunk Works," he said, "we have developed articles on a classified basis for about 60% of the cost of developing a system on a non-classified basis, and in one-half to two-thirds the time. Same company. Same technologies. The only difference is the management method and freedom from queries that too many times tend to be politically motivated, rather than founded in any abuse of the trust the nation places in our industry." – C.P.

including the 13 unique widespan hardened aircraft shelters and a deep underground avionics and sensor maintenance facility known as "Magic Mountain." The USAF's only hyperbaric chamber in Europe was built for the 17th's Physiological Support Division.

On a typical day, one or two operational missions and a half-dozen training flights would be launched from Alconbury—crosswinds permitting! The ops tempo usually increased in April and September. This was when the Warsaw Pact held its spring and autumn military exercises, and EUCOM wanted more Creek Spectre missions. There were also occasional long photo sorties tasked by SAC and codenamed Senior Look. The 17th wing grew to more than 500 personnel, and the 95th RS had an authorized strength of 18 pilots. The wing helped develop a new flight planning sys-

tem running on a minicomputer, which automated much of the drudgery involved in devising flight tracks. It was the most advanced in the USAF.

On 3 October 1989 the USAF and the Skunk Works celebrated the handover of the last TR-1 (01099) in a ceremony at Palmdale. To the agreement of various assembled three- and four-stars, Ben Rich described the program as "a model of the defense procurement process." After various changes of plan stemming mainly from the protracted development and ultimate cancellation of PLSS, a total of 37 aircraft were built at Palmdale from 1981 to 1989. They comprised 25 TR-1As, two TR-1B trainers, two ER-2s for NASA, and the "black budget" U-2Rs—seven U-2Rs and a single U-2R (T). Three of the first five TR-1As were "converted" to the U-2R configuration.

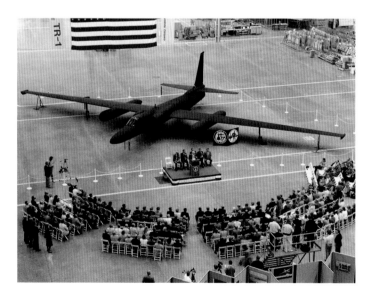

The last TR-1 (01099) was delivered in another ceremony at Palmdale on 3 October 1989. A total of 37 new-production aircraft were built there from 1981-89 (Lockheed 89B-442-11).

Fred Cavanaugh was the U-2/TR-1 program manager in the 1980s, at the end of a long career in the Skunk Works (author).

OLYMPIC TORCH
Steve Brown served tours with Det 2 at Osan during the mid-1980s. He recalls:

It was a nine-hour mission, to provide eight hours on-orbit. We were required to do 30 of these per month, so flying went on through the weekend, too. The usual takeoff was at 0600, but sometimes we did an afternoon launch, as well. There were two standard orbits. The photo one was closest to the DMZ. For SIGINT purposes we flew a "bow-tie" pattern.

We were in constant communication with the ground station. It was just as well. One time, I fell asleep and missed the next orbit turn. The guys below noticed immediately and woke me up!

SHUTTLE MISSION

In 1989 Det 5 at Patrick AFB took up an interesting challenge from NASA. The space agency wanted to find out more about the damage that was occurring to the insulating tiles of the Space Shuttle as it was launched from the Kennedy Space Center. Material dislodged from the nose caps of the Solid Rocket Boosters (SRBs) was suspected. Engineers wanted to view them during the first two minutes of flight. They needed a top-down view!

During the launch of STS-29 in March, a U-2R equipped with the panoramic camera flew a racetrack pattern offset five miles from the Shuttle launch path. But it was tough to position the aircraft at the best downrange point. The U-2 and the Shuttle were moving in different planes.

The scheme was tried again during the launch of STS-30 in May 1989, this time with the H-camera. Again, though, the U-2 could not get into the optimum position for some decent slant-angle imagery. And the PIs could not resolve enough information to tell NASA anything useful about the nose cones. A pity, in view of what happened many years later! – C.P.

- with acknowledgement to Spaceflight magazine, Vol 38, May 1996, p174

The Senior Span satcom antenna pod during flight tests. The modified aircraft acquired the unofficial nickname "Willie the Whale," on account of the large "humpback" that was created (Lockheed via Al Pinkham).

Bye Bye Blackbird

01099 was delivered to Beale a few weeks later. There, the 9th SRW was in the process of closing down the SR-71 operation. The formidable but hugely expensive Blackbird had run out of credit in Washington. "The combination of what you can do with overhead systems today, and what you can do with the TR-1, which also has new sensors on it, gives you a sense that the marginal contributions of the SR-71 are simply not cost-effective," said USAF Chief of Staff General Larry Welch. He was already hated with venom by the Habu camp for his previous attempts to scupper their program. They hotly contested his verdict, but did not prevail. It was not just about sensors, it was about timeliness. The SR-71 did not have a datalink.[5]

Senior Span

The concept of real-time reconnaissance had received a boost from the TR-1 program. But the system that evolved in Europe had one important drawback: the aircraft remained "tethered" to the ground station by the datalink. If a U-2 needed to roam further afield than the 200-250 mile line-of-sight distance to the ground station, the sensor "take" had to be recorded onboard for relay when the aircraft flew back within range of the ground station. Moreover, would political or military circumstances always be such that a ground station could actually be deployed?

Way back in 1975, Skunk Works engineer Bob Anderson had sketched an installation for a satellite antenna on the U-2, which could uplink the data for transmission onwards through space. The U.S. military was now launching its second-generation Defense Systems Communications Satellites (DSCS) with multiple channels. Although satellites were already relaying U-2 data back to the NSA from ground stations in the Senior Stretch program, it was another 10 years before the USAF got around to taking up Anderson's idea, when it approved the Senior Span development. (Anderson eventually became U-2 program manager when Fred Cavanaugh retired).[6]

Bob Anderson (left) replaced Cavanaugh as the U-2 program manager. He is seen here (left) with Skunk Works test pilot Ken Weir (center) and Ben Rich. (Lockheed)

The SYERS nose with glass aperture for the electro-optical sensor could rotate from side to side as required, for stand-off imaging (Lockheed PR2783-45).

Satcom

Lockheed worked with E-Systems and Unisys Government Systems Group to devise the U-2's satcom link. Previously named Sperry, the latter was already providing the U-2 air-ground datalink. The three contractors had to overcome considerable technical challenges to turn the concept into reality.

Unisys provided the buffer into which the aircraft's sensor data could flow and be configured for transmission by an airborne modem. A 30-inch parabolic antenna steerable in both azimuth and elevation at 60 degrees per second, and capable of elevation angles up to 85 degrees was designed. Compared with the air-ground datalink, the antenna pointing angles had to be much-reduced, and the signal filtering much-improved.

The challenge for the Skunk Works was to build a lightweight composite radome for the antenna and mount it so that the U-2's delicate cg was not disturbed, nor its inflight vibration increased; to provide and cool a high-voltage power supply; and to interface the aircraft's INS system.

Secret Configuration

Aerodynamic flight tests of the Senior Span pod began on 80-1071 in 1985. The unpressurized radome was nearly 17 feet long, and the whole system weighed 400 lbs. It was mounted on the upper fuselage immediately aft of the ADF antenna. When someone outside the fence at Palmdale photographed the secret new configuration from a side-on position at some distance, and sent his snap to *Janes' All The World's Aircraft*, the reference book described it as an AWACS development of the U-2!

The program moved slowly forward as the considerable problems were overcome. These included the requirement to constantly track the DSCS satellite through the various aircraft maneuvers: the pointing commands governing the Span antenna depended on extremely accurate positioning data being provided by the aircraft's INS (and on the satellite being in the

Unusual view of a Space Shuttle launch from a U-2R. The imagery was taken in 1989, when NASA requested help in determining how the insulating tiles were being damaged during the launch.

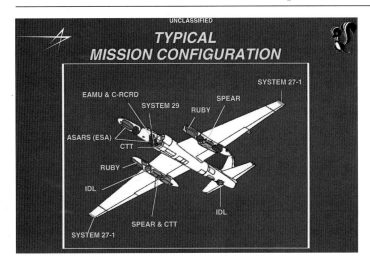

UNCLASSIFIED
TYPICAL
MISSION CONFIGURATION

SYSTEM 27-1
EAMU & C-RCRD
SYSTEM 29
SPEAR
RUBY
ASARS (ESA)
CTT
RUBY
IDL
IDL
SYSTEM 27-1
SPEAR & CTT

Lockheed briefing chart shows an optimum mission configuration, with radar imaging and SIGINT sensors, two datalinks, and defensive system.

expected location at the expected time!). Moreover, the whole set-up had to transmit and receive through a single antenna, since the principle that the sensors could be reconfigured by ground-based operators who received and analyzed the "take" was preserved.

The first deployments with the prototype Senior Span U-2R 10331 were made to Patrick AFB and Suwon AB, South Korea, in late 1986. (Suwon was a relief base for Osan during runway repairs). In March 1989 the first deployment to Europe took place when 80-1070 arrived at Alconbury. Airborne reconnaissance was entering the space age. But it was only a narrowband link, best suited for relaying SIGINT, not imagery.

SYERS

And it was the space age that indirectly provided the U-2 with a new lease on life as an optical imaging platform: the Senior Year Electro-Optic Reconnaissance System, or SYERS. Manufactured by Itek, SYERS was made possible by the new electro-optic (EO) technology, which was invented in the late 1960s.

Itek engineers were among the first to explore EO imaging. They adapted it to a panoramic 70-inch focal lens long-range oblique photographic (LOROP) camera that the company had already designed for the U-2, but which was never ordered into production. As early as 1974 the U-2RL proposal from the Skunk Works included E-O cameras in the two wing pods: one with a wide view, the other a LOROP. A 25-inch datalink antenna faced down from the rear of each pod.

But it was a reconnaissance satellite that first proved the operational utility of long-range E-O imaging and datalinking. The revolutionary and top-secret KH-11 was launched in 1976, the product of 10 years of R&D by the CIA. The KH-11 used light-sensitive semiconducting silicon. The silicon was arranged in arrays of charged-coupled devices (CCDs), which transformed the light energy into electrical charges, ready to be amplified and transmitted as a string of numbers.

In the early 1980s, Itek won the secret competition for a new EO sensor to go on the U-2, together with a ground station to process the imagery. SYERS was born.

Lockheed and Itek engineers then worked together on a radical new nose-mounted installation. The Skunk Works dusted off the old drawings for a revolving U-2 nose section, which had been designed way back in 1963 to house a sensor for the tracking of reentry vehicles. The new nose had an optical glass aperture in the first four feet, which was rotated by a servo to "look" left, right, or below the aircraft flight path. The camera's mirror system was housed here, while its body remained fixed within the rest of the nose section.

After flight testing, the prototype E-O system was deployed for operational testing at Det 2 in Korea, for comparison with the "wet-film" H-camera, which was also a sideways-looking system. By now, the "H" was much more reliable and flexible, compared to the early days. It had an automatic mode, or the pilot could preset a depression angle. There was also a stereo mode.

The prototype ground station, codenamed Senior Blade, was also deployed for the E-O tests. This performed similar functions to that of the ASARS ground station for radar imaging: control of the sensor, processing, and display and reporting of the imagery. As with ASARS, an onboard recorder was also provided so that the U-2 could record E-O imagery when it flew beyond the line-of-sight to the ground station. It took about a minute to downlink an image.

Unfortunately, the first Itek E-O system for the U-2R was destroyed in one of the 1984 crashes at Det 2. But more were built, and they could return usable imagery at roughly twice the range of the H-camera. Of course, the resolution was not as good—but the analysts didn't have to wait for the plane to return and the film to be processed! SYERS was approved for production.

By the end of the 1980s, the U-2 had evolved into a truly flexible, multipurpose reconnaissance platform. It could provide SIGINT, radar imaging, electro-optical imaging—all in near-real-time. The Dragon Lady could also act as a data relay platform, and for specialized requirements, it could still carry very high-resolution film cameras. No wonder Larry Welch preferred it to the SR-71!

32

Desert Shield and Storm

When Iraq invaded Kuwait in August 1990, the call to Beale was not long coming. On 7 August the 9th SRW was tasked to deploy two U-2s as soon as possible. Threatened from the north, Saudi Arabia agreed to host friendly forces, and suggested the airbase at Taif, on the plateau facing the Red Sea.

Fortunately, the wing was preparing to open a new detachment at Howard AFB, Panama, to boost coverage of the Caribbean and Latin America. The deployment support package was quickly expanded, then airlifted to the Middle East. Taif was designated OL-CH, which was officially short for Crested Harvest. By the time the two U-2s arrived on 17 August, an initial supply of JP-TS fuel had been flown in. Two days later the first two Olympic Flare missions were airborne.[1]

The value of the latest U-2 innovations (Senior Span and SYERS) was immediately proven. 01070 was deployed from Beale in the Spear/Ruby configuration, plus the prototype satellite uplink, and could therefore perform SIGINT-collecting flights without installing a TGIF in Saudi Arabia. 01076, deployed from Patrick AFB, FL, in the SYERS configuration, could provide real-time imagery of the Iraqi forces now occupying Kuwait from an orbit over the northern Saudi desert. Even before the U-2s arrived at Taif a Senior Blade van was airlifted to Riyadh. This location allowed the SYERS aircraft to remain "on-tether" during the early months of Operation Desert Shield.[2]

National Assets

Although Desert Shield was a CENTCOM operation, SAC refused to cede operational control of the U-2. According to Offutt, they were "national assets." SAC sent an advisory team to CENTCOM at Riyadh and created the 1700th Strategic Wing (Provisional). Lt Col Ash Lafferty, the 17th RW Assistant Director of Operations, was sent to Riyadh to smooth the process of U-2 tasking and scheduling. The operation at Taif became the 1704th RS (Provisional). The U-2 troops there preferred OL-CH, and took to calling it "OL-Camel Hump!"[3]

It was quickly decided to send TR-1s from Alconbury to boost the operation. Although it had only begun operational testing in March, the mobile TRAC ground station to process ASARS imagery was airlifted from Germany and set up next to the Blade van in the compound of the U.S. Training Mission (USTM) at Riyadh. The antennas were set up on the roof. It was not ideal: clutter from surrounding buildings reduced the range of the datalink to the U-2 by 20 miles. (The ground stations for the RC-135 Rivet Joint ELINT aircraft and the JSTARS were in the same compound, which led to considerable overcrowding! There was also the TADMS, another new mobile U-2 ground station that was designed to supply ASARS data to NATO forces. It was also deployed to Riyadh).[4]

A pair of 17th RW TR-1As arrived on 23 August, and the first ASARS mission was flown six days later. The 17th RW was tasked to support OL-CH by performing phase maintenance on the deployed aircraft, and so a steady shuttle of personnel and aircraft developed between Alconbury and Taif. Another SYERS-equipped U-2R was sent from Korea to the desert on 11 October.[5]

By the end of November the five aircraft at Taif had performed 204 missions, some of them lasting 11 hours. They were flown under normal peacetime rules, which required that the flight tracks be no closer than 15 miles to the Iraqi border. Even so, from 70,000 feet and above the SYERS and ASARS sensors could image most of southern Iraq, while the SIGINT

An unprecedented number of planes and crews was deployed to the Saudi airbase at Taif for Operations Desert Shield and Storm. This is the pilot group, with some of the combined fleet of U-2Rs from the 9th SRW and TR-1s from the 17th RW in the background. (via Mike Masucci)

"The JRC (in Washington) would notify the SRC (at Offutt) of the requirement. The SRC then gave the planners at Taif a box within which the mission was to fly, and asked them to devise the best track. Working with an intelligence planner, they created a flight track within the box that allowed the sensors to operate at optimum angles. The mission planners then relayed the proposed track to the SRC, who coordinated it with the JRC. After they both approved it, SRC would notify the 1704th RS (P) to fly the mission.

Initially tracks changed often, and each change meant redoing the track. Later the tracks became more standard and required fewer changes. As time drew near for the air war, however, the number of track and schedule changes greatly increased."
- *Coy Cross, "The Dragon Lady Meets The Challenge," 9RW, 1996, Chapter 5*

THE AARDVARKS ARRIVE AT TAIF

"Amid the confusion of the OL-CH bed-down, the 48th TFW's F-111s arrived at Taif. The 48th became the host unit. Members of OL-CH perceived that the F-111 organization considered them 'second-class citizens,' since the U-2 did not carry bombs. Relations quickly deteriorated. 48th commander Colonel Lennon ordered the OL-CH enlisted people out of the Al Gaim housing compound. Then, after Lt Col Lafferty had found two refueling trucks to replace the 'safety nightmares' that OL-CH was using, Col Lennon insisted they should go to the 48th TFW. This characterized relations between the two units until family health problems forced OL-CH commander Lt Col 'Bubba' Lloyd to return to the U.S. Lt Col Steve Peterson, his replacement, came to Taif with orders to 'fix' the relations between the two units."
- *Coy Cross, "The Dragon Lady Meets The Challenge," 9RW, 1996, Chapter 5*

U-2 imagery of burning oilfields was taken by the SYERS electro-optical sensor. (USAF via Tim Ripley)

sensors on the Span bird covered most of Iraq, including Baghdad. The usual routine was to fly a SYERS mission every day, an ASARS mission every night, and a Span mission every second day.

MiG-25 fighters

Iraq "painted" the U-2 flights with its air defense radars, and in mid-September began launching MiG-25 fighters in response. They flew along the border, parallel to the U-2 and 5,000 feet below. In response, the System 20 IR warning pod, which had not been regularly used on the U-2 for some years, was reactivated. A direct voice link to the USAF E-3A AWACS was established for the first time—in Europe, all communications from the U-2 pilot to the outside world were channeled via Metro Tango. F-15 fighters were tasked to fly "MiGCAP" sorties to protect the U-2 flights.[6]

CENTCOM commanders liked what they saw from the U-2, but those planning the air war in the "Black Hole" at Riyadh wanted more, including hard copy photos. (The ground stations could print ASARS and SYERS imagery, but it was a protracted process). The call went back to Beale for camera-equipped aircraft and photo processing vans. The 9th Reconnaissance Technical Squadron (RTS, or "recce-tech") scrambled to bring the 15-van Mobile Intelligence Processing Element (MIPE) back into service. It had been mothballed when the SR-71 was deactivated. The MIPE deployed to Riyadh in mid-December, and the 9th deployed U-2Rs with IRIS III and H-cameras to Taif in late December and early January. Saudi Arabia raised objections to the all-seeing IRIS being flown over its territory and imposed restrictions on the flight tracks.[7]

Taif was also the base for the F-111Fs of the 48th TFW from RAF Lakenheath. Their pilots and mission planners approached the U-2 squadron directly for target information, trying to short-circuit the system. The solution was to send a 48th pilot to the ground station at Riyadh, where he could view the imagery on-screen and interpret it for his colleagues. In the last week of December the Aardvaark/Dragon Lady alliance was cemented when an exercise confirmed the practicality of relaying target information derived from SYERS and ASARS to airborne F-111s, via the TRAC, TACC (Theatre Air Control Center), and ABCCC aircraft. Within 10 minutes of a target being imaged its coordinates were in the TACC's hands.

As the United Nations deadline for an Iraqi withdrawal approached, CENTCOM made plans to send the U-2 over Iraq if war broke out. A second Senior Blade van was requested, to be deployed closer to the border. The U-2's reconnaissance capabilities, and potential additional roles as an airborne data relay and a "high-altitude FAC" were explored and explained to CENTCOM planners, most of whom had no knowledge of Dragon Lady operations! When the air war started, SAC was obliged to "chop" operational control of the U-2s to CENTAF, where Ash Lafferty assumed the authority to approve the missions.[8]

Desert Storm

As Desert Storm began in the small hours of 17 January, Captain Chris McDonald had a great view of the action from his ASARS orbit south of the Iraqi border. The view did not seem so great a few minutes later, when his radar warning system activated and an SA-2 missile exploded slightly above his altitude! But it was 10 miles away—the mission planners had drawn his track far enough away from the threat.

As soon as there was enough light for SYERS on 17 January, Major Blaine Bachus flew the first U-2R mission across the border. His task was to image the fixed Scud missile sites at H2 and H3 airfields, and to perform

The Iraqi airbase at Tallil as seen by the H-camera on a U-2 passing by (USAF via Tim Ripley).

bomb damage assessment (BDA) from the initial F-117 attacks. The Scuds were a high-priority target, given their potential for Chemical Warfare, and they soon became the major priority when Iraq began firing them at Israel.[9]

Mission planners drew up flight tracks to try and ensure that Bachus, and those who followed, avoided known SAM sites. But there were conflicting opinions over where the U-2 could safely fly: the threat databases maintained by DIA, SAC, and CENTCOM seldom agreed! Moreover, the exigencies of war quickly intervened. Many U-2 flights during Desert Storm were retasked when airborne. This required pilots to replot their own tracks and make critical judgements about whether to fly near or over SAM sites.

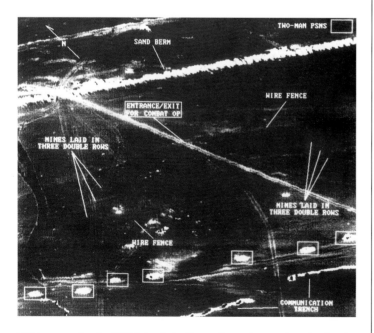

U-2 imagery of an Iraqi SAM site during Desert Storm. In a wartime situation, the Dragon Lady was sometimes sent in harm's way. However, no aircraft were lost to enemy fire in DS—or in any of the subsequent flights over Iraq. (USAF via Tim Ripley)

SLEEPLESS IN TAIF

"On 15 January, Lt Col Peterson moved squadron personnel on base to protect them from possible terrorist attack. Pilots had rooms in hardened aircraft shelters. This provided them a dark, quiet place to sleep. Unfortunately, four people had to share a room. Major Dave Wright, operations officer, tried to schedule everyone in a room to fly either day or night sorties, but this was not always possible. Pilots often had to rely on Restoril sleeping medication. The only available accomodations for eveybody else—including civilian contractors—were tents next to the flight line. They had no protection from nearby jets. Since most F-111 sorties were at night, day shift workers seldom got more than one or two hours of uninterrupted sleep."

- Coy Cross, "The Dragon Lady Meets The Challenge," 9RW, 1996, Chapter 6

FIRST TIME OUT...IN THE SPAN BIRD...AROUND BAGHDAD!
Captain David Miller had been flying the U-2 for just one year when he was sent to Taif in January 1991 to join Operation Desert Storm:

They wanted to warm me up in the combat zone with an easy one, so they tasked me for an ASARS patrol along the border. I studied the mission and was ready to go. It was a night takeoff about midnight, and I was prebreathing when someone tapped me on the faceplate and said, "there's been a change." The prime pilot for another mission had gone sick. They gave me new maps and boards...I was now going all the way round Baghdad. I was told: "Don't worry, they've not got much left that can get you, and the bombers will be taking out the bad guys anyway!"

My eyes were wide. Then they told me I'd be flying the Span bird, the one with the radome on top. The Lockheed techrep explained how to operate this system I had never even seen it before, let alone flown it. It had different operating limits. "It lands quite differently from the one you're used to flying, so be sure to give us a call on the ops frequency as you return so we can brief you on how to recover," he added.

I took off, and muddled through. I saw a lot of fire, a lot of rockets. I only oversped the jet about three times, including takeoff and coming home....

- remarks at the 4080th SRW reunion, Del Rio, 1993

DIRECTING FIRE FROM 70,000 FEET

One of the things we ad-libbed during the war was flying along with that electro-optical camera, and sending the information back to the ground station, which was in direct contact with Army artillery units. The U-2 knew where its position was to within a very few feet; so did the artillery units know their position. One of our pilots was in the ground station with an artillery officer, and between us we had the whole system of bearings, which we kept refining all day long. It was one shot, one kill, back and forth. The Iraqis never knew I was up there spotting for them.

- Captain David Miller, 1704th RS, Taif, remarks at the 4080th SRW reunion, Del Rio, 1993

DESERT STORM: INTELLIGENCE FAILURES?

After the war was over, the intelligence functions in Desert Shield/ Storm came in for significant criticism. A Congressional study said that field commanders did not get the quantity and type of products that they required. But it was a systemic problem, and no fault of the operators:

"When Desert Shield began, CENTCOM had one person on the J-2 staff with U-2 experience, and CENTAF had none. Lt Cols Dave Bonsi, Ash Lafferty, and Mark Spencer (were then deployed). They used their connections at the JRC, SRC, and the 1704th RS to overcome the hurdles and make the system work.

Despite these efforts, some in-theater commanders grumbled that the U-2 was not responsive to their needs. Few commanders appreciated the difference between the U-2 and fighter aircraft. Conflicting opinions over where the U-2 could safely fly caused frustrations.

Pilots and commanders did not like the targeting reports (generated by SYERS and ASARS). While the Blade and TRAC vans could produce hard copy images, the process took about 20 minutes for one print...There was no sensor available to provide both high resolution and broad area coverage.

In response to the ever-increasing demand for photographs, the U-2 flew more camera missions. The U-2 output quickly overwhelmed the processing capability...."

— Coy Cross, "The Dragon Lady Meets The Challenge," 9RW, 1996, Chapter 7

The H-camera found new use in Desert Storm as a very high-resolution tool for Bomb Damage Assessment (BDA), looking straight down. This image from before DS, showing Det 5 in Florida from 70,000 feet, gives an idea of the capability.

Lethal range

In fact, the U-2's supposed vulnerability to SAMs did not prevent the aircraft from providing valuable intelligence on them. Some missions were specifically flown to pinpoint SAMs, such as one flown by Captain Bryan Anderson on 22 January that identified multiple SA-2, SA-3, and AAA sites in western Iraq. Lt Col Steve Peterson (the 1704th RS commander) and Major James Milligan both flew missions that were deliberately routed within lethal range of known SAM sites. Moreover, the pilots knew that the U-2's radar warning and jamming systems had not been updated for many years.

An estimated 15 fixed Scud sites were identified from U-2/TR-1 imagery and eliminated during the first week of the war. Ten of them were assessed as destroyed by one strike package, which launched on the sec-

ond day of the war, less than one hour after they were identified by a TR-1 flown deep into northern Iraq flown by Lt Col James Burger.

But *mobile* Scud sites were a more difficult proposition. The U-2 had to go "off-tether" in order to cover the more distant parts of Iraq, although the installation of the second Senior Blade van at King Khalid Military City in northern Saudi Arabia helped increase real-time SYERS processing. There was a time delay while the U-2 returned within range of the ground stations to download ASARS imagery. The Iraqis learned to hide their Scud Transporter/Erector/Launchers (TEL) by day, and quickly move into place, fire, and withdraw by night.

When it was all over..the 1704th Provisional Reconnaissance Squadron displays the statistics for February 1991 (via Bill Bonnichsen).

Lt Col Steve Peterson was the commander at Taif during Desert Storm. He is seen at a subsequent Blackbirds reunion, where he received a trophy from Hughes to mark the 1704th's stellar achievements during the conflict. (author)

Days before the war broke out, the troops at Taif were visited by U.S. Vice-President Dan Quayle, seen here to left of Saudi flag. (via Steve Peterson)

CENTAF responded by coordinating the nighttime patrols of a U-2R and an F-15E. When the ASARS sensor located a suspected TEL the Strike Eagle was primed to destroy it. Several mobile Scud kills were claimed with this technique, but subsequent analysis showed that the "kills" were of decoys, shorter-range FROG missiles, or ordinary trucks!

Some of this analysis is disputed, and U-2s were certainly responsible for some TEL kills. These include the one that misfired a Scud on the night of 22 February, which detonated just three miles from a TR-1 flown by Captain Chris McDonald! (In fact, U-2 pilots observed most of the Scud launches from their lofty perch.) Undoubtedly, too, the Iraqi mobile Scud crews knew they were being hunted. As a result, their launch rate and accuracy declined significantly.

Conflicting traffic

When Desert Storm began the 1704th had nine aircraft at Taif, and another three were quickly added. At least five missions were flown each day during the air campaign, rising to eight on some days during the land campaign. For the first time ever, U-2 pilots had to worry about conflicting traffic at 70,000 feet! Most missions lasted more than eight hours, and some were voluntarily extended by their pilots to 11 hours when the need arose.

More units sent pilots or artillery officers to the U-2 ground stations, from where they could convey exactly what they saw on the screens to their flight crews or gunners. On one occasion, a B-52 bombardier in the TRAC van spotted a likely bomb dump and diverted a B-52 strike inbound

ASARS-equipped aircraft regroup at Palmdale after the end of Desert Storm (Lockheed PR501-13).

Flying Dragon tail art on 01086 at Taif. (via Steve Peterson)

The camel and the palm trees on the tail of 01081 leave no doubt as to the location. (via Steve Peterson)

from Diego Garcia to hit it, with spectacular results. Towards the end of the war U-2 pilots became "high-altitude FACs" by identifying tank concentrations and relaying the coordinates for attack by allied artillery. On many occasions, U-2 pilots coordinated search-and-rescue attempts for downed pilots.

When the ground forces attacked on 24 February, a TR-1 provided hour-by-hour imagery updates of precise Iraqi front-line armour and troop movements. Coalition troops advanced more quickly than expected, and another TR-1 mission the next day proved invaluable in keeping CENTCOM commanders abreast of the fluid situation, so they could cut off the Iraqi retreat.

The day after the war ended, a U-2 equipped with the IRIS camera flew back and forth across large parts of the battlefield to take a synoptic view of the carnage below. When this film was eventually analyzed back in Washington, it indicated that CENTCOM had seriously overestimated the number of Iraqi weapons that had been destroyed in the air campaign.[10]

Wet film sensors

U-2 photography had itself been used for BDA during the war. With so many "smart" missiles and bombs flying through windows and air vents to destroy buildings, a very high-resolution sensor was often needed to confirm a kill. The U-2 mission planners worked with Hycon techrep John Mueller to modify the H-camera mode of operation so that it could shoot pictures looking straight down. The resolution was fantastic—only six inches! But it was a nightmare to plan the flight lines—they were only 2.4 miles apart, because the swath width was so narrow. There were other prob-

lems with "wet film." The take from both H-camera and IRIS III missions had to be flown from Taif to Riyadh on a C-21 courier aircraft for processing at the MIPE. There, it could take all day just to handle a single IRIS mission with its 10,000 feet of film!

The overall contribution that the U-2 made to Desert Storm was substantial. The 1704th RS flew 260 missions totaling over 2,000 hours, with 80% of this time spent above Iraq or occupied Kuwait. The vast majority of missions took off when scheduled. According to USAF assessments, the U-2 supplied over 50% of all imagery intelligence and 90% of the Army's targeting intelligence. So much for reconnaissance satellites! They were often defeated by haze, smoke, or bad weather, and when they did take useful images, the product was simply not available to the right people at the right time.[11]

The air war commander confirmed the value of U-2 radar imagery: Said General Chuck Horner: "With ASARS, my aircraft hit the target. Without it, they just hit sand. Eighty percent of the targets produced by ASARS were at the stated coordinates when strike assets arrived on station, and 70% of these targets resulted in secondary explosions."[12]

When it was all over, most of the plaudits went to JSTARS, the hugely expensive battlefield radar flown in two converted Boeing 707s, which was still under development. This had a Moving Target Indicator (MTI), as well as a Synthetic Aperture Radar (SAR) mode, with the data also downlinked to ground stations. Partly because the Span and SYERS sensors were still classified, and partly because JSTARS needed boosting to secure more funds from Congress, the U-2 remained an unsung hero in the first desert war.

33

New World Disorder

It was not only the end of the Gulf War, it was the end of the Cold War. And, moreover, the end of the Soviet Union. Behind the fallen Berlin Wall, the Group of Soviet forces in Germany was left high and dry. Their withdrawal to Russia was negotiated, and then funded by massive handouts from the newly-unified Germany. The role of the TR-1 in Europe was redundant.

In June 1991 the 17th RW was deactivated. But SAC kept the 95th squadron and five TR-1s at Alconbury, as a direct report to the 9th SRW at Beale. The base was much quieter now, and most of the massive, newly-built reinforced concrete shelters were empty. In Germany work on the hardened TRIGS ground station was halted. Within a year, the trailers and mobile vans at Metro Tango were on their way back to the U.S., to be repackaged as a deployable system named the Contingency Airborne Reconnaissance System (CARS).

For a while, it seemed that some of the TR-1s would go into storage. Continuing instability in southern Europe, the Gulf, the Korean Peninsula, and elsewhere soon forced a rethink. In the "New World Order," the U-2 capability was obviously still needed. But Desert Storm had proven that the old way of tasking and controlling "national" reconnaissance assets like the U-2 could not continue. Theater commanders demanded that they no longer should go through bureaucratic hoops in Washington and Omaha to get a mission flown.

SAC reacted by creating the 2nd Air Force at Beale AFB. It would control all of the command's reconnaissance aircraft, and be the "executive agent" for global reconnaissance operations. Former RC-135 pilot and 55th Wing commander Brig Gen Larry Mitchell was given command. "Obviously, SAC's No 1 mission is nuclear deterrence, but as we look at the changing world order...conventional support to the theater commander is SAC's No 2 priority," he said.[1]

UNSCOM

In Saudi Arabia, the 1704th RS was renumbered the 4402nd RS. Four aircraft remained there, instead of returning to the U.S. It became clear that the Iraqi regime was not going to fully cooperate with the United Nations Special Commission (UNSCOM), which was set up to hunt down Saddam Hussein's weapons of mass destruction. In mid-1991 the U.S. offered the U-2 to the UN as an airborne inspector. The offer was accepted, and the Olive Branch missions began, using the OBC and IRIS III cameras. One or two were flown each week from Taif, with the reluctant agreement of Iraq. The imagery was flown straight to Washington and processed. NPIC forwarded copy negatives to the UN in New York.[2]

In June and July 1992 there were sweeping changes in the USAF command structure, as the post-Cold War realities sunk in. The mighty Strategic Air Command was deactivated, and its assets were combined

A massive amount of concrete was poured at Alconbury in the 1980s, to protect the 17th RW and its TR-1 fleet from an aerial attack by the Warsaw Pact. By the time that the work was finished, the Cold War was over! (author)

One of the five aircraft of the 95th RS that remained at Alconbury in the early 1990s, inside one of the custom-built widespan hardened shelters. (author)

UNSCOM, WHITE U-2s, AND BAND AID

In the early 1990s, former U-2 pilot Major Chuck Wilson was working at the Joint Reconnaissance Center (JRC) in the Pentagon when the idea of using the U-2 to support the weapons inspectors in Iraq first came up:

I went to New York for the coordination meetings with the United Nations Special Commission (UNSCOM). They wanted the U-2 painted all-white, with "UN" marked on the tail in blue. They also asked if they could have their own observer onboard during the flights!

In Akrotiri, we didn't even paint "UN" on the tails of our black airplanes for the Olive Harvest flights. But that was a lower-profile operation, and was flown with the full support of the countries being overflown. Iraq was different, of course. We agreed to paint a white "UN" on the tail before every flight for UNSCOM. We didn't need to dedicate an aircraft, because the missions were notified 96 hours in advance to ourselves and the Iraqis. Every time, the U.S. issued a formal warning to Iraq not to interfere with the flight.

But in January 1993 there was a strong Iraqi air defense reaction to a flight. General Powell (JCS) asked me what defensive systems were carried by the U-2. I had to tell him, "not much!" He immediately called General McPeak (USAF C-in-C), who obviously had to do something about it.

That was the first impetus for the "Band Aid" upgrade to the U-2 defensive system. Shortly thereafter I was promoted to Lt Col, and was reassigned back to the 9th RW. After requalification, I was posted straight to Taif as the Det commander. On my first UN mission over Iraq, the warning lights lit up like a Christmas tree! Next day, I copied General Powell on my mission report. I guess that really got the ball rolling, because "Band Aid" was quickly funded, at a cost of some millions. - *interview with author*

A THANK-YOU FROM UNSCOM

17 December 1992

Dear General Powell,

I should like to take the occasion of the completion of the 100th Olive Branch mission to express our gratitude and appreciation for the efforts and dedication of all the personnel involved in this most successful operation...

The material produced by this operation is central to the commission's efforts to eliminate Iraq's weapons of mass destruction...the flights of the UN U-2 aircraft are a major deterrent to Iraq conducting illegal activities. The photography produced is used routinely to plan inspections and has, on occasion, provided "smoking-gun" evidence of Iraqi non-compliance with its obligations....

Yours Sincerely,
Rolf Ekeus
Executive Chairman, UNSCOM

with those of TAC to form the new Air Combat Command (ACC). Cold War warriors from SAC were appalled, as TAC doctrines prevailed in the ACC after the merger. "Normalization" was the new mantra. According to ACC, while the U-2 was a valuable asset, there would be no more special treatment.

ACC insignia

There were visible signs of the change. U-2 pilots had to give up their distinctive orange flight coveralls and wear the standard olive-drab garb. Their coveted "Towards the Unknown" and "Blackcat" patches also had to go. The ACC insignia and a TAC-style tailcode "BB" was painted on the tails of the aircraft. After the 9th RW joined ACC, the flying side was controlled by the 9th Operations Group OG, comprising the 1st RS for training, and the 99th RS for operational missions launched from Beale, and support of the far-flung deployments. The 9th OG also controlled the 9th Intelligence Squadron, which produced and stored all domestic U-2 imagery. Operational tasking of the overseas U-2 deployments was now "chopped" to the relevant theater command: CENTCOM (for the 4402nd RS at Taif); EUCOM (for the 95th RS at Alconbury and Det 3 at Akrotiri); PACOM (for Det 2 at Osan); and SOUTHCOM (for Det 4 at Howard AFB, Panama).

The TR-1 designation had already been dropped, in October 1991. All U-2s became...well, they became U-2s! The end of this ultimately pointless subterfuge in nomenclature also marked a new drive to standardize the airframes. Unlike the U-2Rs, the TR-1s had never been wired for some "national" missions, such as sampling.

Three more Senior Span uplinks had been procured. But although they were adequate for relaying SIGINT, they were power-hungry—and it took an eternity to transmit imagery. Lt Col Curt Osterheld was serving on the staff of OSD in the Pentagon. A former SR-71 RSO, he was aware of an aborted attempt codenamed Senior King, to develop an uplink from the Blackbird to carry ASARS data. Osterheld pushed the idea of adapting this

The Senior Spur configuration provided for the timely relay of ASARS radar imagery by satellite for the first time (Lockheed 91A-045-16).

to the U-2. Instead of using the low-date-rate military DSCS satellites, the uplink was adapted to use a higher-bandwidth alternative.

A prototype of the new uplink system was deployed to Europe in early 1992. It was codenamed Senior Spur. It went first to Alconbury, but soon moved on to NAS Sigonella, Italy, just as heavy fighting broke out in Bosnia. Later, it was tested in Korea.

New engine
A less visible, but equally significant upgrade to the U-2 was in flight test at Palmdale—a new engine. Ever since the last F-106 fighter was retired a year earlier, the U-2R had been the sole remaining aircraft in the USAF inventory that was powered by the P&W J75. The support costs threatened to become unaffordable. Moreover, the weight of new sensor and datalink systems was restricting the aircraft's operating performance. Often, the aircraft could not be fully fueled due to the maximum gross weight restriction.

Lockheed selected the General Electric F101-GE-F29 turbofan as a potential replacement for the J75 in the late 1980s. This was a low bypass ratio (0.8:1) unit with a three-stage low pressure compressor and a nine-stage high pressure compressor. It was being developed for the then still-secret B-2 Stealth bomber. Rated at 18,300 lbs st, the GE powerplant offered equivalent thrust for the U-2R, but a significant weight reduction and improved fuel consumption. And it was a good fit!

A refurbished ground test engine from the B-2 program was released to the Skunk Works in 1988. It was fitted to 01090, and made its first flight with Lockheed test pilot Ken Weir at the controls on 23 May 1989. This was four months before the B-2 first flew, incidentally.

Over the next 15 months 82 flight hours were logged. Initial flights were limited to engine-out gliding distance of Edwards AFB, because unlike the J75 turbojet, the new turbofan could not be restarted inflight by windmilling. An emergency airstart system was then added, comprising compressed air and jet fuel that was ignited in a two-stage compressor. This was heavy, however, so a hydrazine system capable of spooling the engine up to 45% core rpm was developed instead.

Before the pre-production flight tests started in late 1991 the GE powerplant was redesignated F118-GE-101, and the re-engined aircraft was

After Desert Storm, the U-2s stayed on at Taif as the 4402nd Reconnaissance Squadron. This group photo from 1992 uses an aircraft painted for the new United Nations monitoring mission as a backdrop.

Colored dots on this ASARS radar map depict vehicles moving along a highway. The Moving Target Indicator (MTI) enhancement to ASARS was first fielded in Korea. (Hughes)

designated U-2S. A host of evaluations were addressed in the next 38 flights. For instance, whether vibrations from this different engine would affect sensor or INS performance, and whether the 9th stage bleed air that provided the pilot's pressure suit cooling was satisfactory!

Weight and fuel saving

The flight test results showed a weight saving of 1,300 lbs and an average fuel saving of 16%, compared with the J75. These translated into an increase in maximum altitude of 3,500 ft, an increased payload, and a 1,220 nautical mile increase in range, or increased time on station. There were other benefits, including increased reliability and maintainability, an improved cg, and a digital engine control. This provided linear thrust with engine stall-free operation throughout the flight envelope. It throttled back automatically during the U-2's ascent through the "Badlands." Those famous U-2 flameout incidents were about to become history, it was hoped!

At the same time, further weight was saved for payload by replacing some airframe components with composite materials. The rudders, elevators, speed brakes, landing gear doors, and the leading edge of the vertical tail were all swapped during depot overhauls.[3]

The first production U-2S conversion was 01071, which flew with the new engine for the first time on 12 August 1994. Delivery ceremonies for the first three conversions were held at Palmdale and Beale. (The other two aircraft were two-seaters 80-1064 and 80-1078. The latter was built as a single seater, but was damaged in a landing accident at Alconbury and rebuilt as a fourth trainer). The entire U-2R fleet was converted to U-2S as major overhauls became due—every 3,400 hours or five years. The last aircraft (01068) was re-engined in 1998.[4]

Sensor improvements

Some improvements to the imaging sensors were also funded. The venerable H-camera was given solid-state electronics. SYERS became a dual-band sensor with the addition of infrared. Of most significance, perhaps, the USAF finally approved the addition of Moving Target Indicator (MTI) capability to every ASARS set.

Hughes had spent its own money to adapt the ASARS to show moving as well as fixed targets in 1988. This entailed adding components to the receiver/exciter and processor control unit in the aircraft, and software changes in the ground station. The USAF was unwilling to fund further

development, in case the new capability should overshadow JSTARS, which was first and foremost an MTI system—and needed very large amounts of money. Then the Gulf conflict interrupted operational tests of the ASARS-MTI prototype by the 17th RW in Europe.

In the ground station, the ASARS MTI showed the speed and location of moving targets in search or spot modes, against either a cartographic or synthetic aperture radar map background. While Grumman loudly proclaimed the virtues of JSTARS, Hughes quietly but firmly insisted that ASARS was "the most advanced reconnaissance radar in the world." The ASARS MTI prototype was eventually sent to the 5th RS in Korea. Meanwhile, the original ASARS ground station in Korea, built by Hughes, was upgraded and moved into PACOM's hardened Korean Combat Operation Information Center (KCOIC).

The MTI capability was a big hit with PACOM. The E-Systems Commanders' Tactical Terminal (CTT) was added to the U-2 airplanes in Korea. This was a "broadcast" system that could relay processed MTI data from the ground station to Army commanders in the field via the U-2. Two more ASARS MTI add-ons were trickle-funded in the mid-1990s and sent to Korea.

Skunk Works U-2 program manager Bob Anderson surveys paperwork, with Ben Rich (left) and Jack Gordon (right) looking on. Rich retired in 1990. Gordon became the "chief skunk" a few years later, but he was the last head of the company at Palmdale, before it was consolidated within the Lockheed Martin Aeronautics Company in 2000. (Lockheed PI9021-6)

One of the keys to the success of ASARS on the U-2 was the navigation data interface. For years, the Litton LN-33 INS was used, updated periodically by the Northrop NAS-21 astro-inertial 'star-tracker." The advent of the Global Positioning System (GPS) and its lightweight receivers allowed Lockheed to dispense with the excellent but complicated NAS-21. The GPS receiver was faired into the U-2's left wing trailing edge.

A new Common Data Link (CDL) replaced the long-serving L51/L52 (AN/UPQ-3A) on the U-2. A second CDL could now be carried in the Q-bay, providing more flexibility.

DARO

The U-2 had strong support from the theater commanders, from most of the intelligence community, and from Congress. But in late 1993 a new Defense Airborne Reconnaissance Office (DARO) was established in the Office of the Secretary of Defense (OSD). DARO was created as a response to some recent development fiascos, notably the billion dollar top-secret project to replace the SR-71 with a stealthy, high-altitude, long-endurance platform. DARO's charter was to oversee upgrades to existing platforms and make investment decisions for the future. It was run by Brig Gen Ken Israel, and he was a strong proponent of Unmanned Aerial Vehicles (UAVs). So were the key civilian appointees in the Pentagon, John Deutsch and Larry Lynn.

Soon, the U-2 and RC-135 Rivet Joint procurement accounts were being raided to fund the accelerated development of new UAVs. A SIGINT

Farnborough Air Show 1996. Lockheed's chief of ISR systems Garfield Thomas (left), and U-2 business development manager Curt Osterheld displayed their proposal for the UK's ASTOR program. Instead, though, the British MoD eventually chose a business jet as its new platform for radar imaging. (author)

upgrade for the U-2 was put on hold, but DARO wanted to spend more on a controversial multi-platform SIGINT system named Senior Smart.

A debate raged over the utility, maturity, and total cost of unmanned aircraft. DARO's priorities were challenged by the operating community, represented by Bg Gen Larry Mitchell. "Larry Lynn is a certified technocrat with a lifelong love of UAVs. DARO is the worst thing that has happened to the Air Force in the last 10 years!" railed Mitchell. Those with long memories recalled the same debate over the relative merits of Compass Cope and the U-2 in the mid-1970s![5]

Brig Gen Ken Israel was the controversial head of DARO—the Defense Airborne Reconnaissance Office in the Pentagon. He advocated boosting funding for UAV programs, at the expense of the U-2 and other manned systems.

Lt Col Chuck Wilson commanded the 5th RS in 1995-96. He flew the first operational mission in the re-engined U-2S aircraft from Osan, in October 1995. (via Chuck Wilson)

"The performance parameters published for the UAVs and their sensors to date do not approach what the U-2 already has in many cases," noted Garfield Thomas, the vice-president for reconnaissance systems at the Skunk Works. He added: "Weather avoidance, flexibility, ground support systems, and logistics support have not received a great deal of attention from the UAV proponents to date, and when they are honestly included in the trade studies, the result may shock some people!"[6]

Hard-pushed

Meanwhile, the U-2 was as busy as ever. The 9th RW was hard-pushed to support the deployments, and its people were pulling very long TDYs. The aircraft had now operated continuously out of Korea and Cyprus for 20 years. Flights over the Caribbean were conducted from time to time by Det 4 out of Panama, for instance, after the coup in Haiti in July 1994.

At Osan, Det 2 became a fully-fledged squadron in October 1994. But the 5th RS was still known as the "Blackcats," keeping alive the long tradition of the U-2 in East Asia. The 5th RS was the first outfit to fly the

new U-2S models operationally, from October 1995. The mission was much the same as before: standard orbits along the DMZ. But the North Korean regime was as obtuse as ever. This was the year that its nuclear weapons reactor at Yongbyon was first discovered on satellite photography.[7]

By early 1993, the 95th RS was flying regular nine-hour roundtrips from the UK to Bosnia, where a grim civil war was unfolding. A Senior Span-configured aircraft was deployed permanently to Alconbury from early April. It could provide SIGINT coverage of the Balkans from off-tether orbits over the Adriatic Sea. In mid-September 1993 the 95th RS was deactivated. Henceforth, the three-aircraft operation at Alconbury was manned on a TDY basis from Beale, as OL-UK.

When Alconbury finally closed in March 1995, the three aircraft of OL-UK were moved temporarily to Fairford. In December of that year they were moved again to Istres, the big airbase in southern France. OL-FR took up residence in a huge hangar owned by Dassault. The new location offered a shorter transit time to the area of interest, and therefore lighter fuel loads and higher altitudes. France was a full partner in the UN and

At Osan airbase, Korea, Det 2 became a fully-fledged squadron—the 5th RS—in 1994. (Peter R. Foster)

The Black Cat tradition was alive and well at Osan, as evidenced by this tail art in 1992. (via Chris Wheatley)

NATO attempts to deter the warring factions in Bosnia. But a combination of weak Western resolve and ancient Balkan enmities served to prolong and worsen the conflict.

In mid-1995 a U-2 collected OBC imagery of the Srebrenica area of Bosnia. The PIs noticed earthworks on a football field. The imagery was compared with satellite coverage from a few days earlier. There were hundreds of people in the field then. The earthworks were mass graves—the single biggest war crime in Europe since the Second World War.[8]

The drive to get U-2 sensor information quickly to the people that really mattered was ongoing. In a test exercise in 1995, ASARS imagery was transmitted from a U-2 via a ground station and a GBU-15 datalink to the rear cockpit of an F-15E. The Strike Eagle's weapons system operator then used it to cue his own APG-70 radar and lock on to the target. This was a simulated Scud missile, and it was destroyed. In mid-1996 this Rapid Targeting System (RTS), codenamed Gold Strike, was deployed over Bosnia.

MOBSTR

Before that, though, a new trailer-based data relay system codenamed Mobile Stretch (MOBSTR) was introduced to Europe. It was developed by the Warner-Robins Air Logistics Center, which was home to the USAF's U-2 Program Directorate. MOBSTR was deployed to Rimini, Italy, in November 1995. That was just too late to aid U-2 operations during NATO Operation Deliberate Force over Bosnia, which forced a fragile peace and the Dayton Peace Accords.

MOBSTR received downlinked imagery and ELINT from U-2s flying the Creek Torch mission over the Balkans, and compressed it into a format suitable for onward transmission by narrow-band satellites. From now on, the take from an orbiting U-2R was routinely relayed to the U.S. for exploitation and dissemination. A second CARS ground station was set up at Beale, and could operate exactly as it would if deployed in the field. The two-way link with the U-2 was maintained so that, for instance, if the SIGINT sensors picked up a radar, the same aircraft could immediately be tasked to image the location and determine if missiles were present.[9]

The term "Reachback" was coined to describe this use of modern communications technology. A second MOBSTR was installed in Saudi

DETECTING MISSILE RADARS IN BOSNIA – OR NOT
Here are three short items from Aviation Week after an F-16 was shot down. Take your pick!

12 June 1995: Gen John Shalikashviri, chairman of the JCS, insisted in Congressional testimony that even though (F-16 pilot) O'Grady was shot down by a Bosnian Serb mobile SA-6 surface-to-air missile, "We had absolutely no intelligence...For months there had never been an air defense site detected in that area."

3 July 1995: According to Pentagon and industry officials, a U-2R aircraft picked up SA-6 missile radar transmissions on and off for 2 hr. 48 min. before the shootdown. The information was automatically relayed to a ground station, but for some reason it was not passed on.

9 September 1996: By strictly controlling radar and voice emissions from the SA-6 until just before the launch, the Bosnian Serb missile crew was able to surprise O'Grady and destroy his F-16.

BOSNIA SPYPLANE PILOT DIES IN RAF BASE CRASH

London: Thirty-five years ago, the U-2 affair was an emblem of the Cold War years. A descendant of that early spy plane crashed yesterday in an English cornfield. The U-2R was destined for Bosnia, and its wreckage now serves as sculpture of our failure in that savage conflict.

This man-made albatross, wide-winged and subsonic, has been in Britain in support of "Operation Deny Flight". Although awkward in appearance, it has on board the most intricate intelligence-gathering technology yet conceived. The U-2R can pinpoint areas on the ground below with disconcerting clarity. It was from the images gathered by just such a craft that the mass graves of Srebrenica came recently to light, where thousands of murdered Bosnian Muslims lie crudely interred. The cruel irony of that discovery is apparent: man's technical advancement served there only to uncover man's descent into the barbarism of an older, tribal age.

- editorial in The Times, 30 August 1995

In 1993, nine-hour roundtrips were flown from Alconbury to monitor the deteriorating situation in Bosnia. (author)

Arabia in July 1997. Data from the missions now being flown by the 4402nd RS in support of Operation Southern Watch could be similarly relayed to the first CARS, which was situated at Langley AFB, VA.

MOBSTR could be deployed by only 17 troops using two C-141s, and set up within 24 hours. The complete CARS configuration needed six C-5 transports to deploy, as well as 120 troops. Although the CARS were also known as the Deployable Ground Stations, they never moved from Langley (DGS-1) or Beale (DGS-2). Not only was MOBSTR now available, but an enhanced version of the U.S. Army's more mobile TRAC ground station was now being manufactured by Westinghouse. This could be carried in two C-130s and set up in the field to receive the ASARS downlink in only 90 minutes! The E-Systems Commander's Tactical Terminal (CTT) was also integrated with the U-2, so that the aircraft could rebroadcast intelligence reports and other data sent from the U-2 ground stations (or other parties).[10]

Iraq harassment

In September 1996 the southern no-fly zone over Iraq that was established by coalition forces after the Gulf War was extended to the 33rd parallel. Iraq objected, of course, and its air defense system stepped up harassment of U.S. and British fighters. Despite sanctions, Iraq had managed to rebuild and refine its air defense system, including SA-2/3/6/8 SAMs and fiberoptic links between radar sites and control rooms. In Operation Desert Strike, the U.S. launched cruise missiles against Iraqi SAM sites and command bunkers.

U-2s flying from Taif were operating in the zone, helping to identify Iraqi air defense developments. They were protected by coordinating the sorties with the patrols of RC-135 Rivet Joint aircraft. The RJ could detect and analyze missile and interceptor threats with its more comprehensive SIGINT suite, and broadcast them to the higher-flying U-2.

U-2s were also flying north of the zone, including over Baghdad itself, on the separate Olive Branch missions for UNSCOM. By early 1996, some 280 such missions had been flown, each one notified to the Iraqi ambassador to the UN two days in advance in respect of entry and exit points, but not the exact time of the flight, nor the course to be flown once inside the country. The imagery from these flights helped the UNSCOM

inspectors track movements of banned weapons from suspected sites. The Iraqis resented the U-2 flights, of course, and foreign minister Tariq Aziz complained in March 1996 about the "material and psychological damage caused by the violations of our airspace by this aircraft."

Graybeard panel

In the eight years before ACC took over the U-2 operation, there was not a single Class A mishap. In the five years following the ACC takeover, the 9th RW lost five U-2s and four pilots in accidents. Two more aircraft were badly damaged. ACC commissioned a team of six old U-2 hands to examine why. In particular, was the "normalization" process to blame? The team was known as the GrayBeard panel.[11]

The run of accidents started on 15 January 1992 when a U-2R from Osan crashed into the East Sea. Captain Marty McGregor was killed. On 13 December 1993 an aircraft taking off from Beale went out of control. Captain Richard Schneider, an experienced U-2 IP, ejected but did not survive. In August 1994 Captain Cholene ("Chuck") Espinoza survived a landing crash in thick fog at Osan. (She was the second woman pilot to train in the U-2 and, like all new graduates, was making her operational debut in Korea).

On 29 August 1995, Captain David Hawkens was killed at Fairford at the start of a Senior Span mission when a pogo hung up on takeoff. He returned to the airfield to try and shake it loose. But he descended too low, and allowed the speed of the maximum gross weight aircraft to drop. The aircraft stalled, and crashed into a field adjacent to the runway.[12]

In February 1996 a student pilot on his first high flight declared an emergency on climbout with apparent loss of engine power. He managed a flamed out approach but landed long, ran off the runway, and hit obstacles. The pilot was not hurt, but the damage cost $6 million to repair. On 7 August 1996 a Functional Check Flight from Beale ended in disaster when a fire developed at 20,000 feet. Unaware of the problem, Captain Randy Roby entered a spin and fought to regain control. At 10,000 feet he initiated ejection, but the sump tank exploded just as his seat rode up the rails, damaging the separation mechanism. The aircraft crashed into a parking lot in Oroville, killing one person on the ground. Roby was found dead in his ejection seat two city blocks away. He was an experienced IP, taking his last U-2 flight.

When Alconbury closed, the three U-2s remaining in the UK flew instead from RAF Fairford. In this view, Captain Dave Hawkens is acting as mobile for the launch of yet another sortie to the Balkans. Sadly, Hawkens was killed a few days later, in the crash of 10338 at the British base. (author)

From Fairford, the U-2s moved to Istres airbase in southern France, and became OL-FR. There was plenty of room in the huge hangar there! (author)

Concerns

The GrayBeard Panel could not identify any single major issue linking the accidents. But it had a large number of concerns about the U-2 operation. It found that the maintenance organization was too decentralized and lacking in experience. Because of the U-2's non-mil-standard specs and technical documentation, airmen, NCOs, and officers needed longer to familiarize themselves with the aircraft. As soon as they were up to speed their tour was over, and ACC moved them on to other weapons systems. (In the SAC days, tours in the U-2 could be extended almost indefinitely). Moreover, the civilian tech reps provided by the contractors were being sidelined; their valuable experience was under-utilized.

On the operations side, the panel noted that there was no well-defined career path for U-2 pilots. It was not an attractive assignment anyway, with a high TDY rate that kept many pilots away from young families for months at a time. Learning to fly the Dragon Lady was not a career-enhancing move, compared with being a fighter jock. For instance, since ACC took over, the three top command positions in the 9th RW had almost always gone to officers who had never previously been involved with the U-2. That sent a negative message to new and potential recruits.

The panel could not resist a dig at the new way of managing U-2 reconnaissance. "What was once a tightly-controlled, almost over-managed secret program, is now a strategic asset managed by tactical thinkers," the panel wrote. There were too many requirements, and the theater CINCs who now specified when the U-2s should fly needed to re-examine their priorities and reduce the tasking.[13]

Some of the Graybeard panel's recommendations were implemented. But 9th RW commander Bg Gen Charles Simpson took the criticisms personally. ACC ignored most of the ones relating to maintenance. The Lockheed techreps were still barred from the flight line at Beale.

Iraqi objections

In the Middle East, as tensions mounted over the increasingly-intrusive UNSCOM inspections, the Iraqi regime stepped up its objections to the U-2 flights. This culminated in Baghdad making overt threats to shoot them down in late October 1997. It was a twitchy time for the U-2 pilots whenever a UN mission took off and headed north of the no-fly zone.

During that same month, the U-2s moved to join the rest of U.S. airpower in Saudi Arabia that was concentrated at Al Kharj, near Riyadh, also known as Prince Sultan Air Base (PSAB). There, the U-2s eventually became part of the 363rd Expeditionary Air Wing, as the 363rd ERS. Despite Iraq's objections, the Olive Branch flights continued at an average weekly interval, until Iraq stopped cooperating at all with UNSCOM in August 1998. Operation Desert Fox, a four-day bombing campaign, followed in December 1998.

The series of U-2 accidents in the 1990s included this one, when 10338 crashed and burned in a cornfield next to RAF Fairford. (Duncan Adams)

The U-2 pilot TDY rates for the past several years is between 135 and 150 days. Last year, one individual was TDY over 200 days, with a substantial number at the 180 day mark. The desired Air Force maximum goal of 120 days TDY will probably never be met by pilots of this unit....

Safety is affected not only by the high TDY rate. The physiological wear on the pilot's body is a major concern while flying at the deployed location. Recent changes at the 5th RS now have pilots flying shorter sortie lengths to maximize scheduling effectiveness. By limiting the flights to less than 6.5 hours, pilots may be scheduled for a flight one day, ground duty the next, then a flight the next day, etc. Recently, an officer pulled this duty cycle for 24 days before he had a break. The break was caused by weather, not scheduling. Theoretically, his duty cycle could have continued for the entire 60-day TDY.

- U-2 GrayBeard Panel 1997, section 4.7

WEATHER LIMITS

U-2 aircraft are often put at risk due to marginal weather conditions. Allowable conditions for take-off on operational missions is 1000 feet RVR, and for landing 2400 feet RVR. No ceiling limit is imposed. Single engine, single seat fighter aircraft at the same operating locations are not allowed to fly in weather conditions this low. U-2s operate on a daily basis at what should probably be considered a wartime weather limit. Considering this is a single seat, single engine aircraft, whose risk factor is compounded by a long duration, pressure suit environment, the exposure to risk seems obvious. One mishap has already occurred under these conditions. Flying in these weather conditions should be reserved for only the highest priority missions, not intelligence routine database updates or to meet a sortie count.

- U-2 GrayBeard Panel 1997, section 4.9

Meanwhile, the tragedy of the Balkans continued to play out. In 1998 the 400th U-2 Creek Torch mission to monitor compliance with the Dayton Peace Accords was flown. Serb paramilitary forces stepped up a campaign of repression in the semi-autonomous Yugoslav province of Kosovo. U.S. and NATO countries pressured President Slobodan Milosevic into accepting photo reconnaissance flights over the province. "I've got U-2s in one hand, B-52s in the other. Which is it to be?" Lt Gen Mike Short asked Serbian Premier Milosevic. The first U-2 mission over Kosovo was flown on 16 October 1998 by the 99th ERS, temporarily based at Aviano while the runway was resurfaced at Istres, France. It was a panoramic camera sortie to get maximum coverage.[14]

Operation Allied Force

But the situation on the ground deteriorated, and on 24 March 1999 NATO launched Operation Allied Force (OAF) to evict Serb forces from Kosovo. During the 78-day campaign the 99th ERS flew 189 missions with five airplanes, and provided over 1,300 hours of collection time. By flying out of NAS Sigonella, Italy, instead of Istres, the U-2s were closer to the ac-

SAY THAT AGAIN !

Here is a selection of comments by U-2 pilots who were invited to air their view to the GrayBeard panel in 1997:

"On the road too much; was told TDYs would slow down after 18 months

"Though I was passed over for Lt Col, I've loved every minute."

"I've lost leave every year I've been here."

"There's nothing wrong at Beale that can't be solved by a few good fighter pilots."

"How many times have we flown Bosnian sorties where the tape couldn't get picked up, and nobody really cared? Too many."

"The iron majors at J-3 in Ramstein and Riyadh always think and schedule as though every mission will discover new atrocities, or catch the Republican Guard moving south again...."

"When I was in France I asked an intel officer if they ever got anything useful out of B-H (Bosnia-Herzegovina). He replied, 'Yes, we got something useful about a month ago.' 30-35 missions a month for *one* useful piece of intel!?"

"We are only one of a few programs who must hand select our pilots (and for good reasons), yet we are given absolutely no priority to receiving good pilots from FPC."

"Old defensive system—can't handle today's threats."

"The intangible benefits of being considered special undoubtedly helped recruiting, retention, and morale."

"I'm so tired of being told 'You're not special, and neither is your jet.'"

"This airplane will kill you in a heartbeat, and it often takes every bit of skill I have to deal with its quirks. If you want to get a bunch of guys killed, send us some copilots or new graduates from flight training."

"It is still a great mission with the best guys in the world!"

OAF KOSOVO – THE VIEW FROM THE ISARC

Former U-2 pilot Major John Bordner was the chief of the ISARC (Intelligence, Surveillance, and Reconnaissance Cell) at NATO's 5th ATAF during Operation Allied Force:

In the beginning, all our collection went towards fixed target development. Then emphasis moved towards mobile targets and fielded forces. Towards the end, it was nearly all flexible targeting.

From stand-off range, the U-2 looked at the IADS and high-value targets in Serbia proper. It produced two to three attackable radar sites every night, from SIGINT fused with imagery—a thing of beauty! But we did not always have the assets to strike them....

There were a few cues from the Rivet Joint...but the only usable SIGINT that I got for targeting was from the U-2.

Lessons Learned? We have collection assets, but we lack analysts and an automated system to track targets. Multiple communications systems and classifications made it difficult to pass data in a timely manner.

- presentation to the HSA ISTAR Conference, London, March 2000

OAF KOSOVO - REACHBACK IN ACTION

I walked into the ships' intelligence center, and a specialist petty officer was talking to a sergeant at Beale AFB via secure telephone, and they were driving a U-2 over the top of this spot. The U-2 snapped the picture and fed it back to Beale, from where that young sergeant told my petty officer, we have confirmation. I called Admiral Ellis, he called General Clark, and about 15 minutes later we had three Tomahawk missiles enroute, and we destroyed those three Serbian early warning radars.

- Admiral Daniel Murphy, commander U.S. Sixth Fleet, testimony to Congress 26 October 1999

ANOTHER THANK-YOU FROM UNSCOM

TO: The U.S. Ambassador to the UN
8 June 1998

The Special Commission has benefited greatly during most of its existence from the use of U-2 aircraft provided by your government. We know that the product of our U-2 missions, which is very important to UNSCOM's inspection and monitoring responsibilities, is the result of hard work by a great many people.

In addition to the monthly briefings and photo product sets brought to us by your experts, we know that they work hard in mission planning to put the aircraft where we ask it to go, and often at specific times when we ask that it be overhead. In the six months from October 1997 to March 1998, your experts flew and processed for us 25 U-2 missions...

We know it has taken a huge amount of effort to support our requests for analysis of historical imagery to help us verify or disprove Iraqi claims of unilateral weapons destruction. This work gives UNSCOM a credible, factual basis for dialogue with Iraq, and is immensely useful.

Richard Butler
Executive Chairman, UNSCOM

---

tion, and could therefore increase their time-on-station within a standard nine-hour mission. And with cloud over the region so often, plus some mountainous territory to be covered, images from the high-flying U-2's ASARS radar sensor proved vital in identifying targets.

The MOBSTR was moved to Brindisi so that all U-2 missions were within datalink range, all the time. And all the U-2 exploitation and dissemination in OAF was done by DGS-2 at Beale, half a world away! The lack of physical presence did not seem to make much difference. During one mission, over 100 ad-hoc collection requirements from the CAOC in Vicenza abruptly displaced the preplanned targets. Although it had never been done before, planners at DGS-2 were able to reprogram the U-2 mission "on the fly" while the aircraft was airborne.[15]

Predator UAVs and JSTARS grabbed most of the publicity during the air action over Kosovo. But "the U-2 was the backbone of our ISR architecture," noted USAFE's Director of Operations, Maj Gen William Hobbins. "We never dropped a bomb on a target without having the U-2 take a look at it," he continued. Although Serbian air defenses were never completely eliminated, 39 radars and 28 aircraft were destroyed after being identified by U-2 missions. Moreover, this conflict demonstrated a significant speed-up of the "sensor-to-shooter" cycle, which had become a key aim in U.S. air combat doctrine.[16]

LJUBIZDA, SR
GEO COORD=42°017'N/20°112'E
DOI 13 NOV 98

N

POSSIBLE CHECK POINT

During Operation Allied Force over Kosovo in 1999, "we never dropped a bomb on a target without having the U-2 take a look at it," said a USAFE General. (USAF via Tim Ripley)

Closeup of this U-2S cockpit reveals the new single-piece windscreen, which formed part of the Power-EMI upgrade developed in the late 1990s. (Lockheed Martin PR3832-43)

Rapid Targeting

From the mid-1990s, Beale-based U-2s and other U.S. reconnaissance platforms had participated in various exercises to develop the Rapid Targeting System (RTS) and Real-Time Information to the Cockpit (RTIC). By using powerful computer hardware and software, imagery and SIGINT data from multiple sources, including satellites, was matched or "fused" to provide target locations with enough accuracy for precision attack. Selected imagery frames from the U-2 or JSTARS were annotated and transmitted via JTIDS links from the ground to an E-3 AWACS, and on to an F-15E, allowing the data to cue the Strike Eagle's APG-70 radar.

During the Kosovo conflict, the U-2 provided 66 RTS (Rapid Targeting System) packages to strike aircraft. Moreover, because it could carry SIGINT as well as imaging sensors, the U-2 proved to be a "one-stop shop" for providing the targeting data. On one U-2 mission, the Senior Ruby

By the time that Ben Rich retired at the end of 1990, the Lockheed Advanced Development Company (LADC, aka the Skunk Works) was heading for trouble. Revenues from design and production of the F-117 had peaked. Design and test flights of the YF-22 had been completed. Production of the TR-1 was over. The Air Force had just retired the SR-71, which reduced the company's support revenues.

Rich's successor was Sherm Mullin, a systems engineer who had played key roles on the F-117 and YF-22. He commissioned a "Looking Forward" study, which identified three promising areas for research and development. These were unmanned autonomous aircraft, low-cost access to space, and intercontinental cargo transport systems. But despite considerable investment, all three concepts foundered.

In fact, the major unmanned aircraft program during the early 1990s was a total bust. The Skunk Works and other contractors (including Boeing) spent $1.5 billion of government "black" money to develop a very large, very stealthy, very long-endurance high-altitude reconnaissance vehicle that never even got airborne. It was an NRO project, identified at one stage by the cryptonym Quartz. Known within Palmdale as the "B-project," it did not meet the stringent range or radar cross-section design goals during component testing. When operational commanders were belatedly consulted, they didn't want it.

Out of this fiasco emerged a less ambitious requirement, which the Skunk Works attempted to meet with the strange-looking Darkstar UAV. This ran into technical problems, and one of the prototypes crashed. Before long, the Pentagon determined that it was too small anyway, and canceled it!

Despite these setbacks investment in new facilities continued, as LADC completed the move from its old home at Burbank to Plant 10, in the southwest corner of Palmdale airfield. On the other side of the huge airfield, the U-2 was still a prime source of revenue, since Lockheed continued to perform upgrades and depot-level maintenance at Site 2. The USAF U-2 Flight Test team, officially part of the U-2 program Directorate at Warner-Robins ALC, was also located at Site 2.

In 1996 Lockheed merged with Martin Marietta. But the biggest change at Palmdale was the separation of "routine" activities like the U-2 from the Skunk Works. The Skunk Works returned to its roots as a small organization charged with leading-edge R&D.

In 2000, the separate Lockheed Martin Skunk Works company ceased to exist. The activities at Palmdale—including the U-2 program—became part of the Lockheed Martin Aeronautics Company (LM Aero), headquartered in Fort Worth, TX. – *C.P.*

ELINT sensor operator in the ground station at Beale AFB detected a mobile SA-6 SAM radar. He quickly took another direction-finding "cut,' and passed the information to his colleagues nearby who were controlling the ASARS sensor. The U-2 pilot was ordered to reverse track so that imagery could be obtained. This imagery was then passed to the CAOC in Vicenza, Italy, and from there to an F-15E that struck the radar. Total elapsed time was 42 minutes.[17]

After the Serbs were evicted from Kosovo, the 99th ERS continued to monitor the Balkans with three U-2s from Sigonella. In June 2000 the 1000th Sentinel Torch mission was flown. Each one of them had involved the relay of sensor data all the way back to Beale.

Global Hawk

But while the Dragon Lady was firmly part of the Intelligence, Surveillance, and Reconnaissance (ISR) revolution, it was not the poster child. That distinction went to UAVs like the Predator, which was used intensively during Operation Allied Force. Then there was the Global Hawk, the big-wing high-altitude drone that was now flying as a technology demonstrator, carrying smaller versions of the U-2's ASARS and SYERS imaging sensors.

In fact, some USAF leaders had fallen in love with the Global Hawk. They now described the U-2 as "a sunset system." This played well in the technical journals, but not with the theater CinCs. They were not willing to forgo the U-2's proven performance for projections of future UAV performance. The purse-holders on Capitol Hill took a similar view. Even the former DARO head and UAV enthusiast Bg Gen Ken Israel was now a convert. "The U-2 will be around for 40 years. It can overcome the incipient shadowing of Global Hawk," he told a 1998 symposium.[18]

The UAV camp complained about a "Congressional U-2 mafia," but by the end of the 1990s major upgrades to the Dragon Lady had been approved, as well as significant improvements to the U-2's three most important sensor systems.

To take advantage of the increased electrical generating capability of the F118, a new "power distribution backbone" was designed. Using new copper wiring and the latest fiberoptic cables, the new system replaced bundles of old wiring that had been dedicated to specific sensors. This saved some weight, and made it much easier to swop sensors on the airframe. The total generator power was increased to 45 kVA, of which about 36 kVA was available to the sensors. Moreover, electro-magnetic interference (EMI) from the aircraft's power system was much reduced through better shielding and grounding. This was of particular value to the U-2's SIGINT systems, which could now "listen" from a much quieter airborne environment.

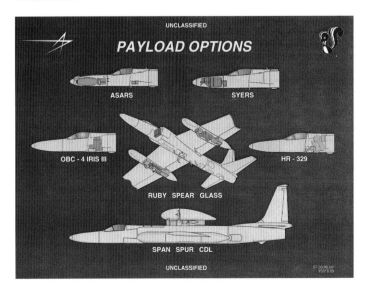

The sensor options that were available on the U-2 in the mid-late 1990s are shown on this Lockheed briefing chart.

Power-EMI upgrade

In a six-year effort costing $140 million, the Power-EMI upgrade would be done as each U-2 entered depot maintenance at Palmdale. At the same time, three other improvements were to be incorporated. There was a new single-piece windscreen with a better anti-icing system. The wing-mounted Trimble GPS was replaced by the USAF's standard Garmin model in a new installation behind the Q-bay, and integrated with the INS. Provision was made for a SIGINT upgrade. The resulting aircraft would be designated U-2S Block 10 (the original re-engined U-2S standard was retrospectively designated Block 0).

Lockheed's Jim Carter led the Power-EMI upgrade at Palmdale. The prototype installation was flying on 80-1090 by the end of 1998. Conversions of the fleet began in 2000, as 80-1078 and 80-1095 entered depot maintenance. The first deployment of Block 10 took place in September 2002, to the 5th RS in Korea.[19]

Very little money had been spent on the U-2's SIGINT systems during the 1990s, partly because they were supposed to be replaced by the Joint SIGINT Avionics Family (JSAF), a common system for the RC-135, EP-3, and U-2. But JSAF proved technically difficult, especially to adapt to the high-altitude U-2. Meanwhile, black boxes were proliferating on the U-2, and they required frequent swop-outs to cover new threat frequencies. Moreover, complications such as that found in the Iraqi air defense system, where Soviet missiles were netted to French and Chinese radars, could defeat the automated detection techniques used by the U-2's ELINT sensor.

RAS-1

Some improvements to the Spear and Ruby systems were funded so that they could all be brought to the Senior Glass configuration. Raytheon had bought E-Systems, which provided both the SIGINT systems on the U-2. Raytheon's company designation for the combined U-2 SIGINT suite was Remote Avionics System 1 (RAS-1). The first digital receivers were added in 1993, along with the flexibility to uplink and downlink from the U-2. This was the RAS-1A system.

Ever since it was introduced in the early 1980s, ASARS-2 had been the leading radar reconnaissance sensor in the U.S. inventory. Early refinements to the system included electronic scanning of the antenna (in azimuth), and the addition of the Moving Target Indicator (MTI) mode.

AIP

In June 1996 work began on a major upgrade to ASARS. The program name was Senior Dart, but it became known as the ASARS-2 Improvement Program, or AIP. Using commercially-available hardware, Hughes (subsequently acquired by Raytheon) replaced the Receiver/Exciter and

UNMANNED U-2 PITCHED AT PENTAGON

Washington – Lockheed Martin Skunk Works is studying an unmanned variant of the U-2. The firm outlined its concept in an unsolicited proposal to the USAF in March. The U-2U variant would augment the U-2S for very-long-duration, high-risk missions.

The proposal is to fit the flight management system originally developed for the Darkstar low-observable UAV. The U-2U design would also allow manned flights. The development cost was pegged at $85 million, and each U-2U would cost $35 million to build, including engine and avionics, but not sensors.

- Flight International, 23 April 1997

FOR THE RECORD, 1998

It was an initiative of the Lockheed U-2 Program Office to try for new world records for time-to-climb and altitude with the U-2 in October 1998. The publicity would help to gain funding for a new round of upgrades—particularly the glass cockpit. The USAF cooperated, but only up to a point. The service refused to declassify the maximum altitude of the aircraft. The security guide stated "above 70,000 feet." This rather defeated the purpose of the record attempts. Nevertheless, they went ahead. The maximum altitude claimed was 68,700 feet by Jim Barrileaux in a NASA ER-2. The maximum payload was 4,400lbs flown to 66,800 feet by Major Alan Zwick, a 9th RW IP at Beale. Two other obscure FAI records were claimed for a flight out of Palmdale by Major Bryan Galbreath. Still, the records helped the re-engined U-2S to win the 1998 Collier Trophy, and the upgrades were duly funded. – C.P.

Left: 079 returns to Taif after another mission for UNMOVIC. The Iraqis resented the flights to monitor their compliance with United nations sanctions, and frequently threatened to shoot them down. (via Chuck Wilson)

the big telescope housed in the U-2's nose. Five of them were built by Itek, which was subsequently sold to Hughes, itself later bought by Raytheon. They produced excellent imagery in good weather, but frequent cloud cover and haze over Europe and the Korean peninsula restricted the number of days on which SYERS could usefully be used there, especially if it meant replacing the ASARS.

SYERS upgrade

Thought was given to redesigning SYERS so that it could fit in the Q-bay, thereby leaving the U-2 nose free for ASARS and allowing both sensors to be carried on the same mission. But there was not enough room. Instead, funding was approved for a multi-spectral upgrade to the four SYERS sensors, and the purchase of an additional two.

The upgraded SYERS-2 had five new collection wavebands, making seven in total (three visible, two shortwave IR, and two mediumwave IR). The use of color in the visible bands would improve the identification of targets, while shortwave IR would cut through haze. The medium wave IR waveband would improve nighttime resolution. The combination of bands would help defeat the increasingly sophisticated camouflage and concealment techniques that were out there. As with ASARS, the upgrade also offered much greater area coverage, and improved geolocation. (Goodrich bought Raytheon's high-end EO systems business in 2001, and therefore took over manufacture and support of SYERS).

In order to cope with the increased data produced by these improved imaging sensors, the U-2's line-of-sight link to the MOBSTR relay station was upgraded to a capacity of nearly 300 mb/sec, and redesignated as the Interoperable Airborne Data Link II (IADL-II). A second line-of-sight system could also be carried by the U-2 for communication with mobile imagery exploitation systems in the field (the Dual Data Link, or DDL).

There was not much of a role left for the U-2's traditional, wet-film cameras. They could not provide timely data for fast-paced military scenarios, and the chemicals required for processing could not be easily flushed away under modern environmental legislation. The U-2's excellent Optical Bar Camera (OBC), the 30-inch lens panoramic system, was retained for UN missions and other survey tasks. But the IRIS III, the very-high-resolution H-camera, and a mapping camera designated F489 were all placed in storage at the end of 1999. So was the 35mm tracker camera. It had been used to establish "ground truth" for both operational and training sorties. Now it was retired because student navigation training sorties could be evaluated from a GPS readout.

Controller boxes with a combined REC, and added an onboard processor for the first time (in the Q-bay). A new Asynchronous Transfer Mode (ATM) connected the radar boxes to each other and to the datalink.

The payoff was a dramatic improvement in both resolution and coverage. Three-foot resolution was now achieved in the best search mode (versus 10 foot previously), and one-foot resolution was possible in "spot" mode. The area covered by these modes was increased by 1500% and 900%, respectively, yet thanks to the powerful new onboard processor there was less bandwidth required on the datalink. Since the U-2's new GPS/INS installation pinpointed the aircraft's location, the improved radar could now be used for precision targeting and digital terrain mapping.

Flight tests of the upgraded radar were completed in late 1998, and the first of 12 AIP sensors was delivered in September 2000. This time MTI modes were to be included in all the systems. There were some problems with the new onboard commercial processor, a Power PC. But it was still "a giant stride forward," according to veteran ASARS manager Bob Chiota. "All that functionality that used to be in six-foot racks on the ground was put into a 2.5 foot-square box. Amazing!" he noted.[20]

ASARS was the Rolls-Royce of radar systems, and SYERS was the Cadillac of camera systems. The EO sensor was originally a dual-band system, offering visible and infrared modes and very long range, thanks to

The last overseas detachment to swop the U-2R for the re-engined U-2S was OL-FR at Istres, France. The new and the old are seen lined up there in February 1997.

34

New Century, Same Solution

On 5 December 2000, Lockheed Martin test pilot Eric Hansen climbed into 10336 and took off from Palmdale on the maiden flight of the "Glass Dragon." In front of him, instead of the familiar round dials and the prominent viewsight cone, the instrument panel was dominated by three large screens. All of the 40-year-old instruments and switches were gone. The U-2 was heading into the 21st century with a cockpit to match.

Until now, very little had changed in the U-2 cockpit since the first flight of the U-2R in 1967. Yet by the mid-1990s, the Dragon Lady was carrying some of the most sophisticated sensors known to man. The contrast with the profoundly low-tech U-2 cockpit was acute. If the U-2 was to remain the nation's premier airborne reconnaissance collection asset, something had to be done. Meanwhile, the difficulty of sourcing spares for those old-fashioned instruments was growing by the month.

In October 1998, therefore, Lockheed Martin (LM) was awarded a $93 million contract for the U-2 Reconnaissance Avionics Maintainability Program (RAMP)—a new "glass cockpit." This major development was led by Jim Kaplan, and later by Bryan Swords, as the Lockheed Martin project managers. Former 9th SRW pilots Stormy Boudreaux and Major Mike "Sooch" Masucci also played key roles. Boudreaux was a flight test manager for Lockheed at Site 2, Palmdale. Masucci was commander of the U-2 test force at Palmdale, and therefore the USAF's chief U-2 test pilot. But the RAMP managers sought the active participation of many others in the U-2 community. That included the operational pilots, whose views were collected and represented by the 9th RW's RAMP project officer, Major Ed McGovern.

An integration rig was set up at Palmdale. The new cockpit would use a standard MIL1553B database: a new main avionics processor (based on the Power PC) would convert analog signals from the airframe to digital. Three 6 x 8-inch flat panel multi-function displays (MFDs) would dominate the new layout, plus an upfront control and display panel that would conveniently group all the vital switches together. (In the old cockpit, vital controls such as radio and navigation were housed in awkward-to-reach locations in the lower side panels).

Off-the-shelf

Although off-the-shelf hardware was used (the MFDs came from the C-5, C-130J, and T-38 upgrades, for instance), everything had to be adapted for high-altitude flight. For instance, the glass panels had to be tested to ensure that they would not explode if the cockpit decompressed at high alti-

tude. The touch controls were spaced so that a pilot wearing the bulky gloves of the pressure suit could easily operate them.

The result was much-improved situational awareness. Information that pilots of other military aircraft took for granted was now available to the U-2 drivers for the first time! The groundspeed and wind vector were now displayed throughout the flight; the fuel panel accurately reflected the actual system layout; and flight plan tracks and waypoints could be displayed on the moving map. An angle-of-attack indicator with aural as well as visual warnings was another first—useful for those final few feet before land-

The new "glass cockpit" introduced in the U-2 Reconnaissance Avionics Maintainability Program (RAMP) swept away all the old round-dial instruments from the 1960s-era (top). (Lockheed Martin)

U-2 MISSION PLANNING

The complex task of planning a U-2 reconnaissance mission just got easier with the Mission Planning System-Five (MPS-V) computer and software. A U-2 mission may have 400-500 data requests, and the camera, radar, and electronic intelligence sensors have their own limitations, such as range and sun angle. The software integrates the Aircraft/Weapons/Electronics module that creates the route with the Common Sensor Planner module that controls sensor activation, as well as with other requirements. MPS-V writes the flight plan on a disk for transfer to the aircraft, as well as producing paper charts and documents for the pilot. MPS-V is 19 times faster than the 1995-era system it replaces, and fits in a 70-lb box, instead of 13 cases that occupied two shipping pallets.

- Aviation Week and Space Technology, 4 June 2001, p21

As commander of Det 2 at Palmdale, Lt Col Mike Masucci was the chief USAF test pilot for the RAMP upgrade. (via Mike Masucci)

ing on the bicycle gear, when the Dragon Lady must be persuaded to quit flying by touching down close to the stall speed.

The new cockpit design retained the familiar large control yoke, the sunshade, and even the rear view mirror. But there was no room for the viewsight (or driftsight) that used to dominate the main panel. Generations of U-2 drivers had scanned the viewsight optics to answer such vital questions as: are there fighters below me? Am I contrailing? Is the landing gear really down and locked? Or even, where am I?!

After six months of flight tests the new cockpit was approved. It was subsequently to be incorporated in each aircraft as it returned to Palmdale for depot maintenance. 01082 was the first production modification. It was redelivered to Beale after a suitable ceremony on 15 April 2002. The RAMP aircraft were designated U-2S Block 20.

Operation Enduring Freedom

After the 9-11 outrage in 2001 the U.S. took aim at its perpetrators. Inevitably, the U-2 was called to action again. But while many countries lent support to the campaign against the Taleban and Al Qaeda in Afghanistan, Saudi Arabia was not among them. It refused to let the Kingdom's airbases be used for Operation Enduring Freedom (OEF).

The United Arab Emirates was more cooperative. In late September, the two U-2s at Sigonella were flown to Al Dhafra airbase, near Abu Dhabi. They were joined by others from Akrotiri and Beale. On 5 October the new Det 4 of the 9th RW flew its first mission over Afghanistan. Two aircraft assigned to the 363rd ERS at Al Kharj, in Saudi Arabia, remained there to support Operation Southern Watch.

Although the new base in the UAE was closer to Afghanistan, the geography of the new conflict had two significant impacts on U-2 operations. First, in order to provide the lengthy on-orbit times required by CENTCOM, pilots had to fly 12-hour missions. Second, data from the U-2's sensors could not first be downlinked to MOBSTR before relay to the U.S. by satellite for processing and analysis. Instead, the U-2 had to operate "off-tether" using its own satellite relay system.

Fortunately, after a period in the 1990s when such systems were under-funded, new versions had been procured from L-3 Communications. The original Senior Span had limited bandwidth, and proved suitable only

The 5th RS continued to fly along the DeMilitarized Zone separating the two Koreas, as it had done since 1976. (Katsumi Ohno)

A U-2S with the Power-EMI upgrade was tested in the Benefield Anachoic Chamber at Edwards AFB. "A significant reduction in aircraft noise levels" was confirmed.

OPERATION ENDURING FREEDOM
VIEWS FROM THE COCKPIT

- The average sortie length was 11 hours, and we flew every three days. We had never flown such long sorties on an intensive basis before. Many pilots experienced serious decompression problems.
- My first mission was along the Pakistan border...we had not yet got the clearance to go over Afghanistan. But there wasn't much of an air defense threat there anyway. I was more worried about flying over the Navy ships in the Gulf, in case they mis-identified me!
- Fighter pilots would ask us, what's the cloud cover like over the west of Afghanistan? Only we could see that far.
- We were flying over mountains reaching 22,000 feet. But if we had to eject, the seat was set to separate at 15,000 feet! There was no direction from the U.S. on this. So we decided amongst ourselves that we would pull the D-ring when we felt the pressure suit start to deflate—at about 35,000 feet.
- There was plenty of turbulence over Pakistan, thanks to temperature inversions. Then over Afghanistan, we encountered some *serious* mountain waves. It was particularly scary at night. Sometimes, it was so bad I couldn't read any instruments!
- Due to turbulence, my INS failed when I was close to the Afghan/ Iran border. I flew all the way home using one of the hand-held Garmin GPS sets that we bought with squadron funds. We would plug them in to the spot where the cockpit fan fits. These sets served as our very own moving map display...they also did ETAs and fuel computations. We even loaded our DPs into it. Not bad for $500 each!

- authors' interviews with Det 4 pilots, 2003

for the relay of SIGINT. Now, though, four Senior Spur systems were in service. They provided a full bandwidth link to a classified U.S. satellite architecture, so that ASARS or SYERS imagery could also be transmitted across continents. Spur was now referred to as the Extended Tether Program (ETP).

However, the first task over Afghanistan was to provide the ground forces with some good maps. The best way to do that quickly was to fly the OBC camera, with its wide swath, over the area. Two OBC missions were flown, with the film being rapidly downloaded and flown back to Europe for processing and readout. After that, the SYERS plus SIGINT configuration was used more often than ASARS plus SIGINT. There were two missions on most days.

Global Hawk deploys

Bandwidth was a huge issue in OEF, thanks especially to the heavy use of UAVs. The Predator was flying all over the place, and everyone from Secretary Rumsfeld down wanted to look at its video feed. The conflict in Afghanistan also marked the first deployment of the Global Hawk. It was another communications-intensive platform, hence the nickname "Global Hog!" Three of these autonomous UAVs were operated by a combined team from Northrop Grumman and ACC HQ that took up residence at Al Dhafra, in the other end of the U-2 hangar. The team was led by Col Ed Walby, a former 99th RS commander.

The go-ahead for Global Hawk development and production had been given a year earlier. It had since been decided to base the big drone alongside the U-2 at Beale. But a debate was raging over whether—or to what extent—the Global Hawk could replace the U-2. It had a smaller payload, less electrical power to drive the sensors, and could climb only slowly to a maximum 65,000 feet. However, the GH could stay airborne for more than 30 hours, and that was good...very good. "Combat persistence" was now a favorite term in the military's lexicon! Over Afghanistan during OEF, the three Global Hawks flew 65 operational sorties and logged about 1,200 hours. But two of them crashed, one of them on the Afghan/Pakistan bor-

An ASARS-equipped U-2 at Beale AFB. In 2001, and again in 2003, most of the 9RW's fleet was deployed away from home base, and playing a vital role over Afghanistan and Iraq. (author)

PENTAGON PRESS BRIEFING 11 MARCH 2002

Q: What can you tell us about the aborted U-2 missions today in Iraq?

Secretary Rumsfeld: UNMOVIC wants them resumed. We believe that we had clearance. DoD talks to State. State talks to UNMOVIC. UNMOVIC talks to the Iraqis. Where the breakdown occurred is not clear to me. We supplied the aircraft, and at some moment the Iraqis asked UNMOVIC to cancel because there were two instead of one or something. I would not put that on the cooperation side of the ledger for Iraq.

- In fact, what happened here is that UNMOVIC tried to catch the Iraqis off-guard, by mounting two U-2 inspection flights at the same time. This had never been done before. UNMOVIC was obliged to inform Iraq of the location and time of U-2's entry and exit points—but no more! The two aircraft took off and flew to the same IP, and then diverged to different flight tracks. The Iraqis radar-tracked them both, and immediately demanded an end to the flights. The aircraft were recalled. – C.P.

der. Some useful reconnaissance photographs of the wreckage were taken—by the OBC camera from a U-2!

OEF once again stretched U-2 resources to their limit: pilots, maintainers, airframes, and sensors. Sigonella was closed in favor of consolidation with Akrotiri, which became the 99th ERS. Missions in support of Operation Northern Watch were flown from the Cyprus base. The squadron's two to three aircraft also flew a monthly mission over the Balkans using the OBC camera, to meet a national U.S. requirement. (The Det 1 designation at Akrotiri remained, but now referred only to the maintenance operation. Aircraft from the two U-2 locations in the desert could be inspected here every 400 hours as required, without ferrying back to the U.S.)

On the other side of the world, the 5th RS was still watching the North Koreans, as it had done nearly every day since 1976. Osan was still the first assignment for newly-qualified U-2 pilots, because the flight tracks were standard. After a 60-day tour here they were ready for worldwide deployments.

Despite the economic decline of the Pyongyang regime, its military forces were still arrayed in threatening concentrations, less than 70 miles from Seoul. Frog tactical missiles, long-range artillery, and tanks were kept in extensive tunnels and caves all along the North's side of the ceasefire line. Intelligence analysts were having a hard time keeping track of it all. From high altitude, the U-2 offered a superior "look angle" across the mountainous terrain of the DMZ.

President visits the Black Cats
On 21 February 2002 President George W. Bush and Secretary of State Colin Powell visited the Blackcats at Osan, as part of a six-day trip to Asia. It was the second time that a U.S. commander-in-chief had reviewed the 5th RS operation: President Clinton had also been there. Bush gave a speech thanking the squadron and the other units at Osan while his national security team viewed U-2 operations.

Nearly a year later the 5th RS was back in the headlines, for the wrong reason this time. A U-2S crashed into a suburb of Seoul after the pilot ejected. He survived, but three people on the ground were injured. The F118 engine had quit at high altitude after the number four bearing failed. The engine seized, so the restart system could not work. Descending through bad weather, both batteries failed, and ice accumulated on the pitot tube. Denied his key airspeed and altitude references, the pilot was unable to maintain control.

Unfortunately, this was not the first time that the new GE engine had malfunctioned at high altitude. On 14 October 2001 Major Jeff Oleson was flying over southern Iraq from PSAB in support of Operation Southern Watch when he experienced "rollbacks"—momentary but severe losses of thrust. Following the SOP he selected Secondary engine mode, but now the engine vibrated severely and threatened to seize. Reselecting primary mode reduced the vibrations, but the rollbacks continued. The idle power setting was the only reliable one. Oleson selected an airfield in Kuwait and made an immaculate deadstick landing. He won the 2003 Kolligian Award for this save.

UNMOVIC
North Korea was one "axis of evil" to President Bush; Iraq was another. As far as his administration was concerned, the policy of containing Iraq through sanctions and no-fly zones had failed. Saddam Hussein had to go. The U.S. sought support from the United Nations. Intense pressure was put on Baghdad to re-admit the weapons inspectors. UNSCOM was now UNMOVIC—the United Nations Monitoring, Verification, and Inspection Commission (UNMOVIC). The inspectors returned to Iraq in November 2002, but Baghdad imposed "unacceptable" conditions on the resumption of U-2 flights, according to UNMOVIC chief Hans Blix.

Of course, the Iraqis knew that the U-2 also played a key part in Operations Northern and Southern Watch. In fact, they nearly bagged one in July 2001 when an SA-2 that the Iraqis had fired unguided exploded below and behind the aircraft during a mission over the southern no-fly zone. It was a lucky escape. Of course, without any radar guidance signals to alert the Rivet Joint there was no warning passed to the U-2 pilot.

The connectivity of the modern battlefield prompted these concepts from Lockheed of additional missions that could be performed by the U-2. All of them became reality, in the skies over Afghanistan and Iraq.

The incident followed a similar attack on a Navy E-2C Hawkeye AEW aircraft a week earlier. Iraq was using Chinese early-warning radars, mixing and matching various target acquisition and missile guidance radars, moving SAMs in and out of the no-fly zone, and netting its air defenses with fiberoptic links. That also made it more difficult for U.S. SIGINT sensors to detect and warn of missile attacks on the high-flyers.

The pressure on Saddam Hussein mounted. U.S. and British troops massed in Kuwait. Iraq now said the safety of U-2 flights for UNMOVIC could not be guaranteed if they flew at the same time that U.S. and British warplanes conducted air patrols in the "no-fly" zones. Then it caved in, and the U-2 flights began on 17 February 2003 with a four-hour mission.[1]

But State Department spokesman Richard Boucher said Iraq's toleration of the flights and other signs that seemed to suggest increased cooperation were "not worth getting excited about." U-2 pilots were plenty excited, though, as they once more flew over central Iraq, not really knowing if they were safe from attack! Neither the flights, nor the renewed inspections on the ground, uncovered any firm evidence that the Saddam regime still possessed weapons of mass destruction.

Operation Iraqi Freedom (OIF)

The U.S. lost patience with the weapons inspection process and launched Operation Iraqi Freedom (OIF) less than a month later. Once again, U-2s played a vital—if unheralded—part in providing the ISR picture. But there was plenty of competition: eighty ISR aircraft took part in the war altogether. Collectively, they produced a staggering 42,000 battlefield images, 2,400 hours of SIGINT collection, and 1,700 hours of MTI data.

No fewer than 15 jets flown by 31 pilots clocked up 169 missions in OIF. It was the biggest-ever deployment for the Dragon Lady. 10 aircraft flew out of Al Dhafra (UAE), two out of Al Kharj (PSAB, Saudi Arabia),

Ever since 1976 the 99th RS has been the operational U-2 squadron based at Beale, and providing crews and aircraft for the overseas locations. (Lockheed Martin PR2853)

Unlike other warplanes, we can *talk* on the crypto links. That made us invaluable as a command and control tool. We were the only line-of-sight show in town! We were involved in the F-14 crash, the POW rescue, and the special forces actions. We cleared fighters into kill boxes, we talked to AWACS...we were pilot-in-the-middle.

We flew a unique "dual" mission a few times. An OBC camera in one aircraft, an ASARS in the other, along the same flight track.

It was dynamic retasking all the time. Lots of alternative DPs. Lots of BDA.

In the ATO, there were *hopes* for the Global Hawk, but *expectations* for the U-2.

- author's interviews with 363 ERS and Det 4 pilots, 2003

U-2 HELPS BRING POWs HOME

A U-2 Dragon Lady aircraft provided critical "situational awareness" that allowed U.S. Marines to safely recover seven U.S. Army soldiers who were taken prisoner-of-war near Samarrah, Iraq. Marines learned about the seven POWs from Iraqi military officers who had deserted their unit. The U-2 communicated with the marines and with the Combined Air Operations Center. The pilot monitored radio transmissions and passed messages between key parties who were otherwise out of communications range. The U-2 also gathered information that insured that no Iraqi air defense or ground troops were in the area to threaten the Marine helicopters that recovered the POWs.

- Air Force Link, 17 April 2003

PHYSICAL TOLL

The average duration of a flight over Iraq (in OIF) was close to 10 hours and could extend to 11 hours. By regulation, we have to have 48 hours out of the pressure suit after nine hours of flying. Every pilot was flying every three to four days. The long durations and frequency take a physical toll. The U-2's cabin is pressurized to the equivalent of 30,000 feet the entire sortie. So OIF pilots were sitting on top of Mount Everest sucking 100% oxygen in a fish bowl every third day.

- Major Brian Farrar, quoted in Code One magazine, 1Q 2004

INFORMATION OVERLOAD

We were not airframe or pilot-limited for the first time we have employed this aircraft in combat. We typically had four to five U-2s in the air at one time. The limitations in OIF were a function of our ability to move and exploit the information. The limits were set by the photo-interpreters and our intel collectors on the back end. They had to receive a huge volume of data, digest it, make it actionable information, and then push it back to the commanders. At one point the intelligence community said, "We're maxed out. We can't possibly move any more electrons for you."

- Lt Col Troy Devine, 99th SRS commander, quoted in Code One magazine, 1Q 2004

were swamped by the sheer amount of data streaming back to them for analysis.

The challenge of generating sorties under wartime conditions was heightened by the various modification states of the airplanes, and the sensors. In this respect, OIF could not have come at a worse time for the U-2. The U-2S fleet comprised "original" Block 0 aircraft, Block 10s with the Power/EMI upgrade, and the first half-dozen Block 20s with the glass cockpit. The new RAMP aircraft stayed at Beale, but the Block 10s went to war, despite some doubts over the availability of their sensor upgrades.

Once again, the Global Hawk operated alongside the U-2 at Al Dhafra. Once again, Northrop Grumman made sure that the GH role in OIF was heavily briefed and publicized. But there was no denying its achievements. The single UAV deployed flew 16 times during the 25-day air action—and it didn't crash! It carried an E-O sensor at the same time as a radar sensor—the U-2 could not do that. The mission planners proved that the Global Hawk vehicle could be "dynamically retasked" inflight, just like the U-2. "Our guys had more situational awareness in their van than a U-2 pilot in the cockpit," alleged Ed Walby, now retired from the Air Force and gone to work for Northrop Grumman.[2]

At the end of OIF, the 363rd ERS at Al Kharj was closed, as the remaining USAF aircraft were withdrawn from Saudi Arabia. The U-2 had been based in the Kingdom for nearly 13 years. But Saudi political support for the U-2 missions, and for U.S. policy in general, had been equivocal. Future missions over Iraq, and in support of Operation Enduring Freedom over Afghanistan, would be flown from Det 4.

Most of the aircraft were returned to Beale via Akrotiri, Fairford (the UK airbase which is regularly used by the 9th RW as a ferry stop), and Pease AFB, NH.

At last, the wing could begin to catch up on deferred maintenance—and deferred family matters. The punishing TDY rates were still taking their toll.

Construction was underway at Beale on new facilities to house the Global Hawks. A new squadron (12th RS) was formed to operate them. The first production Global Hawk finally arrived at Beale on 16 November 2004. After 15 years of ruling the roost—since the Blackbird retired—the Dragon Lady had competition again.

and three from Akrotiri (Cyprus). The U-2s were tasked to provide three H24 orbits over the North, South, and West of Iraq. But one day six aircraft flew at the same time. Throughout the 14 days of major conflict at least one U-2 was always airborne.

There was a MOBSTR deployed at Al Jabbour, Kuwait, to receive downlinked imagery, but the ETP/Spur birds from Det 4 provided the off-tether capability.

Countless hours were spent looking for mobile Scud missile launchers, especially in the western deserts of Iraq. The U-2s were joined in this task by three Canberra PR9s from the UK Royal Air Force, which also carried the SYERS sensor and downlinked it to the RAF's own ground station. Intelligence analysts were convinced that the Iraqis still had about 20 Scud TELs, which could possibly launch chemical warheads at Israel. The intel was wrong. None were found.

According to the number-crunchers, the U-2 provided 88% of all battlefield imagery during OIF. ASARS proved particularly useful during the thunderstorms and sandstorms that prevailed during the first week of the war. The biggest problem was that the analysts back in the ground stations

The first production RAMP upgrade was 082, seen here with a patriotic backdrop for the redelivery ceremony in April 2002. (Lockheed Martin)

Parity

Of course, this was not stated in public. Officially, the two platforms were "complementary." However, the UAV camp was just waiting for the day when it could kiss the Dragon Lady goodbye. For that to happen, USAF officials suggested that the Global Hawk must reach "parity" with the U-2 in terms of its sensor fit and collection capability. But it was still a matter of hot debate when—or if—that day would come. First, Northrop Grumman had to boost the payload and electrical generation of the Global Hawk. Then, the big UAV had to overcome the objection that, no matter how clever the software routines were, it was always better to have a "man-in-the-loop" at high altitude.

Fortunately, the days when U-2 procurement accounts were robbed for funds to boost the UAVs were over, for the time being. There were more improvements and additions for the Dragon Lady in the pipeline.

The new Advanced Defensive System (ADS) was top priority, as far as the pilots were concerned. For too many years they had been sent in harm's way without the same degree of self-protection as the USAF's fighters and bombers. Or, the missions had been scrubbed if an RC-135 Rivet Joint and escort fighters were not available. But there was a problem. Flying at high altitude, the U-2 could be within line-of-sight of many more radars than a low-flyer.

Sanders—the traditional supplier of defensive systems for the U-2—was now part of BAE Systems North America. The company's lightweight radar warning receiver and jammer for the AH-64 Apache helicopter was chosen for the U-2 and adapted. Designated AN/ALQ-221, it was a wideband system that could detect search, tracking, and missile launch radars, and jam the latter two types. On the RAMP aircraft it was much easier to integrate. Flight tests began in 2002, and the production installations followed in 2004.[3]

Installation of the ALQ-211 could pave the way for the addition of a fiberoptic towed decoy (FOTD). An FOTD is an extra, last-ditch measure of protection against radar-guided missiles. BAE's ALE-55 FOTD was modified with special fins for high-altitude flight, and test-flown on a U-2 in 1999. It was mounted in the pod on the trailing-edge of the left wing, which was originally added to the U-2 to house the GPS.[4]

RUSSIAN FIGHTERS TRACK U.S. SPY PLANE ALONG BORDER

Moscow – U-2 spyplanes have been spotted near Russian borders again. This time the aircraft was operating in Georgia's airspace. Russian Air Force Commander Col-Gen Vladimir Mikhailov said that a U-2S flew along the same route on 27 February and 7 March at a distance of 20-25 km from the Russian border. Another sustained U-2 flight along the border was registered on 22 March.

The U.S. side claims that the missions have been performed in order to identify international terror bases. The Russian Ministry of Foreign Affairs insist that activities of this kind are likely to cause further tension in the region. The Russian military said that the flight of the U.S. spy aircraft was monitored from the ground, and two Su-27 fighters were called on to prevent possible violation of the state border.

- Air Fleet magazine, Moscow, March 2003

RAYTHEON ON THE U-2 SIGINT SYSTEM

"The new U-2 SIGINT system does a tremendous amount of processing in the air, and sends down, for most signal types, fully processed data. What we have done with our SIGINT systems is basically design a very large software radio that digitizes great amounts of frequency bandwidth, then runs it through DSPs (Digital Signal Processors) and starts working on it to derive all sorts of information.

Our new systems are fully software reprogrammable, even in flight. If a new type of threat signal comes along, we can update the system's software, not its hardware. Or we can dynamically reprogram the DSPs to focus processing on signals of interest that are of greater volume than anticipated."

- John Nannen, v-p business development, Raytheon C3I Systems, quoted in ISR Journal 2002/Issue 3

The ability to transmit reconnaissance imagery from anywhere to virtually anywhere by means of the satellite uplink, made the U-2 indispensible over Afghanistan during Operation Enduring Freedom. (Lockheed Martin PR2781-10)

HITTING A MOVING TARGET

Washington - Northrop Grumman has been selected to develop the Affordable Moving Surface Target Engagement (AMSTE) concept...The heart of AMSTE is the fusion of data simultaneously from two long-range, ground surveillance radars that can immediately be passed on to a missile-firing fighter. Such radars—in use on U-2s, Global Hawk UAVs, and E-8 Joint-STARS aircraft—have good range resolution, but less precise azimuth readings. However, combining the data from two or three aircraft can give measurements accurate to within 30 feet. The data is fused into a common reference frame that includes the exact position of the radar aircraft, the launch aircraft, the missile, and the target. As the missile flies to its target, data links provide GPS-based, target-location updates.

- *Aviation Week & Space Technology*, 10 September 2001, p33

The men and women of the 363rd ERS pose for the camera at the conclusion of OIF. The Saudi-based squadron was deactivated as soon as the conflict was over. The patch and slogan superimposed on this image was designed by TSgt Mike Polenske in 1995.

Sitting in the new glass cockpit, many U-2 pilots missed the familiar viewsight. Goodrich came up with a small electro-optic camera that could fit in the old viewsight bubble below the fuselage. Images from the camera could be displayed on one of the big new screens. The view of below was fantastic! But the bean counters did not want to fund it.

Climbing out of Al Dhafra one night during OIF, one pilot suspected from the climb performance that his landing gear had not retracted, despite no indication from his warning lights that this was the case. Over Qatar there was enough reflected light from the city below for him to peer through the viewsight and confirm that the gear was indeed down! He returned to base. When they put the aircraft on jacks and recycled the landing gear, it retracted for two seconds—then the doors fell open and the wheels fell down again.

The value of preserving the view below was confirmed. The money was found for the Goodrich Electro-Optic View Sight (EOVS), and it was being added to the aircraft during 2005.

One of the biggest constraints to deploying the U-2 around the world has always been its fuel. The logistics effort to pre-position the unique JP-TS (Jet Propellant, Thermally Stabilized) fuel was considerable. Moreover, it cost three times as much per gallon as standard military JP8! In the late 1990s studies began on how JP8 could be adapted to the re-engined U-2S. The ideas included transferring heat from the engine oil circuit to heat

On its way back to the U.S. from OIF, 089 is towed inside at a rainy RAF Fairford. (Jeff Jungemann)

A U-2S gets airborne for yet another mission during Operation Iraqi Freedom, April 2003. (USAF)

exchangers in the outboard fuel tanks, and/or reducing the freeze point of JP8 through additives. But funding for operational trials proved elusive.

DDL

A new datalink system for the sensors was devised by L-3 Communications—the latest sign on the door of the company in Salt Lake City that had provided the U-2's downlinks and uplinks for 30 years. In 2001-03, a common airborne modem assembly was developed to replace the single-purpose boxes that were previously dedicated to the three different types of U-2 datalink, namely the IADL (standard up/downlink), DDL (eg the Span satcom system), and ETP (eg Spur). New nine-inch antennas were fitted in the Q-bay and tail. The new system was designated DDL-II. It provided the U-2 with multiple communications options: two line-of-sight (LOS) links; or one LOS plus one ETP (satellite) link; or one LOS plus an air-to-air (ATA) link; or the ETP plus the ATA. For connectivity, that was hard to beat!

A new SIGINT system was also in prospect. The multi-platform JSAF program was canceled in 2001—the low-band part of it did not work. Anyway, it was too heavy and too expensive to put on the U-2. Instead, Raytheon received funding to upgrade the U-2's SIGINT suite to the RAS-1R configuration. This introduced commercial off-the-shelf digital technology, and the receivers could be reprogrammed from the ground station during a mission, instead of having to swap black boxes before a flight. The frequency coverage was also broadened.

For the longer term, Northrop Grumman was selected to provide the ASIP (Advanced Signals Intelligence Package) for both the U-2 and the Global Hawk. This was a scaleable system for the low-band frequencies (RFINT, including some early-warning radars) that could be integrated with the High Band Sub System (HBSS—this was the part of JSAF that did work). The HBSS was provided by TRW, which was subsequently acquired by Northrop Grumman).

Data Deluge

On the ground, the dream of having a common ground station that could process data from a variety of reconnaissance platforms was becoming a reality. Already, DGS-2 at Beale was doing Global Hawk and Predator stuff, as well as U-2. But would the problem of "data deluge" ever be solved? A shared information network was emerging: the "war-fighters" would "pull" the data that they really needed from the intelligence system, rather than have it "pushed" at them indiscriminately.

Then there was Network-Centric Collaborative Targeting (NCCT). A small group of former E-Systems engineers devised a scheme to network sensors on various airborne platforms together, using "smart agents" to automate the complicated process of cross-cueing. They formed a new company named Comcept to push the idea. In one scenario, the U-2 SIGINT system would make the first detection of a target, then a Predator UAV might take an image to corroborate, and the combined data would provide the geolocation for a strike weapon. Comcept was soon bought by L-3 which—through its prime role as the U-2 datalink provider—knew a few things about network communications.

Meanwhile, the scientists and engineers were working on more leading-edge ISR technology that was suitable for the U-2. A hyperspectral sensor with onboard automatic target detection that could detect camoflaged targets. A synthetic aperture radar using VHF instead of X-band to penetrate foliage. An airborne laser terminal to send recce data up to satellites at much higher rates.[5]

The potential of the improved ASARS radar was yet to be fully exploited: the quality of radar data now streaming from the U-2 allowed for various additional manipulation techniques to be performed in the ground stations. These could lead to coherent change detection and automatic target recognition/cueing. And more improvements to SYERS were possible.

75,000 hours

In the late nineties, Lockheed Martin fitted strain gauges and accelerometers to some U-2s to measure how the airframes were doing, fatigue-wise. The surprising conclusion was that the U-2S has a fatigue life of 75,000 hours! Even the highest-time airframes are only just approaching 30,000 hours. And yet the U-2 has always been characterized as a delicate aircraft, which skimped on milspecs in order to reach the high altitudes.

The fact is, the U-2 spends most of its time in a benign high-flight environment, where stress on the airframe from turbulence and gusts is minimal. (Pilots flying over the mountains in Korea would not entirely agree, but no matter!). There were some other factors that also contribute to the U-2 airframe longevity. These were summarized a few years ago by

Over the past few years, some U-2s deployed to the desert have been decorated with nose art in chalk. Major John Cabigas poses next to his own creation, "Eye in the Sky." (Jeff Jungemann)

Canvas shelters had to be erected at Al Dhafra to house all the U-2s that were deployed there for OIF. (John Bordner)

083 is nearly ready to depart from Al Dhafra for another mission, equipped with the SYERS nose and the satcom datalink. (Jeff Jungemann)

Fred Carmody, the Lockheed field service manager who spent 25 years helping to maintain the Dragon Lady: "The key is good initial design, maturity of the design, and proper maintenance."[6]

So at the current rates of utilization, the U-2 is good for at least another 150 years of service, if required! Instead though, will it be replaced in only a few years' time by the Global Hawk—that plastic computer-in-the-sky? If you look back at 50 years of U-2 history, the odds on this happening begin to lengthen. The Blackbird has come and gone. The satellites have come, and stayed. But so has the U-2. It's not over while the Dragon Lady sings.

The pilots of the 99th ERS who flew in Operation Iraqi Freedom from Al Dhafra.

Flying the Early Articles

Flying a U-2 sortie without incident in the early days was triumph of hope over expectation. Not only was it a challenging airplane to fly at high altitude, and then land, there was also the small matter of engines that kept flaming out, autopilots and fuel controls that did not work properly, and a life support system that was still in the development phase, if the truth be told.

In the first three years of the program 11 U-2 pilots lost their lives and 13 aircraft were destroyed. There were many more serious incidents that could have resulted in loss of plane, pilot, or both. Lessons were learned, often the hard way. Mostly they were applied. Sometimes they were not. Inevitably, perhaps, in a program that has lasted so long, some errors by early U-2 pilots were repeated by those who followed, sometimes decades later.

Hung Pogo

The very first fatal accident was caused by a hung pogo. At the Ranch on 15 May 1956, trainee CIA pilot Billy Rose "failed to maintain adequate airspeed and altitude" as he tried to release it, according to an accident summary. Nearly 40 years later, another U-2 and its pilot were lost under similar circumstances at RAF Fairford, in the UK.[1]

The second U-2 loss occurred at night, when another trainee pilot at the Ranch apparently pulled the nose up too high upon takeoff. At about 50 feet, the left wing dropped and the aircraft stalled into the ground. Frank Grace was fatally injured. "The probable cause was pilot error, with possible loss of night vision as a contributing factor," it was concluded.[2]

Pilots are human, and will therefore make errors. But few of the early U-2 "drivers" had ever encountered such an unforgiving flying machine. Even renowned Lockheed test pilot Tony Levier struggled to land the Article the first time. The SAC training group led by Colonel Bill Yancey devised a checkout syllabus, in which the T-33 trainer was used to instruct prospective U-2 pilots before they climbed into the real thing. The group also devised the "mobile" system, in which a second, fully-trained U-2 pilot attended each flight to provide assistance on the ground, including the calling-out of heights and instructions during the landing phase, from a chase car speeding alongside the Article.

But the T-bird could not replicate the Article's wily ways. To provide some experience in landing a tail-dragger, trainee pilots flew in an L-20 Beaver lightplane. Nevertheless, two trainee pilots survived serious landing accidents at the Ranch: Carmine Vito from the first CIA group, and Tony Bevacqua from the first Air Force group. "It was my first landing on the runway," recalled Bevacqua. "I approached the threshold OK, but then the damned wing dropped, and I applied power to go around. But the mobile called to shut it down, and I hit and slewed off the tarmac at an angle. The gear sheared off when I hit a ditch. Of course, that wouldn't have happened if I had landed on the lakebed. It wasn't so much of a problem, going off to the side a bit there...."[3]

Wing drop

Bevacqua said that the aircraft that he was flying had a history of wing drop. Certainly, each of the hand-built aircraft exhibited slightly different

Because it flew so high, the U-2 was nicknamed the Angel in the earliest days. But it hardly flew like one, in the unforgiving high-altitude regime. (Lockheed U2-91-028-3)

THE RIGHT STUFF

The crews who flew and maintained the U-2 took an unproved airplane, and flew it into an unknown world. They explored the high-altitude world for those who came later. It was trial-and-error, one step forward and two steps backward at a time. Their combat was with the unknown, where one mistake could result in death. Those of us who lived through those early days, when many of our friends perished, never felt that they died without cause. Their heritage was a fierce determination to make it work, safely. They really had the "Right Stuff," long before the term became fashionable.

- Colonel Donald James, 4080th SRW, 1957-1965

U-2 CHECKOUT SYLLABUS IN 1956
This was the training syllabus devised for the early U-2 pilots. Three flights in the T-33—and then they were on their own, in the Article!

Missions 1 and 2: T-33 flights, 1 hour 45minutes each
Local area familiarization; simulated U-2 patterns and landings, jet penetration, flameout and airstart procedures
Mission 3: T-33 flight, 2 hours
Instrument check (hooded)
Mission 4: U-2, 1 hour
Taxi aircraft to get feel; Takeoff at 85% RPM, retain pogos and leave gear down; Climb to 20,000 feet, remain within 15 nm of base; level off, retract gear; practice turns; extend gear and speed brakes, practice stalls; practice gust control operation; descend to pattern altitude and make four touch-and-go landings; on fifth takeoff retract flaps, drop pogos, make a pattern and full stop landing
Mission 5: U-2, 2 hours
Takeoff and make four touch-and-go landings with pogos; drop pogos on fifth takeoff and climb to 30,000 feet for familiarization with aircraft, radio compass, autopilot, driftsight, sextant and instruments; make five celestial observations; make jet penetration plus one or two practice flameout patterns

Mission 6: U-2, 3 hours
Takeoff, retain pogos and climb to 45,000 feet; fly in local area for (further) familiarization for 1 1/2 hours; make 10 celestial observations; climb to 60,000 feet, and remain there approx 20 mintes; descend extending dive flaps, gear and actuating gust control; make a jet penetration on local beacon; enter pattern and make four touch-and-go landings with pogos on; drop pogos on fifth takeoff; stay in pattern and make full-stop landing
Mission 7: U-2, 4 hours
Takeoff, drop pogos and camera covers, and turn on (tracker) camera; climb to 65,000 feet; during remainder of mission cruise-climb but do not exceed 68,000 feet; make three photo runs on assigned targets and routes; make five celestial observations; one hour before intended landing time, begin briefed letdown; make one or two practice flameout patterns
Mission 8: U-2, 1 hour
First landings on the runway, plus instrument and GCA approach practice
Mission 9 & 10: U-2, 6 and 7 hours, respectively
High Altitude navigation and photography. Do not exceed 70,000 feet
Mission 11: U-2, 1 hour
Second runway landing stage, plus GCA approach practice
Mission 12: U-2, 2 hours
Night check-out
Missions 13, 14 & 15: U-2, 8 hours each
Integrated Night-Day navigation and photography. Do not exceed 70,000 feet
Mission 16: U-2, 8 hours
Standardization Check: climb on briefed route to 64,000 feet; cruise-climb to 68,000 feet, maintain 68M and IAS until power is at minimum; continue cruise-climb with minimum power as IAS requires (do not exceed 70,000 feet); accomplish one night celestial leg; accomplish one day celestial leg; accomplish photography as briefed; make jet penetration, GCA and final landing

---

tendencies as it approached the stall. Lockheed made various refinements to compensate: stall strips in 1957; spoilers in 1964; and retractable stall strips in 1965. They helped, but pilots still ignored one basic truth at their peril: the potential for losing control of the Article at low altitude and low speed was great, if the fuel in those long wings was not properly balanced.

Moreover, the rate of roll was low, even with full aileron deflection. Pilots had to exert significant force on the yoke and rudder pedals to maintain directional stability.

Just 17 days after the first U-2s were flown into Laughlin AFB in June 1957, a 4080th SRW pilot on his second checkout ride killed himself through not appreciating all this. Lt Ford Lowcock took off at 0845 and was supposed to make touch-and-go landings, followed by a climb to medium altitude for familiarization.

Instead, eight minutes after takeoff, eye witnesses in Del Rio saw the aircraft make two descending turns to the right from 1,500 feet and crash one mile northeast of the town. The aircraft struck the ground in a steep angle of bank, slightly nose-high. Accident investigators determined that

A pilot and his mobile, in front of a U-2A. The need for a fully-qualified assistant to attend all flights, was recognized from the very start. The pogo supporting the left wing can be seen. A hung pogo upon takeoff led to the first fatal U-2 accident—and another one 40 years later. (NARA KKE 47590)

Lowcock was trying to perform a fly-by for his wife's benefit! "The turns were executed to try and find her house. The final turn was a 50-degree bank, and the pilot was unable to bring the low wing up in time," they reported. Twenty years later, another example of flying indiscipline led to the loss of control and crash upon takeoff of a U-2 at RAF Akrotiri, which killed bystanders as well as the pilot.[4]

Some early fatal accidents in the U-2 were never properly explained. Two hours after Lowcock's crash the SAC wing suffered another setback when Lt Leo Smith's aircraft crashed near Abilene, TX. This was Smith's sixth checkout ride, a four-hour cross-country sortie. There may have been an autopilot or trim malfunction. Or Smith may have allowed the fuel to become unbalanced, so that the left wing dropped when he made a scheduled turn over the Abilene VOR beacon.[5]

Disintegration

The disintegration of Howard Carey's aircraft when climbing out over Germany on 17 September 1956 may have been caused by the jet wash from the formation of four Canadian F-86 fighters that were flying close by. The U-2 was not stressed to fly through severe turbulence. According to the recall of CIA Project Director Richard Bissell, Kelly Johnson determined that the cause was overpressure in the wing tanks during a very steep climb. The solution was to install a simple relief valve. One of Carey's fellow pilots theorized that the accident was caused by an uncommanded extension of the flaps.[6]

This was probably the cause of Major Jack Nole's accident on 26 September 1957. The commander of the SAC U-2 squadron was climbing

The health and physical fitness of U-2 "drivers" was carefully monitored. There was a medical check before each flight. The CIA pilots additionally underwent a stringent examination at the Lovelace Clinic every two years. (Lockheed C88-1447-73)

LAKEBED RESCUE

In early 1956, trainee pilot Carmine Vito landed badly on the lakebed and his landing gear collapsed. His mobile, Captain Hank Meierdierck, recalled:

He was knocked unconscious. The engine was running, and fuel was pouring out of the wings. I dragged him out of the cockpit and onto the lakebed. But the oxygen hose was still attached to the plane. I had to lay him down, run back to the plane, unplug it, then drag him further away in case of an explosion. Then Bob Murphy and the Lockheed crew drove up. Bob shut the engine down: I was afraid to, in case I caused a spark and an explosion.

THE LOVELACE CLINIC

Those pilots chosen for the CIA's Project Aquatone were obliged to undergo a stringent medical examination at the world-renowned Lovelace Clinic in Albuquerque, NM. They were the guinea pigs for a whole series of unpleasant tests, some of which were later given to the Mercury and Apollo astronauts. But the U-2 pilots were the pioneers. Moreover, the Agency made them retake the Lovelace medical every two years. Jim Cherbonneaux recalled:

In every visit to the Lovelace clinic we were subjected to new tests. Yet if we wanted to keep our jobs, we had to pass every one of them. In addition to their standard up-the-rectum examinations, the tortures took the form of psychological hand/eye coordination evaluations, along with some tests in which they put radioactive particles in our bloodstream. We spent six and a half days at the clinic one year.

When we were finished, they sent us to Wright Patterson AFB for the heat chamber, the altitude chamber, and the centrifuge tests. Yet we hardly needed training in high G conditions! After all, the U-2 was limited to plus 3 and minus 1.5 Gs....

---

through 53,000 feet, and had just shifted the flaps from the gust to the faired position when the nose began to drop. Nole tried to retrim, but to no avail. The U-2 went out of control. The pilot made the highest-yet escape from an aircraft. Lockheed determined that grounding within the flap microswitch had caused the flaps to deploy.[7]

However, an alternative explanation was offered. Nole could have accidentally bumped the flap switch to the down position during his climb. This switch was located alongside the throttle. While the flaps were in the gust position this action would have no immediate effect. But when the pilot canceled the gust position, the flaps would seek the position of the flap switch.

The gust control position of the flaps was designed to reduce aerodynamic loads on the lightly-constructed wing and tail in turbulent air. It was routinely used during climbout. Lockheed recommended shifting back to the faired position at 30,000 feet. But because turbulence had not been ruled out as the cause of Carey's accident in 1956, pilots were subsequently advised to leave the flaps in the shifted position until 55,000 feet.[8]

Such were the uncertainties of technique, and of technology, during the early U-2 days. The pilot's handbook and checklists were frequently revised.

THE PARTIAL PRESSURE SUIT

The very earliest U-2 pilots had to wear an MC-3 suit consisting only of capstans, long tubes running from the shoulders to the wrist, and down the body and legs. When inflated, oxygen compressed to 5 psi held the capstans against the body, so that the occupant's body fluids would not expand if he were exposed to the low air pressures of the upper atmosphere. So the suits had to be really tight-fitting to be worth wearing at all. Despite being individually tailored to each pilot, partial-pressure suits were exceedingly uncomfortable, especially on a long flight. They stretched doubly tight across joints, such as elbows and knees, creating pressure points that could become intensely irritating as the hours wore on.

The MC-3 was later modified as the MC-3A to include a bladder on the torso and upper legs (pressurised to 1 psi), as well as the chest. This allowed the suit to be somewhat less tightly laced than was necessary when the capstans and chest bladder were providing the only constriction. The extra bladders also improved the air conditioning properties of the suit, since ventilation air circulated through them to rather greater effect than through the capstans. Despite this, most pilots perspired freely while wearing the pressure garment, and the long underwear that they wore beneath the suit was frequently soaking wet by the end of the flight. Some reckoned to lose a full pound of body weight this way, for each hour that they were confined within the suit.

To add to the general level of discomfort, there was a tight cork seal that fitted around the neck, over which was placed an MA-2 pressure helmet. Frank Powers described the neck seal as feeling like one was wearing a badly shrunk collar around which a tie was fastened too tight. Pilots often returned from long U-2 missions with the skin around their neck chafed red and raw. There were also special gloves with a pressure bladder stitched in, these being attached to the suit, and put on after the pilot had first donned a pair of white silk glove liners. Completing the outfit, there was an outer garment containing water flotation collar, parachute harness and seat pack, and protective coveralls on top of that. Heavy boots were worn to offset the lack of pressure protection for the feet. – C.P.

Oxygen leak

Problems with the life support system for the U-2 pilots caused three, possibly four accidents. On 19 December 1956, trainee CIA pilot Bob Ericson suffered a leak in his oxygen system during one of his final checkout flights from the Ranch. Early in the flight, he noticed that his oxygen consumption was greater than forecast on his "green card." The card was carried on all flights, and provided projected consumption curves for fuel and oxygen against which the pilot made hourly plots of his actual consumption. Ericson failed to heed the warning as his oxygen plot began to fall below the projection curve.

After four and a half hours of flight Ericson became hypoxic, and lost control during an emergency descent over Arizona. He was flying an aircraft still equipped with one of the "smoky" -37 engines, and fumes in the cockpit did not help as he removed his faceplate upon reaching 35,000

feet. As the aircraft oversped, Ericson struggled to jettison the canopy and bail out. Luckily he survived, and flew U-2s with the CIA and NASA for another 30 years![9]

A summary of official report into the accident that killed Lockheed test pilot Bob Sieker on 4 April 1957 noted that "the cause...was hypoxia from an undermined cause. Engine flameout due to hydraulic system failure and subsequent loss of cabin pressurization, malfunctioning cockpit seals, oxygen system and/or personal equipment were considered the most probable reason for the hypoxia." However, DPD Assistant Chief Jim Cunningham noted the report's revelation that Sieker took several candy bars aloft with him, which were never found. "He also had a known habit of opening his faceplate at altitude when he became hungry, and suffered from a lack of energy of the sort that sugar would correct. An open faceplate seal could have also been a contributing cause to the accident," Cunningham added.[10]

If correct, this was not the first time, nor the last, that U-2 pilots would remove their helmet faceplates in flight. How else would you scratch an itching nose!?

Hypoxia

Hypoxia caused two fatal accidents at the 4080th wing on successive days in July 1958. The first killed trainee RAF pilot Squadron Leader Chris Walker on 8 July. Walker was six hours into a high-altitude navigation training flight and over Amarillo, TX, when something went wrong. He

Colonel Jack Nole bailed out of a U-2 at 53,000 feet, deployed his parachute at high altitude, and lived to tell the tale. It was a long, slow trip down!

JACK NOLE'S GREAT ESCAPE

Seven years after he escaped from an out-of-control U-2 at 53,000 feet over Texas, Colonel Jack Nole described the incident in an article for Reader's Digest magazine.

"Suddenly, the plane's nose began to drop. There was no sound, no warning. I pulled the stick back into my lap, trying to bring the nose back up. But there was no control. In the far left corner of the instrument panel, the wing-flap position indicator told the story: the wing flaps were full down. I hadn't actuated the flaps to put them down—but there they were."

Nole found himself looking at the earth far below as the aircraft entered a dive. Despite extending the landing gear and the speed brakes, then shutting the engine off, he could not pull out. Then the tail section broke off. The crippled U-2 gyrated through one outside loop after another.

"With each huge somersault," said Nole, "I would fall out of my seat, and my helmet would crash against the canopy. When the plane turned upside down for the fourth time, my helmeted head smashed the canopy assembly loose."

Nole managed to contact the command post at Laughlin AFB to tell them he was bailing out. He unfastened the seat belt. As his head smashed against the canopy again, it sailed away into space and the pilot nearly followed, but his seat pack snagged against the ledge of the cockpit, and the fierce slipstream pinned him there for what seemed like an eternity: "There I was, bent over backwards against the fuselage, and the plane going end over end. I was afraid it might break up completely at any time, and I had better be free when it happened! I thrashed around, kicked and pulled, and finally came free."

Now he faced another life or death decision. During his struggles in the cockpit, Nole had been unable to locate the "green apple," a small ball valve that turned on the emergency oxygen supply from seat-pack to the pressure suit. "Normally, the valve was on your left side, tucked into the crease between your thigh and your hip," he recalled. "But the valve is green, the pressure suit is green, and the inside of the cockpit is green...."

With no emergency oxygen feeding the pressure suit, it was slowly beginning to deflate, and Nole detected the first signs of hypoxia as his vision began to fade. "Dimly, I realised I had two alternatives," he recalled. "The first was to let myself fall until my parachute opened automatically at the preset 14,000 feet. But it would take more than two minutes to free-fall those seven and a half miles; by that time, there was a good chance I'd have suffocated. The suit's made to force oxygen into you under pressure; it's not like breathing in air on the ground. In the suit, you open your mouth, oxygen flows in, and you have to make an effort to exhale. If I was unconcious when the chute opened, I would not be able to open the face plate of my helmet and breathe naturally. The suit is made to hold air inside, not to let it in from the surrounding atmosphere!"

The second alternative was to immediately open his parachute, and hope that he could then find the emergency oxygen valve to sustain him through what would be a lengthy descent. But this would entail a terrible risk; in just a few seconds, a body dropping through the thin air at his height could accelerate to 375 mph. A parachute snapping open to arrest such a descent could be torn to shreds in the slipstream, or else deploy with such force that the body to which it was attached could be ripped apart from the shock of its opening!

If by good fortune that didn't happen, the extreme cold would pose another threat to the pilot's survival, since it would take him half-an-hour to descend all the way from 53,000 feet with the parachute deployed. "Into my dimming vision floated the release ring of my parachute ripcord," said Nole. He took the risk and pulled it.

Miraculously, Nole's parachute opened gently, without a trace of shock. Accident investigators later surmised that since the pilot had been flung from the aircraft as it curved upward in an outside loop, his body had described a similar upward arc. Nole must have pulled the ripcord just as he reached the apex of this arc, and before he started to fall towards the earth at an ever-quickening pace.

"It opened so gently that I was perfectly horizontal in the air, at a level even with my chute," Nole continued. "Then I swung back like a giant pendulum until I was even with the chute on the other side." The giant oscillations continued in the thin air, with Nole apparently powerless to stop them: "Each time I swung, I was afraid that air would spill from the chute's high side and that it would collapse, dropping me like a stone. I began pulling the shroud lines at the top of each swing, in an effort to stop the oscillation." By now, the pilot had located and pulled the "green apple," but the exertion of trying to stop the giant swings was exhausting his emergency oxygen supply quite quickly. He would have to get outside air soon.

"Usually it's a simple matter to locate and pull the string, just below the chin, that releases the faceplate from the helmet," said Nole. Not this time, however! Nole had to painstakingly peel the pressure glove off his right hand before he was able to get the faceplate off. He was now at 20,000 feet, and still swinging wildly from side to side. For the first time in 17 years' of military flying, the veteran pilot was hideously airsick. "I threw up over half of Texas," he recalled.

By now Nole had company. Two other U-birds were airborne from Laughlin, along with a Cessna U-3 chase plane. Fellow pilots Dick Atkins, Warren Boyd and Dick Leavitt located the descending parachute and flew slow circles around it. Nole approached the ground, still oscillating violently. But luck was still on his side: "I came right down over one of those small, rolling Texas hills. On the one side of it was this big, flat-topped rock. As I drifted over the hill, my body swung back, and my dangling seat pack caught on the rock, and jerked me to a stop in the air, so that I fell backwards to the ground without injury."

Jack Nole had survived by far the highest parachute escape in history. It had taken 22 minutes. He was later told that it should have taken another 11 minutes, but those giant swings had spilled air from the chute and sped him down. Otherwise, he might not have descended to thicker and warmer air before his oxygen ran out. "We can only conclude that Colonel Nole survived through an act of God," the accident board reported.

- details from "I Bailed Out Ten Miles Up!" by Col Jack Nole, Reader's Digest, September 1964; "U-2 Pilot Bares Tale of Fantastic Parachute Jump," Del Rio News Herald, 26 September 1963; and 4080 SRW History, February 1958

HYPOXIA – A NEAR-FATAL INCIDENT, 1958

Every aspect of the life support system had to work properly—the high-altitude regime was unforgiving of errors. Pat Halloran recalls what happened when his oxygen hose was not properly connected before takeoff:

On a routine training flight I detected signs of hypoxia shortly after leveling off at about 64,000 feet. We had been trained in the altitude chamber to learn our individual warning signs of hypoxia. That training paid off in this case. I began to feel signs of heat and flushing on my face, followed shortly by an onset of hyperventilation. My helmet bladder collapsed around my head, and I experienced difficulty in breathing as I lost pressurized oxygen inside my helmet.

Realizing what was happening I quickly checked the oxygen system controls, but found nothing amiss. As I frantically evaluated my options (there weren't any) my vision rapidly began to close down. I happened to glance in one of the cockpit mirrors and saw my face plate breathing hose dangling loose from the connection cluster on the lower right side of my pressure suit. This area cannot normally be seen due to the restrictions of the pressure suit— which is one reason the mirrors were installed. I was able to grab the cluster connection in one hand and the breathing hose in the other and reconnect them, but I was fading fast.

I remember thinking that this was my last shot! But relief was immediate, as pressurized oxygen surged into my helmet. It was later determined that the initial connection of the hose on the ground by the life support technicians had been faulty, and it somehow came loose in flight. A modification to the system followed by installing small, safety clips on the hoses so as to preclude their accidental disconnecting. During the short time I was operating without pressure suit oxygen I was breathing the ambient cockpit pressurized air of 29,000 feet, so time of useful consciousness was extremely short.

THE SILENT BIRDMAN CLUB

On the wall of the Heritage Room at Beale AFB hangs a board containing a long list of names of those pilots who have found themselves returning to land in a U-2 without the benefit of an engine. Many of their stories are told elsewhere in this book. Here are some more:

Captain Jim Qualls: after four successive flameouts in the course of a seven-hour flight, the SAC pilot made a forced landing at a dirt airstrip 80 miles northeast of Laughlin AFB in September 1957
Captain Pat Halloran: wing tanks failed to feed due to maintenance error; sump tanks emptied before pilot made it back to Laughlin, for heavy and silent landing, 1957
Captain Art Leatherwood: autopilot problems caused high-altitude flameout over Texas and deadstick into Biggs AFB after six failed attempts to relight, March 1961
Major Pat Halloran (again!): after coasting-out of Cuba, March 1963, fuel control failure forced engine shutdown followed by a quiet landing at Eglin AFB
Captain Chuck Stratton: a blown oil seal caused a flameout and an early unpowered return to Laughlin AFB, April 1963
Bill Park: the Lockheed test pilot was another victim of closed fuel valves, leaving him with only sump tank fuel and a silent return to beautiful downtown Burbank
Major Ward Graham: made it safely into the small airfield at Flagstaff, Arizona, with only partial flaps and no drag chute in September 1965 after a 50-minute glide

---

called Mayday and "aircraft descending out of control." An eye witness saw him eject at medium-altitude, but the pilot never separated from the seat, and was killed when it hit the ground. Captain Al Chapin was killed 24 hours later over New Mexico on a similar high-altitude sortie.

Autopilot failures leading to loss of control were suspected in both accidents, until accident investigators checked the oxygen systems on other U-2s at Laughlin AFB and discovered excessive moisture. They concluded that ice had formed in the oxygen systems of the two aircraft that crashed. SAC restricted its U-2 fleet to 20,000 feet until various corrective actions could be implemented. The CIA did not follow suit, apparently more confident in the quality of its life support system maintenance, which was all performed by experienced tech reps from the Firewel company.[11]

An unfortunate feature of Walker's accident was that he failed to survive, despite using the ejection seat. The U-2 entered service in 1956 without one, to save weight. But in the accidents that killed pilots Sieker and Smith, it was obvious that they might have survived if a better means of escape had been provided. Smith was actually dangling from his aircraft as it hit the ground, encumbered by the various umbilical cords attached between his pressure suit and the bottom of the cockpit floor.

Still prebreathing from a portable oxygen cylinder, a U-2 pilot is helped into the cockpit where he will be hooked up to the aircraft's life support system. Problems with the oxygen supply led to serious incidents, and at least two fatal accidents, in the early days. (Lockheed C88-1447-87)

Lightweight ejection seat

Lockheed proposed fitting the lightweight seat from the Lockheed T2V Navy jet trainer. In August 1957 the Air Force agreed to install it for "training and other non-critical operations." The CIA was not keen on the idea, but did eventually follow suit. Before the seat could be added, another pilot made an unsuccessful attempt to bail out of a crippled U-2. Captain Benny Lacombe was killed 13 miles southeast of Laughlin on the night of 28 November 1957.[12]

But when Walker attempted to use the new ejection system in July 1958, the automatic lap belt failed to release because the mechanism was distorted from catapult and wind blast forces, according to the accident report. A "more reliable" initiator was fitted, but many pilots did not trust the rudimentary seat to work properly. And they were right. The subsequent problems with the U-2 ejection seat and oxygen system are discussed elsewhere in this book. Suffice it to note here that, between 1957 and 1965, Lockheed issued no fewer than 15 Service Bulletins describing modifications and upgrades to the U-2 escape system. In the same period, another 15 SBs were issued to cover changes to the life support system...oxygen regulators and valves, helmet faceplates and tie-downs, quick-disconnect features, and so on.

Landing accidents

Landing accidents continued to take their toll of U-2 pilots. The 4080th SRW introduced an airborne chase aircraft to fly in formation with novice pilots on their first few flights in the Dragon Lady. It was an L-27, the military version of the Cessna 310 twin-turboprop. The U-2 instructor pilot would radio instructions and encouragement from the L-27 (which was later redesignated U-3). Unfortunately, the chase plane could not prevent the fatal crash of trainee U-2 pilot Lt Paul Haughland on approach to Laughlin on 6 August 1958. He rolled rapidly to the left at 200 feet and struck the ground in a near-vertical attitude. The accident report noted that the flight manual did not sufficiently highlight the unusual stall characteristics.[13]

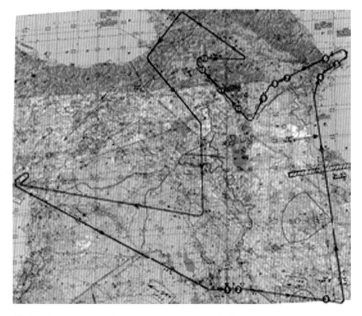

Mission planners supplied annotated maps that told U-2 pilots where to go, and when to turn their cameras on and off. This one shows the route of a shallow penetration of the Soviet Union's southern border with Turkey and Iran on 20 November 1956 by Frank Powers.

Learning to land the U-2 was a serious business. Usually, a near-stall at touchdown would do the trick. Unfortunately, each one of the Articles had slightly different stall characteristics! The Air Force used drag chutes for some landings. (NARA KKE 12287)

It was vital for U-2 pilots to establish the correct speed as they approached the threshold. But some pilots did not like to go around, if they found themselves at the wrong speed coming down the approach. Full nose-up trim was required for landing, and a rapid throttle movement to initiate a go-around could easily lead to an uncontrollable nose-up condition, followed by a stall and crash.[14]

On 13 September 1961, Det G pilot Buster Edens was returning to North Base after a long test flight. On final all seemed to be well until close to the threshold, when the aircraft suddenly stalled and dropped 100 feet like a stone. The main gear collapsed backwards into the fuselage and broke the sump tank. Fuel sloshed out, and also from where the wings had broken from the fuselage upon impact. Two small fires started.

Jim Cherbonneaux was mobile for this flight, and was quickly on the scene. Edens was concussed and in shock. Cherbonneaux got the canopy released and began unhooking the pilots' suit hoses and other straps (this was in the days before a quick disconnect system was provided). Then there was an explosion in the left wing, and the flames began spreading. Pilot and mobile were lucky to escape. "It seemed to take an eternity before I got everything undone," recalled Cherbonneaux. The two men scrambled clear just as the right wing and fuselage blew up. Edens swore that he had flown the correct speed schedule, and that's the way it looked to Cherbonneaux, too. According to the latter, there never was a proper investigation of the accident. Both he and Edens reckoned it had been caused by windshear.[15]

Spectacular incidents

In the 1960s the SAC wing began filming each landing at home base for postflight analysis. The camera caught some spectacular incidents, which were duly spliced together on video and shown as a warning to new pilots. The first such film was shot by accident; maintenance men were running a U-2 tracker camera on a test bench outside the hangar at Davis-Monthan at the very moment on 18 September 1964 when Major Robert Primrose stalled 2,000 feet short of the runway and slammed into the ground. The tracker lens was pointing in that direction and recorded the incident. "Pinky" Primrose was an experienced pilot, but according to the accident report, he was attempting a steep turn onto finals. The wind was gusting around the desert airbase at the time, and it forced Primrose to overshoot the turn.[16]

GREAT U-2 SAVES

ROGER COOPER, 1960

On 15 March 1960, Captain Roger Cooper of the 4080th wing was on the return leg of a U-2 sampling flight from Minot AFB to Great Bear Lake and back. He had risen to almost 70,000 feet above the desolate landscape. As he passed through 56 degrees north, almost above the middle of Sakatchewan, his electrical system began to malfunction. He began losing engine instruments, and so began a slow descent while reducing power to avoid an overtemp. Soon thereafter the engine flamed out, and thick white smoke filled the cockpit, almost obscuring the instrument panel. Cooper managed to radio a warning on HF to his mobile in the command post at Minot AFB, almost 500 miles to the southeast, before he also lost battery power.

He was nearly 13 miles above the frozen wastes. The odds were stacked against a successful ejection at such a height, and yet if he stayed with the aircraft, there was the imminent possibility of an electrical fire taking serious hold. He opened the ram air position to clear the smoke, hoping that the lack of oxygen at this height would cause the fire to go out. Luckily, it did. He continued to descend, but turned 180 degrees to his reciprocal heading, since he knew the weather was better to the north. There were two possible emergency landing fields within reach to the south, but Cooper knew that there was a low overcast with blowing snow at both. Instead, he decided to try for a deadstick landing on one of the many frozen lakes beneath his flightpath.

As yet, however, he could not see one. There was a solid overcast beneath him, but since he still had airspeed, rate of climb, and turn and bank instruments, he felt confident that the cloud could be successfully penetrated. But as he glided slowly towards the tops of the clouds at 25,000 feet the turn and bank indicator stopped working! In the murk, he would have to resort to using the magnetic compass as a bank indicator. Fearing disorientation, he prepared to eject if the aircraft got out of control, but the clouds were surprisingly smooth, and he emerged into the clear at 15,000 feet with wings still level.

Now he had difficulty in seeing the ground, because the canopy and most of the windscreen were covered in frost. He tried to jettison the canopy, but it merely flipped into the open position. Now he could not read his maps because of the wind blast, but he did notice a frozen lake below with a sawmill on one shore. He prepared to land by installing the ejection seat pin, tightening his seat belt and shoulder harness, and manually extending the gear.

At 7,000 feet he noticed a radio station off to his right, and decided to fly over it to attract attention. This meant selecting another lake, but there were plenty to choose from, and he eventually made an almost textbook approach, and a two-point landing in the snow. The U-bird rolled 300 feet to a gentle stop, and Cooper quickly evacuated. But there was no more sign of fire, or of any other external damage. The pilot was just beginning to unpack his emergency survival equipment when a rescue helicopter appeared and carried him off to warm safety. The aircraft was later flown off the lakebed, and Cooper was cited for his "sense of responsibility and calm, professional airmanship."

DEKE HALL, 1960

On 13 October 1960, Captain Robert "Deacon" Hall was ferrying a U-2A from Laughlin AFB to Hickam AFB as part of the first Crowflight deployment to Australia by the 4080th SRW. Two more U-2s were flying some way ahead of him, at the same optimum altitude for long-range ferry—60,000 feet.

Hall was almost exactly halfway between California and Hawaii when he heard a dull thud, and the hydraulic gauge began to wind down. Since the drive motor that boosted fuel to the engine above 40,000 feet worked off the hydraulic system, the engine soon flamed out. Hall declared an emergency on HF, which was picked up by a passing Pan Am airliner and relayed to Hickam. He drifted down to 35,000 feet in order to get a relight, but had already worked out that the engine would quit on him again if he attempted to rise above 40,000 feet.

Hall did some rapid calculations. Now confined to a maximum 39,000 feet, Hall's U-2 was heading smack against a strong eastbound jetstream. He concluded that he did not have enough fuel to reach Hickam. However, Hall reckoned that he might be able to glide in from 200 miles out of Hickam, if the fuel supply lasted that long.

He later described a comic exchange with the Pan Am pilot who acted as radio relay: "I asked the guy to tell Hickam I had lost my engine, and was declaring an emergency. He asked me how many engines I had. I told him just one. There was a pause. 'You really have got an emergency!' came the reply. Later, after I had relit, he asked me for all the usual information—souls on board, ETA, fuel remaining, and so on. I told him between two and a half and three hours fuel onboard, with ETA Hickam three to three and a half hours. Another long pause. 'You're not going to make it!' he exclaimed."

But Hall did indeed make it. The fuel finally ran out with 150 miles to go, but the aircraft arrived overhead Hickam in perfect shape, at 3,000 feet and 100 knots. During training flights, U-2 pilots practiced frequently for such an engine-out approach, and Hall was now at what they termed the "high key point." From here, the pilot was supposed to turn into a downwind leg with flaps at 25 degrees and landing gear down, reaching 1,500 feet at the "low key point" and 800 feet as he turned onto finals. Then he could also extend the speed brakes.

But Hall's aircraft had no hydraulics, and although the gear had manually extended, he had no flaps or speedbrakes. Also, as he pointed out, "we never practised with no fuel on board!" By the time he reached low key he was going much too fast, and with not enough altitude left to bleed off speed in a turn, he had no option but to dive for the end of the runway and hope that the brake chute did its stuff. He crossed the threshold at 120 knots instead of 80, but the chute popped, and he came to an uneventful halt. As he climbed out of the cockpit, he turned to the other two ferry pilots and called for the customary welcoming beer. Captains Bobby Gardiner and Bob Powell had landed more than an hour earlier. "We're sorry, Deke," they replied. "We figured you've been gone so long that you weren't gonna make it. So we drunk it!"

MORE GREAT U-2 SAVES

JIM CHERBONNEAUX, 1961

After passing over the northern coast of Cuba the autopilot went completely beserk. It did its best to pull the wings off in a sudden, climbing turn. I quickly disengaged it and took the next couple of minutes in getting everything back on an even keel. When I tried to reengage the autopilot, nothing happened. Then I found what I had previously missed on the sun-drenched instrument panel—the "generator out" light was on.

I checked the switch and all the circuit breakers. After going through my emergency checklist a second time, I finally realized the generator was dead. I knew I had to save what was left of the battery for my faceplate heat, so that it would not frost over while I was in Cuban airspace. I turned north and continued until reaching Key West, then west onto a heading that would get me back to Laughlin. With my faceplate staying relatively clear and all the non-electrical stuff working, I figured I could make it across the Gulf before having to descend. I knew the weather was clear all the way back to Laughlin, so I pressed on to the west for about an hour. How dumb I was! The faceplate did start frosting around the edges. So I turned back towards Key West—and then it frosted over completely! Heading west the sun had been in my face, and it must have been helping the weak battery keep the faceplate clear.

What now? It is almost impossible to hand-fly a U-2 at altitude while looking cross-eyed at the tip of your nose. I felt the aircraft begin to shudder and shake. I had to do something drastic if I did not want to become shark bait in the waters below. There was no other choice but to open the faceplate to see enough to fly the aircraft. I kept it open until I started getting hypoxic, then I snapped it back in place. I kept on descending in this manner until I could see a coastline ahead. Then I began letting down. At 40,000 feet, my cockpit was pressurized to 18,000 feet and I could breath naturally.

As I approached Key West, the off-center position of the yoke told me that I had a heavy right wing, and at 10,000 feet I did a stall series to check out the handling characteristics and the no-flap stall speed. The right wing stalled out violently at 90 knots. I rolled into a steep left bank, hoping that gravity would transfer fuel out of the right wing, through the fuselage tank, and into the left wing. I kept that bank up for about 15 minutes, but it was a self-defeating proposition. To keep the nose up, I had to use extra power, and that was using more fuel out of the fuselage tank than was coming in from the high wing.

The fuselage tank got down to half full: it was decision time. Either eject, or get the landing right first time. I flew down to initial approach OK—one thousand feet. But when I pulled the throttle to near idle, it reduced the flow of hot air to the canopy, and all the humidity in the cockpit condensed. I managed to rub off enough to line up on the runway. With no flaps or dive brakes I was low and fast. At the threshold I shut down the engine. When my wheels hit the ground, it was all I could do to keep the right wing up with the ailerons. I used most of the runway before it stalled out and fell to the ground. When the skid hit, it dragged the aircraft off the right side of the runway. When we finally stopped, I sat still for a while and let my heartbeat get back to normal.

FORREST WILSON, 1962

Flying south on a sampling mission out of Eielson AFB, Alaska, on 9 October 1962, Lt Col Forrest Wilson experienced a generator failure almost 300 miles from the nearest land. Most of the instruments failed, together with the autopilot and communications. Wilson turned around, set course for Kodiak, and began an emergency descent.

Having set up a descent, Wilson was faced with the prospect of navigating from an uncertain position to a suitable landing field, with only a stand-by magnetic compass and altimeter to guide him. In the Arctic darkness, he had to read these instruments with a hand-held flashlight, peering through the frost that was building up on the faceplate of his pressure helmet after the cockpit heating failed.

Wilson's body was going numb from the extreme cold, which began penetrating his pressure suit. Fatigue developed as he fought to maintain pressure on the control yoke—he had no power to correct the out-of-trim condition that had developed. The pilot arrived overhead Kodiak, having reached an altitude at which he could remove his faceplate. But the runway lights were not turned on, and despite flying over the field three times at 500 feet, Wilson was unable to attract any attention from below.

Rather than trying to land on an unlit field, he climbed back to 27,000 feet and flew 200 miles more to reach Elmendorf AFB. Approaching the base, he found that there was only enough power in the battery to extend the flaps a few degrees and provide a small amount of nose trim. He repeated the process every 10 minutes until he had 20-degrees of flap and the proper trim for landing.

Wilson made a safe landing, three and half hours after his difficulties began. He won the Kolligian Trophy for this epic flight. – C.P.

According to the book, a U-2 was not to be landed in crosswinds of more than 15 knots. This was a significant constraint on U-2 operations. Sometime in the early 1960s, Lockheed test pilots demonstrated U-2 landings in gusts of 32 knots and 90 degrees of crosswind component. The trick was to lower the downwind wing, so as to drag it on the runway, to counter the cross wind effect. The demonstration was spectacular, but the Air Force decided not to increase the crosswind limit as standard procedure.[17]

Over the years there were various proposals to solve the crosswind problem, such as a ventral fin beneath the nose, or a steerable main wheel. None were ever adopted. When the U-2R came along the limit was raised to 20 knots for a time, but later it was reduced to 15 knots again. This remains the limit today (12 knots for touch-and-goes).

T-speed

There were two keys to a successful landing in the U-2. The first was to accurately compute the necessary speed over the threshold, which depended on the aircraft's weight and the amount of flap to be used. This "T- speed" was a minimum 12 percent above stall speed, and the pilot added 30 knots more to arrive at his pattern entry speed, 20 knots more for the correct downwind speed, and another 10 knots for the start of finals. Ideally, this last 10 knots would bleed off down the final approach so that the aircraft arrived at the threshold at T-speed, at an altitude of 10 feet.

The second key to a good landing was to ensure that the fuel was precisely balanced in the long wings. The recommended procedure was to slow to landing approach speed while at 20,000 feet, and before making the standard instrument letdown. If one wing dropped early as the speed was cut back, then fuel had to be transferred to the other wing by an electric pump. A final check for lateral trim was supposed to be accomplished on the downwind leg. A simple mechanical device helped the process: a pointer and plate was attached to the control yoke. Pilots noted the extent to which the pointer was off-center during their after take-off check. It would be in the same position for landing if the fuel was correctly balanced.

A U-2A of the 4080th SRW flies over Texas. The SAC wing lost seven aircraft and six pilots in its first two years. (NARA KKE 13567)

Landing the U-2 was a particular problem for the Nationalist Chinese pilots, who entered the program from 1959. Sometimes they failed to get the fuel balance right before making an approach. Other times they managed this, but simply could not hack the final few feet before touchdown, when the plane had to be virtually stalled onto the runway. Lockheed suggested an adjustment to the fixed stall strips on the inboard wing leading edge for their benefit. But this adjustment made it difficult for the pilots to distinguish the stall from the mach buffet at altitude.

The retractable stall strips that were added in 1965-66 helped keep the wings level during the crucial final moments of landing. The pilot pulled a T-handle by his right knee that extended them from the leading edge by a half-inch. But the landing accidents continued. On 17 October 1966 Major Leslie White stalled on final approach during his first flight. "The pilot survived, but the airplane was washed out," noted Kelly Johnson drily. He blamed the crash on poor training procedures and inexperienced instructors.[18]

The partial pressure suit, made by the David Clark company and modeled here by Frank Powers in 1963. It had to be tight-fitting, if it was to protect the pilot from a cockpit depressurization, or a high-altitude escape from the aircraft. (Lockheed U2-91-0001C)

At this point in the approach the U-2 pilot is hoping that he calculated the T-speed correctly, and that no unexpected crosswind will complicate the last few moments before touchdown. (via Mick Roth)

Chinese pilots

The Chinese pilots attracted more than their fair share of criticism, especially after Steve Sheng destroyed two Articles at D-M within six months in 1964, and Captain Andy Fan wrote off another one on 22 March 1966. Fan ejected safely from his aircraft and was allowed to continue training.

But the CAF also supplied some "hot sticks" who could not be faulted. Major Pete Wang was one of these, and his American colleagues were devastated when he perished in the crash off Taiwan on 22 October 1965. "He was one of the best, always studying the ops manuals and following the correct procedures," noted one CIA cable after the accident.

Wang had just completed a 180-degree turn at high altitude. Eyewitnesses on the shoreline saw the plane hit the water, but no parachute. Analysis of the strip chart from Birdwatcher showed that the plane had first exceeded max mach and positive g limits. Then came alternating negative and positive g readings, and fluctuating fuel pressure, which were symptoms of a wildly-tumbling aircraft that had probably lost its horizontal tail and wings. Loss of cockpit pressurization and other indications of a flameout followed as the altitude channels showed a rapid descent through 60, 50, and 40,000 feet. After 40 seconds of this the transmissions had ceased, probably because the wire antenna had been ripped off as the plane spun towards the sea.

There was no indication that the pilot had ejected, nor that he had jettisoned the canopy prior to a bailout. An extensive search was nevertheless mounted, but all that was discovered were two of the aircraft's oxygen bottles. Wang had presumably been pinned in the cockpit by heavy g-forces.

Kelly Johnson disputed the Accident Board's conclusion that a "hardover" autopilot signal was to blame for Wang's loss of control at high altitude. "For the last 15 years, all LAC aircraft have been designed so that the pilot can readily overpower the autopilot," he cabled Project HQ. Yet another debate ensued about the capability of the U-2 autopilot. OSA directed a detailed examination of the system. This found a number of deficiencies, especially the precession rates of the gyro platform. Lockheed was asked to provide a fault monitoring system that would alert the pilot when an autopilot malfunction occurred.[19]

Deke Hall ejects

Whatever the cause, Wang's accident proved that the U-2 was not built to survive a major upset. On 25 February 1966, Deke Hall confirmed this in

---

FATAL CHANGE OF MIND

On 17 February 1966, Captain Charlie Wu Tse Shi was on a high altitude training flight over the middle of Taiwan when his EGT indicator rose sharply. When it pegged at 950 degrees Wu suspected an engine fire, shut down the J75, and began a descending glide. Much of the country was covered in cloud, but he decided to head for the long runway at Chiang Ching Kuo airbase, near Taichang. At 40,000 feet he was nicely set up for CCK, and as the descent continued, he reported the 12,000 foot runway in sight. For some reason, though, he decided to land at the much smaller Taichung airport. Bad move! Although it was slightly closer to his present position, the runway was only 4,900 feet, and he would have to land downwind. Battling a 15-knot following wind, Wu overshot the threshold and drifted right. He touched down on the grass halfway down the field, bounced twice, and crashed into a farmhouse beyond the far end of the runway. The pilot and one person in the farmhouse was killed; another four were injured.

Accident investigators recovered the EGT indicator and were able to bench-test it. It operated normally until a spurious voltage was applied, which drove the needle off the maximum end of the scale. It seemed that some errant arcing—perhaps from the HF antenna tuner—had caused a false EGT indication. There was nothing wrong with the engine!

The final accident report found the primary cause to be "the pilot's failure to accomplish a satisfactory flameout landing, complicated by weather, cockpit fogging, and possible disorientation." – C.P.

---

spectacular fashion over Edwards. After refueling practice he pulled up and away from the KC-135 tanker. The left wing broke off at the root. Hall ejected and landed safely.

There were plenty of eyewitnesses. The tanker crew saw it, including the boomer and an extra passenger, Flt Lt Alastair Sutherland, the RAF navigator attached to Det G. So did Det G pilot Tom McMurtry, who was observing the refueling from one of the T-33s assigned to the CIA unit.

The characteristic yoke, by which a U-2 pilot worked the (unboosted) flight controls. In emergency situations, he had to wrestle with it to regain control, before the aircraft stalled or oversped.

This head-on view shows the smaller intake of the original, J57-powered U-2A version.

PILOT TRAINING THEORIES

Opinions on how to check out new pilots in the U-2 were many and varied, especially before the two-seat trainer finally came along in 1972. Here are some extracts from a 1968 report dealing with the training of nationalist Chinese pilots at Edwards North Base. Two years earlier, Project HQ had taken on this task from SAC, which simply did not have enough Articles left to do the job at D-M.

The 10 T-33 transition missions designed to familiarize the students with the local flying area, voice procedures etc was not excessive. To assist in voice procedures evaluation, a mic-actuated tape recorder in the T-33s would be of great assistance...Although a new student is considered completely "checked out" at the completion of T-33 training, the first solo flight is accomplished in the U-2. It is therefore recommended that the initial solo flight be scheduled in the T-33 which would be an IFR round-robin flight...

The first three U-2 missions require a U-3 chase which should be continued. The first mission also requires a U-2 chase, if available, and the second a T-33 chase. Both of these missions were flown with a T-33 chase, which worked out very satisfactory. Mission #3 requires a pressure suit for familiarization. The (trainee pilot) experienced difficulty from a comfort standpoint, as this mission requires considerable time in the traffic pattern...Mission #4 – Recommend that engine shutdown be accomplished at 55,000 feet in order that the pilot experience more realistic suit inflation. The current syllabus requires suit inflation at 45,000 feet.

During initial transition missions requiring touch and go's, the U-2 flap position is left up to the IP. For (Chinese) training it is recommended that touch and go's be executed with flaps in order to avoid an excessive trim change...We used a maximum of 8 knots as a limiting crosswind landing factor...TV coverage of all takeoffs and landings was, without a doubt, an invaluable training aid and should be continued.

For all training missions requiring flight lines, an accurate tracker film plot was accomplished, which included an assessment of percentage error. As an incentive "gimmick" these results were plotted on a mission board posted in the trailer.

HEAD ON VIEW OF IMPACT DAMAGE

One of the many early-model U-2s that did not make it back in one piece. Of the 55 that were built, 37 were destroyed in accidents, and another seven were shot down. (via Bob Birkett)

The Accident Report found that Hall's application of aileron, at the same time as positive "G" was being applied in the climb, applied a twisting moment that the wing could not sustain. A CIA cable noted Hall's comment that the "G" forces that he applied were less than those encountered at take-off. "This is understandable where control forces are smoothly applied, and serves to underline the ease with which destructive forces can be applied."[20]

On 1 June 1967 Captain Sam Swart of the 100th SRW learned this the hard way. He was climbing out of Barksdale AFB for his first overflight of Cuba. The weather was poor, with thunderstorms and turbulence. At 45,000

It was not until 1972 that a two-place trainer was finally built, after yet another landing accident persuaded the Air Force. 66953 was the first "two-headed goat." (Lockheed C-1057-03)

LEARNING TO LAND THE U-2, 1974

After the U-2CT was introduced, the training of new U-2 pilots was a less haphazard exercise. But there were still some anxious moments, especially on that nerve-wracking IQ1 mission. Captain Glenn Perry, who made that flight on 18 October 1974, later described it in detail for Air Force Magazine:

We proceed to the end of the runway to do a high-speed taxi exercise. I am congratulating myself for exceptional performance in handling my first tail-dragger when the IP barks "Fly the wings!," and I realize that the left pogo is on the ground. At airspeeds of about 10 knots the wings are flyable, even though the aircraft is not. Proper technique demands that the wings be held absolutely level throughout the ground roll. That is no easy task when all other controls are being worked feverishly in order to track down the runway!

I am trying to avoid a ground loop when we finally come to a stop. All this effort, and I'm not even airborne yet! The IP takes the bird and demonstrates a maximum performance take-off. In only a few hundred feet we leap off the ground and climb nearly straight up. I keep waiting for the back side of a loop, but it never comes....

The first touch and go—a demonstration by the IP—shows graphically what kind of learning situation I am about to face. The IP sets a fine example as he reaches the end of the runway at between five and 10 feet altitude and exactly on computed threshold speed. Then the throttle comes to idle, and he continues a steady descent as the Mobile vehicle dashes madly down the runway beside us, with the officer calling off our height.

I suddenly realize how tough it's going to be to see out of this thing. The glare shield and instrument panel obscure everything except side vision and a tiny glimpse of the far end of the airfield. "Eight feet...six feet...four...two...one foot...holding one foot...tail's coming down...one foot...hold it off!" The U-2 shakes violently, stalls completely, and slams sharply onto the runway. I am informed over the intercom that that was a perfect textbook landing.

The next landing is mine. My pattern is rough and crude, and I am impressed with the effort needed to fly the U-2. It is like a headstrong child: it demands constant attention to make it obey. Somehow, I manage to maneuver to the landing threshold at approximately the correct airspeed and altitude. I put the throttle to idle and listen for Mobile's calls. "Eight feet...six...four...two...one...hold it off." Sloppy, but I luck out. It is nowhere near the desired full stall, but at least it is close to two points, and the bird does not come back off the runway.

But once I'm on the runway, my problems have only just begun. All my briefing and determination to the contrary, I allow the stick to go forward in an obvious gesture of relief at being on the ground in one piece. The tail breaks loose and starts to do its own thing from one side to the other. I desperately jab at the rudders and finally reduce the oscillations to something more manageable. The unavaoidable impression is that any minute now this thing is going to swap ends.

"Raise your right wing!" I have completely forgotten about the wings and am rolling along on the right pogo. "Raise your left wing." Wings-level eludes me completely as I bounce from one pogo to the other. "Flaps are up. Reset trim and go when ready." One glance inside the cockpit to check the trim, and I'm headed off the runway again. I slam the rudder, add power, and breathe easier as we end that torment by becoming airborne.

The remainder of my landings are a little better, but my control on the runway does not improve at all. It seems all I have learned is how to recover from one disastrous situation after another. Finally we make a full stop, and I realize how exhausted I am. Taxiing back to the parking ramp, I look inside the cockpit for an instant, and the plane wanders off the center line. Even at 10 knots, the beast wants to destroy me!

- from "Learning to Land the U-2" by Capt Glenn Perry II, Air Force Magazine, January 1976

---

feet he heard a thump and started a descending turn to return to base. But the aircraft broke up and he ejected. Examination of the wreckage showed that the wings failed in similar fashion to Hall's accident over Edwards.[21]

On 21 May 1968 there was another inflight breakup of a U-2C when Major Vic Milam lost control at 42,000 feet over Arizona and was obliged to eject. He was lucky not to collide with wreckage from the disintegrating aircraft on the way down. But Hall, Swart, and Milam all successfully ejected from their crippled U-2s, proving at least that the seat did now work.

At this time, the improved and enlarged U-2R was being introduced with a zero-zero ejection seat. Lockheed studied the addition of a similar seat to the remaining early models. Anticipating the phaseout of the U-2C by 1970, the Air Force elected not to proceed.

But 1970 came, and six of the early models were still flying. At Davis-Monthan, the 100th SRW was using 66952 and 66953 for training. At North Base, Article 383 (66716) performed similar duties for Det G. Three more were still flying with the AFFTC at South Base. The idea of replacing the

The U-2CT proved very popular, and a second one was converted in 1976. The two trainers were not retired until 1987. (NARA KKE 58310)

seats was raised again. After all, as one memo from OSA noted, "a new and inexperienced pilot is placed in the most hazardous configuration possible when he is asked to learn to fly using the U-2C."[22]

Two-place trainer

Year after year, someone in the U-2 program would call for a two-place trainer to be built. Somehow, the calls went unheeded until a series of events forced the issue in 1971-72.

On 18 November 1971, trainee pilot Captain John Cunney was killed at D-M in 66952. He landed heavily, wing low, and tried to go around, but stalled and crashed onto the runway. In early 1972, the U-2C was chosen as the platform for the ALSS project, which meant pulling the six other early models out of storage—and training more pilots to fly them. This move was in process when, in early May 1972, Captain Usto Schultz bounced 66953 heavily on one of his first landings and stalled during the rebound. The aircraft hit left wingtip and tail-first, the main gear collapsed, and the sump tank caught fire.[23]

The badly-damaged aircraft was trucked to Palmdale. Kelly Johnson quoted $1 million to rebuild it. Two weeks later 15th Air Force commander General P.K. Carlton sent Colonel Tony Martinez to Lockheed to discuss making 66953 into a trainer. "It's very late to do this," Johnson remarked, but Martinez explained the serious training problem that SAC was running into. Lockheed estimated $5-6 million to do the job, and the Air Force gave the go-ahead.[24]

In typical Skunk Works fashion, the job was done in five months. Ed Baldwin led the conversion team. Parts from three other crashed aircraft were used. Major George Worley was the project leader from the 100th SRW, advising on which controls and gauges should be replicated in the raised second cockpit, where the instructor pilot would sit. Lockheed chief test pilot Bill Park made the first flight of the converted U-2CT on 13 February 1973. Eleven days later, Worley flew it from Palmdale to D-M with crew chief TSgt Jose Ortiz in the front seat. It was the first time an enlisted man had ever flown in a U-2.[25]

With the strange-looking "two-headed Goat" safely delivered to D-M, Worley led a redesign of the training syllabus. New pilots would make five accompanied flights in the U-2CT before going solo. First, though,

they would be given one hour's taildragger experience in a Bellanca Decathlon at nearby Ryan Airport, Tucson.

The U-2CT proved very popular. The Cessna U-3 used for chasing new pilots on their first U-2 flights was phased out. Det G requested that the next two Chinese pilots that were due to be checked out in the U-2R at North Base be given four rides in the SAC trainer first. The request was granted. In 1976 a second U-2CT was added, a conversion of 66692. The two trainers moved to Beale with the rest of the U-2s in 1976, and were not finally retired until 1987.

But the landing problems did not go away completely. In 1973, Captain Dan Riggs was blamed when the gear of a U-2C collapsed on landing after a bad bounce. Fortunately, the aircraft was not badly damaged. 100th SRW commander Don White contested the Accident Board verdict, and when test pilot Bill Park experienced a similar bounce, Kelly Johnson realized that the proper operation of the U-2C landing gear's anti-porpoise valve had been affected by changed maintenance procedures.[26]

After that affair, the rejuvenated U-2C fleet flew without incident until 29 June 1975, when Captain Terry Rendleman experienced flight control problems at high altitude over Germany during the Constant Treat deployment of the ALSS. The aircraft entered Mach tuck and Rendleman ejected safely.

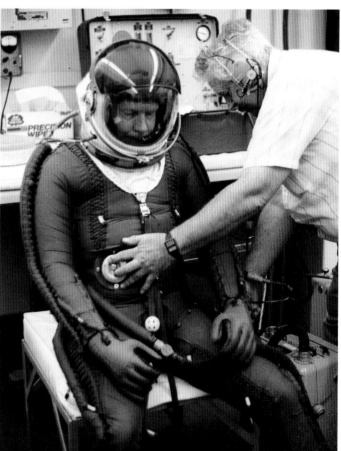

The first U-2CT on approach to Davis-Monthan AFB.

In the 1970s, the early-model U-2 life support system was modified so that a more comfortable helmet from the full-pressure suit could be worn with the partial-pressure suit.

Remarkable

Saving the best till last, this chapter ends with one of the most remarkable of all U-2 accidents. On 31 January 1981, Captain Edward Beaumont was in the early stages of checkout at Beale AFB, having made his first trip in the U-2CT only nine days earlier. This day, he was flying one of the U-2C models shortly before they were retired. On a bright winter's day he performed a number of touch-and-gos, and then climbed out for some work at medium altitude. After this he reported descending through 14,000 feet. Some time later, his mobile control officer on the ground at Beale was surprised to hear Beaumont key the mike, but make no transmission. Instead, all that could be heard was a heavy breathing sound as the U-2 pilot's transmitter remained open, but silent. The tower was alerted, and a T-37 trainer that was also flying locally was instructed to rendezvous with the errant U-2 and attract Beaumont's attention.

As the two pilots in the T-37 drew alongside they could hardly believe their eyes. The U-2 pilot appeared to be slumped at the controls, with the aircraft in a gentle, turning descent. Beaumont had had a catatonic seizure, and was completely unconscious. With the accompanying pilots in the T-37 powerless to intervene, the U-2 floated slowly towards the Sierra foothills north of Oroville. As it neared the sloping ground, some high voltage power transmission lines barred the way. The T-37 pilots braced themselves for a searing explosion as the black airframe flew into the 230,000-kilovolt wires.

It never happened. Incredibly, the U-2 clipped the bottom two wires with a wingtip, but failed to incinerate. In fact, the contact with the power lines had the effect of rolling the aircraft into the correct attitude for a forced landing in an adjacent cow pasture. Had its wingtip not been flipped up in this way, the aircraft would have cartwheeled as it impacted the gently sloping terrain with one wing low. As the astonished T-37 pilots orbited overhead, the U-bird flopped into the muddy field and ground to a halt with the engine running. Fuel began spilling from a ruptured tank, but it ran downhill and therefore failed to ignite.

The sudden arrival on terra firma revived the stricken pilot. Although confused, he managed to shut the engine down. But the drama was not yet over. As the still-groggy Beaumont began to extricate himself from the aircraft, his foot slipped and caught in the D-ring of the ejection seat, which

One of the last U-2C models flown by the 9th SRW is returning to the ramp at Beale in 1979. In 1981, Captain Edward Beaumont made one of the most remarkable of all U-2 pilot escapes from one of these aircraft.

ROLLING THE U-2

...was not recommended, but it did happen. Captain Ronnie Rinehart was on one of his first high flights in 1972 when he began encountering what he thought was the Mach buffet. He slowed down, but the buffet continued, so Rinehart eased off on the throttle a little more. This failed to correct the condition, so he repeated the process. The aircraft suddenly stalled, snap-rolled, and entered a high-speed spin. Somehow the aircraft did not come apart, and Rinehart managed to regain control. When he got down, they could tell he had survived some extraordinary maneuvers by examining the film from the aircraft's tracker camera—every few frames, the view of the ground was replaced by one of the sky!

During their long careers flying U-2s for the CIA, Marty Knutson and Barry Baker also spun and rolled in the aircraft, yet managed to bring them home.

So did Captain Don Evans, a test pilot with the "Smokey Joe" unit at Edwards. Unlike the others, though, he had an airborne witness, since he was flying the two-place U-2D with Captain Bill Frazier behind him as observer. Frazier recalled:

"Don was bending down to change a radio frequency or something, and the nose dropped. I felt this god-awful buzz and saw the altimeter unwinding. But I had no attitude instruments in the back. I said: 'what's going on?' He said: 'Hang on!' The next thing I knew we were upside down. We did a complete roll and bottomed out at about 50,000 feet. Don later told me that we had gotten to a 90-degree bank and he didn't dare stop it. So we just completed the roll, but we pulled Gs and just about lost it. Don was a small guy, and he had to put his feet up on the instrument panel to gain enough leverage to pull the yoke back. We popped rivets in the tail, and the aircraft was grounded for a fortnight for inspections and repair."

Possibly as a result of a trainee pilot damaging the tail during landing, this U-2CT at Beale AFB in the early 1980s had temporarily "borrowed" one from a black-painted single-seater.

he had failed to make safe. It fired through the canopy, flinging the pilot upwards with it. Beaumont's body described a somersault, but he landed on his feet to one side of the aircraft, while the seat thudded into the ground nearby. His only injury was a chipped tooth! When the preliminary acci-

dent report was circulated, SAC Generals and Lockheed managers alike thought that someone had made up the whole story as a joke. Not surprisingly, Beaumont was scrubbed from the U-2 program on medical grounds. The U-2C that ended its flying days in a cow pasture (66714) is now on display at Beale, outside the 9th RW headquarters.

36

Flying the Larger Models

When the larger U-2R flew in 1967, it was the product of many lessons learned from the original version of the U-2. Moreover, there was a significant input during the design stage from pilots and maintainers. But the R-model was still the Dragon Lady. The basic airplane characteristics remained the same. Prolonged flight at high altitude was still far from routine; the margin between mach and stall buffet was still only 15 knots at the highest altitudes. Landings were still a challenge. Flameouts and electrical and autopilot malfunctions were rarer now, but if they happened, a significant amount of flying skill, plus physical and mental endurance, was required to bring the U-bird home safely.

In some respects, the U-2R was more of a handful than its predecessor, especially because of that 100-foot wing. The very first U-2R accident in November 1968 was caused by a failure to appreciate just how important it was to have the fuel correctly balanced before making an approach. Trainee Chinese pilot David Lee ground-looped at Edwards North Base after his left wing dropped rapidly just before touchdown. Lee had not taken enough notice of a previous write-up on the aircraft: "excessive fuel transfer required left to right in the outboards."[1]

One month later, RAF Flt Lt Dick Cloke also ground-looped at North Base. He was making an emergency landing after his canopy unlatched during climbout! The plexiglass shattered and some was ingested into the engine, but the frame remained hanging on the left side of the Article. The British pilot dumped fuel and requested a landing on the lakebed. He noted a slight right yoke position during a pre-landing slow-speed test, which he attributed to wing or aileron damage. Unfortunately, the real cause was unbalanced fuel again. On approach the yoke moved further. Five seconds after the main gear made contact, the left wing dropped rapidly to the lakebed and the aircraft made a slow, graceful ground loop.[2]

First loss

A landing accident also caused the first loss of a U-2R and its pilot. On 24 November 1970, CAF pilot Denny Huang Chi Hsien was returning to Taoyuan after a routine, high-altitude training flight. At touchdown, he skipped slightly and began drifting to the right. A 12-knot crosswind didn't help. The aircraft left the runway, and Huang applied power to go around. But before the engine could spool up, the aircraft struck a 6-foot high runway marker. It then started a slow, left climbing turn, but the nose was high and the aircraft stalled. It fell to the ground and burst into flames. The Accident Board recommended that the Dash One pilot's handbook be amended to emphasize that a go-around should not be attempted after loss of directional control upon landing.[3]

The second loss of a U-2R was on 15 August 1975, when Captain John Little ejected from an aircraft he was ferrying back to the U.S. from U-Tapao. In company with another U-2R and a KC-135, Little took off from the Thai base on a very dark night. The group had not been airborne long when his plane developed autopilot problems, and Little lost control as it oversped. The tail came off, and Little ejected into the Gulf of Thailand, where he bobbed around in his life raft until being picked up by a fishing boat the next morning. He never flew the U-2 again, as was the SAC tradition in those days.

Rumor control was very active after this crash. The story was that a package of drugs had been concealed in the tail, to be retrieved in the U.S. This caused the controls to bind, and thus, the crash. The OSI investigated for several months, but found nothing to support the story. A few months after the crash a Thai fisherman recovered the tail. Accident Board member and U-2 pilot Dave Young bought it back from him. No package was found.[4]

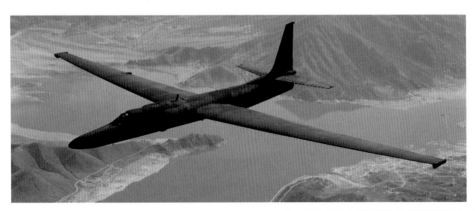

The U-2R improved the breed—but could still be a handful to fly, especially at low altitude. (Lockheed PI8870)

With the U-2R came the full pressure suit. The entire assembly was produced by the David Clark company. The first version was the S1010A, in which the regulator providing breathing oxygen, together with communications gear, parachute harness, and flotation device, were all mounted integrally. For the first two years of the U-2R, the suits were custom-made to fit each pilot, just like the early partial pressure suits.

Then came the S1010B, which was produced in 12 standard sizes, with adjustments to fit individual pilots. The communications and oxygen regulator were moved to the helmet, while the flotation gear and parachute formed part of a separate harness worn over the top of the suit.

In the early 1970s, David Clark designed the S100 system for use in the early-model U-2s. This added the helmet from the full-pressure suit to the partial pressure suit. It was used by pilots of the few remaining NASA and USAF U-2C and CT models, until they were retired in the late 1980s.

The next round of improvements to the full pressure suit resulted in the S1031, introduced in 1980-81 when the new TR-1s were being produced. An exposure garment is built in, to provide an inch-thick layer of thermal air if the pilot should end up in the water. These suits were again hand-tailored to individual pilots, costing around $30,000 to make, and each pilot had two of them.

No more new suits were funded for many years. Instead, they were refurbished every four to six years.

In the mid-1990s new suits designated S1034 were eventually purchased to replace the existing stock. They featured a new neck ring and connectors for the gloves, and a new oxygen supply for improved comfort and safety. – *C.P.*

many, he noticed a low-frequency vibration of increasing intensity. Then the engine RPM began to unwind. Faber turned towards Ramstein airbase as his flamed-out descent began. He tried two airstarts at 46,000 and 37,000 feet without success. Luckily, he was now overhead Ramstein and made a spiral descent. At 15,000 feet he lowered the gear and made one last attempt to restart. A slow ignition was obtained, but the engine vibrations returned, and Faber eventually decided to shut down and make a deadstick landing. (Three months later Faber was in trouble again over Germany with a complete electrical failure, but again safely brought the TR-1 down to Ramstein.)[5]

Flameout patterns

All U-2 pilots practice simulated flameout patterns on each training mission. It's so important to get the "high key" point correct for the weight of the airplane, and the airspeeds correct for downwind and approach. A year after Faber's silent landing, Major Bruce Jinneman had cause to thank that training, when he was obliged to deadstick back into Alconbury after his first nine-hour Creek Spectre sortie in 1985. The problem this time was trapped fuel in the outboard wing tanks. Jinneman was still over the North Sea when his engine quit, but he calculated correctly that by immediately cleaning the aircraft up he was within gliding distance of home base, even

After the U-2s were consolidated with the SR-71s under the 9th SRW at Beale in 1976, the sole U-2 squadron (now the 99th SRS) remained responsible for pilot training. The two U-2CT trainers were kept busy, and the remaining five U-2C models were also used for training, when they were not being used on test flights to support the continuing ALSS and PELSS programs.

Dedicated squadron

In 1981, the arrival of the TR-1 boosted the numbers of new pilots required. The 9th SRW therefore established a dedicated training squadron at Beale. Lt Col Doyle Krumrey was the first commander of the 4029th SRTS, also known as the "Dragon Tamers." The new squadron led a complete overhaul of the training syllabus. One of the first tasks was to advise the Skunk Works on development of the TR-1B trainer. This was, of course, the first time that a two-cockpit training version of the U-2 had been ordered as part of a production run. The first two trainers arrived in March and May 1983. Meanwhile, the very first computer-driven Cockpit Procedures Trainer (CPT) for the U-2/TR-1 was installed at Beale in October 1982. Before the CPT arrived trainee U-2 pilots would simply read the Dash One, then go and sit in the jet on the ramp, to familiarize themselves!

Major Larry Faber was one of the first pilots assigned to the 17th RW at Alconbury. On 20 February 1985, after three hours on-station over Ger-

In the U-2R, pilots could wear a full pressure suit for the first time. This one is hooked up to the portable oxygen supply that provides continuity in the pre-breathing process, when the pilot is walking out to the aircraft. (Chris Ryan)

though his mission-configured aircraft was as heavy as they come. As a precaution, Jinneman raised his high-key altitude by 1,000 feet.

Inevitably, a crosswind complicated the planning for final approach, and there were some clouds over Alconbury. This caused one heart-stopping moment for Jinneman, who had only just arrived at the 17th RW, when he mistook the runway at nearby RAF Wyton for Alconbury, and wondered why it was covered in trucks—the RAF was resurfacing the runway! Still, the TR-1 pilot eventually arrived overhead Alconbury with enough altitude for two 360-degree turns. "From then on, it was almost anticlimactic," he reported.[6]

In 1989 Captain Bryan Anderson also experienced the trapped fuel phenomenon, which was caused by faulty reinstallation of tank valves. Andesron's engine did not actually flameout until he was rolling out on final approach. However, the pilot had positioned the aircraft for this eventuality—the fuel low-level light had been on throughout his descent.[7]

Remarkable save

In some respects, landing a flamed-out U-2 is less complicated than landing one with some sort of control problem. In 1986 a remarkable save of a U-2R was recorded by Captain Jonathan George of the 9th SRW. He was flying his first operational mission out of Osan when the autopilot disconnected and the pitch trim ran full nose down. The aircraft pitched over and exceeded allowable Mach, but George managed to grab the yoke and somehow pull the bird out of a steep dive before the airframe failed. But try as he might, he could not reset the trim. The fledgling pilot lowered the gear and started a slow descent to base, during which he was forced to "bear-hug" the yoke, exerting up to 50 lbs back pressure to prevent the aircraft from pitching over. After an hour of this he arrived overhead the airfield, but due to the tremendous fatigue, muscle cramps, and other physiological problems caused by such heavy exertion while completely enclosed in his full pressure suit, George was unable to properly configure the aircraft for landing without losing control. He therefore executed a spiraling approach and flew a perfect no-flap approach to a full-stop landing. They had to carry him from the aircraft and send him to hospital, where he was treated for severe muscle strain and exhaustion.[8]

The speed brakes are deployed in this photo of the first TR-1. Together with the landing gear, they were extended at high altitude to dump enough lift for the descent. (Lockheed PR1332-11)

Extracts from informal guidance to pilots, compiled at Beale AFB, 1990s:
Our objective is to place the aircraft over the threshold (T) at the proper altitude (less than 10 feet), at the proper airspeed (T-speed) and descent rate (flight path)...The two variables that we all should take care of early in the approach are fuel balance and configuration...Power is a variable that many of us could manage better – how many times have you pulled power off only to add it back almost immediately? Convince yourself that pitch (trim) controls airspeed and that power controls descent rate (glide path), though this is contrary to Air Force teaching.

One of the most obvious things that sets the U-2 apart from other aircraft is yaw control. At approach speeds, the Deuce does some directional hunting which is most pronounced with the flaps down. Most pilots make no attempt to control this until in the flare. Since Lockheed did not provide the airplane with a yaw damper, it is up to the pilot to handle it. The way to hold a heading in this airplane is to level the wings and then hold the heading constant with short period, *small* rudder control inputs...

Due to the bicycle gear, the airplane will not gracefully accept any crab or drift at touchdown. You must control heading with your feet, and drift with roll control inputs. Many pilots...experience difficulty determining the difference between crab and drift. The most common mistake is using rudder in the flare to keep your body over the centreline. This action creates crab at touchdown and usually causes mobile to call for opposite rudder. If you ignore mobile you land in a crab. If you merely step on the called-for rudder, you will touchdown in a drift. Neither of these situations are preferred, so how do you prevent the problem?...With the rudder you keep the longitudinal axis of the airplane parallel to the runway centreline. Now keep your body over the centreline using roll control. Sounds simple enough, doesn't it? But you must also flare and achieve the proper touchdown attitude...

Now that we have flown a stable approach followed by a two-point landing with no crab and no drift, are we through? An emphatic NO! The Deuce is still flying even though the wheels are rolling down the runway. Keep the Yoke coming aft. Raise the flaps to ease wing and directional control and put maximum weight on the tailwheel. Don't relax until you are stopped!

CHUCK WILSON ON GOING...AND COMING BACK
Taxiing the U-2 is challenging. Turning into the wind, the radius is about 189 feet. Turning away from the wind, the radius can exceed 300 feet. The pilot must judge turns carefully or get stuck and need the aircraft to be repositioned by ground crew. No easy task either.

The U-2 is, without doubt, the most difficult aircraft in the inventory to land...Keep in mind, our pilot has been in a hazardous physiological environment for over nine hours. He is dehydrated, fatigued, and has a skewed depth perception from the high altitude.

To successfully land this aircraft, the pilot must achieve a full stall at two feet above the runway. The maneuver looks graceful to onlookers, but tends to feel violent inside the cockpit, as the pilot feels the stall, touches down, and struggles to keep the wings level. But, it is not over yet. The pilot still has to "fly" the wings until the aircraft can stop. - *comments posted on John Stone's Blackbirds website*

Captain Roger Mostar also had to use brute strength to recover a TR-1 over Germany in 1991. This time, a hydraulic system failure caused the autopilot to stick in full nose-up trim. Mostar had to use his knees to push against the yoke, after his arms tired of the constant effort to keep the aircraft from stalling. With the loss of all hydraulics, the landing gear provided the only drag to get the aircraft down from high altitude. It took Mostar an hour and a half to make the emergency descent towards Ramstein. There, he had to make a no-flap landing in which the correct T-speed is critical if the aircraft is not to float down the runway and maybe run off the other end. Mostar was unable to slow the aircraft enough on his first approach, but wisely elected to go around despite his fatigue. He made it safely down on the second attempt.[9]

In a no-flap landing, the final approach path cannot be greater than two degrees. Pilots also practice them frequently during initial training, recurrency, and requalification. What cannot be practiced is the additional complications that can turn a minor emergency into a major one, for example, bad weather in the descent or at the recovery airfield, or the loss of pressure suit ventilation leading to overheating. It is always so much more difficult to execute recovery maneuvers in a bulky pressure suit.

Falling retention
In 1993, a record 25 new U-2 pilots were graduated by the training squadron at Beale, by now renumbered as the 1st RS. The extra numbers were needed to overcome the falling retention rates, as qualified high-flyers deserted the Air Force for a more attractive career with the airlines. The long TDYs, long duty days, and the poor promotion prospects afforded to U-2 pilots by the Air Force were was taking their toll. So many of them left for United Airlines, which the group jokingly designated as OL-UA!

The pilot shortage also affected the 1st RS, as it attempted to retain qualified instructors. However, the problem was eased in 1997 when a contractor was brought in to handle classroom and cockpit procedures training. Reflectone Training Systems hired some retired U-2 pilots and a mission planner, who provided valuable experience and continuity. The contract continues in force, and is currently operated by Crew Training International (CTI).

The 9th RW was still anxious to maintain standards. Traditionally, 60% of those applying to become U-2 pilots were not successful. But the

Captain Roger Mostar enjoys a well-earned beer after a long mission from RAF Alconbury. His emergency landing in 1991 after a hydraulic failure was one of many skillful and determined recoveries made by U-2 pilots. (author)

When pulling duty as "mobile," U-2 pilots get to drive a high-powered chase car. In the 1950s, these Chevrolet Camaeros were used. (author)

pool of talent from which to select was declining, year by year. A website was set up to try and encourage new applicants. In 1999, the required previous experience level was lowered from 1,500 hours to 800 hours for fighter pilots, and the commitment period was reduced from five to three years. In 2003, the required experience was further lowered to 500 hours for fighter pilots, and from 1,500 to 1,300 hours for those applying from "crewed" aircraft, eg transports and bombers. Instructor pilots with 800 hours on the T-37, T-38, etc. were also welcome to apply. So too were pilots from the other U.S. armed services.

"Flying the U-2 isn't for everybody," noted 1st RS commander Lt Col Walt Flint. "It's hard enough asking them to climb into a full space suit and helmet; then we ask them to strap into one of the most challenging aircraft to fly in the U.S. military."

Glass Dragon
However, the introduction of the "Glass Dragon" from 2002 finally meant that the new pilot recruits did not have to make a mental leap back into the past, and fly in a 1960s-era round-dial airplane. Some annoying deficiencies were also put right for the first time in the RAMP architecture. For instance, the fuel panel now faithfully reflected the actual tank configuration of the airplane. A new real-time wind sensor ensured that the aircraft's groundspeed and wind vector was accurately displayed at all times.

A Ford Mustang chase car at Beale in 1999. (author)

THE PROBLEM WITH 099

After a depot overhaul in August 1998, the last U-2 built (80-1099) exhibited a directional control problem. When in the flare to land, it behaved as though it was landing in a full 15-knot right crosswind, requiring full left rudder to compensate. Attempting a landing with any real right crosswind bordered on unsafe and uncontrollable.

After six months, the 9th RW returned the aircraft to Flight Test at Palmdale for investigation. Were the flight controls incorrectly rigged? After thorough investigation and re-rigging, it seemed not. Instead, Flight Test determined that the right wing was stalling well before the left, with the drag rise causing the yaw.

Optical and laser tools and computer programs were used to compare the profiles of both wings. The left wing was slightly thicker than the right, with small depressions on the upper and lower surface just outboard of mid-span.

So, tufts were placed on the upper surface of the wings to enable a viewing of the true air flow separation pattern. A Cessna 195 belonging to Lockheed Martin U-2 test pilot Eric Hansen was used as the chase/video aircraft. Major Mike Masucci flew the U-2. Sure enough, the tufts revealed clear asymmetry of each wing in the airflow separation and pattern of stall progression. A few knots before the left wing showed any sign of tuft activity, flow separation of the right tip was easily seen, followed by an inboard progression of that flow separation. The right wing stalled well before the left. Moreover, it stalled from the outboard to the inboard, regardless of flap setting. (This characteristic of the U-2—all of them, not only 099—was a surprise to all concerned, since most airplanes stall inboard to outboard).

After a study of how to remedy the problem at the least cost, Lockheed Martin made a cuff for the *right* wing to match the fatness of the left wing. Thereafter, the difference in stall speeds between the right and left wings was less than 1 knot.

This whole exercise proved—yet again—that the production of hand-made airplanes can result in barely measurable but significant aerodynamic differences. – C.P.

TINY BUBBLES

The U-2 is a physically demanding aircraft to fly. Breathing 100% oxygen sucks the moisture out of your lungs faster than you can replace it by drinking water. The pressure suit is cumbersome. The more you move around, the more fatigued you get. The suit's fabric does not breathe, so heat tends to build up. Sitting in one position for long periods of time can cause stagnant hypoxia—blood pools in the lower extremeties. Unless you really enjoy tube food, your state of nourishment might not be so good. You may experience some intestinal discomfort if you've eaten anything that produces any kind of bubbles. Those bubbles will expand to 10 times their normal size at 30,000 feet.

- Major Cory Bartholomew, as quoted in
Code One magazine, First Quarter 2004

THE U-2 DIET

Tube foods range from main course meals, like turkey a la king, beef and gravy, and spaghetti, to smaller meals, like clam chowder. We have tube desserts, such as apple or cherry pie, or butterscotch pudding. On long missions, we carry six to eight quarts of water, and up to eight of these tube foods. We pop them in a little heater in the cockpit, so we can get a nice warm meal.

A lot of guys will pace their eating, like one an hour, to give them something to do. On a busy combat mission, we might not eat any of them. On slower missions, we might eat them all before the halfway point.

- Major Tom Parent, as quoted in Code One
magazine, First Quarter 2004

AT LAST – AN ANGLE-OF-ATTACK INDICATOR!

U-2 pilots waited 20 years for a trainer. But they waited nearly 50 years for an Angle-of-Attack (AoA) indicator! It was only in 2003 that this stall warning instrument was finally installed. Surprising, really, since the U-2 operates within 5 knots of the stall speed during most phases of flight. When it was introduced, some U-2 pilots found the audio warning to be a distraction in the landing phase. But most are now used to it. - *C.P.*

VIP RIDES

About once a month during the 1990s, the 9th RW gave a familiarization trip in the U-2 trainer to a VIP approved by higher headquarters. Usually, this was some important Congressman or General, but a few invitations were also extended to the media. The author of this volume was fortunate enough to get a ride in 1995 (see chapter 40). Apart from some problems with the intercom to my IP, Major Brandon King, in the front cockpit, my flight went smoothly. That was not the case a few years later, when television reporter Joan Lunden of ABC News flew:

"We were supposed to be up for three hours. At about 63,000 feet my pilot said, "we've lost our AC." I said, "that's OK, I don't mind if I get a little hot." But he didn't mean the air conditioning! He meant the alternating current, our main power supply. He said that we had about 30 minutes to get back on the ground, or there was the danger of an engine fire.

So as we started down. He went to extend the landing gear to give us more drag, and our gauges said it did not go down. I was amazed at how calm I was. And it taught me something, that these people are so highly trained and experienced, they can stay calm in a crisis. I really learned a lot and saw how they conduct themselves on a daily basis."

- the aircraft landed safely.

In the 1990s, a record number of new Dragon Lady pilots was being trained each year—but record numbers were also leaving, discouraged by long TDYs and the perceived lack of promotion prospects for U-2 drivers. (Lockheed PI 9307)

Along with the Block 20-upgraded aircraft came a second cockpit procedures trainer, in the RAMP configuration. It included an earth model with navigation aids, so that pilots at Beale could practice, for instance, an approach to Osan airbase, Korea.

(The desirability of having U-2 pilots trained in a full-motion simulator had been debated for years. Apart from the expense, there were doubts about whether such a machine could ever accurately replicate the aircraft's unique "feel" and landing characteristics. The idea was eventually dropped.)

Pilot Selection

The pilot selection process involves a two-week visit to Beale, during which the prospective high-flyer has a physical, followed by a pressure suit acclimatization test. Then comes three familiarization rides in the backseat of the U-2S trainer. The applicant also flies one of the dozen T-38 proficiency trainers belonging to the 1st RS.

In 1990, Captain Troy Devine (right) became the first female pilot to qualify in the U-2. She is seen here in 1994 after flying Secretary of the Air Force Sheila Widnall on a VIP ride. Devine later returned to Beale as a Lt Col and commanded the 99th RS during Operation Iraqi Freedom.

The third new-build trainer was added in 1988. Since then two more have been added, by converting operational single-seaters. (Lockheed)

Once accepted, the new pilots start on the T-38 for the first month, then do a month's ground school. The next month is spent doing landings and pattern work in the two-seat U-2 trainer. The third and fourth months consist of high-altitude training flights, including the first solo. The last two months of the training program cover the flying and operation of reconnaissance payloads.

After that, it's off to either the 5th RS or Det 4 for the first 60-day operational TDY. The 5th RS operation out of Osan still involves relatively standard orbits and procedures, and is thus a good place to start. However, the current U-2 pilots must be prepared for a much more dynamic environment than their predecessors. They must learn to adjust their flight plans in-the-air, in order to meet emerging collection requirements. And they must be prepared to act as high-altitude airborne command posts or communications relays. Not many books are taken upstairs to read, these days!

Fantastic view

Still though, there is the fantastic view to enjoy. This leaves a marked impression on nearly every U-2 driver. Shaped in the military mold, and also needing to be heavily self-reliant in the particular flying job that they do, many of them are relatively gruff and taciturn individuals. They are not given to flights of fancy, or poetic visions. Even so, few manage to avoid being affected by "the breakaway phenomenon," a strange sort of reverie experienced by those who fly for prolonged periods at extreme altitudes. Some describe it as a sense of detachment, a shaking- loose of all earthly concerns and responsibilities, but others are affected in different ways.

"I get a personal feeling of serenity" explained Major Thom Evans, who flew U-2s from 1975-1985 and became the high-time Air Force pilot. "Yet at the same time a feeling of power. You realize that you're up there by yourself, entirely alone, doing something that not many others can do."

When he tires of gazing at the earth below, the Dragon Lady pilot need only look at the sky all around him for further amazement. "The sky is a very brilliant blue at the horizon, and gets darker and darker as you look up until directly overhead it's almost black, even at midday," noted Evans.

"I'm sure that I'll never get over the thrill I experienced of flying high in the U-2, especially when the sun is coming up or going down. It's an

ELECTRICAL FAILURE

Beale AFB – Flying above 70,000 feet in a two-seat U-2 Dragon Lady, Major Mike Means and Captain Steve Rodriguez had less than 10 minutes to respond to an impending electrical systems failure, an emergency never before encountered in the aircraft.

About four hours into their training mission...digital airspeed and altitude read-outs disappeared, followed by the loss of fuel quantity and gear position indicators, and radio and navigation equipment. Even emergency back-up systems were not immune.

Sensing an imminent electrical failure, the crew shut down all electrical equipment in an attempt to preserve emergency battery power. While the intercom still functioned, they quickly briefed ATC and then turned off the battery.

With only a magnetic compass, Major Means successfully navigated back to Beale. "We had a nose down trim situation, which meant a very heavy stick," he said. The inability to dump fuel and reduce weight, and lower flaps to reduce speed, also compounded their difficulties.

As Means gathered his strength for landing, Rodriguez—on only his second high-altitude sortie and unable to communicate with his instructor—ran all checklists. This included manually lowering the landing gear. The failed electrical system prevented indications that the wheels were locked.

As the aircraft neared the runway Means turned the battery back on. It was dead. Consequently, the crew had no intercom, and no way to communicate with a chase car. He settled the aircraft onto the runway, turned the engine off to help slow it, and dragged a wingtip on the runway to stop it.

- 9 RW Public Affairs Office for ACC
News Service, 27 November 2002

Every aircraft flies a little different, it was said. Certainly, this was true of 01099, seen here during test flights from Palmdale in 1998 that confirmed that a slightly thicker left wing kept flying, after the right wing had stalled. (USAF)

The 9th RW has 12 T-38 trainers that are used at Beale AFB in the training program, and to maintain pilot proficiency. (author)

The trainers were painted black to match the rest of the fleet in the late 1980s. They are now designated U-2ST. (author)

incredible view," said Lt Col Ken Tupper. He spent 15 years in the 9th RW before retiring from the Air Force in 2002. He still works at Beale as a government employee, ensuring that training and systems expertise is passed on to the next generation of U-2 pilots.

According to Doyle Krumrey, who flew for the USAF and then for NASA, U-2 pilots "get to see things that someone who has never flown the airplane can never fully appreciate or understand. I remember back in Southeast Asia when we were sitting out over the Gulf of Tonkin, or running up the Chinese coast on those SIGINT sorties. We would launch after dark and come home early in the morning...very boring flying, with not much activity going on. But you could sit over the Gulf and look down south, and see stars in a way you had never seen before. They would twinkle, but they would also turn color—greens, blues, reds. We were looking at them through the diffraction of the earth's atmosphere; it was wonderfully pretty to me."

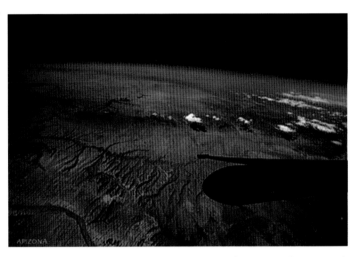

Black sky above, blue at the curved horizon, and a sense of detachment from the earth below. A view of Arizona from the cockpit of a U-2 at high altitude. (Jeff Olesen)

As part of the new TR-1 production, three twin-cockpit trainers were built. This is the first TR-1B in the original all-white color. (Lockheed PI 873)

A U-2S with "clean" superpods flies over the main Lockheed Martin site at Palmdale. (Lockheed PR 381415)

Thom Evans liked the sunsets best: "They are unique. You see what we call a "terminator" every time. That's the line between light and dark. It starts out on the eastern horizon, which turns a strange and fuzzy grey. This brilliant line forms at the very edge of the horizon like a miniature compressed rainbow. It gradually works its way up towards the vertical and over towards the west. Behind the terminator is darkness and the stars. As it approaches the western horizon, it becomes more brilliant—oranges, reds, and blues. Then all of a sudden it is night."

Marty Knutson, who clocked up 3,800 hours in the U-2 over nearly 30 years, agreed that sunrise and sunset provided the most beautiful scenes of all. He also referred to the almost metaphysical experience that high-altitude flying can provide. "Views like that," he said, "give you an entirely different perspective on life."

In the "Heritage Room" at Beale, the 9th RW keeps memorabilia, and a stock of beer for after-work relaxation. Posted on the walls are the names of all those who have flown the Article. (author)

37

Smokey Joe and Other Test Projects

When the Air Force ordered its own fleet of U-2s in early 1956, three of the 29 aircraft were allocated to the Air Research and Development Command (ARDC) from the outset. After all, no airplane entered the USAF inventory without the flight test engineers, and test pilots of the Air Force Flight Test Center (AFFTC) having a hand in it!

But the prospect of the U-2 being flown from Edwards AFB posed a big security problem, according to the CIA. In the fall of 1956 Project Aquatone's deputy director, Colonel Jack Gibbs, wrote: "Regardless of how securely they house the aircraft, within a matter of days every U.S. aircraft manufacturer's representative operating from Edwards will know quite accurately the altitude, climb, endurance, and functional capabilities." Gibbs recommended that the USAF's U-2 test aircraft be securely based out of sight, at the Ranch.[1]

The first ARDC aircraft (66701) was delivered to the secret base in the spring of 1957. But it was soon flying from Edwards after all, since the resumption of nuclear testing by the AEC forced closure of the Ranch in June 1957. However, for the first few years the U-2s belonging to ARDC and operated by AFFTC were based at the remote North Base site, at the edge of the Rogers Dry Lake. It was not until Gary Powers was shot down in 1960 that the veil of secrecy over the operation was lifted, and it was moved to the main base at Edwards. (The U-2s of the CIA's own test squadron, which in 1960 became an operational unit designated Det G, remained at North Base).

Special Projects Branch

The AFFTC assigned Major Robert Carpenter to run what it euphemistically called the "Special Projects Branch." He recruited an engineering project officer, Captain Dick Miller, and four test pilots, who all checked themselves out in the U-2 at Edwards. The research tasks fell into three categories: weather, human factors, and Infrared (IR). But IR research was the most important task.

In the early days of U-2 development, Trevor Gardner had recognized the aircraft's potential as a high-altitude platform for IR sensors. The Secretary of the Air Force for R&D advised Kelly Johnson to explore the possibilities of adapting the aircraft. Ever-keen to find new business opportunities for the Skunk Works, Johnson set to work.[2]

A meeting of the USAF Scientific Advisory Board on 13 November 1956 heard Kelly Johnson propose a version of the U-2 equipped with an infrared sensor that could detect the exhaust plumes of jet aircraft many thousands of feet below. A similar IR sensor was also being proposed to provide early warning of a Soviet missile attack from space. It was one of the potential payloads for the WS-117L satellite system, for which Lockheed's Missile Systems Division in Sunnyvale, CA, received an Air Force development contract in October 1956.

66701 was the first U-2A delivered to the Air Force Flight Test Center in 1957. (AFFTC)

The first U-2 to be equipped with an InfraRed sensor for tracking aircraft or missiles was 66722, a single-seater. (Lockheed Report SP-112)

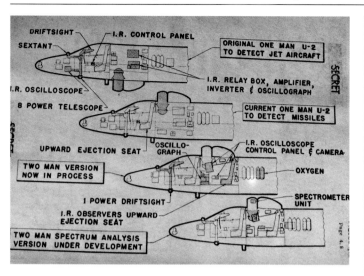

The design progression from 1957 to 1959 of the U-2 equipped with the IR sensor can be seen here. It was soon realized that the pilot could not safely fly the plane, monitor the oscilloscope, and operate the sensor, all at the same time! (Lockheed Report SP-112)

The CIA's radical new spyplane had only been flying for a few weeks when the U.S. Air Force began plans to acquire some of the "Special Aircraft" for itself. At a procurement conference in Washington on 26 September 1955 chaired by General Albert Boyd of ARDC, eight senior officials decided to procure 29 of them. Twenty of these would be for reconnaissance, and another three for R&D. The remaining six would be three prototypes each of the Long-Range Intruder (LRI) and Air Defense versions that Kelly Johnson was proposing at the time.

Within two months, however, Johnson recommended against building the interceptor version, and it seems likely that the CIA squashed the idea of building the LRI (eg nuclear bomber) on political grounds. When the contract was eventually let in January 1956 it still comprised 29 airplanes, at a cost of $23 million (excluding engines and other equipment). A thirtieth airplane was later added, and in 1959 a further five were built to replace those already lost in accidents. – C.P.

IR sensor

In spring 1957, the Skunk Works received a contract to modify one of the U-2A models being built for the ARDC with an IR sensor. This was designated AN/AAS-8, and would be co-developed by Lockheed and Baird-Atomic, the company which had provided the U-2's sextant. (Meanwhile, Aerojet General worked separately on the IR sensor for the proposed satellite).[3]

But there were delays with the AN/AAS-8. It was not test-flown by Lockheed until December 1957, on the third U-2A destined for ARDC, 66722. The sensor was housed in a large rotating barrel pressurized by dry nitrogen that protruded from the bottom of the U-2's equipment bay. The barrel contained a mirror that could be tilted in order to focus infrared energy, via a second reflector, onto a lead sulphide detector. An infrared oscilloscope was added to the optical path within the U-2's combined sextant/driftsight, so that the data from the IR sensor could be presented to the pilot without installing a new display in the cramped cockpit. The telescope function of the driftsight was made twice as powerful, to achieve x8 magnification and allow the pilot a chance of identifying large intruding aircraft below him.[4]

Lockheed delivered the IR-modified aircraft to the Special Projects Branch in March 1958. In this "AIRSearch" configuration, the aircraft was designed only to detect aircraft, as a possible supplement to Airborne Early Warning (AEW) aircraft and the Distant Early Warning (DEW) line of radars. These guarded the airspace over which Soviet bombers would have to fly in any attack on North America. However, fears of a mass Soviet bomber attack were receding, thanks in no small part to the intelligence provided by early U-2 overflights of the USSR. But as the fears of missile attack grew, infrared detection of exhaust plumes remained a subject of great interest.

On 2 April 1958, Captain Pat Hunerwadel flew the modified aircraft to Ramey AFB for the start of Project Low Card. Flying from Ramey, the sensor's performance could be assessed during the test-launch of U.S. ballistic missiles from Cape Canaveral down the Eastern Test Range. Unfortunately, the aircraft ran off the runway in early June, badly damaging the downwards-protruding sensor. It was airlifted back to Edwards from Ramey for repair, and since the focus of attention was now missiles rather than aircraft, it was decided to rehouse the sensor at the top of the equipment bay. 66722 was quickly modified and returned to Ramey in September. By

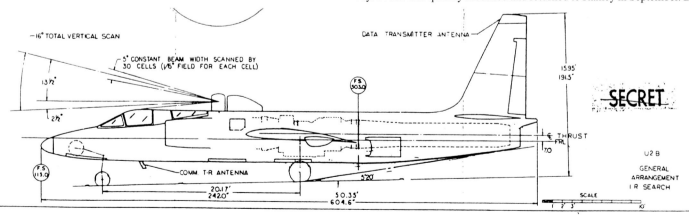

The U-2B, as proposed for production by Kelly Johnson, would have featured a longer fuselage, a relocated IR search sensor, and a tricycle undercarriage. (Lockheed Report SP-112)

THE U-2B PROPOSAL FOR A MISSILE WARNING PATROL
The following details are taken from Lockheed Report SP-112 for an "ICBM Detection System" dated January 1959:

To cover all the areas of the USSR from which ICBMs might be launched, three widely separated U-2 patrol areas would be required, with a total of 15 aircraft airborne *at any one time*. Six aircraft each would be launched from Tromso, Norway, and Nome, Alaska, and a further three from Misawa, Japan. They would fly 3,000-nautical mile missions in prescribed loops across the Arctic and the Sea of Japan. The need to maintain line-of-sight UHF communication between each aircraft determined the very large number that must be airborne at any one time (the option of longer-range HF communications was rejected as too unreliable). It took over 1,300 personnel to fly, operate, and maintain the 84 U-2 aircraft that would be required in total. Another 200 people would operate computer centers at the three bases, which would analyze any target data picked up and relayed down the line by the U-2s.

The basic U-2B model provided for a pilot, the observer's position, the IR sensor, an astro-inertial navigation system, and the UHF data link. A conventional tricycle landing gear replaced the U-2A model's unique bicycle configuration; the cost was 884lbs in weight, but "the expected gain in overall operations by lessening landing accidents outweighs this," said the Skunk Works. Even so, the overall empty weight of the U-2B was only 1,500 lbs more than a standard U-2A, at just over 12,000 lbs. Range was cut by nearly 25%, but the U-2B could still reach 70,000 feet. The fuselage length and wingspan were unaltered. To meet the objection to operating a single-engine aircraft so intensively over such hostile terrain, the Skunk Works provided an option to add the small Pratt & Whitney JT-12 turbojet. This provided an emergency get-me-home capability at 35,000 feet, if the standard J57-31 failed and could not be restarted. The JT-12 was housed in the aft fuselage, with the intakes and exhaust covered by aerodynamic fairings to minimize the drag. These fairings had to be ejected before the small turbojet could be lit.

TRAINING AS A U-2 OBSERVER

I was the second observer to arrive at Edwards. Ray Oglukian was the first. I had been a radar intercept officer in F-89s and F-94s, but those skills were not of much use in this operation. Oglukian taught me how to operate the IR sensor. He sat me in the back seat one night and had the airplane towed out to a remote part of the base. Then he stood some distance away and lit a cigarette lighter. I had to detect this heat source by operating the IR sensor, and then follow his movements with it.

- Captain Jim Eastlund, interview with author

November 1958, when the U-2 was flown back to Edwards, it had tracked 11 of the 12 successful missile launches from the Cape since April.

By now fears of a surprise Soviet ballistic missile attack on the U.S. were growing. The Pentagon established the Missile Defense and Alarm System (MIDAS) as a separate program to warn of attack from space. But MIDAS could not be operational until July 1961 at the earliest.[5]

Astonishing scheme

Capitalising on the "missile gap" fears, Kelly Johnson nearly managed to sell an astonishing scheme to the Pentagon. The Skunk Works and Baird Atomic team quickly wrote two reports describing the performance of the AN/AAS-8 sensor in these test flights; missile detection ranges of over 1,000 miles had been demonstrated. In mid-November, Johnson and Walter Baird presented the reports to the Pentagon, and proposed that a fleet of U-2s should be kept on constant airborne patrol around the Soviet borders, to warn of any impending missile attack on the U.S. The "ICBM Detection System" suggested to the USAF by the Skunk Works would have required the building of over 80 more aircraft, in a new version designated U-2B.[6]

The Generals in the Pentagon liked the idea. Johnson was asked to fly immediately to Wright Field for further discussions with ARDC. From there, he returned to Burbank with approval to modify three more airplanes to the IR search configuration. But the USAF officials had doubts about the communications links and navigational accuracy of the proposed U-2 patrols, especially since the aircraft would be operating within the Arctic Circle. Moreover, they worried about the safety and reliability of the single-engined U-2 in this role.

The U-2B incorporated the "lessons learned" from the 1958 series of IR test flights. One of these was that it was asking too much of the pilot to find and track targets with the sensor, as well as fly the airplane. The idea of carrying a second crew member to operate the sensor had already been raised. He would have to fit into the equipment bay behind the cockpit, where the camera was carried by reconnaissance U-2s. Before it was delivered, the Skunk Works fitted a downward ejection seat to the ARDC's second U-2 (66710). The USAF had just decided to provide all U-2 pilots with an ejection seat, and 66710 apparently tested the means of escape for a second crewmember or observer.[7]

Major Robert Carpenter (right) was the first commander of the Special Projects Branch at Edwards. He was succeeded in 1960 by Major Harry Andonian (left). Behind them is 66954, the first U-2D. (AFFTC)

One of the rear-seat observers stands astride the converted Q-bay in which he was confined during a mission in the U-2D aircraft. His right hand rests on the rotating dome of the IR sensor, otherwise known as the "Pickle Barrel." (AFFTC)

Two U-2A models belonging to the Special Projects Branch fly over the dry lake at Edwards during the early 1960s. (Lockheed PR 1187)

The first recorded flight of a two-place U-2 was on 7 January 1958, when Lockheed test pilot Bob Schumacher flew 66710 with flight test engineer Glen Fulkerson in the Q-bay. Unfortunately, this aircraft was lost in a crash at Edwards on 11 September 1958 that killed AFFTC test pilot Pat Hunerwadel. While trying to land in gusty conditions and with improperly-balanced fuel the wingtip hit hard. Captain Hunerwadel applied power to go around, not knowing that the skid had been buckled and the aileron balance mechanism damaged. He lost control, and the aircraft spiraled into the ground. Fortunately no observer was on board. The skid was shortened to prevent it jamming the aileron, if it should be deformed.[8]

A second U-2 modified with an observer's position was flying by January 1959. This aircraft (66954) was one of the five extra U-2s that Lockheed built as a supplement to the original 50. The observer was seated facing the relocated oscilloscope, which now also featured a camera, and the control panel, which was relocated from the pilot's cockpit. The downward ejection seat, having apparently proved unsatisfactory, was replaced with a more conventional, upwards-operating escape system.

Revised proposal

At the end of January 1959, Johnson submitted a revised proposal for the operational ICBM warning system. It was the cheapest and earliest-available solution to the requirement, he wrote. Still, it would have cost $200 million to set up, and another $50 million each year to run.[9]

The Lockheed proposal won the support of the early warning panel of the President's Science Advisory Committee (PSAC). This panel met on 11-12 March 1959 to review progress on the Ballistic Missile Early-Warning System (BMEWS) radar and the MIDAS satellite. The development of MIDAS had been accelerated, but the first test-launch was still many months away. Lockheed had promised to have the first U-2 patrol (out of Alaska) operational just 18 months after go-ahead, and all three patrols in service by two years. The panel urged "immediate procurement" of the U-2B system as a complement to BMEWS.[10]

The PSAC was probably attracted by the quick development promised by the Skunk Works, and also by the retention of a man-in-the-loop in

any missile warning system—in this case, the U-2 observer. These were early days for IR detection sensors, and their reliability was still suspect. Moreover, Baird-Atomic was promising that the IR sensor on the U-2 could soon be sensitive enough to track missiles even after they had burned out. That offered the prospect of determining the missile's re-entry point over U.S. territory, since just three azimuth and elevation measurements by the observer in one U-2 would be enough to compute a free ballistic trajectory.

But other government advisors were less enthusiastic about the U-2 warning scheme. Moreover, as we have seen, the CIA was not buying the

Although they were home-based at Edwards, the U-2s of the Special Projects Branch were frequently to be found at Patrick AFB, FL, close to the Eastern Test Range. 66682 is outside the hangar there in 1963. (NARA KKE 50754)

SMOKEY JOE AT EDWARDS

Your first view of the 6512 Test Group, and of ARDC's Special Projects Test Branch, is Smokey Joe, a paunchy cigar-smoking Indian cartoon mascot. He is the unofficial greeter for the very few visitors to enter the home of the U-2 fliers, a small two-room office in the corner of the Flight Test Operations building....

Life is lonely and can suddenly become dangerously short for the U-2 pilot who flies to the far corners of the globe at extreme altitudes that would make Mt. Everest look like a mound....

Mounted between the pilot and the observer in the U-2D is the "Pickle Barrel"—a tube-shaped protrusion that houses the spectrometer or radiometer. The lens, or "hot-eye," faces forward and acts as the search light for picking up infrared radiation from the missile exhaust. The radiometer scans that portion of the color spectrum being studied while the hot-eye swings back and forth in a search mode.

The spectrometer gives a picture of the continuous spectrum, rather than a small portion of it, and can give more information faster. All data is stored on an oscillograph mounted below the feet of the observer. To his left front there is a cathode ray scope for studying magnetic fields....

One silver hangar is earmarked for the U-2 mission, and the maintenance team goes with the planes. Nobody else in the Air Force ever touches them....

The reason that the U-2 enjoys number one takeoff priority at Edwards is because it is simply too damn uncomfortable to stay on the ground longer than absolutely necessary....

Members of the U-2 team must have 2,000 hours of flying time. They fly a minimum of one time a week, and are required to make 15 landings per month. After ground training at Del Rio, Texas—home of the SAC base—the pilots return to Edwards to fly 10 hours at low altitude while waiting for their special pressure suits to be tailor-made. After that, they spend 30 hours on high altitude flights.

- extracts from an article by Walt Keeshen, Jr., in Western Aviation Missiles and Space magazine, February 1961

CAPTAIN BILL FRAZIER – SMOKEY JOE OBSERVER

Flying in the back seat of the U-2D to operate the IR sensor was no picnic. Bill Frazier joined the Special Projects Branch in 1960 and flew on many of the missile-detecting missions. He recalled:

The psychological aspects of flying in that back seat could not be discounted. It was a miserable environment! Because of all the equipment, you couldn't stretch your legs. When I first arrived, the Q-bay canopy windows were teeny things, and the observer could not see anything through them except straight up, which wasn't much good. We held a mirror up to the window so that we could get a view of the outside during taxiing and takeoff. After a few months, Ray Oglukian and myself had had enough. We told them: give us bigger windows or find some other guys to fly! Lockheed gave us bigger windows....

The IR equipment was very difficult to operate, because the sweep was very slow. The missile could go screaming away if you didn't raise the elevation in time. We'd only get a single pip from the radiometer, which was set to a single frequency. Whereas if we threw the switch to move the prisms for the spectrometer into the optical path, it would give multiple indications every time you scanned across the missile's flight path.

It was also not very reliable at times. The sensor had to be cooled by liquid nitrogen, and sometimes this would not flow properly. Sometimes we'd comeback with nothing, which was terribly frustrating.

And the flights could be very long. We would pre-breathe for two hours, get the airplane cranked up, take off—and then call the Cape, only to find that they had halted the countdown at T-minus 10 minutes, and were estimating a two-hour delay. We could do nothing except fly around the sky, waiting for them to launch.

We always took off with full fuel, in case there was a delay. If the missile got off on time, or the launch was canceled, we had to fly for three hours with the gear down and the speedbrakes out, to burn off enough fuel to land.

To pass the time I would try to read, but with the weight of the helmet your neck gets sore. So we came up with the idea of taking two copies of the same book. The pilot would read one page, then I would read the next, and so on....

We flew against every type of U.S. missile...Atlas, Pershing, Polaris, and Titan. I tracked Alan Shepherd on his first Mercury sub-orbital mission with the radiometer. We tracked the Apollo launches, too.

- interview with author

USAF's theory that the Soviets were indeed preparing to launch a pre-emptive strike by long-range nuclear missiles. Another technology suggested by the early warning advisory panel—ionospheric propagation—was already helping the CIA analysts to confirm missile launches. The U-2B proposal was not given an immediate go-ahead, as Kelly Johnson had hoped.

However, the testing of IR sensors on the Edwards-based U-2s continued. A second two-place IR research aircraft joined the test fleet in late 1959. It was serial number 66721, transferred from SAC after its landing accident in August 1959 and modified by Lockheed. The spectral analysis of IR radiation emitted by aircraft or missiles was begun with a lightweight spectrometer that was also developed by Baird-Atomic, and combined in the optical path with the radiometer.

U-2B to U-2D
But as time slipped by, the desperate need to get something—anything—deployed for ICBM detection diminished. The Soviet missile threat was downgraded, and BMEWS became operational. The U-2B proposal with-

Film from the top-secret Corona reconnaissance satellites was ejected and returned to Earth in re-entry capsules. 66722 was converted to carry and drop two dummy capsules, to train the recovery crews. (NARA KKE 22564)

Formation flight of three Edwards test birds in April 1964, the month that they moved from the Main to the South base at Edwards. U-2D 66954 is in the foreground, with U-2As 66682 and 66722 beyond. (AFFTC)

ered on the vine, and was never built. However, the pair of two-seat U-2s continued to fly from Edwards as testbeds for further development of the IR sensors. For a while, they were unofficially known as U-2Bs. But by 1961 they were formally designated as U-2Ds.

By the time that Major Harry Andonian took over as chief of Special Projects in November 1960, an average 100 hours per month was being flown on six projects, with four more coming up. The Branch had seven test pilots and three back-seat observers assigned.

The ICBM detection and tracking research program was now nicknamed Smokey Joe, after the cartoon character. To track missiles launched down the Atlantic Missile Range from Cape Canaveral, the three U-2s fitted with IR sensors now deployed frequently to Patrick AFB. When Vandenberg was the launch base, the sorties could be flown from Edwards.

During missile launches, both two-seaters would be airborne if they were serviceable. Having taken off at least an hour before the missile launch, they would climb to 60,000 feet and take up a heading in line with the planned launch azimuth of the missile, about 200 miles from the launch pad. Sometimes both aircraft were positioned uprange; on other occasions, one would fly downrange to be underneath the missile's trajectory. Once the missile was launched, the observer could monitor the operation of the revolving turret head, which was nicknamed the "Pickle Barrel." This could be scanned through 180-degrees horizontally, while in the vertical plane there was enough movement to follow the missile until its trajectory exceeded 30-degrees above the aircraft.

On the U-2, the observer could operate the system manually if required. On the MIDAS satellite still in development the process would have to be automatic, with the scanner operating in search mode until the missile plume was detected, whereupon it would lock-on and focus the radiant energy onto the detector. There were high hopes for the system; it was expected to distinguish different types of missile launches, and deliver staging and trajectory information to ground stations below.

Part of the task involved measuring solar and other background radiation, so that developers could refine the missile-detecting sensor for MIDAS to discriminate against false alarms—such as sunlight reflected from high clouds. In 1961 there were two test launches of MIDAS satellites, but reliability of detection was a major concern. The urgency to deploy an opera-

tional system was reduced by the successful introduction of the BMEWS radars, and the downgrading of the Soviet missile threat by intelligence analysts. MIDAS remained stuck in R&D, renamed as Program 461. The Smokey Joe U-2s provided much of the test data needed to refine the sensors.[11]

The Smokey Joe aircraft also flew from Hickam AFB, Hawaii, during the recovery of film capsules that were ejected from the Corona reconnaissance satellites. The IR sensor was used in an attempt to detect and track the capsules, and direct the recovery teams. These teams flew in C-119s (later C-130s) and attempted to snatch the capsules in mid-air. If they failed, more recovery teams were deployed on ships in the predicted splashdown area. But the IR sensor on the U-2 was not sensitive enough to pick out the capsule's re-entry signature.[12]

In 1961, the Smokey Joe U-2Ds flew alongside the B-52 mothership that launched the X-15 rocket plane. The observers would track the rocket plume as the X-15 soared upwards into near-space.[13]

Dummy capsules

The Special Projects Branch was also responsible for a B-47 that dropped dummy capsules from high altitude to help the Corona recovery crews practice for the real thing. The U-2s would fly chase and record the drops. By late 1961, the single-seat U-2A 66722 had been modified from Smokey Joe configuration into a second film capsule drop aircraft. It provided a

Another view of 66682, which was used for camera and film trials from 1960 to 1964. (AFFTC)

The HiCAT aircraft flies over the B-70 at Edwards in the mid-1960s.

better test for the recovery crews on the C-119—they could not see the U-2, whereas the lower-flying B-47 was often visible, especially when it contrailed! The B-47 also served as a navigation escort and communications relay aircraft when the U-2s flew from Edwards to Hickam, and on other long excursions.[14]

Meanwhile, 66701 was dedicated to meteorological research. The Air Force Cambridge Research Laboratory (AFCRL) was the major investigator. It used the U-2 to study atmospheric structure, cosmic radiation, cloud cover, and thunderstorms. In October 1961 this aircraft made the Branch's first trip to another country, deploying across the Pacific for weather re-

In 1964, 66722 was modified for a study of turbulence at high altitude named Project HiCAT. The gust probe on the nose was nicknamed the "Barber's Pole." (Lockheed LA 3562-5)

search flights across the Antarctic ice cap from Australia. Nicknamed the "Saint," 66701 spent a lot of time deployed to the AFCRL's main base at Hanscom Field, near Bedford, MA. In one test series, the Saint investigated mountain waves; during one flight over the lee of the High Sierras, a smooth but strong updraft carried the Saint and its surprised pilot from 68,000 feet to 69,500 feet in a matter of minutes.[15]

A fifth U-2 (66682) joined the Special Projects Branch later in 1960. This was another U-2 that had been damaged in a forced landing and returned to Lockheed for repair. It was introduced as a test platform for satellite camera systems and Army mapping cameras. It flew the Tiros 1 and Nimbus weather satellite sensors before they were committed to orbit. In 1963, 66682 flew an infrared reconnaissance sensor, and was also used in the High Altitude Sky Background Measurement Program. But in 1964 this aircraft was reclaimed from the Air Force by the CIA and converted to an operational reconnaissance aircraft once again.

Project HiCAT

In early 1964, 66722 was modified again for Project HICAT. This was a fresh study of high-altitude clear air turbulence sponsored by the Air Force Flight Dynamics Laboratory. The purpose was to ensure that future fast and high-flying aircraft could be designed to the appropriate structural criteria. The AFFDL had studied the previous data on turbulence above 50,000 feet, which was almost entirely derived from the weather package carried on the CIA U-2s during training flights pre-1960.

This time a more sophisticated instrumentation package was designed. Lockheed designed and built a special gust probe with fixed vanes that was stuck on the nose of the U-2. It was painted in red and white stripes, and so inevitably became known as the "Barber's Pole." The vanes sensed vertical and lateral gusts, while longitudinal gusts were sensed by a pressure transducer in the aircraft's pitot-static tube. As the vanes moved in rough air, they generated electrical signals that were recorded on magnetic tape. Since the aircraft itself was bound to move as it encountered the rough air, this was measured by accelerometers and gyros placed in the Q-bay, so that the appropriate corrections could be made.

66721 carrying photo-resolution markings for yet another test project in the late 1960s.

On display at an Edwards open house, 66721 was the second two-seat U-2D. In the late 1960s, the protracted effort to develop a missile launch warning satellite was reaching fruition, and the latest sensors were test-flown first on the AFFTC's U-2s.

The HiCAT research program extended over the next four years, although for the first year or so the HiCAT aircraft was also tasked with other duties, so that the accumulation of data was slow. In October 1965 the aircraft was fitted with new digital instrumentation, and was henceforth dedicated to HiCAT. The bird was now deliberately flown into regions where clear air turbulence was predicted, resulting either from jetstreams, weather fronts, temperature inversions, or mountain waves. An average of three flights were made each week, with the aircraft airborne for four hours each time.

Eight years earlier, the early U-2 pilots would have been aghast at the idea of deliberately seeking out turbulence in this way. It would be inviting structural trouble! Yet serial 66722 was to survive nearly 55 hours of flight in high-altitude turbulence over the four years of the HiCAT project, during which time a grand total of 285 sorties and 1,221 flying hours were logged! The aircraft flew out of Edwards, Hickam, Ramey, Hanscom, and Elmendorf AFB, in Alaska. In June 1966 it was deployed to New Zealand to sample conditions over the South Pacific, and moved on to Australia the following month. In March 1967 the research was extended to Europe. The aircraft flew from the UK test airfield at Thurleigh, near Bedford, over the eastern Atlantic and the Scottish Highlands. Two sorties over the French and Italian Alps were made in mid-April. Then it was back to the eastern U.S., with 66722 deployed to Barksdale, Loring, Albrook (Panana), and Patrick AFBs in succession. The project ended at Edwards in February 1968.[16]

New IR sensors
By 1965, the two U-2D aircraft had carried a variety of IR sensors to high altitude: new radiometers that operated in a wider spectral range, or with greater sensitivity at the target wavelengths. Background measurements were made with a spectrometer designed by A.D. Little, and another package designed by the Jet Propulsion Laboratory. A General Electric IR Vidicon (television) detector was also flown. But it was trial and error all the way—especially since the new generation of solid-fueled ballistic missiles propellants burned cooler than the early liquid-fueled missiles, and the radiation signatures of ascending missiles changed according to their altitude.

Early in 1966, Harry Andonian completed his tour in charge of the Special Projects Branch, and handed over to Lt Col J.K. Campbell. Also in 1966, with the operational U-2 fleet dwindling, AFFTC was obliged to give up two of its four remaining aircraft. 66701 and 66954 were sent to the Lockheed depot at Van Nuys, where they were converted to J75 power and transferred to SAC as U-2C models. That left U-2D 66721 and U-2A 66722 to continue as test birds at Edwards. They never were re-engined, and soon became the only remaining U-2s powered by the J57.

The effort to develop a reliable space-based ICBM launch detection system lasted throughout the 1960s. New long wavelength IR and visible light sensors were developed. Lockheed lost the integration contract for the spaceborne missile warning system, which was now designated Program 949, to TRW. In May 1968 new instrumentation was installed in 66721, and it flew 31 test missions in support of Program 949 from Hanscom Field and Patrick AFB by October.

In June 1968, a former CIA U-2F was added to the Edwards fleet. 66692 flew a variety of missions that year, as did 66722 after the HiCAT

From 1971-74, 66692 flew in this heavily-modified configuration during Project TRIM, with two IR tracking domes above the fuselage. (Lockheed PR 1186)

The surviving U-2D, 66721, at Edwards in the mid-1970s. Like its sister ship 66722, it retained the J57 engine until they were both retired in 1978.

project ended in February. Project codenames included Senior Girl, Have Echo II, and Meteor. The various tasks continued in 1969 and 1970, including a helium-cooled sensor built by North American Autonetics for detecting satellites that was flown at night to provide the optimum conditions.

By the end of the 1960s, an operational missile launch warning satellite was finally in prospect. The first Defense Support Program (DSP) satellite was launched in November 1970, and the second in May 1971. The Edwards U-2s still flew out of Patrick AFB testing the IR sensors whenever U.S. missile launches were scheduled on the Eastern Test Range. The DSP system was declared operational in December 1973.

Project TRIM

In May 1971, 66692 was returned to Lockheed for a major modification. It emerged from the Palmdale depot in November that year with a huge dorsal spine, housing two tracking domes containing 36- and 24-inch IR detectors that rotated in synchro. 66692 spent the next two-and-half years on

Project TRIM (Target Radiation Intensity Measurement). The aim was to determine whether specific types of propulsion could be determined by measuring missiles' launch plumes, and also to measure the radiation characteristics of re-entry vehicles.

After the TRIM project finished in June 1974, 66692 was demodified to U-2C standard and re-issued to SAC for the ALSS program. This again left just the two J57-powered U-birds at Edwards. 66721 and 66722 were kept in the inventory for another four years. They were repainted in a smart white color scheme with a red cheat line, and used to chase the Compass Cope long-endurance UAVs.

The U-2s were sometimes made available to students of the Test Pilots School at Edwards as part of their course. After all, they had heard about the aircraft's challenging flight characteristics, and budding test pilots were naturally keen to have a go in the Dragon Lady. Newcomers were first flown in the back seat of the U-2D; throughout the 21 years that U-2s were operated by AFFTC, the flight test organization always trained its own pilots.

Towards the end of their flight test careers, the last two AFFTC aircraft were repainted in a smart red-and-white color scheme. This is 66722, the single-seat U-2A. (Lockheed LN 6296)

NASA

On 3 June 1971, a U-2 touched down at Moffett Field, CA, and taxied to the NASA Ames Research Center. It was newly-painted in white and gray, and carried blue NASA markings and civilian registrations. Another one followed a few days later. The pair of former spyplanes—and their pilots—were being recycled into a new career as "Earth Resources Survey Aircraft."

By the late 1960s, it was obvious that the huge U.S. national investment in high-altitude reconnaissance aircraft and sensors could have valuable civilian applications. The CIA had already made provision for other federal agencies to access some classified overhead photography. Both the SAC and the CIA U-2 units flew missions in support of civilian agencies, but only when their busy schedule allowed.

In 1968 Art Lundahl, the NPIC Director and imagery analysis guru, recommended the creation of a "White Center," where aerial photography could be used for emergency management purposes. The idea gained traction when a few early-model U-2s became available, after they were replaced by the U-2R. In 1970 NASA drafted a plan to take over two of the aircraft.[1]

Knutson

At the CIA, Deputy Director for Science and Technology Carl Duckett reviewed the plan. He found that it lacked a proper appreciation of just how complicated it could be to operate the unique and temperamental U-2. In December 1970 he attended a lecture at Langley by Marty Knutson, one of the original pilots, who was now retiring from the Agency after flying the U-2 for 15 years and 4,000 hours. Knutson had other plans for his future. But over a drink-fueled lunch Duckett, together with veteran OSA managers John McMahon and John Parangosky, persuaded him to lend expertise to the NASA project.[2]

At NASA HQ, Knutson helped officials redraft their U-2 plan. The proposed base was changed from the Rome Air Development Center in upstate New York to Ames. The prospect of living and working in the Bay Area persuaded Knutson to sign up as project manager. Lockheed was contracted to overhaul the two U-2G models that were in storage at North Base, and to provide pilots and the entire field maintenance, including physiological support. Kelly Johnson hired three of Knutson's veteran colleagues from the CIA's Project Idealist to fly the airplanes: Jim Barnes, Bob Ericson, and Ivor "Chunky" Webster. Between them, this trio contributed another 40 years of U-2 flying experience! (Frank Powers also applied, but was told that his notoriety precluded selection. Senior officials at NASA wanted

to downplay the connection between their new operation and the U-2's spyplane past as much as they possibly could).

At the Palmdale depot, Skunk Works engineers removed the carrier-landing modifications from Articles 348 and 349, and some other items, which reduced their zero fuel weight to 13,800 lb. They were given the civilian registrations N708NA and N709NA. Then Chunky Webster flew them both to Ames, where familiarization flights were followed by the first data acquisition flight on 31 August 1971.

Landsat

The initial purpose of the NASA project was to acquire small scale, low resolution, multispectral photography over selected representative ecosystems to simulate the Return Beam Vidicon (RBV) data system, which would be aboard the forthcoming Earth Resources Technology Satellite (ERTS, or Landsat 1). Four 70 mm Vinten framing cameras were mounted vertically in the Q-bay to simultaneously image the same ground area. Equipped with 1 1/2-inch focal length lenses, the first three cameras were flown with black and white emulsion film, spectrally filtered to image the green, red, and near infrared portions of the electro-magnetic spectrum, with the fourth camera loaded with color infrared film.[3]

The two U-2s flew over five "control" areas chosen for their particular ecological interest. Four of the areas were in California and Arizona, and were therefore reached easily from the Moffett Field base, but the fifth

At Palmdale in 1971, Lockheed modified the two surviving U-2G models for their new role as "Earth Survey Aircraft" with NASA. (Lockheed U2-91-019-9)

ONCE TOP SECRET SPY PLANE IN NEW CIVILIAN ROLE

The famous U-2 spy plane has left the "black Air Force" for NASA's civilian fleet to probe the ecological secrets of the U.S....NASA has indefinite possession of two U-2s for earth surveys.

Martin Knutson, manager of the Earth Resources Aircraft program at NASA Ames, says the aircraft is a "natural" for earth surveys. "In my personal opinion, it is the most stable platform man has ever designed."

- *Aerospace Daily, 17 September 1971*

HIGH ALTITUDE PERSPECTIVE (NASA SP-427)

The unusual (U-2) aircraft that is the subject of this descriptive booklet...can scan shorelines, measure water levels, help fight forest fires, collect mapping data, assess flood damage, and sample the stratosphere. Over the oceans it can make sensitive measurements of water color and current; over land it can provide a form of "ground truth" that is valuable in calibrating the rich store of information from our satellites. Because it can do these things so well, it deserves attention for the service it is providing.

Anthony Calio
Associate Administrator
NASA Space and Terrestrial Applications

Inflight view of NASA 708 reveals the seven windows of the B-camera hatch in the Q-bay. (Lockheed U2-91-019-5)

was the Chesapeake Bay region of the eastern U.S. seaboard, which required a deployment to the NASA airfield at Wallops Island, Virginia.

For the first time, details of the U-2 payload specifications and cameras were made freely available through NASA, which needed to acquaint the wider scientific community with the research possibilities that the high-altitude aircraft now offered. In 1972-73, the U-2's original Hycon 24-inch cameras from 1956 were made available in the A-1, A-2, and A-3 configurations. A Wild-Heerbrug RC-10 metric mapping camera was also added, and this could also be flown with one of the 24-inch A-cameras (to make the A-4 configuration). The B-camera arrived from North Base when the CIA finally quit flying the U-2 in 1974.

Multispectral

Additionally, a multispectral scanner built by NASA's Goddard Space Flight Center was integrated into the aircraft, to provide a full simulation of the Landsat capability. After the delayed launch of the first Landsat, the NASA U-2s staged "underflights" along the satellite's track at 65,000 feet, to provide a means of comparison with the imagery being relayed from space.

Landsat 2 was not launched until January 1975. Long before this time, the NASA U-2 operation had been extended and placed on a more permanent basis. The High Altitude Missions Branch was established within Ames. In November 1973 the aircraft were recruited into NASA's long-term Stratospheric Research Program. They carried a variety of sensors to 60,000 feet or higher to measure various gases and particles, such as ozone, nitric oxide, and man-made pollutants.

The first of what became an annual series of deployments to Eielson AFB, Alaska, took place in summer 1974. There was a month-long deployment to Hickam AFB, Hawaii, later that year, followed by visits to Howard AFB, Panama Canal Zone, and Loring AFB, Maine. By 1977 the two U-birds had sampled the stratosphere from the eastern U.S. coast to 1,000 miles west of Hawaii, and from 10 degrees south latitude to the North Polar region.

The sampling devices on the NASA U-2 were more sophisticated than those carried by the SAC aircraft in previous decades. There was an Ames-designed Q-bay sampler weighing 500 lbs that used chemiluminescent reactions to continuously measure gases in situ. An alternative Q-bay payload, also designed at Ames, consisted of four cryogenically-cooled sam-

Lockheed provided the maintenance and physiological support for the new NASA U-2 operation under contract. (Lockheed U2-91-019-11)

PHOTO-MAPPING PROJECTS: ARIZONA AND ALASKA

A cooperative program between the state of Arizona, the U.S. Geological Survey, and NASA resulted in the acquisition of black and white panchromatic metric photography by the U-2 in summer 1972. This was utilized by the Geological Survey to produce 7.5 minute, 1:24,000 scale orthophoto quadrangle sheets. Using new orthophoto compilation techniques, full quadrangle compilation could be accomplished from a single stereo model, eliminating the extra step of photographically mosaicing separate models into quad sheet representations. This was the first demonstration of the use of high altitude aircraft data for quadrangle map production over a large area.

Faced with the administration, mapping, surveying, and conveyance of federal lands in Alaska to the State and native corporations, a consortium of Federal and State agencies requested NASA's assistance in acquiring high altitude black and white and color infrared photography of the entire state. Over eight years from 1978, flights were conducted resulting in 95% of Alaska being photographed with color infrared and black and white films with less than 10% cloud cover.

The U-2s from Ames were joined in Alaska by the WB-57F operated by NASA Houston, and in the first year of the program they photographed 25,000 line miles of the state at a cost of $496,000. It worked out at less than $20 per data mile, which the bureaucrats reckoned was very good value, compared with trekking through the tundra or hiring a lightplane and zig-zagging about at low level. During the mapping of Alaska, the U-2s flew at between 60,000 and 65,000 feet with the dual RC-10 camera configuration. The 6-inch camera was loaded with black and white film, and the 12-inch one with color infrared film. The flights could only be conducted in the short summer season when the snows had melted and vegetation was flourishing. – *C.P.*

"BIG BANG" THEORY CHALLENGED

In 1976 a team of astrophysics researchers from Berkeley designed and placed an "Aether Drift" radiometer in the U-2, which looked upwards rather than downwards. A special Q-bay hatch top with two sensor ports was fabricated to accomodate the ultra-sensitive microwave device. It measured the cosmic radiation that had been discovered in 1965 to be still coming from the most distant parts of space.

The pilots had to fly the U-2 level to within one-half a degree, because only then would the effects of the earth's atmospheric microwave radiation be canceled out, thereby allowing the sensor to accurately detect the very-low-frequency light radiation coming from way beyond the quasars in outer space. "Chunky" Webster flew most of the 11 highly-demanding night flights over the western U.S. at 65,000 feet for this experiment. "Actually, we did better than required," he told Lockheed's company newspaper. "The U-2's lateral displacement was plus or minus one-sixth of a degree—that's just about as straight and level as you can fly an airplane."

The Aether Drift radiometer was, in effect, a camera that built up an image part by part spread over the 11 flights, but the frequency of the signal that the scientists were trying to detect was 20,000 times lower than the frequency of visible light! Thanks to plane and pilot, the flight criteria were met—an on-board measurement system indicated that average lateral displacement of the U-2 during Webster's flights was only plus or minus one-sixth of a degree!

From the data collected, the Berkeley scientists challenged the "Big Bang" theory of evolution. They concluded that far from being a cataclysmic explosion, this event was a very smooth, almost serene process, with matter and energy uniformly distributed and expanding at an equal rate in all directions. Not only that, they discovered that the entire Milky Way galaxy was streaking through the universe at a velocity greater than one million miles per hour, and that the universe was probably not spinning, contrary to currently-accepted theory. – *C.P.*

An impressive line-up of the sensors that could be carried by the NASA U-2s by the late 1970s. The special Q-bay hatch containing the upward-looking Aether Drift Radiometer is in front of the nose. (NASA)

plers, plus two whole air samplers to collect gases for laboratory analysis after landing. There was also an Ames version of the traditional filter paper type sampler for collecting aerosol and halogen particles.

Declassified

More payloads were added. The Itek Optical Bar Camera was declassified in 1974 so that the NASA U-2s could fly it. This was followed in early 1975 by the HRB Singer thermal scanner and Goddard Space Flight Center's Heat Capacity Mapper.

During 1979 the Daedalus Multispectral Scanner was integrated onto the aircraft, and was the first digitally-recorded multispectral scanner to become available.[4]

In February 1977 another U-2 veteran joined the NASA team. Former CIA pilot Jim Cherbonneaux had spent 11 years at Project HQ, and helped to close down Project Idealist in 1974. Then he worked at NPIC for a couple of years before moving to Ames as the non-flying head of the High Altitude Missions Branch. By the time he arrived the two aircraft had acquired imagery from all 50 U.S. states, covering some 35 percent of their total surface area. The imagery had proved useful in nearly all the earth science disciplines. Forest diseases and insect infestations had been detected and timber harvesting practices improved; photographic data of watersheds had indicated where pollution needed to be tackled; large-area coverage provided "the big picture" on population and agricultural trends to state and local government land-use planners. NASA U-2 photography had also proved invaluable in assessing the effects of natural disasters, such as fires and floods. In rapid-response missions for the State of California, the aircraft were dispatched to the scene of forest fires. The photographs taken showed the extent of the inflagration, possible access routes for firefighters, and potential firebreak locations. During the 1975-76 drought, U-2 photos helped ensure that water levels were managed in rivers and reservoirs.

"What this is, is classic plowshare technology," noted Cherbonneaux, referring to the aircraft's (and his own) origins. "You know what I mean? Beating swords into plowshares?"

Not everyone saw it that way. To some California citizens, the NASA U-2 was still a spy in the sky. In 1977 the state Coastal Conservation Commission commissioned a photo survey to help its wastelands management program. But the photos also served another purpose. Unlicensed construction in the coastal zone had recently been prohibited, and licences were hard to get. The survey was flown with the big 24-inch cameras, and therefore provided high resolution 9 x 18 negatives from which it was possible to determine whether landholders had defied the ban on construction. Citizens of the town of Bolinas got particularly vocal about it; a resident attorney summed up local feelings: "I do have this gut reaction to this eye in the sky able to look at all the little things in people's backyards. It's a feeling of distaste, you know, that this is just one more step on the road to 1984."

All the imagery that the NASA U-2s collected was available for public inspection at Ames, via a computerized image retrieval system. Anyone could purchase full-scale reproductions of any frame from a huge data bank in South Dakota.

A color infrared photograph of the Hubbard Glacier in Alaska, taken by the RC-10 survey camera of a NASA U-2 in August 1978. Since each object on the ground reflects and absorbs different wavelengths, this type of film can reveal features that go unrecorded by ordinary black and white or natural color film. (NASA ACC-50193-2546)

Marty Knutson ended his long U-2 flying career in 1985, but continued working for NASA at Ames and Dryden for another 12 years. (via Marty Knutson)

Upgraded model

When Lockheed won the contract in 1978 to restart U-2 production as the TR-1, NASA quickly signed up for the upgraded model. At NASA Houston, the three WB-57F aircraft also in use for earth resource surveys were getting old. Although they carried a larger payload, the U-2 beat them on range, altitude, and above all, stability.

The maximum payload of the new U-bird for NASA would be 2,600 lbs. That still did not match the 4,000 lbs offered by the WB-57F. But the greater volume offered by the superpods, larger Q-bay, and detachable nose would be very useful, and the ability to combine sensors and experiments on different parts of the ER-2 during the same flight meant that the cost could be shared amongst a number of researchers.

The new aircraft for NASA was designated ER-2. It was the very first aircraft built on the reopened production line at Palmdale. Smartly painted as N706NA, the ER-2 was first flown by Skunk Works test pilot Art Peterson on 11 May 1981. Marty Knutson delivered it to Moffett Field on 10 June.

In 1982 Chunky Webster was the first of the veteran pilots to retire from NASA. When Marty Knutson was promoted and gained additional responsibilities at NASA's Dryden Flight Research Center in 1985, he also finally quit flying the U-2. Bob Ericson retired at the same time, leaving Jim Barnes as the sole survivor from the early days. Barnes finally hung up his pressure suit in late 1988, after flying the Deuce (he never called it the Dragon Lady!) for 31 years. He amassed a remarkable 5,760 hours in the U-2, a record that is unlikely ever to be matched. At about the same time Jim Cherbonneaux also retired. His replacement as chief of the High Altitude Missions Branch was John Arvesen.

Demand

The demand for new surveys continued. There were also continuing deployments to Wallops Island in Virginia. In the summer of 1984, a U-2 flew from there to photograph more than 80,000 square miles in five eastern states, in order to survey the damage being caused to standing trees by the gypsy moth caterpillar, and assess whether spraying programs were having the desired effect. The following year, the ER-2 flew over Florida

Jim Barnes retired in 1988, after flying U-2s for the CIA and NASA for an uninterrupted span of 32 years. During that time, he clocked up an amazing 5,862 flying hours in the aircraft, a record that will likely stand unmatched in U-2 history. (NASA AC89-0093-18)

in a major survey of the state's citrus trees for the Department of Agriculture. In both surveys, the Itek Iris II panoramic camera was used, loaded with color infrared film. The Iris was becoming a favorite tool for regulatory agencies, thanks to its high resolution and wide coverage. The Environmental Protection Agency used it to check up on illegal dumping of waste.

Although NASA was not keen to publicize it, there were also a number of missions being flown by the U-2 and ER-2 aircraft in support of Department of Defense projects. The most notable of these was Teal Ruby, a satellite that would detect and track aircraft from space by measuring their infrared signature. It formed part of the Air Force's Air Defence Initiative (ADI) to defend U.S. airspace against future missile and bomber threats. While these could currently be detected by radar, alternative forms of detection might be necessary if the USSR developed stealth technology. The Teal Ruby concept was made possible by advances in charged-coupled devices and cryogenic cooling of sensors. The satellite would carry a six-foot tall infrared telescope that "stared" down at the earth's surface and registered disruptions to the normal background signal return (caused by an aircraft) on a mosaic of thousands of focal-plane detectors.

It was complex technology, and one of the problems was establishing a database of background measurements. The NASA ER- 2 was enlisted to fly a similar multiwavelength infrared sensor as part of a Teal Ruby support effort codenamed Hi-CAMP (Highly-Calibrated Airborne Measurements Program). This provided an atmospheric, terrestrial, and oceanic background database, making precise measurements of the clutter that Teal Ruby would have to deal with. The ability of the Hi-CAMP sensor to pick out aircraft from the ER-2's 65,000 feet cruising height was also tested. In a year-long series of highly coordinated flights over the western U.S. and Europe (the latter while the ER-2 was deployed to Mildenhall airbase in the UK during the spring of 1985), a variety of U.S. Air Force aircraft ranging in size from a T-38 to a C-5 were flown against the Hi-CAMP sensor. The Teal Ruby satellite itself was ready for launch by 1986, but the Challenger shuttle disaster forced a three-year postponement.

The trip to the UK with the ER-2 was the first to non-U.S. territory by the High Altitude Missions Branch. The second came in January 1987 when the same aircraft was deployed to Darwin, northwest Australia. It was engaged in the Stratosphere-Troposphere Exchange Project (STEP), a continuation of earlier atmospheric studies by the Ames-based U-2s. NASA and the National Oceanic and Atmospheric Administration (NOAA) funded STEP to obtain yet more data on the mechanisms and rate of transfer of particles, trace gases, and aerosols from the troposphere into the stratosphere. Darwin was chosen as a suitable launch point for flights into the region, where the world's coldest and highest tropopause was to be found, as well as the largest and highest cumulonimbus clouds.[5]

The Ozone hole

But the most important deployment ever carried out by NASA came in 1987. It also involved the most hazardous flying—long hours over inhospitable terrain, from which rescue in the event of an accident might prove impossible. But the stakes were very high. In August and September 1987 the ER-2 flew 12 times across deepest Antarctica from Punta Arenas, southern Chile. Its mission was to take detailed measurements in the recently-discovered hole in the ozone layer that was developing over the South Pole every winter.

Over 170 scientists, NASA managers, and support crews descended on the desolate area at the southernmost tip of South America; in addition to the ER-2, NASA also deployed the Ames Research Center's converted DC-8 airliner. Between them, the two aircraft carried no fewer than 21 separate scientific payloads to measure every conceivable variable that might be linked to the alarming phenomena of ozone depletion. The whole effort cost $10 million, but it soon became apparent that it was worth every penny.

Conditions at the windswept Punta Arenas airfield were rudimentary. Before the deployment, the taxiways had to be resurfaced to prevent damage to the ER-2's delicate landing gear. Even basic office accommodation had to be specially built in the draughty military hangar allocated to the NASA team. Under difficult conditions the scientists labored to perfect their experimental payloads, and then crossed their fingers as they watched the ER-2 soar into the mostly grey and turbulent skies over the Magellan strait. The missions lasted well over six hours.

Aerial view of the NASA Ames Research Center shows the U-2/ER-2 fleet and hangar in 1989, with the wind tunnels and other research facilities behind. (NASA AC89-0215-4)

The new and the old. NASA acquired a former USAF TR-1A on loan in 1988 as N708NA. In the background is N709NA, the last of the early models still flying. (NASA AC88-0755-6)

CONFIRMING THE OZONE HOLE

The ozone hole was first discovered by a team of scientists from the British Antarctic Survey in 1985. Their measurements taken on the ground prompted NASA to recompute data from the Nimbus 7 satellite, which carried an ozone mapping spectrometer. Sure enough, the hole showed up: a 40 percent reduction in the amount of ozone over Antarctica during late winter and early spring.

The findings seemed to support a controversial theory advanced some years earlier by two California scientists. They figured that 99% of the man-made chlorofluorocarbons (CFCs) were rising into the stratosphere. Once there, ultraviolet radiation from the sun could break down CFCs into their constituent parts—including chlorine. This very reactive chemical could then attack the ozone layer. The chemical industry poured scorn on their findings, but the U.S. government was sufficiently impressed to ban the use of CFCs as spray can propellant in 1978.

The Europeans were not so impressed, even when the hole over Antarctica was discovered in 1985. They pointed out that meteorological conditions there were unusual and extreme: very cold temperatures at all levels, and strong upcurrents from the troposphere. After all, the hole was known to disappear each November, when a vortex of winds over the pole breaks up, allowing air to flow in laterally from elsewhere in the stratosphere. Maybe the ozone was being pushed out of the stratosphere every September by a natural effect that was simply part of cyclical global weather variations. Maybe solar flares were responsible. Maybe the distinctive clouds which form at record altitudes in the polar stratosphere were somehow responsible. And so on. Some American scientists suspected that European doubts were motivated by the fact that the chemical industries there had more to lose if CFCs were banned.

NASA's mission to the Antarctic was designed to settle these questions, once and for all. While the DC-8 would fly at the lowest extremities of the hole, with some of its sensors peering upwards, the ER-2 would fly right through the very center of it. It would carry some payloads from the recent STEP series of atmospheric sampling flights, but also some specially-designed experiments. Altogether, there would be 14 separate sensors carried in the nose, Q-bay, and wing pods (the shorter "Spear" type, rather than superpods, were to be used for these missions).

The most important of these, if those blaming CFCs for the ozone hole were to be vindicated, was a chlorine monoxide detector designed by Harvard chemistry professor James Anderson. But, as Anderson himself pointed out, "there isn't a single instrument on either plane that, in the long run, won't be crucial. Every chemical that can be measured must be measured, and measured precisely. If there is any ambiguity in our findings, our impact will be weakened. The burden of proof is enormous."

During the ER-2 flights over the Antarctic, Anderson's chlorine monoxide detector measured levels up to 500 times the normal concentration. The edge of the hole was found to have extended further north this year than ever—as far as Punta Arenas, in fact! Meteorological factors peculiar to the region could not be entirely discounted, but they were not themselves the cause of so much ozone depletion. Even as the scientists and airmen strived to gather this vital data, a UN convention of 30 nations in Montreal agreed to a 50 percent reduction in CFC production by 1999. When the results of NASA's expedition to southern Chile were published in early 1988, the case for a complete ban on CFCs was greatly strengthened.

After the NASA team deployed to northern Europe and measured the same depletion in the ozone layer over the Arctic in winter 1988-89, ministers and officials from 120 nations met in London to discuss the crisis. It was already clear that the Montreal agreement was inadequate; the U.S. and European countries now declared they would phase out CFCs completely. – C.P.

It was not good flying weather down there. At ground level, fronts and surface winds of up to 60 knots could develop rapidly. At altitude, the polar vortex caused winds of up to 200 knots, and temperatures as low as minus 95 degrees centigrade were experienced. Dual VHF radios and INS were fitted to aid with navigation and communications. The pilots took arctic survival courses before they left the U.S. All the same, they figured their chances of surviving an ejection onto the icecap were very slim. Unlike an earlier generation of U-2 pilots, who had flown to the North Pole on sampling flights in the early sixties, the NASA pilots did not have the comfort of an accompanying C-54 rescue aircraft with paramedics. But the flights were uneventful, and the data take was excellent. The scientists found that the hole was bigger than ever, and proved beyond doubt that man-made chlorofluorocarbons (CFCs) were to blame.

Polar vortex

Could the same phenomena of ozone depletion be occurring over the North Pole? A field investigation to the Arctic suggested it could, and so in late December 1988 the DC-8 and ER-2 were dispatched from Moffett Field to

N709NA climbs from Edwards during the record-setting flight on 17 April 1989. A few days later, it made the final flight of an early-model U-2, to a final resting place at the Robins AFB museum. (Lockheed Pl 9002)

Jerry Hoyt (left) and Ron Williams were the pilots for the record-setting flights in the last U-2C at Edwards in April 1989. (Lockheed PI 9017-16)

ABOVE THE SKY

Tugging on a zipper, Lockheed life support technician Walt Prouty struggles to close pilot Ron Williams' mustard-yellow pressure suit. "There isn't as much material here as there used to be," Prouty mutters, playing the insolent valet. Williams, silver-haired and a little paunchy, just growls....

At 58, Ron Williams may be a bit weathered for a hot-shot aviator, but he and five other retired Air Force spy pilots are still flying high. They operate civilian deriritives of the legendary U-2. The ER-2s carry only scientific experiments, and none of them is classified.

"We travel all over the world with these (aircraft)," says NASA's chief engineer for the U-2, Andy Roberts. "We give tours to politicians and military pilots overseas. Afterwards they'll take us aside and say, 'What are you *really* using it for?'"

While the payload is often the last word in sophistication, the platform carrying it is simple to the extreme. Willie Horton, a genial, heavyset ex-U-2 pilot and Lockheed's on-site manager, wouldn't have it any other way. "Among all this high-tech, we've got a barbershop fan and a manual fog scraper," he says approvingly.
- *by Doug Stewart, extracted from Air & Space magazine, August/September 1993*

Stavanger, in Norway. Each aircraft flew 14 times into the polar vortex over the next two months. The ER-2 missions lasted up to eight hours, going as far as 80 degrees North, and ranging from the Barents Sea to Greenland. For safety's sake, the flight tracks were kept to within 250 nautical miles of emergency landing strips, so that the ER-2 could glide in from 65,000 feet if it encountered trouble. The precaution was not necessary; the ER-2 performed flawlessly once again, although the pilots had a hard time navigating and landing because of the strong prevailing winds.

While the ER-2 was ranging far and wide on these vital missions, the two U-2C models were ending their 30-year flying careers. N708NA was retired at Moffett Field in mid-1987 when it reached 10,000 hours. To replace it, NASA acquired the former USAF TR-1A 80-1069 on loan as the new N708NA.

As time ran out on N709NA in the spring of 1989, Lockheed secured USAF permission to retire the last of the original U-2s in style. It was flown to Edwards so that a record-breaking flight could be made, and duly measured on the Flight Test Center's range. Of course, everyone involved with the aircraft had always known that it could smash the world time-to-climb and sustained altitude records for its weight category. But the aircraft's maximum performance had always been shrouded in official secrecy. Now, the veil would be lifted.

On 17 April 1989, with observers from the Federation Aeronautique Internationale (FAI), the press, and television looking on, Jerry Hoyt took off from Edwards with only 395 gallons on board. Those who were unfamiliar with a high-performance U-2 take-off gasped as Hoyt climbed away almost vertically.

Records

From the control room at NASA's Dryden Research Facility at the edge of the lakebed, Hoyt's progress was tracked by radar. The old time-to-climb records in the FAI's C-1F Group III weight category were all held by a Lear Jet, the hottest of the small business jets. Predictably enough, the U-2C broke them by a very wide margin. It reached 3 kilometers altitude (9,842 feet) in 52 seconds, compared with one minute 48 seconds for the Lear Jet. At six, nine, and 12 kilometers, the performance gap widened still further. N709NA reached 15 kilometers (49,212 feet) in six minutes 15 seconds, almost three times faster than the previous record. The Lear jet

had eventually reached 54,370 feet, but Hoyt had a way to go yet. He passed 20 kilometers (65,617 feet) in 12 minutes 13 seconds, and finally rounded out at 73,700 feet after just 16 minutes.

Hoyt brought the bird back down and taxied up to the NASA hangar. Ben Rich and most of the Skunk Works managers and test pilots were on hand to greet him, including Tony LeVier. The spritely 76 year-old who had made the first flight in a U-2 almost 34 years earlier was, as usual, in a voluble mood. "It's a hell of an airplane," he told reporters. "That damn plane may have kept us out of World War III." Rich said the record flight would pay tribute to all those who had been associated with the aircraft over the years.

The Thematic Mapper Simulator was widely-flown in the 1980s and 1990s. Digital data from this multispectral scanner could be manipulated with a computer classification algorithm to produce maps of land use, such as this one of Santa Cruz, CA, in which 12 classes of land cover are differentiated. (NASA)

The next day Ron Williams made another measured flight, this time with the aircraft fully-fueled to give a gross takeoff weight of 20,900 lb. This time, records in the higher weight C-1G category were broken. Then Williams flew the short distance to Palmdale, where Lockheed repainted the aircraft black at the request of its new owners-to-be, the air museum at Robins AFB in Georgia. On 26 April 1989 Doyle Krumrey had the honor of piloting the last of the original U-2s to its final resting place.

A second purpose-built ER-2 was delivered to NASA in 1989 from Palmdale, and became the new N709NA. The NASA ER-2 fleet numbered three until 1996, when the USAF reclaimed N708NA after a nine-year loan.

Busy schedule

In June 1991, N706NA returned to Europe for a series of flights out of RAF Alconbury using the AVIRIS, TMS, and RC-10 camera sensors. A busy schedule of deployments continued for the next three years. ER-2s flew out of Eielson AFB, Bangor, ME, and Christchurch, New Zealand, to study the winter polar stratosphere.

In 1992, NASA began investigations to determine whether a future fleet of commercial supersonic transports (SSTs) would also reduce the ozone layer. The ER-2 took measurements of the known ozone depletion catalysts from 60-65,000 feet in the 15-60 deg N latitudes where most SSTs would fly. In one 1993 sortie, the ER-2 took samples from the wake of a specially-flown Air France Concorde over New Zealand. The scientists concluded that SSTs would have little impact on the ozone layer.[6]

The ER-2 then participated in the SUCCESS project (SUbsonic aircraft: Contral and Cloud Effects Special Study) to measure the effect on cirrus cloud formation of the growing world fleet of subsonic airliners. Unusually, this sometimes required the NASA pilots to fly at lower levels—around 40,000 feet.

In early 1993 an ER-2 was flown out of Townsville, Australia, as part of the highly-coordinated TOGA COARE project to explore the formation of tropical storms over the unique "warm pool" of water in the Pacific Ocean, northeast of Papua New Guinea. This was done by measuring the heat radiating from the earth's surface, as well as with atmospheric measurement. No fewer than nine sensors were carried during the flights. The ultimate goal was to develop satellite sensors that could help predict storm formations and movement.

Laser system

A laser-based system weighing 1,000 lbs was carried by the ER-2, starting in 1994. The Lidar Atmospheric Sensing Experiment (LASE) was built by NASA Langley at a cost of $20 million to operate autonomously, and flights were conducted from NASA's Wallops Island airfield in Virginia in coordination with other lidars on the Space Shuttle and NASA's lower-flying Electra. It fired 20-megawatt bursts of laser light straight down from the Q-bay to analyze water vapor in the atmosphere. The LASE would eventually go into orbit, but like many satellite sensors before it, the high-flying capability of the U-2 was invaluable for proving flights.[7]

For the airborne monitoring of critical payloads such as LASE, the ER-2 had a rudimentary, one-channel, omni-directional telemetry system transmitting at 1 Mb/s. But in 1995, the NASA High Altitude Missions Branch secured a loan from the Pentagon of the prototype U-2 Senior Spur satcom system. It was renamed STARLink (Satellite Telemetry and Return Link) and added to N709NA. STARlink offered the possibility of getting

urgent imagery—of floods, hurricanes, or wildfires, for instance—transmitted in near real time from the ER-2 to the ground. There was also a command uplink that would enable scientists to control their research payloads from the ground.[8]

In theory, STARLink made it possible for the payload scientists to stay at home, rather than accompany the ER-2 to remote airfields throughout the world. In practice, the satcom link was best used for environmental emergencies. For instance, the ER-2 would fly over forest fires and transmit images showing hotspots, which firefighters at the scene could download via the Internet. STARLink was used for four years, but did not find enough funding from NASA to justify retention of such a sophisticated system.

Although the entire USAF fleet of U-2s was being re-engined with the GE F118 turbofan, NASA did evaluate keeping the J75 on its pair of ER-2s. In the end, however, it signed up for the conversion. N706NA was re-engined in October 1996, and N709NA followed six months later. The aircraft designation did not change.

In 1997 Marty Knutson finally retired as chief of flight operations at Ames, after 47 years of service to the USAF, CIA, and NASA. At the end of the same year, the pair of ER-2s moved from Ames to the Dryden Flight Research Center at Edwards AFB as part of a cost cutting exercise at NASA.

From their new base the aircraft were as busy as ever, with experiments related to Earth resources, celestial observations, atmospheric chemistry and dynamics, oceanic processes, satellite calibration and data vali-

In the 1990s, NASA flew three ER-2 aircraft—until the USAF reclaimed N708NA in 1996. (NASA AC96-0106-1)

A U-2 satcom datalink was modified and renamed STARLink and flown on N709NA from 1995-98. (NASA)

dation, and so on. By now, NASA's ER-2s and the predecessor U-2Cs had flown over 4,000 missions. More experiments were coordinated with NASA's DC-8, such as the 1998 deployment to Patrick AFB, Florida, when an ER-2 flew over Hurricane Bonnie at 65,000ft while the DC-8 flew into the storm.

LM contract

Lockheed Martin continued to provide four pilots, plus maintainers and physiological support to the NASA ER-2 operation under contract. A fifth pilot, Jim Barrilleaux, was employed directly by NASA, and was now the veteran of the operation, having signed on in 1986. The five pilots did their own mission planning; there was no specialist navigator assigned.

The most-flown ER-2 sensor was now the AVIRIS hyperspectral scanner, but data derived from the wet-film RC-10 camera was still in demand. A modified multi-spectral scanner built by Daedalus Enterprises and NASA (MODIS - Moderate Resolution Imaging Spectrometer) was also added. This recorded 50 channels of 16-bit data in the visible, near infrared, mid-infrared, and thermal portions of the spectrum. An X-band pulsed-Doppler radar was specially designed for the ER-2 to measure cloud formations.

Monitoring of the ozone layer remained a key task. In early January 2000, N809NA (ex N709NA) deployed with the DC-8 to a very cold and very dark Kiruna airbase, Sweden, for research on ozone depletion inside the Arctic Circle. The SOLVE (SAGE III Ozone Loss and Validation Experiment) campaign required the ER-2 to fly to the North Pole. During the campaign, NASA also made the first flight by a U-2-type aircraft over Russia since the downing of Gary Powers 40 years earlier!

North Pole

NASA pilot Dee Porter flew the first SOLVE mission to the North Pole in total darkness. For navigation in this hostile environment, a backup GPS/INS system named PARS (Platform Attitude Heading Reference) was added to the ER-2, supplementing the primary system, which integrates GPS with the Litton LTN-92 INS. Porter was able to maintain communication with Kiruna via the commercial Iridium satellite system, using a blade antenna on the ER-2. In view of the very low temperatures, extra precautions were

STARLINK

An airborne satcom system developed by Unisys Corporation for military use has been modified, and is being integrated into an Ames Research Center ER-2 aircraft. This equipment will support multiple data rates up to 43 Mb/s each for an aggregate rate of 274 Mb/s via the TDRS Ku-band satellite. The data stream from the ER-2 will be downlinked to the White Sands Complex, and then relayed via Domsat to Ames. The data will then be demultiplexed and transferred to a workstation having 64 MB memory and interfaced to an 18 GB storage array.

The Airborne Element consists of an Airborne Data Recorder...an Airborne Modem Assembly...transceiver...TWT Amplifier, and a 30-inch steerable parabolic antenna. The TDRSS element consists of the TDRSS constellation and the Second TDRSS Ground Terminal....

The Ground Station Element at Ames allows investigators to use telephone modems, Internet, or private on-site Local Area Network (LAN) for access to their data...A full duplex voice channel is embedded...and allows constant communication with the ER-2 pilot.

- NASA Ames Research Center, High
Altitude Missions Branch paper

THE ER-X PROPOSAL

In 1995, NASA and Lockheed explored the possibility of boosting the aircraft's maximum altitude. With the existing J75 powerplant, the ER-2 could take a 2,000 lb payload to 65-70,000 feet. That was higher than some of the alternative aircraft available to researchers, such as the WB-57F and Myasischev M-55 (65,000 feet), or Grob Egrett (55,000 feet). But two new propeller-powered and turbocharged high altitude research aircraft now promised to reach 80, 000 feet: the Grob Strato-2C in Germany, and Aurora Flight Sciences Perseus UAV that NASA was already funding.

Some scientists specializing in atmospheric chemistry wanted to fly their research payloads as high as possible. When re-engined with the F118, the ER-2 would be able to reach 74-76,000 feet. By extending the wingtips of the ER-2 to increase the aspect ratio from 10.7 to 12.9, and flying with no wing pods and a reduced payload and fuel load, the F118-powered ER-2 could reach 76-78,000 feet. Lockheed did preliminary design of removable extended wingtips, which would be supported by new wingtip skids, in addition to the mid-wing pogos.

In a Lockheed/NASA Ames briefing dated 1 December 1995, the modification was dubbed ER-X, and described as minimal risk. It would be accomplished during the re-engining of the NASA aircraft.

The ER-X proposal was not taken up. In any case, the "rival" high-altitude platforms failed to make good on their promise. For practical purposes, the ER-2 remained the highest-altitude air-breathing platform available to atmospheric researchers. – *C.P.*

WEATHER FLIGHTS FROM EGLIN

Although it is not the Space Shuttle, NASA is launching an unusual aircraft at Eglin for the next few weeks...NASA researchers, along with universities including Texas A&M, are using the ER-2 aircraft to collect data about storms and temperatures around Houston. The equipment costs about $25 million, which is about the same as a basic U-2.

Gary Shelton, the ER-2 program director, said the group used Eglin because if the weather is poor in Houston, they can't take off...The purpose of the tests is to make weather forecasting technology more accurate.

"And the bigger, the badder the weather, the better it is for the scientists' equipment," said ER-2 pilot Bill Collette. He said that they gear up for a flight when the meteorologists report a big storm heading towards Texas. About an hour (after takeoff) the pilot reaches the Houston area at the target altitude of 65,000 feet. "They say about 90% of the earth's atmosphere is below us," said Collette....

The aircraft and researchers plan to be at Eglin for at least another two weeks. Other experiments include tracking the amount of rainfall along the Texas Coast through microwave and infrared sensors.

- extracted from Eglin Express, special edition, undated

PORTER RECOUNTS FLIGHT THROUGH RUSSIAN AIRSPACE

On 27 January 2000 Dee Porter, a Lockheed Martin pilot under contract to NASA's Dryden Airborne Science program, became the first pilot to fly a U-2-type aircraft through Russian airspace since Francis Gary Powers was downed by Soviet missiles in 1960....

Porter, apprehensive about overflight safety, asked a Russian Air Force general if all air traffic control centers and air defense systems would be notified in advance. The general assured him: "There will not be a second incident."

With the flight plan filed with Moscow, Porter piloted the ER-2 across the Finnish-Russian border. The aircraft was loaded with more than a ton of scientific equipment, and Porter was responsible to switch it on at various locations designated by SOLVE's team of 250 scientists. Some 17 different environmental experiments were performed during the flight....

Porter began flying the U-2 with the Air Force in 1980, and has some 3,200 flight hours in that aircraft—more than any other active U-2 pilot....

Porter's first mission out of Kiruna during the SOLVE deployment was to fly the single-engine ER-2 to the North Pole and back. Prior to the flight, Arctic survival instructors had warned that if he had to eject at altitude—with an outside air temperature of minus 83 degrees centigrade—survival would not be an issue. He would be frozen before hitting the ground. Porter explained, "that's when you say, GE and Lockheed Martin, don't fail me now!" He added, "But true to form, the engine and the airplane performed superbly."

- extracted from LM Aero Star, Palmdale, 30 March 2000

INDEX OF INSTRUMENTS

The following list of instruments that are currently cleared for use on the ER-2 gives an idea of the variety and scale of the NASA operation. The list does not include the three standard camera systems that can also be carried, eg the RC-10 mapping camera, the HR-732 24-inch focal length framing camera, and the IRIS 24-inch panoramic camera.

Airborne Chromatograph For Atmospheric Trace Species (ACATS)
Airborne Laser Induced Atmospheric Sensor (ALIAS)
Advanced Microwave Precipitation Radiometer (AMPR)
Airborne Tunable Laser Absorption Spectrometer (ATLAS)
Airborne Visible - InfraRed Imaging Spectrometer (AVIRIS)
Cloud LIDAR System (CLS)
Condensation Nucleus Counter (CNC)
Harvard Carbon Dioxide Experiment (Harvard CO2)
Composition and Photo-Dissociative Flux Measurement (CPFM)
ER-2 Doppler Radar (EDOP)
Focused Cavity Aerosol Spectrometer (FCAS)
High Resolution Interferometer Sounder (HIS)
Harvard Hydroxyl Experiment (HOx)
Large Area Collectors (LAC)
Lidar Atmospheric Sensing Experiment (LASE)
Lightning Instrument Package (LIP)
Microwave Imaging Radiometer (MIR)
Meteorological Measurement System (MMS)
Microwave Temperature Profiler (MTP)
MIT Millimeter-Wave Temperature Sounder (MTS)
NASA Aircraft Satellite Instrument Calibration (NASIC)
NOAA Water Vapor Experiment (H2O)
Reactive Nitrogen Experiment (NOy)
Harvard Ozone Experiment (O3)
Quartz Crystal Microbalance/Surface Acoustic Wave (QCM/SAW)
Radiation Measurement System (RAMS)
Whole Air Sampler (WAS)
Harvard Water Ozone Experiment (WOX)

ER-2 pilots at NASA Ames in the mid-1990s. From left to right (standing): Jan Nystrom, Bill Collette Ron Williams, and Jim Barrilleaux; (kneeling): Doyle Krumrey and Ken Broda.

taken with the fuel; the JP-TS was specially refined, and temperature probes were added to the tanks.

Porter also flew the first mission into Russia on 27 January—a 6-hour straight line southeast past Moscow to a point near the Ukraine border and back. Russian scientists helped gain the necessary approvals, but Porter had to enter at strictly-defined waypoints. Some 17 different experiments were performed during the flight. A second 8-hour flight into Russia on 5 February was more complicated, involving an outbound leg to Spitsbergen before turning to cross the Barents Sea and fly over northern Russia. A team of 250 scientists on the ground at Kiruna were devising new flight paths throughout the deployment, since the ozone-depletion vortex is dynamic, moving south to east. In a second series of SOLVE flights during March 2000, NASA pilot Jan Nystrom also flew into Russia.[9]

Despite sweeping budget cuts elsewhere, NASA kept the two ER-2s flying into the new decade. The world's environmental problems made sure of that. Global warming was now a reality, leading to melting ice caps, the increased incidence of forest fires, and so on. Ozone depletion remained a serious concern. In Fiscal 2004, the two ER-2 aircraft flew 400 hours on five major campaigns.

But like the Air Force, NASA was eyeing the new generation of high-altitude, long-endurance UAVs as an alternative platform. For the first time, NASA began taking money from the ER-2 budget to fund rival developments, notably the General Atomics Altus and Altair. Scientists were encouraged to plan their experiments for these vehicles. When long-serving

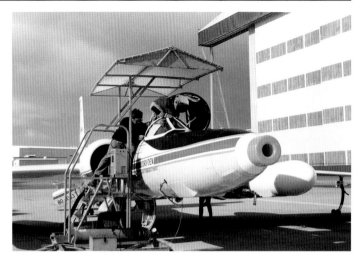

In late 1997, the two ER-2s moved to the NASA Dryden Research Center at Edwards AFB. N806NA is seen here with a nose job. (Lockheed PR2789-23)

ER-2 pilot Jim Barrilleaux retired in late 2004 he was not replaced. Support contracts were cut back, and holes appeared in the future schedule. But NASA continued to advertise the availability of this premier airborne science aircraft. As stated on the Dryden website, the ER-2 was still "an extremely versatile aircraft well-suited to multiple mission tasks."[10]

39

Management and Maintenance

The U-2 is a unique aircraft. Therefore, it is not surprising that the arrangements for managing and maintaining it have always been unusual. The need for complete secrecy in the early days resulted in a unique procurement and security control system. Unlike a military operation, the CIA's Project Aquatone relied largely on contractors to maintain the aircraft and its systems in the field. Even after the USAF bought its own U-2s, the degree of contractor support to SAC's 4080th wing was greater than that to a normal military flying wing.

The fact that the CIA—and not the Air Force—was the original customer for the U-2A, U-2C, and the U-2R models resulted in an aircraft that was not built according to strict military specifications. This was the key to the U-2's outstanding performance, but it led to problems through the years. Military maintenance personnel grappled with hundreds of non-standard technical documents. When it took delivery of its own U-2s in 1957, SAC soon realized that the only way to keep the Dragon Lady flying was to allow airmen and maintenance officers to extend their tours to gain the necessary experience.

"Black" contracts

Soon after Project Aquatone was launched in early 1955, the CIA set up its own procurement team within DPS, led by George Kucera. The Agency also set up a supply depot for the U-2 in a secure warehouse at Cheli AFS, in the Los Angeles suburb of Maywood. The location was chosen for its proximity not only to the Lockheed Skunk Works, but also to the key systems subcontractors Perkin Elmer (cameras) and Ramo Wooldridge (SIGINT systems). The Agency wrote "black" contracts with these and other suppliers, such as Baird Associates for the sextant, Firewel for the pilots' life support systems, and REECO for the construction of Watertown Strip, aka the Ranch.

Meanwhile, the USAF organized its support for the Project under the codenames Oilstone and Shoehorn. This support was directed from HQ USAF by a small team led by Colonel Leo Geary. It included the supply of the Pratt & Whitney engines, which were an Air Force responsibility from the outset. Geary's office, later designated AFCIG-5, provided assistance to the CIA's various covert aircraft operations, including selection and temporary transfer of Air Force personnel, airlift, refueling, and other logistics support.

Lockheed has always done the major overhauls on the U-2. A reworked U-2C model is seen here outside the hangar at Van Nuys, where the Skunk Works performed all inspections, repairs, and conversions from 1964 to 1969. (Lockheed)

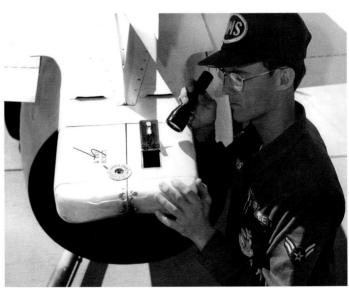

An airman from SAC inspects the U-2 drag chute housing sometime in the 1960s. Six-year tours were not uncommon in those days. (Lockheed)

In June 1956 the CIA's General Counsel, Larry Houston, wrote to DCI Allen Dulles explaining in detail the contracting arrangements for Project Aquatone. He concluded:

The administration of the contracts has not followed normal service practices, as for security reasons it was decided to limit the number of contract officers to the minimum....However...all contracts and changes thereto have been reviewed by the General Counsel or his deputy, and specific approvals on policy or fiscal matters have been obtained...Again, granting that this system may work only when dealing with companies which are themselves competent in the running of their business...Under the circumstances surrounding this Project, we believe the procurement system adequately protected the government, and through its efficiency and simplicity was economical for the Government.

SUMMARY OF SUPPORT OPERATION
This report was given to the Weapons Phasing Group Meeting for Project Dragon Lady in HQ USAF on 6 August 1957

Mr Bill Denard discussed his operation at WRAMA. The support center has been set up in a secure warehouse in which all depot functions are performed. Access to the warehouse is limited to certain designated supervisory personnel, and those assigned duty within the warehouse.

Requisitions are received by a sterile teletype line directly from Laughlin AFB. All materiel is processed to the final stage of shipment within the secure warehouse, including sterile method of packing.

Action is being taken in support of the sampler mission to establish a flyaway kit to support three aircraft.

Mr Denard reported the current status of prime equipments...and presented the current status of aircraft engines and spare parts deliveries...24 J57-P-37 engines in the supply system...in addition there are 16 J/YJ57-P-31A engines, which will be supplemented by 24 more....

The electrical generators were unreliable for a time in the 1960s, and had to be replaced on numerous occasions. (Lockheed)

PARTIAL PRESSURE SUITS
A whole separate book could be written about the U-2 pressure suits. Suffice it to say here, that the maintenance of a life support system for U-2 pilots has involved enormous effort and dedication by a huge number of people, civilian contractors, and military physiological support specialists over the years.
The original T-1 partial pressure suits and K-1 helmets were soon improved to the MC-3 and MA-1, respectively. The suits were designed and manufactured by the David Clark Company. Dave Clark recalled:

We were told of the need for some partial pressure suits comfortable enough to be worn for 12 hours unpressurized, and as long as four hours pressurized. The selected pilots would be sent to our factory to be measured carefully, then notified when we were ready for a trial fit. We tried to make them comfortable enough to sleep in, yet fitted enough to tighten all over the body when the capstans were inflated to 15 psi. After the first few pilots were fitted, Colonel Phil Maher complimented us and asked us to try improving the helmet. We inserted about two inches of "Link-net," our own invention, in the neck section. That allowed some easier turning (of the head).

I gave the responsibility for the secrecy of the project over to Joe Ruseckas. I did not wish to know where we might be sending people to maintain or repair suits....

(But) I can remember meeting one of the pilots who had come back to be fitted with a new suit because he had gained weight. He said: "Dave, this suit has saved my life and let me bring my ship home more than eight times."

- from "The Development of the Partial Pressure Suit" by David Clark, published by the David Clark company in 1992

When the USAF decided to acquire its own fleet of U-2s in January 1956 they were procured via the CIA. However, the service set up its own U-2 Weapon System Project Office (WSPO) within Air Materiel Command (AMC) at Wright-Patterson AFB, headed by Lt Col Sid Brewer.

Brewer and his team provided the executive and logistics management for Project Dragon Lady. They wrote requirements that were specific to the USAF U-2s, and participated in operational conferences with SAC and CIA; accident investigations; and new design and construction matters. The WSPO also included a small group from the Air Research & Development Command (ARDC), headed by Col R.M. Herrington.[1]

The USAF designated the Warner-Robins Air Materiel Area (WRAMA) as its prime supply depot for the U-2. However, to maintain security, the service initially agreed to use the CIA supply system that had already been established. All support equipment was therefore shipped through the Maywood depot, and only a small number of WRAMA people were cleared into the Project and sent to Los Angeles on TDY. But in June 1957, as the USAF U-2s moved from the Ranch to their new base at Del Rio, in Texas, a Weapons System Support Center (WSSC) was set up at Warner-Robins.[2]

The FOG
To further preserve secrecy in the early days, suppliers were told to refer to the CIA as "Customer One" and the Air Force as "Customer Two." At Lockheed and the CIA, the USAF U-2 operation was often referred to as

the "Follow-On Group," or FOG. For years the two programs were kept separate, to such an extent that supplies destined for the USAF U-2s had to be sanitized so that no one could formally link them with the CIA U-2 Project.[3]

Initially, the USAF planned to overhaul its U-2s at Warner-Robins. But the idea was soon dropped, in favor of depot maintenance by the Skunk Works. Lockheed has performed this task ever since.

The first cadre of SAC maintainers was trained by Lockheed at the Bakersfield (Oildale) production facility, prior to proceeding to the Ranch to work on the FOG airplanes as they were delivered. It was not long before SAC was complaining that there were no illustrated parts breakdowns, and other types of standard maintenance documentation! In planning meetings during 1957, Lt Col Brewer cautioned that because of the peculiarities of the U-2, SAC should not try to organize the maintenance on the standard wing-base concept.

Meanwhile, the CIA was relying on Lockheed not only for field maintenance, but also for every modification that required an aircraft to be returned to Burbank. These included the Rainbow project to add radar-evading devices in 1956-57, and the first conversions to J75 power in 1959.

IRAN

In January 1960, upon reaching 1,000 hours, the first USAF U-2A was sent to Lockheed for the Phase I IRAN (Inspect and Repair As Necessary). This process included modernization of the aircraft's communications and navigation equipment, and some much-needed modifications for reliability and ease of maintenance. The program started at Edwards North Base, but was transferred within months to Building 351 at Burbank. The Phase II IRAN program followed from June 1961. This included a structural inspection for corrosion and fatigue, and a modernization of the electrical system. The Phase III IRAN from June 1963 included many modifications, including the new autopilot, a new compass system, and refurbished cockpit.[4]

In the middle of Phase III, Lockheed decided to move U-2 overhauls from Burbank to Van Nuys airfield, 20 miles to the west. This was spurred primarily by the need to find more space at the Skunk Works for SR-71

The early U-2s were not a maintenance-friendly design! A Lockheed mechanic inspects wiring bundles in the Q-bay during major maintenance on a NASA aircraft. (author)

TECH REPS IN THE FIELD – EARLY DAYS
Freed from the rigid constraints of tech orders and military manning, a "can-do" mentality prevailed at the CIA detachments in the early days, as these comments by Lockheed tech reps convey:

Frank Dewar: I was an electrician, the youngest person deployed by Lockheed to Japan with Det C. Even younger than Bob Murphy—and he was my boss! They must have liked me, though, because when Stan Beerli was posted from there to Det B in Turkey, he got some of us (including Bob Murphy and me) transferred with him.

I specialized in the autopilots, but the key to the operation was versatility. We did sheet metal, airframe, hydraulics, whatever. And we checked each others' work. Many times, we would work round-the-clock to get the job done.

Bob Murphy: I was only 27 years old when they sent me to run Det C. Frank Bertelli was supposed to go, but his clearance was late in coming, so off I went. I had 13 people there.

Sometimes, we developed modifications in-the-field, and then they wrote the Service Bulletins after the fact. That was the style of the program! The rear-view mirror was an example. I did that in Turkey when the Det B pilots asked for a means of detecting whether they were contrailing or not. Not long after (U-2 program manager) Art Bradley called from Burbank and told me that this was a new requirement. I told him, "don't worry, it's already done!"

Jim Wood: Things were pretty basic, especially during the Quick Move deployments from Det B. We built a canvas shelter to push over the aircraft so that nobody could see us loading or unloading the camera when we did the practice deployments to the UK. Peshawar was better: we had a hangar there, and we did all the work inside, including refueling and oxygen and nitrogen replenishment.

- interviews with author

USAF U-2 PROGRAM HISTORY BRIEFING POINTS – FEBRUARY 1958

First aircraft delivered September 1956 (eight months after go ahead)
30th aircraft delivered in December 1957
All contracting and funding handled thru special procedures at HQ USAF
WSPO given responsibility for overall program
All channels of normal weapons system programs were and are by-passed
No AMC control other than WSPO
No AMC depot responsibility other than supplies through WSSC
No AMC Depot maintenance
No WADC Labs
No standard handbooks, data etc.
Contractors given design and performance responsibility
Special security procedures

MAINTENANCE NIGHTMARES

The early U-2s may have been wonderful flying machines, but they were designed and built in a hurry. Maintenance concerns were not a high priority. TSgt Glenn Chapman was a camera systems technician in the 4080th SRW from 1958 to 1966. He recalls:

To purge the driftsight we had to undo the entire left access panel. That was 20-plus fasteners. And we might have to do this pre-takeoff, on the ramp, with the engine running. The potential for FOD was great! Eventually, they provided a smaller access panel below the big one, with only one fastener....

Every airplane was different. Some were good to maintain...683, 705, and 716, were great. But 692 and 700 were lousy! Then there were the different mod states to consider. For instance, the aileron counter-balance was on top in airplanes 951 through 955. Those were the supplementary batch produced in 1958-59. I think they learned from one of the early accidents not to put it inside the wingtip skid.

The engine fit was so tight, that after we removed one, we lined the fuselage with plastic sheeting so that we could slide it back in afterwards.

- interview with author

NEPHO AND SFERICS AT THE 4080th WING

Each of us in the Nephography Shop—as the photo repair facility was known—had our units that we loved or hated. Some liked the (Hycon) 73B camera, others liked the A-1 or A-2. I did enjoy working on the tracker camera, but my speciality was the driftsight and hand control.

Every time that (SIGINT) System IV flew, we also had to install the tracker camera. However, we had to wrap it in aluminum foil so the stray electromagnetic energy did not interfere with System IV. It was extremely difficult wrapping this foil as directed...then you had to install it on the lower hatch, taking care not to tear the foil. If you did, you started all over again.

System IV missions were so secret that the shop maintaining the equipment was given a cover name, much like our Nepho shop. They were known as Sferics. I have no idea what it was supposed to mean, and I never asked.

- from "Me and U-2" by Glenn Chapman, self-published book, 1999

THE GLOCKENSPIEL

There were times when the Dragon Lady had a reason to fly with no mission system installed....for instance, a functional check flight, or a ferry flight. But the aircraft still needed to have 475 pounds or so strategically placed on the airframe in order to maintain her weight and balance. Kelly Johnson came up with a unique way to do this....

The "glockenspeil" was nothing more than two pieces of heavy steel tubing about two inches in diameter that were welded together at one end and held apart by another tube (at) the other ends. Across this array of steel tubing were a series of steel ingots that weighed about 50 pounds each. When one looked at it from the top, it resembled the glockenspiel that the guy in the band played...

To install the glock into the Q-bay the hatches were removed, and the bomb hoist was attached to the upper rails. The rear legs were installed into the split brackets at the aft of the Q-bay, and the nose end was fastened to the forward bulkhead.

- from "Me and U-2" by Glenn Chapman, self-published book, 1999, p205

THE CREW CHIEF

The hardest job of any belonged to the aircraft crew chief...He was responsible for initiating work orders for all kinds of specialists to perform repairs, alignments, and preventative maintenance...

These guys also had to perform refueling, put nitrogen in the tires, meet the pilot when he came out to fly, recover the aircraft, and go to the debriefing to find out that multitudes of problems had arisen during the flight. The crew chief was also responsible for the aircraft forms, making sure they were right, that all the work had been done, weight and balance was correctly calculated, and the aircraft time logged and annotated properly.

Believe me, no one caught hell as much as a Dragon Lady crew chief, and most of the time they did not deserve it at all.

- from "Me and U-2" by Glenn Chapman, self-published book, 1999, p246

production. The Van Nuys facility was in use for five years before Lockheed moved the U-2 depot to Palmdale in 1969.

On 1 January 1961, Warner-Robins became the single supply depot for the U-2, including the support of Project Idealist, the new name for CIA operations. The driving factor behind the consolidation was that the CIA's own facility (Mira Loma, since 1958) was becoming the depot for the CIA's even more-classified A-12 Oxcart aircraft. Of course, there was also a cost saving by consolidating the U-2 supply chain. From then on, funding for "Customers 1 and 2" came from a common pool, approved ultimately by the NRO in Washington.

Ground crew from the 100th SRW move a U-2C to the hangar after a mission. (author)

THE FIREWEL COMPANY

One of the less well-known companies in the U-2 program, Firewel was actually the main contractor responsible for life support at the CIA detachments. The David Clark Company was a subcontractor to Firewel, providing the pilots' pressure suits. Two Firewel tech reps recall:

Ennio Ripa: Firewel was a furnace company in Buffalo, NY, that got into oxygen work, and therefore into regulators. We built an altitude chamber—which the David Clark company did not have. So that's how we got into life support for the U-2 and other "black" programs. In only a few years, we went from 50 to 500 people. I went to Det B in 1957 as a tech rep, and did that job for the next 20 years on the A-12 and SR-71, as well as the U-2. The company was bought by ARO, which continued the U-2 contract through to the 1970s.

Ralph "Lucky" Lewis: I was a safety equipment tech rep at Det H in the 1960s. We provided a standard survival kit for training flights, but when we prepared for operational missions, the seat kit was customized. We would put in the type of clothes worn on the Chinese mainland, farmers' shoes and so on, and communist currency. We provided gold rings that the pilots could barter.

Each pilot had his own oxygen breathing schedule, so he could check the depletion rate during a long mission....

We were quite well paid, and we had some fun out there in Taiwan! We all stayed in the hostel on base—that was a security requirement—but everyone had girlfriends downtown and kept some clothes there.

- interviews with author

U-2 FUEL

Moving barrels of the specially-refined fuel to support far-flung U-2 operations was always an issue. In the first few years sealed steel drums were used, and the temperature in transit was closely monitored. Later, tank trucks were used within the U.S., but this practice came under scrutiny after the Air Force experienced fuel contamination incidents in early 1959, and again in 1962.

Actually, there were two U-2 fuels. LF-1A was used by the CIA (and was preferred by Pratt & Whitney). JP-TS was used by the Air Force because it met milspecs. That proved to be of little advantage during the early 1960s, when U-2 fuel manifolds and engine nozzles were being clogged by "cracking" of the fuel at the high operating temperatures. Sabotage was suspected, but in reality, JP-TS was not proving to be so thermally stable after all. Three point testing of the fuel was instigated (at the points of manufacture, shipment, and usage).

Some fuel statistics from Desert Storm in 1991 show the magnitude of the logistics effort required to keep the Dragon Lady flying. By the time the war started, the 9th RW had almost 450,000 gallons of JP-TS on hand at Taif. Based on a sortie rate of five per day, that was enough for four weeks of operations. But the sortie rate then went up to seven per day. Despite the arrival of more fuel by ocean tanker, and by C-130 airlift, the total on hand dwindled to 100,000 gallons by mid-February. – C.P.

FROM KELLY JOHNSON'S DIARY

1 February 1962: I have had to shake up our U-2 inspection and shop personnel because of poor workmanship and inspection on two airplanes out of IRAN.

14 August 1962: Our workload on the airplane remains very high, and we are looking for new pilots.

17 September 1962: Gary Powers came out with John McMahon, and I agreed to hire him to fly U-2s, at least during the time he is getting a divorce. Gen. LeMay and Jim Cunningham want very much that we should do this, and I have lived up to my promise to him that I made when he first came back from Russia.

November 1962: The U-2 program at this time is in quite a shambles and, as it is being operated by the Air Force, using many CIA airplanes, nobody quite knows who is running the show.

19 May 1964: There is a very noticeable change in management from the days of Dick Bissell. Wheelon wants to do a good job and is highly competent, but their whole organization back there is subject to a great deal of mismanagement. Talking to Wheelon, he asked what we could do to get back more on the former operating basis. I suggested a monthly meeting in Burbank, where we can tell him things we can't begin to put in wires.

5 August 1964: To Van Nuys to accelerate delivery of two aircraft for HQs, and also to straighten out some loose operation that developed since we moved from Building 351. Ralph Plue is working to unscramble the shop end, and I took on engineering and inspection.

20 September 1966: Had our first fatigue cracks in the U-2. These were in a fuselage bulkhead after 4,000 hours. Also had our first sign of corrosion on a non-alclad doubler in a fuel tank. No important problems.

25 January 1967: We discussed the increasingly poor quality of the flying of the U-2s by SAC. Have set up a meeting to talk to Major Boyd, now our SPO at Wright Field, and a number of U-2 groups. I will have to give some lessons in elementary aerodynamics.

19 October 1967: We have encountered cracks around rivets near the wing attachment on the U-2C. And one airplane had an 11-inch crack on the bottom surface. We instituted a program for repair.

But there were many items of U-2 equipment that were peculiar to the Agency's aircraft, such as SIGINT systems and the J75 engine. This materiel was still directly contracted by the Materiel Branch within the Agency's DPD, and it was still warehoused by the CIA Office of Logistics, and supplied direct to the CIA U-2 detachments from there. Meanwhile, all the U-2 tooling, jigs, and fixtures were retained at Mira Loma, because it was close to Lockheed at Burbank. (The U-2R tooling was also stored after use—a wise decision, since it enabled the start of TR-1 production in the late 1970s at a reduced cost.)[5]

In 1962, the creation of the top-secret NRO sparked changes in the Air Force headquarters direction of the U-2 program. Colonel Geary became dual-hatted as head of AFCIG-5 and Program D of the NRO, which controlled "black budget" spending on military reconnaissance aircraft, notably the Lockheed R-12 (eg what became the SR-71 Blackbird), but also the Air Force U-2 program. Geary's deputy at AFCIG-5, Colonel Clay Saunders, took over primary responsibility for USAF support to the CIA's U-2 Project Idealist. When Geary finally left the Pentagon in 1966 after 10 years working on the "black" programs, Saunders stepped up to become director of Program D.

Wright-Patterson SPO

By 1963 Lt Col Wayne Freas succeeded Sid Brewer as the chief of the U-2 WSPO at Wright-Patterson, now part of the Aeronautical Systems Division (ASD). Bill Denard still ran the depot at WRAMA, reporting to the WSPO. In 1965 Freas reported that the SPO was controlling 29 active contracts, that the U-2 fleet had flown a total 106,000 hours, and that the average maintenance man/hours per flying hour was 24.6. The management concept was "minimum personnel/maximum experience; mutual trust, and minimum paper." Apart from Freas, the SPO consisted of only two engineers, a production specialist, and a secretary!

By the mid-1960s, though, the Air Force fleet of U-2s was dwindling, and the SR-71 was on the way in. At Wright-Patterson, the four long-serving U-2 SPO staff members had been consolidated within the growing SR-71 management operation at Wright-Patterson, which was known as Advanced Systems. Major Warren Boyd took care of U-2 management (10 years earlier he had been one of the first SAC pilots to train on the U-2). Colonel Bellis from Advanced Systems sat on the U-2R Configuration Control Board, but the CIA had total acquisition responsibility for the new U-2 version.

It was decided to move the U-2 management functions into a single field office to be colocated with the supply and warehouse activity at WRAMA. In 1967, therefore, the four staff positions were transferred from AFSC at Wright-Patterson to AFLC at Warner-Robins, where a new Senior Year Program Office (SYPO) was created, commanded by Col Frank Shipley.[6]

When Lockheed delivered its proposal for the U-2R, it was careful to specify that although 13 key Military Specifications had been used as design guides, "full compliance (was) not attempted due to the radical nature of (the) development." The company claimed that reliability was a prime design consideration. Ease of access for maintenance and repair were also taken into account. Many more items were interchangeable, compared with the original U-2 models.[7]

Warner-Robins

By 1971, the SYPO and depot at Warner-Robins employed 78 people. It was directed by the Program D office of the still-secret NRO in Washington, which was also responsible for managing the two key Air Force U-2R development programs, namely the Senior Book COMINT system and the Senior Lance radar.

The Program D office now coordinated the USAF support to Project Idealist. It was run by Colonel Frank Hartley from 1967 until his retirement in 1972. By then, the NRO was looking forward to the end of the CIA's U-2 operation. In September 1972 AF/IGJ was created in the Pentagon, essentially to bring Program D out of the "black" world. Still, though, "program reporting and documentation will remain limited in scope and distribution," noted the official order that created this new staff office. From 1972-74 Colonel Bernard Bailey was "dual-hatted" as the head of this office, as well as Program D. In 1973 AF/IGJ took control of all the Air Force-operated U-2s.

This left the five aircraft that were still operationally-controlled by the CIA in Project Idealist. In 1974, however, the CIA did finally get out of the U-2 business. AF/IGJ in the Pentagon was now the Office of Primary Responsibility (OPR) for the U-2 (and the SR-71). It controlled the SYPO and depot at Warner Robins, now a 100-strong team.

There was an inevitable debate over whether to keep a streamlined management and support structure directed from HQ USAF, or whether to instead "normalize" the U-2 (and SR-71) using routine AFLC procedures. The Air Staff recommended a middle course, but General Rogers of AFLC

Close-up of the famous pogos. The ground crew attend each launch and recovery of a U-2, to collect and re-install them. (Lockheed)

Lockheed crews performed field maintenance at Akrotiri until the late 1990s, a legacy from the CIA days. Tech reps Rich Waide (under the wing) and Bill Bonnichsen are changing a hydraulic pump on a U-2R in 1983. (via Bill Bonnichsen)

had other ideas. Eventually, AFLC's Special Projects Office at Wright-Patterson assumed control of the SYPO at Robins AFB, which became Det 8 of the 2762nd Logistics Squadron.

At the same time, a USAF review questioned why military pilots were not assigned to Palmdale for functional check flights of U-2s coming out of the depot after IRAN. Det 8 subsequently assumed responsibility from Lockheed test pilots for these FCFs.

While Lockheed's primacy in overhauling the U-2 fleet was never seriously challenged, in the mid-1980s the USAF changed the 20-year old IRAN system to Periodic Depot Maintenance (PDM). Lockheed now had to quote a fixed price for each aircraft. Previously, the IRANs were done on a cost-plus-fixed fee basis.[8]

LR

After the last TR-1 was completed in 1989, the USAF's Aeronautical Systems Division relinquished some management responsibility that it had assumed during the production run. However, Wright-Patterson AFB continued to house the U-2 System Program Directorate (SPD, coded RA).

Det 8 Warner Robins was still the U-2 depot and Senior Year program office, however. It was run by Air Force Colonel Richard Scuderi for many years, but consisted largely of government civilian specialists and administrators. In 1994 Det 8 was redesignated as the U-2 Management Directorate, coded LR. The mission of LR was to provide depot support, supply, distribution, system and inventory management, system engineering and maintenance, budget and financial management, security, flight test, acquisition, and contracting functions. The task included not only the U-2 airframe and sensors, but all the associated systems, such as ground stations.[9]

The fatigue life of the U-2R was originally envisioned as 20,000 hours, but in August 1994 68-10338 became the first aircraft to pass that milestone with no problems. A new limit of 30,000 hours was set. By now, aircraft were being returned to Lockheed at Site 2, Palmdale, for PDM every 3,400 hours, or five years. Phase inspections were scheduled every 400 hours for aircraft that were deployed on operational missions, and therefore spending most of their time at high altitude. For aircraft at Beale that

Aerial view of Site 2, where depot maintenance and flight test of the U-2 has been performed since 1969. When this photo was taken, the SR-71 was still in service. (Lockheed PR 1237-18)

The whole atmosphere in the 9th RW has changed dramatically over the past few years. The recent increase of U-2 mishaps and crashes have dictated this change. Now, everybody's a bit gun-shy to make simple maintenance decisions. I guess it is better to be safe than sorry, but sometimes it gets a bit hysterical. I guess it's a good thing I retired, because I don't think I could have put up with the new management styles much longer. What was really scary to me was the implementation of the new Quality Assurance Program (QAP) throughout the Air Force. What that did was create more paperwork and less oversight. In the old program, QA was manned with many highly experienced mechanics and technicians. With the new program, emphasis is placed on processes and not individual accountability.

- MSgt Christopher Bennett (retd), comments posted on www.blackbirds.net, 1997

CLASS A MISHAP AT OSAN

The mishap occurred 30 March 1999 on an operational reconnaissance mission, when the U-2S experienced a hydraulic failure in flight and lost hydraulic pressure. The pilot attempted an emergency release of the main landing gear; however, there was not enough airflow pressure to bring the main landing gear to a down and locked position. When the aircraft landed the landing gear collapsed, and the aircraft skidded approximately 1,500 feet on the runway before coming to a stop. There were no injuries associated with the mishap; however, the aircraft sustained extensive damage to the lower forward fuselage.

The report concluded that...the right roll spoiler actuator cylinder developed a fatigue crack, causing a loss of hydraulic fluid.

- Air Force News Release, 8 July 1999

NASA ER-2 aircraft undergoing routine maintenance at Moffett Field. Phase maintenance is required every 400 hours, or every 200 hours for aircraft that have been used mainly at low-level for training. (Lockheed PI 8768)

were used mostly for training, and were therefore spending more of their time at low altitude, the phase interval was every 200 hours.

New engine

The arrival of the U-2S and its new GE F118 engine eased the maintenance burden considerably. It was easier to install and remove. The hydraulic components were easier to access, and the new gearbox was mounted on the airframe. Even with the engine removed the aircraft's hydraulic and electrical systems could still be operated. Troubleshooting capabilities were improved, and sophisticated new test equipment was provided. The downside to the new engine was its hydrazine system for emergency restart at high altitude. Special handling procedures had to be introduced for this highly toxic, yet colorless and odorless substance.[10]

Accidents

The series of accidents that afflicted the U-2 wing in the 1990s led to much debate over the maintenance organization. There was an average one Class A mishap every year from 1991 to 1999. Those in 1996 and 1997 were clearly maintenance-related. In the accident that killed Captain Randy Roby

Inside the hangar at Site 2, Lockheed employees are at work on one of the trainers. Aircraft are returned here for PDM every 3,400 hours. (Lockheed PR 847.2)

To change a sump tank, the engine must be removed. To remove an engine, the tail must be removed.... (author)

Postflight scene at Beale, as the maintenance crew waits to learn whether their jet is still "Code One." (Lockheed CBS 3286-7)

Two young airmen contemplate a Dragon Lady at Beale. After a series of accidents in the 1990s, an independent panel recommended that tours be extended so that maintenance technicians could gain extra experience in the unique aircraft. (author)

at Beale in August 1996, a clamp had not been reinstalled after a phase inspection, allowing very hot engine bleed air to escape and start a fire that spread quickly and severed hydraulic and control lines. A similar error at Osan the following year nearly caused the loss of another airplane, which had to be airlifted back to Palmdale for repair after an emergency landing.[11]

The Graybeard panel found that maintenance experience levels had significantly decreased in the 9th RW, as in some other USAF wings at the time. It recommended four to six year tours instead of the normal one to three years. The panel called for improved technical data to be funded, and better training in how to read the non-standard blueprints and aperture cards that had always been used in the U-2 program, in lieu of Illustrated Parts Breakdowns (IPBs). The panel also called for a return to the SAC concept of centralized maintenance, which had been abandoned when ACC assumed control of the 9th RW in 1992.[12]

Teamwork keeps the show on the road: pilot and crew chief in mutual harmony at an overseas detachment. (author)

The 9th RW was already implementing a "Get Well Plan," and the panel's findings on maintenance were not welcomed. In particular, the issue of how much reliance should be placed on contractor support in the field was controversial. ACC had already decided to turn the field maintenance of the ASARS radar sensor over to the manufacturer, Hughes (later Raytheon), from 1997. Lockheed's expertise was also being tapped to a greater extent at RAF Akrotiri, Cyprus. Here, the company was still providing all the field maintenance—a legacy from the CIA days in 1974. In the late 1990s, blue-suiters took over the flightline at Akrotiri. But Lockheed took responsibility for the 400-hour phase inspections on all U-2s deployed to Europe and the Middle East, rather than have the 9th RW deploy extra blue-suiters from Beale to do the job.[13]

Contractors

In July 1999, LR awarded a five-year fixed-price contract worth $260 million to Raytheon for the consolidated field support of all U-2 sensors, data links, and ground stations. (By now Raytheon had bought Hughes, Itek, and E-Systems, respectively responsible for the U-2's ASARS, SYERS, and SIGINT sensors). The single contract replaced 10 separate support contracts that had never previously been competed. But the new arrangement got off to a shaky start when Raytheon's chosen subcontractor for the datalink support (Harris Corporation) had to be replaced after only a few months. The task was taken on by the original U-2 datalink supplier, an activity which was sold in 1999 by Unisys to L-3 Communications. (Raytheon retained the contract when it was rebid in 2004, but this time on a cost-plus-incentive basis).[14]

The U-2 System Program Directorate at Wright-Patterson considered going further, by having a contractor assume the "Total System Performance Responsibility" (TSPR) for the U-2. Lockheed was already doing this for the F-117 Stealth Fighter. Lockheed and Raytheon drafted competing proposals for a U-2 TSPR. Then the two companies joined forces and added L-3 for a combined effort. But if the U-2 program went the same way as the F-117, a large number of government jobs would be eliminated at LR Warner-Robins, where the head count had now risen to 250. The

The U-2 has always been supported in the field by a higher proportion of contractor tech reps than is usual on other USAF airplanes. Bill Cook of Lockheed is in conversation with enlisted maintenance crew at OL-UK, RAF Fairford, 1995. (author)

On display during an open house at Warner-Robins AFB, this aircraft carries the two-letter designation of the U-2 Management Directorate, which was based there. (Mike Masucci)

supply depot would move, and the TSPR contractors would also take over all the systems integration and engineering.[15]

The TSPR concept foundered in 2000 over the scope of the changes, who would pay for the bidding costs, and whether the ground stations should be included. Instead, the U-2 Management Directorate at Warner-Robins continued to manage 23 separate contracts spread among 13 different contractors. But 95% of the total still went to the "big three" U-2 suppliers: Lockheed Martin, Raytheon, and L-3.[16]

In the late 1990s, a Systems Integration Laboratory (SIL) for the U-2 was completed at Warner-Robins. The aim was to accomplish as much integration testing as possible on the ground, rather than in the air on the two aircraft that were now dedicated to flight test at Palmdale. It was completed in time to help introduce the Power/EMI upgrade and the RAMP glass cockpit.[17]

The Power/EMI upgrade helped U-2 maintainers in various ways. Not only did it increase the electrical load shedding abilities and standard-

The long TDYs away from home affect the maintenance troops, as well as the flight crew. A U-2S receives attention in a hangar at one of the desert bases during Operation Iraqi Freedom. (Jeff Jungemann)

The "WR" tailcode is worn by one of the two U-2s that are permanently assigned to Flight Test at Palmdale. This indicates that they "belong" to the U-2 Management Directorate at Warner-Robins, rather than to the 9th RW at Beale. (Lockheed PR 3899.4)

Pilots and their crew chiefs at Det 4 pause for the camera after OIF. (Jeff Jungemann)

Lt Col Steve Peterson recalled an issue with the bleed valves that resulted in a flameout landing while he was the commander at Osan:

Jack Smith was getting ready to come down after his mission. Standard procedure on the R-model was to open the bleed valves and then pull the throttle back. Care had to be taken on descent to maintain a minimum EPR (Engine Pressure Ratio) or the engine would flame out. Opening the bleed valves allowed a lower EPR. Not opening the Bleed Valves and then using the Bleed Valve open EPR settings would result in a flameout, so we tended to be very careful about that.

Jack opened the bleed valves, and pulled the throttle back to the bleed valve open EPR setting (lower than the bleed valve closed EPR setting for descent). He promptly flamed out. Weather was not pleasant. He went into the tops of the clouds near 30K. Weather at Osan was around 1500 overcast. This is just barely enough to do a flame out landing. That's *if* you come out of the clouds right over the base.

As Jack got down lower, we went through the engine start procedure and got the engine started once we got down to around 25K. Jack then flew a flawless SFO and landed uneventfully.

I flew an FCF (Functional Check Flight) the next day to try and find out what went wrong. Maintenance had not found anything. When I got up to altitude, I opened the bleed valves and noted the appropriate EPR drop. This is our indication in the cockpit that the bleed valves had opened. I also noted, after several operations, that after I opened them and noted the prescribed drop, that the EPR went back up. I came down using the bleed valve closed EPR schedule and landed without incident.

It turns out one of the bleed valves had been installed incorrectly during major maintenance on the engine and was in backwards. This meant that one bleed valve was always open and one was always closed. When the bleed valve switch was activated, it closed one and opened the other. This resulted in too much pressure in the compressor section of the engine to use the bleed valve open EPR schedule for descent. When the switch was first activated though, half way through the movement, both were open for a little while. This showed the right EPR drop and had fooled the pilots. It got fixed and we had no more problems.

- letter to the author

ize the power interfaces, it swopped one of the aircraft's troublesome silver-zinc batteries for a maintenance-free rechargeable lead-acid battery. The new windscreen was a single piece of glass-composite material that was easy to replace. The old three-panel design took days to remove and reseal in place. Moreover, the new windscreen contained an integrated antifog coating, which substantially reduced the drain on the battery during an emergency descent.[18]

The introduction of the "Glass Dragon" in 2002 promised an end to the "vanishing vendor" problem affecting the supply of old-fashioned round-dial instruments. It was also expected to further ease the maintenance training task, as avionics technicians transferring to the 9th RW from other USAF wings would be more familiar with the new technology.

One-of-a-kind

However, the U-2 remains a one-of-a-kind breed, and some things never change. For instance, the old subtractive-type fuel counter is still the main indication to the pilot of the aircraft's fuel state. This has important implications for piloting, especially when maintenance screws up. A few years ago, an aircraft was released to the flight line without the sump tank valves having been safety-wired open. Over the years, this particular error had been made quite a few times. But no one spotted it during preflight inspections.

The student pilot took off, but soon realized that there was some type of fuel feed problem. However, he misinterpreted the information on the subtractive counter, and the separate needle which shows the fuel level in the sump tank. Luckily, the mobile for this flight was experienced enough to realize that there was a serious problem. He advised the pilot to make the speediest possible return. The aircraft landed with just four usable gallons remaining in the sump tank.

The regime of flight has always been unforgiving of technical error. This is especially true of the U-2, whose pilots venture into the high-altitude regime, and return many hours later, to make landings in the USAF's only tail-dragger. More than most aviators, these pilots rely on the best possible support from those who remain on the ground, be they specialists in airframe, avionics, or physiological support.

More than most aircraft, the Dragon Lady requires dedication from those who attend it, in all weathers, at all hours. (author)

40

Riding the Dragon Lady

This chapter first appeared as an article with the same title in the United States Air Force Yearbook, 1997. It describes the author's flight in a U-2ST in 1995.

We had been airborne for almost 50 minutes before I really appreciated just how high we were! As we cruised steadily across California's San Joaquin Valley, I glanced down and to the right. Way below, an airliner leaving a thick contrail was intersecting our flight track. As it passed underneath us, that jet seemed no bigger to the naked eye, than if I had been looking up at it from ground level.

In fact, this was no illusion. He was at 35,000 feet, whereas we were above 70,000 feet! We were 50 minutes out of Beale AFB, and I was riding backseat in U-2ST trainer 80-1064, callsign *Pinon 72*. From the front cockpit, my instructor pilot Major Brandon King explained that the Pinon grows at higher elevations than any other tree. The U-2 Dragon Lady is similarly found at higher altitudes than any other flying machine, except the occasional SR-71 Blackbird from the same stable, Lockheed Martin's famous Skunk Works.

When the U-2 was first conceived back in 1954, the rationale for flying 13 or more miles high was to escape detection by the radars of the Soviet Union, and interception by its fighters and missiles. Although the first aim was never really achieved, for four glorious years the U-2 did soar above the USSR and other "denied territory" with impunity. Once Gary Powers was shot down in 1960, the nature of the game changed somewhat. The Blackbird and reconnaissance satellites invaded the U-2's patch.

Forty years after the U-2 took off on its first operational flight, however, the aircraft has never been busier. The 9th Reconnaissance Wing maintains four overseas detachments, which perform around 1,000 operational missions each year. The 99th Reconnaissance Squadron provides the crews for these detachments, and also flies in support of U.S.-based exercises, disaster relief efforts, and even the occasional search-and-rescue mission.

Enlarged and Improved

The enlarged and improved U-2R model which first flew in 1967, proved to be an unrivalled platform for a new generation of reconnaissance sensors. It offered a stable environment for sensitive, long-range side-looking cameras, radars and signals-gathering devices. They could listen and look further from the U-2's lofty perch, than if they were carried on more conventional craft. Most importantly, the U-2 could hang around—operational

flights usually last for more than nine hours. Blackbirds, satellites and unmanned aerial vehicles come and go, but no-one has yet devised a more cost-effective method of airborne intelligence-gathering.

Such are the rewards of long-endurance, high-altitude flight. But there are also penalties - and I was wearing one of them. The S1031 pressure suit and helmet. It's bulky and inconvenient—40 pounds of cumbersome restriction to the everyday movements that one takes for granted (including bodily functions!). It's also a virtually complete barrier to sensible communication with the outside world, save through the intercom system. But if you want to survive a cockpit depressurization at high altitude, you don't leave the ground without it.

U-2 pilots learn to live with it, and I seemed to be coping quite well too, thanks to the previous day's very thorough induction into the strange world of pressurized protection at Beale's Physiological Support Division (PSD).

Following a stringent medical, I had first been introduced to the S1 ejection seat. This is a zero-zero device for low-altitude escape, but if a

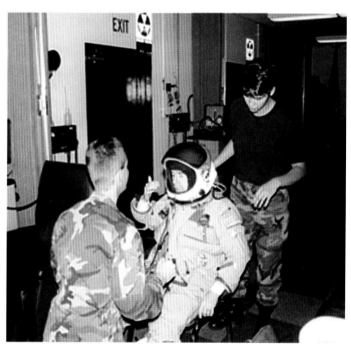

PSD checks that the author is suited-up correctly, and ready to go "on the hose." (via author)

In the altitude chamber at Beale. Here, pressure suits—and their pilots—are checked to ensure they can survive an explosive decompression. (via author)

high-altitude ejection is ever required, it is designed to descend from the heavens with its occupant still attached, who thus benefits from a continuing supply of oxygen for breathing and suit pressure from two emergency cylinders. At 15,000 feet, aneroids automatically command release of the body-restraining straps, and one floats free as the parachute deploys.

Pressure suit

Then I was invited to change into long white underwear, and don the suit itself. This procedure requires the active cooperation of two PSD technicians, who do most of the tugging, stretching, attaching and zipping. From the inside out, the suit consists of a nylon inner layer, a polyurethane-coated pressure layer, a restraint layer of adjustable mesh-patterned nylon, an immersion layer, and an exterior cover of yellow-colored nomex.

Supervised by Dick Cook, a veteran PSD supervisor, my assistants pulled on my boots and clip-fitted the gloves to the suit's rigid metal attachment rings. Then I squeezed my head with some difficulty into the goldfish-bowl helmet. This too was attached to the suit, and now I was

ready to go "on the hose." I flopped into a semi-reclined leather chair next to the oxygen console.

Nothing really prepares you for the sense of detachment which ensues once the faceplate has been latched down and the oxygen starts flowing. People carried on conversations a few feet in front of me, but I couldn't hear them. They sometimes moved out of my limited field of vision. I found that I could only follow their movements by raising my arms to the helmet and physically pushing or pulling the helmet sideways. The sound of my breathing was amplified through the built-in headset, and soon became monotonous.

According to Major King, some prospective U-2 pilots never get past this initial suit-up. A member of the 1st Reconnaissance Squadron (Training), King manages the recruitment of the 20 or so pilots who join the wing each year. "One in ten of them feel uncomfortable and get claustrophobic. Hearing their own breathing gets them disconcerted—we call it the Darth Varder syndrome," he told me.

The selection process is rigorous. Applicants must have 1,500 hours of flying time, and the skills necessary to transition from (for instance) an electric jet such as the F-16 to the unboosted cable controls of the U-2. Even the most confident jet jockey can come unstuck as he tries to handle a powered glider with a 104-foot wingspan and a bicycle undercarriage for landing! Each newcomer is given three checkrides in the U-2ST by Major King or one of his fellow IPs, who have been known to "wash out" five candidates in a row!

Altitude Chamber

My "indoctrination" at PSD continued with a visit to the altitude chamber. I was installed within and the "climb" began. At 20,000 feet Cook invited me to remove the faceplate for a demonstration of the insidious effects of hypoxia. Then the ascent continued to 70,000 feet, then down to 55,000 feet, whereupon Cook simulated an explosive decompression. The chamber fogged over, though I could still see the glass of water that had been placed on a nearby ledge, and which was now boiling vigorously. My body fluids would have met the same fate, had I not been protected by the pressure suit, which had now inflated to hold my arms and legs in a vice-like grip. I wondered how a U-2 pilot could physically manage flying the jet, if this should ever happen for real.

Still, Major King gave every reassurance when we met later to discuss the next day's flight. After discussing my few essential tasks (pulling the pins, sealing the canopy etc.), he proffered some culinary advice. On long flights, U-2 pilots take sustenance by squeezing pureed food up a tube

On the ramp at Beale, the U-2 trainer awaits another rookie pilot and his instructor. (Lockheed Pl-8738)

A superb, high-altitude view of the San Francisco bay area. (Stuart Brose)

he fully reclined his chair and fell asleep! When the appointed time came, our oxygen supply was switched to portable containers, and we waddled out of PSD onto the van which took us to the flightline.

After negotiating the steps up to the cockpit with some difficulty, I gingerly lowered myself inside, one leg either side of the huge, old-fashioned control column. A long process of connecting man with machine ensued...oxygen hoses, communications cord, seat harnesses, boot stirrups and so on. According to standard procedure, I was a helpless spectator throughout the process, which was carried out by two PSD technicians and Capt. Reed.

In the four dual-control U-2 trainers, the rear cockpit occupies the space known as the Q-bay on operational aircraft, where cameras or other sensors may be carried. The instruments are conventional, with a large attitude indicator at centre-front. Unfortunately, I was denied the use of a unique U-2 feature: the driftsight, which affords pilots a splendid view of the territory beneath them. Shielded by a rubber cone protruding from above the attitude indicator, the viewing optics for this are at head-level—but in the two-seaters, only the front cockpit is so equipped.

With some difficulty thanks to the heavy helmet, I glanced down and sideways. Throttle and trim wheel to the left, with radio and oxygen controls aft, next to a recess where Reed had placed my food tubes and drink bottles. Navigation and some environmental controls to the right. Somewhere behind me were a whole raft of circuit breakers, which could surely only be manipulated by feel.

On the intercom, I heard Major King call for engine start. The brand-new General Electric F118-GE-101 turbofan wound into action. All 38 remaining Dragon Ladies are having their venerable Pratt & Whitney J75 turbojets replaced with the F118, a variant of the engine which powers the B-2 bomber. In the process, they are redesignated from U-2R to U-2S (except for two flown by NASA which remain known as ER-2s). The new motor is marginally more powerful than the J75 at 18,300 lbs st, and offers modern technology, a weight saving of 1,300 lbs, and 16% less fuel consumption.

We set off for a holding point on the taxiway which intersects Beale's 12,000-foot runway at the halfway point. No need to take the full length in this bird! The departure performance is so impressive that each mission is said to "launch" rather than "take-off." And for today's two-hour flight, we would be "launching" with only a half fuel load.

We taxied onto the runway and paused to allow the groundcrew to extract the locking pins from the outrigger wheels, known as pogos. Then King selected 80% power, released the brakes, and we surged forward. In

which is inserted into the helmet through a pressure port. King recommended "Peach and Pear," and suggested that I also take at least two bottles of liquid along, to help prevent dehydration.

The day of the flight dawned, cloudier than I had hoped. At the met office, King introduced me to Captain Steve Reed, another 1st RS pilot who would be our "mobile" today. He would preflight the black jet while its two prospective pilots were suiting-up and pre-breathing. He would also assist the heavily-encumbered King and myself into the aircraft, and generally supervise the ongoing flight.

Pre-breathing

Off we went to suit-up. A one-hour period of pre-breathing is necessary to reduce the proportion of nitrogen in the blood, and prevents decompression sickness. King demonstrated a useful procedure for passing the time:

Above: The trainer flares for landing at Beale, having reached the threshold at the correct speed. (Jeff Olesen) Left: Heading for the heavens. The runway below recedes as the U-2 climbs steeply (Jeff Olesen).

no time at all we were rotating into a steep climb that took us to 6,000 feet before we reached the end of the runway!

Breathtaking

King had prepared me for this, but it was still breathtaking to watch the altimeter wind up at such a rate. We passed 20,000 feet after only three minutes, and King soon engaged the autopilot in pitch mode. The 30-degree climb attitude seemed more like 60 degrees to me as we turned north to our first waypoint above the Sierras. "Climbout is much simpler with the new engine than the R-model, where we had to follow a strict EGT regime," King explained over the intercom. "Now we can set full throttle and the engine does the rest."

As we neared 50,000 feet, King decreased the pitch so that we could establish a speed schedule of Mach 0.72, then re-engaged the autopilot. We were about to enter the cruise-climb, and henceforth the aircraft would rise steadily but more slowly as fuel was burned off. King bid goodbye to Sacramento control, and checked in with Oakland Center on a special frequency that had only another U-2 flying from Beale to keep us company. After 18 minutes of flight we passed through 60,000 feet.

We turned south over Reno, Nevada, and I caught a glimpse of Lake Tahoe below as the overcast thinned. Right now, though, it was more interesting to look above and to the side. The sky had turned darker as we climbed, and directly overhead it was now almost black, with the stars visible. The blue had retreated towards the horizon, where it resided as a thin line separating earth from sky. This horizon seemed a long way distant, and I could now discern the curvature of the earth quite clearly.

It was all rather peaceful and beautiful, but my reverie was interrupted as Major King invited me to take the controls. I accepted a trifle reluctantly, having heard plenty and written some about the dreaded "coffin corner," or "throat." This is a condition known to all high-flyers as they approach the top left hand corner of the envelope. Put simply, the slowest that the aircraft can go comes close to the fastest that it can go, as the margin between stall speed and Mach buffet steadily erodes.

In the original, smaller U-2 versions, that margin could be a mere five knots under certain conditions. Right now our margin was a generous 30 knots, but King warned that we were only a few knots from overspeed, and told me to maintain 100 knots IAS, Mach 0.71. I tried a few gentle turns, and the big-winged bird responded well. It seemed at home up here.

Now King fell silent on the intercom, and my sense of isolation grew. I could not actually see him in the cockpit forward and below mine, because the interior was obscured by its large black sliding sunshade. Some minutes later, I learned that his microphone was malfunctioning intermittently. In the meantime, though, I began to experience something of the "out of this world" feeling that has been described by so many U-2 pilots.

In order to re-establish some relationship with Mother Earth, I peered downwards over the canopy rail. The altostratus had cleared, and we were approaching our next turn point at Monterey, on the California coast. I had a superb view all the way up the San Francisco Bay. King re-established contact, and after we rolled out of the turn he checked our fuel balance. Soon it would be time to start the descent.

The U-2 is the only flying machine where you routinely extend the landing gear at 70,000 feet. Plus the speed brakes. The throttle is brought back to idle, the flaps are set to the gust position, and with luck the aircraft may now be persuaded to quit the heavens and start a slow descent. King set a direct course back to Beale, but although the base was more than 100

Instructor pilot Major Brandon King with the author at the successful conclusion of the flight, which took place on 1 June 1995. (USAF)

miles distant, we were not coming down quickly enough. A lazy 360-degree turn helped us lose 15,000 more feet.

As we passed through 30,000 feet I took control again. In contrast to its earlier performance at altitude, the aircraft now handled like a truck in the thick lower air. I handed it back to the instructor, and since we were now safely below 20,000 feet, unlatched my faceplate and turned the oxygen supply off. For the first time in this entire exercise, I could smell real airplane!

At 5,000 feet King retracted the speed brakes, faired the gust control, and trimmed the bird for landing. This can be the most challenging phase of flight, especially for novice pilots. The correct procedure is to cross the runway threshold at 10 feet, and the correct speed for the aircraft's configuration. With 600 gallons remaining, our T-speed today should (would, dammit!) be 76 knots.

Our mobile came up on the radio, ready to talk us through the landing and chase us down the runway in one of those ostentatious five-liter Ford Mustangs. We arrived overhead the field and turned downwind at 105 knots. Flaps and speedbrake were extended once again.

The powers-that-be had rejected King's request to perform a touch-and-go, so we performed one low approach before repositioning for a full-stop landing. King told me that on hot afternoons in summer, strong thermals rising from the cornfields that surround Beale can wreak havoc with even the most carefully-flown approach. No such drama today, though. With the appropriate adjustments for yaw, pitch, and power, we reached the threshold in good shape.

King flared for landing. "Five feet, four, two" called Reed from the mobile. As we touched down, King retracted flaps and speed brakes, but continued making yaw and pitch inputs until the aircraft slowed to near-walking pace. Many a U-2 pilot has relaxed upon touchdown, only to find himself skipping, porpoising, or heading sideways for the grass.

Groundcrew reinserted the pogos, and we headed back to the ramp. A small reception committee awaited. Later, I was required to seal my initiation into the world of the high flyers by drinking a yard of ale in the so-called "Heritage Room." A less distinguished flying outfit would merely describe this place as their bar. But no other wing has a drinking establishment that can boast wall plaques listing every pilot who has ever qualified on type. Even after all these years, the U-2 drivers are still a select band.

Abbreviations

ABM	Anti-Ballistic Missile	DGS	Deployable Ground Station
ACC	Air Combat Command	DIA	Defense Intelligence Agency
ADF	Air Direction-Finding	DMZ	De-Militarized Zone
ADIZ	Air Defense Identification Zone	DOD	Department of Defense
ADC	Air Defense Command	DPD	Development Projects Division, CIA
ADP	Advanced Development Projects organization at Lockheed	DDI	Deputy Director (or Directorate) for Intelligence, CIA
		DDL	Dual Data Link
AEC	Atomic Energy Commission	DDP	Deputy Director (or Directorate) for Plans, CIA
AEW	Airborne Early Warning	DEW	Distant Early Warning
AFDAP	Air Force Development and Advanced Planning office	DME	Distance Measuring Equipment
AFFTC	Air Force Flight Test Center	DPS	Development Project Staff, CIA
AFLC	Air Force Logistics Command	DSCS	Defense Systems Communications Satellites
AFOAT	Air Force Office of Atomic Testing	ECM	Electronic CounterMeasures
AFSS	Air Force Security Service	EG&G	Edgerton, Germeshausen & Grier
AFSWP	Armed Forces Special Weapons Project	EGT	Exhaust Gas Temperature
AFTAC	Air Force Technical Applications Center	ELINT	Electronic Intelligence
ALSS	Advanced Location and Strike System	ERS	Expeditionary Reconnaissance Squadron
AMC	Air Materiel Command	ESC	Electronic Security Command
ARC	Ad-hoc Requirements Committee, CIA	ETP	Extended Tether Program
ARDC	Air Research and Development Command	EUCOM	European Command
ASD	Aeronautical Systems Division	FCLP	Field Carrier Landing Practice
ASARS	Advanced Synthetic Aperture Radar System	GCI	Ground-Controlled Intercept
ATIC	Air Technical Intelligence Center	GD	General Dynamics
AWACS	Airborne Warning & Control System	GE	General Electric
BDA	Bomb Damage Assessment	GPS	Global Positioning System
BMEWS	Ballistic Missile Early Warning System	GRU	Soviet Military Intelligence
BOB	Bureau of the Budget	HASP	High Altitude Sampling Program
BRIXMIS	British Mission to Soviet Forces in Germany	HEDCOM	Headquarters Command, USAF
CAF	Chinese Air Force (Taiwan)	HUMINT	Human Intelligence
CAOC	Combined Air Operation Center	IADL	Integrated Airborne Data Link
CARS	Contingency Airborne Reconnaissance System (ground station)	ICBM	Intercontinental Ballistic Missile
		IG	Inspector General, CIA
CENTCOM	Central Command	INS	Inertial Navigation System
CCK	Chiang Ching Kuo	IPIR	Initial Photo-Interpretation Report
CDL	Common Data Link	IRAN	Inspect and Repair As Necessary
CINC	Commander in Chief	IRBM	Intermediate-Range Ballistic Missile
CKS	Chiang Kai Shek	IOT&E	Initial Operational Test and Evaluation
COMINT	Communications Intelligence	ISP	Intelligence Systems Panel of SAB
COMOR	Committee on Overhead Reconnaissance, CIA	ISR	Intelligence, Surveillance & Reconnaissance
COMIREX	Committee on Imagery Requirements and Exploitation, CIA	JCS	Joint Chiefs of Staff
		JP-TS	Jet Propellant, Thermally Stabilized
DARO	Defense Airborne Reconnaissance Office	JRC	Joint Reconnaissance Center
DASA	Defense Atomic Support Agency	JSTARS	Joint Surveillance & Target Attack Radar System
DCI	Director of Central Intelligence, CIA	JTIDS	Joint Tactical Information Distribution System
DDCI	Deputy Director of Central Intelligence, CIA	LAC	Lockheed Aircraft Company
DDR	Deputy Director (or Directorate) for Research, CIA	LMSC	Lockheed Missiles & Space Company
DDS&T	Deputy Director (or Directorate) for Science & Technology, CIA	LOROP	Long-Range Oblique Photographic
		LSO	Landing Signals Officer, U.S. Navy

MAAG	Military Aid and Assistance Group
MACV	Military Assistance Command Vietnam
MIDAS	Missile Defense and Alarm System satellite
MIPE	Mobile Intelligence Processing Element
MIT	Massachusetts Institute of Technology
MLP	Mirror Landing Practice
MOBSTR	Mobile Stretch data relay system
MRBM	Medium-Range Ballistic Missile
MTI	Moving Target Indicator
NACA	National Advisory Committee for Aeronautics
NASA	National Aeronautics and Space Administration
NATO	North Atlantic Treaty Organisation
NavPIC	Naval Photographic Intelligence Center
NEFA	North East Frontier Agency
NIE	National Intelligence Estimate
NORAD	North American Air Defense Command
NPIC	National Photo-Intelligence Center, CIA
NRO	National Reconnaissance Office
NSA	National Security Agency
NSC	National Security Council
OAF	Operation Allied Force
OBC	Optical Bar Camera
OEF	Operation Enduring Freedom
OEL	Office of ELINT, CIA
OIF	Operation Iraqi Freedom
OL	Operating Location
ONR	Office of Naval Research
ORD	Office of Research and Development, CIA
OSD	Office of the Secretary of Defense
OSI	Office of Scientific Intelligence, CIA
OSA	Office of Special Activities, CIA
PACAF	Pacific Air Forces
PACOM	Pacific Command
P&W	Pratt & Whitney
PBCFIA	President's Board of Consultants on Foreign Intelligence Activities
PELSS	Precision Emitter Location and Strike System
PIC	Photo Interpretation Center, CIA
PID	Photo Intelligence Division, CIA
PLAAF	People's Liberation Army Air Force (mainland China)
PMR	Pacific Missile Range
PSD	Physiological Support Division
PSAC	President's Scientific Advisory Council
PVO	Soviet Air Defense Troops
RADAN	Radar Air Navigation
RAF	Royal Air Force, UK
RAMP	Reconnaissance Avionics Maintainability Program
RFINT	Radio-Frequency Intelligence
ROC	Republic of China (Taiwan)
RPV	Remotely-Piloted Vehicle
RTASS	Remote Tactical Airborne SIGINT System
RTS	Reconnaissance Technical Squadron
SAB	Scientific Advisory Board, USAF
SAC	Strategic Air Command
SAM	Surface-to-Air Missile
SAMOS	Space And Missile Observation System satellite
SCT	Shuang Cheng Tzu (missile test site)
SEI	Scientific Engineering Institute
SIGINT	Signals Intelligence
SLAR	Side-Looking Airborne Radar
SOUTHCOM	Southern Command
SRS	Strategic Reconnaissance Squadron
SRTS	Strategic Reconnaissance Training Squadron
SRW	Strategic Reconnaissance Wing
SSB	Single Side-Band (radio)
SSM	Surface-to-Surface Missile
SYERS	Senior Year Electro-Optical Reconnaissance System
SYPO	Senior Year Program Office
TAC	Tactical Air Command
TADMS	TR-1 ASARS Data Manipulation System
TCP	Technological Capabilities Panel
TDY	Temporary Duty or Tour of Duty
TEL	Transporter/Erector/Launcher
TELINT	Telemetry Intelligence
TGIF	Transportable Ground Intercept Facility
TRAC	Tactical Radar Correlator
TRIGS	TR-1 Ground Shelter
UAV	Unmanned Aerial Vehicle
UNMOVIC	United Nations Monitoring, Verification and Inspection Commission
UNSCOM	United Nations Special Commission
USAFE	United States Air Forces in Europe
USCM	Unit Simulated Combat Maneuvers
USIB	United States Intelligence Board
USSR	Union of Soviet Socialist Republics
VHF	Very High Frequency
WADC	Wright Air Development Center
WRAMA	Warner-Robins Air Materiel Area
WSMR	White Sands Missile Range
WSPO	Weapon System Project Office

Appendix A:
Aircraft Data

Airplane Basic Dimensions

Model	wingspan	wing area	aspect ratio	Fuselage length	Tail height
U-2A/C	80ft	600 sq ft	10.67	49ft 8in	15ft 6in
U-2R/S	104ft	1,000 sq ft	10.67	63ft 1in	16ft 2in

Engine ratings

Model	dry weight	Thrust sl	Max EGT	Max PR
P&W J57-P-37	4,050 lbs	10,500 lbs	640 deg C	3.07
P&W J57-P-31	3,615 lbs	11,200 lbs	610 deg C	3.24
P&W J75-P-13	4,900 lbs	15,800 lbs	630 deg C	3.3
P&W J75-P-13B	4,900 lbs	17,000 lbs	665 deg C	3.3
GE F118-GE-101	3,220 lbs	18,500 lbs		3.4

Weights and Performance Summary

Note: The values shown below for maximum range, endurance and altitude could not be achieved on the same mission, since different flight profiles were required. Atmospheric conditions and other variables also affect performance. Range and endurance is to zero fuel. Usable fuel can be up to 50 gals less than values shown. Cruise speed for all variants was Mach 0.72/410 knots.

Sources: Lockheed Reports SP-109 (U-2A), SP-179 (U-2C in 1959), U-2C Flight Manual (U-2C in 1966), SP-3051 (U-2R); SAC History FY1978-81 (TR-1A); NASA Dryden website (ER-2); Senior Year Security Classification Guide (U-2S)

Model	MTOGW lbs	Fuel gals	Range nm	Endurance	Altitude ft
U-2A [1]	20,080	1,335	3,775	9h	72,000
U-2A [2]	19,665	1,335	4,000	10h	72,500
U-2C [3]	23,040	1,545	4,600	11h30m	76,000
U-2C [4]	24,270	1,520	3,700	9h15m	74,000
U-2R [5]	37,585	2,950	6,300	15h	75,500
TR-1A [6]	40,000	2,950	5,000	12h+	70,000+
ER-2 [7]	34,750	2,950	3,000	8h	73,000+
U-2S [8]	40,000	2,950	7,000+	14h+	70,000+

[1] With original J57-P-37 engine in 1955-56
[2] With definitive J57-P-31 engine from 1957.
[3] With original J75-P-13 engine from 1959, with slipper tanks
[4] With J75-P-13B engine from 1966, with slipper tanks
[5] in 1968, clean aircraft (no pods)
[6] in 1981
[7] with J75-P-13B engine, with superpods, NASA-imposed MTOGW, range and endurance limitations
[8] with F118-GE-101 engine

Additional References

Most of the previously-published technical books about the U-2 are out of print. Unfortunately, this includes *Aerograph 3: Lockheed U-2* by Jay Miller (Aerofax Inc, Austin, TX, 1983) which served as a standard reference to model-makers and others looking for three-view drawings, close-up photographs etc.

A less ambitious book, *Lockheed U-2 Dragon Lady* by Dennis R. Jenkins (Volume 16, Warbird Tech Series, Speciality Press, MN, 1998) has drawings, photographs and a brief history.

Readers seeking details of the U-2R/S airframes, but not the earlier U-2 models, should consult *Black Jets* (AIRtime Publishing, CT, 2003). The author contributed the U–2 pages to this book, and they contain many detailed illustrations which were beyond the scope of the volume that you are now reading.

Fortunately, model-makers do have an alternative reference available. Meteor Productions of Merrifield, VA, has produced four sheets of U-2 decals, which are accompanied by three-views and other useful information.

Of course, a number of non-specialist books have covered various aspects of the U-2 story. This author recommends *The Black Watch: The Men Who Fly America's Secret Spy Planes* by Ernest K. Gann (Random House, NY, 1989) which can still be found in used bookstores, and *Operation Overflight* by Francis Gary Powers, which was republished in 2004 by Potomac Books, VA.

Appendix B:
Systems Data

Imaging Systems– early models

A-1 Configuration

One Hycon HR731 camera with 24-inch focal length f6 lens on rocking mount to provide left, right and vertical options, plus HR732 film magazine, format 9 x 18 inch x 700 or 1,800 feet. Plus three Hycon HR730 cameras with 6-inch focal length f16.3 lens in fixed trimetrogen mount, film format 9 x 18 inch x 390 feet. Weight 350 lbs
All aircraft, specialist mapping applications only

A-2 Configuration

Three Hycon HR731 with 24-inch focal length f6 lenses fixed at vertical, 37 degrees left and right, plus HR732 film magazines, format 9 x 18 inch x 700 or 1,800 feet. Weight 360 lbs
All aircraft. Used on 1956 overflights, pending arrival of B-configuration. Retained and used as alternative. Also used on early U-2R

A-3 Configuration

Three Hycon HR731 with 24-inch focal length lenses all fixed in vertical position
All aircraft, specialist applications only, mainly NASA in 1970s

B-camera

One Hycon HR73B1 camera, 36-inch focal length, f10, shutter aperture 3.6 inches, with seven 'stop-and-shoot' positions (left and right 1,2,3 plus vertical). Four modes of operation (1 - all positions; 2 - L1, R1, vertical only; 3 - L1,2,3 plus vertical only; 4 - R1,2,3 plus vertical only). Normal stereo overlap 55 degrees. Film format 2 x contra-winding 9.5 x 18-inch rolls x 4,000 or 6,500 feet, to obtain image format of 18 x 18-inch. Flight weight 520 lbs when fully loaded with 2 x 6,500 feet film.
HR73B2 was lightweight version (455 lbs) produced mid-1960s
HR73B3 was larger shutter (f8) version produced early-1970s
All aircraft. The workhorse camera for overflights from 1957. Also used on early U-2R.

C-camera

One Perkin Elmer/Hycon 180-inch folding focal length LOROP camera. Three operating modes. Film format 13 x 13-inch x 5,300 feet
343, 56-6712, 56-6721 only. Technical problems: never used operationally. Withdrawn in 1959

D-package

Westinghouse APQ-56 side-looking radar, Ka-band, plus ASN-6/RADAN system for improved navigation accuracy.
349, 350/56-6683, 56-6708 and 56-6955 only. Dubious operational utility; withdrawn in 1961

Delta camera

Itek adaptation of Corona satellite 24-inch focal length f3.5 lens panoramic camera. Film format 70mm x 29-inch x 5,000 or 7,800 feet. Weight over 500 lbs
Delta I (aka System 112A) was the prototype, one only, monoscopic, with 70-degree scan
Delta II (aka System 112B) was twin cameras mounted at 30-degree angle for stereo. Four built.
Delta III was rebuild of two Delta IIs for lighter weight (430 lbs) and flush-fit in Q-bay
Most aircraft. Used mainly by CIA 1963-1969

FFD infrared camera

Texas Instruments FFD-2 infrared linescan system. Later improved as FFD-3 and FFD-4.
Used only by CIA, 1964-late 1960s

H-camera

Hycon HR-329 66-inch focal length f5 lens LOROP camera. Four modes provided 24-85% overlap. Maximum oblique angle 70 degrees. Film format 4.5 x 4.5-inch x 2,000 feet. Weight 666 lbs. Three built. Two modified with lightweight mounts (- 90 lbs) and other improvements early 1970s
SAC developed 1964-65, but mainly used by CIA until 1975. Thereafter improved version used by SAC U-2R

Mark I (T-1) Tracker Camera

One Perkin Elmer 3-inch focal length lens panoramic camera, f8, film format 70mm x 9.5-inch x 1,000 feet. 180-degree scan. Stereo overlap capability. Weighed 55lbs when film loaded.
Original tracker used until mid-1960s, carried on Q-bay

T-35 Tracker camera

One Perkin Elmer 3-inch focal length lens panoramic camera, f2.8, film format 35mm x 50mm x 700 feet. 180-degree scan. Stereo overlap capability. Weight 12 lbs.
Replacement, lighter-weight tracker from mid-1960s, also on U-2R in nose

Imaging Systems – Later Models

IRIS-II

Itek 24-inch focal length f3.5 lens rotating bar panoramic camera. Mono or stereo modes (selectable pre-flight only) 140-degree scan. Format 4.5-in x 35 or 58-inch x 6,500 or 10,500 feet. Weight 395 lbs. Twelve built.
On all CIA and SAC U-2R aircraft from 1969, and NASA U-2C and ER-2 aircraft. Withdrawn late 1990s except ER-2

IRIS-III
Improved version of IRIS-II
On SAC U-2R aircraft from mid-1970s and U-2S until withdrawn in 1999

OBC
Itek 30-inch focal length Optical Bar Camera (apochromatic panoramic). Format 4.5-in x 73-inch x 5,000 feet. Weight 505 lbs
On SAC U-2R aircraft from mid-1970s. Still in service.

F489
Fairchild 6-in focal length mapping camera. Film format 9 x 9-inch x 663 feet.
Former SR-71 camera used on U-2R/S for survey work in 1990s

RC-10
Wild Heerbrugg 6 or 12-inch focal length f4 lens mapping camera. Film format 9 x 9-inch
On NASA ER-2 aircraft

ASARS
Hughes Advanced Synthetic Aperture Radar System. High-power X-band imaging radar. Search and spot modes. 12 built. Moving Target Indicator (MTI) (search and spot modes) added to three systems. Electronically-scanned antenna added to all systems. Hughes sold to Raytheon.
Improved ASARS-2A version with onboard processor, Enhanced MTI, better coverage, resolution and geolocation.
On TR-1A and U-2R from 1984, improved version from early 2000s

SYERS
Itek Senior Year Electro-optical Reconnaissance System. Dual-band EO/IR high-resolution oblique/panoramic scanning sensor offering search, spot and stereo coverage in both visible and medium-wave IR bands simultaneously or individually. Itek sold to Hughes, then Raytheon, then Goodrich. Improved SYERS-2 version with five additional collection bands for multispectral collection (three visible, two short-wave IR, and two medium-wave IR), plus better coverage, resolution and geolocation.
On U-2R from late 1980s, improved version from early 2000s

SIGINT and Defensive Systems

System 1
Ramo Wooldridge ELINT receiver. Preset, crystal-video receivers covered S/X-bands. Antennas in nose.
Improved System 1A from 1965.
All aircraft except 66705, 66714, 66715, 66716, 66717, 66718. Used from 1956 until 1960 (CIA) and late-1960s (SAC)

System 3
Ramo Wooldridge COMINT receiver, covered VHF band. Antenna originally in long radome beneath nose. From 1958 antenna in nose or on tailfin (SAC aircraft), lower ventral scimitar antenna inside radome (CIA aircraft). SAC adopted latter, mid-1960s.
All aircraft. Used from 1956 until mid-1960s

System 4
Ramo-Wooldridge multiband SIGINT search receiver, covered G-K bands. Occupied entire Q-bay, weighed 570lbs. Belly-mounted antenna, replaced by "ram's horns" on upper rear fuselage in 1961, and by lower ventral scimitar antenna inside radome, mid-1960s.
System 4A extended coverage to VHF early 1960s.
CIA aircraft from 1957-1958 only, SAC aircraft from 1958, used until late 1960s

System 5
Ramo-Wooldridge multiband SIGINT search receiver. Occupied entire Q-bay. Belly-mounted antenna
CIA aircraft 1956-57 only

System 6
Ramo Wooldridge (STL) multiband SIGINT receiver, covered VHF - K bands. Antennas in nose, Q-bay and lower ventral scimitar antenna inside radome.
System 6A improved VHF coverage, mid-1960s, two blade antennas above rear fuselage replaced ventral scimitar mid-1960s
System 6B for U-2R with flush-mounted antennas
CIA aircraft only. Replaced System 1 from 1958, used until late 1960s (System 6B until early 1970s)

System 7
HRB Singer TELINT (missile telemetry intercept) system. Most equipment was in Q-bay. Antennas were 'ram's horns' above rear fuselage.
Used by some CIA aircraft at Det B only, 1959-60

System 8
Never installed on U-2

System 9
Granger Assocs (later, ATI) deceptive jammer to counter air intercept radars. Carried in small box at base of tail.
System 9A improved version in 1963
System 9B much-improved version 1964, all-quadrant coverage, higher-power. Antennas below nose, fuselage and tail. Cockpit display integrated with System 12B
System 9C/D further minor improvements
Systems 9/9A on all CIA aircraft 1959-1964. System 9B on all CIA aircraft from 1965 and all SAC aircraft from 1966 as part of defensive upgrade; System 9D on early U-2R

System 10
HRB Singer TELINT system. Intended as replacement for System 7 in 1961-62. Never installed on U-2

System 11
Originally-intended designation for what became System 4A

System 12
ATI surface-to-air missile fire control radar warning system. Antenna in nose.
System 12A intended to display range as well as direction, not deployed.
System 12B improved version. Cockpit display integrated with System 9B.
System 12C improved direction-finding.
System 12E improved correlation with other defensive systems
System 12E on U-2R
System 12F on U-2C modified for ALSS
System 12 added to all CIA aircraft early 1963, installed then removed from some SAC aircraft 1963, re-installed on SAC aircraft 1964-65. System 12B installed on all aircraft 1964-65. System 12C on CIA aircraft 1968. System 12E on early U-2R. System 12F on U-2C 1972-80

System 13
Sanders surface-to-air missile fire control radar jamming system. Adaptation of US Navy ALQ-19 system, which covered S-band, in later 1962. Carried in modified U-2 slipper tanks.
System 13A designation used for the redevelopment and down-sizing in 1965 of Systems 13/14/15 to (eventually) both C and S-bands, carried in box below rear tail.
System 13B designation not used.
System 13C with new antennas and correlation with OS system
On some CIA aircraft. System 13A on CIA aircraft from 1965 and SAC aircraft from 1966 as part of defensive upgrade; System 13C on CIA aircraft from mid-1966 and SAC aircraft from 1972

System 14
Sanders surface-to-air missile fire control radar jamming system. Adaptation of US Navy ALQ-49 system, which covered C-band, in early 1963. Carried in modified U-2 slipper tanks.
On some CIA aircraft 1963, added to SAC aircraft 1964, replaced by System 13A 1965-66

System 15
Sanders surface-to-air missile fire control radar jamming system. Adaptation of US Navy ALQ-51 system, which covered S-band, in early 1963. Carried in modified U-2 slipper tanks.
On some CIA aircraft 1963, added to SAC aircraft 1964, replaced by System 13A 1965-66

Oscar Sierra (OS)
HRB Singer SA-2 surface-air-missile command guidance link warning system. Antenna on Q-bay hatch. TRW took over contract.
Mk II improved version.
Mk III further improvements including cockpit display integrated with other systems
on all CIA aircraft from 1965 and SAC aircraft from 1966 as part of defensive upgrade, Mk III on early U-2R and SAC U-2C from 1972

System 16
Proposed SIGINT receiver, not developed

System 17
TRW multiband SIGINT search receiver, with direction-finding capability in wingtip and horizontal tail antennas. Occupied entire Q-bay.
Repackaged as System 17B for detachable U-2R nose, with flush-mounted antennas
On CIA aircraft late 1966, on CIA U-2R from 1969

System 18
Proposed ELINT receiver, not developed

System 192
TRW ELINT receiver with direction-finding capability in wing pod antennas
System 192A improved version, antennas relocated to Q-bay hatch
On some SAC aircraft on experimental basis 1963-64, System 192A on all SAC and two CIA aircraft from 1966-1972

System 20
Sanders infrared missile approach warning system. Sensor housed on right wing in rearward-facing fairing
On CIA aircraft from 1968, and SAC aircraft from 1972. On U-2R and TR-1 aircraft until mid-1990s

System 21
TRW? COMINT receiver, covered VHF band. Antennas in intake cheeks.
Replaced System 3 on CIA aircraft 1967. On CIA U-2R

System 22
Infrared missile jamming system also known as HIRAMS. Carried in small box at base of tail. Developed but not deployed?
Tested on one CIA aircraft 1967, provisions to install on SAC aircraft 1968

Systems 23-26
Not much known. System 24 was deployed on CIA U-2R aircraft in 1970.
Systems 25 and 26 were potential warning system upgrades, discontinued

System 27
Dalmo-Victor (later, Litton) ALR-46 digital radar warning receiver. Antennas on wingtip extensions and below wing root.
System 27-1 improved version.
On U-2R and TR-1A late 1970s onwards

System 28
ITT ALQ-117 radar jamming system. Antennas below tail.
Intended for TR-1A, not deployed

System 29
Sanders surface-to-air missile radar jamming system. Antennas below fuselage.
System 29-1, 29-2, 'Band Aid', 29E (for low band) and 29F: various improvements. Sanders now BAE Systems
Replaced System 13 on U-2R early 1980s, on TR-1A, still in service

System 30
Proposed wide-spectrum radar jammer. Development abandoned.

ALSS

Advanced Location and Strike System (ELINT).
SAC U-2Cs were development testbeds 1972-80. Never deployed.

P(E)LSS

Precision (Emitter) Location and Strike System (ELINT)
SAC U-2Rs were development testbeds 1984-88. Never deployed.

Senior Book

E-Systems COMINT receiver system. Antennas on fuselage
On SAC U-2R 1971 - early 1980s

Senior Spear

E-Systems (Melpar Division) COMINT receiver system. Antennas on fuselage and in wing pods
Later Raytheon, with company designations RS-4, RS-5, RS-6.
On SAC U-2R and TR-1A 1974 onwards.

Senior Ruby

E-Systems (Garland Division) ELINT receiver system. Antennas on fuselage and in wing pods. Later Raytheon, with company designations RA-1, RA-2.
On SAC U-2R and TR-1A 1978 onwards

RAS-1

Raytheon SIGINT receiver systems, combination of Spear and Ruby. Aka Senior Glass
RAS-1A part digital system
RAS-1R full-digital system
On U-2R/S from 1993, RAS-1R from 2001

AN/ALQ-221 Advanced Defensive System (ADS)

BAE Systems wideband radar warning receiver/jammer for search, track and launch detection capability and track and launch jamming.
On U-2S from 2004

Sampling Systems

A-Foil

first U-2 sampling system consisting of four 16-inch diameter filter papers rotated through duct leading from small opening at the tip of the aircraft's nose.
Six SAC aircraft (66705, 66714, 66715, 66716, 66717, 66718) used 1957-64

F-2 Foil

second U-2 sampling system, also to capture air particles. Used six of the 16-inch filter papers fed by air from intake duct faired onto left side of special Q-bay hatch.
All aircraft, used by CIA 1957-58 then only by SAC. Used in conjunction with:

P-2 Platform

also known as the "ball sampler," consisting of six 13-inch diameter spherical receptacles for air (gas) sampling. Each had 944 cu inch capacity, and was filled with air compressed to 2,000 psi from the engine bleed.
P-3 in 1961 and P-4 in 1970s were improved versions
All aircraft, used by CIA 1957-58 thereafter only by SAC.

Other Systems

System 2

Ramo-Wooldridge HF communications and navigation system. Development abandoned in 1956
Never deployed

Ivory Tower I/II/III

Q-bay hatch-mounted weather reconnaissance instrumentation
All early-model aircraft, CIA and SAC

US Mule

Q-bay hatch for leaflet dropping.
CIA early-model aircraft only. Believed never used operationally

Appendix C:
Unit Histories

CIA Projects Aquatone and Chalice 1955-1960

Project HQ

Development Project Staff (DPS) established December 1954 reporting directly to the Director of Central Intelligence (DCI). Became part of the new Development Projects Division (DPD) in February 1959, reporting to the Deputy Director for Plans (DDP).

Richard Bissell	Special Assistant to DCI for Planning and Co-Ordination (SA/PC/DCI), December 1954> Deputy Director for Plans (DDP) January 1959>
Col Ozzie Ritland	military deputy to SA/PC/DCI, August 1955>
Col Jack Gibbs	military deputy to SA/PC/DCI, May 1956>
Col Bill Burke	military deputy to SA/PC/DCI, May 1958> acting chief, DPD, January 1959>
Herb Miller	executive officer 1955-56
Jim Cunningham	director of administration, 1956>
Col Marion Mixson	director of operations, 1956>
Col Paul Gremmler	director of operations, 1958>
Col Stan Beerli	director of operations, 1959>

U-2 Test Unit

established at Watertown Strip (Groom Lake) 1955, moved to North Base, Edwards AFB, May-June 1957. Cover designation at Edwards was Weather Reconnaissance Squadron (Provisional) - 4 (WRSP-4)

Col Dick Newton	base/unit commander 1955>
Col Landon McConnell	base/unit commander 1956>
Lt Col Cy Perkins	unit commander 1957>
Lt Col Walter Rosenfield	unit commander 1957>

Detachment A

established at Watertown Strip January 1956, to Lakenheath April 1956, to Wiesbaden June 1956, to Giebelstadt October 1956, closed November 1957. Cover designation was Weather Reconnaissance Squadron (Provisional) - 1 (WRSP-1)

Col Fred McCoy	unit commander 1956>
Col Marion Mixson	unit commander July 1957>

Detachment B

established at Watertown Strip spring 1956, to Incirlik (Adana) August 1956. Flying suspended May 1960 but not closed until December 1961. Cover designation was Weather Reconnaissance Squadron (Provisional) - 2 (WRSP-2). Also known as Det 10-10, TUSLOG.

Col Ed Perry	unit commander 1956>
Col Stan Beerli	unit commander November 1957>
Col William Shelton	unit commander August 1959>

Detachment C

established at Watertown Strip August 1956, to Atsugi Febraury 1957, closed June 1960
cover designation Weather Reconnaissance Squadron (Provisional) - 3 (WRSP-3)

Col Stan Beerli	unit commander 1956>
Col Marion Mixson	unit commander November 1957>

4070th Support Wing

This was the designation used by the group which SAC established in later 1955 to provide U-2 training and support to the CIA at Watertown Strip. The group was officially based at March AFB, CA.

Col Bill Yancey	unit commander 1955-1957

USAF Project Dragon Lady 1956 - 1966

4080th Strategic Reconnaissance Wing (SRW)

Activated at Turner AFB, GA on 1 April 1956. The first mission was to operate the RB-57Ds of Project Black Knight, for which purpose the 4025th SRS was assigned to the wing in May 1956. The second mission was to operate the U-2s ordered by SAC under Project Dragon Lady, and the 4028th SRS was created for this purpose. Prior to receiving the U-2s, the 4080th wing moved to Laughlin AFB, TX during February-April 1957.

A second U-2 squadron, the 4029th SRS, was assigned in expectation that the CIA Project Aquatone would end, and the aircraft be turned over to SAC. This never happened, and the 4029th SRS was never equipped. The wing moved to Davis-Monthan AFB in 1963.

Wing Commanders:	
Col Gerald Johnson	May 1956>
Col Hub Zemke	April 1957>
Bg Gen Austin Russell	November 1957>
Col Andrew Bratton	December 1958>
Col William Wilcox	July 1960>
Col John DesPortes	July 1961>
Col Julius Baughn	June 1965>

CIA Project Idealist 1960-1974

Project HQ

The Development Projects Division (DPD) continued to run the CIA U-2 program until July 1962, when it was renamed the Office of Special Activities (OSA). The Office was closed at the end of 1974

Col Stan Beerli	Chief DPD, then Director of Special Activities, June 1960>
Col Jack Ledford	Director of Special Activities, September 1962>
Col Paul Bacalis	Director of Special Activities, August 1966>

Bg Gen Gene Ross	Director of Special Activities, July 1968>
Bg Gen Harold Knowles	Director of Special Activities, June 1970>
Bg Gen Wendell Bevan	Director of Special Activities, July 1971>
Jim Cunningham	Asst Chief DPD then Deputy Director OSA, 1960>
John Parangosky	Deputy Director OSA 1966>
Bob Singel	Deputy Director OSA 1969>
Jim Cherbonneaux	Deputy Director OSA 1972>
Col Don Songer	Chief, Operations, then Director, Field Activities 1960>
Col Bill Shelton	Director, Operations 1966>
Col Bill Burnett	Director, Operations 1969>
Col George Nakis	Director, Operations 1970>

Detachment G, Edwards North Base, California

(cover designation Weather Reconnaissance Squadron (Provisional) - 4 (WRSP-4) until mid-1969, thereafter 1130th Air Tactical Training Group (ATTG). This was the base for the CIA's U-2 operations throughout Project Idealist, where training, development and maintenance activities took place.

Col Bill Gregory	unit commander 1960>
Col Miles Doyle	unit commander 1965>
Col R.A. Schamber	unit commander 1967>
Col Roger Cooper	unit commander 1972>

CIA/CAF Project Tackle 1961-1974

Detachment H / 35th Squadron Taoyuan AB, Taiwan
Established at Taoyuan AB near Taipei in January 1961, as a joint operation between the CIA and the nationalist Chinese Air Force (CAF). The unit was nicknamed "The Black Cat Squadron", and was jointly commanded by a CAF and a USAF officer. The unit closed in August 1974.

Lt Col Denny Posten	U.S. commander 1961>
Lt Col Bob Tomlinson	U.S. commander 1962>
Lt Col Hugh Slater	U.S. commander 1963>
Lt Col Walt Meyler	U.S. commander 1964>
Lt Col Bill Shelton	U.S. commander 1965>
Col Duke Rowdon	U.S. commander 1967>
Col Cy Perkins	U.S. commander 1969>
Col John Ludwig	U.S. commander 1970>
Col Warren Boyd	U.S. commander 1972>
Col Lu Si Liang	CAF commander 1961>
Col Yang Shi Chuen	CAF commander 1963>
Col Wang Tai Yu	CAF commander 1969>
Col Liu Jai Chuang	CAF commander 1970>
Col Wang Tao	CAF commander 1973>

USAF Senior Year Program 1966 - date
100th Strategic Reconnaissance Wing

The 100th SRW was created at Davis-Monthan AFB, Arizona in June 1966 by a renumbering of the 4080th SRW. The U-2 squadron was renumbered from 4028th SRS to the 349th SRS. The 100th wing also controlled the 350th SRS which operated the Ryan RPVs and the associated DC-130 launch and CH-3 recovery aircraft.

In November 1972 the 99th SRS was created as a permanent squadron for the U-2 operation already in place at U-Tapao airbase, Thailand

Wing Commanders:	
Colonel William Kyle	February 1966>
Colonel Marion Mixson	August 1966>
Colonel Ray Haupt	August 1970>
Col Don White	June 1972>
Col Chuck Stratton	May 1974>

9th Strategic Reconnaissance Wing

On 1 July 1976, SAC decided to consolidate U-2 operations with that of the SR-71, under the 9th SRW at Beale. The 1st SRS remained the SR-71 squadron, while the U-2 squadron was numbered 99th SRS.

The 4029th Strategic Reconnaissance Training Squadron (SRTS) was activated at Beale in August 1981 to train all U-2 and TR-1 pilots. It was redesignated the 5th SRTS in 1986, and again redesignated in July 1990 to the 1st SRS (T), after the end of SR-71 operations.

Wing commanders:	
Col John Storrie	June 1975>
Col Lyman Kidder	September 1977>
Col Dale Shelton	February 1979>
Col Dave Young	July 1980>
Col Tom Pugh	July 1982>
Col Hector Freese	August 1983>
Col Dave Pinsky	January 1985>
Col Rich Graham	July 1987>
Col James Savarda	December 1988>
Col Thomas Keck	June 1990>

17th Reconnaissance Wing

The 17th RW was activated in October 1982 at RAF Alconbury, UK to operate the TR-1 in Europe. The operating squadron was designated the 95th RS. The squadron survived the deactivation of the 17th RW in June 1991, remaining at Alconbury under the control of the 9th Wing at Beale. However, it was reduced in size, and eventually deactivated in September 1993, when Alconbury became a TDY location of the 9th Wing.

Wing commanders:	
Col George Freese	October 1982>
Col Tom Lesan	July 1983>
Col James Wrenn	August 1985>
Col Art Saboski	July 1987>
Col John Sander	June 1989>
Col Doug Cole	February 1991>

9th Reconnaissance Wing

The 9th SRW was redesignated as the 9th Wing in September 1991. After SAC was deactivated in June 1992, the wing joined Air Combat Command (ACC), and the "BB" tailcode was henceforth carried on all its aircraft. It was redesignated as the 9th Reconnaissance Wing in 1994.

Wing commanders:	
Col Richard Young	November 1991>
Col Larry Tieman	June 1993>
Bg Gen John Rutledge	July 1994>
Bg Gen Bob Behler	September 1995>
Bg Gen Charles Simpson	April 1997>
Bg Gen Kevin Chilton	June 1999>
Bg Gen Stan Gorenc	September 2000>
Bg Gen Thomas Wright	March 2003>
Col Larry Wells	August 2004>

Appendix D:
Aircraft Histories

Original production batch for CIA

341 was delivered to the test site on 24 July 1955 and was first flown 1 August 1955. Used for test and development flights at Groom Lake. Crashed on 4 April 1957 north of the Nevada Test Range, during Project Rainbow test flight, killing Lockheed test pilot Bob Sieker.

342/56-6675 was delivered 11 September 1955 to the CIA. Damaged in landing accident 21 March 1956 (pilot Carmine Vito). Repaired. In early 1959, was allocated for conversion as the prototype U-2C. First flew as U-2C on 13 May 1959. Remained as the U-2C test aircraft through the end of 1959. Landing accident in late 1959 (Ray Goudey). Repaired. Prototype for U-2F version in May 1961. Damaged on landing at Charbatia, India in May 1964 (pilot Bob Ericson). Flying again by September 1964. Crashed on 25 February 1966 during aerial refueling practice over Edwards AFB. Pilot Robert "Deke" Hall successfully ejected.

343/56-6676 was delivered 16 October 1955 to the CIA. Probably used in the pilot training program during 1956. Believed damaged in early 1957. Repaired, then did test/development work June-November 1957. Converted to U-2F in mid 1961. Loaned to USAF in October 1962 during the Cuban Missile Crisis. Shot down over Cuba on 27 October 1962 killing SAC's Major Rudolph Anderson.

344/56-6677 was delivered 20 November 1955 to the CIA. Engaged in test and development work through most of 1956. Repaired after landing accident 1 June 1956 (pilot Bill Strickland). Converted to U-2F by October 1961. Crashed 1 March 1962 near Edwards during aerial refueling training of SAC pilot Captain John Campbell, who was killed.

345/56-6678 was delivered 16 December 1955 to the CIA. Crashed at Groom Lake on 15 May 1956, killing CIA pilot Billy Rose.

346/56-6679 was delivered 13 January 1956 to the CIA. Crashed on 17 September 1956 during climb-out from Wiesbaden, Germany, killing pilot Howard Carey.

347/56-6680 was delivered 8 February 1956 to the CIA. Transferred to SAC in late 1957. Modified to 'ferret' aircraft and also converted to U-2E in mid-1962. First SAC U-2 to be painted black in fall 1964. Converted to U-2F in 1966. Flyable storage at D-M 1969. Returned to U-2C configuration for ALSS project, 1972. Stored at Palmdale in May 1980. Placed on display at the National Air and Space Museum in Washington, DC in 1985.

348/56-6681/N708NA was delivered 5 March 1956 to the CIA. Deployed with Det A in late April 1956. Returned to US by November 1957. Transferred to SAC but retained by Lockheed through January 1959 as part of the test/development effort. Returned to CIA in mid-1963 and converted to U-2G by January 1964. Flyable storage at Edwards North Base from 1969 until transferred to NASA in spring 1971. Based at Ames Research Center, NAS Moffett Field as N708NA from June 1971 till retired in August 1987. Displayed at Ames Research Center.

349/56-6682/N709NA was delivered 29 March 1956 to the CIA. Damaged in forced landing in Thailand April 1960. After repair, was transferred to USAF Air Research and Development Command at Edwards AFB. Returned to CIA in mid 1964, converted to U-2H by 6 October 1964. In flight refueling mod removed August 1965 and aircraft redesignated U-2G. Flyable storage at Edwards North Base from 1969 until transferred to NASA in spring 1971. Based at Ames Research Center, NAS Moffett Field as N709NA from June 1971 till retired in April 1989. Final flight to the Museum of Aviation at Robins Air Force Base, Georgia, that same month.

350/56-6683 was delivered 24 April 1956 to the CIA. Transferred to SAC in fall 1957. Involved in flight test activity May-November 1962. Returned to CIA and converted to U-2F by spring 1963. Loaned to SAC for Cuba overflight missions and crashed in the Gulf of Mexico 40 miles northwest of Key West on 20 November 1963. Captain Joe Hyde Jr killed.

351/56-6684 was delivered 18 May 1956 to the CIA. Project Rainbow flight tests early 1957, then deployed. Converted to U-2C by July 1959. Crashed at Taoyuan 19 March 1961, killing Major Yao-Hua Chih.

352/56-6685 was delivered 13 June 1956 to the CIA. Converted to U-2C by September 1959. With Lockheed and Det G for most of 1963 on test and systems development flying. Crashed on a training flight offshore Taiwan on 22 October 1965, killing Major Pete Wang.

353/56-6686 was delivered 6 July 1956 to the CIA. Was still a U-2A when it was destroyed in a landing accident at Edwards North Base on 14 September 1961. CIA pilot Buster Edens escaped serious injury.

354/56-6687 was delivered 27 July 1956 to the CIA. Crashed at Groom Lake 31 August 1956, killing pilot Frank Grace.

355/56-6688 was delivered 16 August 1956 to the CIA. Damaged on landing at Groom Lake 30 August 1956. Repaired. Converted to U-2C by September 1962 and deployed to Det H in November. Shot down on 1 November 1963. Major Robin Yeh survived.

356/56-6689 was delivered 5 September 1956 to the CIA. Transferred to SAC in November 1957. Damaged by typhoon at Guam late 1962, then transferred back to CIA and converted to U-2F by March 1963. Crashed in Taiwan Straits 23 March 1964, killing Major Sonny Liang.

357/56-6690 was delivered 21 September 1956 to the CIA. Crashed in Arizona on 19 December 1956. Pilot Bob Ericson successfully bailed out.

358/56-6691 was delivered 8 October 1956 to the CIA. At factory for test/development flight activity from September 1958 – August 1959. Converted to U-2C by July 1959. Shot down over China on 10 January 1965. Major Jack Chang survived.

359/56-6692 was delivered 22 October 1956 to the CIA. Transferred to SAC in December 1960. Returned to CIA in July 1962, converted to U-2F by November 1962. Loaned to SAC in later 1963 for Cuba missions. Used as test aircraft for U-2R configrations 1965-67. Transferred to USAF Systems Command at Edwards in July 1968. Heavily modified for Project TRIM 1972 – 1974. Returned to U-2C configuration for ALSS project, 1974. Returned to Lockheed in August 1975 and converted to U-2CT two place trainer, delivered January 1976. After final flight in December 1987, airlifted to RAF Alconbury February 1988 for use as battle damage repair training airframe. Restored to U-2C configuration and put on display at the Imperial War Museum, Duxford, England in 1992.

360/56-6693 was delivered 5 November 1956 to the CIA. Test and development work 1957 till May 1959. Converted to U-2C by 18 August 1959. Damaged in belly landing in Japan September 1959 (pilot Tom Crull unhurt). After factory repair, deployed to Det B and on 1 May 1960, was shot down near Sverdlovsk, USSR. Pilot Francis Gary Powers became a guest of the USSR.

These aircraft were built at Burbank under contract SP-1913. The Lockheed model number was L-185. The aircraft were originally identified only by their Lockheed production number eg the Article number. They were assigned USAF serial numbers (and the designation U-2A) in early 1956. However, the CIA never used serial numbers to identify its aircraft.

First USAF production batch

361/56-6694 was delivered in September 1956 to USAF at Groom Lake, out of sequence and ahead of the last three CIA aircraft. Moved to 4080th SRW Laughlin AFB in June 1957. Crashed on maintenance test flight 26 September 1957. Colonel Jack Nole bailed out successfully.

362/56-6695 was delivered in November 1956 to USAF at Groom Lake. Moved to 4080th SRW Laughlin AFB in June 1957. Transferred to CIA in mid-1963 and converted to U-2G by December. Shot down over southern China on 7 July 1964, killing Lt. Col. Terry Lee.

363/56-6696 was delivered in December 1956 to USAF at Groom Lake. Damaged in a landing accident in early 1956, it was repaired by July, and sent to 4080th SRW at Laughlin AFB. With SAC until 22 March 1966 when it crashed near Tucson. Captain Andy Fan (CAF) ejected successfully.

364/56-6697 was delivered in January 1957 to USAF at Groom Lake. Moved to 4080th SRW Laughlin AFB in June 1957. Crashed there on 6 August 1958, killing Lt Paul Haughland.

365/56-6698 was delivered in January 1957 to USAF at Groom Lake. Moved to 4080th SRW Laughlin AFB in June 1957. Crashed in New Mexico on 9 July 1958, killing Captain Al Chapin Jr.

366/56-6699 was delivered in February 1957 to USAF at Groom Lake. Moved to 4080th SRW Laughlin AFB in June 1957. Crashed days later on the 28th in New Mexico. Lt Leo Smith killed.

367/56-6700 was delivered in February 1957 at Groom Lake under the Air Force contract, but apparently transferred to the CIA by June 1957. Transferred to SAC in fall 1960. Converted to U-2C by October 1966. Flyable storage at D-M 1969. Configured for ALSS project, 1972. Crashed in Germany on 29 May 1975. Captain Robert Rendleman escaped unhurt.

368/56-6701 was delivered in March 1957 to USAF at Groom Lake. Used by Special Projects Branch of ARDC at Edwards until transferred to SAC in 1966. Converted to U-2C by November 1966. Flyable storage at D-M 1969. Configured for ALSS project, 1972. After last flight in late 1980, delivered to the SAC Museum at Offutt AFB, Nebraska. Now in the new SAC museum near Offutt.

369/56-6702 was delivered in March 1957 to USAF at Groom Lake. Moved to 4080th SRW Laughlin AFB in June 1957. Crashed on 28th of that month at Del Rio, killing Lt. Ford Lowcock.

370/56-6703 was delivered in April 1957 to USAF at Groom Lake. Moved to 4080th SRW Laughlin AFB in June 1957. Modified as 'ferret' aircraft by mid-1959. Converted to U-2E in August 1962. Destroyed in landing accident at Davis-Monthan AFB on 18 September 1964 which killed Major Robert Primrose.

371/56-6704 was delivered to USAF in April 1957. Moved to 4080th SRW Laughlin AFB in June 1957. Crashed near there on 28 November 1957. Captain Benny Lacombe killed.

372/56-6705 was delivered in April 1957 to USAF at Groom Lake. Moved to 4080th SRW Laughlin AFB in June 1957. Was the prototype "hardnose" fallout sampling aircraft. Transferred to CIA in October 1964; converted to U-2F by May 1965 and assigned to Det G. Deployed to Det H November 1965. Crashed at Taichung, Taiwan on 17 February 1966, killing Captain Charlie Wu.

373/56-6706 was delivered in May 1957 to USAF. Assigned to 4080th SRW Laughlin AFB. Transferred to CIA in August 1966 and converted to U-2C by November. Shot down over China on 9 September 1967, killing Captain Tom Hwang.

374/56-6707 was delivered in May 1957 to USAF. Assigned to 4080th SRW Laughlin AFB. Modified as ferret aircraft by mid-1959. Converted to U-2E in mid 1962. Converted to U-2F by November 1966. Flyable storage at D-M 1969. Converted back to U-2C and configured for ALSS project, 1972. Stored at Palmdale in 1980. Moved to Laughlin AFB, Texas for display at main gate.

375/56-6708 was delivered in June 1957 to USAF. Assigned to 4080th SRW Laughlin AFB. Converted to U-2C in March 1966. Destroyed in crash near Barksdale AFB, Louisiana 1 July 1967. Captain Sam Swart successfully ejected.

376/56-6709 was delivered in June 1957 to USAF. Retained at factory through November 1957 for development of SAC 'ferret' (SIGINT) configuration. Crashed in Mississippi on 2 January 1962. Captain Chuck Stratton survived.

377/56-6710 was delivered in June 1957 to USAF. Assigned to ARDC Special Projects Branch at Edwards AFB. Modified to two-place configuration. Crashed at Edwards on 11 September 1958, killling Captain Pat Hunerwadel.

378/56-6711 was delivered in July 1957 to the CIA, although built under the Air Force contract. Test and development aircraft. Converted to U-2C by February 1962. Shot down over China on 9 September 1962 killing Lt Col Chen-Huai Sheng.

379/56-6712 was delivered in July 1957 to USAF. Assigned to 4080th SRW Laughlin AFB. Crashed on 18 December 1964 near Tucson after CAF Captain Steve Sheng bailed out.

380/56-6713 was delivered in July 1957 to USAF. Assigned to 4080th SRW Laughlin AFB, and configured as a 'ferret' aircraft. Crashed in Texas on 8 July 1958, killing RAF Sqn Ldr Christopher Walker.

381/56-6714 was delivered in August 1957 to USAF. Assigned to 4080th SRW Laughlin AFB as a 'hard-nose' sampling aircraft. Transferred to CIA and converted to U-2G in mid 1965. Transferred to SAC. Flyable storage at D-M 1969. Returned to U-2C configuration for ALSS project, 1972. Damaged on landing at D-M 2 May 1974. Repaired. Written off after crash of 31 January 1980 (Captain Edward Beaumont survived). Put on display at 9th SRW headquarters at Beale AFB.

382/56-6715 was delivered in August 1957 to USAF. Assigned to 4080th SRW Laughlin AFB as a 'hard-nose' sampling aircraft. Transferred to CIA in mid 1964 and converted to U-2G by February 1965. Det G pilot "Buster" Edens was killed at Edwards North Base in the 26 April 1965 crash.

383/56-6716 was delivered in September 1957 to USAF. Assigned to 4080th SRW Laughlin AFB as a 'hard-nose' sampling aircraft. Transferred to CIA in June 1965 and converted to U-2C by August. Relegated to test/training flights only in 1969. Transferred to SAC in 1971 and returned to U-2C configuration for ALSS project, 1972. Stored at Palmdale May 1980. Moved to Davis-Monthan AFB, Tucson, for display at main gate.

384/56-6717 was delivered in September 1957 to USAF. Assigned to 4080th SRW Laughlin AFB as a 'hard-nose' sampling aircraft. Transferred to CIA in June 1964 and converted to U-2C by June 1965. Crasked off Taiwan on 21 June 1966, killing Major Mickey Yu.

385/56-6718 was delivered in September 1957 to USAF. Assigned to 4080th SRW Laughlin AFB as a 'hard-nose' sampling aircraft. Transferred to CIA in August 1964 and converted to U-2G by February 1965. Crashed into Yellow Sea on 5 January 1969, killing Major Billy Chang.

386/56-6719 was delivered in October 1957 to USAF. Assigned to 4080th SRW Laughlin AFB as a 'ferret' aircraft. Crashed in Bolivia 28 July 1966, Captain Robert Hickman killed.

387/56-6720 was delivered in October 1957 to USAF. Assigned to 4080th SRW Laughlin AFB as a 'ferret' aircraft. Crashed 14 July 1960 in Texas, Major Raleigh Myers ejected safely.

388/56-6721 was delivered in October 1957 to USAF. Assigned to 4080th SRW at Laughlin AFB. Forced landing at Cortez, Colorado on 5 August 1959. Aircraft repaired, transferred to ARDC, and modified to two-place configuration. Delivered to Edwards AFB by early 1960. Later designated U-2D. Never received J-75 engine. Still based at Edwards in 1976. Retired in 1978 and moved to March AFB museum. Transferred to AFFTC Museum and moved to Palmdale. First at Lockheed gate, then after restoration at the Blackbird Air park.

389/56-6722 was delivered in November 1957 to USAF. Assigned to ARDC as first aircraft to carry IR-sensor. Remained a single-seat and J57-powered U-2A, throughout long test career at Edwards. Retired in 1978 and moved to USAF Museum, Wright-Patterson AFB, Ohio.

390/56-6690 was delivered in December 1957 to USAF. Assigned to 4080the SRW. Converted to U-2C by April 1966. Crashed in South Vietnam on 8 October 1966. Major Leo Stewart ejected successfully.

These aircraft were built at Oildale under contract SP-1914. This contract originally comprised 29 aircraft. A 30th aircraft was added later, and may have been constructed using parts from crashed aircraft. For some unknown reason, the USAF serial number 56-6690 was re-assigned to this last aircraft, having previously been allocated to Article 357, a CIA aircraft which crashed in December 1957.

Supplementary USAF production

391/56-6951 was delivered by December 1958 to USAF. Assigned to the 4080th SRW at Laughlin AFB. Crashed at D-M on 17 October 1966 in a non-fatal accident (pilot Captain Leslie White).

392/56-6952 was delivered in January 1958. Assigned to the 4080th SRW at Laughlin AFB. Converted to U-2C by November 1966. Relegated to training flights at D-M 1969. Destroyed there on 18 November 1971 in landing accident which killed Captain John Cunney.

393/56-6953 was delivered in February 1959 to USAF. Assigned to the 4080th SW at Laughlin AFB. Converted to U-2C by October 1966. Flyable storage at D-M 1969. Assigned as training aircraft August 1971. Badly damaged in landing accident at D-M May 1972 (Captain Usto Schultz unhurt). Rebuilt as first U-2CT trainer. First flight 13 February 1973. Retired in 1987 and originally assigned to AFFTC Museum at Edwards. Reassigned to Cold War Museum at Bodo, Norway in 1994. Moved to there, and restored to U-2C configuration for display.

394/56-6954 was delivered in March 1959 to USAF. Built as a two-place aircraft for ARDC at Edwards AFB. Later redesignated U-2D. Transferred to SAC in 1966 and converted to U-2C by January 1967. Crashed near Tucson on 31 May 1968. Major Vic Milam ejected successfully.

395/56-6955 was delivered to USAF in March 1959. Assigned to the 4080th SRW. Crashed near Bosie, Idaho, on 14 August 1964. CAF Captain Steve Sheng ejected safely.

Although these aircraft were not ordered until 1958, they were assigned Fiscal 1956 serial numbers

Original U-2R Production

051/68-10329 First flight 28 August 1967 as N803X, unpainted. Subsequently reworked to production standard and delivered to CIA March 1969. Re-allocated to flight test by 1974. To 9th SRW by 1981. Converted to U-2S and redelivered May 1995.

052/68-10330 First flight 29 December 1967 as N809X. Delivered to 100th SRW 25 July 1968. Testbed for Senior Lance and US Navy EP-X trials. To 9th SRW 1976. Crashed at at Akrotiri on 7 December 1977 (Capt Robert Henderson killed).

053/68-10331 First flight 17 February 1968 as N800X. Delivered to CIA 22 November 1968. To 100th SRW mid-1974. To 9th SRW 1976. Converted to U-2S and redelivered August 1996.

054/68-10332 First flight 29 March 1968 as N810X. Delivered to CIA. To 100th SRW mid-1975. To 9th SRW 1976. Crashed off Korean coast on 15 January 1992 (Capt Marty McGregor killed).

055/68-10333 First flight 8 May 1968 as N812X. Delivered to CIA 28 May 1968. To 100th SRW mid-1974. To 9th SRW 1976. Damaged at Akrotiri on 24 April 1980. Repaired. Crashed at Osan on 22 May 1984 (Capt David Bonsi survived).

056/68-10334 First flight 18 May 1968. (N814X allocated). Delivered to 100th SRW 10 June 1968. Crashed in Gulf of Thailand on 15 August 1975 (Capt Jon Little survived).

057/68-10335 First flight 30 July 1968 as N815X. Delivered to CIA 29 August 1968. Crashed at Taoyuan on 24 November 1970 (Maj Denny Huang killed).

058/68-10336 First flight 20 August 1968. (N816X allocated). Delivered to 100th SRW 29 August 1968. To 9th SRW 1976. Returned to Det 8/Flight Test at Palmdale for ASARS trials. Remained there for test and development work. Converted to U-2S and remained with Combined Test Force at Palmdale (Det 2, WR-ALC).

059/68-10337 First flight on 9 September 1968. (N817X allocated). Delivered to 100th SRW 21 September 1968. Damaged at U-Tapao on 16 May 1975. Repaired. To 9th SRW 1976. Damaged at Patrick on 24 May 1988. Repaired. Converted to U-2S and redelivered June 1998.

060/68-10338
First flight on 2 October 1968. (N818X allocated). Delivered to 100th SRW 17 October 1968. To 9th SRW 1976. First aircraft to reach 20,000 hours, in August 1994. Crashed at Fairford on 29 August 1995.

061/68-10339
First flight 22 October 1968. (N819X allocated). Delivered to USAF 22 October 1968 but retained for trials. Delivered to 100th SRW by early 1972. To 9th SRW 1976. Crashed at Beale on 13 December 1993 (Capt Rich Snyder killed).

062/68-10340
First flight 26 November 1968. (N820X allocated). Delivered to 100th SRW 19 December 1968. To 9th SRW 1976. Crashed in Korea on 5 October 1980 (Capt Cleve Wallace survived).

New production 1981-89

063/80-1063/N706NA First of new-batch aircraft to fly, 1 May 1981. Delivered as ER-2 to NASA Ames Research Center June 1981. Re-engined with F118 but retained ER-2 designation, redelivered October 1996. Re-registered N806NA upon move from Ames to Dryden (Edwards) in 1998.

064/80-1064 Delivered as TR-1B to 9th SRW March 1983. Converted to TU-2S and redelivered on 28 October 1994.

065/80-1065 Delivered as TR-1B to 9th SRW May 1983. Converted to TU-2S and redelivered August 1995.

066/80-1066 Second new-batch aircraft to fly, 1 August 1981. Delivered as TR-1A to 9th SRW September 1981. Converted to U-2S and redelivered November 1997.

067/80-1067 Delivered as TR-1A to 9th SRW July 1982. Returned to flight test at Palmdale in 1989. Remained there for test and development work. Converted to U-2S and remained with Combined Test Force at Palmdale (Det 2, WR-ALC).

068/80-1068 Delivered as TR-1A to 9th SRW July 1982. First aircraft to 17th RW February 1983. To 9th SRW April 1987. Converted to U-2S and redelivered July 1998. Converted to U-2ST trainer in 2004.

069/80-1069/N708NA Delivered as TR-1A to 9th SRW July 1982. To 17th RW July 1983. Damaged by vehicle collision at Alconbury October 1983. Repaired. Converted to ER-2 and loaned to NASA, March 1987. Returned to 9th RW 1995. Converted to U-2S and redelivered September 1997.

070/80-1070 Delivered as TR-1A to 9th SRW October 1982. To 17th RW February 1983. To 9th SRW May 1988. Converted to U-2S and redelivered February 1995.

071/80-1071 Delivered as U-2R to 9th SRW November 1983. Returned to flight test as first Senior Span aircraft 1985. Returned to 9th SRW by late 1988. First U-2S production conversion, redelivered on 28 October 1994. Damaged at Beale February 1996. Repaired

072/80-1072 Delivered as TR-1A to 17th RW November 1993. To 9th SRW March 1984. Crashed at Beale on 18 July 1984 (Capt Tom Hubbard survived).

073/80-1073 Delivered as TR-1A to 9th SRW February 1984. To 17th RW January 1991. To 9th RW September 1992. Converted to U-2S and redelivered in February 1996.

074/80-1074 Delivered as TR-1A to 9th SRW February 1984. PLSS configuration 1984-85. To 17th RW December 1990. To 9th SRW October 1992. Converted to U-2S and redelivered May 1996.

075/80-1075 Delivered as U-2R to 9th RW 1984. Crashed in Korea on 8 October 1984 (Capt Tom Dettmer survived).

076/80-1076 Delivered as U-2R to 9th SRW 1984/5. Converted to U-2S and redelivered August 1997. Damaged at Osan 30 March 1999. Repaired.

077/80-1077 Delivered as TR-1A to 17th RW March 1985. To 9th SRW November 1989. Converted to U-2S and redelivered June 1996.

078/80-1078 Delivered as TR-1A to 17th RW March 1985. Damaged at Alconbury 24 April 1990 and returned to Lockheed for storage. Re-engined, converted to TU-2S trainer and delivered 28 October 1994.

079/80-1079 Delivered as TR-1A to 17th RW March 1985. To 9th SRW January 1991. Converted to U-2S and redelivered May 1997.

080/80-1080 Delivered as TR-1A to 9th RW May 1985. Damaged at Beale 25 May 1988. Repaired. Converted to U-2S and redelivered in March 1997.

081/80-1081 Delivered as TR-1A to 17th RW October 1985. To 9th SRW August 1991. Converted to U-2S and redelivered October 1996.

082/80-1082 Delivered as TR-1A to 9th SRW November 1985. Converted to U-2S and redelivered January 1997.

083/80-1083 Delivered as TR-1A to 17th RW March 1986. To 9th SRW December 1991. Converted to U-2S and redelivered September 1996.

084/80-1084 Delivered as TR-1A to 17th RW April 1986. Damaged by vehicle collision at Alconbury December 1987. Repaired. To 9th SRW 1988/9. Converted to U-2S and redelivered March 1998.

085/80-1085 Delivered as TR-1A to 17th RW August 1986. To 9th SRW February 1991. Converted to U-2S and redelivered June 1997.

086/80-1086 Delivered as TR-1A to 9th SRW 1986/7. To 17th RW April 1987. To 9th SRW August 1991. Converted to U-2S and redelivered December 1997.

087/80-1087 Delivered as TR-1A to 9th SRW by May 1987. Converted to U-2S and redelivered February 1998.

088/80-1088 Delivered as TR-1A to 17th RW December 1987. To 9th SRW August 1991. Crashed near Beale 7 August 1996 (Capt Randy Roby killed).

089/80-1089 Delivered as U-2R to 9th SRW 1988. Converted to U-2S and redelivered December 1995.

090/80-1090 Built as TR-1A 1988 and retained by flight test at Palmdale. Prototype U-2S re-engined aircraft, first flight 23 May 1989. Delivered to 9th RW.

091/80-1091 Delivered as TU-2R to 9th SRW March 1988. Converted to TU-2S and redelivered December 1998.

092/80-1092 Delivered as TR-1A to 17th RW April 1988. To 9th SRW December 1991. Converted to U-2S and redelivered September 1998.

093/80-1093 Delivered as TR-1A to 17th RW June 1988. To 9th RW April 1992. Converted to U-2S and redelivered June 1995.

094/80-1094 Delivered as TR-1B to 17th RW September 1988. To 9th RW December 1991. Converted to U-2S and redelivered June 1995.

095/80-1095 Delivered as U-2R to 9th SRW 1988. Converted to U-2S and redelivered January 1996. Crashed in Korea 26 January 2003.

096/80-1096 Delivered as U-2R to 9th SRW by April 1989. Converted to U-2S and redelivered in April 1996.

097/80-1097/N709NA Delivered as ER-2 to NASA Ames Research Center in 1989. Re-engined with F118 but retained ER-2 designation, redelivered March 1997. Re-registered N806NA upon move from Ames to Dryden (Edwards) in 1998.

098/80-1098 Delivered as U-2R to 9th SRW 1989. Crashed on landing at Osan in August 1994 (Capt Chuck Espinoza survived).

099/80-1099 Delivered as TR-1A to 9th SRW in final delivery ceremony 3 October 1989. To 17th RW March 1990. To 9th Wg December 1991. Converted to U-2S and redelivered August 1995.

In the mid-1970s, some USAF aircraft were repainted with false serials such as 10342 and 10345. These came from a batch of serials (68-10341 through 10353) which had been allocated for additional U-2R production, which never materialized.

The remaining TR-1 aircraft were redesignated U-2R in October 1991.

Appendix E:
Pilots

* "Be it known to all men, that those whose names appear thus have made the supreme sacrifice for the mission and the welfare of mankind"
(those listed in *italics* did not complete training, or did not qualify to fly operationally)

Lockheed

1955
Tony Levier
Bob Matye
Ray Goudey
Bob Sieker *
Bob Schumacher

After this original cadre, the following Lockheed test and engineering test pilots are also known to have flown the Article: 1957 *Ted Limmer*, 196x *Bill Park*, 1962 *Frank Powers*, 1967 *Art Petersen*, 1972 *Darryl Greenamyer, Ken Weir*, 1976 *Dave Bittenbinder*, 1978 *Robert Reidenauer*; 1983 *Dave Kerzie, Skip Holm*; 1993: *Rob Rowe,* 1997 *Eric Hansen*

Project Oilstone

1955
Maj	*Louis Garvin*
Capt	*Hank Meirdierck*
Maj	*Bob Mullin*
Lt. Col	*Phil Robertson*
Capt	*Lou Setter*
Col	*Bill Yancey*

Project Aquatone

1956	
Jim Allison	Frank Powers
Glen Dunaway	*Billy Rose**
Jacob Kratt	Sam Snyder
Marty Knutson	Barry Baker
Carl Overstreet	Jim Barnes
Hervey Stockman	Jim Cherbonneaux
Carmine Vito	Tom Crull
Tom Birkhead	Bob Ericson
Howard Carey *	*Frank Grace**
Buster Edens *	*Russ Kemp*
Bill Hall	Al Rand
E.K. Jones	Lyal Rudd
Bill McMurry	Al Smiley
	John Shinn
	Frank Strickland

Among those Air Force personnel seconded to Project Aquatone, the following are known to have flown the Article: 1956 *Col Stan Beerli, Lt Col Chet Bohart, Capt Harry Cordes, Col Ed Perry, Lt Col Cy Perkins,* 1957: *Col Marion Mixson*

Project Chalice

1958	1959	
Flt Lt John MacArthur (RAF)	*Flt Lt*	*Bunny Austin (RAF)*
Flt Lt David Dowling (RAF)	*Flt Lt*	*Brian Cox (RAF)*
Flt Lt Michael Bradley (RAF)		
Sqn Ldr ChrisWalker (RAF)*		
Sqn Ldr Robbie Robinson (RAF)		

Project Low Card ("Smokey Joe")

1957	1960-63
Capt Loren Davis	Capt Weldon Armstrong
Capt Norris Hanks	Maj Fred Cuthill
Capt Pat Hunerwadel*	Capt Norvin Evans
Maj Donald Sorlie	Lt Bill Frazier (observer)
	Capt Henry Gordon
1958	Maj James King
Capt Robert Jacobson	Maj John Ludwig
Lt Ray Oglukian (observer)	Capt Bobby Lynn (observer)
Maj Phil Smith	Capt Lachlan Macleay
	Lt Charles Manske (observer)
1959	Lt Charles Nyquist (observer)
Maj Harry Andonian	Capt Charles Rosburg
Capt James Eastlund (observer)	Capt Wendell Shawler
Capt Don Evans	Capt Robert Titus
Capt Merv Evenson	Capt Ken Weir, USMC
Capt Budd Knapp	Capt James Williams (observer)
Capt Rial Lowell	

Amongst those test pilots who flew the U-2 for the Special Projects Branch at Edwards after 1964 are: 1966 Maj Tom Smith, 1967 Maj Joe Basquez, Maj Ken Mason, Capt Roy Palmer, 1969 Capt Ralph Cunningham. Also in the 1960s: Theodore Angle, Wayne Frye, Richard Lawyer, George Lyddane, George Meyers, plus observer Bill Sung. And in the 1970s: Michael Clarke, Richard Cooper, Dave Ferguson, Mel Hayashi, Walter Hersman, Thomas Higgins, Skip Holm, James Manley, David Peterson, Robert Riedenauer, Joseph Spiers, B.C. Thomas, Jim Thomas, Robert Zang.

Project Dragon Lady

1956		1957	
Col	Jack Nole	Capt	Dick Atkins
Maj	Joe Jackson	Capt	Warren Boyd
Maj	Floyd Herbert	Maj	Ray Haupt
Maj	Hank Nevett	Capt	Joe King
Maj	Howard Cody	Capt	Steve Heyser
		1/Lt	Mike Styer
		Capt	Dick Leavitt
		Capt	Benny Lacombe*
		Capt	Skip Alison

1/Lt	Tony Bevacqua	Capt	Robert "Deke" Hall	Capt	Keith Spaulding		1968
1/Lt	Jack Graves	Lt. Col	Ken McCaslin	Capt	Earle Smith	Maj	Johnny Shen Chung Li
Capt	Ed Emerling	Capt	Jack Carr	Capt	Les Powell	Maj	Tom Wang Tao
Capt	Richard McGraw	Maj	J.B. Reed	Capt	John Amundson		
Capt	John Campbell*	Maj	Raleigh Myers	Capt	Ed Rose		1970
1/Lt	Ken Alderman			Capt	Don Wright	Lt Col	Simon Chien Chu
1/Lt	*Leo Smith**		1960				
1/Lt	*Ford Lowcock**	Capt	Bob Wilke		1966		1971
Capt	Linus "Buck" Lee	Capt	Bob Spencer	Capt	Bob Birkett	Lt Col	Mike Chiu Sung Chou
1/Lt	*Alfred Chapin* *	Capt	Don Crowe	Capt	Bob Hickman *	Maj	*Chai Shen Sheng*
1/Lt	Jim Sala	Capt	Rex Knaak	Capt	Harold Swanson		
Capt	Scott Smith	Maj	Tony Martinez	Capt	Jim Hoover		1972
Capt	Jim Qualls	Maj	Hank McManus	Capt	Lonnie Liss	Lt Col	Joe Wei Chen
Capt	Roger Cooper	*Lt. Col*	*Dave Gammons*	Capt	Jim Whitehead		1973
Capt	Pat Halloran	*Col*	*William Wilcox*	Capt	Dave Patton	Lt Col	Chris I Chi Chang
1/Lt	Frank Stuart	Capt	Leo Stewart	Capt	Sam Swart	Maj	"Mory" Tsai Sheng
Capt	Jim Black	Capt	Robert "Pinky"	Capt	Don Aitro		Hsiung
Capt	Ed Perdue		Primrose*	Capt	Les White		
Capt	Roger Herman	Capt	Ed Hill	Capt	Richard Woodhull		**Project Idealist**
Capt	Bobbie Gardiner	Capt	Joe Hyde*				1961
Capt	Marv Doering	Capt	Dave Ray		**Project Tackle**	Sqn Ldr	Charles Taylor, RAF
Col	*Nat Adams*	Capt	Cliff Beeler		1959	Sqn Ldr	Ivor "Chunky" Webster,
Maj	Hayden "Buzz" Curry			Maj	Chen Huai*		RAF
Maj	Forrest Wilson		1961	Maj	Chih Yao Hua		
1/Lt	Roy St Martin	Capt	Chuck Maultsby	*Maj*	*Hsu Chung Kuei*		1964
Capt	James "Snake" Bedford	Capt	Chuck Kern	Maj	Mike Hua Hsi Chun		Robert "Deke" Hall
Capt	Rudy Anderson	Capt	Willie Lawson III	Maj	"Tiger" Wang Tai Yu		Dan Schmarr
Capt	John McElveen	Capt	George Bull	Lt Col	"Gimo" Yang Shih Chu	Sqn Ldr	Martin Bee, RAF
Capt	Ed Dixon	Capt	Don Webster			Sqn Ldr	Basil Dodd, RAF
1/Lt	Bob Pine	Capt	Eddie Dunagan		1963	LCDR	Tom McMurtry, USN
Capt	Earl Lewis	*Col*	*John A. DesPortes*	Lt Col	Terry Lee Nan Ping*		
Capt	Wes McFadden	Capt	Dan Schmarr	Maj	Robin Yeh Chang Ti		1968
Capt	Cozy Kline	Capt	John Wall	Maj	"Sonny" Liang Teh Pei*	Sqn Ldr	Dick Cloke, RAF
		Capt	Dick Bouchard	Lt Col	Johnny Wang Shi Chuen	Flt Lt	Harry Drew, RAF
	1958						Ben Higgins
Capt	Don James		1962		1964		Dan Wright
B/Gen	*Austin Russell*	Maj	Art Leatherwood	Maj	Jack Chang Li Yi		
Maj	Adrian Acebedo	Capt	Jim Rogers	*Maj*	*Yang Hui Chia*		1970
Capt	Bill Rodenbach	Capt	Don McClain	*Capt*	*Steve Sheng Shi Hi*		Dave Young
Capt	Bob Wood	Capt	Clair McCombs	Maj	Pete Wang Chen Wen*		
1/Lt	Bob Ginther	Capt	Ed Smart	Capt	Charlie Wu Tse Shi*		1971
1/Lt	*Paul Haughland**					Sqn Ldr	Ian McBride, RAF
Maj	Ken Van Zandt		1963		1965		Tom Lesan
Maj	Horace "Bo" Reeves	Capt	Vic Milam	Capt	"Spike" Chuang Jen		Jerry Shilt
Capt	Dick Callahan	Capt	Ward Graham		Liang		
Capt	Buddy Brown	*Col*	*Julius Baughn*	Lt Col	Terry Liu Jai Chuang		1972
Maj	John Boynton	Capt	Ron Stromberg	Maj	Mickey Yu Ching Chang*	Sqn Ldr	Ron Shimmons, RAF
Col	*Andrew Bratton Jr.*	Capt	Ken Somers				
		Capt	Gene O"Sullivan		1966		1973
	1959			Maj	Billy Chang Hseih*		Dan Nesbitt
Capt	Ron Hendrick		1964	Capt	Andy Fan Huang Ti		Gerry West
Maj	Harold Melbratten	Capt	Theodore Baader	*Capt*	*Yang Erh Ping*		
Capt	Gerry McIlmoyle	Capt	Jack Fenimore	Maj	Eddy Chu Yen Chun		**Senior Year Program**
Capt	Bill Stickman			Maj	Tom Huang Lung Pei*		1967
Maj	Dick Rauch		1965			Capt	Jerry Chipman
Capt	Floyd Kifer	*Col*	*Ken Diehl*		1967	Capt	Carl "Lash" LaRue
Col	*T.J. Jackson*	Capt	Jerry Davis	Maj	Denny Hwang	Capt	Frank Ott
Capt	Chuck Stratton	Capt	George Worley		Chi Shien*	Capt	Roy Burcham
Capt	Bob Schueler	Capt	Arnie Strasheim	Maj	David Lee Pao Wei	*Col*	*Dale Kellam*
Capt	Bob Powell	Capt	Bill Copeman				

1968
Capt Frederick Banks
Capt George "Hector" Freeze
Capt Jim Phielix
Capt Curt Behrend
Capt Doyle Krumrey
Capt Ron Williams
Capt Ken Chisholm
Capt Ray Samay
Capt Jerry Wagnon
Capt Stan Lawrence

1969
Capt Thomas Block
Capt Willie Horton

1970
Capt Dick Davies
Capt Jim Terry
Capt Jim Wrenn

1971
Capt Phil Daisher
Capt Sid Head
Capt Jerry Sinclair
Capt John Cunney*

1972
Capt Frank "Fuzzy" Furr
Capt Don Schreiber
Capt Usto Schulz
Capt Terry Nelson
Capt Dan Riggs
Capt Ronnie Rinehart

1973
Capt Richard Rice
Capt Art Saboski
Capt Robert Armstrong
Capt Charles Smyth
Maj Rich Drake
Maj Jerry Hoyt
Capt Robert Henderson*
Capt John Kent
Capt Dale Hudler
Capt Howard Bayne
Capt Jim Pinson
Capt John Sander
Capt Ken Stanford
Capt Chuck Crabb
Capt Tom Doubek
Lt Col John A. Dale
Capt Denny Gagen

1974
Capt Jack Stebe
Capt Don Hahn
Capt John Cantwell
Capt Augustine "Hoho" Hoenninger

Capt Dick Whitaker
Capt Denny Thisius
Capt Mike Lemmons
Capt James Martin
Capt Glenn Perry
Capt Terry Rendleman
Capt Warren "Snake" Pierce
Capt Donald "Muff" Heckhert
Capt Dave Dickerson

1975
Capt Stanley Rauch
Capt Jim Barrilleaux
Capt Bob Gaskin
Capt James Wilson
Capt Bill Kopplin
Capt Jim Madsen
Capt Jon Little
Capt Michael Phillips
Capt James Evans
Capt Don Hatten
Capt Richard Boyer
Capt Dick Keylor
Capt Thom Evans
Capt Dave Kantrud
Capt Ron Friesz
Capt Jimmy Myer
Capt Kit Busching
Capt John Swanson
Capt Anthony McGarvey

1976
Capt James Winans
Capt Larry Driskill
Capt Ken Bassett
Capt Chuck Voxland
Col Mike Kidder
Capt Dave Bateman

1977
Capt Mike Kelly
Capt Richard Fossum
Capt Fred Kishler
Col John Storrie
Capt Wally Drage
Capt Dave Bittenbinder

1978
Capt Jimmy Carter
Capt Raymond Wilson
Capt Bob McCrary
Capt Billy Ely
Capt Mark Fischer
Capt Warren "Bill" Williams
Capt Bob Munger
Capt Paul Roberts
Capt Mick Uramkin
Capt Doug Morin
Capt Bill Collette

1979
Capt Dale Smith
Capt Mike Musholt
Capt Rick Bishop
Capt Cecil Snyder
Capt Charles "Butch" Hinkle
Capt Rich Snow
Capt Bob Johnson
Capt Bill Burk
Capt Steve Brown
Capt Don Feld
Capt Mike Dannielle
Capt Dave Ebersole
Capt Pete Balzli
Capt Lionel "Stormy" Boudreaux
Capt Dave Bechtol
Capt Kirt Lindeman
Capt Jimmie McLean
Capt Bob Ray
Capt Tim Lyle

1980
Capt Paul Cross
Capt Jan Nystrom
Capt Edward Beaumont
Capt Mark Spencer
Capt Larry Faber
Capt Steve Barber
Capt James Nicol
Capt Cleve Wallace
Capt John Petersen
Capt Grant Gordon
Capt Bruce Cucuel

1981
Capt Bill Earnest
Capt Dee Porter
Capt Lou Campbell
Capt Ken Broda
Capt Dan House
Capt Bill Kemmer
Capt Ken Womack
Capt Ron Blatt
Capt Jim Kippert
Capt Glen Johnson
Capt Bobby Fairless

1982
Capt Rob Bateson
Capt Marty Decker
Capt Bill Gilbert
Capt James "Bubba" Lloyd
Capt Bruce Carmichael
Capt Sam Ryals
Capt James O"Neal
Capt Ash Lafferty
Capt Bruce Jinneman
Capt Joe Crawley

Capt Steve Randle
Capt Robert Heath
Capt Dan David
Capt Tim Cox
Capt Marty Guthierrez

1983
Capt Jimmy Milligan
Capt Dave Hensley
Capt Dan Kelly
Capt Mark Benda
Capt William Walker
Capt Alan Kopf
Capt Howard Johnson
Capt Dave Bonsi
Capt Joe Mudd
Capt James Sonnhalter
Capt Alan Popwell
Capt Dewayne Rudd
Capt Ken Sasine

1984
Col Dave Pinsky
Capt Tom Dettmer
Capt Joe Fusco
Capt Todd Hubbard
Capt Steve Benningfield
Capt Clifford Napolitano
Capt Bob Uebelacker
Capt James Perkins
Capt James "Bob" Roberts
Capt Don Merritt
Capt Robert Johnson
Capt Pete Lemaire
Capt Bob Dunn
Capt Jim Burger
Capt John Zermer
Capt Al Crawford

1985
Capt David Floyd
Capt Ralph Balzli
Capt Craig Gardner
Capt Steve Peterson
Capt Mark Mitchell
Capt Bob Gaylord
Capt Joe Marquardt
Capt Bill Carrington
Capt Stephen Nicholes
Capt Joe Muus
Capt Jonathan George
Capt David Weaver
Capt Michael Phillips
Capt Terry Gruber

1986
Capt Ed Walby
Capt Kenneth Schopper
Capt Eddie Dejarnette

Capt	Bradley Jones	Capt	Chris McDonald	**1992**		Capt	Mark Tirrell
Capt	Dave Vrabel			Capt	Paul Nelson	Capt	Bruce Ellis
Capt	Robert Rowe	**1989**		Capt	Dewie Shook	Capt	Lars Hoffman
Capt	Paul Castle	Capt	John Bauer	*Col*	*Richard Young*	Capt	Fred Berg
Col	*James Savarda*	Maj	Mike McWilliams	Capt	Chris Wheatley	Capt	Cory Bartholomew
Capt	Scott Mefford	Capt	Mario Buda	Capt	Dave McCabe	Capt	David Hawkens*
Capt	Ernest Ward	Capt	John Roush	*Capt*	*Andy Jones*	Capt	Jeff Fletcher
Capt	Henry Sahut	Capt	Chuck Braymer	Capt	Timothy Cordner	Capt	Dave Prewitt
Capt	Leslie Vanheeswyk	*Capt*	*Stan Clayton*	Capt	Kevin Vaille	Maj	Frank Gebert
Capt	Domenic Eanniello	Capt	Craig Scott	Capt	Greg Nelson	Maj	Ran Shelley
Capt	Pete Szyjka	Capt	Greg Lamb	Capt	Jeff Stout	Capt	Craig Nowicki
Capt	Jack McGirr	Capt	Kyle Lampela	Capt	Cholene "Chuck"	Capt	Erik Eliel
Capt	John Bowen	Capt	Scott Koehler	Espinoza			
Capt	Larry Jones	Capt	Gregg Dotter	Capt	Don Ellis	**1995**	
Capt	George Marshall	Capt	Dan Sanders	Capt	Mark Brandt	Capt	Beth Martin (Larson)
Capt	Heinz Weissenbuehler	Capt	Joe Thomas	Capt	Greg Kern	Capt	Jeremy Parisi
Capt	Jason Barlow	Capt	Dave Markl	Capt	J.T. Taylor	Col	James Shambo
Capt	Mike Rampey	Capt	Jeff Gruver	Capt	Rob "Crash" Creedon	Capt	Lance Barker
Capt	James Crossley	Capt	Tim Feldman	Maj	Dana Purifoy	Capt	Brian Peck
		Capt	Jon Huggins	Capt	Mark Cole	Capt	Jamie Toombs
1987				Capt	Jerome Mestman	Capt	Willam Been
Capt	Gary Edelblute	**1990**		Capt	Lee Brumley	Maj	Jonathan Holmes
Capt	Buddy Leach	Capt	Steve Feldman	Capt	Bart Langland	Capt	Michael Mack
Capt	Terry Barrett	Capt	Dave Miller	*Col*	*Bob Behler*	Capt	William Gremp
Capt	Chuck Wilson	Capt	Carl Trout	Capt	Al Williams	Capt	Pete Lewis
Capt	John Smith	*Lt Col*	*Doug Cole*	Capt	Jeff Jungemann	Capt	Forrest Green
Maj	Ken Tupper	Capt	Richard "Scoop" Jackson			Capt	John Mitchell
Capt	Fred Doug Dillard	Capt	Mark Lilley	**1993**		Capt	John Bordner
Capt	Kevin Riebsam	Capt	Mike "Sooch" Masucci	Capt	Rob King	Capt	James Stewart
Capt	John Feda	Capt	Steve Abrams	Capt	John Cabigas	Capt	John Tomjack
Capt	Glen Whicker	Capt	Steve Reed	Capt	Tom Holder	Maj	Mark Greising
Capt	Edmund Barnette	*Capt*	*Jose Pacheco*	Capt	Al Zwick	Capt	David Hosley
Capt	James Christy	Maj	Bryan Galbreath	Capt	Al Cobb	Capt	John Scott Winstead
Capt	Kevin W. Briggs (e-mail)	Capt	Rich Schneider*	Capt	Steve Hoogasian	Capt	Jeff Klosky
Capt	Gregg A. Matous	Capt	Rusty Nelson	Capt	Dave Rogelstad		
Capt	Edward Laux	Capt	Chuck Cunningham	Capt	Brad Kenwisher	**1996**	
Capt	Jeffrey Price	Capt	Troy Devine	Capt	Mike Smith	Capt	Ralph Baker
Capt	Greg Augst	Capt	Vince Sergi	Capt	Soren Jones	Capt	Duane Dively
Capt	Roger Mostar	Capt	Steve Silver	Capt	Randy Roby*	Capt	Sean Jones
Capt	James Ownbey	Capt	Brandon King	Capt	Walt Flint	Maj	Douglas Hill
				Capt	Arnie Gaus	Maj	Edgar Knouse
1988		**1991**		Capt	George Smith	Capt	Paul Britton
Capt	Brian Long	Capt	Keith "Spike" Gentile	Capt	Vinnie Bachelier	Capt	Brad Berry
Capt	Blaine Bachus	Capt	Jon Guertin	Capt	Dave Claxton	Capt	Jimmy Donohue
Capt	Patrick Davis	Capt	Glenn Roberts	Capt	Eric Nuss	Maj	Bob Gardner
Capt	Paul Memrick	Capt	Don Pickenpaugh	Capt	Fred Bower	Capt	Rob Hess
Capt	Jake Jacobson	Capt	Brian Heyne	Capt	Ed McGovern	Capt	Michael Means
Capt	Joe Pacheco	Capt	Kevin Nielan	Capt	Pete Vanpelt	Capt	Tim Decker
Maj	Samuel Crouse	Capt	Ken Mautino	Capt	Pat Wrynn	Capt	Jack Hirlinger
Capt	J.J. Jackson	Capt	Mike Colaco	Capt	Todd Ansty	Capt	Timothy Williams
Capt	Bryan Anderson	Capt	Darryl "Egg" Smith	Capt	John Larson	Capt	Scott Hoffman
Capt	Dave Wright	Capt	Philip Bass	Capt	Sandy Balkan		
Capt	Larry Bill	Capt	Marty McGregor*	Capt	Steve Conner	**1997**	
Capt	Garry Baccus	*Col*	*Thomas J. Keck*			Lt Col	James Hunt
Capt	Thad Fuller	Capt	Craig Roebuck	**1994**		Maj	Bob Yahn
Capt	Doug Bissell	Capt	Dave Larson	*Capt*	*Warren Trout*	Capt	Michael Godwin
Capt	Kevin Henry	*Col*	*Larry W. Tieman*	Capt	Paul Schaefer	Capt	Dean Neeley
Capt	Ken Bray	Capt	Gary Diekema	Capt	Chris Coffland	Capt	Michael Fleck
Maj	Tom Danielson	Capt	Ed Venner	Capt	Matt Sanning	Maj	Bill Schlecht
Capt	Nate Green	Capt	Jim Chandler	Capt	Darrell Dearman	Maj	Steven Mundine

Capt	Kelvin Blake Smith	Capt	Mark Marshall	Maj	Jerry Lavely	Maj	James Mark Hogge
Capt	Don Yu	Capt	Dave Russell	Capt	Joe Santucci	Maj	Kevin Quamme
Capt	Rod Harrell	Capt	Tim Schultz	Maj	Thom Ryan	Maj	Gary MacLeod
Capt	Joseph Pokoski	Maj	James Al Marshall	Maj	Curtis Walker	Maj	Jeffery Wright
Col	*Chuck Simpson*	Lt. Col	Daniel Baltrusaitis	Capt	Thomas Anderson	Capt	Ralph Shoukry
Maj	Guy Neddo	Capt	Chris McCann	Maj	Donald Temple	Maj	Kirt Stallings
				Maj	Doug Morse	Maj	Deric Kraxberger
1998		**2000**		Capt	Jeff Cook	Maj	Richard Mehl
Maj	Greg Barber	Capt	Quinn Gummel	Capt	Steve Rodriguez	Lt. Col	Stuart Broce
Capt	Rob Haines	Maj	Dennis Davoren	Capt	Tom Engle	Capt	Greg Hafner
Capt	Shawn Dunsmoor	*Capt*	*Gary Witover*	Capt	John Glass		
Capt	Darrell Dunn	Maj	Jeff Olesen	Capt	John Samuel-Burnett	**2004**	
Maj	Bert Garrison	*Capt*	*Brian McLaughlin*	Maj	Jerry Barnett	Maj	Rob Wehner
Capt	Paul Cook	Capt	James Greg Kimbrough	Capt	Ralph Bill Booth	Capt	Mike Colson
Capt	Monte Anderson	Capt	Eliot Ramey			Maj	Brian Maddocks
Capt	Byron Mathewson	Capt	Joe Vasile	**2002**		Capt	Dan Hayenga
Capt	Matthew Roller	Capt	Spence Thomas	Lt. Col	Tom Plumb	Capt	Bill Evans
Capt	Larry McCreary	Capt	Tom Parent	Capt	Michael Clavenna	Lt Col	David Bourke Milligan
Col	*Kent Traylor*	Lt. Col	Jon Engle	Capt	Alberto Cruz	Maj	Jeff Starr
		Capt	John Long	Capt	Todd Hunter Boatman	Maj	Blane Kilpper
1999		*Col*	*Alan Vogel*	Capt	Steve Spiegel	Maj	John Chris Merten
Capt	Andrew Werner	Maj	Joseph Mason Gaines	Capt	Suzanna Moore	Capt	Mikko LaValley
Capt	Chris Burns	Capt	William Skeeters	Maj	Shane Johnson	Maj	Howard Robinson
Capt	Todd Kalish	Maj	David Sandige	Maj	Joey Medlin	Capt	Merryl David
Capt	*Marc Caudill*	Capt	Joel Boswell	Capt	Dan St. Clair	Maj	Ramsey Sharif
Capt	Dave Blazek	Capt	Brian Dickinson	Capt	Ray Simmons	Capt	Alex Castro
Capt	Vince Catich	Lt. Col	Randall Schermerhorn	Capt	Mike Sovitsky	Capt	Richard Todd Hornbuckle
Col	*Jon Stroberg*	Maj	Pat Baumhover			Maj	Scott Proffitt
Maj	Denis Steele			**2003**		Maj	Stan Wilson
Capt	Mike Glaccum	**2001**		Maj	Mark Mount	Maj	Todd Ernst
Capt	Brian Farrar	Capt	Mike Wheeler	*Maj*	*Christian Dollwet*	Capt	Karl Frederick
B/Gen	*Kevin Chilton*	Capt	Steve Hamlin	Capt	Jeremy Potvin		

Comments, Sources, & Acknowledgments

This project got bigger as it progressed. I suppose this was inevitable, given the length and breadth of the U-2 story. However, I resisted the temptation to extract extensively from previously-published work on the history of this amazing airplane - other than from my own writings! Instead, the 'raw materials' for this book were mainly official documents that have become available in recent years; memoirs, briefings and other unpublished material made available to me; and notes from interviews that I have conducted over a 20-year period.

During the writing process, I made a few policy decisions to which purists may object. To improve the appearance of the text, cryptonyms appear in lower-case only. I gave up trying to distinguish between nicknames and codenames. Soviet defense systems are identified by their Western reporting names and designations. Chinese names are rendered into English using the Wade-Giles system that was most widely used in the US, Europe and Taiwan, during the period under discussion.

This is one of the first books to make extensive use of documents declassified by the CIA as part of its 25-Year Review Program, which was mandated by Executive Order 12958. In the past five years, the CIA has released about 10 million pages in electronic form to the US National Archives facility at College Park, MD. This sounds impressive, until you realize that many of these pages deal with mundane administrative matters. Of the remainder, many have been heavily redacted (eg censored). Those who venture to research these pages must have the time and the patience to sort the few ears of wheat, from the mountains of chaff! Then, they must try to decipher the meaning of those sections where redactions have been made!

However, I do not wish to be churlish about the work of the CIA Declassification Center. It has provided some valuable material that will, I suspect, be used by intelligence analysts and historians for many years to come.

Ironically, I learnt as much about the early years of the Air Force U-2 program from the CIA documents, as I did from official USAF sources. Despite various formal and informal requests, the response of the Air Force History Support Office and Historical Research Agency was disappointing.

A book like this could not have been compiled without the help of many people. But I especially want to thank Joe Donoghue. He labored tirelessly at the National Archives to identify documents that were relevant to the CIA's overhead reconnaissance activities. Moreover, his deep understanding of the U-2 program was invaluable. Dwayne Day and Jeff Richelson also provided significant help, based on their own archival research. The National Security Archive in Washington was another great source, where thanks are due to Bill Burr and Tom Blanton.

I must also thank some fellow authors, historians, photographers and researchers: Duncan Adams, Matthew Aid, Chang Wei Bin, Dr Coy Cross, Victor Drushlyakov, Nigel Eastaway, Pete Foster, Albert Gibb, Yefim Gordon, Dr Cargill Hall, Dr Gerald Haines, Paul Lashmar, Liu Wen Hsiao, Lu Der Yuen, Georgi Mikhailov, Alex Orlov, Pete Merlin, Jay Miller, Alfred Price, Tim Ripley, Mick Roth, Jim Rotramel, Chris Ryan, Rolf Tamnes, Dave Wilton, and Dr Jim Young.

I have enjoyed a great deal of help from people who have been associated with the U-2 program, or their close relatives. Special thanks are due to Buz Carpenter and Pat Halloran, for their encouragement and support over a number of years. I would also like to thank: Bob Anderson, Art Andraitis, Dr Jim Baker, Ed and Bob Baldwin, Paul Bacalis, Jim Barrilleaux, Jim Barnes, Martin Bee, Stan Beerli, Tony Bevacqua, Bob Birkett, Bill Bonnichsen, John Bordner, Tom Bowen, Lionel Boudreaux, Mike Bradley, Stuart Broce, Buddy Brown, Steve Brown, Dino Brugioni, Bill Burke, Fred Carmody, Jim Carter, Glenn Chapman, Kay Cherbonneaux, Bob Chiota, Spike Chuang, Orville Clancey, Marjorie Cline, Dick Cloke, Henry Combs, Harry Cordes, Brian Cox, Bill Crimmins, Tom Crull, Phil Daisher, John Dale, Dick Davies, Frank Dewar, David Dowling, Harry Drew, Bob Dunn, James Eastlund, Arne and Bob Ericson, Walt Flint, Bill Frazier, Frank Furr, Arnie Gaus, Leo Geary, Jim Gibbs, Fred Gilligan, Joe Giraudo, Mike Glaccum, Bill Gregory, Deke Hall, Bill Hall, Steve Hamlin, Ray Haupt, Robb Hoover, Mike Hua, Matt Huber, Jon Huggins, Ken Israel, Don Jackson, Don James, Ernie Joiner, Jeff Jungemann, Chuck Kern, Helen Kleyla, Cozy Kline, Bob Klinger, Marty Knutson, Doyle Krumrey, Jim Lacey, Ash Lafferty, Torrey Larsen, Dick Leavitt, Jack Ledford, Richard Leghorn, Ralph Lewis, Denny Lombard, Gerry Losey, Michael Lu, John MacArthur, Chris McCann, Jerry McIlmoyle, Norm Mackie, Tom McMurtry, Will Main, Ed Martin, Tony Martinez, Mike Masucci, Bob Matye, John Mabey, Hank Meierdierck, Dick Miller, Vic Milam, Marion Mixson, Gene Monihan, John Mueller, Charlie Murphy, Joe Murphy, Bob Murphy, Mike Musholt, Jacques Naviaux, Ed Naylor, Norm Nelson, Jeff Olesen, Curt Osterheld, Jude Pao, Dave Patton, Steve Peterson, Al Pinkham, Ellsworth Powell, Sue Powers, Gary Powers Jr, Frances Pudlo, John Raines, Elaine and David Rand, Bob Ray, Dave Ray, Ben Rich, Ennio Ripa, Phil Robertson, Robert Robinson, Herb Rodgers, Lyal Rudd, Joe Ruseckas, Norm Sakamoto, Jim Sether, Lou Setter, Johnny Shen, John Shinn, Earl Shoemaker, Art Schuetz, Bob Schumacher, Tom Shepherd, Bob Singel, Hugh Slater, Ed Smart, Earl Smith, Rich Smith, Don Songer, Bob Spencer, Hervey Stockman, Chuck Stratton, Alastair Sutherland, John Swanson, Larry Tart, Lowell Taylor, Jim Terry, Garfield Thomas, Jack Thomas, Jack Thornton, Mory Tsai, John Tsao, John Turner, Carmine Vito, Ed Walby, Bill Walker, Tiger Wang, Jerry West, John Weston, Bud Wheelon, Don White, Chuck Wilson, Jim Wood, George Worley, Robert Yang, Robin Yeh, Dr Herb York, and Dave Young.

This book did not benefit from any official sponsorship or review. Therefore, all errors are my responsibility.

These days, not many publishers are equipped for, or inclined to persevere with, specialist works such as this one. I am therefore grateful to Peter Schiffer of Schiffer Publishing, and his editors Bob Biondi and Ian Robertson, for keeping the faith!

Finally, I would like to thank my wife Meng, and daughters Nicola and Melanie, for tolerating my frequent travels—and travails. Without their support and understanding, this book would never have been completed.

Chris Pocock
Uxbridge, UK
February 2005

Footnotes

Chapter 1:
[1] Lockheed memo from J.H.Carter to L.E.Root, 30 November 1953
[2] Bud Wienberg interviewed by Cargill Hall, March 1995
[3] author's interview with Richard Leghorn
[4] for a comprehensive review of such US and British missions in the early to mid-fifties, see a long article by Cargill Hall, "Cold War Overflights: Military Reconnaissance Missions Over Russia before the U-2" in Colloquy, April 1997, Vol 18, Number 1. More detail on the RAF flights, and on SAC RB-47 flights in 1955-56, can be found in Paul Lashmar's substantial book, "Spy Flights of the Cold War", Sutton Publishing, UK 1996
[5] letter from John Seaberg to NASA historian John Sloop, 25 June 1976. Sloop subsequently incorporated Seaberg's comments in his NASA History Report SP-4404, "Liquid Hydrogen as a Propulsion Fuel 1945-1959", 1978. In his letter, Seaberg claims that he and Lamar originated the concept of a specialized reconnaissance aircraft in late 1952. However, the weight of evidence suggests otherwise, including the fact that Wienberg and Leghorn both served at WADC in 1951-52.
[6] Kelly Johnson, "Log for Project X". Hereafter Johnson Log. This is Johnson's personal diary of progress on the U-2 project. A sanitized version of this diary has been released by Lockheed, but all references in this book are to the unexpurgated version which was made available to the author by another source. The first entry in the log (December 1953) suggests that Johnson may have been aware of the new requirement before Carter and Root approached him. Robert Amory (CIA Deputy Director for Intelligence at the time) states in an oral history interview conducted for the JFK Library in 1966, that Johnson was tipped off by the CIA's Philip Strong (see later this chapter). The author has assessed this evidence, and considers it unlikely.
[7] Lockheed Report LR-9732. The full report is reproduced in Jay Miller, "Lockheed's Skunk Works", Aerofax, US, 1993
[8] the XF-104 flew with an interim Wright J65 engine, however
[9] Miller "Skunk Works" book
[10] patent filing by Kelly Johnson for Span Load Distribution Control on 6 September 1955, provided to the author by Lockheed Martin Skunk Works. Ironically, Johnson may not have had an exclusive on gust control. The Fairchild M-195 design submitted to ARDC in the Bald Eagle competition (see later this chapter) featured a similar device.
[11] Seaberg letter, as above
[12] Wienberg interview, as above. On 8 May 1954, a SAC RB-47E was attacked by MiG-17s during a deliberate daylight overflight of the Kola Peninsula. Despite LeMay's bravado, not even his latest jet bomber could properly perform this type of mission.
[13] Johnson Log, 7 June 1954.
[14] NIE-6-54, "Soviet Capabilities and Probable Programs in the Guided Missile Field", released 5 October 1954, declassified in 1993.
[15] Jim Baker interviewed by author, 1995. In the UK, the RAF told Baker that they had attempted to get photographs of the Kapustin Yar missile test site from a Canberra some months earlier. In his oral history interview (see footnote 5), DDCI Robert Amory relates how this aircraft had been intercepted by Soviet fighters and nearly shot down. Despite extensive research by Lashmar, see note 4, the full story has still not emerged.
[16] Greg Pedlow and Don Welzenbach, "The CIA and the U-2 Program", CIA History Staff, 1998, p14-16, p24. This is a declassified but still partially redacted version of a history of the CIA's U-2 and A-12 programs, which was written in 1989-90 and published with a Secret classification in 1992. In this account, the authors relate that Strong carried details of the CL-282 from the Pentagon to Richard Bissell in May 1954. They cite an interview with Bissell as one of their sources for this. Although Bissell states in all of his published writings, that he was not aware of the project until just after it was given the go-ahead in late November 1954, the best evidence suggests otherwise.
[17] The other members Land chose were mathematician John Tukey from Princeton; nuclear chemist Joseph Kennedy; and Allan Latham, a former Polaroid colleague of Land who was now with the Arthur D. Little consultancy.
[18] Leghorn interview, plus Don Welzenbach, "Din Land: The Patriot from Polaroid" in Optics and Photonics News, US, 1994. This is an excellent account of Land's role in the birth of the U-2.
[19] Baker interview
[20] Pedlow and Welzenbach, p25-26. However, the assertion by these CIA authors that only the CL-282 was designed to low (eg non-milspec) load factors is incorrect. According to Jay Miller, "The X-Planes", Aerofax/Orion Books, US, 1988, which has a detailed description of the X-16, Bell's design had a maneuvering load factor of 3g, only 0.5g more than the CL-282. Pedlow and Welzenbach are also mistaken in their belief that the USAF insisted on defensive armament. See the "Design Study Requirements" for the Bald Eagle project, also in Miller's book.
[21] Baker interview
[22] "Memo for the DCI: A Unique Opportunity for Comprehensive Intelligence", 5 November 1954. This three-page memo was accompanied by a two-page summary and a covering letter.
[23] James Killian, "Sputnik, Scientists and Eisenhower", The MIT Press, US, 1977, p82.
[24] Seaberg letter
[25] Johnson Log, 19 November 1954
[26] Johnson Log, 19-23 November 1954

Chapter 2:
[1] Ritland papers, in AFFTC History Office, Edwards AFB
[2] Richard Bissell, "Reflections of a Cold War Warrior", Yale University Press, 1996, p92-. Bissell's memoirs were completed after his death by his personal assistant in later life, Frances Pudlo, and researcher Jonathan Lewis. Hereafter Bissell memoirs. Readers will find significant differences between this author's account of events, and those as related by the Bissell memoir. It should be noted that neither Bissell, nor his co-authors, had access to classified or declassified documents.
[3] Johnson Log, 15-17 December 1954
[4] Henry Combs interview by author, and remarks at "The U-2: A Revolution in Intelligence" conference, Washington D.C, September 1998, hereafter "U-2 conference"

[5] patent filing on "Droppable Stabilizing Gear for Aircraft", dated 6 September 1955, provided by Lockheed Martin Skunk Works

[6] Ed Baldwin interviewed by author

[7] Baldwin interview

[8] Sloop NASA history, p127; "Military Jet Fuels 1944-1987", Aero Propulsion Lab, Wright-patterson AFB. During the flight test program, it was determined that standard JP-4 could be used in the U-2 at low-medium altitudes for ferry purposes, with a restricted rate of climb, but not above 50,000 feet.

[9] letter from Flickenger to the David Clark Company, 1987, reproduced in the company's David Clark memoirs, 1992

[10] Johnson log, February 1955. Ben Koziol interviewed by author. Ben Rich "Skunk Works", Little Brown and Co, 1994

[11] soundtrack to the film "The Inquisitive Angel", made by the CIA in 1957 and obtained by the author

[12] Jim Baker interviewed by author, and U-2 conference, plus technical manual SP-0045 for the B-camera

[13] Formally, Perkin-Elmer (P-E) subcontracted Hycon and Baker for this work. Effectively, Baker did the most important work on the early U-2 lenses, including the final grounding, and P-E ordered the glass from by the German company Schott, per Baker's recommendation

[14] Johnson log, 12-13 April 1955; Maj Gen Osmand Ritland, USAF oral history interview K239.0512-722.

[15] The Project Oilstone office in the Pentagon was disguised as AFCIG-5, "Special Assistant to the Inspector General for Special Projects"

[16] Leo Geary interviewed by author.

[17] Ben Rich and Leo Janos, "Skunk Works", Little, Brown & Co, US 1994

[18] Johnson diary, May 1955

[19] Baldwin interview

[20] Bissell memoirs and "Origins of the U-2" article-cum-interview with Bissell in Air Power History, winter 1989, hereafter Bissell article; Ritland papers; Geary interview

[21] Combs, Baldwin, interviews

[22] Johnson diary

[23] Bob Murphy interview

[24] flight test reports as reprinted in "Secret First Flight of Article 001", Spyplanes, vol 2, 1988. However, for much of the subsequent technical details in this chapter on flight testing, the author has used Lockheed Report No SP-109, "Flight Test Development of the Lockheed U-2 Airplane", 4 November 1958, declassified and made available to the author, 1999.

[25] contrary to other accounts, LeVier did not fly the U-2 to high altitude

[26] Rich/Janos book, p138

[27] Johnson diary entries for 6 and 22-26 August; Baldwin interview; drawings of a design carrying small nuclear bombs on underwing pylons, discovered in Lockheed ADP archives by the late Richard Abrams

[28] Johnson diary, October/November; Geary interview

[29] author interview with anonymous source; Project Ostiary has never been declassified

[30] Geary interview; DPS memo 29 December 1955

[31] Hank Meierdierck, Phil Robertson and Lew Setter interviews by author. This group were officially part of the 4070th Support Wing, which SAC formed at March AFB to provide logistics support to the early U-2 program.

[32] Robertson interview

[33] Meierdierck, Robertson, Geary interviews

[34] Kilgore was at The Ranch for the early test flights, where he provided medical supervision for the Lockheed test pilots. "Lovelace Doctor Had Secret Role," Albuquerque Journal, 2 August 1987, pA1.

[35] Lew Setter, Phil Robertson interviews

[36] Johnson log, 1 December 1955; soundtrack to "The Invisible Angel"; Jack DeLapp interviewed by author

[37] Col Phil Robertson subsequently claimed an unofficial world altitude record of 74,500 feet during a 10 hour 5 minute flight on 10 May. He flew all the way north to the Great Bear Lake on Canada's Arctic Circle, in a flight designed to measure the effect of high-altitude wind patterns. Returning the way he'd come in a straight line, he arrived overhead The Ranch with plenty of fuel left. So he flew on to San Diego and back. The record was not beaten (again unofficially) until the re-engined U-2C flew in 1959. Robertson interview. (Six days after Robertson's flight, test pilot Bob Schumacher flew for 10 hours 15 minutes, which is the longest-recorded flight of a U-2A model).

[38] Hank Meierdierck note to author

[39] Marty Knutson interview

[40] Pedlow/Welzenbach p78-79.

Chapter 3:

[1] PRO file AIR19/826

[2] as above

[3] Johnson diary, 17 May 1956

[4] Knowledge of the upper atmosphere was indeed still in its infancy, as the early U-2 pilots sometimes found to their cost during flights from The Ranch. One was flying at 68,500 feet near Reno when the aircraft rapidly climbed 2,000 feet, almost exceeding the g-limits. It had been pushed upwards by the Sierra Wave, which meteorologists at the time believed was thoroughly dissipated above 45,000 feet. Another encountered unexpectedly strong head-on jetstreams after a flameout, which destroyed his ability to glide to the nearest available runway for a deadstick landing. Fortunately, he eventually managed to relight his engine - just above the rim of the Grand Canyon! However, NASA eventually concluded from the VGH recorder carried on the U-2 that clear-air turbulence was a rare occurrence above 60,000 feet. See NASA Technical Note D-548, October 1960

[5] Pedlow/Welzenbach, p94

[6] Johnson diary, 18 May 1956

[7] Johnson diary, 19 May 1956, PRO file AIR19/826

[8] Pedlow/Welzenbach, p95/97. This contradicts the Bissell article, where he recalls visiting the German Chancellor *before* the aircraft were moved to Germany

[9] As the pilots gained experience, the CIA detachments dispensed with the need for a 'mobile' chase upon landing. But the USAF deemed this procedure essential, and it continues to this day, no matter how experienced the mission pilot.

[10] Dino Brugioni, "Eyeball to Eyeball", Random House, NY 1990, Bissell book p104, and Bill Crimmins interview. According to Lundahl, interviewed for the Bissell book, the inspiration for the AUTOMAT codename came from the convenience stores in New York city, which were open around the clock, and where various items could be purchased from automatic vending machines. Because a classified codename could not begin with a vowel, the initials of Lundahl's security officer Henry Thomas were prefixed to the name, hence HTAUTOMAT.

[11] UK Joint Intelligence Committee (JIC) report (56) 23, in PRO file CAB158/24

[12] Pedlow/Welzenbach, p101

[13] map of flights from Lockheed Skunk Works Star, 24 May 1996

[14] most flight data from Hervey Stockman, interviewed by author

[15] Bissell article

[16] Charles Ahern, "The Yo-Yo Story: An Electronic Analysis Case History", CIA Studies in Intelligence, Volume 5, Winter 1961, declassified 1997

[17] this is the Kaliningrad north of Moscow, later renamed, and not the port city on the Baltic which still bears this name

18 some flight data from Carmine Vito, interviewed by author

19 Col-Gen Yu.V.Votintsev, "Unknown Troops of the Vanished Superpower", Voyenno-Istoricheskiy Zhurnal, No 8, 1993, hereafter Votinsev article. The CIA's Office of Scientific Intelligence (OSI) eventually concluded in 1958 that the S-25 system (designated SA-1 and nicknamed GUILD by the West) was a major technological advance with good capability at low-medium altitude against multiple targets. see Ahern article. However, the USSR chose to develop mobile SAM systems instead, and the costly, fixed-site S-25 system was not deployed elsewhere.

20 Pedlow/Welzenbach, p106, plus Goodpaster's Memorandum for Record, 10 July 1956, White House Office of the Staff Secretary, Alpha series, in the Eisenhower Presidential Library, hereafter Goodpaster memo plus date

21 Pedlow/Welzenbach, p108; Mission 2021 data; Sergei Khrushchev interview

22 G.A.Mikhailov and A.S.Orlov, "Mysteries of the Closed Skies", New and Newest History, Moscow, June 1992, hereafter Mikhailov/Orlov. Welzenbach/Pedlow p109 mistakenly conclude that the USSR did not realize that Moscow had been overflown.

23 the Soviet Union was probably confusing the U-2 with the USAF's RB-57A, which was now based in Europe. This mistake allowed the US to formally deny that the USSR had been overflown. "No US military planes...at the time of the alleged overflights could possibly have strayed so far from their known flight plans," was the State Dept's formal response to the Soviet protest.

24 Rich and Janos, p165

25 Wayne Jackson, "Allen Welsh Dulles as DCI," a CIA history declassified in 1994, Volume II, p28-30

26 Bill Crimmins interview

27 Lt Gen Eugene Tighe, "Imagery and Reconnaissance Reminiscences" in American Intelligence Journal, Winter/Spring 1992

28 Nigel West, "The Friends: Britian's Post-War Secret Intelligence Operations", Wiedenfelt & Nicholson, London 1988, p112

29 crash details from Robertson interview

30 It is known that two US and four Canadian F-86 interceptors were flying in the vicinity. Carey might have been trying to avoid them and lost control, it was surmised. According to Bissell, book p108, Kelly Johnson determined that the cause of this accident was overpressure in the wing tanks as the aircraft approached operating altitude after a very steep climb. This led to structural failure of the wing. The solution was to install a simple relief valve. However, members of the original U-2 flight test team insisted to this author that the overpressure problem was identified and solved a year earlier during the very first flight tests. The Lockheed U-2A flight test development report (SP-109) shows that to correct an unacceptably low rate of fuel transfer from the wings to the sump tank, the original system of unpressurized tanks relying on a gravity feed system was replaced by pressurization to 1.5psi by engine compression bleed air. However, a Service Bulletin dated November 1958 did make changes in the fuel system "to prevent excessive pressure in the wing tanks". An alternative explanation for Carey's crash was offered by fellow pilot Marty Knutson (interview). This is that there was an uncommanded wing flap extension, which led quickly to loss of control.

31 Pedlow/Welzenbach, p114-6; Charles Cogan, "From the Politics of Lying to the Farce at Suez: What the US Knew" in Intelligence and National Security, Vol 13, No 2 (Summer 1998), Brugioni p33.

32 Brugioni, p34. Another version of this story, from the Amory interview, JFK Library, attributes a similar remark to an RAF intelligence officer who was also shown this imagery. But Pedlow/Welzenbach note, p114, that the only U-2 imagery from the Suez Crisis that was shown to the UK, was during the 8 September briefing mentioned earlier.

33 Pedlow/Welzenbach, p124

34 Pedlow/Welzenbach, p124 states that a secret Soviet protest was made after this flight, but none has been revealed by State Dept archives

35 radar details from Bill Griffiths, former Westinghouse engineer, in letter to author.

36 During 1955-56, a substantial number of penetration overflights of the USSR and Eastern Europe were carried out by SAC RB-47Es, and by specially-modified RB-57As and F-100As assigned to USAFE and PACAF. In recent years, historians employed by the US government have claimed that these flights were always performed under an authority properly delegated by the White House, through the JCS, to the commanders of SAC, USAFE and PACAF. See for instance, "Cold War Overflights: Military Reconnaissance Missions over Russia Before the U-2" by Cargill Hall, in Colloquy, April 1997. This author has not yet seen any declassified memoranda to support this claim. Whatever the truth, it is certain that the 'Vladivostok incident' ended such military flights over the USSR. From now on, the White House approved only CIA U-2 flights, and these only sparingly.

37 personnel from Det C told the author that the US government assured Japan, that no overflights would be conducted from Japanese bases by the U-2. According to Pedlow/Welzenbach, p134, Japan "had no control over US military bases in Japan," and the hold-up was caused by the difficult search for accommodation in the area.

38 The USAF subsequently ordered a 30th aircraft - see Appendix Five

39 Pedlow/Welzenbach, p127-8

Chapter 4:

1 Jack Gibbs remarks, relayed to author through Jim Gibbs

2 Johnson log, 16-17 August 1956

3 Richard N. Johnson, "Radar Absorbent Materiel: A Passive Role in an Active Scenario", The International Countermeasures Handbook, 11th Edition 1986, EW Communications Inc, Palo Alto, CA

4 Robertson, Klinger interviews

5 Matye, Setter interviews

6 History of the 4080th Strategic Reconnaissance Wing, filed at AF Historical Research Agency, Maxwell AFB, April-May 1957, hereafter 4080th history

7 "Open letter on 'Black Jet' Relayed to US commanders", Mainichi, 1 December 1959

8 accident report, 4080th history, October 1957

9 as quoted in Rich and Janos book, p154

10 DPD U-2 Mission list

11 the unintentional overflight took place on 18 March 1957, but the USSR did not make a formal protest

12 Cherbonneaux memoir; Missions 4030/4033 data

13 Mission 4036 data

14 Pedlow/Welzenbach, p134; interview with Jim Barnes

15 Mission 4035 data

16 the author has not been able to confirm the version of the first U-2 flight over Tyuratam as related by Bissell book, p119, namely that the pilot saw the launch site off his nose, and altered course to fly directly overhead. Bissell is certainly wrong to suggest that the existence of the launch site "had not even been suspected."

17 Dino Brugioni, "The Tyuratam Enigma", Air Force Magazine, March 1984

18 Henry Lowenhaupt, "Mission to Birch Woods", CIA Studies in Intelligence, Fall 1968, declassified 1997

19 Mission 4039 data

20 Misions 4049 and 4050 data

21 Tsering Shakya, "The Dragon in the Land of the Snows", Pimlico Books, UK 1999; William M. Leary, "Secret Mission to Tibet" in Air & Space

magazine, December 1997/January 1998

[22] Timothy Varfolomyev, "Soviet Rocktry that Conquered Space", Spaceflight, Vol 37, August 1995, p261

[23] According to Varfolomyev, see previous footnote, this launch may have been an unsuccessful first attempt to launch the Sputnik satellite, rather than an ICBM test

[24] Mission 4058 cable

[25] Mission 6008 cable

[26] Henry Lowenhaupt, "Ravelling Russia's Reactors", CIA Studies in Intelligence, Vol 16, Fall 1972

[27] Cherbonneaux memoir

[28] Mission 4059 data; Bill Hall interview

[29] Mission 4061 data

[30] Stephen Zaloga, "Soviet Air Defense Missiles" .

[31] According to Zaloga, p37, a prototype SA-2 system was deployed to the Kala airport at Baku as early as late 1956. It may therefore have been overflown by U-2 Mission 4016 flown by Frank Powers on 20 November that year, which routed directly over Baku.

Chapter 5:

[1] Zaloga, "Target America", p 176-181

[2] Don Welzenbach and Nancy Galyean, "Those Daring Young Men and Their Ultra-High Flying Machines," CIA Studies in Intelligence, Fall 87

[3] Welzenbach/Galyean article, Pedlow/Welzenbach, p150

[4] Rolf Tamnes, "The United States and the Cold War in the High North," Dartmouth Publishing, VT, 1991; interview with Vidar Ystad. The Welzenbach/Galyean article, written earlier, states that permission to overfly Norway *had* been granted, but this author prefers the information provided by Tamnes and Ystad. Tamnes is a government historian who consulted the official records in Oslo. Ystad interviewed Evang.

[5] 4080th History, September 1957

[6] 4080th History, February 1958

[7] Moreover, it had even become possible to identify the Krypton 85 isotope which was produced and vented into the atmosphere from Soviet reactors which were producing plutonium. By this means, US intelligence could estimate the other side's rate of nuclear weapons production.

[8] from a history of AFTAC (the successor to AFOAT), quoted in Aviation Week and Space Technology, 3 November 1997, p53, 57

[9] White House Memo for Record, 26 October 1957

[10] Jackson's CIA history of Dulles as DCI, Volume IV, p28-31

[11] notes on special meeting, January 1958, unsigned, White House records

[12] Foreign Relations of the USA, 1958-1960, Volume X, Part 1, USGPO 1993

[13] Welzenbach/Pedlow, p263

[14] the specification was actually ANA color 607, "Non-Spectacular Sea Blue". Today, the equivalent specification is FSN 35045.

Chapter 6:

[1] AIR19/826 file, PRO

[2] CAB159/25 file, JIC meeting with Mr H.S. Young, 18 October 1956

[3] author's interview with Dino Brugioni; AIR19/826 file, PRO

[4] Pedlow/Welzenbach, p114

[5] WH Memo by Goodpaster, 26 October 1957

[6] WH Memo by Goodpaster, 26 October 1957; Ranelagh, p332. Brugioni says that the British PM was persuaded by President Eisenhower himself

[7] According to Pedlow/Welzenbach, p215, another three missions were flown over China in August 1958. However, these are not listed in other declassified records; FRUS Volume XIX, items 27, 79 and 228.

[8] WH memo by Goodpaster, 9 September 1958

[9] Johnson log, August 1958. However, none of the maintenance officers of the 4080th wing at the time, recall any such investigation. It's worth noting that the number of accidents and incidents suffered by the SAC wing was a reflection of its far greater flying schedule than the CIA detachments

[10] 4080th history, July 1958

[11] 4080th history, August-September 1958

[12] Lockheed Report SP-117 "Stability and Control Evaluation", dated 1 May 1959; Bob Klinger interview

[13] as above

[14] Zaloga, Target America, p150; sidebar on the history of Plesetsk from an article on Soviet Astronautics, Spaceflight, Vol 38, June 1996, p207

[15] WH memo by Goodpaster, 3 September 1958. Despite the deliberately obscure description - 'a northern operation' - the author believes that this refers to an overflight of the suspected new USSR missile base. This was also the recollection of detachment commander Stan Beerli, interviewed by author.

[16] Rolf Tamnes, "The United States and the Cold War in the High North," Dartmouth Publishing, Brookfield, VT, 1991, p176; Olav Riste, "The Norwegian Intelligence Service 1945 – 1970", Frank Cass, London, 1999 p67

[17] Riste p67, Tamnes, p175

[18] Tamnes, p133 and Ericson interview. Tamnes asserts that both the 9 and 25 October U-2 missions out of Bodo were sampling flights, but the author prefers Ericson's account.

[19] Tamnes, p176

[20] Tamnes p176, Bissell memoirs p121, John Shinn interview. Shin n does not recall flying over Eastern Europe during this flight

[21] Zaloga, "Target America", p150; Varfolomyev, p262. Unlike the USSR, the US chose to launch its first satellites on much smaller boosters.

[22] Jackson's CIA history of Dulles as DCI, volume V, section II

[23] as above. The analyst's name has been withheld from the CIA history, as declassified.

[24] CIA "Memorandum to Holders of NIE 11-5-58" dated 25 November 1958. It is not clear how the CIA interpreted the first three Soviet attempts to launch a rocket to the moon between September and December 1958, presuming that these attempts were detected. The Luna program also relied on the SS-6 design, to which a third stage was added. The Luna launches on 23 September, 12 October and 4 December 1958 flew for 92, 100 and 245 seconds respectively, before failing. See Asif Siddiqi, "Major Launch Failures in the Early Soviet Space Program", Spaceflight, Vol 37, November 1995, p393

Chapter 7:

[1] Ranelagh, p328-9

[2] CIA Notice No 1-120-2, "Organization and Functions, Office of the DDP", 18 February 1959, declassified 1990

[3] CIA Notice No 1-130-5, "Office of the DDI - PIC", 19 August 1958, declassified 1990; interviews with Bill Crimmins, Art Andraitis

[4] Dwayne Day, John Logsdon, Brian Latell, "Eye in the Sky - The Story of the CORONA Spy Satellites", Smithsonian Institution Press, Washington, 1998, p5-6

[5] interview with Orville Clancey

[6] Christopher Robbins, "Air America", Avon Books, New York, 1985, p74-76

[7] author's interviews with Lyle Rudd, Tom Crull.

[8] William Leary, "Secret Mission to Tibet" in Air & Space magazine, December 1997/January 1998

[9] Brugioni book, p39

Chapter 8:

[1] Lockheed Report SP-179, "Flight Test Development of the U-2C Airplane", I July 1960 declassified 1999

[2] White House Office of the Staff Secretary, Memorandum of Conference with the President, 22 December 1958, by John D. Eisenhower

[3] White House Office of the Staff Secretary, Memorandum for the Record, 12 February 1959, by John D. Eisenhower.

[4] White House memo, 4 March 1959; Varfolomeyev, p263

[5] these are approximate figures. For the exact data, see Appendices

[6] Seymour Hersh, "The Samson Option", Random House, NY 1991, p52-58

[7] Bruce Bailey, "A Crow's Story", unpublished manuscript 1992, posted on 55th SRW Association's website 1998, p5

[8] Pedlow/Welzenbach, p162. These authors suggest that the other aircraft involved in this successful telemetry interception was a USAF RB-57D, rather than an EB-47TT. However, no RB-57D was deployed to the area at this time.

[9] White House Office of the Staff Secretary, Memorandum for the Record, 7 July 1959; and Memorandum of Conference with the President, 8 July 1959, by Andrew Goodpaster

[10] Beerli interview

[11] Beerli, Knutson interviews.

[12] Memo to the DCI from the Ad-Hoc Panel on the Status of the Soviet ICBM Program, 25 August 1959, declassified by the DDEL.

[13] as above

[14] 4080th wing history, November/December 1959

[15] 4080th wing history, July 1959

[16] information from White House memo, supplied by Dwayne Day

[17] Memo to DCI from Ad-Hoc Panel

[18] Ericson, Knutson, Robinson interviews

[19] One of the weather flights out of Watton didn't go according to plan, because the aircraft had a hydraulic failure over the Bay of Biscay, and had to divert into the USAF base at Brize Norton near Oxford.

[20] Bissell book, p116-117, maintains that the separate chain of approval really did exist. This author can find no evidence of this, even after interviewing RAF officers who were involved with the U-2 project at the command level. See next footnote

[21] author interviews with Wg Cdrs Norman Mackie and Colin Kunkler. Mission codename is from the title of three yet-to-be-declassified files in the UK Ministry of Defence

[22] Zaloga, "Target America", p150-151

[23] Jackson, volume 5, p87-90

[24] White House memo by Goodpaster, 8 February 1960

[25] RAF Air Intelligence Review, April 1962, declassified as file AIR40/2556 in the PRO

[26] NIE 11-5-60, "Soviet Capabilities in Guided Missiles and Space Vehicles", approved 3 May 1960 noted that there was "limited evidence pointing to two Soviet cities as possible production sites" for the ICBM

[27] X interview. Incidentally, although much of the terrain imaged by MacArthur's flight was covered in deep snow, that did not entirely negate the intelligence value of the imagery. As Dino Brugioni explained to a conference on the CORONA satellite program in 1995, photo-interpreters learned much from the snow clearance patterns adopted by the USSR. For instance, the paths and roads to the headquarters buildings of any given complex were always the first to be cleared!

[28] Pedlow/Welzenbach, p167

[29] Dwayne Day, "The Development and Improvement of the CORONA Satellite" p57, in "Eye in the Sky, The Story of the CORONA Spy Satellites," Smithsonian Institution Press, Washington , 1998.

Chapter 9:

[1] memo from COMOR, "List of Highest Priority Targets", 18 August 1960, in CIA Corona documents, p49-52

[2] author's interview with Col Stan Beerli

[3] Pedlow/Welzenbach, p172

[4] DPD Memo 10 March 1960; Lockheed Skunk Works report SP-179, "Flight Test Development of the Lockheed U-2C Airplane," 1 July 1960

[5] Pedlow/Welzenbach, p170-171; DPD memos 16 and 19 February 1960

[6] Herbert York, "Making Weapons, Talking Peace", Basic Books, New York 1987, p123, and author's correspondence with York; DPD memo 19 February 1960, which suggests that DDCI Gen Pierre Cabell may also have been at this White House meeting.

[7] Pedlow/Welzenbach, p168

[8] For clarity, I have used the word 'battery' to describe the individual firing sites of the SA-2 system, rather than the Soviet term 'battalion'. Confusingly, the Russian word for a battalion is 'diviziony'. The Russian word 'diviziya' describes the next-highest level of command, namely the regimental headquarters!

[9] Zaloga, "Soviet Air Defense", p39-47; Col-Gen S. Mironov, "Several Questions on Evaluating the Effectiveness of the Basic Means of AntiAir Defense of a Front, and its Organizational Structure," Voyennaya Mysl (Military Thought), circa 1960, p7. Amongst the readers of this top-secret Soviet military journal was Col Oleg Penkovsky, who passed a copy of this and many other articles to CIA, whose translation is used here.

[10] author's italics

[11] NIE 11-3-60, "Sino-Soviet Air Defense Capabilities Through Mid-1965", 29 March 1960, declassified 1996

[12] Michael Beschloss, "MayDay", Harper and Row, New York, 1986, p178

[13] Ray Garthoff, comments at CIA U-2 conference, Washington DC, September 1998

[14] Tony Geraghty, "BRIXMIS", Harper Collins, London 1996 p90

[15] NIE 11-5-59, "Soviet Capabilities in Guided Missiles and Space Vehicles" approved 3 November 1959, declassified

[16] CIA Corona documents, p193

[17] details of Chinese shootdown (related here in English for the first time) are from "Dangdai Zhongguo Kongjun" eg History of the Chinese Air Force, published in the China Today series, China Aviation Industry Press, Beijing, 1989. Confirmation that US intelligence did not know that a SAM had shot down the RB-57D is from NIE 11-3-60 dated 29 March 1960, p12 ("there is no evidence that any surface-to-air missiles have been given to any other Soviet Bloc nation"). It was probably the Soviet spy Penkovskiy who finally tipped off the West about Soviet missiles to China. During the course of an extensive grilling on the SA-2 in 1961, he told his interrogators from MI6 and CIA that the Chinese had been given "all the types of guided rocket that are in production."

[18] Pedlow/Welzenbach, p170, 174

[19] NIE 11-3-60, p10,12

[20] exactly what that distance should be, was disputed. The US held that sovereign airspace extended only three miles from the coast, but the USSR insisted it was 12 miles. It wasn't until 1988 that the US unequivocally accepted the 12-mile limit.

[21] 4080th wing history, May 1960, Dixon notes

[22] Leavitt notes

[23] Pedlow/Welzenbach, p168, 170, 172. Mysteriously, White House records recording these decisions have not been found or declassified. In correspondence with the author, Herbert York recalls learning in later years, of Eisenhower's request that no notes be taken of these most sensitive discussions in spring 1960. The authors of the CIA's history used references to these White House meetings, which were contained within the individual U-2 mission folders. These folders still exist - but have not been declassified.

[24] Votintsev article, part 2

[25] Mikhailov and Orlov article, Khrushchev book

[26] Khrushchev book. Mikhailov and Orlov have an alternative version of this story. They say that the missiles themselves were not actually at the launch pad, that troops rushed to move them there from the storage depot, but did not get there in time.

[27] Mikhailov and Orlov article; notes provided to author by Yefim Gordon

[28] Votintsev article, part 2; CIA transcript of a debriefing of Col Oleg Penkovsky by CIA and MI6, 27 April 1961, paragraph 85

[29] CIA Corona volume, p195

[30] Zaloga, "Target America", p151-157, 194

[31] see, for example, NIE 11-4-60 "Main Trends in Soviet Capabilities and Policies 1960-1965", approved 1 December 1960, declassified

[32] Khrushchev book; Mikhailov and Orlov article, implies that both of Det B's 1959 overflights were detected.

[33] Pedlow/Welzenbach, p170

[34] U-2 incident chronology sent by DCI John McCone to ex-President Eisenhower in the mid-1960s (Eisenhower requested the information to help in writing his memoirs). According to Leonard Moseley, "Dulles - A Biography of Eleanor, Allen and John Foster Dulles and their Family Network", Hodder & Staughton, London 1978, p453, Bissell, Dulles, Herter and Hugh Cumming (who ran the State Department's Bureau of Intelligence & Research) all met in the White House on 13 or 14 April to discuss U-2 flights. Bissell, in memoirs p125, does not recall meeting Eisenhower personally at this time. He says that Andrew Goodpaster relayed his request for an extension to the overflight deadline to the President

[35] Pedlow/Welzenbach, p172; White House memo, 25 April 1960; U-2 incident chronology

[36] Pedlow/Welzenbach, p170

[37] The authors reconstruction of the sequence of events which led up to the launch of the final U-2 overflight is based on many sources. They include Powers book and prison diary, Tamnes book, Pedlow/Welzenbach CIA history, and interviews with Bob Ericson, Stan Beerli, Glen Dunaway, John Shinn, and Jim Woods. Where appropriate, travel orders and pilot's flight records have also been consulted

[38] The investigation which Norwegian authorities conducted following the abortive U-2 flight into Bodo suggests that Beerli told Evang that plans for the US operation had changed, and would now only involve C-130 flights. See Tamnes, p178. The USAF did indeed operate C-130s in Europe for SIGINT purposes. However, it cannot be discounted that Evang did not tell the whole truth to the investigation, about what he knew of the U-2 operation, and when he knew it.

[39] The author has not been able to determine who made the change of plan. Stan Beerli, the operations chief in Project HQ, says he knew of no such plan to ferry the aircraft to and fro before he left Washington for Norway on 26 April. The decision may have been taken by Colonel Shelton of Det B himself, although Colonel Bill Burke in project HQ should also have been aware

[40] According to testimony given by DDCI Gen Pierre Cabell to Congress after the Powers shootdown, meteorological records showed that there were only six days in the entire April-September period when weather conditions were ideal for aerial photography across such a large area of the USSR

[41] author's interviews, plus 4080th wing histories, August 1959, March/April 1960

[42] Skunk Works engineers will, to this day, point out that even when zero gallons were indicated on the fuel counter, there was a further 45 of usable fuel remaining - author interview with Bob Klinger

[43] 4080th history, May 1960, Dixon notes

[44] Dick Leavitt interview. Powers, in book p67, alleges that he and others in the U-2 program knew that SAMs were being fired at the later CIA U-2 overflights eg in 1959-60. However, the author has spoken to the pilots of all four successful overflights in those years, and none recalls such an event.

In evidence to the Senate Foreign Relations Committee on 31 May 1960, DDCI General Pierre Cabell quickly and unequivocally corrected DCI Allen Dulles, when the latter suggested that missiles had been fired at earlier overflights. It's not clear whether the intelligence derived from the imagery from SAC's U-2 flight past Anadyr, eg that a SAM had been fired, was available to the CIA project before Powers' mission was launched

[45] Allen Dulles' testimony to Senate Committee on Foreign Affairs, Executive Session, 31 May 1960

[46] Powers prison diary, Ericson interview. (In his autobiography written in 1970, Powers wrote that he knew the details of his route over the USSR some days earlier, and that he had complete trust in the aircraft. However, the author has preferred to rely on the diary that Powers wrote while imprisoned in the USSR. This was written six months after the event, not ten years later)

[47] On a flight over Bulgaria in December 1956, Det A Carmine Vito nearly mistook the cyanide capsule for a lemon drop. Vito occasionally removed his faceplate temporarily during a long mission, to suck one of his favorite sweets, although this was against orders. Fumbling for one of the sweets in his coveralls, he discovered that the ground crew had slipped the cyanide capsule into the same pocket. According to Pedlow/Welzenbach, p125, Vito didn't discover his mistake until he actually sucked on the capsule. However, Vito has assured this author that this story has grown with the telling, and the capsule never actually reached his mouth before he discovered what it was!

[48] After this fact emerged at Powers' trial in Moscow, the neutral Finns were embarrassed - and rather puzzled. Sodankylas airfield had been destroyed by the Germans during the Second World War. All that remained was a 2,500-feet gravel runway, which would have been a tough landing for the U-2!

[49] Pedlow/Welzenbach, p176. According to Powers (book), Shelton told him that the delay was because they were awaiting approval from the White House. This was not correct, although Shelton may have said this, for reasons unknown. As Allen Dulles made clear in his testimony to the Senate Foreign Relations Committee on 31 May 1960, he personally took the decision to proceed, "after consultation with (DDCI) General Cabell and other qualified advisors"

Chapter 10:

[1] Mikhailov and Orlov article

[2] Mikhailov and Orlov article

[3] Mironov article, p6-7

[4] Lockheed Report SP-179, p188

[5] Powers book, p81

[6] Lt Col V. Samsonov, "Eight Missiles for Powers", Motherland (the magazine of the PVO Moscow Air Defence District) 30 August 1992; Col Mikhail Voronov, "The Shooting Down of Powers", abridged from Komsomolets Kubani newspaper in Sputnik: Digest of the Soviet Press, April 1991. Samsonov was in the district command post on 1 May, and Voronov in the first missile battery to engage the U-2. In another article ("U-2: How It Was", HBO - Independent Military Review, No 28, 1998), Igor Tsisar (who was an officer in Voronev's battery at Sverdlovsk) alleges that the radar officer at the Chelyabinsk battery was drunk, and the soldier who was supposed to check the fuses was incompetent.

[7] from an article in Popular Science, August 1994, p58

[8] Mentyukov later speculated that his radar screen had been affected by interference from his own, tail-mounted ECM (electronic countermeasures) system. However, it is possible that the small 'Granger' ECM box on Powers' U-2 really did work as hoped against airborne intercept radar! (In Rich and Janos, p162, Rich notes that Kelly Johnson suspected after the shootdown, that the Granger may have acted in the opposite manner to that

intended eg as a homing device for the SAMs that were subsequently fired at Powers. There is no evidence to support this speculation and (sadly) much of the rest of the U-2 story as related by Rich and Janos is inaccurate)

[9] Lt Col Anatoly Dokuchaev, "Duel in the Stratosphere - How the Spy Flight of Francis Powers was stopped," Krasnaya Zvezda (Red Star) 29 April 1990; Dokuchaev, "Flap of the Overflight Mission", Air Fleet Herald, Moscow, November-December 1998. In an interview with Trud newspaper in October 1996, Mentyukov claimed that he managed to reach the U-2's altitude, and as he overtook it, the U-2 was upset by wake turbulence from the interceptor. This led to the spyplane's break-up and descent. This claim is highly suspect, and Mentyukov did not repeat it when interviewed again for the Air Fleet Herald article. The author prefers the more convincing evidence offered by the 'official' Red Star version cited in this footnote, Powers' own account, and other non-official Russian accounts which are cited here.

[10] Voronov and Tsisar articles, and Penkovsky debrief, as above, where the spy notes that "Powers would have escaped if he had flown 1 or 1.5 kilometers to the right of his flight(path)." Tsisar says that he fabricated his official report, as to why two of the battery's three missiles didn't fire. The story that they were prevented from firing because the antenna on the battery's radar cabin obstructed their line of fire, is not correct, he says. By reporting this as fact, he presumably hoped to draw attention away from the battery's slow reaction to the target, which caused the U-2 to be out-of-range by the time that the second and third missiles were ready to launch

[11] Powers book

[12] Zaloga book; Penkovsky debrief, NSA 315, p10; Mikhailov, interviewed by Indigo Films for The History Channel, 1999. Mikhailov estimated that the warhead exploded 20 meters behind the U-2

[13] Powers book

[14] Tsisar article

[15] Samsonov and Tsisar articles

[16] Boris Ayvazyan, interviewed by Indigo Films for "Mystery of the U-2", a film documentary for The History Channel, 1999. In this detailed account, Ayvazyan contradicts earlier-published accounts (Dokuchaev, Samsonov articles), that he saw Shugayev's missile(s) coming, and instigated his dive without instruction from the ground controllers.

[17] Samsonov article

[18] Pedlow/Welzenbach, p178

[19] Mikhailov and Orlov article, Powers book, Khrushchev book

[20] according to Beschloss p38, the NSA duty officer also sent word of the incident to his opposite numbers at State, FBI, USAF, Army and Navy, although Bissell had stipulated that such intelligence would be sent only to DPD, to preserve U-2 project security.

[21] Beschloss, p32-33

[22] In a telephone conversation with DCI John McCone, transcript published in Beschloss, p404, Eisenhower named Dulles and Bissell as the ones who informed him that the pilot would not survive. Dulles, the 'gentleman spy' was not a technical man, and may thus have believed this himself. Bissell was not technically trained either, but his reputation for assimilating such detail was awesome. He therefore had less excuse for misleading the President. Equally, as a former soldier, one might have expected Eisenhower to have queried the assertion.

[23] Mikhailov and Orlov article

[24] According to MiG-19 flight leader Ayvazyan, interviewed for the History Channel (see above), the truth is more complicated than that. As flight leader, he was supposed to keep his IFF turned on, while his wingman turned his off. But during their refueling at Koltsovo, the two MiG pilots swopped aircraft. After the pair took off to intercept the target, there was confusion as to which aircraft was 'squawking' the IFF code. Ayvazyan

turned his on, then off again, since it seemed (to him) that the ground controllers *were* seeing a squawk, from his wingman. Ayvazyan surmised that this caused the ground controllers to mistake him for the target and his wingman as the pair of MiGs in pursuit (as we have seen, Safronov fell some distance behind Ayvazyan, which made this mistake more likely). According to this theory, when the pair were told that the target was "only 5 km away", the 'target' was actually Ayvazyan's (non-squawking) aircraft. As he approached Koltsovo, Ayvazyan says that he did warn ground controllers that his IFF was turned off. But it seems that the missile controllers (in a different room, as noted already) were not informed. They continued to 'tag' Ayvazyan as the intruder and eventually Shugayev's battery was cleared to fire.

[25] Khrushchev book; Samsonov and Tsisar articles. The author has not been able to determine why the account of 14 missiles being fired, gained widespread currency. It seems to this author and his advisers, including a Russian air defense source, that the Samsonov article ("Eight Missiles for Powers") is the most detailed and reliable of the Russian accounts which have been published.

[26] The standing instructions to pilots before an overflight mission at this time were that they could "tell the full truth about their mission with the exception of certain technical specifications of the aircraft."

[27] Powers, p 305-6

[28] Many contemporary accounts claim that this was a fake, but this is incorrect, according to Automat photo-interpreter Bill Crimmins, interviewed by author. He recognized the airfield in Khrushchev's photo by the row of elderly Tu-4 Bull bombers lined up there. Marty Knutson's flight ten months earlier had flown over the same airfield, south of Sverdlovsk. The Soviets had quickly recovered and developed the B-camera film. However, they had not yet understood the camera's unconventional design, which required the film to be printed emulsion side-up. The photograph which was given to Khrushchev for display, had been printed back-to-front!

[29] Dick Leavitt, Ed Dixon notes and interviews

[30] According to later reports and various Soviet memoirs, Khrushchev did not expect Eisenhower to admit unequivocally that he had authorized the U-2 flights. After he did, though, it is said that the Soviet leader was unable to continue dealing with him, because of the loss of face this would have entailed

[31] reaction of Pakistan and Iran from Beschloss, p268

[32] Tamnes book. According to Beerli, interview, Evang was under such pressure, that DPD's Jim Cunningham even considered 'evacuating' him to the US and arranging a new career for him there.

[33] Robinson interview; Hansard 11 May 1960, col 398. The next day, suspicious MPs tabled more questions to the Prime Minister. Replying on MacMillan's behalf, Home Secretary 'Rab' Butler told them that "it has never been our practice to disclose either the nature or the scope of intelligence activities" (Hansard, 12 May 1960, cols 619-622)

[34] Brugioni, p47-48

[35] Memorandum of Discussion at the 445th Meeting of the National Security Council, 24 May 1960, as reproduced in Foreign Relations of the US (FRUS) 1958-60, Volume X, document 153

[36] According to Powers book, the delay was set for 70 seconds.

[37] memo of NSC discussion, FRUS volume as above

[38] Memorandum of Conversation, 26 May 1960, FRUS volume as above, document 154

[39] Executive Sessions of the Senate Foreign Relations Committee, Vol 12, SuDocs Ref Y4.F 76/2: Ex3/2/v.2

[40] In fact, these headlines were from one of the more informed reports, in the St Louis Post Dispatch on 7 June 1960, p10

[41] The quotes are from Kelly Johnson's diary, 24 June 1960. The report itself was SP-173, "Engineering Investigation of Airplane 360 Mission

Failure", 21 June 1960, declassified and made available to the author, 1999.
[42] White House Memo for the Record, 2 June 1960
[43] "Reconnaissance Flights 1956-57" AIR19/827 file in PRO (the file is mistitled: it actually covers 1960 as well)
[44] Hansard, 12 July 1960, col 1171
[45] AIR19/827 as above
[46] from the USAF Oral History program interview with General Twining, date unknown, p134-5. This may be the basis for the story in Rich and Janos, p158, that Twining had reviewed the last few overflight plans in advance and called Allen Dulles to personally urge changes
[47] author interview with Bill Burke
[48] Powers book, p151
[49] Jerrold Schecter and Peter Deriabin, "The Spy Who Saved the World", Charles Scribner's Sons, New York, 1992 p6-7. The author does not believe that as many as 14 missiles *were* actually fired - see footnote 26
[50] "The Trial of the U-2", Translation World Publishers, Chicago 1960
[51] True, The Man's Magazine, September 1960, p76
[52] S-13 details from Nikolay Yakubovich, "Turnover Spy" in Kryl'ya Rodiny, Moscow, October 1996

Chapter 11:
[1] CIA transcript of Penkovsky debriefs, 20 and 23 April 1961, declassified IRONBARK materials, made available by the National Security Archive, Washington DC, reference NSA286. The transcript shows that Penkovsky's knowledge of the Powers shootdown was not accurate in every detail, such as the number of missiles fired; his main informant was a Major General who headed the Political Directorate of the PVO.
[2] Board of Inquiry report, as above.
[3] Pedlow/Welzenbach, p185; Thomas Power, "The Man Who Kept The Secrets", Alfred Knopf, 1979, note 4 to Chapter 6, p379; CIA General Counsel memo 24 March 1962
[4] Pedlow/Welzenbach, p186. Ironically, none of the pilots was allowed to retain the Medal when it was first awarded. Two years later, this decision was rescinded for those pilots who were no longer flying for CIA. In fact, the first Medal given for retention in 1965 was the one given to Powers. Powers never did receive the USAF's Distinguished Flying Cross, which was awarded to all his contemporaries in the U-2 program in 1968. But in 1987, Leo Geary finally persuaded HQ USAF to correct the wrongdoing. The retired Brigadier-General spent ten years from 1956 to 1965 as the Pentagon's chief liaison officer for the CIA U-2 program. He presented the medal to Powers' second wife and widow, Sue, at a reunion of U-2 and A-12 veterans in Las Vegas.
[5] In "Oswald and the CIA", Carroll and Graf, 1995, author and conspiracy theorist John Newman devotes an entire chapter to a confused and inaccurate account of Det C operations, what Oswald may have known, what the CIA knew about what Oswald may have known, and so on.
[6] Victor Sheymov, "Tower of Secrets", Naval Institute Press, 1993, p137
[7] Burke, Beerli interviews
[8] Powers refers to the go-code being transmitted from Germany to Turkey by open telephone line, following problems in passing the signal by the usual radio means. CIA records show that the difficulty in transmission was between Turkey and Pakistan, and the solution was to use a different HF frequency (Pedlow/Welzenbach, p175-6)
[9] author's interviews with CIA 'commo' operators.
[10] Col Alex Orlov, remarks posted to the website of the CIA/Center for the Study of Intelligence, after the 1997 conference. In "The Samson Option", as above, p51 note, author Seymour Hersh asserts that the USSR *did* deduce when U-2 overflights were scheduled, from message traffic analysis. Hersh says that USAF communications technicians themselves monitored "the extensive and poorly masked preflight communications between Wash-

ington and the U-2 airfields." Hersh gives no sources for this information. Hersh further alleges that the USSR routinely grounded all their air traffic whenever a U-2 was overflying , to make the task of detection and tracking easier. This did indeed happen on 1 May 1960, but this author has not been able to verify that it happened on any other occasion
[11] author interview
[12] author interview with Jim Woods. On 17 May 1960, the US embassy in Kabul was informed by the Afghan foreign minister that during his wait at Peshawar, Powers had been "entertained socially by his Pakistani officer opposite numbers, who knew all about his mission." Since the foreign minister's source for this information was the USSR, this author believes this was disinformation, and gives it no credence
[13] author interview with Stan Beerli
[14] Pedlow/Welzenbach, p163, confirmed by U-2 Mission List 1956-68, declassified OSA document
[15] According to Mikhailov/Orlov (article), the PVO stood down a V-75 (SA-2) regiment at the prime target of Tyaratam for the holiday. Why would they have done that, if they knew for certain that a U-2 overflight was about to be launched?

Chapter 12:
[1] Cherbonneaux memoir
[2] memo for DDP 16 May 1960, CLJ Diary 24 June 1960
[3] DDR memo for DCI 26 March 1962
[4] memo for DDP 23 May 1960, memo to Branch Heads 27 May 1960
[5] memo for Acting DDP 26 May 1960, memo for record 30 June 1960
[6] Future of the Agency's U-2 Capability, version dated 7 July 1960 in White House Office of the Staff Secretary files; version dated 15 July 1960 in CREST 2000 release. The latter contains the (redacted) reference to plans for a detachment on Taiwan.
[7] CIA memos for Acting Chief, 21 July 1960 and 25 August 1960
[8] Cherbonneaux memoir, CIA memo to Col Geary 12 August 1960.
[9] Cherbonneaux memoir
[10] 4080SW history, July 1960
[11] Lockheed Change Proposal LAC-93 of 30 November 1960
[12] 4080SW history, July, August/September and October 1960
[13] in early September 1960, the wing also mounted a short deployment to Alaska in order to photograph Mt McKinley with the A-2 camera system
[14] unpublished paper, "A Perspective of the Joint Reconnaissance Center" by Col Tom Shepherd (retd) 1996; Gen Maxwell Taylor oral history, JFK Library, p32
[15] WRSP-IV Operations Plan 15-60 and various DPD cables 16 October 1960 onwards
[16] memo for Acting Chief DPD 7 December 1960; DPD memo 5 December 1960, November Commanders Report
[17] Marty Knutson interview
[18] DPD memos 2, 14, 15, 21, 28 November 1960 and 8 February 1961
[19] DPD Staff Meeting Minutes 15 November 1960

Chapter 13:
[1] Chinese names are presented here with surname (family name) first, followed by forenames. Most of the Chinese pilots adopted (or were given) a Christian name; when these are cited, the Christian name is given first, followed by the surname and Chinese forenames. In this book, the Wade-Giles system of romanisation is used, since this was commonly used during the period under discussion. Thus, the capital of the People's Republic of China is rendered as Peking, rather than Beijing.
[2] 4080th wing history, August-September 1958
[3] Phil Robertson interview
[4] OSA Chronology 12 December 1958

[5] "The Black Cat Squadron" by Mike Hua Hsi Chun, Air Power History, spring 2002, p6

[6] do, p7

[7] 4080th wing history, August 1959

[8] DPD memo 8 July 1959

[9] undated DDP memo shortly after 8 July 1959

[10] FRUS 1958-1960, Vol XIX, p572-4

[11] "U-2 Spyplane in Taiwan" memoir by Jude Pao

[12] "Piercing The Bamboo Curtain" by Lu Si Liang and Liu Wen Shiao, Wings of China, Taipei, 1996

[13] "Chiang Ching-Kuo Remembered" by Ray Cline, US Global Strategy Council, Washington DC, 1989, p86

[14] Pao, op.cit.

[15] DPD staff meeting minutes, 15 November 1960

[16] Pao, op.cit.

[17] Hua, op.cit.

[18] Pao, op.cit.

[19] DPD memos 1 and 7 February 1961

[20] DPD memo 6 March 1961

[21] Hua, op.cit, Lu and Liu, op.cit, DPD cable 22 March 1961

[22] FRUS 1961-63, Volume XXII, entry 39

[23] DPD memos 3 and 26 July 1961

[24] DPD cable 22 September 1961, FRUS 1961-63 Volume XXII

[25] DPD report 1 December 1961

[26] Cline, op.cit, and "The CIA Under Reagan, Bush & Casey" by Ray Cline, Acropolis Books, 1981, p201

[27] "Nuclear Weapons Development in China" by Lewis Frank, Bulletin of the Atomic Scientists, January 1966

[28] NPIC report R-36/62 on the SCT Missile Center

[29] NIS 39A Communist China Air Forces, January 1962

[30] Pao op.cit;, MCI and IPIR for GRC-100

[31] Pao op.cit., Cline op.cit

[32] DPD cable 15 January 1962, HQ PACAF Ops Plan 15 January 1962

[33] DPD cables 1 and 2 February 1962, Cherbonneaux memoir; Bob Ericson interview

[34] MCI and IPIR for GRC-102; NIE 13-2-62

[35] MCI and IPIR for GRC-104 and GRC-106, det H report to DPD 4 April 1962, Cherbonneaux memoir

[36] Det H report to DPD 4 April and 2 May 1962; DPD memo 8 May 1962,

[37] MCI and IPIR for GRC-112 and 113, Cherbonneaux memoir

[38] FRUS Volume XXIII, doc 122

[39] DPD memo 25 June 1962, Dave Ray, Ed Dixon interviews

[40] various DPD cables early June, MCI and IPIR for GRC-117/119/120/123, COMOR memo for USIB 20 August 1962

[41] Hua, op.cit.

[42] "Fight to Protect the Motherland's Airspace" by Lt Gen Lin Hu, PLAAF retd., Beijing 2001, Part 3

[43] DPD cable 6 September 1962; ONE memo for DCI 27 July 1961; "The Generalissimo's Son" by Jay Taylor, Harvard University Press, 2000, p265

[44] Lin, op.cit; IPIR for GRC-126

[45] Lin, op.cit.

Chapter 14:

[1] Cherbonneaux memoir; Commanders report, undated, DPD document

[2] According to Jim Cherbonneaux, memoir, contrails were still produced on the later, successful missions, but contrary to instructions he and his fellow pilots decided not to abort, otherwise no photos would ever have been obtained on this deployment!

[3] Various MCIs and OXYs for Missions 3018 thru 3026

[4] ELINT report, Mission 3025

[5] Jim Barnes interview

[6] Chernonneaux memoir, various DPD memos

[7] MCI Mission 3035

[8] Cherbonneaux memoir

[9] DPD memos 23 March, 12 June, 21 August, 30 August, 11 October and 18 December 1961 and cable 6 December 1961

[10] DPD memo 29 November 1961

[11] JACKSON detachment reports Sep/Oct 1961

[12] DPD memos 30 August 1960, 22 September 1961

[13] CLJ Diary October 1960 and April 1961, DPD Memo 30 January 1961

[14] DPD memos 15 June and 23 October 1961

[15] "Eyeball to Eyeball" by Dino Brugioni, Random House, 1991, p74

[16] DPD memo 24 July 1961

[17] Pedlow/Welzenbach, p222, OSA Chronology

[18] 4080th wing histories.

[19] "Moscow's Biggest Bomb" by Viktor Adamsky and Yuri Smirnov, CWIHP Bulletin No 4

[20] 4080 Wing histories for 1961; Haupt, Brown interviews

[21] Vance Mitchell interview

[22] Draft memo to Special Assistant to the President for National Security Affairs

[23] NIE 11/8/1-61, amplified by CIA history of Allen Dulles as DCI, Vol V, pages 132 onwards

[24] Memo of Conference with President Kennedy, 20 September, item 44 in in FRUS 1961-1963, Volume VIII

[25] CLJ Diary, 21 September 1961

[26] CLJ Diary, 14 September 1961, DPD memo from Johnson, 25 September 1961

[27] DPD memo 30 August 1960

[28] CLJ Diary, 21 September 1961

[29] Clancey, Powell interviews

[30] COMOR memo for USIB 25 September 1961

[31] 4080th wing history, September 1961

[32] DPD memo 28 September, DDP memo undated, early October?

[33] USIB memo for The Special Group, 5 October 1961

Chapter 15:

[1] "The Wizards of Langley" by Jeffrey Richelson, Westview Press 2001, p40; "Science & Technology: Origins of a Directorate" by Donald Welzenbach, from Studies in Intelligence. 4080th wing history, January 1962

[2] DPD undated memo "Problems on GF62-01"; Air Force Oral History interview with Ellsworth Powell in 1996.

[3] 4080th wing history; McIlmoyle interview

[4] 4080th wing history; DDR memo for DCI 21 March 1962

[5] 4080th wing history; pilot interviews

[6] 4080th wing history for January 1962; Stratton interview

[7] from press cuttings in the AFFTC Edwards History Office

[8] DPD memo 14 March 1962, 4080SW History August 1962

[9] "The Oxcart Story" by John Parangosky, written for Studies in Intelligence, Vol 26, No 2, summer 1982 under the pseudonym Thomas P. McInich.

[10] Undated 1962 description "Office of Deputy Director (Research)"

[11] DPD memo 21 June 1962, OSI memo 17 January 1962

[12] DPD memo 3 April 1962

[13] Inspector General's Survey of Air Activities, February 1962, part-contained within OSA cable 29 January 1969

[14] DPD memos, 19 February 1962 and 25 June 1962; 4080SW monthly histories

Chapter 16:

[1] Brugioni, op.cit, p79-80

[2] OSA cable 21 September 1962

[3] as quoted by Brugioni, op.cit., p88

[4] Brugioni, op.cit., p67-70

[5] DPD memo 17 April 1962

[6] "One Hell of a Gamble" by Aleksander Fursenko and Timothy Naftali, W.W.Norton & Co, 1997, p191; NSA Cuban Missile Crisis collection, 22 June 1962

[7] for the sake of clarity, the Western reporting nomenclature for Soviet military equipment is used in this chapter. The Soviet designation for the SS-4 was R-12, and for the SS-5 was R-14. The SA-2 SAM system was S-75 V750K.

[8] "Soviet Deception in the Cuba Missile Crisis" by James Hansen, Studies in Intelligence, 2002

[9] Fursenko and Naftali, op.cit., p139, 167,188; "The Hot Front of the Cold War" by Col Orlov, Geopolitical Security No2, 1994, Moscow, p26

[10] according to "The Missiles in Cuba: The Role of SAC Intelligence" by Capt Sanders Laubenthal, SAC Project Warrior Study, May 1984, photo-interpreters at SAC Offutt AFB did discern scars on thre ground character-istic of preparations for an SA-2 site, by now.

[11] "Cratology Pays Off" by Thaxter Goodell, Studies in Intelligence, Vol 8, Fall 1964

[12] Laubenthal, op.cit., p9, Goodell, op.cit. p6

[13] OSA memos for Acting DCI, 4 September 1962, and for DCI 27 September 1962, and OSA cables

[14] mission map in Pedlow/Welzenbach, p 202

[15] "The San Cristobel Trapezoid" by John Hughes with A Denis Clift, Studies in Intelligence, Winter 1992; John McCone oral history in JFK Library

[16] Memo for DCI 27 February 1963

[17] Bob Spencer interview; X interview

[18] OSA memo 10 September 1962

[19] FRUS Volume X, Cuba 1961-62, item 421; Brugioni p136-8

[20] according to Brugioni, p151-3, U-2 mission planners were now con-fused as to exactly what type of mission, peripheral or penetrating, had been approved by higher authority. This is supported by a DDR memo on 10 September, but not reflected in OSA and other CIA documents declas-sified since Brugioni's book was published. Incidentally, these documents do refute Brugioni's thesis that the political caution advocated by Bundy and Rusk was the sole reason why so little U-2 coverage of Cuba was obtained in September and early October.

[21] Various OSA cables September 1962

[22] OSA report undated "CIA Cuban Overflights"

[23] SNIE 85-3-62

[24] Pedlow/Welzenbach, p205; Brugioni, p121-2, OSA report undated "CIA Cuban Overflights"
The "coastal defence missile" was the SSC-2 Samlet (Soviet designation S-2 Sopka). US intelligence was previously only aware of a convention-ally-armed version of this cruise missile, used for coastal defence. In fact, there was also a nuclear-armed version (Soviet designation FKR-1 Me-teor) used as a tactical surface-surface missile and more of these (80) were deployed to Cuba than the former (32). This did not become clear until 1994 (correspondence from Steven Zaloga and Raymond Garthoff to CWIHP Bulletin, Issue 12/13)

[25] Hughes op.cit, p45; Laubenthal, op.cit, p16. Brugioni, p165, insists that there were no SAMs deployed in a so-called trapezoidal pattern near San Cristobal.

[26] DCI memo 28 February 1963

[27] Brugioni, p155; Laubenthal, p16

[28] Joe Jackson and Ellswoth Powell oral history interviews, USAF History Program

[29] Brugioni, p157, Various OSA cables 1-8 October 1962

[30] Pedlow/Welzenbach, p206, various OSA cables.

[31] Various OSA cables, OSA memo 11 October

[32] Pedlow/Welzenbach, p206-7. However, Brugioni (p166) says that the COMOR recommendation was for three more north-south missions, if the first one was successful.

[33] Jack Ledford interview; Pedlow/Welzenbach, p207

[34] Pedlow/Welzenbach p207-9, OSA report undated "CIA Cuban Over-flights", OSA cable 12 October, Ellsworth Powell oral history interview, USAF History program, 1966, Laubenthal p13, Don Songer interview

[35] Laubenthal p17, Powell interview

[36] Laubenthal, p18

[37] Mission 3101 recital; Brugioni p182-6

[38] NSA Cuban Missile Crisis collection

[39] Brugioni p191-9

[40] Brugioni p199-217

[41] Brugioni, p218-232

[42] OSA memo 29 October 1962

[43] Laubenthal p26

[44] Laubenthal p26, 4080 SW history September & October 1962, Brugioni p303

[45] Brugioni, p234-5 and p274, Cherbonneaux memoir; author interview with Tony Martinez

[46] Laubenthal p32; Martinez interview

[47] SNIE 11-18-62; Brugioni p281

[48] Cherbonneaux memoir

[49] Gen Anatoli Gribkov and Gen William Smith, "Operation Anadyr", Edi-tion Q, 1994, p52 & 57

[50] Gribkov & Smith, p62; "The SAM-2 versus the Lockheed U-2" in Krasnaya Zvezda, 24 November 1990 (translation); CIA Daily Summary "The Situation in Cuba" 27 October 1962

[51] author interview with Jerry McIlmoyle. This incident of SAM firing has not been reported in Soviet sources.

[52] Gribkov & Smith, p66

[53] Tony Martinez interview

[54] Buddy Brown interview; Martinez interview

[55] Krasnaya Zvezdda article; message, Malinovsky to Khrushchev 28 Oc-tober 1962, from CWIHP website. The story that Fidel Castro himself was visiting the SAM site as it engaged the U-2, and actually ordered the mis-siles fired himself, is a complete fiction.

[56] Martinez interview; letter to author from K.P.Kilpatrick

[57] Krasnaya Zvezdda article, Gribkov & Smith p66-67

[58] Kilpatrick; NSA Cuban Misile Crisis collection; Brugioni p461

[59] Excom transcript 27 October 1962 in JFK Library, Brugioni p463-4

[60] "Soviet Union Overflight – Accidental" unpublished memoir by Chuck Maultsby

[61] as quoted by Robert Kennedy, "Thirteen Days", p210

[62] Excom transcript; 4080SRW history October 1962

Chapter 17:

[1] Brugioni p488-491

[2] Brugioni, p492-511, DDR memo 31 October 1962. Brugioni says that SecDef Macnamara vetoed the resumption of U-2 flights at this stage

[3] CIA Daily Summary 28 October

[4] Kern interview; Spencer interview

[5] Author correspondence with Tony Martinez, Chuck Kern and Jerry McIlmoyle

[6] from Russian Presidential Archives, as reproduced in CWIHP Bulletin 14/15, Document 8

7 Kern corr, CIA Daily Summary 5 & 6 November

8 Kern corr

9 OSA cable 8 October 1962, OSA memo 12 October 1962

10 OEL memo 25 September 1962, OSA memo 19 November 1962, "The Saga of the 2.3 FT3 Box" unpublished paper by Ed Ward, Sanders Associates

11 CLJ diary 25 October 1962, OSA memo 1 November 1962, draft DDR memo 2 November 1962, OSA memo 5 November 1962

12 CLJ diary 5 November 1962, Lockheed U-2 Service Bulletins 681 and 691

13 OSA JACKSON detachment report 3 December 1962

14 "New Evidence on the Cuban Missile Crisis" by Raymond Garthoff, CWIHP Bulletin 11

Chapter 18:

1 OSA memo 30 January 1963

2 Hua, p10

3 USIB memo 12 December 1962, MCI for GRC-133

4 MCIs and MCPs for missions GRC-128/134/135/136, OSA cable 27 December 1962, Hua letter

5 Mission 3206 analysis

6 Robert McMahon, "The Cold War on the Periphery", Columbia University Press 1994, p272-287

7 X interview

8 Joe Giraudo interview

9 OSA memo 8 February 1963; MCIs and MCPs for Missions 3202/3203/3205

10 OSA cable 10 January 1963, OSA memo 12 December 1962; Shekhar Gupta, "Charbatia: Secret Base" in India Today, 31 December 1983, p16

11 DDR memo 23 January 1963, OSA memo 24 January 1963OSA memos

12 CLJ diary February 1963, OSA memo 6 February 1963

13 OSA memos 6 and 19 February 1963

14 CLJ Diary 20 March 1963

15 OSA memos 6 February and 4 March 1963

16 4080SW history February 1963, Ed Dixon tape

17 OSA memos 19 and 26 February 1963, 5 June 1963

18 Hua, p10, Lin translation para 10, Wang interview

19 FRUS 1961-63 Vol XXII item 168, OSA memo 10 April 1963

20 NPIC memo 28 March 1963

21 SNIE 13-2-63 of 24 July 1963

22 Hua p11, Lin para 10

23 USIB memo "Chinese Communist Ground Threat Against India from Tibet and Sinkiang" 17 April 1963

24 4080SW history May 1963; OSA cable 2 May 1963

25 FRUS 1961-63 Volume XI, item 389, 4080th wing history June/July 1963

26 OSA memo 24 June 1963

27 4080th wing history June/July 1963

28 4080th wing history, August 1963, Bill Gerber interview

29 4080th wing history August, September 1963

30 various OSA cables, plus MCI for Mission GRC-169

31 OSA memo 26 August 1963

32 Slip Slater interview

33 Lin translation, para 12

34 OSA memo 16 October 1963

35 OSA cable re GRC-176 25 September 1963

36 OSA activity report 1 October 1963

37 Lin translation, para 12

38 Lin translation, paras 15-16

39 OSA memo 11 February 1963, LAC U-2 Service Bulletin 713

40 Itek summary notes; OSA memos 26 April, 21 May, 15 and 20 August 1963

41 OSA memos 3, 19 and 29 October 1963

42 OSA memos 5 and 23 December 1963

43 DDR and DepSecDef memos 18 November 1963

Chapter 19:

1 CLJ Diary June 1957, CIA document "U-2 Aircraft Carrier Operation" December 1964

2 Ledford interview

3 Johnson letter to Scoville 24 April 1963

4 CIA document

5 RADM Martin Carmody, "The U-2 Carrier Caper" in Foundation, the magazine of the National Museum of Naval Aviation, Spring 1991, p32

6 OSA memos 26 November and 18 December 1963, CLJ Diary 9 August 1963 and January 1964

7 Cherbonneaux memoir

8 Cherbonneuax memoir

9 OSA memo 17 February 1964, CLJ Diary 12 May 1964

10 Bill Gregory interview, OSA memos 26 October and 18 November 1964

11 OSA Directive 7 February 1966; pilot interviews

12 OSA cables 27 April and 5 May 1965

13 CLJ Diary 26 April 1965

14 X memoir, Schumacher interview

15 CLJ Diary March 1966

16 various OSA cables late May 1967

17 do

18 Hall interview, various OSA cables late May/early June 1967

19 do

20 Various OSA cables early June 1967, X interview, Losey interview

Chapter 20:

1 CIA Preliminary Evaluation of Missions 6070/6071, 6 January 1964

2 4080 SW history, February 1964, Stratton. McIlmoyle interviews

3 OSA memo for DCI 18 March 1964

4 OSA memo 21 April 1964

5 Lt Col George Bennett, "A Study of the Use of the RB-57 and U-2 Aircraft in Southeast Asia, 1965-167", Air War College Research Report N0 3566, April 1968

6 SNIE 85-2-64

7 4080SRW history Jul-Sep1964

Chapter 21:

1 4080 SRW history December 1963/January 1964

2 CLJ Diary 18 February and July 1964

3 Mission C024C documents

4 OSA memo 4 December 1963, Itek unpublished history

5 OSA trip report, 20 July 1964

6 OSA cable 14 May 1964; Jerry Losey interview

7 OSA cable 24 May 1964; Ericson interview

8 OSA cables 25 May

9 A year later, however, a solution was found, by adding an Engine Pressure Ratio (EPR) gauge and devising an EPR schedule for climb and descent, instead of EGT. Because of the Reynolds Number effect, it was deduced that on a very cold day, a pilot could retard the throttle to a lower EGT setting, and yet the engine would still produce the same amount of thrust.

10 Lin translation, para 18

11 OSA cables for mission C184C, Hua p12

12 CLJ diary 7 July 1964

[13] William Wagner, "Lightning Bugs and other Reconnaissance Drones", Aero Publishers, 1982, p54-61

[14] 4080 SRW history Jul-Sep and Oct-Nov 1964

[15] FRUS Volume XXX, China 1964-68, item 50; SNIE 13-4-64 of 26 August 1964

[16] FRUS as above, item 55

[17] Mission C224C documents, Hua p12, Lin translation para 19

[18] OSA cable 11 September 1964

[19] R.E.Lawrence and Harry Woo, "Infrared Imagery in Overhead Reconnaissance", CIA Studies in Intelligence, Summer 1967

[20] Mission C284C cables, X memoir

[21] Lin translation, para 19

[22] Lin translation, para 19

[23] Mission C304C cables, X memoir

[24] Lin translation, para 20

[25] NIE 13-2-65 p11

[26] OSA cables 10, 15, 16 December 1964, various MCI, IPIR etc Missions T314A/T324A/T344A, OSA report 8 January 1965; Ericson interview

[27] Donoghue memoir

[28] Mission C374C cables

[29] Mission C015C cables, Lawrence & Woo, p29

[30] Mission C025C cables, memos

[31] Chang interview, Hua p13

[32] Lin translation paras 21/22

[33] Chang interview, Hua p13

Chapter 22:
[1] OSA memo 30 August 1963

[2] OSA memo 26 April 1965, Itek history

[3] Donoghue memoir

[4] Donoghue memoir

[5] OSA cables 19 March and 16 April 1965, CLJ Diary 16 March and 12 May 1965

[6] CLJ diary 16 March 1965

[7] article in CWIHP Bulletin 6-7, p36

[8] OSA cable 17 May 1965, Missions C325C, C405C, C425C, C475C, C495C data

[9] Donoghue memoir, OSA memos 20 December 1965

[10] OSA memo 30 December 1965

[11] mission C185C and C355C cables; The Gioi Publishers, "The 30-Year War 1945-1075", Hanoi, April 2001, Vol II, p157

[12] Wagner, p93-96

[13] Martinez interview

[14] OSA memos 2 February and 13 April 1966

[15] Wagner, p101-102

[16] Bennett; Ward Graham, letter to Air Force magazine, January 1999, Spencer interview

[17] USIB memo 25 March 1966, Pedlow/Welzenbach

[18] mission C126C data

[19] OSA report, May 1966; Chuang interview

[20] OSA report May 1966; OSA memos 2 November 1965 and 21 April 1966

[21] NIE 13-2-66, p11; Lin translation, para 25

[22] CIA Intel memo SC 09518/66; C076C mission data

[23] Lockheed Service Bulletins 1100/1116/1138

[24] various OSA cables June/July 1966

[25] various OSA cables Feb/Mar 1966

[26] Chuang interview, OSA summary 6 September 1966

[27] OSA cable 26 August 1966

[28] OSA memo 31 August 1966

[29] Kern, Martinez interviews

Chapter 23:
[1] CLJ Diary 31 October 1963

[2] CLJ Diary 6 February and April 1964

[3] CLJ Diary 19 May 1964, Richelson p96

[4] NRO memo 22 March 1965, OSA Chronology 21 June 1965

[5] NRO memo 17 August 1965

[6] CLJ Diary June to October 1965

[7] Ben Koziol, "The U-2 Aircraft Engine" at The U-2 History Symposium, CSI, September 1998

[8] CLJ Diary 12 October 1965

[9] CLJ Diary 18 January 1966

[10] do, OSA memo 4 February 1966, Cherbonneaux memoir

[11] CLJ U-2R Log 17 May 1966

[12] Cherbonneaux memoir, CLJ U-2R log 15 August 1967

[13] NRO memo 1 September 1966, OSI memo 22 March 1967, CLJ U-2R Log 9 February 1966 and 18 January 1967

[14] OSA memo 2 November 1966

[15] Lockheed Report SP-1125

[16] Bob Anderson interview

[17] CLJ U-2R Log 24 October 1966

[18] OSA memo 2 December 1966

[19] CLJ U-2R Log 17 March, 19 April 1967, and June 1967

[20] CLJ U-2R Log 28 August 1967

[21] OSA memo 7 March 1968, OSA summary 4 April 1968 and 19 July 1968

[22] OSA summary 19 July 1968, PFIAB sumbission 30 June 1968

[23] Lockheed U2R Report SP3051; OSA working paper 1969

[24] Cherbonneaux memoir

[25] NIE 11-3-67, p10, 27

[26] undated CIA memo from A/D/DCI/NIPE; Welzenbach/Pedlow p253

[27] briefing guide for OL-19, undated

[28] OSA memo 14 October 1968; OSA summary 16 January 1969; OSA memo 28 January 1970

[29] History of SAC Reconnaissance Operations, FY72, p61

Chapter 24:
[1] NIS39A Communist China Armed Forces, September 1968, Fig 23

[2] SNIE 13-8-66 of 3 November 1966

[3] Lin translation, para 24. NPIC cable 5 May 1967

[4] Wheelon interview; X interview

[5] OSA memo 3 May 1966; X interview, Knutson interview

[6] OSA summary 6 December 1966

[7] OSA memo 2 November 1966

[8] FRUS Volume XXX, China 1964-1968, item 222

[9] OSA memo 29 December 1966; Mission C216C data

[10] OSA memo 3 February 1967; DST memo undated, Duckett to DCI

[11] OSA memo 27 January 1967

[12] various OSA cables January-March 1967, OSA memo 2 February, OSA summary 9 February

[13] OSA cable 17 and 24 February 1967, OSA summary for February

[14] United States-Chinese "Project Razor" Agreement, dated 17 March 1967

[15] Missions C117C, C147C and C157C data

[16] OSA cable 20 March 1967

[17] various OSA cables April 1967

[18] OSA cable 5 May 1967

[19] various OSA cables Mission C167C May 1967, Chuang interview

[20] Chuang interview

[21] Mission C167C cables; Chuang interview

[22] OSA cable 5 May 1967

[23] X interview; Chuang interview

[24] ORD cables 14 and 17 May 1967; NIE 13-2-66, 1 July 1966

[25] OSA cables 23 June, 6, 14 July 1966

[26] various OSA cables, inc Mission C287C, early August 1966

[27] do

[28] do

[29] OSA cable 31 August 1967

[30] Lin translation, para 26. Curiously, the compilers of a subsequent intelligence assessment of the Chinese air defense system, did not list the site that attacked Billy on their maps of known SA-2 deployments (NIS39A, Communist China Armed Forces, Air Forces, September 1968)

[31] OSA cable 31 August 1967

[32] information displayed at ROCAF Museum, Kang Shan AB

[33] Lin translation, para 27

[34] According to Lin translation, para26, the U-2 ECM system succeeded in defeating the guidance radar of only one of the sites that attacked the aircraft. At the other site, the "anti-jamming circuit" worked and three missiles were launched in the expectation of success. Then, however, "the operator reached for the wrong switch and accidentally turned off the electric power. All of the missiles were out of control and self-destructed."

[35] Lin translation, para 28; OSA cable and memo 8 September

[36] COMIREX memo to DCI 10 March 1969

Chapter 25:

[1] CLJ Diary 8 February 1967, OSA memo 15 May 1969

[2] CLJ Diary 20 September 1966 and 19 October 1967; OSA memo 30 October 1967, OSA cable 6 November 1967

[3] SAC Reconnaissance History January 1968-June 1971, p69; Ray Haupt interview

[4] OSA memo 7 November 1968

[5] OSA cable 5 July 1968

[6] OSA cable 15 January 1969

[7] Lockheed SB1190, Mission C228C data, OSA memo 1 November 1968, OSA Review 3Q,1969

[8] Mission C259C data

[9] Birkett interview

[10] JCS memo for NRO and DIA, 26 April 1969

[11] NRO memo 29 April 1969

[12] Jim Terry interview

[13] OSA memos 9 September 1968, 16 November 1968

[14] OSA memo 20 February 1968

[15] OSA memos 7 March and 9 April 1968

[16] OSA Chronology

[17] X interview

[18] OSA memo 3 April 1969, OSA cable 11 April 1969

[19] OSA memos 3 April 1969 and 19 May 1969

[20] Dale Weaver info via John Dale

[21] Lockheed report SP-1528

[22] Det G activity report November 1969

[23] OSA memo for DCI 28 November 1969

[24] OSA memo 2 June 1970

[25] NRO memo 1 July 1971; DepSecDef memo 8 December 1969; 303 Cttee Minutes 20 December 1969; NSC memo for President 29 December 1969; OSA cable 25 December 1969

[26] Henry Kissinger, "The White House Years", Little, Brown 1979, Chapter XVI

[27] do

[28] Pedlow/Welzenbach, p256

[29] do; Birkett interview

[30] Ericson interview

[31] Knutson interview; X interview

[32] X interview, Pedlow/Welzenbach p256

[33] Kissinger, Chapter XII

[34] Pedlow/Welzenbach p253

[35] Marty Knutson interview

[36] OSA Report to PFIAB 1 July 1971, X interview, Knutson interview

[37] NROI memo 1 July 1971

Chapter 26:

[1] "A History of SAC Reconnaissance Operations FY1972," HQ SAC, p33

[2] Lightning Bugs, p166-171

[3] Lightning Bugs, p170; John Mabey interview

[4] "A Brief History of the Air Intelligence Agency", HQ AIA, p21

[5] AIA History, p23; Mark Clodfelter, "The Limits of Air Power", The Free Press, 1989, p165

[6] SAC History, FY1972, p33; FY73 p14

[7] SAC History, FY1973, p57, 100th Wing History, Jan-Mar1973

[8] SAC History, FY1973, p44

[9] Clodfelter, p188-198

[10] SAC History, FY1974, p61

[11] SAC History, FY1974, p62

[12] SAC History, FY1975, p43

[13] SAC History, FY1976, Appendix II

[14] SAC History Jul75-Dec76, p129

[15] SAC History, FY1972, p77-78; CLJ Diary 28 March 1972, NRO memo 25 July 1972

[16] SAC History, FY1973, p93; Service Bulletins 1340 to 1474

[17] SAC History, FY1973, p94

[18] ALSS IOT&E Final Report, USAF TAWC, Eglin AFB, December 1973

[19] ALSS Dem/Val Final Report, USAF TAWC, Eglin AFB, February 1976

Chapter 27:

[1] Mission C011C, C031C data

[2] Hua, p17; CIA memo 8 January 1970

[3] DDI memo 26 March 1971

[4] OSA cable 11 June 1971, ROC U-2 Mission Lists; OSA memos 22 June and 1 July 1971

[5] OSA cable 19 October 1971

[6] Al Pinkham interview

[7] Itek briefing sheet

[8] undated NRO memos

[9] OSA cable 16 March 1973

[10] ROC U-2 mission lists; OSA cable 13 March 1973

[11] OSA cable 16 March 1973, OSA summaries 11 April 1973, 15 October 1973; Dave Young interview

[12] NRO memos 31 July 1973, 24 May 1974, Pedlow/Welzenbach, p257

[13] Patrick Tyler, "A Great Wall", The Century Foundation, New York, 1999, p167

[14] OSA summary, 14 January 1974; Pedlow/Welzenbach, p256

[15] SAC History, FY1974, p30; OSA cable 14 May 1974

[16] SAC History, FY1975, p59-61

[17] OSA cables 1 March, 10 May and 20 June 1974

[18] Jerry West interview; Phil Daisher interview

Chapter 28:

[1] George Stimson, "Introduction to Airborne Radar", Hughes Aircraft Company, 1983, p524

[2] 100th SRW wing histories 1973; Dave Patten interview

[3] do

[4] interview, Fred Carment

[5] Barry Miller, "Lockheed to Flight Test U-2 for Navy Surveillance Role", AWST 29 January 1973, p17-18

[6] Carment interview

[7] Miller article, CLJ diary June 1973, NRO undated memo

[8] 100SRW histories 1973

[9] undated NRO memos

[10] Carment interviw

[11] Ben Rich and Leo Janos, "Skunk Works", p9-11

[12] Bob Anderson interview

Chapter 29:

[1] X interview

[2] SAC History, 1978-1980, p196-205

[3] SAC History, 1Jan-31Dec 1977, p119-121

[4] SAC History, 1978-1980, p187-191

[5] SAC Histories, FY1976, p150; Jul75-Dec76, p149; and 1978-1980 p187; Doyle Krumrey interview

[6] SAC History 1Jan-31Dec1977, p100

[7] SAC History 1978-1980, p 211-215

[8] Lowell Taylor interview

[9] do, p215-218

[10] do, p229

Chapter 30:

[1] Quoted in Robert Futrell, "Ideas, Concepts, Doctrines. Basic Thinking in the USAF 1961-1984" Vol II, Air University Press, 1989, p545

[2] Futrell, p545

[3] Aerospace Daily, 28 June 1978, p306

[4] Rich & Janos, p15; AW&ST 28 August 1978, p16

[5] SAC History 1978-1980, p68

[6] ALSS Dem/Val Final Report, USAF TAWC, Eglin AFB, February 1976

Chapter 31:

[1] Dave Young interview

[2] 17RW unclassified history summary; Bob Ray interview

[3] Bob Anderson interview, Bill Walker interview; Steve Brown interview

[4] do

[5] Quoted in Paul Crickmore, "Lockheed SR-71 – The Secret Missions Exposed", Osprey, 1993, p178

[6] Bob Anderson interview

Chapter 32:

[1] Coy Cross, "The Dragon Lady Meets The Challenge", 9RW, 1996, Chapter 2

[2] Cross, Chapter 3; Dave Wilton, "The U-2 in the United Kingdom", British Aviation Research Group, 1996

[3] Cross, Chapter 4

[4] X interview

[5] Wilton

[6] Cross, Chapter 5

[7] do; X interview

[8] Cross, Chapter 6

[9] Cross, Chapters 6 and 7

[10] "Intelligence Successes and failures in Operations Desert Shield/Storm", US Congress 71-430 CC, 1993, p20

[11] Cross, Chapter 7

[12] quote via Mike Rip

Chapter 33:

[1] AWST 19 August 1991, p61

[2] Peter Boyer, "Scott Ritter's Private War", The New Yorker, 9 November 1998

[3] AWST article 4 June 1990, p23

[4] AWST article 4 June 1990, p23

[5] Mitchell speech to Blackbirds Association reunion, Reno, May 1995

[6] letter to Defense News, 23 October 1995

[7] 5th RS history from www.osan.af.mil

[8] "Jeffrey Richelson, "High Flying Spies", Bulletin of the Atomic Scientists, Sep/Oct 1996

[9] WR-ALC History FY 1997, Chapter 3

[10] do

[11] U-2 GrayBeard Panel, SAIC, 20 November 1997. The panel comprised Maj Gen Pat Halloran (retd), Lt Col Ken Broda (retd), Maj Chris Wheatly, Maj Stormy Boudreaux, CMSgt Steve Earlich, and CMSgt Fred Carmody

[12] Accident Report, via Gavin Payne

[13] GrayBeard Panel, section 4.8

[14] 31st AEW press release; Maj Gen Glen Schaeffer, remarks, 22 February 2001

[15] Skunk Works Star, 30 September 1999;

[16] letter from USAFE to Lockheed Martin, 12 August 1999

[17] Bg Gen Kevin Chilton briefing to DLA Reunion, Reno, May 2000

[18] Royal International Air Tattoo, UK, July 1998

[19] WR-ALC History FY1999, Chapter 3

[20] Bob Chiota interview

Chapter 34:

[1] UNMOVIC report S/2003/232

[2] presentation and remarks at IQPC Conference, London, 26 March 2004

[3] PE0305202F RDT&E Schedule, February 2004

[4] AWST 8 March 1999, p64

[5] AFRL "A New Sensor Suite for an Old Lady", October 2004

[6] Space Sentinel, Beale AFB, 30 September 1994

Chapter 35:

[1] Undated DPD memo for DCI late December 1961 or early January 1962; USAF report on accident at RAF Fairford, 29 August 1995

[2] DPD memo as above

[3] Tony Bevacqua interview

[4] 4080th SRW history, February 1958; author interviews

[5] as above

[6] DPD memo as above; Richard Bissell with Jonathan Lewis, "Reflections of a Cold War Warrior" p108; Marty Knutson interview

[7] 4080th SRW history, February 1958; DPS memo 18 October 1957

[8] DPS memo 18 October 1957

[9] DPD memo as above; Bob Ericson interview

[10] DPD memo as above; DPD memo 3 January 1962

[11] 4080th SRW history, July and August-September 1958; DPS memos 18 July and 18 August 1958

[12] Summary of meeting at HQ USAF, 6 August 1957, found in DPD archives

[13] 4080th SRW history, August-September 1958

[14] Jim Cherbonneaux memoir

[15] Jim Cherbonneaux memoir

[16] Tucson newspaper article, 19 September 1964; Tony Bevacqua letter to authot

[17] Bob Schumacher interview

[18] CLJ Diary 17 October 1966

[19] OSA summaries 3 December 1965 and 3 January 1966; OSA memo 20 December 1965

[20] Accident Report, in OSA archives; OSA cable 24 March 1966

[21] OSA cable 20 June 1967

[22] OSA memo 5 February 1970

[23] information from George Worley; Ray Haupt intertview

[24] CLJ Diary 19 may and 7 June 1972; George Worley info

[25] 100th SRW history, Jan-Mar1973

[26] infor from Don White

Chapter 36:

[1] OSA cables 13 November 1968, 14 January 1969

[2] OSA cable 18 December 1968

[3] OSA cable 1 December 1970

[4] Dave Young interview

[5] 17RW CC nomination letter

[6] Combat Crew magazine, June 1987; Bruce Jinneman interview

[7] Combat Crew magazine, 1989

[8] Combat Crew magazine

[9] Combat Crew magazine

Chapter 37:

[1] DPS memo 25 October 1956

[2] CLJ Diary 19 June 1955

[3] N.W.Watkins, "The MIDAS Project", Journal of the British Interplanetary Society, Vol 50, 1997

[4] Lockheed Report SP-112

[5] Watkins, p218

[6] CLJ Diary 13-14 November 1958

[7] Summary of meeting at HQ USAF, 6 August 1957, found in DPS archives

[8] Bill Frazier interview

[9] SP-112

[10] Report of the PSAC Early Warning Panel, 13 March 1959, found at DDEL

[11] "Edwards Becomes Space Recovery Center", Aviation Week & Space Technology, 25 September 1961

[12] Bill Frazier interview

[13] Jim Eastlund interview

[14] Walt Kesheen Jr, "The U-2 Today Scores..." in Western Aviation Missiles and Space, February 1961; AWST article op cit

[15] AWST article, 11 November 1963, p78-79; History of the AFFTC 1Jan-30Jun1964, p61

[16] Crooks, Hoblit, Mitchell et al, "Project HiCat", Air Force Flight Dynamics Laboratory (AFFDL) technical report 68-127, November 1968

[17] Major Barkley Sprague, "Evolution of the MIDAS", Air University Report 85-2580 ; History of the AFFTC 1Jan-30Jun1968 p98 and 1Jul-31Dec1968 p135

Chapter 38:

[1] Dino Brugioni and Robert McCort, "Arthur C Lundal", Photogrammatic Engineering and Remote Sensing, February 1988

[2] Knutson interview

[3] NASA ER-2 program history at http://www.nasa.gov/centers/dryden/research/AirSci/ER-2/history.html

[4] NASA ER-2 history

[5] NASA ER-2 history

[6] AWST article, 21 November 1994, p88

[7] Doug Stewart, "Above The Sky", Air & Space magazine, August/September 1993

[8] Andrew Roberts and Claude Hashem, STARLink description, NASA Ames Research Center

[9] Dee Porter, Dave Wright interviews

[10] Jim Barrilleaux interview; www.nasa.dfrc.gov

Chapter 39:

[1] Minutes of 9 May 1956 meeting, from DPS files

[2] Minutes of 3 April 1956 meeting, from DPS files; Project Dragon Lady presentation at HQ AMC, February 1958, from DPS files

[3] DPS memo 11 September 1956

[4] The Air Force U-2, report dated 25 March 1960 in DPD files; USAF briefing, 1965, in OSA files

[5] CIA memo to DDP 12 October 1960

[6] Advanced Systems memo dated 3 April 1968; Donn Byrnes & Kenneth Hurley, "Blackbird Rising" Appendix A; Jerry Moncree, "HABU and Dragon Lady", p171

[7] Lockheed Report SP-1125

[8] Big Safari Program History; Bob Anderson interview

[9] Moncree, p172 and 264

[10] "Newly re-engined U-2s arrive today", Space Sentinel, 28 October 1994; "9th Maintenance Squadron : Unsung professionals, leading the way" High Flyer, 16 November 2001

[11] "U-2 FY97 in Review", Flying Safety magazine, December 1997; author's interviews

[12] U-2 Graybeard Panel report to ACC, 20 November 1997, Section 3

[13] author's interviews

[14] Raytheon news release July 1999; author's interviews; WR-ALC history, FY2000, Chapter 3, from www.robins.af.mil

[15] author's interviews; WR-ALC history, FY2001, Chapter 3

[16] WR-ALC history FY2000 and FY2001, Chapter 3

[17] WR-ALC history FY1999, Chapter 3

[18] from WR-ALC History, FY2000, Chapter 3

Index

The Advanced Synthetic Aperture Radar System (ASARS) was introduced on the U-2 in the mid-1980s. This very high-resolution imaging radar was subsequently improved by adding a Moving Target Indicator (MTI). It was then upgraded as ASARS-2A, with onboard processing, increased coverage and improved geolocation. A high-resolution search mode map is shown here. ASARS-2A is produced by Raytheon Space and Airborne Systems.